Precious Remedies
Against
Satan's Devices
&
The Covenant of Grace

Precious Remedies
Against
Satan's Devices
&
The Covenant of Grace

Thomas Brooks

Sovereign Grace Publishers, Inc.
P.O. Box 4998
Lafayette, IN 47903
2001

Printed In the United States of America
By Lightning Source, Inc.

CONTENTS

A WORD TO THE READER

Solomon tells us to buy the truth (Prov. 23:23), but he does not tell us what it costs — yet we must get it however costly it may be. We must love it both shining and scorching. Every parcel of truth is precious, like filings of gold. We must either live with it, or we must die for it. As Ruth said to Naomi, 'Where you go I will go, and where you stay I will stay, and nothing but death shall divide you and me' (Ruth 1:16); so must gracious spirits say, Where truth goes I will go, and where truth is I will be, and nothing but death shall divide me and the truth. A man may lawfully sell his house, land, and jewels, but truth is a jewel that exceeds all price, and it must not be sold. It is our heritage, 'I have taken Your testimonies as a heritage forever' (Ps. 119:111). It is a legacy that our forefathers have bought with their blood, which should make us willing to lay down anything, and to lay out anything, that with the wise merchant we may purchase this precious pearl (Matt. 13:45), for it is worth more than heaven and earth. It will cause a man to live happily, die comfortably and reign eternally. And now, if you please, read the work and receive counsel from me:

1. You must know that every man cannot be excellent, yet he may be useful. An iron key may unlock the door of a golden treasure; yea, iron can do things gold cannot do!

2. Remember that it is not hasty reading, but serious meditation on holy and heavenly truths, that makes them prove sweet and profitable to the soul. It is not the mere touching of the flower by the bee that gathers honey, but her abiding for a time on the flower that draws out the sweet. It is not he that reads most, but he that meditates most .that will prove to be the choicest, sweetest, wisest and strongest Christian.

3. Know that it is not the knowing, nor the talking, nor the reading man, but the doing man that at last will be found the happiest man. If you know these things, blessed and happy are you if you do them (John 16:14) — 'Not every one that says Lord, Lord, shall enter into the kingdom of heaven, but he that does the will of my Father' (Matt. 7:21). Judas called Christ Lord, Lord, yet he betrayed Him. Ah! How many Judases we have in these days, those that kiss Christ yet betray Him; that in their words profess Him, but in their works deny Him; that bow their knee to Him, and yet in their hearts despise Him; that call Him Jesus, and yet they will not obey Him for their Lord.

Reader, if it is not strong on your heart to practice what you read, then why do you read? Do you do it to increase your own condemnation? If your light and knowledge is not turned into practice, the more you know the more miserable you will be in the day of recompense; your light and your knowledge will torment you more than all the demons in hell. Your knowledge will be the rod that will eternally lash you, the scorpion that will be forever biting you, the worm that will everlastingly gnaw on you. Therefore read, and labor to know, so that you may do. Otherwise, you will be undone forever (as Luther said, God loves not the questioner, but the runner). When Demosthenes was asked what was an orator's first part, what the second, what the third, he answered, Action! I may say the same, if any should ask me what is the first, second and third part of a Christian, I must answer, Action! That man who reads so that he may know, and also labors to know so that he may do, will have two heavens — a heaven of joy, peace and comfort on earth, and a heaven of glory and happiness after death.

4. If while you read you will cast a serious eye toward the margin, you will find many sweet and precious notes that will oftentimes give light to the things you read and thus pay you for your pains. So, desiring that you may find as much sweetness and advantage in reading this treatise as I have found, by the overshadowings of heaven, in the studying and writing of it, I recommend you 'to God, and to the word of His grace, which is able to build you up, and to give you an inheritance among those who are sanctified' (Acts 20:32)

The servant of your soul in every office of the Gospel,

THOMAS BROOKS

PRECIOUS REMEDIES AGAINST SATAN'S DEVICES.

Lest Satan should get an advantage of us: for we are not ignorant of his devices.—2 Cor. II. 11.

In this fifth verse, the apostle shews, that the incestuous person had by his incest sadded those precious souls that God would not have sadded.[1] Souls that walk sinfully are Hazaels to the godly, 2 Kings viii. 12, *et seq.*, and draw many sighs and tears from them. Jeremiah weeps in secret for Judah's sins, Jer. ix. 1 ; and Paul cannot speak of the belly-gods with dry eyes, Philip. iii. 18, 19. And Lot's righteous soul was burdened, vexed, and racked by the filthy Sodomites, 2 Peter ii. 7, 8.[2] Every sinful Sodomite was a Hazael to his eyes, a Hadad-rimmon to his heart, Zech. xii. 11. Gracious souls use to mourn for other men's sins as well as their own, and for their souls and sins who make a mock of sin, and a jest of damning their own souls. Guilt or grief is all that gracious souls get by communion with vain souls, Ps. cxix. 136, 158.

In the 6th verse, he shews that the punishment that was inflicted upon the incestuous person was sufficient, and therefore they should not refuse to receive him who had repented and sorrowed for his former faults and follies. It is not for the honour of Christ, the credit of the gospel, nor the good of souls, for professors to be like those bloody wretches, that burnt some that recanted at the stake, saying, 'That they would send them into another world whiles they were in a good mind.'[3]

In the 7th, 8th, 9th, and 10th verses, the apostle stirs up the church to forgive him, to comfort him, and to confirm their love towards him, lest he should be 'swallowed up with over much sorrow,' Satan going about to mix the detestable darnel, Mat. xiii. 25, of desperation with the godly sorrow of a pure penitent heart. It was a sweet saying of one, 'Let a man grieve for his sin, and then joy for his grief.'[4] That sorrow for sin that keeps the soul from looking towards the mercy-

---

[1] 'Saddened.'—G.

[2] καταπονούμενον, ἰβασάνιζιν.

[3] [Foxe.] Acts and Mon. fol. 1392 [Cf. Under Cranmer and Recantation. ed. 1631. Vol. iii. 667, 668.—G.]

[4] Doleat et de dolore gaudeat.—*Jerome.*

seat, and that keeps Christ and the soul asunder, or that shall render the soul unfit for the communion of saints, is a sinful sorrow.

In the 11th verse, he lays down another reason to work them to shew pity and mercy to the penitent sinner, that was mourning and groaning under his sin and misery; *i. e.* lest Satan should get an advantage of us : for we are not ignorant of his devices. A little for the opening of the words

Lest Satan should get an *advantage* of us ; lest Satan over-reach us. The Greek word πλεονεκτηθῶμεν, signifieth to have more than belongs to one. The comparison is taken from the greedy merchant, that seeketh and taketh all opportunities to beguile and deceive others. Satan is that wily merchant, that devoureth, not widows' houses, but most men's souls.

' We are not ignorant of Satan's *devices*,' or plots, or machinations, or stratagems, Νοήματα. He is but a titular Christian that hath not personal experience of Satan's stratagems, his set and composed machinations, his artificially moulded methods, his plots, darts, depths, whereby he outwitted our first parents, and fits us a pennyworth still, as he sees reason.

The main observation that I shall draw from these words is this:

Doct. That Satan hath his several devices to deceive, entangle, and undo the souls of men.

I shall, 1. Prove the point.

2. Shew you his several devices ; and,

3. The remedies against his devices.

4. How it comes to pass that he hath so many several devices to deceive, entangle, and undo the souls of men.

5. I shall lay down some propositions concerning Satan's devices.

I. For the *proof of the point*, take these few Scriptures: Eph. vi. 11, 'Put on the whole armour of God, that ye may be able to stand against the *wiles* of the devil.' The Greek word that is here rendered 'wiles,' is a notable emphatical word.

(1.) It signifies such snares as are laid behind one, such treacheries as come upon one's back at unawares. It notes the methods or way-layings of that old subtle serpent, who, like Dan's adder 'in the path,' biteth the heels of passengers, and thereby transfuseth his venom to the head and heart.[1] The word Μεθοδίας signifies an ambushment or stratagem of war, whereby the enemy sets upon a man *ex insidiis*, at unawares.[2]

(2.) It signifies such snares as are set to catch one in one's road. A man walks in his road, and thinks not of it ; on the sudden he is catched by thieves, or falls into a pit, &c.

(3.) It signifies such as are purposely, artificially, and craftily set for the taking the prey at the greatest advantage that can be. The Greek μεθοδίας, being derived from μετὰ and ὁδὸς, signifies properly a waylaying, circumvention, or going about, as they do which seek after

---

[1] Cf. Genesis xlix. 17. Misprinted originally ' Pan's,' and so has been usually transmitted.—G.

[2] Spelled ' anawares,' which is to be noted along with the earlier form ' anonywar.' Cf. Richardson *sub voce.*—G.

their prey. Julian, by his craft, drew more from the faith than all his persecuting predecessors could do by their cruelty. So doth Satan more hurt in his sheep's skin than by roaring like a lion.

Take one scripture more for the proof of the point, and that is in 2 Tim. ii. 26, 'And that they might recover themselves out of the snare of the devil, who are taken captive by him at his will.' The Greek word that is here rendered recover themselves, 'Ανανη-ψωσιν, signifies to awaken themselves. The apostle alludeth to one that is asleep or drunk, who is to be awakened and restored to his senses; and the Greek word that is here rendered 'taken captive,' signifies to be taken alive, ἐζωγρημένοι. The word is properly a warlike word, and signifies to be taken alive, as soldiers are taken alive in the wars, or as birds are taken alive and ensnared in the fowler's net. Satan hath snares for the wise and snares for the simple ; snares for hypocrites, and snares for the upright ; snares for generous souls, and snares for timorous souls; snares for the rich, and snares for the poor; snares for the aged, and snares for youth, &c. Happy are those souls that are not taken and held in the snares that he hath laid !¹

Take one proof more, and then I will proceed to the opening of the point, and that is in Rev. ii. 24, 'But unto you I say, and unto the rest in Thyatira, as many as have not this doctrine, and which have not known the depths of Satan, as they speak, I will put upon you no other burden but to hold fast till I come.' Those poor souls called their opinions the depths of God, when indeed they were the depths of Satan. You call your opinions depths, and so they are, but they are such depths as Satan hath brought out of hell. They are the whisperings and hissings of that serpent, not the inspirations of God.

II. Now, the second thing that I am to shew you is, his *several devices;* and herein I shall first shew you the several devices that he hath to draw the soul to sin. I shall instance in these twelve, which may bespeak our most serious consideration.

His first device to draw the soul to sin is,

Device (1). *To present the bait and hide the hook;* to present the golden cup, and hide the poison ; to present the sweet, the pleasure, and the profit that may flow in upon the soul by yielding to sin, and by hiding from the soul the wrath and misery that will certainly follow the committing of sin. By this device he took our first parents: Gen. iii. 4, 5, 'And the serpent said unto the woman, Ye shall not surely die : for God doth know, that in the day ye eat thereof, then your eyes shall be opened; and ye shall be as gods, knowing good and evil.' Your eyes shall be opened, and you shall be as gods ! Here is the bait, the sweet, the pleasure, the profit. Oh, but he hides the hook, —the shame, the wrath, and the loss that would certainly follow !²

There is an opening of the eyes of the mind to contemplation and joy, and there is an opening of the eyes of the body to shame and

¹ Cf. [Daniel] Pareus *in loc.* 1 Tim. iv. 1. [Works, 3 vols. folio, 1647.—G.]
² So to reduce Dr [Rowland] Taylor, martyr, they promised him not only his pardon, but a bishopric. Acts & Mon. fol. i. 86. [Foxe. ed. 1631. Vol. iii. p. 176.—G.]
. . . . Inest peccatum cum delectaris : regnat si consentis. [Augustine in Ps. l.—G.]

confusion. He promiseth them the former, but intends the latter, and so cheats them—giving them an apple in exchange for a paradise, as he deals by thousands now-a-days. Satan with ease puts fallacies upon us by his golden baits, and then he leads us and leaves us in a fool's paradise. He promises the soul honour, pleasure, profit, &c., but pays the soul with the greatest contempt, shame, and loss that can be. By a golden bait he laboured to catch Christ, Mat. iv. 8, 9. He shews him the beauty and the bravery of a bewitching world, which doubtless would have taken many a carnal heart; but here the devil's fire fell upon wet tinder, and therefore took not. These tempting objects did not at all win upon his affections, nor dazzle his eyes, though many have eternally died of the wound of the eye, and fallen for ever by this vile strumpet the world, who, by laying forth her two fair breasts of profit and pleasure, hath wounded their souls, and cast them down into utter perdition. She hath, by the glistering of her pomp and preferment, slain millions; as the serpent Scytale,[1] which, when she cannot overtake the fleeing passengers, doth, with her beautiful colours, astonish and amaze them, so that they have no power to pass away till she have stung them to death. Adversity hath slain her thousand, but prosperity her ten thousand.[2]

Now, the remedies against this device of the devil are these:

Remedy (1). *First, Keep at the greatest distance from sin, and from playing with the golden bait that Satan holds forth to catch you;* for this you have Rom. xii. 9, 'Abhor that which is evil, cleave to that which is good.' When we meet with anything extremely evil and contrary to us, nature abhors it, and retires as far as it can from it. The Greek word that is there rendered 'abhor,' is very significant; it signifies to hate it as hell itself, to hate it with horror.[3]

Anselm used to say, 'That if he should see the shame of sin on the one hand, and the pains of hell on the other, and must of necessity choose one, he would rather be thrust into hell without sin, than to go into heaven with sin,' so great was his hatred and detestation of sin. It is our wisest and our safest course to stand at the farthest distance from sin; not to go near the house of the harlot, but to fly from all appearance of evil, Prov. v. 8, 1 Thes. v. 22. The best course to prevent falling into the pit, is to keep at the greatest distance; he that will be so bold as to attempt to dance upon the brink of the pit, may find by woful experience that it is a righteous thing with God that he should fall into the pit. Joseph keeps at a distance from sin, and from playing with Satan's golden baits, and stands. David draws near, and plays with the bait, and falls, and swallows bait and hook with a witness. David comes near the snare, and is taken in it, to

---

[1] Scytale : Solinus, c. xxvii. and xl.—G.

This world at last shall be burnt for a witch, saith one. . . . Multi amando res noxias sunt miseri, habendo miseriores.—*Aug*[*ustine*] in Ps. xvi. Many are miserable by loving hurtful things, but they are more miserable by having them. . . . Men had need pray with Bernard, Da Domine ut sic possideamus temporalia, ut non perdamus æterna. Grant us, Lord, that we may so partake of temporal felicity, that we may not lose eternal.

[2] ἀποστυγουντες. The simple verb imports extreme detestation, which is aggravated by the composition.—*Chrys*[*ostom*].

the breaking of his bones, the wounding of his conscience, and the loss of his God.[1]

Sin is a plague, yea, the greatest and most infectious plague in the world ; and yet, ah ! how few are there that tremble at it, that keep at a distance from it ! 1 Cor. v. 6, ' Know ye not that a little leaven leaveneth the whole lump ?' As soon as one sin had seized upon Adam's heart, all sin entered into his soul and overspread it. How hath Adam's one sin spread over all mankind ! Rom. v. 12, ' Wherefore as by one man sin entered into the world, and death by sin, and so death passed upon all men, for that all have sinned.' Ah, how doth the father's sin infect the child, the husband's infect the wife, the master's the servant ! The sin that is in one man's heart is able to infect a whole world, it is of such a spreading and infectious nature.[2]

The story of the Italian, who first made his enemy deny God, and then stabbed him, and so at once murdered both body and soul,[3] declares the perfect malignity of sin ; and oh ! that what hath been spoken upon this head may prevail with you, to stand at a distance from sin !

The second remedy is,

Remedy (2). To consider, *That sin is but a bitter sweet.* That seeming sweet that is in sin will quickly vanish, and lasting shame, sorrow, horror, and terror will come in the room thereof: Job xx. 12–14, 'Though wickedness be sweet in his mouth, though he hide it under his tongue, though he spare it, and forsake it not, but keep it still within his mouth, yet his meat in his bowels is turned, it is the gall of asps within him.' Forbidden profits and pleasures are most pleasing to vain men, who count madness mirth, &c. Many long to be meddling with the murdering morsels of sin, which nourish not, but rent and consume the belly, the soul, that receives them. Many eat that on earth that they digest in hell. Sin's murdering morsels will deceive those that devour them. Adam's apple was a bitter sweet ; Esau's mess was a bitter sweet ; the Israelites' quails a bitter sweet ; Jonathan's honey a bitter sweet ; and Adonijah's dainties a bitter sweet. After the meal is ended, then comes the reckoning. Men must not think to dance and dine with the devil, and then to sup with Abraham, Isaac, and Jacob in the kingdom of heaven ; to feed upon the poison of asps, and yet that the viper's tongue should not slay them.[4]

When the asp stings a man, it doth first tickle him so as it makes him laugh, till the poison, by little and little, gets to the heart, and

---

[1] It was a divine saying of a heathen, ' That if there were no God to punish him, no devil to torment him, no hell to burn him, no man to see him, yet would he not sin for the ugliness and filthiness of sin, and the grief of his own conscience.'—*Seneca.* [De Beneficiis, l. iv. 23, and often in his ' Letters.' Cf. *sub Conscientia.*—G.]

[2] Sin is like those diseases that are called by physicians, *corruptio totius substantiæ.*

[3] Told in Wanley's *Wonders*, with authorities, b. iv. c xii.—G.

[4] When the golden bait is set forth to catch us, we must say as Demosthenes the orator did of the beautiful Lais, when he was asked an excessive sum of money to behold her, ' I will not buy repentance so dear ;' I am not so ill a merchant as to sell eternals for temporals. If intemperance could afford more pleasure than temperance Heliogabalus should have been more happy than Adam in paradise.—*Plutarch.*

then it pains him more than ever it delighted him. So doth sin ;
it may please a little at first, but it will pain the soul with a witness
at last ; yea, if there were the least real delight in sin, there could
be no perfect hell, where men shall most perfectly be tormented with
their sin.

The third remedy against this device of Satan is,

Remedy (3). Solemnly to consider, *That sin will usher in the
greatest and the saddest losses that can be upon our souls.* It will
usher in the loss of that divine favour that is better than life, and the
loss of that joy that is unspeakable and full of glory, and the loss of
that peace that passeth understanding, and the loss of those divine
influences by which the soul hath been refreshed, quickened, raised,
strengthened, and gladded, and the loss of many outward desirable
mercies, which otherwise the soul might have enjoyed.[1]

It was a sound and savoury reply of an English captain at the loss
of Calais, when a proud Frenchman scornfully demanded, When will
you fetch Calais again, replied, When your sins shall weigh down
ours.[2] Ah, England ! my constant prayer for thee is, that thou
mayest not sin away thy mercies into their hands that cannot call
mercy mercy, and that would joy in nothing more than to see thy
sorrow and misery, and to see that hand to make thee naked, that
hath clothed thee with much mercy and glory.

The fourth remedy against this device of Satan is,

Remedy (4). Seriously to consider, *That sin is of a very deceitful
and bewitching nature.*[3] Sin is from the greatest deceiver, it is a
child of his own begetting, it is the ground of all the deceit in the
world, and it is in its own nature exceeding deceitful. Heb. iii. 13,
' But exhort one another daily, while it is called To-day, lest any
of you be hardened through the deceitfulness of sin.' It will kiss
the soul, and pretend fair to the soul, and yet betray the soul for
ever. It will with Delilah smile upon us, that it may betray us into
the hands of the devil, as she did Samson into the hands of the
Philistines. Sin gives Satan a power over us, and an advantage to
accuse us and to lay claim to us, as those that wear his badge; it is
of a very bewitching nature, it bewitches the soul, where it is upon
the throne, that the soul cannot leave it, though it perish eternally
by it.[4] Sin so bewitches the soul, that it makes the soul call evil good,
and good evil ; bitter sweet and sweet bitter, light darkness and darkness light ; and a soul thus bewitched with sin will stand it out to the
death, at the sword's point with God ; let God strike and wound,
and cut to the very bone, yet the bewitched soul cares not, fears not,
but will still hold on in a course of wickedness, as you may see in
Pharaoh, Balaam, and Judas. Tell the bewitched soul that sin is a
viper that will certainly kill when it is not killed, that sin often kills

---

[1] Isa. lix. 2, Ps. li. 12, Isa. lix. 8, 2 Chron. xv. 3, 4, Jer. xvii. 18. Jer. v. 2.

[2] Quando peccata vestra erunt nostris graviora.

[3] In Sardis there grew an herb, called *Appium Sardis*, that would make a man lie
laughing when he was deadly sick ; such is the operation of sin.

[4] Which occasioned Chrysostom to say, when Eudoxia the empress threatened him,
Go tell her, ' Nil nisi peccatum timeo,' I fear nothing but sin.

secretly, insensibly, eternally, yet the bewitched soul cannot, nor will not, cease from sin.

When the physicians told Theotimus that except he did abstain from drunkenness and uncleanness, &c., he would lose his eyes, his heart was so bewitched to his sins, that he answers, 'Then farewell sweet light ;'[1] he had rather lose his eyes than leave his sin. So a man bewitched with sin had rather lose God, Christ, heaven, and his own soul than part with his sin. Oh, therefore, for ever take heed of playing or nibbling at Satan's golden baits.

The second device of Satan to draw the soul to sin is,

Device (2). *By painting sin with virtue's colours.* Satan knows that if he should present sin in its own nature and dress, the soul would rather fly from it than yield to it ; and therefore he presents it unto us, not in its own proper colours, but painted and gilded over with the name and show of virtue, that we may the more easily be overcome by it, and take the more pleasure in committing of it. Pride, he presents to the soul under the name and notion of neatness and cleanliness, and covetousness (which the apostle condemns for idolatry) to be but good husbandry ;[2] and drunkenness to be good fellowship, and riotousness under the name and notion of liberality, and wantonness as a trick of youth, &c.

Now, the remedies against this device of Satan are these,

Remedy (1). *First,* consider, *That sin is never a whit the less filthy, vile, and abominable, by its being coloured and painted with virtue's colours.* A poisonous pill is never a whit the less poisonous because it is gilded over with gold ; nor a wolf is never a whit the less a wolf because he hath put on a sheep's skin ; nor the devil is never a whit the less a devil because he appears sometimes like an angel of light. So neither is sin any whit the less filthy and abominable by its being painted over with virtue's colours.

The second remedy against this device of Satan is,

Remedy (2). *That the more sin is painted forth under the colour of virtue, the more dangerous it is to the souls of men.* This we see evident in these days, by those very many souls that are turned out of the way that is holy—and in which their souls have had sweet and glorious communion with God—into ways of highest vanity and folly, by Satan's neat[3] colouring over of sin, and painting forth vice under the name and colour of virtue. This is so notoriously known that I need but name it. The most dangerous vermin is too often to be found under the fairest and sweetest flowers, and the fairest glove is often drawn upon the foulest hand, and the richest robes are often put upon the filthiest bodies. So are the fairest and sweetest names upon the greatest and the most horrible vices and errors that be in the world. Ah ! that we had not too many sad proofs of this amongst us.[4]

---

[1] Vale lumen amicum. —*Ambrose.*   [2] 'Thrift,' 'economy.'—G.

[3] Careful, clever.— G.

[4] Turpiora sunt vitia quæ virtutum specie celantur.—*Jer*[ome.] .... Thus the *Illuminates* (as they called themselves) a pestilent sect in Arragon, professing and affecting in themselves a kind of angelic purity, fell suddenly to the justifying of bestiality, as many have done in these days.

The third remedy against this device of Satan is,

Remedy (3). *To look on sin with that eye* [*with*] *which within a few hours we shall see it.* Ah, souls! when you shall lie upon a dying bed, and stand before a judgment-seat, sin shall be unmasked, and its dress and robes shall then be taken off, and then it shall appear more vile, filthy, and terrible than hell itself; then, that which formerly appeared most sweet will appear most bitter, and that which appeared most beautiful will appear most ugly, and that which appeared most delightful will then appear most dreadful to the soul.[1] Ah, the shame, the pain, the gall, the bitterness, the horror, the hell that the sight of sin, when its dress is taken off, will raise in poor souls! Sin will surely prove evil and bitter to the soul when its robes are taken off. A man may have the stone who feels no fit of it. Conscience will work at last, though for the present one may feel no fit of accusation. Laban shewed himself at parting. Sin will be bitterness in the latter end, when it shall appear to the soul in its own filthy nature. The devil deals with men as the panther doth with beasts; he hides his deformed head till his sweet scent hath drawn them into his danger. Till we have sinned, Satan is a parasite; when we have sinned, he is a tyrant.[2] O souls! the day is at hand when the devil will pull off the paint and garnish that he hath put upon sin, and present that monster, sin, in such a monstrous shape to your souls, that will cause your thoughts to be troubled, your countenance to be changed, the joints of your loins to be loosed, and your knees to be dashed one against another, and your hearts to be so terrified, that you will be ready, with Ahithophel and Judas,[3] to strangle and hang your bodies on earth, and your souls in hell, if the Lord hath not more mercy on you than he had on them. Oh! therefore, look upon sin now as you must look upon it to all eternity, and as God, conscience, and Satan will present it to you another day!

The fourth remedy against this device of Satan is,

Remedy (4.) Seriously to consider, *That even those very sins that Satan paints, and puts new names and colours upon, cost the best blood, the noblest blood, the life-blood, the heart-blood of the Lord Jesus.*[4] That Christ should come from the eternal bosom of his Father to a region of sorrow and death; that God should be manifested in the flesh, the Creator made a creature; that he that was clothed with glory should be wrapped with rags of flesh; he that filled heaven and earth with his glory should be cradled in a manger; that the power of God should fly from weak man, the God of Israel into Egypt; that the God of the law should be subject to the law, the God of the circumcision circumcised, the God that made the heavens

---

[1] Tacitus speaks of Tiberius, that when his sins did appear in their own colours, they did so terrify and torment him that he protested to the Senate that he suffered daily. [*Ann.* vi. 51.—G.]

[2] Satan, that now allures thee to sin, will ere long make thee to see that *peccatum est deicidium*, sin is a murdering of God; and this will make thee murder two at once, thy soul and thy body, unless the Lord in mercy holds thy hands.

[3] 2 Sam. xvii. 23, and Mat. xxvii. 5.—G.

[4] Una guttula plus valet quam cœlum et terra.—*Luther;* *i. e.* one little drop (speaking of the blood of Christ) is more worth than heaven and earth.

working at Joseph's homely trade; that he that binds the devils in
chains should be tempted; that he, whose is the world, and the fulness
thereof, should hunger and thirst; that the God of strength should
be weary, the Judge of all flesh condemned, the God of life put to
death; that he that is one with his Father should cry out of misery,
' My God, my God, why hast thou forsaken me?' Mat. xxvii. 46; that
he that had the keys of hell and death at his girdle should lie imprisoned in the sepulchre of another, having in his lifetime nowhere
to lay his head, nor after death to lay his body; that that head,
before which the angels do cast down their crowns, should be crowned
with thorns, and those eyes, purer than the sun, put out by the darkness of death; those ears, which hear nothing but hallelujahs of saints
and angels, to hear the blasphemies of the multitude; that face, that
was fairer than the sons of men, to be spit on by those beastly wretched
Jews; that mouth and tongue, that spake as never man spake, accused
for blasphemy; those hands, that freely swayed the sceptre of heaven,
nailed to the cross; those feet, ' like unto fine brass,' nailed to the
cross for man's sins; each sense annoyed: his feeling or touching, with
a spear and nails; his smell, with stinking flavour, being crucified
about Golgotha, the place of skulls; his taste, with vinegar and gall;
his hearing, with reproaches, and sight of his mother and disciples
bemoaning him; his soul, comfortless and forsaken; and all this for
those very sins that Satan paints and puts fine colours upon! Oh!
how should the consideration of this stir up the soul against it, and
work the soul to fly from it, and to use all holy means whereby sin
may be subdued and destroyed ![1]

After Julius Cæsar was murdered, Antonius brought forth his
coat, all bloody and cut, and laid it before the people, saying, ' Look,
here you have the emperor's coat thus bloody and torn:' whereupon
the people were presently in an uproar, and cried out to slay those
murderers; and they took their tables and stools that were in the
place, and set them on fire, and run to the houses of them that had
slain Cæsar, and burnt them. So that when we consider that sin
hath slain our Lord Jesus, ah, how should it provoke our hearts to be
revenged on sin, that hath murdered the Lord of glory, and hath done
that mischief that all the devils in hell could never have done ?[2]

It was good counsel one gave, ' Never let go out of your minds the
thoughts of a crucified Christ.'[3] Let these be meat and drink unto
you; let them be your sweetness and consolation, your honey and
your desire, your reading and your meditation, your life, death, and
resurrection.

The third device that Satan hath to draw the soul to sin is,

---

[1] One of the Rabbins, when he read what bitter torments the Messias should suffer
when he came into the world, cried out, *Veniat Messias et ego non videam*, *i.e.* Let the
Messias come, but let not me see him! Dionysius being in Egypt at the time of
Christ's suffering, and seeing an eclipse of the sun, and knowing it to be contrary to
nature, cried out, *Aut Deus naturæ patitur, aut mundi machina dissolvitur*, Either the
God of nature suffers, or the frame of the world will be dissolved.

[2] It is an excellent saying of Bernard, *Quanto pro nobis vilior, tanto nobis charior*.
The more vile Christ made himself for us, the more dear he ought to be to us.

[3] *Nolo vivere sine vulnere cum te video vulneratum*. O my God! as long as I see thy
wounds, I will never live without wounds, said Bonaventura.

Device (3). *By extenuating and lessening of sin.* Ah ! saith Satan, it is but a little pride, a little worldliness, a little uncleanness, a little drunkenness, &c. As Lot said of Zoar, ' It is but a little one, and my soul shall live,' Gen. xix. 20. Alas ![1] saith Satan, it is but a very little sin that you stick so at. You may commit it without any danger to your soul. It is but a little one ; you may commit it, and yet your soul shall live.

Now the remedies against this device of Satan are these :

Remedy (1). First, Solemnly consider, *That those sins which we are apt to account small, have brought upon men the greatest wrath of God,* as the eating of an apple, gathering a few sticks on the Sabbath day, and touching of the ark. Oh ! the dreadful wrath that these sins brought down upon the heads and hearts of men ![2] The least sin is contrary to the law of God, the nature of God, the being of God, and the glory of God ; and therefore it is often punished severely by God ; and do not we see daily the vengeance of the Almighty falling upon the bodies, names, states, families, and souls of men, for those sins that are but little ones in their eyes ? Surely if we are not utterly left of God, and blinded by Satan, we cannot but see it. Oh ! therefore, when Satan says it is but a little one, do thou say, Oh ! but those sins that thou callest little, are such as will cause God to rain hell out of heaven upon sinners as he did upon the Sodomites.

The second remedy against this device of Satan is,

Remedy (2). Seriously to consider, *That the giving way to a less sin makes way for the committing of a greater.* He that, to avoid a greater sin, will yield to a lesser, ten thousand to one but God in justice will leave that soul to fall into a greater. If we commit one sin to avoid another, it is just we should avoid neither, we having not law nor power in our own hands to keep off sin as we please ; and we, by yielding to the lesser, do tempt the tempter to tempt us to the greater. Sin is of an encroaching nature ; it creeps on the soul by degrees, step by step, till it hath the soul to the very height of sin.[3] David gives way to his wandering eye, and this led him to those foul sins that caused God to break his bones, and to turn his day into night, and to leave his soul in great darkness. Jacob and Peter, and other saints, have found this true by woful experience, that the yielding to a lesser sin hath been the ushering in of a greater. The little thief will open the door, and make way for the greater, and the little wedge knocked in will make way for the greater. Satan will first draw thee to sit with the drunkard, and then to sip with the drunkard, and then at last to be drunk with the drunkard. He will first draw thee to be unclean in thy thoughts, and then to be unclean in thy looks, and then to

[1] Brooks uses ' alas' much as Sibbes does.

[2] Draco, the rigid lawgiver, being asked why, when sins were not equal, he appointed death to all, answered, he knew that all sins were not equal, but he knew the least deserved death. So, though the sins of men be not all equal, yet the least of them deserves eternal death.

[3] Ps. cxxxvii. 9, ' Happy shall he be that taketh and dasheth thy little ones against the stones.' Hugo's gloss is pious, &c , *Sit nihil in te Babylonicum,* Let there be nothing in thee of Babylon ; not only the grown men, but the little ones must be dashed against the stones ; not only great sins, but little sins must be killed, or they will kill the soul for ever.

be unclean in thy words, and at last to be unclean in thy practices. He will first draw thee to look upon the golden wedge, and then to like the golden wedge, and then to handle the golden wedge, and then at last by wicked ways to gain the golden wedge, though thou runnest the hazard of losing God and thy soul for ever ; as you may see in Gehazi, Achan, and Judas, and many in these our days. Sin is never at a stand: Ps. i. 1, first ungodly, then sinners, then scorners. Here they go on from sin to sin, till they come to the top of sin, viz. to sit in the seat of scorners, or as it is in the Septuagint—$\tau\tilde{\omega}\nu$ $\lambda o\iota\mu\tilde{\omega}\nu$—to affect the honour of the chair of pestilence.

Austin, writing upon John, tells a story of a certain man, that was of an opinion that the devil did make the fly, and not God. Saith one to him, If the devil made flies, then the devil made worms, and God did not make them, for they are living creatures as well as flies. True, said he, the devil did make worms. But, said the other, if the devil did make worms, then he made birds, beasts, and man. He granted all. Thus, saith Austin, by denying God in the fly, became to deny God in man, and to deny the whole creation.[1]

By all this we see, that the yielding to lesser sins, draws the soul to the committing of greater.[2] Ah! how many in these days have fallen, first to have low thoughts of Scripture and ordinances, and then to slight Scripture and ordinances, and then to make a nose of wax of Scripture and ordinances, and then to cast off Scripture and ordinances, and then at last to advance and lift up themselves, and their Christ-dishonouring and soul-damning opinions, above Scripture and ordinances. Sin gains upon man's soul by insensible degrees : Eccles. x. 13, 'The beginning of the words of his mouth is foolishness, and the end of his talking is mischievous madness.' Corruption in the heart, when it breaks forth, is like a breach in the sea, which begins in a narrow passage, till it eat through, and cast down all before it. The debates of the soul are quick, and soon ended, and that may be done in a moment that may undo a man for ever. When a man hath begun to sin, he knows not where, or when, or how he shall make a stop of sin. Usually the soul goes on from evil to evil, from folly to folly, till it be ripe for eternal misery. Men usually grow from being naught to be very naught, and from very naught to be stark naught, and then God sets them at nought for ever.

Remedy (3). The third remedy against this third device that Satan hath to draw the soul to sin, is solemnly to consider, *That it is sad to stand with God for a trifle.* Dives would not give a crumb, therefore he should not receive a drop, Luke xvi. 21. It is the greatest folly in the

---

[1] An Italian having found his enemy at advantage, promised him if he would deny his faith, he would save his life. He, to save his life, denied his faith, which having done, he stabbed him, rejoicing that by this he had at one time taken revenge both on body and soul. [See authorities, Note 8, page 14.—G.]

[2] A young man being long tempted to kill his father, or lie with his mother, or be drunk, he thought to yield to the lesser, viz. to be drunk, that he might be rid of the greater ; but when he was drunk, he did both kill his father, and lie with his mother. [Related, with authorities, in Wanley's *Wonders*, book iv. c. xviii. : probably a reference to an extraordinary legend of Judas Iscariot. See Mrs Jameson's *Sacred and Legendary Art*, vol. i. p. 235 ; but cf. the old Italian legend of St John Chrysostom, *ibid.*, p. 317.—G.]

world to adventure the going to hell for a small matter. 'I tasted but a little honey,' said Jonathan, 'and I must die,' 1 Sam. xiv. 29. It is a most unkind and unfaithful thing to break with God for a little. Little sins carry with them but little temptations to sin, and then a man shews most viciousness and unkindness, when he sins on a little temptation. It is devilish to sin without a temptation; it is little less than devilish to sin on a little occasion. The less the temptation is to sin, the greater is that sin.[1] Saul's sin in not staying for Samuel, was not so much in the matter, but it was much in the malice of it; for though Samuel had not come at all, yet Saul should not have offered sacrifice; but this cost him dear, his soul and kingdom.

It is the greatest unkindness that can be shewed to a friend, to adventure the complaining, bleeding, and grieving of his soul upon a light and a slight occasion. So it is the greatest unkindness that can be shewed to God, Christ, and the Spirit, for a soul to put God upon complaining, Christ upon bleeding, and the Spirit upon grieving, by yielding to little sins. Therefore, when Satan says it is but a little one, do thou answer, that often times there is the greatest unkindness shewed to God's glorious majesty, in the acting of the least folly, and therefore thou wilt not displease thy best and greatest friend, by yielding to his greatest enemy.

Remedy (4). The fourth remedy against this device of Satan, is seriously to consider, *That there is great danger, yea, many times most danger, in the smallest sins.* 'A little leaven leaveneth the whole lump,' 1 Cor. v. 6. If the serpent wind in his head, he will draw in his whole body after. Greater sins do sooner startle the soul, and awaken and rouse up the soul to repentance, than lesser sins do. Little sins often slide into the soul, and breed, and work secretly and undiscernibly in the soul, till they come to be so strong, as to trample upon the soul, and to cut the throat of the soul. There is oftentimes greatest danger to our bodies in the least diseases that hang upon us, because we are apt to make light of them, and to neglect the timely use of means for removing of them, till they are grown so strong that they prove mortal to us. So there is most danger often in the least sins. We are apt to take no notice of them, and to neglect those heavenly helps whereby they should be weakened and destroyed, till they are grown to that strength, that we are ready to cry out, the medicine is too weak for the disease; I would pray, and I would hear, but I am afraid that sin is grown up by degrees to such a head, that I shall never be able to prevail over it; but as I have begun to fall, so I shall utterly fall before it, and at last perish in it, unless the power and free grace of Christ doth act gloriously, beyond my present apprehension and expectation. The viper is killed by the little young ones that are nourished and cherished in her belly: so are many men eternally killed and betrayed by the little sins, as they call them, that are nourished in their own bosoms.[2]

[1] It was a vexation to king Lysimachus, that his staying to drink one small draught of water lost him his kingdom; and so it will eternally vex some souls at last that for one little sin, compared with great transgressions, they have lost God, heaven, and their souls for ever. [Plutarch. Cf. Bp. Jeremy Taylor, vol. iv. p. 457 (Eden).—G.]

[2] Cæsar was stabbed with bodkins. Pope Adrian was choked with a gnat. A

I know not, saith one, whether the maintenance of the least sin be not worse than the commission of the greatest : for this may be of frailty, that argues obstinacy. A little hole in the ship sinks it; a small breach in a sea-bank carries away all before it; a little stab at the heart kills a man; and a little sin, without a great deal of mercy, will damn a man.[1]

Remedy (5). The fifth remedy against this device of Satan, is solemnly to consider, *That other saints have chosen to suffer the worst of torments, rather than they would commit the least sin, i. e.* such as the world accounts.[2] So as you may see in Daniel and his companions, that would rather choose to burn, and be cast to the lions, than they would bow to the image that Nebuchadnezzar had set up. When this *pecchaddillo*,[3] in the world's account, and a hot fiery furnace stood in competition, that they must either fall into sin, or be cast into the fiery furnace, such was their tenderness of the honour and glory of God, and their hatred and indignation against sin, that they would rather burn than sin; they knew that it was far better to burn for their not sinning, than that God and conscience should raise a hell, a fire in their bosoms for sin.[4]

I have read of that noble servant of God, Marcus Arethusius, minister of a church in the time of Constantine, who in Constantine's time had been the cause of overthrowing an idol's temple ; afterwards, when Julian came to be emperor, he would force the people of that place to build it up again. They were ready to do it, but he refused; whereupon those that were his own people, to whom he preached, took him, and stripped him of all his clothes, and abused his naked body, and gave it up to the children, to lance it with their pen-knives, and then caused him to be put in a basket, and anointed his naked body with honey, and set him in the sun, to be stung with wasps. And all this cruelty they shewed, because he would not do anything towards the building up of this idol temple; nay, they came to this, that if he would do but the least towards it, if he would give but a halfpenny to it, they would save him. But he refused all, though the giving of a halfpenny might have saved his live ; and in doing this, he did but live up to that principle that most Christians talk of, and all profess, but few come up to, viz., that we must choose rather to suffer the worst of torments that men and devils can invent and inflict, than to commit the least sin, whereby God should be dishonoured, our consciences wounded, religion reproached, and our own souls endangered.

scorpion is little, yet able to sting a lion to death. A mouse is but little, yet killeth an elephant, if he gets up into his trunk. The leopard being great, is poisoned with a head of garlic. The smallest errors prove many times most dangerous. It is as much treason to coin pence as bigger pieces.

[1] One little miscarriage doth, in the eyes of the world, overshadow all a Christian's graces, as one cloud doth sometimes overshadow the whole body of the sun.

[2] *Melius mori fame quam Idolothytis vesci.—Augustine.* It is better to die with hunger, than to eat that which is offered to idols.

[3] The early form of this at the time scarcely accepted word ; but the context indicates a reminiscence of Boskierus (*Codrus Evang.*), who uses the term and preceding illustrations of little sins.—G.

[4] Many heathens would rather die than cozen or cheat one another, so faithful were they one to another. Will not these rise in judgment against many professors in these days, who make nothing of over-reaching one another?

Remedy (6). The sixth remedy against this device of Satan is, seriously to consider, *That the soul is never able to stand under the guilt and weight of the least sin, when God shall set it home upon the soul.* The least sin will press and sink the stoutest sinner as low as hell, when God shall open the eyes of a sinner, and make him see the horrid filthiness and abominable vileness that is in sin. What so little, base, and vile creatures as lice or gnats, and yet by these little poor creatures, God so plagued stout-hearted Pharaoh, and all Egypt, that, fainting under it, they were forced to cry out, ' This is the finger of God,' Exod. viii. 16, x. 19. When little creatures, yea, the least creatures, shall be armed with a power from God, they shall press and sink down the greatest, proudest, and stoutest tyrants that breathe.[1] So when God shall cast a sword into the hand of a little sin, and arm it against the soul, the soul will faint and fall under it. Some, who have but projected adultery, without any actual acting it ; and others, having found a trifle, and made no conscience to restore it, knowing, by the light of natural conscience, that they did not do as they would be done by ; and others, that have had some unworthy thought of God, have been so frightened, amazed, and terrified for those sins, which are small in men's account, that they have wished they had never been ; that they could take no delight in any earthly comfort, that they have been put to their wits' end, ready to make away themselves, wishing themselves annihilated.[2]

Mr Perkins mentions a good man, but very poor, who, being ready to starve, stole a lamb, and being about to eat it with his poor children, and as his manner was afore meat, to crave a blessing, durst not do it, but fell into a great perplexity of conscience, and acknowledged his fault to the owner, promising payment if ever he should be able.

Remedy (7). The seventh remedy against this device is, solemnly to consider, *That there is more evil in the least sin than in the greatest affliction;* and this appears as clear as the sun, by the severe dealing of God the Father with his beloved Son, who let all the vials of his fiercest wrath upon him, and that for the least sin as well as for the greatest.

' The wages of sin is death,' Rom. vi. 23 ; of sin indefinitely, whether great or small.[3] Oh ! how should this make us tremble, as much at the least spark of lust as at hell itself ; considering that God the Father would not spare his bosom Son, no, not for the least sin, but would make him drink the dregs of his wrath !

And so much for the remedies that may fence and preserve our souls from being drawn to sin by this third device of Satan.

[1] The tyrant Maximinus, who had set forth his proclamation engraven in brass for the utter abolishing of Christ and his religion, was eaten of lice. [Maximinus II., Euseb. H. E. viii. 14, ix. 2, &c.—G.]

[2] *Una guttula malæ conscientiæ totum mare mundani gaudii absorbet ; i. e.* one drop of an evil conscience swallows up the whole sea of worldly joy. How great a pain, not to be borne, comes from the prick of this small thorn, said one.

[3] Death is the heir of the least sin ; the best wages that the least sin gives his soldiers is, death of all sorts. In a strict sense, there is no sin little, because no little God to sin against.

The fourth device that Satan hath to draw the soul to sin is,

Device (4). *By presenting to the soul the best men's sins, and by hiding from the soul their virtues; by shewing the soul their sins, and by hiding from the soul their sorrows and repentance :* as by setting before the soul the adultery of David, the pride of Hezekiah, the impatience of Job, the drunkenness of Noah, the blasphemy of Peter, &c., and by hiding from the soul the tears, the sighs, the groans, the meltings, the humblings, and repentings of these precious souls.

Now, the remedies against this device of the devil are these :

Remedy (1). The first remedy against this device of Satan is, seriously to consider, *That the Spirit of the Lord hath been as careful to note the saints' rising by repentance out of sin, as he hath to note their falling into sins.* David falls fearfully, but by repentance he rises sweetly : 'Blot out my transgressions, wash me throughly from my iniquity, cleanse me from my sin ; for I acknowledge my transgressions, and my sin is ever before me. Purge me with hyssop, and I shall be clean ; wash me, and I shall be whiter than snow; deliver me from blood-guiltiness, O God, thou God of my salvation.' It is true, Hezekiah's heart was lifted up under the abundance of mercy that God had cast in upon him; and it is as true that Hezekiah humbled himself for the pride of his heart, so that the wrath of the Lord came not upon him, nor upon Jerusalem, in the days of Hezekiah. It is true, Job curses the day of his birth, and it is as true that he rises by repentance : 'Behold, I am vile,' saith he ; 'what shall I answer thee? I will lay my ·hand upon my mouth. Once have I spoken, but I will not answer; yea twice, but I will proceed no further. I have heard of thee by the hearing of the ear, but now mine eye seeth thee ; wherefore, I abhor myself, and repent in dust and ashes,' Job xl. 4, 5 ; xlii. 5, 6.[1] Peter falls dreadfully, but rises by repentance sweetly ; a look of love from Christ melts him into tears. He knew that repentance was the key to the kingdom of grace. As once his faith was so great that he leapt, as it were, into a sea of waters to come to Christ; so now his repentance was so great that he leapt, as it were, into a sea of tears, for that he had gone from Christ. Some say that, after his sad fall, he was ever and anon weeping, and that his face was even furrowed with continual tears. He had no sooner took in poison but he vomited it up again, ere it got to the vitals ; he had no sooner handled this serpent but he turned it into a rod to scourge his soul with remorse for sinning against such clear light, and strong love, and sweet discoveries of the heart of Christ to him.[2]

Clement notes that Peter so repented, that all his life after, every night when he heard the cock crow, he would fall upon his knees, and, weeping bitterly, would beg pardon of his sin.[3] Ah, souls, you can easily sin as the saints, but can you repent with the saints !

[1] Tertullian saith that he was (*nulli rei natus nisi pœnitentiœ*) born for no other purpose but to repent.

[2] Luther confesses that, before his conversion, he met not with a more displeasing word in all his study of divinity than *repent*, but afterward he took delight in the word. *Pœnitens de peccato dolet et de dolore gaudet*, to sorrow for his sin, and then to rejoice in his sorrow.   [3] In Hefele's *Patrum Apostolicarum Opera*. 1847. 8vo.—G.

Many can sin with David and Peter, that cannot repent with David and Peter, and so must perish for ever.

Theodosius the emperor, pressing that he might receive the Lord's supper, excuses his own foul fact by David's doing the like ; to which Ambrose replies, Thou hast followed David transgressing, follow David repenting, and then think thou of the table of the Lord.[1]

Remedy (2). The second remedy against this device of Satan is, solemnly to consider, *That these saints did not make a trade of sin.* They fell once or twice, and rose by repentance, that they might keep the closer to Christ for ever. They fell accidentally, occasionally, and with much reluctancy ;[2] and thou sinnest presumptuously, obstinately, readily, delightfully, and customarily. Thou hast, by thy making a trade of sin, contracted upon thy soul a kind of cursed necessity of sinning, that thou canst as well cease to be, or cease to live, as thou canst cease to sin. Sin is, by custom, become as another nature to thee, which thou canst not, which thou wilt not lay aside, though thou knowest that if thou dost not lay sin aside, God will lay thy soul aside for ever ; though thou knowest that if sin and thy soul do not part, Christ and thy soul can never meet. If thou wilt make a trade of sin, and cry out, Did not David sin thus, and Noah sin thus, and Peter sin thus ? &c. No ; their hearts turned aside to folly one day, but thy heart turns aside to folly every day, 2 Peter ii. 14, Prov. iv. 16 ; and when they were fallen, they rise by repentance, and by the actings of faith upon a crucified Christ ;[3] but thou fallest, and hast no strength nor will to rise, but wallowest in sin, and wilt eternally die in thy sins, unless the Lord be the more merciful to thy soul. Dost thou think, O soul ! this is good reasoning ? Such a one tasted poison but once, and yet narrowly escaped ; but I do daily drink poison, yet I shall escape. Yet such is the mad reasoning of vain souls. David and Peter, &c., sinned once foully and fearfully ; they tasted poison but once, and were sick to death ; but I taste it daily, and yet shall not taste of eternal death. Remember, O souls ! that the day is at hand when self-flatterers will be found self-deceivers, yea, self-murderers.

Remedy (3). The third remedy against this device of Satan is, seriously to consider, *That though God doth not, nor never will, disinherit his people for their sins, yet he hath severely punished his people for their sins.* David sins, and God breaks his bones for his sin : ' Make me to hear joy and gladness, that the bones which thou hast broken may rejoice,' Ps. li. 8. ' And because thou hast done this, the sword shall never depart from thy house, to the day of thy death,' 2 Sam. xii. 10. Though God will not utterly take from them his loving-kindness, nor suffer his faithfulness to fail, nor break his covenant, nor alter the thing that is gone out of his mouth, yet will he ' visit their transgression with a rod, and their iniquity with stripes,'

---

[1] Theodoret, Hist. l. iv. c. xvii.

[2] The saints cannot sin (*voluntate plena sed semi-plena*) with a whole will, but, as it were, with a half will, an unwilling willingness ; not with a full consent, but with a dissenting consent.

[3] Though sin do (*habitare*) dwell in the regenerate, as Austin notes, yet it doth not (*regnare*) reign over the regenerate ; they rise by repentance.

Ps. lxxxix. 30, 35. The Scripture abounds with instances of this kind. This is so known a truth among all that know anything of truth, that to cite more scriptures to prove it would be to light a candle to see the sun at noon.[1]

The Jews have a proverb, 'That there is no punishment comes upon Israel in which there is not one ounce of the golden calf;' meaning that that was so great a sin, as that in every plague God remembered it; that it had an influence into every trouble that befell them. Every man's heart may say to him in his sufferings, as the heart of Apollodorus in the kettle, 'I have been the cause of this.'[2] God is most angry when he shews no anger. God keep me from this mercy; this kind of mercy is worse than all other kind of misery.

One writing to a dead friend hath this expression: 'I account it a part of unhappiness not to know adversity; I judge you to be miserable, because you have not been miserable.'[3] It is mercy that our affliction is not execution, but a correction.[4] He that hath deserved hanging, may be glad if he scape with a whipping. God's corrections are our instructions, his lashes our lessons, his scourges our schoolmasters, his chastisements our advertisements;[5] and to note this, both the Hebrews and the Greeks express chastening and teaching by one and the same word (*Musar, Paideia*[6]), because the latter is the true end of the former, according to that in the proverb, 'Smart makes wit, and vexation gives understanding.' Whence Luther fitly calls affliction 'The Christian man's divinity.'[7] So saith Job (chap. xxxiii. 14–19), 'God speaketh once, yea, twice, yet man perceiveth it not. In a dream, in a vision of the night, when deep sleep falleth upon men, in slumberings upon the bed; then he openeth the ears of men, and sealeth their instruction, that he may withdraw man from his purpose, and hide pride from man. He keepeth back his soul from the pit, and his life from perishing by the sword.' When Satan shall tell thee of other men's sins to draw thee to sin, do thou then think of the same men's sufferings to keep thee from sin. Lay thy hand upon thy heart, and say, O my soul! if thou sinnest with David, thou must suffer with David, &c.

Remedy (4). The fourth remedy against this device of Satan is, solemnly to consider, *That there are but two main ends of God's recording of the falls of his saints.*

And the one is, to keep those from fainting, sinking, and despair, under the burden of their sins, who fall through weakness and infirmity.

And the other is, that their falls may be as landmarks to warn others that stand, to take heed lest they fall. It never entered into the

---

[1] Josephus reports that, not long after the Jews had crucified Christ on the cross, so many of them were condemned to be crucified, that there were not places enough for crosses, nor crosses enough for the bodies that were to be hung thereon. [The Jewish War and Antiq.—G.]   [2] The tyrant of Cassandreia.—G.

[3] *Qui non est cruciatus non est Christianus*, saith Luther, There is not a Christian that carries not his cross.

[4] Ps. xciv. 12; Prov. iii. 12, 13, 16; Obad. 6, 13; Isa. ix. 1, *et seq.*

[5] Admonitions.—G.

[6] That is, מוּסָר, Prov. iii. 11; and παιδεία, Heb. xii. 5, 7, 8, 11.—G.

[7] Theologium Christianorum. . . . . Afflictiones Benedictiones, Afflictions are blessings.—*Bernard.*

heart of God to record his children's sins, that others might be encouraged to sin, but that others might look to their standings, and to hang the faster upon the skirts of Christ, and avoid all occasions and temptations that may occasion the soul to fall, as others have fallen, when they have been left by Christ. The Lord hath made their sins as landmarks, to warn his people to take heed how they come near those sands and rocks, those snares and baits, that have been fatal to the choicest treasures, to wit, the joy, peace, comfort, and glorious enjoyments of the bravest spirits and noblest souls that ever sailed through the ocean of this sinful troublesome world; as you may see in David, Job, Peter, &c. There is nothing in the world that can so notoriously cross the grand end of God's recording of the sins of his saints, than for any from thence to take encouragement to sin; and wherever you find such a soul, you may write him Christless, graceless, a soul cast off by God, a soul that Satan hath by the hand, and the eternal God knows whither he will lead him.[1]

The fifth device that Satan hath to draw the soul to sin is,

Device (5). *To present God to the soul as one made up all of mercy.* Oh! saith Satan, you need not make such a matter of sin, you need not be so fearful of sin, not so unwilling to sin; for God is a God of mercy, a God full of mercy, a God that delights in mercy, a God that is ready to shew mercy, a God that is never weary of shewing mercy, a God more prone to pardon his people than to punish his people; and therefore he will not take advantage against the soul; and why then, saith Satan, should you make such a matter of sin?

Now the remedies against this device of Satan are these:

Remedy (1). The first remedy is, seriously to consider, *That it is the sorest judgment in the world to be left to sin upon any pretence whatsoever.* O unhappy man! when God leaveth thee to thyself, and doth not resist thee in thy sins.[2] Woe, woe to him at whose sins God doth wink. When God lets the way to hell be a smooth and pleasant way, that is hell on this side hell, and a dreadful sign of God's indignation against a man; a token of his rejection, and that God doth not intend good unto him. That is a sad word, 'Ephraim is joined to idols: let him alone,' Hosea iv. 17; he will be uncounsellable and incorrigible; he hath made a match with mischief, he shall have his bellyful of it; he falls with open eyes, let him fall at his own peril. And that is a terrible saying, 'So I gave them up unto their own hearts' lusts, and they walked in their own counsels,' Ps. lxxxi. 12. A soul given up to sin, is a soul ripe for hell, a soul posting to destruction. Ah Lord! this mercy I humbly beg, that whatever thou givest me up to, thou wilt not give me up to the ways of my own heart; if thou wilt give me up to be afflicted, or tempted, or reproached, &c., I will patiently sit down, and say, It is the Lord; let him do with me what seems good in his own eyes. Do anything

---

[1] I have known a good man, saith Bernard, who, when he heard of any that had committed some notorious sin, he was wont to say with himself, ' *Ille hodie et ego cras*,' he fell to-day, so may I to-morrow.

[2] *Humanum est peccare, diabolicum perseverare, et angelicum resurgere.—Aug*[ustine]; *i.e.* It is a human thing to fall into sin, a devilish to persevere therein, and an angelical or supernatural to rise from it.

with me, lay what burden thou wilt upon me, so thou dost not give me up to the ways of my own heart.[1]

Remedy (2). The second remedy against this device of Satan is, solemnly to consider, *That God is as just as he is merciful.* As the Scriptures speak him out to be a very merciful God, so they speak him out to be a very just God. Witness his casting the angels out of heaven, 2 Peter ii. 4–6, and his binding them in chains of darkness[2] till the judgment of the great day ; and witness his turning Adam out of paradise, his drowning of the old world, and his raining hell out of heaven upon Sodom ; and witness all the crosses, losses, sicknesses, and diseases, that be in the world ; and witness Tophet, that was prepared of old ; witness his 'treasuring up of wrath against the day of wrath, unto the revelation of the just judgments of God ; but above all, witness the pouring forth of all his wrath upon his bosom Son, when he did bear the sins of his people, and cried out, ' My God, my God, why hast thou forsaken me ?' Mat. xxvii. 46.

Remedy (3). The third remedy against this device of Satan is, seriously to consider, *That sins against mercy will bring the greatest and sorest judgments upon men's heads and hearts.* Mercy is Alpha, Justice is Omega. David, speaking of these attributes, placeth mercy in the foreward, and justice in the rearward, saying, ' My song shall be of mercy and judgment,' Ps. ci. 1. When mercy is despised, then justice takes the throne.[4] God is like a prince, that sends not his army against rebels before he hath sent his pardon, and proclaimed it by a herald of arms : he first hangs out the white flag of mercy ; if this wins men in, they are happy for ever ; but if they stand out, then God will put forth his red flag of justice and judgment ; if the one is despised, the other shall be felt with a witness.[5]

See this in the Israelites. He loved them and chose them when they were in their blood, and most unlovely. He multiplied them, not by means, but by miracle ; from seventy souls they grew in few years to six hundred thousand ; the more they were oppressed, the more they prospered. Like camomile, the more you tread it, the more you spread it ; or to a palm-tree, the more it is pressed, the further it spreadeth ; or to fire, the more it is raked, the more it burneth. Their mercies came in upon them like Job's messengers, one upon the neck of the other : He put off their sackcloth, and girded them with gladness, and 'compassed them about with songs of deliverance ;' he ' carried them on the wings of eagles ;' he kept them 'as the apple of his eye,' &c.[6] But they, abusing his mercy, became the greatest objects of his wrath. As I know not the man that can reckon up

---

[1] *A me, me salva Domine ;* Deliver me, O Lord, from that evil man myself.—*Aug-* [*ustine*].

[2] God hanged them up in gibbets, as it were, that others might hear and fear, and do no more so wickedly.　　　　[3] Cf. Rom. ii. 5 ; but it is the sinner, not God.—G.

[4] *Quanto gradus altior, tanto casus gravior ;* the higher we are in dignity, the more grievous is our fall and misery.

[5] *Deus tardus est ad iram, sed tarditatem gravitate pœnæ compensat ;* God is slow to anger, but he recompenseth his slowness with grievousness of punishment. If we abuse mercy to serve our lust, then, in Salvian's phrase, God will rain hell out of heaven, rather than not visit for such sins.

[6] Ps. xxxii. 7 ; Exod. xix. 4 ; Deut. xxxii. 10.—G.

their mercies, so I know not the man that can sum up the miseries that are come upon them for their sins. For as our Saviour prophesied concerning Jerusalem, 'that a stone should not be left upon a stone,' so it was fulfilled forty years after his ascension, by Vespasian the emperor and his son Titus, who, having besieged Jerusalem, the Jews were oppressed with a grievous famine, in which their food was old shoes, old leather, old hay, and the dung of beasts. There died, partly of the sword and partly of the famine, eleven hundred thousand of the poorer sort; two thousand in one night were embowelled; six thousand were burned in a porch of the temple; the whole city was sacked and burned, and laid level to the ground; and ninety-seven thousand taken captives, and applied to base and miserable service, as Eusebius and Josephus saith.[1] And to this day, in all parts of the world, are they not the off-scouring of the world? None less beloved, and none more abhorred, than they.[2]

And so Capernaum, that was lifted up to heaven, was threatened to be thrown down to hell. No souls fall so low into hell, if they fall, as those souls that by a hand of mercy are lifted up nearest to heaven. You slight souls that are so apt to abuse mercy, consider this, that in the gospel days, the plagues that God inflicts upon the despisers and abusers of mercy are usually spiritual plagues; as blindness of mind, hardness of heart, benumbedness of conscience, which are ten thousand times worse than the worst of outward plagues that can befall you. And therefore, though you may escape temporal judgments, yet you shall not escape spiritual judgments: 'How shall we escape, if neglect so great salvation?' Heb. ii. 3,[3] saith the apostle. Oh! therefore, whenever Satan shall present God to the soul as one made up all of mercy, that he may draw thee to do wickedly, say unto him, that sins against mercy will bring upon the soul the greatest misery; and therefore whatever becomes of thee, thou wilt not sin against mercy, &c.

Remedy (4). The fourth remedy against this device of Satan, is seriously to consider, *That though God's general mercy be over all his works, yet his special mercy is confined to those that are divinely qualified.*[4] So in Exodus xxxiv. 6, 7, 'And the Lord passed by before me, and proclaimed, The Lord, the Lord God, merciful and gracious, longsuffering, and abundant in goodness and truth, keeping mercy for thousands, forgiving iniquity, transgression, and sin, and that will by no means clear the guilty.' Exodus xx. 6, 'And shewing mercy unto thousands of them that love me, and keep my command-

---

[1] Vespasian brake into their city at Kedron, where they took Christ, on the same feast day that Christ was taken; he whipped them where they whipped Christ; he sold twenty Jews for a penny, as they sold Christ for thirty pence.—*S. Andr. Cat.* [*Sic* in all editions; but qu. St Augustine, De Civitate Dei?—G.]

[2] Men are therefore worse, because they ought to be better; and shall be deeper in hell, because heaven was offered unto them; but they would not. *Ingentia beneficia, flagitia, supplicia.* Good turns aggravate unkindnesses, and men's offences are increased by their obligations. [Eusebius, Eccl Hist. *sub* Jerusal. Josephus, Jewish War, Book vi. 5, *et alibi.*—G.]   [3] ἐμιλήσαντες. Shift off, disregard.

[4] Augustus, in his solemn feasts, gave trifles to some, but gold to others that his heart was most set upon. So God, by a hand of general mercy, gives these—poor trifles —outward blessings, to those that he least loves; but his gold, his special mercy, is only towards those that his heart is most set upon.

ments.' Ps. xxv. 10, 'All the paths of the Lord are mercy and truth, unto such as keep his covenant, and his testimonies.' Ps. xxxii. 10, 'Many sorrows shall be to the wicked ; but he that trusteth in the Lord, mercy shall compass him about.' Ps. xxxiii. 18, 'Behold, the eye of the Lord is upon them that fear him, upon them that hope in his mercy.' Ps. ciii. 11, 'For as the heaven is high above the earth, so great is his mercy toward them that fear him.' Ver. 17, 'But the mercy of the Lord is from everlasting to everlasting upon them that fear him.' When Satan attempts to draw thee to sin by presenting God as a God all made up of mercy, oh then reply, that though God's general mercy extend to all the works of his hand, yet his special mercy is confined to them that are divinely qualified, to them that love him and keep his commandments, to them that trust in him, that by hope hang upon him, and that fear him ; and that thou must be such a one here, or else thou canst never be happy hereafter ; thou must partake of his special mercy, or else eternally perish in everlasting misery, notwithstanding God's general mercy.

Remedy (5). The fifth remedy against this device of Satan is, solemnly to consider, *That those that were once glorious on earth, and are now triumphing in heaven, did look upon the mercy of God as the most powerful argument to preserve them from sin, and to fence their souls against sin, and not as an encouragement to sin.* Ps. xxvi. 3–6, 'For thy loving-kindness is before mine eyes, and I have walked in thy truth ; I have not sat with vain persons, neither will I go in with dissemblers. I have hated the congregation of evil-doers, and will not sit with the wicked.' So Joseph strengthens himself against sin from the remembrance of mercy : 'How then can I,' saith he, 'do this great wickedness, and sin against God ?' Gen. xxxix. 9. He had fixed his eye upon mercy, and therefore sin could not enter, though the irons entered into his soul; his soul being taken with mercy, was not moved with his mistress's impudence. Satan knocked oft at the door, but the sight of mercy would not suffer him to answer or open. Joseph, like a pearl in a puddle, keeps his virtue still.[1] So Paul, 'Shall we continue in sin, that grace may abound ? God forbid. How shall we that are dead to sin, live any longer therein?' Rom. vi. 1, 2. There is nothing in the world that renders a man more unlike to a saint, and more like to Satan, than to argue from mercy to sinful liberty ; from divine goodness to licentiousness. This is the devil's logic, and in whomsoever you find it, you may write, 'This soul is lost.' A man may as truly say, the sea burns, or fire cools, as that free grace and mercy should make a soul truly gracious to do wickedly. So the same apostle, 'I beseech you therefore, brethren, by the mercies of God, that ye present your bodies a living sacrifice, holy, acceptable unto God, which is your reasonable service,' Rom. xii. 1. So John, 'These things I write unto you, that ye sin not,' 1 John ii. 1, 2. What was it that he wrote? . He wrote, 'That we might have fellowship with the Father and his Son ; and that the blood of Christ cleanseth us

---

[1] The stone called *Pontaurus*, is of that virtue, that it preserves him that carries it from taking any hurt by poison. The mercy of God in Christ to our souls is the most precious stone or pearl in the world, to prevent us from being poisoned with sin.

from all sin, and that if we confess our sin, he is just and faithful to forgive us our sins; and that if we do sin, we have an advocate with the Father, Jesus Christ the righteous.' These choice favours and mercies the apostle holds forth as the choicest means to preserve the soul from sin, and to keep at the greatest distance from sin; and if this won't do it, you may write the man void of Christ and grace, and undone for ever.

The sixth device that Satan hath to draw the soul to sin is,

Device (6). *By persuading the soul that the work of repentance is an easy work, and that therefore the soul need not make such a matter of sin.* Why! Suppose you do sin, saith Satan, it is no such difficult thing to return, and confess, and be sorrowful, and beg pardon, and cry, 'Lord, have mercy upon me;' and if you do but this, God will cut the score,[1] and pardon your sins, and save your souls, &c.

By this device Satan draws many a soul to sin, and makes many millions of souls servants or rather slaves to sin, &c.

Now, the remedies against this device of Satan are these that follow:

Remedy (1). The first remedy is, seriously to consider, *That repentance is a mighty work, a difficult work, a work that is above our power.* There is no power below that power that raised Christ from the dead, and that made the world, that can break the heart of a sinner or turn the heart of a sinner. Thou art as well able to melt adamant, as to melt thine own heart; to turn a flint into flesh, as to turn thine own heart to the Lord; to raise the dead and to make a world, as to repent. Repentance is a flower that grows not in nature's garden. 'Can the Ethiopian change his skin, or the leopard his spots? then may ye also do good, that are accustomed to do evil,' Jer. xiii. 23. Repentance is a gift that comes down from above.[2] Men are not born with repentance in their hearts, as they are born with tongues in their mouths:[3] Acts v. 31, 'Him hath God exalted with his right hand to be a Prince and a Saviour, for to give repentance to Israel, and forgiveness of sins.' So in 2 Tim. ii. 25, 'In meekness instructing them that oppose themselves; if God peradventure will give them repentance to the acknowledging of the truth.' It is not in the power of any mortal to repent at pleasure.[4] Some ignorant deluded souls vainly conceit that these five words, '*Lord! have mercy upon me,*' are efficacious to send them to heaven; but as many are undone by buying a counterfeit jewel, so many are in hell by mistake of their repentance. Many rest in their repentance, though it be but the shadow of repentance, which caused one to say, ' Repentance damneth more than sin.'

---

[1] The reference is to the 'scored' or notched sticks by which debt accounts were recorded anciently.—G.

[2] Fallen man hath lost (*imperium suum* and *imperium sui*) the command of himself, and the command of the creatures. And certainly he that cannot command himself cannot repent of himself.

[3] *Da pœnitentiam et postea indulgentiam*, said dying Fulgentius.

[4] It was a vain brag of king Cyrus, that caused it to be written upon his tombstone, πάντα ποιεῖν δυνάμην, I could do all things; so could Paul too, but it was 'through Christ, which strengthened him.' [Cf. Arrian vi. 29 : Plutarch, *Alexander*, 69.—G.]

Remedy (2). The second remedy against this device of Satan is, solemnly to consider *of the nature of true repentance.* Repentance is some other thing than what vain men conceive.[1]

Repentance is sometimes taken, in a more strict and narrow sense, for godly sorrow ; sometimes repentance is taken, in a large sense, for amendment of life. Repentance hath in it three things, viz. :

The act, subject, terms.

(1.) *The formal act of repentance is a changing and converting.* It is often set forth in Scripture by turning. 'Turn thou me, and I shall be turned,' saith Ephraim ; 'after that I was turned, J repented,' saith he, Jer. xxxi. 18. It is a turning from darkness to light.

(2.) *The subject changed and converted, is the whole man ;* it is both the sinner's heart and life : first his heart, then his life ; first his person, then his practice and conversation. 'Wash ye, make you clean,' there is the change of their persons ; 'Put away the evil of your doings from before mine eyes ; cease to do evil, learn to do well,' Isa. i. 16 ; there is the change of their practices. So 'Cast away,' saith Ezekiel, 'all your transgresssions whereby you have transgressed ;' there is the change of the life ; 'and make you a new heart and a new spirit,' xviii. 30 ; there is the change of the heart.

(3.) *The terms of this change and conversion, from which and to, which both heart and life must be changed ; from sin to God.* The heart must be changed from the state and power of sin, the life from the acts of sin, but both unto God ; the heart to be under his power in a state of grace, the life to be under his rule in all new obedience ; as the apostle speaks, 'To open their eyes, and to turn them from darkness to light, and from the power of Satan unto God,' Acts xxvi. 18. So the prophet Isaiah saith, 'Let the wicked forsake their ways, and the unrighteous man his thoughts, and let him return unto the Lord,' lv. 7.

Thus much of the nature of evangelical repentance. Now, souls, tell me whether it be such an easy thing to repent, as Satan doth suggest. Besides what hath been spoken, I desire that you will take notice, that repentance doth include turning from the most darling sin. Ephraim shall say, 'What have I to do any more with idols ?' Hosea xiv. 8. Yea, it is a turning from all sin to God : Ezek. xviii. 30, 'Therefore I will judge you, O house of Israel, every one of you according to his ways, saith the Lord God. Repent, and turn yourselves from your transgresssons ; so iniquity shall not be your ruin.

[1] The Hebrew word for repentance is תשובה, from שוב, which signifies to return, implying a going back from what a man had done. It notes a turning or converting from one thing to another, from sin to God. The Greeks have two words by which they express the nature of repentance, one is μεταμέλειν, which signifies to be careful, anxious, solicitous, after a thing is done ; the other word, μετάνοια, is *resipiscentia*, after-wit, or after-wisdom, the mind's recovering worth of wisdom, or growing wiser after our folly. Ab. ἄνοια *dementia, et μετὰ post*, it being the correction of men's folly, and returning *ad sanam mentem.* True repentance is a thorough change both of the mind and manners ; *optima et optissima pœnitentia est nova vita,* saith Luther, which saying is an excellent saying. Repentance *for* sin is nothing worth without repentance *from* sin. If thou repentest with a contradiction, saith Tertullian, God will pardon thee with a contradiction ; if thou repentest and yet continuest in thy sin, God will pardon thee, and yet send thee to hell ; there is a pardon with a contradiction. Negative goodness serves no man's turn to save him from the axe.

Herod turned from many, but turned not from his Herodias, which was his ruin. Judas turned from all visible wickedness, yet he would not cast out that golden devil covetousness, and therefore was cast into the hottest place in hell. He that turns not from every sin, turns not aright from any one sin. Every sin strikes at the honour of God, the being of God, the glory of God, the heart of Christ, the joy of the Spirit, and the peace of a man's conscience; and therefore a soul truly penitent strikes at all, hates all, conflicts with all, and will labour to draw strength from a crucified Christ to crucify all. A true penitent knows neither father nor mother, neither right eye nor right hand, but will pluck out the one and cut off the other. Saul spared but one Agag, and that cost him his soul and his kingdom, 1 Sam. xv. 9. Besides, repentance is not only a turning from all sin, but also a turning to all good; to a love of all good, to a prizing of all good, and to a following after all good : Ezek. xviii. 21, ' But if the wicked will turn from all the sins that he hath committed, and keep all my statutes, and do that which is lawful and right, he shall surely live, he shall not die ;' that is, only negative righteousness and holiness is no righteousness nor holiness.[1] David fulfilled *all* the will of God, and had respect unto *all* his commandments, and so had Zacharias and Elizabeth. It is not enough that the tree bears not ill fruit; but it must bring forth good fruit, else it must be ' cut down and cast into the fire,' Luke xiii. 7. So it is not enough that you are not thus and thus wicked, but you must be thus and thus gracious and good, else divine justice will put the axe of divine vengeance to the root of your souls, and cut you off for ever. ' Every tree that bringeth not forth good fruit is hewed down and cast into the fire,' Mat. iii. 10. Besides, repentance doth include a sensibleness of sin's sinfulness, how opposite and contrary it is to the blessed God. God is light, sin is darkness ; God is life, sin is death ; God is heaven, sin is hell ; God is beauty, sin is deformity.

Also true repentance includes a sensibleness of sin's mischievousness ; how it cast angels out of heaven, and Adam out of paradise ; how it laid the first corner stone in hell, and brought in all the curses, crosses, and miseries, that be in the world ; and how it makes men liable to all temporal, spiritual, and eternal wrath ; how it hath made men Godless, Christless, hopeless, and heavenless.

Further, true repentance doth include sorrow for sin, contrition of heart. It breaks the heart with sighs, and sobs, and groans, for that a loving God and Father is by sin offended, a blessed Saviour afresh crucified, and the sweet comforter, the Spirit, grieved and vexed.

Again, repentance doth include, not only a loathing of sin, but also a loathing of ourselves for sin. As a man doth not only loathe poison, but he loathes the very dish or vessel that hath the smell of the poison ; so a true penitent doth not only loathe his sin, but he loathes himself,

---

[1] It is said of Ithacus, that the hatred of the Priscilian heresy was all the virtue that he had. The evil servant did not riot out his talent, Mat. xxv. 18. Those reprobates, Mat. xxiii. 2, robbed not the saints, but relieved them not; for this they must eternally perish.

the vessel that smells of it; so Ezek. xx. 43, 'And there shall ye remember your ways and all your doings, wherein ye have been defiled; and ye shall loathe yourselves in your own sight for all your evils that ye have committed.' True repentance will work your hearts, not only to loathe your sins, but also to loathe yourselves.[1]

Again, true repentance doth not only work a man to loathe himself for his sins, but it makes him ashamed of his sin also: 'What fruit have ye of those things whereof ye are now ashamed?' saith the apostle, Rom. vi. 21. So Ezekiel, 'And thou shalt be confounded, and never open thy mouth any more, because of thy shame, when I am pacified toward thee for all that thou hast done, saith the Lord God,' xxxvi. 32. When a penitential soul sees his sins pardoned, the anger of God pacified, the divine justice satisfied, then he sits down and blushes, as the Hebrew hath it, as one ashamed. Yea, true repentance doth work a man to cross his sinful self, and to walk contrary to sinful self, to take a holy revenge upon sin, as you may see in Paul, the jailor, Mary Magdalene, and Manasseh. This the apostle shews in 2 Cor. vii. 10, 11: 'For godly sorrow worketh repentance never to be repented of; but the sorrow of the world worketh death. For behold the self-same thing, that ye sorrowed after a godly sort, what carefulness it wrought in you, yea, what clearing of yourselves, yea, what indignation, yea, what fear, yea, what vehement desire, yea, what zeal, yea, what revenge.'[2] Now, souls, sum up all these things together, and tell me whether it be such an easy thing to repent as Satan would make the soul to believe, and I am confident your heart will answer that it is as hard a thing to repent as it is to make a world, or raise the dead.

I shall conclude this second remedy with a worthy saying of a precious holy man: 'Repentance,' saith he, 'strips us stark naked of all the garments of the old Adam, and leaves not so much as a shirt behind.' In this rotten building it leaves not a stone upon a stone. As the flood drowned Noah's own friends and servants, so must the flood of repenting tears drown our sweetest and most profitable sins.

Remedy (3). The third remedy against this device of Satan is seriously to consider, *That repentance is a continued act.* The word *repent* implies the continuation of it.[3] True repentance inclines a man's heart to perform God's statutes always, even unto the end. A true penitent must go on from faith to faith, from strength to strength; he must never stand still nor turn back. Repentance is a grace, and must have its daily operation as well as other graces. True repentance is a continued spring, where the waters of godly sorrow are

---

[1] True repentance is a sorrowing for sin, as it is *offensivum Dei, aversivum a Deo.* This both comes from God, and drives a man to God, as it did the church in the Canticles, and the prodigal: Ezek. xiii. 22, 23.

[2] Quantum displicet Deo immunditia peccati, in tantum placet Deo erubescentia pœnitentis.—*Ber[nard]: i. e.* So much the more God hath been displeased with the blackness of sin, the more will he be pleased with the blushing of the sinner. They that do not burn now in zeal against sin, must ere long burn in hell for sin.

[3] Anselm in his Meditations confesseth, that all his life was either damnable for sin committed, or unprofitable for good omitted; at last concludes, *Quid restat, O peccator, nisi ut in tota vita tua deplores totam vitam tuam,* Oh, what then remains but in our whole life to lament the sins of our whole life.

always flowing: 'My sins are ever before me,' Ps. li. 3. A true penitent is often casting his eyes back to the days of his former vanity,
and this makes him morning and evening to 'water his couch with
his tears.' 'Remember not against me the sins of my youth,' saith
one blessed penitent; and 'I was a blasphemer, and a persecutor,
and injurious,' saith another penitent.[1] Repentance is a continued act
of turning, a repentance never to be repented of, a turning never to
turn again to folly. A true penitent hath ever something within him
to turn from; he can never get near enough to God; no, not so near
him as once he was; and therefore he is still turning and turning that
he may get nearer and nearer to him, that is his chiefest good and his
only happiness, *optimum maximum*, the best and the greatest.[2] They
are every day a-crying out, 'O wretched men that we are, who shall
deliver us from this body of death!' Rom. vii. 24. They are still sensible of sin, and still conflicting with sin, and still sorrowing for sin,
and still loathing of themselves for sin. Repentance is no transient
act, but a continued act of the soul. And tell me, O tempted soul,
whether it be such an easy thing as Satan would make thee believe,
to be every day a-turning more and more from sin, and a-turning
nearer and nearer to God, thy choicest blessedness. A true penitent
can as easily content himself with one act of faith, or one act of love,
as he can content himself with one act of repentance.

A Jewish Rabbi, pressing the practice of repentance upon his disciples, exhorting them to be sure to repent the day before they died,
one of them replied, that the day of any man's death was very uncertain. 'Repent, therefore, every day,' said the Rabbi, 'and then you
shall be sure to repent the day before you die.' You are wise, and
know how to apply it to your own advantage.

Remedy (4). The fourth remedy against this device of Satan is
solemnly to consider, *That if the work of repentance were such an
easy work as Satan would make it to be, then certainly so many
would not lie roaring and crying out of wrath and eternal ruin
under the horrors and terrors of conscience, for not repenting;
yea, doubtless, so many millions would not go to hell for not repenting, if it were such an easy thing to repent.*[3] Ah, do not poor souls
under horror of conscience cry out and say, Were all this world a lump
of gold, and in our hand to dispose of, we would give it for the least
drachm of true repentance! and wilt thou say it is an easy thing to
repent? When a poor sinner, whose conscience is awakened, shall
judge the exchange of all the world for the least drachm of repentance to be the happiest exchange that ever sinner made, tell me, O
soul, is it good going to hell? Is it good dwelling with the devouring
fire, with everlasting burnings? Is it good to be for ever separated

---

[1] Ps. vi. 6, xxv. 7, 1 Tim. i. 13.—G.

[2] It is truly said of God, that he is *Omnia super omnia*.

[3] If thou be backward in the thoughts of repentance, be forward in the thoughts of
hell, the flames whereof only the streams of the penitent eye can extinguish.—*Tertul-
[lian]*. Oh, how shalt thou tear and rend thyself! how shalt thou lament fruitless
repenting! What wilt thou say? Woe is me, that I have not cast off the burden of
sin; woe is me, that I have not washed away my spots, but am now pierced with
mine iniquities; now have I lost the surpassing joy of angels!—*Basil*.

from the blessed and glorious presence of God, angels, and saints, and
to be for ever shut out from those good things of eternal life, which
are so many, that they exceed number; so great, that they exceed
measure; so precious, that they exceed all estimation? We know it
is the greatest misery that can befall the sons of men; and would they
not prevent this by repentance, if it were such an easy thing to repent
as Satan would have it? Well, then, do not run the hazard of losing
God, Christ, heaven, and thy soul for ever, by hearkening to this device of Satan, viz., that it is an easy thing to repent, &c. If it be so
easy, why, then, do wicked men's hearts so rise against them that
press the doctrine of repentance in the sweetest way, and by the
strongest and the choicest arguments that the Scripture doth afford?
And why do they kill two at once : the faithful labourer's name and
their own souls, by their wicked words and actings, because they are
put upon repenting, which Satan tells them is so easy a thing? Surely,
were repentance so easy, wicked men would not be so much enraged
when that doctrine is, by evangelical considerations, pressed upon
them.

Remedy (5). The fifth remedy against this device of Satan is seriously to consider, *That to repent of sin is as great a work of grace
as not to sin.*[1] By our sinful falls the powers of the soul are weakened,
the strength of grace is decayed, our evidences for heaven are blotted,
fears and doubts in the soul are raised (will God once more pardon
this scarlet sin, and shew mercy to this wretched soul?), and corruptions in the heart are more advantaged and confirmed ; and the conscience of a man after falls is the more enraged or the more benumbed.
Now for a soul, notwithstanding all this, to repent of his falls, this
shews that it is as great a work of grace to repent of sin as it is not
to sin. Repentance is the vomit of the soul ; and of all physic, none
so difficult and hard as it is to vomit. The same means that tends to
preserve the soul from sin, the same means works the soul to rise by
repentance when it is fallen into sin. We know the mercy and loving-
kindness of God is one special means to keep the soul from sin ; as
David spake, 'Thy loving-kindness is always before mine eyes, and I
have walked in thy truth, and I have not sat with vain persons, neither will I go in with dissemblers. I have hated the congregation of
evil doers, and will not sit with the wicked,' Ps. xxvi. 3–5. So by the
same means the soul is raised by repentance out of sin, as you may
see in Mary Magdalene, who loved much, and wept much, because
much was forgiven her, Luke vii. 37–39, &c. So those in Hosea,
'Come, let us return unto the Lord ; for he hath torn, and he will
heal ; he hath smitten, and he will bind us up. After two days he
will revive us, in the third day he will raise us up, and we shall live
in his sight, or before his face,' Hos. vi. 1, 2 ; as the Hebrew [לפניו]
hath it, *i.e.* in his favour. Confidence in God's mercy and love, that
he would heal them, and bind up their wounds, and revive their dejected spirits, and cause them to live in his favour, was that which
did work their hearts to repent and return unto him.

---

[1] Yet it is better to be kept from sin than cured of sin by repentance, as it is better
for a man to be preserved from a disease than to be cured of the disease.

I might further shew you this truth in many other particulars, but this may suffice : only remember this in the general, that there is as much of the power of God, and love of God, and faith in God, and fear of God, and care to please God, zeal for the glory of God, 2 Cor. vii. 11, requisite to work a man to repent of sin, as there is to keep a man from sin ; by which you may easily judge, that to repent of sin is as great a work as not to sin. And now tell me, O soul, is it an easy thing not to sin? We know then certainly it is not an easy thing to repent of sin.

Remedy (6). The sixth remedy against this device of Satan is, seriously to consider, *That he that now tempts thee to sin upon this account, that repentance is easy, will, ere long, to work thee to despair, and for ever to break the neck of thy soul, present repentance as the difficultest and hardest work in the world ;* and to this purpose he will set thy sins in order before thee, and make them to say, ' We are thine, and we must follow thee.'[1] Now, Satan will help to work the soul to look up, and see God angry ; and to look inward, and to see conscience accusing and condemning ; and to look downwards, and see hell's mouth open to receive the impenitent soul : and all this to render the work of repentance impossible to the soul. What, saith Satan, dost thou think that that is easy which the whole power of grace cannot conquer while we are in this world ? Is it easy, saith Satan, to turn from some outward act of sin to which thou hast been addicted ? Dost thou not remember that thou hast often complained against such and such particular sins, and resolved to leave them ? and yet, to this hour, thou hast not, thou canst not ? What will it then be to turn from every sin ? Yea, to mortify and cut off those sins, those darling lusts, that are as joints and members, that be as right hands and right eyes ? Hast thou not loved thy sins above thy Saviour ? Hast thou not preferred earth before heaven ? Hast thou not all along neglected the means of grace ? and despised the offers of grace ? and vexed the Spirit of grace ? There would be no end, it I should set before thee the infinite evils that thou hast committed, and the innumerable good services that thou hast omitted, and the frequent checks of thy own conscience that thou hast contemned ; and therefore thou mayest well conclude that thou canst never repent, that thou shalt never repent. Now, saith Satan, do but a little consider thy numberless sins, and the greatness of thy sins, the foulness of thy sins, the heinousness of thy sins, the circumstances of thy sins, and thou shalt easily see that those sins that thou thoughtest to be but motes, are indeed mountains ; and is it not now in vain to repent of them ? Surely, saith Satan, if thou shouldest seek repentance and

---

[1] Beda tells of a certain great man that was admonished in his sickness to repent, who answered that he would not repent yet ; for if he should recover, his companions would laugh at him ; but, growing sicker and sicker, his friends pressed him again to repent, but then he told them it was too late. *Quia jam judicatus sum et condemnatus:* For now, said he, I am judged and condemned.

As one *Lamachus,* a commander, said to one of his soldiers that was brought before him for a misbehaviour, who pleaded he would do so no more, saith he, *Non licet in bello bis peccare,* no man must offend twice in war ; so God will not suffer men often to neglect the day of grace.

grace with tears, as Esau, thou shalt not find it ; thy glass is out, thy sun is set, the door of mercy is shut, the golden sceptre is taken in, and now thou that hast despised mercy, shalt be for ever destroyed by justice. For such a wretch as thou art to attempt repentance, is to attempt a thing impossible. It is impossible that thou, that in all thy life couldst never conquer one sin, shouldst master such a number-less number of sins ; which are so near, so dear, so necessary, and so profitable to thee, that have so long bedded and boarded with thee, that have been old acquaintance and companions with thee. Hast thou not often purposed, promised, vowed, and resolved to enter upon the practice of repentance, but to this day couldst never attain it ? Surely it is in vain to strive against the stream, where it is so impos-sible to overcome ; thou art lost and cast for ever ; to hell thou must, to hell thou shalt. Ah, souls ! he that now tempts you to sin, by suggesting to you the easiness of repentance, will at last work you to despair, and present repentance as the hardest work in all the world, and a work as far above man as heaven is above hell, as light is above darkness. Oh that you were wise, to break off your sins by timely repentance.[1]

Now the seventh device that Satan hath to draw the soul to sin is,

Device (7). *By making the soul bold to venture upon the occasions of sin.* Saith Satan, You may walk by the harlot's door, though you won't go into the harlot's bed ; you may sit and sup with the drunkard, though you won't be drunk with the drunkard ; you may look upon Jezebel's beauty, and you may play and toy with Delilah, though you do not commit wickedness with the one or the other ; you may with Achan handle the golden wedge, though you do not steal the golden wedge, &c.

Now the remedies against this device of the devil are these :

Remedy (1). The first remedy is, solemnly *to dwell upon those scriptures that do expressly command us to avoid the occasions of sin, and the least appearance of evil :* 1 Thes. v. 22, ' Abstain from all appearance of evil.' Whatsoever is heterodox, unsound, and un-savoury, shun it, as you would do a serpent in your way, or poison in your meat.[2]

Theodosius tare the Arian's arguments presented to him in writing, because he found them repugnant to the Scriptures ; and Austin retracted even ironies only, because they had the appearance of lying.

When God had commanded the Jews to abstain from swine's flesh, they would not so much as name it, but in their common talk would call a sow another thing. To abstain from all appearance of evil, is to do nothing wherein sin appears, or which hath a shadow of sin. Bernard glosseth finely, ' Whatever is of evil show,[3] or of ill report, that he may neither wound conscience nor credit.' We must shun and be shy of the very show and shadow of sin, if either we tender our credit abroad, or our comfort at home.

---

[1] Repentance is a work that must be timely done, or utterly undone for ever. *Aut pœnitendum aut pereundum.*

[2] Epiphanius saith that in the old law, when any dead body was carried by any house, they were enjoined to shut their doors and windows.

[3] *Quicquid est male coloratum.*

It was good counsel that Livia gave her husband Augustus : ' It behoveth thee not only not to do wrong, but not to seem to do so,' &c. : so Jude 23, ' And others save with fear, pulling them out of the fire, hating even the garment spotted by the flesh.' It is a phrase taken from legal uncleanness, which was contracted by touching the houses, the vessels, the garments, of unclean persons.[1] Under the law, men might not touch a menstruous cloth, nor God would not accept of a spotted peace-offering. So we must not only hate and avoid gross sins, but everything that may carry a savour or suspicion of sin ; we must abhor the very signs and tokens of sin. So in Prov. v. 8, ' Remove thy way far from her, and come not nigh the door of her house.' He that would not be burnt, must dread the fire ; he that would not hear the bell, must not meddle with the rope.[2] To venture upon the occasion of sin, and then to pray, ' Lead us not into temptation,' is all one as to thrust thy finger into the fire, and then to pray that it might not be burnt So, in Prov. iv. 14, 15, you have another command : ' Enter not into the path of the wicked, and go not in the way of evil men : avoid it, and pass not by it, turn from it, and pass away.' This triple gradation of Solomon sheweth with a great emphasis, how necessary it is for men to flee from all appearance of sin, as the seaman shuns sands and shelves, and as men shun those that have the plague-sores running upon them. As weeds do endanger the corn, as bad humours do endanger the blood, or as an infected house doth endanger the neighbourhood ; so doth the company of the bad endanger those that are good. Entireness[3] with wicked consorts is one of the strongest chains of hell, and binds us to a participation of both sin and punishment.

Remedy (2). The second remedy against this device of Satan is, solemnly to consider, *That ordinarily there is no conquest over sin, without the soul turns from the occasion of sin.* It is impossible for that man to get the conquest of sin, that plays and sports with the occasions of sin. God will not remove the temptation, except you turn from the occasion. It is a just and righteous thing with God, that he should fall into the pit, that will adventure to dance upon the brink of the pit, and that he should be a slave to sin, that will not flee from the occasions of sin. As long as there is fuel in our hearts for a temptation, we cannot be secure. He that hath gunpowder about him had need keep far enough off from sparkles. To rush upon the occasions of sin, is both to tempt ourselves, and to tempt Satan to tempt our souls. It is very rare that any soul plays with the occasions of sin, but that soul is ensnared by sin.[4] It is seldom that God keeps that soul from the acts of sin, that will not keep off from the occasions of sin. He that adventures upon the occasions of sin is as he that would quench the fire with oil, which is a fuel to maintain it, and

---

[1] Socrates speaks of two young men that flung away their belts, when, being in an idol's temple, the lustrating water fell upon them, detesting, saith the historian, the garment spotted by the flesh. [The ecclesiastical historian, *not* the philosopher.—G.]

[2] One said, As oft as I have been among vain men, I returned home less a man than I was before.   [3] Friendship.—G.

[4] The fable saith, that the butterfly asked the owl how she should deal with the fire which had singed her wings, who counsels her not to behold so much as its smoke.

increase it. Ah, souls, often remember how frequently you have been overcome by sin, when you have boldly gone upon the occasions of sin ; look back, souls, to the day of your vanity, wherein you have been as easily conquered as tempted, vanquished as assaulted, when you have played with the occasions of sin. As you would for the future be kept from the acting of sin, and be made victorious over sin, oh ! flee from the occasions of sin.

Remedy (3). The third remedy against this device of Satan is, seriously to consider, *That other precious saints, that were once glorious on earth, and are now triumphing in heaven, have turned from the occasion of sin, as hell itself ;* as you may see in Joseph, Gen. xxxix. 10, ' And it came to pass, as she spake to Joseph day by day, that he hearkened not unto her, to lie by her, or to be with her.'[1] Joseph was famous for all the four cardinal virtues, if ever any were. In this one temptation you may see his fortitude, justice, temperance, and prudence, in that he shuns the occasion : for he would not so much as be with her. And that a man is indeed, that he is in a temptation, which is but a tap to give vent to corruption. The Nazarite might not only not drink wine, but not taste a grape, or the husk of a grape. The leper was to shave his hair, and pare his nails. The devil counts a fit occasion half a conquest, for he knows that corrupt nature hath a seed-plot for all sin, which being drawn forth and watered by some sinful occasion, is soon set a-work to the producing of death and destruction. God will not remove the temptation, till we remove the occasion. A bird whiles aloft is safe, but she comes not near the snare without danger. The shunning the occasions of sin renders a man most like the best of men. A soul eminently gracious, dares not come near the train, though he be far off the blow. So Job xxxi. 1, ' I have made a covenant with mine eyes ; why then should I think upon a maid ? '[2] I set a watch at the entrance of my senses, that my soul might not by them be infected or endangered. The eye is the window of the soul, and if that should be always open, the soul might smart for it. A man may not look intently upon that, that he may not love entirely. The disciples were set a-gog, by beholding the beauty of the temple. It is best and safest to have the eye always fixed upon the highest and noblest objects : as the mariner's eye is fixed upon the star, when their hand is on the stern. So David, when he was himself, he shuns the occasion of sin : Ps. xxvi. 4, 5, ' I have not sat with vain persons, neither will I go in with dissemblers ; I have hated the congregation of evil doers, and will not sit with the wicked.'

Stories speak of some that could not sleep when they thought of the trophies of other worthies, that went before them. The highest and choicest examples are to some, and should be to all, very quickening and provoking ; and oh that the examples of those worthy saints, David, Joseph, and Job, might prevail with all your souls to shun and

[1] There are stories of heathens that would not look upon beauties, lest they should be ensnared. Democritus plucked out his own eyes to avoid the danger of uncleanness.

[2] ברית ברתי, I cut a covenant. In making covenants, it was a custom among the Jews to cut some beast or other in pieces, and so walk between the pieces, to signify that they desired God to destroy them that should break the covenant.

avoid the occasions of sin! Every one should strive to be like to them in grace, that they desire to be equal with in glory. He that shooteth at the sun, though he be far short, will shoot higher than he that aimeth at a shrub. It is best, and it speaks out much of Christ within, to eye the highest and the worthiest examples.

Remedy (4). The fourth remedy against this device of Satan is, solemnly to consider, *That the avoiding the occasions of sin, is an evidence of grace, and that which lifts up a man above most other men in the world.*[1] That a man is indeed, which he is in temptation; and when sinful occasions do present themselves before the soul, this speaks out both the truth and the strength of grace; when with Lot, a man can be chaste in Sodom, and with Timothy can live temperate in Asia, among the luxurious Ephesians; and with Job can walk uprightly in the land of Uz, where the people were profane in their lives, and superstitious in their worship; and with Daniel be holy in Babylon; and with Abraham righteous in Chaldea; and with Nehemiah, zealous in Damasco, &c. Many a wicked man is big and full of corruption, but shews it not for want of occasion; but that man is surely good, who in his course will not be bad, though tempted by occasions. A Christless soul is so far from refusing occasions when they come in his way, that he looks and longs after them, and rather than he will go without them he will buy them, not only with love or money, but also with the loss of his soul. Nothing but grace can fence a man against the occasions of sin, when he is strongly tempted thereunto. Therefore, as you would cherish a precious evidence in your own bosoms of the truth and strength of your graces, shun all sinful occasions.

The eighth device that Satan hath to draw the soul to sin, is,

Device (8). *By representing to the soul the outward mercies that vain men enjoy, and the outward miseries that they are freed from, whilst they have walked in the ways of sin.* Saith Satan, Dost thou see, O soul, the many mercies that such and such enjoy, that walk in those very ways that thy soul startles to think of, and the many crosses that they are delivered from, even such as makes other men, that 'say they dare not walk in such ways, to spend their days in sighing, weeping, groaning, and mourning? and therefore, saith Satan, if ever thou wouldst be freed from the dark night of adversity, and enjoy the sunshine of prosperity, thou must walk in their ways.[2]

By this stratagem the devil took those in Jer. xliv. 16–18, ' As for the word that thou hast spoken unto us in the name of the Lord, we will not hearken unto thee : but we will certainly do whatsoever thing goeth forth of our mouth, to burn incense unto the queen of heaven, and to pour out drink-offerings unto her, as we have done, we, and our fathers, our kings, and our princes, in the cities of Judah, and

---

[1] Plutarch saith of Demosthenes, that he was excellent at praising the worthy acts of his ancestors, but not so at imitating them. Oh that this were not applicable to many professors in our times!

[2] It was a weighty saying of Seneca, *Nihil est infelicius eo, cui nil unquam contigit adversi,* there is nothing more unhappy than he who never felt adversity. Some of the heathens would be wicked as their gods were, counting it a dishonour to their god to be unlike him.— *Lactantius.*

in the streets of Jerusalem : for then had we plenty of victuals, and were well, and saw no evil.   But since we left off to burn incense to the queen of heaven, and to pour out drink-offerings unto her, we have wanted all things, and have been consumed by the sword and by the famine.'   This is just the language of a world of ignorant, pro-fane, and superstitious souls in London, and England, that would have made them a captain to return to bondage, yea, to that bondage that was worse than that the Israelites groaned under.   Oh, say they, since such and such persons have been put down, and left off, we have had nothing but plundering and taxing, and butchering of men, &c. ; and therefore we will do as we, and our kings, and nobles, and fathers have formerly done, for then had we plenty at home, and peace abroad, &c., and there was none to make us afraid.[1]

Now the remedies against this device of Satan are these that follow :

Remedy (1). The first remedy is, solemnly to consider, *That no man knows how the heart of God stands by his hand.*   His hand of mercy may be towards a man, when his heart may be against that man, as you may see in Saul and others ; and the hand of God may be set against a man, when the heart of God is dearly set upon a man, as you may see in Job and Ephraim.[2]   The hand of God was sorely set against them, and yet the heart and bowels of God were strongly working towards them.   No man knoweth either love or hatred by out-ward mercy or misery ; for all things come alike to all, to the right-eous and to the unrighteous, to the good and to the bad, to the clean and to the unclean, &c.   The sun of prosperity shines as well upon brambles of the wilderness as fruit-trees of the orchard ; the snow and hail of adversity lights upon the best garden as well as the stinking dunghill or the wild waste.   Ahab's and Josiah's ends concur in the very circumstances.   Saul and Jonathan, though different in their natures, deserts, and deportments, yet in their deaths they were not divided.   Health, wealth, honours, &c., crosses, sicknesses, losses, &c., are cast upon good men and bad men promiscuously.   'The whole Turkish empire is nothing else but a crust, cast by heaven's great housekeeper to his dogs.'[3]   Moses dies in the wilderness as well as those that murmured.   Nabal is rich, as well as Abraham ; Ahithophel wise, as well as Solomon ; and Doeg honoured by Saul, as well as Joseph was by Pharaoh.   Usually the worst of men have most of these outward things ; and the best of men have least of earth, though most of heaven.

Remedy (2). The second remedy against this device of Satan is, seriously to consider, *That there is nothing in the world that doth so*

---

[1] It is said of one of the emperors, that Rome had no war in his days, because it was plague enough to have such an emperor.   You are wise, and know how to apply it.   [The allusion, no doubt, is to Charles I., and the agitation for the Restoration of Charles II   Cromwell died Sept. 3. 1658.—G.]

[2] Tully judged the Jews' religion to be naught, because they were so often overcome, and impoverished, and afflicted; and the religion of Rome to be right, because the Romans prospered and became lords of the world ; and yet, though the Romans had his hand, yet the Jews had his heart, for they were dearly beloved though sorely afflicted. [Brooks's reference is found in Cicero, in Orat. Pro L. Flacco 28.—G.]

[3] Nihil est nisi mica panis.—*Luther.*

*provoke God to be wroth and angry, as men's taking encouragement
from God's goodness and mercy to do wickedly.* This you may see
by that wrath that fell upon the old world, and by God's raining
hell out of heaven upon Sodom and Gomorrah. This is clear in Jeremiah xliv., from ver. 20 to ver. 28. The words are worthy of your
best meditation. Oh that they were engraven in all your hearts, and
constant in all your thoughts! Though they are too large for me to
transcribe them, yet they are not too large for me to remember them.
To argue from mercy to sinful liberty, is the devil's logic, and such
logicians do ever walk as upon a mine of gunpowder ready to be blown
up. No such soul can ever avert or avoid the wrath of God. This is
wickedness at the height, for a man to be very bad, because God is
very good. A worse spirit than this is not in hell. Ah, Lord, doth
not wrath, yea, the greatest wrath, lie at this man's door? Are not the
strongest chains of darkness prepared for such a soul? To sin against
mercy is to sin against humanity. It is bestial; nay, it is worse.
To render good for evil is divine, to render good for good is human,
to render evil for evil is brutish; but to render evil for good is devilish;
and from this evil deliver my soul, O God.[1]

Remedy (3). The third remedy against this device of Satan is,
solemnly to consider, *That there is no greater misery in this life,
than not to be in misery; no greater affliction, than not to be
afflicted.* Woe, woe to that soul that God will not spend a rod upon!
This is the saddest stroke of all, when God refuses to strike at all:
Hos. iv. 17, 'Ephraim is joined to idols; let him alone.' 'Why
should you be smitten any more? you will revolt more and more,' Isa.
i. 5. When the physician gives over the patient, you say, 'Ring out
his knell, the man is dead.' So when God gives over a soul to sin
without control, you may truly say, 'This soul is lost,' you may ring
out his knell, for he is twice dead, and plucked up by the roots. Freedom from punishment is the mother of security, the step-mother of
virtue, the poison of religion, the moth of holiness, and the introducer
of wickedness. 'Nothing,' said one, 'seems more unhappy to me, than
he to whom no adversity hath happened.' Outward mercies ofttimes
prove a snare to our souls. 'I will lay a stumbling-block,' Ezek. iii.
20. Vatablus his note there is, 'I will prosper him in all things,
and not by affliction restrain him from sin.'[2] Prosperity hath been a
stumbling-block, at which millions have stumbled and fallen, and
broke the neck of their souls for ever.[3]

Remedy (4). The fourth remedy against this device of Satan is,
seriously to consider, *That the wants of wicked men, under all their
outward mercy and freedom from adversity, is far greater than all
their outward enjoyments.* They have many mercies, yet they want
more than they enjoy; the mercies which they enjoy are nothing to the

---

[1] Such souls make God a god of *clouts*, one that will not do as he saith; but they shall
find God to be as severe in punishing as he is to others gracious in pardoning. Good
turns aggravate unkindnesses, and our guilt is increased by our obligations.

[2] Faciam ut omnia habeat prospera; calamitatibus eum a peccato non revocabo.
[Annot. in Lib. Vet. Test. Paris, 1557.—G.]

[3] *Religio peperit divitias, et filia devoravit matrem;* religion brought forth riches, and
the daughter soon devoured the mother, saith Augustine.

mercies they want. It is true, they have honours and riches, and pleasures and friends, and are mighty in power; their seed is established in their sight with them, and their offspring before their eyes : 'Their houses are safe from fear, neither is the rod of God upon them;' 'They send forth their little ones like a flock, and their children dance. They take the timbrel and harp, and rejoice at the sound of the organ;' 'They spend their days in wealth, their eyes stand out with fatness, they have more than heart can wish : and they have no bands in their death, but their strength is firm; they are not in trouble as other men,' as David and Job speak.[1] Yet all this is nothing to what they want.[2] They want interest in God, Christ, the Spirit, the promises, the covenant of grace, and everlasting glory; they want acceptation and reconciliation with God; they want righteousness, justification, sanctification, adoption, and redemption; they want the pardon of sin, and power against sin, and freedom from the dominion of sin; they want that favour that is better than life, and that joy that is unspeakable and full of glory, and that peace that passes understanding, and that grace, the least spark of which is more worth than heaven and earth; they want a house that hath foundations, whose builder and maker is God; they want those riches that perish not, the glory that fades not, that kingdom that shakes not. Wicked men are the most needy men in the world, yea, they want those two things that should render their mercies sweet, viz., the blessing of God, and content with their condition, and without which their heaven is but hell on this side hell.[3] When their hearts are lifted up and grown big upon the thoughts of their abundance, if conscience does but put in a word and say, It is true, here is this and that outward mercy. Oh, but where is an interest in Christ? Where is the favour of God? Where are the comforts of the Holy Ghost? Where are the evidences for heaven? &c. This word from conscience makes the man's countenance to change, his thoughts to be troubled, his heart to be amazed, and all his mercies on the right hand and left to be as dead and withered. Ah, were but the eyes of wicked men open to see their wants under their abundance, they would cry out and say, as Absalom did, 'What are all these to me so long as I cannot see the king's face?' 2 Sam. xiv. 24, 33. What is honour, and riches, and the favour of creatures, so long as I want the favour of God, the pardon of my sins, an interest in Christ, and the hopes of glory! O Lord, give me these, or I die; give me these, or else I shall eternally die.

Remedy (5). The fifth remedy against this device of Satan is, solemnly to consider, *That outward things are not as they seem, and are esteemed.* They have, indeed, a glorious outside, but if you view

---

[1] Cf. Psalm xlix. 11, lxxiii. 7; Job xxi. 12, &c., &c.—G.

[2] Men that enjoy all worldly comforts may truly say, *Omnes humanæ consolationes sunt desolationes.*

[3] *Nec Christus nec cœlum patitur hyperbolem*, neither Christ nor heaven can be hyperbolised. A crown of gold cannot cure the headache, nor a velvet slipper cannot ease the gout; no more can honour or riches quiet and still the conscience. The heart of man is a three-square triangle, which the whole round circle of the world cannot fill, as mathematicians say, but all the corners will complain of emptiness, and hunger for something else.

their insides, you will easily find that they fill the head full of cares, and the heart full of fears. What if the fire should consume one part of my estate, and the sea should be a grave to swallow up another part of my estate! what if my servants should be unfaithful abroad, and my children should be deceitful at home! Ah, the secret fretting, vexing, and gnawing that doth daily, yea hourly, attend those men's souls whose hands are full of worldly goods!

It was a good speech of an emperor, ' You,' said he, ' gaze on my purple robe and golden crown, but did you know what cares are under it, you would not take it up from the ground to have it.' It was a true saying of Augustine on the 26th Psalm, ' Many are miserable by loving hurtful things, but they are more miserable by having them.'[1] It is not what men enjoy, but the principle from whence it comes, that makes men happy. Much of these outward things do usually cause great distraction, great vexation, and great condemnation at last, to the possessors of them. If God gives them in his wrath, and do not sanctify them in his love, they will at last be witnesses against a man, and millstones for ever to sink a man in that day when God shall call men to an account, not for the use, but for the abuse of mercy.

Remedy (6). The sixth remedy against this device of Satan is, seriously to consider *the end and the design of God in heaping up mercy upon the heads of the wicked, and in giving them a* quietus est, *rest and quiet from those sorrows and sufferings that others sigh under.* David, in Psalm lxxiii. 17–20, shews the end and design of God in this. Saith he, ' When I went into the sanctuary of God, then I understood their end: surely thou didst set them in slippery places, thou castedst them down into destruction. How are they brought into desolation as in a moment: they are utterly consumed with terrors. As a dream, when one awaketh, so, O Lord, when thou awakest, thou shalt despise their image.'[2] So in Ps. xcii. 7, ' When the wicked spring as grass, and when all the workers of iniquity do flourish, it is that they shall be destroyed for ever.' God's setting them up, is but in order to his casting them down; his raising them high, is but in order to his bringing them low: Exod. ix. 16, ' And in very deed, for this cause have I raised thee up, for to shew in thee my power, and that my name may be declared throughout all the earth.' I have constituted and set thee up as a butt-mark,[3] that I may let fly at thee, and follow thee close with plague upon plague, till I have beaten the very breath out of thy body, and got myself a name, by setting my feet upon the neck of all thy pride, power, pomp, and glory. Ah, souls, what man in his wits would be lifted up that he might be cast down; would be set higher than others, when it is but

---

[1] Multi amando res noxias sunt miseri, habendo miseriores.—*Augustine* on Psalm xxvi.—G.

[2] Valens, the Roman emperor, fell from being an emperor to be a footstool to Sapor, king of Persia. Dionysius, king of Sicily, fell from his kingly glory to be a school-master. The brave Queen Zenobia was brought to Rome in golden chains. Valens, an emperor, Belisarius, a famous general, Henry the Fourth, Bajazet, Pythias, great Pompey, and William the Conqueror, these, from being very high, were brought very low; they all fell from great glory and majesty to great poverty and misery.

[3] Arrow-mark or target.—G.

in order to his being brought down lower than others? There is not a wicked man in the world that is set up with Lucifer, as high as heaven, but shall with Lucifer be brought down as low as hell. Canst thou think seriously of this, O soul, and not say, O Lord, I humbly crave that thou wilt let me be little in this world, that I may be great in another world; and low here, that I may be high for ever hereafter.[1] Let me be low, and feed low, and live low, so I may live with thee for ever; let me now be clothed with rags, so thou wilt clothe me at last with thy robes; let me now be set upon a dunghill, so I may at last be advanced to sit with thee upon thy throne. Lord, make me rather gracious than great, inwardly holy than outwardly happy, and rather turn me into my first nothing, yea, make me worse than nothing, rather than set me up for a time, that thou mayest bring me low for ever.

Remedy (7). The seventh remedy against this device of Satan is solemnly to consider, *That God doth often most plague and punish those whom others think he doth most spare and love;* that is, God doth plague and punish them most with spiritual judgments—which are the greatest, the sorest, and the heaviest—whom he least punishes with temporal punishments.[2] There are no men on earth so internally plagued as those that meet with least external plagues. Oh the blindness of mind, the hardness of heart, the searedness of conscience, that those souls are given up to, who, in the eye of the world, are reputed the most happy men, because they are not outwardly afflicted and plagued as other men. Ah, souls, it were better that all the temporal plagues that ever befell the children of men since the fall of Adam should at once meet upon your souls, than that you should be given up to the least spiritual plague, to the least measure of spiritual blindness or spiritual hardness of heart, &c. Nothing will better that man, nor move that man, that is given up to spiritual judgments. Let God smile or frown, stroke or strike, cut or kill, he minds it not, he regards it not; let life or death, heaven or hell, be set before him, it stirs him not; he is mad upon his sin, and God is fully set to do justice upon his soul. This man's preservation is but a reservation unto a greater condemnation; this man can set no bounds to himself; he is become a brat of fathomless perdition; he hath guilt in his bosom and vengeance at his back wherever he goes. Neither ministry nor misery, neither miracle nor mercy, can mollify his heart, and if this soul be not in hell, on this side hell, who is?[3]

Remedy (8). The eighth remedy against this device of Satan is, *To dwell more upon that strict account that vain men must make for all that good that they do enjoy.*[4] Ah! did men dwell more

---

[1] Da Domine, ut sic possideamus temporalia, ut non perdamus æterna. Grant us, Lord, that we may so partake of temporal felicity, that we may not lose eternal.—*Bernard.*

[2] Psalm lxxxi. 12, lxxviii. 26–31, cvi. 15. He gave them their requests, but sent leanness into their soul. It is a heavy plague to have a fat body and a lean soul; a house full of gold, and a heart full of sin.

[3] It is better to have a sore than a seared conscience. It is better to have no heart than a hard heart, no mind than a blind mind.

[4] In this day men shall give an account (De bonis commissis, de bonis dimissis, de malis commissis, de malis permissis) of good things committed unto them, of good things

upon that account that they must ere long give for all the mercies, that they have enjoyed, and for all the favours that they have abused, and for all the sins they have committed, it would make their hearts to tremble and their lips to quiver, and rottenness to enter into their bones; it would cause their souls to cry out, and say, Oh that our mercies had been fewer and lesser, that our account might have been easier, and our torment and misery, for our abuse of so great mercy, not greater than we are able to bear. Oh cursed be the day wherein the crown of honour was set upon our heads, and the treasures of this world were cast into our laps; oh cursed be the day wherein the sun of prosperity shined so strong upon us, and this flattering world smiled so much upon us, as to occasion us to forget God, to slight Jesus Christ, to neglect our souls, and to put far from us the day of our account!

Philip the Third of Spain, whose life was free from gross evils, professed, ' That he would rather lose his kingdom than offend God willingly;' yet being in the agony of death, and considering more thoroughly of his account he was to give to God, fear struck into him, and these words brake from him: ' Oh! would to God I had never reigned. Oh that those years that I have spent in my kingdom, I had lived a solitary life in the wilderness! Oh that I had lived a solitary life with God! How much more securely should I now have died! How much more confidently should I have gone to the throne of God! What doth all my glory profit me, but that I have so much the more torment in my death?' God keeps an exact account of every penny that is laid out upon him and his, and that is laid out against him and his; and this in the day of account men shall know and feel, though now they wink and will not understand. The sleeping of vengeance causeth the overflowing of sin, and the overflowing of sin causeth the awakening of vengeance. Abused mercy will certainly turn into fury. God's forbearance is no quittance. The day is at hand when he will pay wicked men for the abuse of old and new mercies. If he seem to be slow, yet he is sure. He hath leaden heels, but iron hands. The farther he stretcheth his bow, or draweth his arrow, the deeper he will wound in the day of vengeance. Men's actions are all in print in heaven, and God will, in the day of account, read them aloud in the ears of all the world, that they may all say Amen to that righteous sentence that he shall pass upon all despisers and abusers of mercy.[1]

The ninth device that Satan hath to draw the soul to sin is,

Device (9). By presenting to the soul the crosses, losses, reproaches, sorrows, and sufferings that do daily attend those that walk in the ways of holiness. Saith Satan, Do not you see that there are none in the world that are so vexed, afflicted, and tossed, as those that walk more circumspectly and holily than their neighbours?

neglected by them, of evil committed by them, and of evils suffered [allowed] by them. In die judicii plus valebit conscientia pura, quam marsupia plena; then shall a good conscience be more worth than all the world's good.—Bernard.

[1] Hierom [Jerome] still thought that voice was in his ears (Surgite mortui et venite ad judicium), Arise, you dead, and come to judgment. As oft as I think on that day, how doth my whole body quake, and my heart within me tremble.

They are a byword at home, and a reproach abroad; their miseries come in upon them like Job's messengers, one upon the neck of another, and there is no end of their sorrows and troubles. Therefore, saith Satan, you were better walk in ways that are less troublesome, and less afflicted, though they be more sinful; for who but a madman would spend his days in sorrow, vexation, and affliction, when it may be prevented by walking in the ways that I set before him?

Now the remedies against this device of Satan are these:

Remedy (1). The first remedy against this device of Satan is, solemnly to consider, *That all the afflictions that do attend the people of God, are such as shall turn to the profit and glorious advantage of the people of God.* They shall discover that filthiness and vileness in sin, that yet the soul hath never seen.

It was a speech of a German divine[1] in his sickness, 'In this disease I have learned how great God is, and what the evil of sin is; I never knew to purpose what God was before, nor what sin meant, till now.' Afflictions are a crystal glass, wherein the soul hath the clearest sight of the ugly face of sin. In this glass the soul comes to see sin to be but a bitter-sweet; yea, in this glass the soul comes to see sin not only to be an evil, but to be the greatest evil in the world, to be an evil far worse than hell itself.

Again, They shall contribute to the mortifying and purging away of their sins, Isa. i. 15, and xxvii. 8, 9. Afflictions are God's furnace, by which he cleanses his people from their dross. Affliction is a fire to purge out our dross, and to make virtue shine; it is a potion to carry away ill humours, better than all the *benedictum medicamentum*, as physicians call them.[2] Aloes kill worms; colds and frosts do destroy vermin; so do afflictions the corruptions that are in our hearts. The Jews, under all the prophet's thunderings, retained their idols; but after their Babylonish captivity, it is observed, there have been no idols found amongst them.

Again, Afflictions are sweet preservatives to keep the saints from sin, which is a greater evil than hell itself. As Job spake, 'Surely it is meet to be said unto God, I have borne chastisement, I will not offend any more: That which I see not, teach thou me; if I have done iniquity, I will do no more. Once have I spoken foolishly, yea, twice, I will do so no more,' Job xxxiv. 31, 32. The burnt child dreads the fire. Ah! saith the soul under the rod, sin is but a bitter-sweet; and for the future I intend, by the strength of Christ, that I will not buy repentance at so dear a rate.[3]

The Rabbins, to scare their scholars from sin, were wont to tell them, 'That sin made God's head ache;' and saints under the rod have found by woful experience, that sin makes not only their heads, but their hearts ache also.

Augustine, by wandering out of his way, escaped one that lay in

---

[1] Gaspar Olevianus (1586).—G.

[2] In times of peace our armour is rusty, in time of war it is bright.

[3] Salt brine preserves from putrefaction, and salt marshes keep the sheep rom the rot: so do afflictions the saints from sin. The ball in the Emblem saith, *Percussa surgo*, the harder you beat me down in affliction, the higher I shall bound in affection towards heaven and heavenly things.

wait to mischief him.[1]   If afflictions did not put us out of our way, we should many times meet with some sin or other that would mischief our precious souls.

Again, They will work the saints to be more fruitful in holiness: Heb. xii. 10, 11, ' But he afflicts us for our profit, that we might be partakers of his holiness.'   The flowers smell sweetest after a shower; vines bear the better for bleeding; the walnut-tree is most fruitful when most beaten.   Saints spring and thrive most internally when they are most externally afflicted.   Afflictions are called by some ' the mother of virtue.'   Manasseh his chain was more profitable to him than his crown.   Luther could not understand some Scriptures till he was in affliction.   The Christ-cross is no letter, and yet that taught him more than all the letters in the row.   God's house of correction is his school of instruction.[2]   All the stones that came about Stephen's ears did but knock him closer to Christ, the corner-stone.   The waves did but lift Noah's ark nearer to heaven; and the higher the waters grew, the more near the ark was lifted up to heaven.   Afflictions do lift up the soul to more rich, clear, and full enjoyments of God :[3] Hosea ii. 14, ' Behold, I will allure her into the wilderness, and speak comfortably to her' ; (or rather, as the Hebrew hath it) ; ' I will earnestly or vehemently speak to her heart.'[4]   God makes afflictions to be but inlets to the soul's more sweet and full enjoyment of his blessed self.   When was it that Stephen saw the heavens open, and Christ standing at the right hand of God, but when the stones were about his ears, and there was but a short step betwixt him and eternity ?   And when did God appear in his glory to Jacob, but in the day of his troubles, when the stones were his pillows, and the ground his bed, and the hedges his curtains, and the heavens his canopy ?   Then he saw the angels of God ascending and descending in their glistering robes.   The plant in Nazianzen grows with cutting ; being cut, it flourisheth ; it contends with the axe, it lives by dying, and by cutting it grows.[5]   So do saints by their afflictions that do befall them ; they gain more experience of the power of God supporting them, of the wisdom of God directing them, of the grace of God refreshing and cheering them, and of the goodness of God quieting and quickening of them, to a greater love to holiness, and to a greater delight in holiness, and to a more vehement pursuing after holiness.

I have read of a fountain, that at noonday is cold, and at midnight it grows warm ; so many a precious soul is cold God-wards, and heaven-wards, and holiness-wards, in the day of prosperity ; that grow warm God-wards and heaven-wards, and holiness-wards, in the midnight of adversity.

Again, Afflictions serve to keep the hearts of the saints humble and

---

[1] Confessions.—G.   [2] Schola crucis, schola lucis.
[3] Cf. ' Epistle' prefixed to Durant's *Altum Silentium*, by Brooks.—G.
[4] על לבה . . . . ודברתי   *Vedibbartignal libbab.*
[5] It is reported of Tiberius the emperor, that passing by a place where he saw a cross lying in the ground upon a marble stone, and causing the stone to be digged up, he found a great deal of treasure under the cross.   So many a precious saint hath found much spiritual and heavenly treasure under the crosses they have met withal.

tender : Lam. iii. 19, 20, 'Remembering my affliction and my misery, the wormwood and the gall. My soul hath them still in remembrance, and is humbled in me,' or bowed down in me, as the original hath it.[1] So David, when he was under the rod, could say, 'I was dumb, I opened not my mouth ; because thou didst it,' Ps. xxxix. 4.

I have read of one [Gregory Nazianzen], who, when anything fell out prosperously, would read over the Lamentation of Jeremiah, and that kept his heart tender, humbled, and low. Prosperity doth not contribute more to the puffing up the soul, than adversity doth to the bowing down of the soul. This the saints by experience find ; and therefore they can kiss and embrace the cross, as others do the world's crown.[2]

Again, They serve to bring the saints nearer to God, and to make them more importunate and earnest in prayer with God. 'Before I was afflicted, I went astray ; but now have I kept thy word.' 'It is good for me that I have been afflicted, that I might learn thy statutes.' 'I will be to Ephraim as a lion, and as a young lion to the house of Judah. I, even I, will tear and go away : I will take away, and none shall rescue him.' 'I will go and return to my place, till they acknowledge their offence, and seek my face : in their affliction they will seek me early.' And so they did. 'Come,' say they, 'and let us return unto the Lord : for he hath torn, and he will heal us; he hath smitten, and he will bind us up. After two days he will revive us : in the third day he will raise us up, and we shall live in his sight.'[3] So when God had hedged up their way with thorns, then they say, 'I will go and return to my first husband ; for then was it with me better than now,' Hosea ii. 6, 7. Ah the joy, the peace, the comfort, the delight, and content that did attend us, when we kept close communion with God, doth bespeak our return to God. 'We will return to our first husband ; for then was it with us better than now.'

When Tiribazus, a noble Persian, was arrested, he drew out his sword, and defended himself ; but when they told him that they came to carry him to the king, he willingly yielded.[4] So, though a saint may at first stand a little out, yet when he remembers that afflictions are to carry nearer to God, he yields, and kisses the rod. Afflictions are like the prick at the nightingale's breast, that awakes her, and puts her upon her sweet and delightful singing.

Again, Afflictions they serve to revive and recover decayed graces; they inflame that love that is cold, and they quicken that faith that is decaying, and they put life into those hopes that are withering, and spirits into those joys and comforts that are languishing.[5] Musk, saith one, when it hath lost its sweetness, if it be put into the sink amongst filth it recovers it. So do afflictions recover and revive de-

---

[1] יתשוח from שוח.

[2] The more precious odours and the purest spices, are beaten and bruised, the sweeter scent and savour they send abroad. So do saints when they are afflicted.

[3] Ps. cxix. 67, 71. Hosea v. 14, 15 ; vi. 1, 2.

[4] Cf. Diodorus xv. 8–11 : Plutarch, *Artaxerxes*, 24, 27, 29.—G.

[5] Most men are like a top, that will not go unless you whip it, and the more you whip it the better it goes. You know how to apply it. They that are in adversity, saith Luther, do better understand Scriptures; but those that are in prosperity, read them as a verse in Ovid. Bees are killed with honey, but quickened with vinegar. The honey of prosperity kills our graces, but the vinegar of adversity quickens our graces.

cayed graces. The more saints are beaten with the hammer of afflictions, the more they are made the trumpets of God's praises, and the more are their graces revived and quickened. Adversity abases the loveliness of the world that might entice us ; it abates the lustiness of the flesh within, that might incite us to folly and vanity ; and it abets the spirit in his quarrel to the two former, which tends much to the reviving and recovering of decayed graces. Now, suppose afflictions and troubles attend the ways of holiness, yet seeing that they all work for the great profit and singular advantage of the saints, let no soul be so mad as to leave an afflicted way of holiness, to walk in a smooth path of wickedness.

Remedy (2). The second remedy against this device of Satan is, solemnly to consider, *that all the afflictions that do befall the saints, do only reach their worser part ; they reach not, they hurt not, their noble part, their best part.* All the arrows stick in the target, they reach not the conscience : 1 Peter iii. 13, ' And who shall harm you, if ye be followers of that which is good,' saith the apostle. That is, none shall harm you. They may thus and thus afflict you, but they shall never harm you.[1]

It was the speech of an heathen, whenas by the tyrant he was commanded to be put into a mortar, and to be beaten to pieces with an iron pestle, he cries out to his persecutors, ' You do but beat the vessel, the case, the husk of Anaxarchus, you do not beat me.' His body was to him but as a case, a husk ; he counted his soul himself, which they could not reach. You are wise, and know how to apply it.

Socrates said of his enemies, ' They may kill me, but they cannot hurt me.' So afflictions may kill us, but they cannot hurt us ; they may take away my life, but they cannot take away my God, my Christ, my crown.

Remedy (3). The third remedy against this device of Satan is, seriously to consider, *That the afflictions that do attend the saints in the ways of holiness, are but short and momentary.* ' Sorrow may abide for a night, but joy comes in the morning,' Ps. xxx. 5. This short storm will end in an everlasting calm, this short night will end in a glorious day, that shall never have end.[2] It is but a very short time between grace and glory, between our title to the crown and our wearing the crown, between our right to the heavenly inheritance and our possession of the heavenly inheritance. Fourteen thousand years to the Lord is but as one day. What is our life but a shadow, a bubble, a flower, a post, a span, a dream ? &c. Yea, so small a while doth the hand of the Lord rest upon us, that Luther cannot get diminutives enough to extenuate it, for he calls it a very little cross that we bear, το πικρον μικρον. The prophet in Isaiah xxvi. 20, saith the indignation doth not (*transire*) pass, but (*pertransire*) overpass. The sharpness, shortness, and suddenness of it is set forth by

---

[1] The Christian soldier shall ever be master of the day. *Mori posse, vinci non posse*, said Cyprian to Cornelius ; he may suffer death, but never conquest.

[2] There are none of God's afflicted ones that have not their *lucida intervalla*, intermissions, respites, and breathing whiles, under their short and momentary afflictions. When God's hand is on thy back, let thy hand be on thy mouth, for though the affliction be sharp, it shall be but short.

the travail of a woman, John xvi. 21. And that is a sweet scripture, ' For ye have need of patience, that after ye have done the will of God, ye might receive the promise.' ' For yet a little while, he that shall come will come, and will not tarry,' Heb. x. 36, 37. *Tantillum tantillum adhuc pusillum.* A little, little, little while.[1]

When Athanasius's friends came to bewail him, because of his misery and banishment, he said, ' It is but a little cloud, and will quickly be gone.'[2] It will be but as a day before God will give his afflicted ones beauty for ashes, the oil of gladness for the spirit of heaviness ; before he will turn all your sighing into singing, all your lamentations into consolations, your sackcloth into silks, ashes into ointments, and your fasts into everlasting feasts, &c.

Remedy (4). The fourth remedy against this device of Satan, is seriously to consider, *That the afflictions that do befall the saints are such as proceed from God's dearest love.*[3] ' As many as I love, I rebuke and chasten,' Rev. iii. 19. Saints, saith God, think not that I hate you, because I thus chide you. He that escapes reprehension may suspect his adoption. God had one Son without corruption, but no son without correction. A gracious soul may look through the darkest cloud, and see a God smiling on him. We must look through the anger of his correction to the sweetness of his countenance ; and as by the rainbow we see the beautiful image of the sun's light in the midst of a dark and waterish cloud.

When Munster lay sick, and his friends asked him how he did and how he felt himself, he pointed to his sores and ulcers, whereof he was full, and said, ' These are God's gems and jewels, wherewith he decketh his best friends, and to me they are more precious than all the gold and silver in the world.' A soul at first conversion is but rough cast ; but God by afflictions doth square and fit, and fashion it for that glory above, which doth speak them out to flow from precious love ; therefore the afflictions that do attend the people of God should be no bar to holiness, nor no motive to draw the soul to ways of wickedness.

Remedy (5). The fifth remedy against this device of Satan is, solemnly to consider, *That it is our duty and glory not to measure afflictions by the smart but by the end.* When Israel was dismissed out of Egypt, it was with gold and ear-rings, Exod. xi. 3 ; so the Jews were dismissed out of Babylon with gifts, jewels, and all necessary utensils, Ezra i. 7–11. Look more at the latter end of a Christian than the beginning of his affliction. Consider the patience of Job, and what end the Lord made with him. Look not upon Lazarus lying at Dives's door, but lying in Abraham's bosom. Look not to the beginning of Joseph, who was so far from his dream, that the sun and moon should reverence him, that for two years he was cast where he could see neither sun, moon, nor stars ; but behold him at last made ruler over Egypt. Look not upon David, as there was but a step between him and death, nor as he was envied by some, and slighted and

---

[1] 'Ετι γὰρ μικρὸν ὅσον ὅσον.   [2] Nubecula est, cito transibit.—*Athanasius.*

[3] Austin asketh, *Si amatur quo modo infirmatur,* If he were beloved, how came he to be sick ? So are wicked men apt to say, because they know not that corrections are pledges of our adoption, and badges of our Sonship. God had one Son without sin, but none without sorrow.—[Augustine on Rev. iii. 19.—G]

despised by others ; but behold him seated in his royal throne, and dying in his bed of honour, and his son Solomon and all his glistering nobles about him. Afflictions, they are but as a dark entry into your Father's house ; they are but as a dirty lane to a royal palace. Now tell me, souls, whether it be not very great madness to shun the ways of holiness, and to walk in the ways of wickedness, because of those afflictions that do attend the ways of holiness.[1]

Remedy (6). The sixth remedy against this device of Satan is, seriously to consider, *That the design of God in all the afflictions that do befall them, is only to try them ; it is not to wrong them, nor to ruin them, as ignorant souls are apt to think.* 'He knoweth the way that I take : and when he hath tried me, I shall come forth as gold,' saith patient Job, xxiii. 10. So in Deut. viii. 2, 'And thou shalt remember all the way which the Lord thy God led thee these forty years in the wildernesss, to humble thee, and to prove thee, to know what was in thy heart, whether thou wouldst keep his commandments or no.' God afflicted them thus, that he might make known to themselves and others what was in their hearts. When fire is put to green wood, there comes out abundance of watery stuff that before appeared not ; when the pond is empty, the mud, filth, and toads come to light.[2] The snow covers many a dunghill, so doth prosperity many a rotten heart. It is easy to wade in a warm bath, and every bird can sing in a sunshine day, &c. Hard weather tries what health we have ; afflictions try what sap we have, what grace we have. Withered leaves soon fall off in windy weather, rotten boughs quickly break with heavy weights, &c. You are wise, and know how to apply it.

Afflictions are like pinching frosts, that will search us ; where we are most unsound, we shall soonest complain, and where most corruptions lie, we shall most shrink. We try metal by knocking ; if it sound well, then we like it. So God tries his by knocking, and if under knocks they yield a pleasant sound, God will turn their night into day, and their bitter into sweet, and their cross into a crown ; and they shall hear that voice, 'Arise, and shine ; for the glory of the Lord is risen upon thee, and the favours of the Lord are flowing in on thee,' Isa. lx. 1.[3]

Remedy (7). The seventh remedy against this device of Satan is, solemnly to consider, *That the afflictions, wrath, and misery that do attend the ways of wickedness, are far greater and heavier than those are that do attend the ways of holiness.*[4] Oh, the galling, girding, lashing, and gnawing of conscience, that do attend souls

---

[1] Afflictions, they are but our Father's goldsmiths, who are working to add pearls to our crowns. Tiberius saw paradise when he walked upon hot burning coals. Herodotus said of the Assyrians, Let them drink nothing but wormwood all their life long ; when they die, they shall swim in honey. You are wise, and know how to apply it.

[2] The king of Aracam, in Scaliger, tries her whom he means to marry by sweating. If they be sweet, he marries them ; if not, then he rejects them. You may easily make the application.

[3] Dunghills raked send out a filthy steam, ointments a sweet perfume. This is applicable to sinners and saints under the rod.

[4] Sin oftentimes makes men insensible of the wrath of the Almighty. Sin transforms many a man, as it were, into those bears in Pliny, that could not be stirred with the sharpest prickles ; or those fishes in Aristotle, that though they have spears thrust into their sides, yet they awake not. [*Bears*: Pliny, lib. viii. c. 54.—G.]

in a way of wickedness! 'The wicked,' saith Isaiah, 'are like the troubled sea, when it cannot rest, whose waters cast up mire and dirt.' 'There is no peace to the wicked, saith my God.'[1] There are snares in all their mercies, and curses and crosses do attend all their comforts, both at home and abroad. What is a fine suit of clothes with the plague in it? and what is a golden cup when there is poison at the bottom? or what is a silken stocking with a broken leg in it? The curse of God, the wrath of God, the hatred of God, and the fierce indignation of God, do always attend sinners walking in a way of wickedness. Turn to Deut. xxviii., and read from ver. 15 to the end of the chapter, and turn to Levit. xxvi., and read from ver. 14 to the end of that chapter, and then you shall see how the curse of God haunts the wicked, as it were a fury, in all his ways. In the city it attends him, in the country hovers over him; coming in, it accompanies him; going forth, it follows him, and in travel it is his comrade. It fills his store with strife, and mingles the wrath of God with his sweetest morsels. It is a moth in his wardrobe, murrain among his cattle, mildew in the field, rot among sheep, and ofttimes makes the fruit of his loins his greatest vexation and confusion. There is no solid joy, nor lasting peace, nor pure comfort, that attends sinners in their sinful ways.[2] There is a sword of vengeance that doth every moment hang over their heads by a small thread;[3] and what joy and content can attend such souls, if the eye of conscience be but so far open as to see the sword? Ah! the horrors and terrors, the tremblings and shakings, that attend their souls!

The tenth device that Satan hath to draw the soul to sin is,

Device (10). *By working them to be frequent in comparing themselves and their ways with those that are reputed or reported to be worse than themselves.* By this device the devil drew the proud pharisee to bless himself in a cursed condition, 'God, I thank thee that I am not as other men are, extortioners, unjust, adulterers, or even as this publican, &c., Luke xviii. 11. Why, saith Satan, you swear but pretty oaths, as ' by your faith and troth,' &c., but such and such swear by wounds and blood; you are now and then a little wanton, but such and such do daily defile and pollute themselves by actual uncleanness and filthiness; you deceive and overreach your neighbours in things that are but as toys and trifles, but such and such deceive and overreach others in things of greatest concernment, even to their ruin and undoings; you do but sit, and· chat, and sip with the drunkard, but such and such sit and drink and are drunk with the drunkard; you are only a little proud in heart and habit, in looks and words, &c.

Now the remedies against this device of the devil are these :

Remedy (1). The first remedy against this device of Satan is, solemnly to consider this, *That there is not a greater nor a clearer argument to prove a man a hypocrite, than to be quick-sighted abroad and blind at home,* than to see ' a mote in another man's eye,

---

[1] Isa. lvii. 20, and xlviii. 22.

[2] Sin brings in sorrow and sickness, &c. The Rabbins say, that when Adam tasted the forbidden fruit, his head ached. Sirens are said to sing curiously while they live, but to roar horribly when they die. So do the wicked.

[3] Allusion is to Damocles.—G.

and not a beam in his own eye,' Mat. vii. 3, 4; than to use spectacles to behold other men's sins rather than looking-glasses to behold his own; rather to be always holding his finger upon other men's sores, and to be amplifying and aggravating other men's sins than mitigating of his own, &c.[1]

Remedy (2). The second remedy against this device of Satan is, *To spend more time in comparing of your internal and external actions with the Rule, with the Word, by which you must be judged at last, than in comparing of yourselves with those that are worse than yourselves.*[2] That man that, comparing his self with others that are worse than himself, may seem, to himself and others, to be an angel; yet, comparing himself with the word, may see himself to be like the devil, yea, a very devil. 'Have not I chosen twelve, and one of you is a devil?' John vi. 70. Such men are like him, as if they were spit out of his mouth.

Satan is called 'the god of this world,' 2 Cor. iv. 4, because, as God at first did but speak the word, and it was done, so, if the devil doth but hold up his finger, give the least hint, they will do his will, though they undo their souls for ever. Ah, what monsters would these men appear to be, did they but compare themselves with a righteous rule, and not with the most unrighteous men; they would appear to be as black as hell itself.

Remedy (3). The third remedy against this device of Satan is, seriously to consider, *That though thy sins be not as great as others, yet without sound repentance on thy side and pardoning mercy on God's, thou wilt be as certainly damned as others, though not equally tormented with others.*[3] What though hell shall not be so hot to thee as others, yet thou must as certainly to hell as others, unless the glorious grace of God shines forth upon thee in the face of Christ. God will suit men's punishments to their sins; the greatest sins shall be attended with the greatest punishments, and lesser sins with lesser punishments. Alas, what a poor comfort will this be to thee when thou comest to die, to consider that thou shalt not be equally tormented with others, yet must be for ever shut out from the glorious presence of God, Christ, angels, and saints, and from those good things of eternal life, that are so many that they exceed number, so great that they exceed measure, so precious that they exceed estimation! Sure it is, that the tears of heaven[4] are not sufficient to bewail the loss of heaven; the worm of grief gnaws as painful as the fire burns. If those souls, Acts xx. 37, wept because they should see Paul's face no more, how deplorable is the eternal deprivation of the beatifical vision![5]

---

[1] History speaks of a kind of witches that, stirring abroad, would put on their eyes, but returning home they boxed them up again. So do hypocrites.

[2] The nearer we draw to God and his word, the more rottenness we shall find in our bones. The more any man looks into the body of the sun, the less he seeth when he looks down again. It is said of the basilisk, that if he look into a glass he presently dieth; so will sin, and a sinner (in a spiritual sense), when the soul looks into the word, which is God's glass, &c.

[3] As in heaven one is more glorious than another, so in hell one shall be more miserable than another.—*August*[*ine*].　　　　　[4] Qu, 'hell'?—G.

[5] The gate of indulgence, the gate of hope, the gate of mercy, the gate of glory, the gate of consolation, and the gate of salvation, will be for ever shut against them, Mat. xxv. 10.

But this is not all : thou shalt not be only shut out of heaven, but shut up in hell for ever ; not only shut out from the presence of God and angels, &c., but shut up with devils and damned spirits for ever ; not only shut out from those sweet, surpassing, unexpressible, and everlasting pleasures that be at God's right hand, but shut up for ever under those torments that are ceaseless, remediless, and endless.[1] Ah, souls, were it not ten thousand times better for you to break off your sins by repentance, than to go on in your sins till you feel the truth of what now you hear ?

The God of Israel is very merciful.   Ah, that you would repent and return, that your souls might live for ever !   Remember this, grievous is the torment of the damned, for the bitterness of the punishments, but most grievous for the eternity of the punishments.   For to be tormented without end, this is that which goes beyond the bounds of all desperation.   Ah, how do the thoughts of this make the damned to roar and cry out for unquietness of heart, and tear their hair, and gnash their teeth, and rage for madness, that they must dwell in 'everlasting burnings' for ever ![2]

The eleventh device that Satan hath to draw the soul to sin is,

Device (11). *By polluting and defiling the souls and judgments of men with such dangerous errors, that do in their proper tendency tend to carry the souls of men to all looseness and wickedness, as woful experience doth abundantly evidence.*   Ah, how many are there filled with these and such like Christ-dishonouring and soul-undoing opinions, viz., that ordinances are poor, low, carnal things, and not only to be lived above, but without also ; that the Scriptures are full of fallacies and uncertainties, and no further to be heeded than they agree with that spirit that is in *them ;* that it is a poor, low thing, if not idolatry too, to worship God in a Mediator ; that the resurrection is already past ; that there was never any such man or person as Jesus Christ, but that all is an allegory, and it signifies nothing but light and love, and such good frames born in men ; that there is no God nor devil, heaven nor hell, but what is within us ; that there is no sin in the saints, they are under no law but that of the Spirit, which is all freedom ; that sin and grace are equally good, and agreeth to his will,—with a hundred other horrid opinions, which hath caused wickedness to break in as a flood among us, &c.

Now the remedies against this device of Satan are those that follow :

Remedy (1). The first remedy against this device of Satan is, solemnly to consider, *That an erroneous, vain mind is as odious to God as a vicious life.*[3]   He that had the leprosy in his head was to be pronounced utterly unclean, Levit. xiii. 44.   Gross errors make the heart foolish, and render the life loose, and the soul light in the eye of God.   Error spreads and frets like a gangrene, and renders the soul a leper in the sight of God.[4]

[1] It was a good saying of Chrysostom, speaking of hell : *Ne quæramus ubi sit, sed quomodo illam fugiamus,* let us not seek where it is, but how we shall escape it.

[2] Surely one good means to escape hell is to take a turn or two in hell by our dail meditations.   [3] A blind eye is worse than a lame foot.

[4] The breath of the erroneous is infectious, and, like the dogs of *Congo,* they bite though they bark not.

It was God's heavy and dreadful plague upon the Gentiles, to be given up to a mind void of judgment, or an injudicious mind, or a mind rejected, disallowed, abhorred of God, or a mind that none have cause to glory in, but rather to be ashamed of, Rom. i. 28. I think that in these days God punisheth many men's former wickednesses by giving them up to soul-ruining errors. Ah, Lord, this mercy I humbly beg, that thou wouldst rather take me into thine own hand, and do anything with me, than give me up to those sad errors to which thousands have married their souls, and are in a way of perishing for ever.[1]

Remedy (2). The second remedy against this device of Satan is, *To receive the truth affectionately, and let it dwell in your souls plenteously.*[2] When men stand out against the truth, when truth would enter, and men bar the door of their souls against the truth, God in justice gives up such souls to be deluded and deceived by error, to their eternal undoing : 2 Thes. ii. 10–12, ' Because they received not the love of the truth, that they might be saved, God shall send them strong delusions (or, as the Greek hath it, "the efficacy of error," ἐνεργείαν πλανῆς), that they should believe a lie ; that they all might be damned who believed not the truth, but had pleasure in unrighteousness.' Ah, sirs, as you love your souls, do not tempt God, do not provoke God, by your withstanding truth and out-facing truth, to give you up to believe a lie, that you may be damned. There are no men on earth so fenced against error as those are that receive the truth in the love of it. Such souls are not ' easily tossed to and fro, and carried about with every wind of doctrine by the sleight of men and cunning craftiness, wherein they lie in wait to deceive,' Eph. iv. 14.[3] It is not he that receives most of the truth into his head, but he that receives most of the truth affectionately into his heart, that shall enjoy the happiness of having his judgment sound and clear, when others shall be deluded and deceived by them, who make it their business to infect the judgments and to undo the souls of men.

Ah, souls, as you would not have your judgments polluted and defiled with error, 'Let the word of the Lord,' that is more precious than gold, yea than fine gold, 'dwell plenteously in you,' Col. iii. 16.[4] It is not the hearing of truth, nor the knowing of truth, nor the commending of truth, nor the talking of truth, but the indwelling of truth in your souls, that will keep your judgments chaste and sound, in the midst of all those glittering errors that betray many souls into his hands, that can easily 'transform himself into an angel of light,' 2 Cor. xi. 14, that he may draw others to lie in chains of darkness with him for ever.[5] Oh, let not the word be a stranger, but make it your choicest familiar ! Then will you be able to stand in the day wherein

---

[1] Through animosity to persist in error is diabolical ; it were best that we never erred ; next to that, that we amended our error.

[2] The greatest sinners are sure to be the greatest sufferers.

[3] ἰν τῇ κυϐίᾳ, Gr., signifies cogging with a die ; such sleights as cheaters and false gamesters use at dice.

[4] ἰνοικίτω, *i. e.* indwell in you as an ingrafted word incorporated into your souls, so concocted and digested by you, as that you turn it into a part of yourselves.

[5] They must needs err that know not God's ways, yet can they not wander so wide as to miss of hell.

many shall fall on your right hand, and on your left, by the subtlety of those that shall say, 'Lo, here is Christ, or lo, there is Christ.'

There was more wit than grace in his speech that counselled his friends, 'Not to come too nigh unto truth, lest his teeth should be beaten out with its heels.' Ah, souls, if truth dwell plenteously in you, you are happy ; if not, you are unhappy under all your greatest felicity.[1]

'It is with truth,' saith Melancthon, 'as it is with holy water, every one praised it, and thought it had some rare virtue in it ; but offer to sprinkle them with it, and they will shut their eyes, and turn away their faces from it.'

Remedy (3). The third remedy against this device of Satan is, solemnly to consider, *That error makes the owner to suffer loss.* All the pains and labour that men take to defend and maintain their errors, to spread abroad and infect the world with their errors, shall bring no profit, nor no comfort to them in that day, wherein 'every man's work shall be made manifest, and the fire shall try it of what sort it is,' as the apostle shews in that remarkable scripture, 1 Cor. iii. 11–15. Ah, that all those that rise early and go to bed late, that spend their time, their strength, their spirits, their all, to advance and spread abroad God-dishonouring and soul-undoing opinions, would seriously consider of this, that they shall lose all the pains, cost, and charge that they have been, or shall be at, for the propagating of error ; and if they are ever saved, it shall be by fire, as the apostle there shews. Ah, sirs, Is it nothing to lay out your money for that which is not bread ? and your strength for that which will not, which cannot, profit you in the day that you must make up your account, and all your works must be tried by fire ?[2] Ah, that such souls would now at last 'buy the truth, and sell it not,' Prov. xxiii. 23. Remember you can never over-buy it, whatsoever you give for it ; you can never sufficiently sell it, if you should have all the world in exchange for it.

It is said of Cæsar, that 'he had greater care of his books than of his royal robes,' for, swimming through the waters to escape his enemies, he carried his books in his hand above the waters, but lost his robes.[3] Ah, what are Cæsar's books to God's books ? Well, remember this, that one day, yea, one hour spent in the study of truth, or spreading abroad of truth, will yield the soul more comfort and profit, than many thousand years spent in the study and spreading abroad of corrupt and vain opinions, that have their rise from hell, and not from heaven, from the god of this world and not from that God that shall at last judge this world, and all the corrupt opinions of men.

Remedy (4). The fourth remedy against this device of Satan is, *To hate, reject, and abominate all those doctrines and opinions that are contrary to godliness, and that open a door to profaneness,*[4] *and all*

---

[1] *Veritas vincit,* Truth at last triumphs. *Veritas stat in aperto campo,* Truth stands in the open fields ; ay, and it makes those souls stand in whom it dwells, when others fall as stars from heaven.

[2] Error as a glass is bright, but brittle, and cannot endure the hammer, or fire, as gold can, which, though rubbed or melted, remains firm and orient.

[3] Major fuit cura Cæsari libellorum quam purpuræ.

[4] One old piece of gold is worth a thousand new counters, and one old truth of God

such doctrines and opinions that require men to hold forth a strictness above what the Scripture requireth; and all such doctrines and opinions that do advance and lift up corrupted nature to the doing of supernatural things, which none can do but by that supernatural power that raised Christ from the grave; and such opinions that do lift our own righteousness in the room of Christ's righteousness, that place good works in the throne of Christ, and makes them co-partners with Christ, &c. And all those opinions and doctrines that do so set up and cry up Christ and his righteousness, as to cry down all duties of holiness and righteousness, and all those doctrines and opinions that do make the glorious and blessed privileges of believers in the days of the gospel to be lesser, fewer, and weaker, than they were in the time of the law. Ah, did your souls arise with a holy hatred, and a strong indignation against such doctrines and opinions, you would stand when others fall, and you would shine as the sun in his glory, when many that were once as shining stars may go forth as stinking snuffs.[1]

Remedy (5). The fifth remedy against this device of Satan is, *To hold fast the truth.* As men take no hold on the arm of flesh till they let go the arm of God, Jer. xvii. 5, so men take no hold on error till they have let go their hold of truth; therefore hold fast the truth, 2 Tim. i. 13, and Titus i. 9. Truth is thy crown, hold fast thy crown, and let no man take thy crown from thee. Hath not God made truth sweet to thy soul, yea, sweeter than honey, or the honeycomb? and wilt not thou go on to heaven, feeding upon truth, that heavenly honeycomb, as Samson did of his honeycomb?[2] Ah, souls, have you not found truth sweetening your spirits, and cheering your spirits, and warming your spirits, and raising your spirits, and corroborating your spirits? Have not you found truth a guide to lead you, a staff to uphold you, a cordial to strengthen you, and a plaster to heal you? And will not you hold fast the truth? Hath not truth been your best friend in your worst days? Hath not truth stood by you when friends have forsaken you? Hath not truth done more for you than all the world could do against you, and will you not hold fast the truth?[3] Is not truth your right eye, without which you cannot see for Christ? And your right hand, without which you cannot do for Christ? And your right foot, without which you cannot walk with Christ? And will you not hold fast truth? Oh! hold fast the truth in your judgments and understandings, in your wills and affections, in your profession and conversation.

Truth is more precious than gold or rubies, 'and all the things thou canst desire are not to be compared to her,' Prov. iii. 15.[4] Truth is that heavenly glass wherein we may see the lustre and

---

is more than a thousand new errors. True hatred is *εἰς τὸ γίνος*, to the whole kind; it is sad to frown upon one error and smile upon another.

[1] Gideon had seventy sons, and but one bastard, and yet that bastard destroyed all the rest (Judges viii. 13, *et seq.*). One turn may bring a man quite out of the way.

[2] The priests of Mercury, when they ate their figs and honey, cried out (*γλυκῆ ἡ ἀλήθεια*), Sweet is truth.

[3] It is with truth as with some plants, which live and thrive but in warm climates.

[4] Said of 'wisdom.'—G.

glory of divine wisdom, power, greatness, love, and mercifulness. In this glass you may see the face of Christ, the favour of Christ, the riches of Christ, and the heart of Christ, beating and working sweetly towards your souls. Oh! let your souls cleave to truth, as Ruth did to Naomi, Ruth i. 15, 16, and say, 'I will not leave truth, nor return from following after truth ; but where truth goes I will go, and where truth lodgeth I will lodge ; and nothing but death shall part truth and my soul.'[1] What John said to the church of Philadelphia I may say to you, 'Hold fast that which thou hast, that no man take thy crown,' Rev. iii. 11. The crown is the top of royalties : such a thing is truth : 'Let no man take thy crown.' 'Hold fast the faithful word,' as Titus speaks, chap. i. 9.[2] You were better let go anything than truth ; you were better let go your honours and riches, your friends and pleasures, and the world's favours ; yea, your nearest and dearest relations, ay, your very lives, than to let go truth. Oh, keep the truth, and truth will make you safe and happy for ever. Blessed are those souls that are kept by truth.

Remedy (6). The sixth remedy against this device of Satan is, *To keep humble.* Humility will keep the soul free from many darts of Satan's casting, and erroneous snares of his spreading. As low trees and shrubs are free from many violent gusts and blasts of wind which shake and rend the taller trees, so humble souls are free from those gusts and blasts of error that rend and tear proud, lofty souls. Satan and the world have least power to fasten errors upon humble souls. The God of light and truth delights to dwell with the humble ; and the more light and truth dwells in the soul, the further off darkness and error will stand from the soul. The God of grace pours in grace into humble souls, as men pour liquor into empty vessels ; and the more grace is poured into the soul, the less error shall be able to overpower the soul, or to infect the soul.[3]

That is a sweet word in Psalm xxv. 9, 'The meek' (or the humble) 'will he guide in judgment, and the meek will he teach his way.'[4] And certainly souls guided by God, and taught by God, are not easily drawn aside into ways of error. Oh, take heed of spiritual pride ! Pride fills our fancies, and weakens our graces, and makes room in our hearts for error. There are no men on earth so soon entangled, and so easily conquered by error, as proud souls. Oh, it is dangerous to love to be wise above what is written, to be curious and unsober in your desire of knowledge, and to trust to your own capacities and abilities to undertake to pry into all secrets, and to be puffed up with a carnal mind. Souls that are thus a-soaring up above the bounds and limits

[1] Though I cannot dispute for the truth, yet I can die for the truth, said that blessed martyr.

[2] Ἀντιχίμενοι, Hold fast as with tooth and nail, against these that would snatch it from us.

[3] I have read of one who, seeing in a vision so many snares of the devil spread upon the earth, he sat down mourning, and said within himself, *Quis pertransiet ista,* who shall pass through these ? whereunto he heard a voice answering, *Humilitas pertransiet,* humility shall pass through them.

[4] Ps. xxv. 9. עֲנָוִים, Gnanavim, from עָנָה, Gnanah, which signifies the humble or afflicted. The high tide quickly ebbs, and the highest sun is presently declining. You know how to apply it.

of humility, usually fall into the very worst of errors, as experience doth daily evidence.[1]

Remedy (7). The seventh remedy against this device of Satan is, solemnly to consider, *The great evils that errors have produced.* Error is a fruitful mother, and hath brought forth such monstrous children as hath set towns, cities, and nations on fire.[2] Error is that whorish woman that hath cast down many, wounded many, yea, slain many strong men, many great men, and many learned men, and many professing men in former times and in our time, as is too evident to all that are not much left of God, destitute of the truth, and blinded by Satan. Oh, the graces that error hath weakened, and the sweet joys and comforts that error hath clouded, if not buried ! Oh, the hands that error hath weakened, the eyes that error hath blinded, the judgments of men that error hath perverted, the minds that error hath darkened, the hearts that error hath hardened, the affections that error hath cooled, the consciences that error hath seared, and the lives of men that error hath polluted ! Ah, souls! can you solemnly consider of this, and not tremble more at error than at hell itself ? &c.

The twelfth device that Satan hath to draw the soul to sin is,

Device (12). *To affect*[3] *wicked company, to keep wicked society.* And oh ! the horrid impieties and wickedness that Satan hath drawn men to sin, by working them to sit and associate themselves with vain persons.

Now, the remedies against this device of the devil are these :

Remedy (1). The first remedy against this device of Satan is, *To dwell, till your hearts be affected, upon those commands of God that do expressly require us to shun the society of the wicked* : Eph. v. 11, 'And have no fellowship with the unfruitful works of darkness, but rather reprove them ;' Prov. iv. 14-16, ' Enter not into the path of the wicked, and go not in the way of evil men. Avoid it, pass not by it, turn from it, and pass away.' 1 Cor. v. 9-11, 2 Thes. iii. 6, Prov. i. 10-15. Turn to these Scriptures, and let your souls dwell upon them, till a holy indignation be raised in your souls against fellowship with vain men. ' God will not take the wicked by the hand,' as Job speaks, xxxiv. 20, xxx. 24. Why then should you ? God's commands are not like those that are easily reversed, but they are like those of the Medes, that cannot be changed. If these commands be not now observed by thee, they will at last be witnesses against thee, and millstones to sink thee, in that day that Christ shall judge thee.[4]

Remedy (2). The second remedy against this device of Satan is, seriously to consider, *That their company is very infectious and dangerous*, as is clear from the scripture above mentioned. Ah, how many have lost their names, and lost their estates, and strength, and God, and heaven, and souls, by society with wicked men ! As ye shun a stinking carcase, as the seaman shuns sands and rocks, and shelves,[5] as ye shun those that have the plague-sores running upon them, so

---

[1] The proud soul is like him that gazed upon the moon, but fell into the pit.

[2] Errors in conscience produce many great evils, not only *ad intra*, in men's own souls, but also *ad extra*, in human affairs.   [3] ' Choose.'—G.

[4] Non parentum aut majorum authoritas. sed Dei docebit imperium.—*Jerome.* The commands of God must outweigh all authority and example of men.

[5] ' Shoals.'—G.

should you shun the society of wicked men. As weeds endanger the corn, as bad humours endanger the blood, or as an infected house the neighbourhood, so doth wicked company the soul,[1] Prov. xiii. 20.

Bias, a heathen man, being at sea in a great storm, and perceiving many wicked men in the ship, called upon the gods : ' Oh, saith he, forbear prayer, hold your tongues ; I would not have the gods take notice that you are here ; they sure will drown us all if they should.' Ah, sirs, could a heathen see so much danger in the society of wicked men, and can you see none ?

Remedy (3). The third remedy against this device of Satan is, *To look always upon wicked men, under those names and notions that the Scripture doth set them out under.* The Scripture calls them lions for their fierceness, and bears for their cruelty, and dragons for their hideousness, and dogs for their filthiness, and wolves for their subtleness. The Scripture styles them scorpions, vipers, thorns, briers, thistles, brambles, stubble, dirt, chaff, dust, dross, smoke, scum, as you may see in the margin.[2] It is not safe to look upon wicked men under those names and notions that they set out themselves by, or that flatterers set them out by ; this may delude the soul, but the looking upon them under those names and notions that the Scripture sets them out by, may preserve the soul from frequenting their company and delighting in their society. Do not tell me what this man calls them, or how such and such count them ; but tell me how doth the Scripture call them, how doth the Scripture count them ? As Nabal's name was, so was his nature, 1 Sam. xxv. 25, and as wicked men's names are, so are their natures. You may know well enough what is within them, by the apt names that the Holy Ghost hath given them.[3]

Remedy (4). The fourth remedy against this device of Satan, is, solemnly to consider, *That the society and company of wicked men have been a great grief and burden to those precious souls that were once glorious on earth, and are now triumphing in heaven :* Ps. cxx. 5, 6, ' Woe is me, that I dwell in Meshech, that I sojourn in the tents of Kedar ! My soul hath long dwelt with him that hateth peace.' So Jeremiah, ' Oh that I had in the wilderness a lodging-place of wayfaring men, that I might leave my people, and go from them ! for they be all adulterers, an assembly of treacherous men,' Jer. ix. 2. So they ' vexed Lot's righteous soul by their filthy conversation,' 2 Pet. ii. 7 ;[4] they made his life a burden, they made death more desirable to him than life, yea, they made his life a lingering death. Guilt or grief is all the good gracious souls get by conversing with wicked men.[5]

---

[1] Eusebius reports of John the Evangelist, that he would not suffer Cerinthus, the heretic, in the same bath with him, lest some judgment should abide them both.— *Euseb.* l. iii. cap. 25. [Cf. Note in Sibbes, vol. vii. 603.—G.] A man that keepeth ill company is like him that walketh in the sun, tanned insensibly.

[2] 2 Tim. iv. 17, Isa. xi. 7, Ezek. iii. 10, Mat. vii. 6, Rev. xxii. 15, Luke xiii. 32, Isa. x. 17, Ezek. ii. 6, Judges ix. 14, Job xxi. 18, Ps. lxxxiii. 13, Ps. xviii. 42, Ezek. xxii. 18, 19, Isa. lxv. 5, Ezek. xxiv. 6.

[3] Lactantius says of Lucian (*nec diis, nec hominibus pepercit*). he spared neither God nor man ; such monsters are wicked men, which should render their company to all that have tasted of the sweetness of divine love, a burden and not a delight.

[4] Vide Bezam, *i. e.* the Annott. of Beza, *in loc.*—G.

[5] O Lord, let me not go to hell, where the wicked are ; for Lord, thou knowest I never

The second thing to be shewed is,

The several devices that Satan hath, as to draw souls to sin, so to keep souls from holy duties, to hinder souls in holy services, and to keep them off from religious performances.

'And he shewed me Joshua the high priest standing before the angel of the Lord, and Satan standing at his right hand to resist him,' Zech. iii. 1.

The truth of this I shall shew you in the following particulars :

The first device that Satan hath to draw souls from holy duties, and to keep them off from religious services, is,

Device (1). *By presenting the world in such a dress, and in such a garb to the soul, as to ensnare the soul, and to win upon the affections of the soul.* He represents the world to them in its beauty and bravery,[1] which proves a bewitching sight to a world of men.[2] (It is true, this took not Christ, because Satan could find no matter in him for his temptation to work upon.) So that he can no sooner cast out his golden bait, but we are ready to play with it, and to nibble at it ; he can no sooner throw out his golden ball, but men are apt to run after it, though they lose God and their souls in the pursuit. Ah! how many professors in these days have for a time followed hard after God, Christ, and ordinances, till the devil hath set before them the world in all its beauty and bravery, which hath so bewitched their souls that they have grown to have low thoughts of holy things, and then to be cold in their affections to holy things, and then to slight them, and at last, with the young man in the Gospel, to turn their backs upon them. Ah! the time, the thoughts, the spirits, the hearts, the souls, the duties, the services, that the inordinate love of this wicked world doth eat up and destroy, and hath ate up and destroyed. Where one thousand are destroyed by the world's frowns, ten thousand are destroyed by the world's smiles. The world, siren-like, it sings us and sinks us ; it kisses us, and betrays us, like Judas ; it kisses us and smites us under the fifth rib, like Joab. The honours, splendour, and all the glory of this world, are but sweet poisons, that will much endanger us, if they do not eternally destroy us.[3] Ah! the multitude of souls that have surfeited of these sweet baits and died for ever.

Now the remedies against this device of Satan are these,

Remedy (1). The first remedy against this device of Satan is, *To dwell upon the impotency and weakness of all these things here below.* They are not able to secure you from the least evil, they are not able to procure you the least desirable good. The crown of gold cannot cure the headache, nor the velvet slipper ease the gout, nor the jewel about the

---

loved their company here, said a gracious gentlewoman, when she was to die, being in much trouble of conscience.   [1] 'Finery.'—G.

[2] The beauty of the world foils a Christian more than the strength; the flattering sunshine more than the blustering storm. In storms we keep our garments close about us [as in the fable of the sun and wind.—G.].

[3] The inhabitants of Nilus are deaf by the noise of the waters; so the world makes such a noise in men's ears, that they cannot hear the things of heaven. The world is like the swallows' dung, that put out Tobias his eyes. The champions could not wring an apple out of Milo's hand by a strong hand, but a fair maid, by fair means, got it presently.

neck cannot take away the pain of the teeth. The frogs of Egypt entered into the rich men's houses of Egypt, as well as the poor. Our daily experience doth evidence this, that all the honours, riches, &c., that men enjoy, cannot free them from the cholic, the fever, or lesser diseases.[1] Nay, that which may seem most strange is, that a great deal of wealth cannot keep men from falling into extreme poverty : Judges i. 6, you shall find seventy kings, with their fingers and toes cut off, glad, like whelps, to lick up crumbs under another king's table ; and shortly after, the same king that brought them to this penury, is reduced to the same poverty and misery. Why then should that be a bar to keep thee out of heaven, that cannot give thee the least ease on earth ?

Remedy (2). The second remedy against this device of Satan is, *To dwell upon the vanity of them as well as upon the impotency of all worldly good.* This is the sum of Solomon's sermon, 'Vanity of vanities, and all is vanity.' This our first parents found, and therefore named their second son Abel, or vanity. Solomon, that had tried these things, and could best tell the vanity of them, he preacheth this sermon over again and again, 'Vanity of vanities, and all is vanity.' It is sad to think how many thousands there be that can say with the preacher, ' Vanity of vanities, all is vanity,' nay, swear it, and yet follow after these things as if there were no other glory, nor felicity, but what is to be found in these things they call vanity.[2] Such men will sell Christ, heaven, and their souls for a trifle, that call these things vanity, but do not cordially believe them to be vanity, but set their hearts upon them as if they were their crown, the top of all their royalty and glory. Oh let your souls dwell upon the vanity of all things here below, till your hearts be so throughly convinced and persuaded of the vanity of them, as to trample upon them, and make them a footstool for Christ to get up, and ride in a holy triumph in your hearts [3]

Chrysostom said once, ' That if he were the fittest in the world to preach a sermon to the whole world, gathered together in one congregation, and had some high mountain for his pulpit, from whence he might have a prospect of all the world in his view, and were furnished with a voice of brass, a voice as loud as the trumpets of the archangel, that all the world might hear him, he would choose to preach upon no other text than that in the Psalms,' O mortal men, how long will ye love vanity, and follow after leasing? Ps. iv. 2.

---

[1] The prior in Melancthon rolled his hand up and down in a basinful of angels, thinking thereby to have charmed his gout, but it would not do. Nugas the Scythian, despising the rich presents and ornaments that were sent unto him by the emperor of Constantinople, asked whether those things could drive away calamities, diseases, or death.

[2] Gilemex, king of Vandals, led in triumph by Belisarius, cried out, ' Vanity of vanity, all is vanity.' The fancy of Lucian, who placeth Charon on the top of an high hill, viewing all the affairs of men living, and looking on their greatest cities as little birds' nests, is very pleasant.

[3] Oh the imperfection, the ingratitude, the levity, the inconstancy, the perfidiousness of those creatures we most servilely affect. Ah, did we but weigh man's pain with his payment, his crosses with his mercies, his miseries with his pleasures, we should then see that there is nothing got by the bargain, and conclude, ' Vanity of vanities, all is vanity.'

Tell me, you that say all things under the sun are vanity, if you do really believe what you say, why do you spend more thoughts and time on the world, than you do on Christ, heaven, and your immortal souls ? Why do you then neglect your duty towards God, to get the world ? Why do you then so eagerly pursue after the world, and are so cold in your pursuing after God, Christ, and holiness? Why then are your hearts so exceedingly raised, when the world comes in, and smiles upon you ; and so much dejected, and cast down, when the world frowns upon you, and with Jonah's gourd withers before you ?

Remedy (3). The third remedy against the device of Satan is, *To dwell much upon the uncertainty, the mutability, and inconstancy of all things under the sun.* Man himself is but the dream of a dream, but the generation of a fancy, but an empty vanity, but the curious picture of nothing, a poor, feeble, dying flash. All temporals are as transitory as a hasty headlong current, a shadow, a ship, a bird, an arrow, a post that passeth by. ' Why shouldst thou set thine eyes upon that which is not?' saith Solomon, Prov. xxiii. 5. And saith the apostle, 'The fashion of this world passeth away,'[1] 1 Cor. vii. 31. Heaven only hath a foundation, earth hath none, ' but is hanged upon nothing,' as Job speaks, xxvi. 7. The apostle willed Timothy to 'charge rich men that they be not high-minded, nor put their trust in uncertain riches,' 1 Tim. vi. 17.[2] They are like bad servants, whose shoes are made of running leather, and will never tarry long with one master.[3] As a bird hoppeth from tree to tree, so do the honours and riches of this world from man to man, Let Job and Nebuchadnezzar testify this truth, who fell from great wealth to great want. No man can promise himself to be wealthy till night ; one storm at sea, one coal of fire, one false friend, one unadvised word, one false witness, may make thee a beggar and a prisoner all at once. All the riches and glory of this world is but as smoke and chaff that vanisheth ; ' As a dream and vision in the night, that tarrieth not,' Job xx. 8. ' As if a hungry man dreameth, and thinketh that he eateth, and when he awaketh his soul is empty ; and like a thirsty man which thinketh he drinketh, and behold when he is awaked, his soul is faint,' as the prophet Isaiah saith, chap. xxix. 8. Where is the glory of Solomon ? the sumptuous buildings of Nebuchadnezzar? the nine hundred chariots of Sisera ? the power of Alexander? the authority of Augustus, that commanded the whole world to be taxed? Those that have been the most glorious, in what men generally account glorious and excellent, have had inglorious ends ; as Samson for strength, Absalom for favour, Ahithophel for policy, Haman for favour, Asahel for swiftness, Alexander for great conquest, and yet after twelve years poisoned. The same you may see in the four mighty kingdoms, the Chaldean, Persian, Grecian, and

---

[1] 1 Cor. vii. 31 intimateth, that there is nothing of any firmness, or solid consistence, in the creature.

[2] Riches were never true to any that trusted to them ; they have deceived men, as Job's brook did the poor travellers in the summer season.

[3] A phrase meaning, he is given to rambling about. See Halliwell and Wright *sub voce.*—G.

Roman : how soon were they gone and forgotten !¹   Now rich, now
poor, now full, now empty, now in favour, anon out of favour, now
honourable, now despised, now health, now sickness, now strength,
now weakness.   Oh, let not these uncertain things keep thee from
those holy services and heavenly employments, that may make thee
happy for ever, and render thy soul eternally blessed and at ease,
when all these transitory things shall bid thy soul an everlasting fare-
well.²

Remedy (4). The fourth remedy against this device of Satan is,
seriously to consider, *That the great things of this world are very
hurtful and dangerous to the outward and inward man, through
the corruptions that be in the hearts of men.*   Oh, the rest, the peace,
the comfort, the content that the things of this world do strip many
men of !   Oh, the fears, the cares, the envy, the malice, the dangers,
the mischiefs, that they subject men to ! ³   They oftentimes make men
carnally confident.⁴   The rich man's riches are a strong tower in his
imagination.   ' I said in my prosperity I should never be moved,' Ps.
xxx. 6.   They often swell the heart with pride, and make men forget
God, and neglect God, and despise the rock of their salvation.   When
Jeshurun ' waxed fat, and was grown thick, and covered with fatness,
then he forgot God, and forsook God that made him, and lightly
esteemed the rock of his salvation,' as Moses spake, Deut. xxxii. 15.
Ah, the time, the thoughts, the spirits, that the things of the world
consume and spend !   Oh, how do they hinder the actings of faith
upon God ! how do they interrupt our sweet communion with God !
how do they abate our love to the people of God ! and cool our love to
the things of God ! and work us to act like those that are most unlike
to God !   Oh, the deadness, the barrenness that doth attend men
under great outward mercies ! ⁵   Oh, the riches of the world chokes the
word ; that men live under the most soul-searching, and soul-enriching
means with lean souls.   Though they have full purses, though their
chests are full of silver, yet their hearts are empty of grace.   In
Genesis xiii. 2, it is said, that ' Abraham was very rich in cattle, in
silver, and in gold.'   According to the Hebrew (*Chabbedgh*) it is
' Abraham was very weary ;' to shew that riches are a heavy burden,
and a hindrance many times to heaven, and happiness.⁶

¹ The most renowned Frederick lost all, and sued to be made but sexton of the
church that himself had built.   I have read of a poor fisherman, who, while his nets
were a-drying, slept upon the rock, and dreamed that he was made a king, on a sudden
starts up, and leaping for joy, fell down from the rock, and in the place of his imaginary
felicities loses his little portion of pleasures.

² The pomp of this world John compareth to the moon, which *crescit et decrescit*, increaseth and decreaseth, Apoc. xii. 1.

³ Henry the Second hearing Mentz his chief city to be taken, used this blasphemous
speech : I shall never, saith he, love God any more, that suffered a city so dear to me
to be taken from me.

⁴ When one presented Antipater, king of Macedonia, with a book treating on happiness, his answer was (οὐ σχολάζω), I have no leisure.

⁵ That four good mothers beget four bad daughters : great familiarity begets contempt, truth hatred, virtue envy, riches ignorance ; a French proverb.

⁶ Ponacrites bestowed five talents for a gift upon one Anacreon, who for two nights
after was so troubled with care how to keep them, and how to bestow them, as he
carried them back again to Ponacrites, saying, they were not worth the pains which he
had already taken for them. [Query Polycrates ?—G.]

King Henry the Fourth asked the Duke of Alva if he had observed the great eclipse of the sun, which had lately happened ; No, said the duke, I have so much to do on earth, that I have no leisure to look up to heaven. Ah, that this were not true of most professors in these days. It is very sad to think, how their hearts and time is so much taken up with earthly things, that they have scarce any leisure to look up to heaven, or to look after Christ, and the things that belong to their everlasting peace.

Riches, though well got, yet are but like to manna; those that gathered less had no want, and those that gathered more, it was but a trouble and annoyance to them. The world is troublesome, and yet it is loved; what would it be if it were peaceable ? You embrace it, though it be filthy; what would you do if it were beautiful ? You cannot keep your hands from the thorns; how earnest would you be then in gathering the flowers?[1] The world may be fitly likened to the serpent Scytale, whereof it is reported, that when she cannot over-take the flying passengers, she doth with her beautiful colours so astonish and amaze them, that they have no power to pass away, till she hath stung them.[2] Ah. how many thousands are there now on earth, that have found this true by experience, that have spun a fair thread to strangle themselves, both temporally and eternally, by being bewitched by the beauty and bravery of this world.[3]

Remedy (5). The fifth remedy against this device of Satan is, to consider, *That all the felicity of this world is mixed.* Our light is mixed with darkness, our joy with sorrow, our pleasures with pain, our honour with dishonour, our riches with wants. If our lights be spiritual, clear, and quick, we may see in the felicity of this world our wine mixed with water, our honey with gall, our sugar with worm-wood, and our roses with prickles.[4] Sorrow attends worldly joy, danger attends worldly safety, loss attends worldly labours, tears attend worldly purposes. As to these things, men's hopes are vain, their sorrow certain and joy feigned. The apostle calls this world 'a sea of glass,' a sea for the trouble of it, and glass for the brittleness and bitterness of it.[5] The honours, profits, pleasures, and delights of the world are true gardens of Adonis, where we can gather nothing but trivial flowers, surrounded with many briers.

Remedy (6). The sixth remedy against this device of Satan is, *To get better acquaintance and better assurance of more blessed and glorious things.*[6] That which raised up their spirits, Heb. x. and xi., to trample upon all the beauty, bravery, and glory of the world, was the acquaintance with, 'and assurance of better and more durable

---

[1] A recollection of Augustine.—G.

[2] Sicily is so full of sweet flowers that dogs cannot hunt there. And what do all the sweet contents of this world, but make us lose the scent of heaven !

[3] *Scytale :* Solinus cxxvii., xl.—G.

[4] Hark, scholar, said the harlot to Apuleius, it is but a bitter sweet you are so fond of. Surely all the things of this world are but bitter sweets.

[5] Qu. *not* this world ? Cf. Rev. iv. 6, xv. 2, xxi. 18.—G.

[6] Let heaven be a man's object, and earth will soon be his abject. Luther being at one time in some wants, it happened that a good sum of money was unexpectedly sent him by a nobleman of Germany, at which, being something amazed, he said, I fear that God will give me my reward here, but I protest I will not be so satisfied.

things.' 'They took joyfully the spoiling of their goods, knowing in themselves that they had in heaven a better and a more durable substance.' 'They looked for a house that had foundations, whose builder and maker was God.' 'And they looked for another country, even an heavenly.' 'They saw him that was invisible, and had an eye to the recompence of reward.' And this made them count all the glory and bravery of this world to be too poor and contemptible for them to set their hearts upon. The main reason why men doat upon the world, and damn their souls to get the world, is, because they are not acquainted with a greater glory. Men ate acorns, till they were acquainted with the use of wheat. Ah, were men more acquainted with what union and communion with God means, what it is to have 'a new name, and a new stone, that none knows but he that hath it,' Rev. ii. 17 ; did they but taste more of heaven, and live more in heaven, and had more glorious hopes of going to heaven, ah, how easily would they have the moon under their feet.

It was an excellent saying of Lewis of Bavyer, emperor of Germany, 'Such goods are worth getting and owning, as will not sink or wash away if a shipwreck happen, but will wade and swim out with us.'[1] It is recorded of Lazarus, that after his resurrection from the dead, he was never seen to laugh, his thoughts and affections were so fixed in heaven, though his body was on earth, and therefore he could not but slight temporal things, his heart being so bent and set upon eternals. There are goods for the throne of grace, as God, Christ, the Spirit, adoption, justification, remission of sin, peace with God, and peace with conscience ; and there are goods of the footstool, as honours, riches, the favour of creatures, and other comforts and accommodations of this life. Now he that hath acquaintance with, and assurance of the goods of the throne, will easily trample upon the goods of the footstool. Ah that you would make it your business, your work, to mind more, and make sure more to your own souls, the great things of eternity, that will yield you joy in life and peace in death, and a crown of righteousness in the day of Christ's appearing, and that will lift up your souls above all the beauty and bravery of this bewitching world, that will raise your feet above other men's heads. When a man comes to be assured of a crown, a sceptre, the royal robes, &c., he then begins to have low, mean, and contemptible thoughts of those things that before he highly prized. So will assurance of more great and glorious things breed in the soul a holy scorn and contempt of all these poor, mean things, which the soul before did value above God, Christ, and heaven, &c.

Remedy (7). The seventh remedy against this device of Satan is, seriously to consider, *That true happiness and satisfaction is not to be had in the enjoyment of worldly good.* True happiness is too big and too glorious a thing to be found in anything below that God that

---

[1] *Hujusmodi comparandæ sunt opes quæ cum naufrago simul enatent.* There is, saith Augustine, *bona threni*, goods of the throne ; and there are *bona scabelli*, goods of the footstool. When Basil was tempted with money and preferment, saith he, Give me money that may last for ever, and glory that may eternally flourish ; for the fashion of this world passeth away, as the waters of a river that ins by a city.

is a Christian's *summum bonum*, chiefest good.[1]   The blessed angels, those glistering courtiers, have all felicities and blessedness, and yet have they neither gold, nor silver, nor jewels, nor none of the beauty and bravery of this world.   Certainly if happiness was to be found in these things, the Lord Jesus, who is the right and royal heir of all things, would have exchanged his cradle for a crown; his birth chamber, a stable, for a royal palace; his poverty for plenty; his despised followers for shining courtiers; and his mean provisions for the choicest delicates, &c.   Certainly happiness lies not in those things that a man may enjoy, and yet be miserable for ever.   Now a man may be great and graceless with Pharaoh, honourable and damnable with Saul, rich and miserable with Dives, &c.: therefore happiness lies not in these things.   Certainly happiness lies not in those things that cannot comfort a man upon a dying bed.   Is it honours, riches, or friends, &c., that can comfort thee when thou comest to die?   Or is it not rather faith in the blood of Christ, the witness of the Spirit of Christ, the sense and feeling of the love and favour of Christ, and the hopes of eternally reigning with Christ?   Can happiness lie in those things that cannot give us health, or strength, or ease, or a good night's rest, or an hour's sleep, or a good stomach?   Why, all the honours, riches, and delights of this world cannot give these poor things to us, therefore certainly happiness lies not in the enjoyment of them, &c.[2] And surely happiness is not to be found in those things that cannot satisfy the souls of men.   Now none of these things can satisfy the soul of man.   'He that loveth silver shall not be satisfied with silver, nor he that loveth abundance with increase; this is also vanity,' said the wise man, Eccles. v. 10.   The barren womb, the horse leech's daughter, the grave and hell, will as soon be satisfied, as the soul of man will by the enjoyment of any worldly good.   Some one thing or other will be for ever wanting to that soul that hath none but outward good to live upon.   You may as soon fill a bag with wisdom, a chest with virtue, or a circle with a triangle, as the heart of man with anything here below.   A man may have enough of the world to sink him, but he can never have enough to satisfy him, &c.

Remedy (8). The eighth remedy against this device of Satan is, solemnly to consider, *Of the dignity of the soul.*   Oh, the soul of man is more worth than a thousand worlds!   It is the greatest abasing of it that can be to let it doat upon a little shining earth, upon a little painted beauty and fading glory, when it is capable of union with Christ, of communion with God, and of enjoying the eternal vision of God.

Seneca could say, 'I am too great, and born to greater things, than that I should be a slave to my body.'[3]   Oh! do you say my soul is

---

[1] True happiness lies only in our enjoyment of a suitable good, a pure good, a total good, and an eternal good; and God is only such a good, and such a good can only satisfy the soul of man.   Philosophers could say, that he was never a happy man that might afterwards become miserable.

[2] Gregory the Great used to say, He is poor whose soul is void of grace, not whose coffers are empty of money. *Anima rationalis cæteris omnibus occupari potest, impleri non potest;* the reasonable soul may be busied about other things, but it cannot be filled with them.   [3] Epistle xiv.—G.

too great, and born to greater things, than that I should confine it to a heap of white and yellow earth.[1]

I have been the longer upon the remedies that may help us against this dangerous device of Satan, because he doth usually more hurt to the souls of men by this device than he doth by all other devices. For a close, I wish, as once Chrysostom did, that that sentence, Eccles. ii. 11, 'Then I looked on all the works that my hands had wrought, and on the labour that I had laboured to do, and behold all was vanity and vexation of spirit, and there was no profit under the sun,' were engraven on the door-posts into which you enter, on the tables where you sit, on the dishes out of which you eat, on the cups out of which you drink, on the bed-steads where you lie, on the walls of the house where you dwell, on the garments which you wear, on the heads of the horses on which you ride, and on the foreheads of all them whom you meet, that your souls may not, by the beauty and bravery of the world, be kept off from those holy and heavenly services that may render you blessed while you live, and happy when you die; that you may breathe out your last into his bosom who lives for ever, and who will make them happy for ever that prefer Christ's spirituals and eternals above all temporal transitory things.

Device (2.) The second device that Satan hath to draw the soul from holy duties, and to keep them off from religious services, is, *By presenting to them the danger, the losses, and the sufferings that do attend the performance of such and such religious services.* By this device Satan kept close those that believed on Christ from confessing of Christ: in John xii. 42, 'Nevertheless among the chief rulers also many believed on him; but because of the Pharisees they did not confess him, lest they should be put out of the synagogue.' I would walk in all the ways of God, I would give up myself to the strictest way of holiness, but I am afraid dangers will attend me on the one hand, and losses, and happily such and such sufferings on the other hand, saith many a man. Oh, how should we help ourselves against this temptation and device of Satan!

Now the remedies against this device of Satan are these that follow.

Remedy (1). The first remedy against this device of Satan is to consider, *That all the troubles and afflictions that you meet with in a way of righteousness shall never hurt you, they shall never harm you.* 'And who is he that shall harm you, if you be followers of that which is good?' saith the apostle, *i.e.* none shall harm you, 1 Pet. iii. 13.[2] Natural conscience cannot but do homage to the image of God stamped upon the natures, words, works, and life of the godly; as we may see in the carriage of Nebuchadnezzar and Darius towards Daniel. All

---

[1] Plutarch tells of Themistocles, that he accounted it not to stand with his state to stoop down to take up the spoils the enemies had scattered in flight; but saith to one of his followers, Δύνασαι σὺ, γὰρ οὐκ εἶ Θεμιστοκλῆς, You may, for you are not Themistocles. Oh what a sad thing it is that a heathen should set his feet upon those very things that most professors set their hearts, and for the gain of which, with Balaam, many run the hazard of losing their immortal souls for ever.

[2] *Nemo proprie læditur nisi a seipso,* Nobody is properly hurt but by himself, and his own fault.

afflictions and troubles that do attend men in a way of righteousness can never rob them of their treasure, of their jewels. They may rob them of some light slight things, as the sword that is by their side, or the stick in their hand, or of the flowers or ribbons that be in their hats.[1] The treasures of a saint are the presence of God, the favour of God, union and communion with God, the pardon of sin, the joy of the Spirit, the peace of conscience, which are jewels that none can give but Christ, nor none can take away but Christ. Now why should a gracious soul keep off from a way of holiness because of afflictions, when no afflictions can strip a man of his heavenly jewels, which are his ornaments and his safety here, and will be his happiness and glory hereafter? Why should that man be afraid, or troubled for storms at sea, whose treasures are sure in a friend's hand upon land? Why, a believer's treasure is always safe in the hands of Christ; his life is safe, his soul is safe, his grace is safe, his comfort is safe, and his crown is safe in the hand of Christ.[2] 'I know him in whom I have believed, and that he is able to keep that which I have committed unto him until that day,' saith the apostle, 2 Tim. i. 12. The child's most precious things are most secure in his father's hands; so are our souls, our graces, and our comforts in the hand of Christ.

Remedy (2). The second remedy against this device of Satan is to consider, *That other precious saints that were shining lights on earth, and are now triumphing in heaven, have held on in religious services, notwithstanding all the troubles and dangers that have surrounded them.*[3] Nehemiah and Ezra were surrounded with dangers on the left hand and on the right, and yet, in the face of all, they hold on building the temple and the wall of Jerusalem. So Daniel, and those precious worthies, Ps. xliv. 19, 20, under the want of outward encouragements, and in the face of a world of very great discouragements, their souls clave to God and his ways. 'Though they were sore broken in the place of dragons, and covered with the shadow of death, yea, though they were all the day long counted as sheep for the slaughter, yet their hearts were not turned back, neither did their steps decline from his ways.' Though bonds and imprisonments did attend Paul and the rest of the apostles in every place, yet they held on in the work and service of the Lord; and why, then, should you degenerate from their worthy examples, which is your duty and your glory to follow? 2 Cor. vi. 5, Heb. xi. 36.

Remedy (3). The third remedy against this device of Satan is,

[1] Gordius, that blessed martyr, accounted it a loss to him not to suffer many kinds of tortures. He saith tortures are but tradings with God for glory. The greater the combat is, the greater is the following reward. [For above of Gordius, cf. Clarke's 'Martyrologie,' 1677 folio, pages 54, 55.—G.]

[2] That was a notable speech of Luther, Let him that died for my soul see to the salvation of it.

[3] Wil. Fowler (martyr) said that heaven should as soon fall as I will forsake my profession, or budge in the least degree from it. So Santus being under as great torments as you have read of, cries out, *Christianus sum*, I am a Christian. No torments could work him to decline the service of God. I might produce a cloud of witnesses; but if those do not work you to be noble and brave, I am afraid more will not. [For Fowler see Clarke's 'Martyrologie,' as before, pp. 450, 451, and for Sanctus [*not* Santus] page 31.—G.]

solemnly to consider, *That all the troubles and dangers that do attend the performance of all holy duties and heavenly services are but temporal and momentary, but the neglect of them may lay thee open to all temporal, spiritual, and eternal dangers.* 'How shall we escape, if we neglect so great salvation?' Heb. ii. 3. He saith not, if we reject or renounce so great salvation. No; but if we neglect, or shift off so great salvation, how shall we escape?[1] That is, we cannot by any way, or means, or device in the world, escape. Divine justice will be above us, in spite of our very souls. The doing of such and such heavenly services may lay you open to the frowns of men, but the neglect of them will lay you open to the frowns of God; the doing of them may render you contemptible in the eyes of men, but the neglect of them may render you contemptible in the eyes of God; the doing of them may be the loss of thy estate, but the neglect of them may be the loss of God, Christ, heaven, and thy soul for ever; the doing of them may shut thee out from some outward temporal contents, the neglect of them may shut thee out from that excellent matchless glory 'that eye hath not seen, nor ear heard, neither hath it entered into the heart of men,' Isa. lxiv. 4. Remember this, there is no man that breathes but shall suffer more by neglecting those holy and heavenly services that God commands, commends, and rewards, than possibly he can suffer by doing of them.[2]

Remedy (4). The fourth remedy against this device of Satan is, to consider, *That God knows how to deliver from troubles by troubles, from afflictions by afflictions, from dangers by dangers.* God, by lesser troubles and afflictions, doth oftentimes deliver his people from greater, so that they shall say, We had perished, if we had not perished;[3] we had been undone, if we had not been undone; we had been in danger, if we had not been in danger. God will so order the afflictions that befall you in the way of righteousness, that your souls shall say, We would not for all the world but that we had met with such and such troubles and afflictions; for surely, had not these befallen us, it would have been worse and worse with us. Oh the carnal security, pride, formality, dead-heartedness, lukewarmness, censoriousness, and earthliness that God hath cured us of, by the trouble and dangers that we have met with in the ways and services of the Lord!

I remember a story of a godly man, that as he was going to take shipping for France, he broke his leg; and it pleased Providence so to order it, that the ship that he should have gone in, at that very instant was cast away, and not a man saved; so by breaking a bone, his life was saved.[4] So the Lord many times breaks our bones, but it is in order to the saving of our lives and our souls for ever. He gives us a portion that makes us heart-sick, but it is in order to the making us perfectly well, and to the purging of us from those ill humours that

---

[1] ἀμελήσαντες. Disregard, not care for it.

[2] Francis Xavorias [Xavier.—G.] counselled John the Third, king of Portugal, to meditate every day a quarter of an hour upon that text, ' What shall it profit a man to gain the whole world, and lose his soul!'   [3] Periissem nisi periissem.

[4] The 'breaking of his leg' on the way saved the life of the saintly Bernard Gilpin from being sacrificed by Bonner. See Memoir of Dr Airay, prefixed to his 'Philippians,' in the series of 'Commentaries' issued by the Publisher of this.—G.

have made our heads ache, and God's heart ache, and our souls sick, and heavy to the death, &c. Oh therefore let no danger or misery hinder thee from thy duty.[1]

Remedy (5). The fifth remedy against this device of Satan is, solemnly to consider, *That you shall gain more in the service of God, and by walking in righteous and holy ways, though troubles and afflictions should attend you, than you can possibly suffer, or lose, by your being found in the service of God.* 'Godliness is great gain,' 1 Tim. vi. 6. Oh, the joy, the peace, the comfort, the rest, that saints meet with in the ways and service of God! They find that religious services are not empty things, but things in which God is pleased to discover his beauty and glory to their souls. 'My soul thirsts for God,' saith David, 'that I might see thy beauty and thy glory, as I have seen thee in thy sanctuary,' Ps. lxiii. 2. Oh, the sweet looks, the sweet words, the sweet hints, the sweet joggings, the sweet influences, the sweet love-letters, that gracious souls have from heaven, when they wait upon God in holy and heavenly services, the least of which will darken and outweigh all the bravery and glory of this world, and richly recompense the soul for all the troubles, afflictions, and dangers that have attended it in the service of God.[2] Oh, the saints can say under all their troubles and afflictions, that they have meat to eat, and drink to drink, that the world knows not of; that they have such incomes, such refreshments, such warmings, &c., that they would not exchange for all the honours, riches, and dainties of this world. Ah, let but a Christian compare his external losses with his spiritual, internal, and external gain, and he shall find, that for every penny that he loses in the service of God, he gains a pound; and for every pound that he loses, he gains a hundred; for every hundred lost, he gains a thousand. We lose pins in his service, and find pearls; we lose the favour of the creature, and peace with the creature, and haply the comforts and contents of the creature, and we gain the favour of God, peace with conscience, and the comforts and contents of a better life. Ah, did the men of this world know the sweet that saints enjoy in afflictions, they would rather choose Manasseh's iron chain than his golden crown; they would rather be Paul a prisoner, than Paul rapt up in the third heaven. For 'light afflictions,' they shall have 'a weight of glory;' for a few afflictions, they shall have these joys, pleasures, and contents, that are as the stars of heaven, or as the sands of the sea that cannot be numbered; for momentary afflictions, they shall have an eternal crown of glory.[3] 'It is but winking, and

---

[1] Non essem ego salvus nisi ista periissent.—*Anaxagoras.* Had not these things perished, I could not have been safe, said this phliosopher, when he saw great possessions that he had lost.

[2] Tertul [lian], in his book to the martyrs, hath an apt saying (*Negotiatio est aliquid amittere ut majora lucreris*), *i. e.* that's right and good merchandise, when something is parted with to gain more. He applieth it to their sufferings, wherein, though the flesh lost something, yet the spirit got much more.

[3] When the noble General Zedislaus had lost his hand in the wars of the king of Poland, the king sent him a golden hand for it. What we lose in Christ's service he will make up, by giving us some golden mercies. Though the cross be bitter, yet it is but short; a little storm, as one said of Julian's persecution, and an eternal calm follows.

thou shalt be in heaven presently,' said the martyr.[1] Oh, therefore, let not afflictions or troubles work thee to shun the ways of God, or to quit that service that should be dearer to thee than a world, yea, than thy very life, &c.

The third device that Satan hath to hinder souls from holy and heavenly services, and from religious performances, is,

Device (3). *By presenting to the soul the difficulty of performing them.* Saith Satan, it is so hard and difficult a thing to pray as thou shouldst, and to wait on God as thou shouldst, and to walk with God as thou shouldst, and to be lively, warm, and active in the communion of saints, as thou shouldst, that you were better ten thousand times to neglect them, than to meddle with them ; and doubtless by this device Satan hath and doth keep off thousands from waiting on God, and from giving to him that service that is due to his name.

Now, the remedies against this device of Satan are these :

Remedy (1). The first remedy against this device of Satan is, *To dwell more upon the necessity of the service and duty, than on the difficulty that doth attend the duty.* You should reason thus with your souls : O our souls, though such and such services be hard and difficult, yet are they not exceeding necessary for the honour of God, and the keeping up his name in the world, and the keeping under of sin, and the strengthening of weak graces, and so the reviving of languishing comforts, and for the keeping clear and bright your blessed evidences, and for the scattering of your fears, and for the raising of your hopes, and for the gladding the hearts of the righteous, and stopping the mouths of unrighteous souls, who are ready to take all advantages to blaspheme the name of God, and throw dirt and contempt upon his people and ways. Oh, never leave thinking on the necessity of this and that duty, till your souls be lifted up far above all the difficulties that do attend religious duties.[2]

Remedy (2). The second remedy against this device of Satan is, solemnly to consider, *That the Lord Jesus will make his services easy to you, by the sweet discovery of himself to your souls, whilst you are in his service.* 'Thou meetest him that rejoiceth and worketh righteousness, those that remember thee in thy ways,' as the prophet Isaiah saith, Isa. lxiv. 5.[3] If meeting with God, who is goodness itself, beauty itself, strength itself, glory itself, will not sweeten his service to thy soul, nothing in heaven or earth will.

Jacob's meeting with Rachel, and enjoying of Rachel, made his hard service to be easy and delightful to him ; and will not the soul's enjoying of God, and meeting with God, render his service to be much more easy and delightful? Doubtless it will. The Lord will give that

---

[1] Paulisper O senex, oculos claude, nam statim lumen Dei videbis.—*Sozomen*, lib. ii. cap. ii.—G.

[2] The necessity of doing your duty appears by this, that you are his servants by a threefold right ; you are his servants (*jure creationis, jure sustentationis, jure redemptionis*) by right of creation, and by right of sustentation, and by right of redemption.

[3] פֻּנַעְתָּ, *Paganta*, is diversely taken ; but most take the word here, to meet a soul with those bowels of love and tenderness as the father of the prodigal met the prodigal with. God is *Pater miserationum*, he is all bowels ; he is swift to shew mercy, as he is slow to anger.

sweet assistance by his Spirit and grace, as shall make his service joyous and not grievous, a delight and not a burden, a heaven and not a hell, to believing souls.[1] The confidence of this divine assistance raised up Nehemiah's spirit far above all those difficulties and discouragements that did attend him in the work and service of the Lord, as you may see in Nehemiah ii. 19, 20, 'But when Sanballat the Horonite, and Tobiah the servant, the Ammonite, and Geshem the Arabian, heard it, they laughed us to scorn, and despised us, and said, What is this thing that ye do? will ye rebel against the king? Then answered I them, and said unto them, The God of heaven, he will prosper us; therefore we his servants will arise and build: but you have no right, nor portion, nor memorial, in Jerusalem.' Ah, souls, while you are in the very service of the Lord, you shall find by experience, that the God of heaven will prosper you, and support you, and encourage and strengthen you, and carry you through the hardest service, with the greatest sweetness and cheerfulness that can be. Remember this, that God will suit your strength to your work, and in the hardest service you shall have the choicest assistance.

Remedy (3). The third remedy against this device of Satan is, *To dwell upon the hard and difficult things that the Lord Jesus hath passed through for your temporal, spiritual, and eternal good.* Ah, what a sea of blood, a sea of wrath, of sin, of sorrow and misery, did the Lord Jesus wade through for your internal and eternal good![2] Christ did not plead, This cross is too heavy for me to bear; this wrath is too great for me to lie under; this cup, which hath in it all the ingredients of divine displeasure, is too bitter for me to sup off,[3] how much more to drink the very dregs of it? No, Christ stands not upon this; he pleads not the difficulty of the service, but resolutely and bravely wades through all, as the prophet Isaiah shews: 'The Lord God hath opened my ear, and I was not rebellious, neither turned away my back. I gave my back to the smiters, and my cheeks to them that plucked off the hair; I hid not my face from shame and spitting,' chap. l. 6. Christ makes nothing of his Father's wrath, the burden of your sins, the malice of Satan, and the rage of the world, but sweetly and triumphantly passes through all. Ah, souls! if this consideration will not raise up your spirits above all the discouragements that you meet with, to own Christ and his service, and to stick and cleave to Christ and his service, I am afraid nothing will. A soul not stirred by this, not raised and lifted up by this, to be resolute and brave in the service of God, notwithstanding all dangers and difficulties, is a soul left of God to much blindness and hardness.[4]

---

[1] Luther speaks excellently to Melancthon, who was apt to be discouraged with doubts and difficulties, and fear from foes, and to cease the service they had undertaken. 'If the work be not good, why did we ever own it? If it be good, why should we ever decline it? Why, saith he, should we fear the conquered world, that have Christ the conqueror on our side'? [From the Reformer's Letters during the diet of Augsburg, A.D. 1530. Cf. D'Aubigné, Hist. of Ref.; c. xiv. § 10, c. 6.—G.]

[2] It is not fit, since the Head was crowned with thorns, that the members should be crowned with rosebuds, saith Zanch[ius].   [3] Qu. 'sip of'?—Ed.

[4] Godfrey of Bullen [Bouillon], first king of Jerusalem, refused to be crowned with a crown of gold, saying, it became not a Christian there to wear a crown of gold, where Christ for our salvation had sometime worn a crown of thorns. [Cf. Tasso.—G.]

Remedy (4). The fourth remedy against this device of Satan is to consider, *That religious duties, holy and heavenly exercises, are only difficult to the worse, to the ignoble, part of a saint.* They are not to the noble and better part of a saint, to the noble part, the soul, and the renewed affections of a saint. Holy exercises are a heavenly pleasure and recreation, as the apostle speaks : ' I delight in the law of God, after the inward man : with my mind I serve the law of God, though with my flesh the law of sin,' Rom. vii. 22. To the noble part of a saint, Christ's ' yoke is easy, and his burden is light,' Mat. xi. 30.[1] All the commands and ways of Christ (even those that tend to the pulling out of right eyes and cutting off of right hands) are joyous, and not grievous, to the noble part of a saint.[2] All the ways and services of Christ are pleasantness, in the abstract, to the better part of a saint. A saint, so far as he is renewed, is always best when he sees most of God, when he tastes most of God, when he is highest in his enjoyments of God, and most warm and lively in the service of God. Oh, saith the noble part of a saint, that it might be always thus ! Oh that my strength were the strength of stones, and my flesh as brass, that my worser part might be more serviceable to my noble part, that I might act by an untired power in that service, that is a pleasure, a paradise, to me.

Remedy (5). The fifth remedy against this device of Satan is, solemnly to consider, *That great reward and glorious recompence that doth attend those that cleave to the service of the Lord in the face of all difficulties and discouragements.* Though the work be hard, yet the wages is great. Heaven will make amends for all. Ay, one hour's being in heaven will abundantly recompense you for cleaving to the Lord and his ways in the face of all difficulties. This carried the apostle through the greatest difficulties. He had an eye ' to the recompence of reward ;' he looked for ' a house that had foundations, whose builder and maker was God,' and for ' a heavenly country.' Yea, this bore up the spirit of Christ in the face of all difficulties and discouragements : ' Looking unto Jesus, the author and finisher of our faith ; who, for the joy that was set before him, endured the cross, despising the shame, and is set down at the right hand of the throne of God,' Heb. xii. 2.[3]

Christians that would hold on in the service of the Lord, must look more upon the crown than upon the cross, more upon their future glory than their present misery, more upon their encouragements than upon their discouragements. God's very service is wages ; his ways are strewed with roses, and paved ' with joy that is unspeakable and full of glory,' and with ' peace that passeth understanding.' Some degree of comfort follows every good action, as heat accompanies fire,

---

[1] χρηστός, *i.e.* my yoke is a benign, a gracious, a pleasant, a good, and a gainful yoke, opposed to πονηρός, painful, tedious.

[2] As every flower hath its sweet savour, so every good duty carries meat in the mouth, comfort in the performance of it.

[3] Basil speaks of some martyrs that were cast out all night naked in a cold, frosty time, and were to be burned the next day, how they comforted themselves in this manner : The winter is sharp, but paradise is sweet ; here we shiver for cold, but the bosom of Abraham will make amends for all.

as beams and influences issue from the sun : ' Moreover, by them is
thy servant warned, and in keeping of them there is great reward,'
Ps. xix. 11. Not only for keeping, but in keeping of them, there is
great reward.[1] The joy, the rest, the refreshing, the comforts, the contents, the smiles, the incomes[2] that saints now enjoy in the ways of
God, are so precious and glorious in their eyes, that they would not
exchange them for ten thousand worlds. Ah ! if the vails[3] be thus
sweet and glorious before pay-day comes, what will be that glory that
Christ will crown his saints with for cleaving to his service in the face
of all difficulties ; when he shall say to his Father, ' Lo, here am I, and
the children which thou hast given me,' Isa. viii. 18. If there be so
much to be had in a wilderness, what then shall be had in paradise ? &c.

The fourth device that Satan hath to keep souls off from holy exercises, from religious services, is,

Device (4). *By working them to make false inferences from those
blessed and glorious things that Christ hath done.* As that Jesus
Christ hath done all for us, therefore there is nothing for us to do but
to joy and rejoice. He hath perfectly justified us, and fulfilled the
law, and satisfied divine justice, and pacified his Father's wrath, and
is gone to heaven to prepare a place for us, and in the mean time to
intercede for us ; and therefore away with praying, and mourning,
and hearing, &c. Ah ! what a world of professors hath Satan drawn
in these days from religious services, by working them to make such
sad, wild, and strange inferences from the sweet and excellent things
that the Lord Jesus hath done for his beloved ones.

Now, the remedies against this device are these :

Remedy (1). The first remedy against this device of Satan is, *To
dwell as much on those scriptures that shew you the duties and
services that Christ requires of you, as upon those scriptures that
declare to you the precious and glorious things that Christ hath done
for you.*[4] It is a sad and dangerous thing to have two eyes to behold
our dignity and privileges, and not one to see our duties and services. I
should look with one eye upon the choice and excellent things that Christ
hath done for me, to raise up my heart to love Christ with the purest
love, and to joy in Christ with the strongest joy, and to lift up Christ
above all, who hath made himself to be my all ; and I should look with
the other eye upon those services and duties that the Scriptures require
of those for whom Christ hath done such blessed things, as upon that
of the apostle : ' What, know ye not that your body is the temple of
the Holy Ghost, which is in you, which ye have of God ? and ye are not
your own : for ye are bought with a price ; therefore glorify God in
your body, and in your spirit, which are God's,' 1 Cor. vi. 19, 20.
And that : ' Therefore, my beloved brethren, be ye stedfast, unmoveable,
always abounding in the work of the Lord, knowing that your labour

---

[1] This is *præmium ante præmium*, a sure reward of well doing ; *in* doing thereof, not
only *for* doing thereof, there is great reward, Ps. xix. 11.
[2] 'In-comings.'—G.   [3] 'Gratuities.'—G.
[4] Tertullian hath this expression of the Scriptures : *Adoro plenitudinem Scripturarum*,
I adore the fulness of the Scripture. Gregory calls the Scripture, *Cor et animam Dei*,
the heart and soul of God ; and who will not then dwell in it ?

is not in vain in the Lord,' 1 Cor. xv. 58. And that : 'And let us not be weary in well-doing, for in due season we shall reap if we faint not,' Gal. vi. 9. And that of the apostle : 'Rejoice always,' 1 Thes. v. 16, and 'Pray without ceasing,' 1 Thes. v. 17. And that in the Philippians, 'Work out your own salvation with fear and trembling,' ii. 12 ; and that, 'This do till I come,' 1 Tim. iv. 13 ; and that, 'Let us consider one another, to provoke one another to love, and to good works, not forsaking the assembling of ourselves together, as the manner of some is, but exhorting one another, and so much the more as you see the day approaching,' Heb. x. 24, 25. Now, a soul that would not be drawn away by this device of Satan, he must not look with a squint eye upon these blessed scriptures, and abundance more of like import, but he must dwell upon them ; he must make these scriptures to be his chiefest and his choicest companions, and this will be a happy means to keep him close to Christ and his service in these times, wherein many turn their backs upon Christ, under pretence of being interested in the great glorious things that have been acted by Christ, &c.[1]

Remedy (2). The second remedy against this device of Satan is, to consider, *That the great and glorious things that Jesus Christ hath done, and is a-doing for us, should be so far from taking us off from religious services and pious performances, that they should be the greatest motives and encouragements to the performance of them that may be, as the Scriptures do abundantly evidence.* I will only instance in some, as that, 'That we, being delivered out of the hands of our enemies, might serve him without fear, in holiness and righteousness before him all the days of our lives,' 1 Peter ii. 9, Luke i. 74, 75. Christ hath freed you from all your enemies, from the curse of the law, the predominant damnatory power of sin, the wrath of God, the sting of death, and the torments of hell ; but what is the end and design of Christ in doing these great and marvellous things for his people ? It is not that we should throw off duties of righteousness and holiness, but that their hearts may be the more free and sweet in all holy duties and heavenly services.[2] So the apostle, 'I will be their God, and they shall be my people :' 'And I will be a Father unto you, and ye shall be my sons and daughters, saith the Lord Almighty.' Mark what follows : 'Having therefore these promises, dearly beloved, let us cleanse ourselves from all filthiness of the flesh and spirit, perfecting holiness in the fear of the Lord,' 2 Cor. vi. 17, 18, chap. vii. 1 compared. And again : 'The grace of God that bringeth salvation hath appeared to all men, teaching us that, denying all ungodliness and worldly lusts, we should live soberly, righteously, and godly in this present world, looking for that blessed hope, and the glorious appearing of the great God and our Saviour Jesus Christ, who gave himself for us, that he might redeem us from all iniquity, and

[1] The Jews were much in turning over the leaves of the Scripture, but they did not weigh the matter of them : John v. 39, 'You search the Scriptures.' Greek there seemeth to be indicative rather than imperative.

[2] This I am sure of, that all man's happiness here is his holiness, and his holiness shall hereafter be his happiness. Christ hath therefore broke the devil's yoke from off our necks, that his Father might have better service from our hearts.

purify us unto himself a peculiar people, zealous of good works,' Titus
ii. 12–14. Ah, souls! I know no such arguments to work you to a
lively and constant performance of all heavenly services, like those that
are drawn from the consideration of the great and glorious things that
Christ hath done for you ; and if such arguments will not take you
and win upon you, I do think the throwing of hell fire in your faces
will never do it.[1]

Remedy (3). The third remedy against this device of Satan is,
seriously to consider, *That those precious souls which Jesus Christ
hath done and suffered as much for as he hath for you, have been
exceeding active and lively in all religious services and heavenly
performances.*[2] He did as much and suffered as much for David as for
you, and yet who more in praying and praising God than David ?
' Seven times a day will I praise the Lord,' Ps. cxix. 174. Who more
in the studying and meditating on the word than David ? 'The law is
my meditation day and night,' Ps. cxix. 97. The same truth you may
run and read in Jacob, Moses, Job, Daniel, and in the rest of the holy
prophets and apostles, for whom Christ hath done as much for as for
you. Ah, how have all those worthies abounded in works of righteousness and holiness, to the praise of free grace? Certainly Satan hath
got the upper hand of those souls that do argue thus. Christ hath
done such and such glorious things for us, therefore we need not make
any care and conscience of doing such and such religious services as
men say the word calls for. If this logic be not from hell, what is ?
Ah, were the holy prophets and apostles alive to hear such logic come
out of the mouths of such as profess themselves to be interested in the
great and glorious things that Jesus Christ hath done for his chosen
ones, how would they blush to look upon such souls! and how would
their hearts grieve and break within them to hear the language and to
observe the actings of such souls.[3]

Remedy (4). The fourth remedy against this device of Satan is ,
seriously to consider this, *That those that do not walk in the ways
of righteousness and holiness, that do not wait upon God in the
several duties and services that are commanded by him, cannot have
that evidence to their own souls of their righteousness before God, of
their fellowship and communion with God, of their blessedness here,
and their happiness hereafter, as those souls have, that love and delight in the ways of the Lord, that are always best when they are
most in the works and service of the Lord.*[4] ' Little children,' saith

---

[1] *Tace, lingua ; loquere, vita,* talk not of a good life, but let thy life speak. Your actions
in passing pass not away ; for every good work is a grain of seed for eternal life.

[2] The saints' motto in all ages hath been *Laboremus,* let us be doing. God loves.
Curristas, not *Quæristas,* the runner, not the questioner or disputer, saith Luther.

[3] The day is at hand when God will require of men, *Non quid legerint, sed quid egerint.
nec quid dixerint, sed quomodo vixerint.* He that talks of heaven, but doth not the will of
God, is like him that gazed upon the moon, but fell into the pit.

[4] Certainly it is one thing to judge by our graces, another thing to rest or put
our trust in them. There is a great deal of difference betwixt declaring and de-
serving. As David's daughters were known by their garments of divers colours, so
are God's children by their piety and sanctity. A Christian's emblem should be an
house walking towards heaven. High words surely make a man neither holy nor
just ; but a virtuous life, a circumspect walking, makes him dear to God. A tree
that is not fruitful is for the fire. Christianity is not a talking, but a walking with

the apostle, 'let no man deceive you : he that doth righteousness is
righteous, even as he is righteous,' 1 John iii. 7. ' In this,' saith the
same apostle, ' the children of God are manifest, and the children of
the devil ; whosoever doth not righteousness is not of God, neither he
that loveth not his brother,' ver. 10. ' If ye know that he is righteous,'
saith the same apostle, ' ye know that every one that doth righteousness,
is born of him. He that saith, I know him, and keepeth not his commandments, is a liar, and the truth is not in him. But whosoever
keepeth his word, in him verily is the love of God perfected : hereby
know we that we are in him. He that saith he abideth in him, ought
himself also to walk, even as he walked.' ' If we say that we have
fellowship with him, and walk in darkness, we lie, and do not the
truth ; but if we walk in the light, as he is in the light, we have fellowship one with another ; and the blood of Jesus Christ cleanseth us
from all sin,' saith the same apostle, 1 John ii. 4–6, and i. 6, 7. So
James ii. 14, 20, ' What doth it profit, my brethren, though a man
say he hath faith, and have no works ; can faith save him ?' *i. e.* it
cannot. ' For as the body without spirit is dead, so faith without
works is dead also.' To look after holy and heavenly works, is the best
way to preserve the soul from being deceived and deluded by Satan's
delusions, and by sudden flashes of joy and comfort ; holy works being
a more sensible[1] and constant pledge of the precious Spirit, begetting
and maintaining in the soul more solid, pure, clear, strong, and lasting
joy. Ah souls! As you would have in yourselves a constant and a
blessed evidence of your fellowship with the Father and the Son, and
of the truth of grace, and of your future happiness, look that you
cleave close to holy services ; and that you turn not your backs upon
religious duties.

Remedy (5). The fifth remedy against this device of Satan is,
solemnly to consider, *That there are other choice and glorious ends
for the saint's performance of religious duties, than for the justifying
of their persons before God, or for their satisfying of the law or justice
of God, or for the purchasing of the pardon of sin, &c. viz., to testify
their justification.*[2] ' A good tree cannot but bring forth good fruits,'
Mat. vii. 17, to testify their love to God, and their sincere obedience to
the commands of God ; to testify their deliverance from spiritual bondage, to evidence the indwellings of the Spirit, to stop the mouths of the
worst of men, and to glad those righteous souls that God would not have
sadded. These, and abundance of other choice ends there be, why
those that have an interest in the glorious doings of Christ, should,
notwithstanding that, keep close to the holy duties and religious services that are commanded by Christ. And if these considerations
will not prevail with you, to wait upon God in holy and heavenly

God, who will not be put off with words ; if he miss of fruit, he will take up his axe,
and then the soul is cut off for ever.—[Query, ' horse' ? But prefixed to a volume of
1656, called ' Sacred Principles, Services and Soliloquies, or a Manual of Devotions,'
is a singular frontispiece, having this very emblem of a ' house' ascending upward, re-
presentative, as explained in quaint accompanying verse, of the Church. So that the
mixed metaphor belongs to the period.—G.]   [1] ' Conscious.'—G.

[2] It is a precious truth, never to be forgotten, *Quod non actibus, sed finibus pensantur
officia*, that duties are esteemed not by their acts, but by their ends.

duties. I am afraid if one should rise from the dead, his arguments would not win upon you, but you would hold on in your sins, and neglect his service, though you lost your souls for ever, &c.[1]

The fifth device Satan hath to draw souls off from religious services, and to keep souls off from holy duties, is,

Device (5). *By presenting to them the paucity and poverty of those that walk in the ways of God, that hold on in religious practices.* Saith Satan, Do not you see that those that walk in such and such religious ways are the poorest, the meanest, and the most despicable persons in the world? This took with them in John vii. 47–49, 'Then answered the pharisees, Are ye also deceived? Have any of the rulers, or of the pharisees, believed on him? But this people who knoweth not the law are cursed.'

Now the remedies against this device are these that follow :

Remedy (1). The first remedy against this device of Satan is, to consider, *That though they are outwardly poor, yet they are inwardly rich.* Though they are poor in temporals, yet they are rich in spirituals.[2] The worth and riches of the saints is inward. 'The King's daughter is all glorious within,' Ps. xlv. 13. 'Hearken, my beloved brethren, hath not God chosen the poor of this world, rich in faith, and heirs of the kingdom which he hath promised to them that love him?' saith James ii. 5. 'I know thy poverty, but thou art rich,' saith John to the church of Smyrna,' Rev. ii. 4. What though they have little in possession, yet they have a glorious kingdom in reversion. 'Fear not, little flock, it is your Father's pleasure to give you a kingdom,' Luke xii. 32. Though saints have little in hand, yet they have much in hope. You count those happy, in a worldly sense, that have much in reversion, though they have little in possession; and will you count the saints miserable because they have little in hand, little in possession, though they have a glorious kingdom in reversion of this? I am sure the poorest saint that breathes will not exchange, were it in his power, that which he hath in hope and in reversion, for the possession of as many worlds as there be stars in heaven, or sands in the sea, &c.

Remedy (2). The second remedy against this device of Satan is, to consider, *That in all ages God hath had some that have been great, rich, wise, and honourable, that have chosen his ways, and cleaved to his service in the face of all difficulties.* Though not many wise men, yet some wise men; and though not many mighty, yet some mighty have; and though not many noble, yet some noble have. Witness Abraham, and Jacob, and Job, and several kings, and others that the Scriptures speak of. And ah! how many have we among ourselves, whose souls have cleaved to the Lord, and who have swum to his service through the blood of the slain, and who have not counted

---

[1] *Finis movet ad agendum,* the end moves to doing. *Tene mensuram et respice finem,* keep thyself within compass, and have an eye always to the end of thy life and actions, was Maximilian the emperor's motto.

[2] Do not you see, saith Chrysostom, the places where treasures are hid, are rough and overgrown with thorns? Do not the naturalists ell you, that the mountains that are big with gold within, are bare of grass without? Saints have, as scholars, poor commons here, because they must study hard to go to heaven.

their lives dear unto them, that they and others might enjoy the holy things of Christ, according to the mind and heart of Christ, &c.[1]

Remedy (3). The third remedy against this device of Satan is, solemnly to consider, *That the spiritual riches of the poorest saints do infinitely transcend the temporal riches of all the wicked men in the world; their spiritual riches do satisfy them; they can sit down satisfied with the riches of grace that be in Christ, without honours, and without riches, &c.*[2] 'He that drinks of that water that I shall give him, shall thirst no more,' John iv. 13.   The riches of poor saints are durable; they will bed and board with them; they will go to the prison, to a sickbed, to a grave, yea, to heaven with them.   The spiritual riches of poor saints are as wine to cheer them, and as bread to strengthen them, and as cloth to warm them, and as armour to protect them.   Now, all you that know anything, do know that the riches of this world cannot satisfy the souls of men, and they are as fading as a flower, or as the owners of them are, &c.[3]

Remedy (4). The fourth remedy against this device is, seriously to consider, *That though the saints, considered comparatively, are few; though they be 'a little, little flock,' 'a remnant,' 'a garden enclosed,' 'a spring shut up, a fountain sealed;' though they are as 'the summer gleanings;' though they are 'one of a city, and two of a tribe;'*[4] *though they be but a handful to a houseful, a spark to a flame, a drop to the ocean, yet consider them simply in themselves, and so they are an innumerable number that cannot be numbered.* As John speaketh: 'After this I beheld, and lo, a great multitude which no man could number, of all nations, and kindreds, and peoples, and tongues, stood before the throne, and before the Lamb, clothed with white robes, and palms in their hands,' Rev. vii. 9.   So Matthew speaks: 'And I say unto you, that many shall come from the east and west, and shall sit down with Abraham, Isaac, and Jacob in the kingdom of heaven,' Mat. viii. 11.   So Paul: 'But ye are come unto mount Sion, and unto the city of the living God, the heavenly Jerusalem, and to an innumerable company of angels, to the general assembly and church of the firstborn, which are written in heaven, and to God the judge of all, and to the spirits of just men made perfect,' Heb. xii. 22.[5]

Remedy (5). The fifth remedy against this device of Satan is, seriously to consider, *That it will be but as a day before these poor despised saints shall shine brighter than the sun in his glory.*   It will not be long before you will wish, Oh! that we were now among the poor, mean despised ones in the day that God comes to make up his jewels!   It will not be long before these poor few saints shall be lifted up upon their thrones to judge the multitude, the world, as the apostle speaks: 'Know ye not that the saints shall judge the world?' 1 Cor. vi. 2.   And in that

[1] Good nobles, saith one, are like black swans; and [are] thinly scattered in the firmament of a State, even like stars of the first magnitude: yet some God hath had in all ages, as might be shewed out of histories.

[2] Alexander's vast mind inquired if there were any more worlds to conquer.

[3] Crassus was so rich that he maintained an army with his own revenues; yet he, his great army, with his son and heir, fell together, and left his great estate to others.

[4] Luke xii. 32, Isaiah i. 9, Canticles iv. 12, Judges viii. 2, and Jeremiah iii. 14.—G.

[5] When Fulgentius saw the nobility of Rome sit mounted in their bravery, it mounted his meditations to the heavenly Jerusalem.

day, oh! how will the great and the rich, the learned and the noble, wish that they had lived and spent their days with these few poor contemptible creatures in the service of the Lord! Oh! how will this wicked world curse the day that ever they had such base thoughts of the poor mean saints, and that their poverty became a stumbling-block to keep them off from the ways of sanctity.[1]

I have read of Ingo, an ancient king of the Draves, who, making a stately feast, appointed his nobles, at that time pagans, to sit in the hall below, and commanded certain poor Christians to be brought up into his presence-chamber, to sit with him at his table, to eat and drink of his kingly cheer; at which many wondering, he said, 'He accounted Christians, though never so poor, a greater ornament to his table, and more worthy of his company, than the greatest peers unconverted to the Christian faith; for when these might be thrust down to hell, those might be his consorts and fellow-princes in heaven.' You know how to apply it. Although you see the stars sometimes by their reflections in a puddle, or in the bottom of a well, ay, in a stinking ditch, yet the stars have their situation in heaven. So, though you see a godly man in a poor, miserable, low, despised condition for the things of this world, yet he is fixed in heaven, in the region of heaven: 'Who hath raised us up,' saith the apostle, 'and made us sit together in heavenly places in Christ Jesus.' Oh! therefore, say to your own souls, when they begin to decline the ways of Sion because of the poverty and paucity of those that walk in them, The day is at hand when those few, poor, despised saints shall shine in glory, when they shall judge this world, and when all the wicked of this world will wish that they were in their condition, and would give ten thousand worlds, were it in their power, that they might but have the honour and happiness to wait upon those whom for their poverty and paucity they have neglected and despised in this world.

Remedy (6). The sixth remedy against this device of Satan is, solemnly to consider, *That there will come a time, even in this life, in this world, when the reproach and contempt that is now cast upon the ways of God, by reason of the poverty and paucity of those that walk in those ways, shall be quite taken away, by his making them the head that have days without number been the tail, and by his raising them up to much outward riches, prosperity, and glory, who have been as the outcast because of their poverty and paucity.*[2] John,

[1] Mr Fox being once asked whether he knew a certain poor man who had received succour of him in time of trouble, he answered, I remember him well. I tell you I forget lords and ladies to remember such. So will God deal by his poor saints. He will forget the great and mighty ones of the world to remember his few poor despised ones. Though John the Baptist was poor in the world, yet the Holy Ghost calls him the greatest that was born of woman. Ah, poor saints, men that know not your worth, cannot have such low thoughts of you, but the Lord will have as high.

[2] These following scriptures do abundantly confirm this truth: Jer. xxxi. 12; Isa. xxx. 23, lxii. 8, 9; Joel ii. 23, 24; Micah iv. 6; Amos ix. 13, 14; Zech. viii. 12; Isa. xli. 18, 19, lv. 13, lxvi. 6, 7, lxv. 21, 22, lxi. 4, lx. 10; Ezek. xxxvi. 10. Only take these two cautions: 1. That in these times the saints' chiefest comforts, delights, and contents will consist in their more clear, full, and constant enjoyment of God. 2. That they shall have such abundant measure of the Spirit poured out upon them, that their riches and outward glory shall not be snares unto them, but golden steps to a richer living in God.

speaking of the glory of the church, the new Jerusalem that came
down from heaven, Rev. xxi. 24, tells us, 'That the nations of them
which are saved shall walk in the light of it, and the kings of the
earth do bring their glory into it.' So the prophet Isaiah, 'They shall
bring their sons from far, and their silver and their gold with them.
For brass I will bring gold, and for iron I will bring silver, and for
wood brass, and for stones iron,' chap. lx. 17. And so the prophet
Zechariah speaks: chap. xiv. 14, 'And the wealth of all the heathen
round about shall be gathered together, gold, and silver, and apparel,
in great abundance.' The Lord hath promised that 'the meek shall
inherit the earth,' Mat. v. 5 ; and 'heaven and earth shall pass away,
before one jot or one tittle of his word shall pass unfulfilled,' ver. 18.
Ah, poor saints! now some thrust sore at you, others look a-squint
upon you, others shut the door against you, others turn their backs
upon you, and most of men (except it be a few that live much in God,
and are filled with the riches of Christ) do either neglect you or
despise you because of your poverty ; but the day is coming when you
shall be lifted up above the dunghill, when you shall change poverty
for riches, your rags for robes, your reproach for a crown of honour,
your infamy for glory, even in this world.

And this is not all, but God will also mightily increase the number
of his chosen ones, multitudes shall be converted to him : 'Who hath
heard such a thing? who hath seen such things? shall the earth be
made to bring forth in one day? or shall a nation be born at once?
for as soon as Sion travailed, she brought forth children. And they
shall bring all your brethren for an offering unto the Lord, out of all
nations, upon horses, and in chariots, in litters, and upon mules, and
upon swift beasts, to my holy mountain Jerusalem, saith the Lord ;
as the children of Israel bring an offering in a clean vessel into the
house of the Lord,' Isa. lxvi. 8, 19, 20. Doth not the Scripture say,
that 'the kingdoms of this world must become the kingdoms of our
Lord'? Rev. xi. 15. Hath not God given to Christ 'the heathen, and
the uttermost parts of the earth for his possession'? Ps. ii. 8. Hath
not the Lord said, that in 'the last days the mountain of the Lord's
house shall be lifted up above the hills, and shall be established in the
top of the mountains, and all nations shall flow unto it,' Isa. ii. 2 and
liv. 14 and lxi. 9. Pray, read, and meditate upon Isa. lx. and lxvi. and
ii. 1–5, and there you shall find the multitudes that shall be converted
to Christ. And oh! that you would be mighty in believing ; and, in
wrestling with God, that he would hasten the day of his glory, that
the reproach that is now upon his people and ways may cease !

The sixth device that Satan hath to keep souls off from religious
services is,

Device (6). *By presenting before them the examples of the greatest
part of the world, that walk in the ways of their own hearts, and that
make light and slight of the ways of the Lord.*[1] Why, saith Satan,
do not you see that the great and the rich, the noble and the honourable, the learned and the wise, even the greatest number of men, never
trouble themselves about such and such ways, and why then should

---

[1] John vii. 48, 49, 1 Cor. i. 26, 28, Micah vii. 2–4.

you be singular and nice? You were far better do as the most do, &c.

Now, the remedies against this device are these:

Remedy (1). The first remedy against this device of Satan is, solemnly to consider *Of those scriptures that make directly against following the sinful examples of men.* As that in Exodus, 'Thou shalt not follow a multitude to do evil, neither shalt thou speak in a cause to decline after many to wrest judgment,' chap. xxiii. 2. The multitude generally are ignorant, and know not the way of the Lord, therefore they speak evil of that they know not. They are envious and maliciously bent against the service and way of God, and therefore they cannot speak well of the ways of God: 'This way is everywhere spoken against,' saith they, Acts xxviii. 22. So in Num. xvi. 21, 'Separate from them, and come out from among them.' So the apostle, 'Have no fellowship with the unfruitful works of darkness,' Eph. v. 11. So Solomon, 'Enter not into the way of the wicked; forsake the foolish, and live,' Prov. iv. 14 and ix. 6. They that walk with the most shall perish with the most.[1] They that do as the most shall ere long suffer with the most. They that live as the most, must die with the most, and to hell with the most.

Remedy (2). The second remedy against this device of Satan is, seriously to consider, *That if you will sin with the multitude, all the angels in heaven and men on earth cannot keep you from suffering with the multitude.* If you will be wicked with them, you must unavoidably be miserable with them.[2] Say to thy soul, O my soul! if thou wilt sin with the multitude, thou must be shut out of heaven with the multitude, thou must be cast down to hell with the multitude: 'And I heard a voice from heaven saying, Come out of her, my people, that ye be not partakers of her sins, and that ye receive not of her plagues,' Rev. xviii. 4. Come out in affection, in action, and in habitation, for else the infection of sin will bring upon you the infliction of punishment. So saith the wise man, 'He that walketh with wise men shall be wise, but a companion of fools shall be destroyed,' or as the Hebrew hath it, 'shall be broken in pieces,' Prov. xiii. 20.[3] Multitudes may help thee into sin, yea, one may draw thee into sin, but it is not multitudes that can help thee to escape punishments; as you may see in Moses and Aaron, that were provoked to sin by the multitude, but were shut out of the pleasant land, and fell by a hand of justice as well as others.

Remedy (3). The third remedy against this device of Satan is, solemnly to consider, *The worth and excellency of thy immortal soul.* Thy soul is a jewel more worth than heaven and earth. The loss of thy soul is incomparable, irreparable, and irrecoverable; if that be lost, all is lost, and thou art undone for ever. Is it madness and folly in a man to kill himself for company, and is it not greater madness or folly to break the neck of thy soul, and to damn it for company?

---

[1] The way to hell is broad and well beaten. The way to be undone for ever is to do as the most do. *Argumentum turpissimum est turba,* the multitude is the weakest and worst argument, saith Seneca. [*De Vita Beata,* ii.—G.]

[2] Sin and punishment are linked together with chains of adamant. Of sin we may say as Isidore doth of the serpent, *Tot dolores quot colores,* so many colours, so many dolours.   [3] ירוע, *Jeroange,* from רוע, *Ruange,* to be naught.

Suspect that way wherein thou seest multitudes to walk; the multitude being a stream that thou must row hard against, or thou wilt be carried into that gulf out of which angels cannot deliver thee. Is it not better to walk in a straight way alone, than to wander into crooked ways with company? Sure it is better to go to heaven alone than to hell with company.

I might add other things, but these may suffice for the present; and I am afraid, if these arguments do not stir you, other arguments will work but little upon you.[1]

The seventh device that Satan hath to keep souls off from holy exercises, from religious services, is,

Device (7). *By casting in a multitude of vain thoughts, whilst the soul is in seeking of God, or in waiting on God;* and by this device he hath cooled some men's spirits in heavenly services, and taken off, at least for a time, many precious souls from religious performances. I have no heart to hear, nor no heart to pray, nor no delight in reading, nor in the society of the saints, &c. Satan doth so dog and follow my soul, and is still a-casting in such a multitude of vain thoughts concerning God, the world, and my own soul, &c., that I even tremble to think of waiting upon God in any religious service. Oh! the vain thoughts that Satan casts in do so distaste my soul, and so grieve, vex, perplex, and distract my soul, that they even make me weary of holy duties, yea, of my very life. Oh! I cannot be so raised and ravished, so heated and melted, so quickened and enlarged, so comforted and refreshed, as I should be, as I might be, and as I would be in religious services, by reason of that multitude of vain thoughts, that Satan is injecting or casting into my soul, &c.[2]

Now, the remedies against this device of Satan are these:

Remedy (1). The first remedy against this device of Satan is, *To have your hearts strongly affected with the greatness, holinesss, majesty, and glory of that God before whom you stand, and with whom your souls do converse in religious services.* Oh! let your souls be greatly affected with the presence, purity, and majesty of that God before whom thou standest. A man would be afraid of playing with a feather, when he is speaking with a king. Ah! when men have poor, low, light, slight, &c., thoughts of God, in their drawing near to God, they tempt the devil to bestir himself, and to cast in a multitude of vain thoughts to disturb and distract the soul in its waiting on God. There is nothing that will contribute so much to the keeping out of vain thoughts, as to look upon God as an omniscient God, an omnipresent God, an omnipotent God, a God full of all glorious perfections, a God whose majesty, purity, and glory will not suffer him to behold the least iniquity.[3] The reason why the blessed saints and glorious angels in heaven have not so much as one vain thought is, because

---

[1] What wise man would fetch gold out of a fiery crucible, hazard his immortal soul, to gain the world, by following a multitude in those steps that lead to the chambers of death and darkness?

[2] *Vellem servire Domino, sed cogitationes non patiuntur*; Lord, now how fain would I serve thee, and vain thoughts will not suffer me!

[3] When Pompey could not keep his soldiers in the camp by persuasion, he cast himself all along in the narrow passage that led out of it, and bid them go if you will, but you must first trample upon your general; and the thoughts of this overcame them. You are wise, and know how to apply it to the point in hand.

they are greatly affected with the greatness, holiness, majesty, purity, and glory of God.

Remedy (2). The second remedy against this device of Satan is, *To be peremptory in religious services, notwithstanding all those wandering thoughts the soul is troubled with.* This will be a sweet help against them : for the soul to be resolute in waiting on God, whether it be troubled with vain thoughts or not ;[1] to say, Well I will pray still, and hear still, and meditate still, and keep fellowship with the saints still. Many precious souls can say from experience, that when their souls have been peremptory in their waiting on God, that Satan hath left them, and hath not been so busy in vexing their souls with vain thoughts. When Satan perceives that all those trifling vain thoughts that he casts into the soul do but vex the soul into greater diligence, carefulness, watchfulness, and peremptoriness in holy and heavenly services, and that the soul loses nothing of his zeal, piety, and devotion, but doubles his care, diligence, and earnestness, he often ceases to interpose his trifles and vain thoughts, as he ceased to tempt Christ, when Christ was peremptory in resisting his temptations.

Remedy (3). The third remedy against this device of Satan is, to consider this, *That those vain and trifling thoughts that are cast into our souls, when we are waiting upon God in this or that religious service, if they be not cherished and indulged, but abhorred, resisted, and disclaimed, they are not sins upon our souls, though they may be troubles to our minds; they shall not be put upon our accounts, nor keep mercies and blessings from being enjoyed by us.* When a soul in uprightness can look God in the face, and say, Lord, when I approach near unto thee, there be a world of vain thoughts crowd in upon me, that do disturb my soul, and weaken my faith, and lessen my comfort and spiritual strength. Oh, these are my clog, my burden, my torment, my hell ! Oh, do justice upon these, free me from these, that I may serve thee with more freeness, singleness, spiritualness, and sweetness of spirit.[2] These thoughts may vex that soul, but they shall not harm that soul, nor keep a blessing from that soul. If vain thoughts resisted and lamented could stop the current of mercy, and render a soul unhappy, there would be none on earth that should ever taste of mercy, or be everlastingly happy.

Remedy (4). The fourth remedy against this device of Satan is, solemnly to consider, *That watching against sinful thoughts, resisting of sinful thoughts, lamenting and weeping over sinful thoughts, carries with it the sweetest and strongest evidence of the truth and power of grace, and of the sincerity of your hearts, and is the readiest and the surest way to be rid of them,* Ps. cxxxix. 23. Many low and carnal considerations may work men to watch their words, their lives, their actions ; as hope of gain, or to please friends, or to get a name in the world, and many other such like considerations. Oh ! but to watch

---

[1] It is a rule in the civil law, *Nec videtur actum, si quid supersit quod agatur,* nothing seems to be done, if there remains aught to be done. *Si dixisti, Sufficit, periisti,* if once thou sayest it is enough, thou art undone, saith Augustine.

[2] It is not Satan casting in of vain thoughts that can keep mercy from the soul, or undo the soul, but the lodging and cherishing of vain thoughts: 'O Jerusalem. how long shall vain thoughts lodge within thee?' Jer. iv. 14; Heb. ' in the midst of thee.' They pass through the best hearts, they are lodged and cherished only in the worst hearts.

our thoughts, to weep and lament over them, &c., this must needs be from some noble, spiritual, and internal principle, as love to God, a holy fear of God, a holy care and delight to please the Lord, &c.[1] The schools do well observe, that outward sins are of greater infamy, *majoris infamiæ;* but inward heart sins are of greater guilt, *majoris reatus;* as we see in the devil's. There is nothing that so speaks out a man to be thoroughly and kindly wrought upon, as his having his thoughts to be ' brought into obedience,' as the apostle speaks, 2 Cor. x. 4, 5. Grace is grown up to a very great height in that soul where it prevails, to the subduing of those vain thoughts that walk up and down in the soul.[2] Well ! though you cannot be rid of them, yet make resistance and opposition against the first risings of them. When sinful thoughts arise, then think thus, The Lord takes notice of these thoughts ; ' he knows them afar off,' as the Psalmist speaks, Ps. xxxviii. 6. He knew Herod's bloody thoughts, and Judas his betraying thoughts, and the Pharisees' cruel and blasphemous thoughts afar off.[3] Oh ! think thus : All these sinful thoughts, they defile and pollute the soul, they deface and spoil much of the inward beauty and glory of the soul. If I commit this or that sin, to which my thoughts incline me, then either I must repent or not repent ; if I repent, it will cost me more grief, sorrow, shame, heart-breaking, and soul-bleeding, before my conscience will be quieted, divine justice pacified, my comfort and joy restored, my evidences cleared, and my pardon in the court of conscience sealed, than the imagined profit or seeming sensual pleasure can be worth : ' What fruit had you in those things whereof you are now ashamed,' Rom. vi. 21.[4]

If I never repent, oh ! then my sinful thoughts will be scorpions that will eternally vex me, the rods that will eternally lash me, the thorns that will everlastingly prick me, the dagger that will be eternally a-stabbing me, the worm that will be for ever a-gnawing me ! Oh ! therefore, watch against them, be constant in resisting them, and in lamenting and weeping over them, and then they shall not hurt thee, though they may for a time trouble thee. And remember this, he that doth this doth more than the most glistering and blustering hypocrite in the world doth.[5]

Remedy (5). The fifth remedy against this device of Satan is, *To labour more and more to be filled with the fulness of God, and to be enriched with all spiritual and heavenly things.* What is the reason that the angels in heaven have not so much as an idle thought? It is because they are filled with the fulness of God, Eph. iii. 19.[6] Take it for an experienced truth, the more the soul is filled with the fulness of God and enriched with spiritual and heavenly things, the less room

---

[1] Thoughts are the first-born, the blossoms of the soul, the beginning of our strength, whether for good or evil, and they are the greatest evidences for or against a man that can be.

[2] Ps cxxxix. 23 ; Isa. lix. 7, lxvi. 18 ; Mat. ix. 4, xii. 25.

[3] Zeno, a wise heathen, affirmed God even beheld the thoughts. Mat. xv. 15-18.

[4] Tears instead of gems were the ornaments of David's bed when he had sinned ; and so they must be thine, or else thou must lie down in the bed of sorrow for ever.

[5] Inward bleeding kills many a man ; so will sinful thoughts, if not repented of.

[6] The words are an Hebraism. The Hebrews, when they would set out many excellent things, they add the name of God to it: city of God, cedars of God, wrestlings of God. So here, ' That ye may be filled with the fulness of God.'

there is in that soul for vain thoughts. The fuller the vessel is of wine, the less room there is for water. Oh, then, lay up much of God, of Christ, of precious promises, and choice experiences in your hearts, and then you will be less troubled with vain thoughts. 'A good man, out of the good treasure of his heart, bringeth forth good things,' Mat. xii. 35.

Remedy (6). The sixth remedy against this device of Satan is, *To keep up holy and spiritual affections; for such as your affections are, such will be your thoughts.* 'Oh how I love thy law! it is my meditation all the day,' Ps. cxix. 97. What we love most, we most muse upon. 'When I awake, I am still with thee,' Ps. cxxxix., &c. That which we much like, we shall much mind. They that are frequent in their love to God and his law, will be frequent in thinking of God and his law: a child will not forget his mother.

Remedy (7). The seventh remedy against this device of Satan is, *To avoid multiplicity of worldly business.* Oh let not the world take up your hearts and thoughts at other times. Souls that are torn in pieces with the cares of the world will be always vexed and tormented with vain thoughts in all their approaches to God.[1] Vain thoughts will be still crowding in upon him that lives in a crowd of business. The stars which have least circuit are nearest the pole; and men that are least perplexed with business are commonly nearest to God.

The eighth device that Satan hath to hinder souls from religious services, from holy performances, is,

Device (8). *By working them to rest in their performances; to rest in prayer, and to rest in hearing, reading, and the communion of saints,* &c. And when Satan hath drawn the soul to rest upon the service done, then he will help the soul to reason thus: Why, thou wert as good never pray, as to pray and rest in prayer; as good never hear, as to hear and rest in hearing; as good never be in the communion of saints, as to rest in the communion of saints. And by this device he stops many souls in their heavenly race, and takes off poor souls from those services that should be their joy and crown, Isa. lviii. 1–3, Zech. vii. 4–6, Mat. vi. 2, Rom. i. 7.

Now the remedies against this device are these:

Remedy (1). The first remedy against this device of Satan is, *To dwell much upon the imperfections and weaknesses that do attend your choicest services.* Oh the spots, the blots, the blemishes that are to be seen on the face of our fairest duties![2] When thou hast done all thou canst, thou hast need to close up all with this, 'Oh enter not into judgment with thy servant, O Lord,' Ps. cxliii. 2, for the weaknesses that cleave to my best services. We may all say with the church, 'All our righteousnesses are as a menstruous cloth.' Isa. lxiv. 6. If God should be strict to mark what is done amiss in our best actions, we are undone. Oh the water that is mingled with our wine, the dross that cleaves unto our gold!

---

[1] 2 Tim. ii. 4, ἐμπλέκεται, is entangled; it is a comparison which St Paul borroweth from the custom of the Roman empire, wherein soldiers were forbidden to be proctors of other men's causes, to undertake husbandry or merchandise.

[2] Pride and high confidence is most apt to creep in upon duties well done, saith one.

Remedy (2). The second remedy against this device of Satan is, to consider *The impotence and inability of any of your best services, divinely to comfort, refresh, and bear your souls up from fainting, and sinking in the days of trouble, when darkness is round about you, when God shall say to you, as he did once to the Israelites,* 'Go and cry unto the gods that you have chosen ; let them save you in the time of your tribulation,' Judges x. 14. So, when God shall say in the day of your troubles, Go to your prayers, to your hearing, and to your fasting, &c., and see if they can help you, if they can support you, if they can deliver you.[1] If God in that day doth but withhold the influence of his grace, thy former services will be but poor cordials to comfort thee ; and then thou must and will cry out, Oh, 'none but Christ, none but Christ.' Oh my prayers are not Christ, my hearing is not Christ, my fasting is not Christ, &c. Oh ! one smile of Christ, one glimpse of Christ, one good word from Christ, one nod of love from Christ in the day of trouble and darkness, will more revive and refresh the soul than all your former services, in which your souls rested, as if they were the bosom of Christ, which should be the only centre of our souls. Christ is the crown of crowns, the glory of glories, and the heaven of heavens.

Remedy (3). The third remedy against this device of Satan is, solemnly to consider, *That good things rested upon will as certainly undo us, and everlastingly destroy us, as the greatest enormities that can be committed by us.* Those souls that after they have done all, do not look up so high as Christ, and rest, and centre alone in Christ, laying down their services at the footstool of Christ, must lie down in sorrow ; their bread is prepared for them in hell. ' Behold, all ye that kindle a fire, compass yourselves with the sparks : and walk in the light of your fire, and in the sparks ye have kindled. This shall ye have at mine hands ; ye shall lie down in sorrow,' Isa. l. 11. Is it good dwelling with everlasting burnings, with a devouring fire ? If it be, why then rest in your duties still ; if otherwise, then see that you centre only in the bosom of Christ.

Remedy (4). The fourth remedy against this device of Satan is, *To dwell much upon the necessity and excellency of that resting-place that God hath provided for you.* Above all other resting-places himself is your resting-place ; his free mercy and love is your resting-place ; the pure, glorious, matchless, and spotless righteousness of Christ is your resting-place. Ah ! it is sad to think, that most men have forgotten their resting-place, as the Lord complains : 'My people have been as lost sheep, their shepherds have caused them to go astray, and have turned them away to the mountains : they are gone from mountain to hill, and forgotten their resting-place,' Jer. l. 6. So poor souls that see not the excellency of that resting-place that God hath appointed for their souls to lie down in, they wander from mountain to hill, from one duty to another, and here they will rest and there they will rest ; but souls that see the excellency of that resting-place that God hath provided for them, they will say, Farewell prayer, farewell hearing, farewell fasting, &c., I will rest no more in you, but now I will rest

[1] *Omne bonum in summo bono,* all good is in the chiefest good. *Nec Christus, nec cœlum patitur hyperbolem.*

only in the bosom of Christ, the love of Christ, the righteousness of Christ.

III. The third thing to be shewed is,

The several devices that Satan hath to keep souls in a sad, doubting, questioning, and uncomfortable condition.

Though he can never rob a believer of his crown, yet such is his malice and envy, that he will leave no stone unturned, no means unattempted, to rob them of their comfort and peace, to make their life a burden and a hell unto them, to cause them to spend their days in sorrow and mourning, in sighing and complaining, in doubting and questioning. Surely we have no interest in Christ; our graces are not true, our hopes are the hopes of hypocrites; our confidence is our presumption, our enjoyments are our delusions, &c.[1]

I shall shew you this in some particulars, &c.

Device 1. The first device that Satan hath to keep souls in a sad, doubting, and questioning condition, and so making their life a hell, is, *By causing them to be still poring and musing upon sin, to mind their sins more than their Saviour; yea, so to mind their sins as to forget, yea, to neglect their Saviour;* that, as the Psalmist speaks, 'The Lord is not in all their thoughts,' Ps. x. 4. Their eyes are so fixed upon their disease, that they cannot see the remedy, though it be near; and they do so muse upon their debts, that they have neither mind nor heart to think of their Surety, &c.[2]

Now the remedies against this device are these.

Remedy (1). The first remedy is for weak believers to consider, *That though Jesus Christ hath not freed them from the presence of sin, yet he hath freed them from the damnatory power of sin.* It is most true that sin and grace were never born together, neither shall sin and grace die together; yet while a believer breathes in this world, they must live together, they must keep house together. Christ in this life will not free any believer from the presence of any one sin, though he doth free every believer from the damning power of every sin. 'There is no condemnation to them that are in Christ Jesus, who walk not after the flesh, but after the Spirit,' Rom. viii. 1. The law cannot condemn a believer, for Christ hath fulfilled it for him; divine justice cannot condemn him, for that Christ hath satisfied; his sins cannot condemn him, for they in the blood of Christ are pardoned; and his own conscience, upon righteous grounds, cannot condemn him, because Christ, that is greater than his conscience, hath acquitted him.[3]

Remedy (2). The second remedy against this device of Satan is, to

---

[1] Blessed Bradford, in one of his epistles, saith thus, 'O Lord, sometime methinks I feel it so with me, as if there were no difference between my heart and the wicked. I have a blind mind as they, a stout, stubborn, rebellious hard heart as they,' and so he goes on, &c [A frequent plaint by this holy man. See his 'Writings,' consisting mainly of 'Letters,' by Townsend (Parker Society), 1853.—G.]

[2] A Christian should wear Christ in his bosom as a flower of delight, for he is a whole paradise of delight. He that minds not Christ more than his sin, can never be thankful and fruitful as he should.

[3] *Peccata enim non nocent, si non placent,* my sins hurt me not, if they like me not. Sin is like that wild fig-tree, or ivy in the wall; cut off stump, body, bough, and branches, yet some strings or other will sprout out again, till the wall be plucked down.

consider, *That though Jesus Christ hath not freed you from the molesting and vexing power of sin, yet he hath freed you from the reign and dominion of sin.* Thou sayest that sin doth so molest and vex thee, that thou canst not think of God, nor go to God, nor speak with God.[1] Oh! but remember it is one thing for sin to molest and vex thee, and another thing for sin to reign and have dominion over thee. 'For sin shall not have dominion over you, for ye are not under the law, but under grace,' Rom. vi. 14. Sin may rebel, but it shall never reign in a saint. It fareth with sin in the regenerate as with those beasts that Daniel speaks of, 'that had their dominion taken away, yet their lives were prolonged for a season and a time,' Dan. vii. 12.

Now sin reigns in the soul when the soul willingly and readily obeys it, and subjects to its commands, as subjects do actively obey and embrace the commands of their prince. The commands of a king are readily embraced and obeyed by his subjects, but the commands of a tyrant are embraced and obeyed unwillingly. All the service that is done to a tyrant is out of violence, and not out of obedience. A free and willing subjection to the commands of sin speaks out the soul to be under the reign and dominion of sin; but from this plague, this hell, Christ frees all believers.[2] Sin cannot say of a believer as the centurion said of his servants, 'I bid one Go, and he goeth; and to another, Come, and he cometh; and to another, Do this, and he doth it,' Mat. viii. 9. No! the heart of a saint riseth against the commands of sin; and when sin would carry his soul to the devil, he hales his sin before the Lord, and cries out for justice. Lord! saith the believing soul, sin plays the tyrant, the devil in me; it would have me to do that which makes against thy holiness as well as against my happiness; against thy honour and glory, as my comfort and peace; therefore do me justice, thou righteous Judge of heaven and earth, and let this tyrant sin die for it, &c.

Remedy (3). The third remedy against this device of Satan is, *Constantly to keep one eye upon the promises of remission of sin, as well as the other eye upon the inward operations of sin.* This is the most certain truth, that God would graciously pardon those sins to his people that he will not in this life fully subdue in his people. Paul prays thrice, *i.e.* often, to be delivered from the thorn in the flesh. All he can get is, 'My grace is sufficient for thee,' 2 Cor. xii. 9; I will graciously pardon that to thee that I will not conquer in thee, saith God. 'And I will cleanse them from all their iniquity, whereby they have sinned against me, and whereby they have transgressed against me. I, even I, am he that blotteth out thy transgressions for mine own sake, and will not remember thy sins,'[3] Jer. xxxiii. 8, Isa.

---

[1] The primitive Christians chose rather to be thrown to lions without than left to lusts within. *Ad leones magis quam leonem,* saith Tertullian. [Often in his famous 'Apology.'—G.]

[2] It is a sign that sin hath not gained your consent, but committed a rape upon your souls, when you cry out to God. If the ravished virgin under the law cried out, she was guiltless, Deut. xxii. 27; so when sin plays the tyrant over the soul, and the soul cries out, it is guiltless; those sins shall not be charged upon the soul.

[3] Isa. xliv. 22, Micah vii. 18, 19, Col. ii. 13, 14. The promises of God are a precious book, every leaf drops myrrh and mercy. Though the weak Christian cannot open, read, and apply them, Christ can and will apply them to their souls. מוּחַ, an Hebrew

xliii. 25. Ah! you lamenting souls, that spend your days in sighing and groaning under the sense and burden of your sins, why do you deal so unkindly with God, and so injuriously with your own souls, as not to cast an eye upon those precious promises of remission of sin which may bear up and refresh your spirits in the darkest night, and under the heaviest burden of sin?

Remedy (4). The fourth remedy against this device of Satan is, *To look upon all your sins as charged upon the account of Christ, as debts which the Lord Jesus hath fully satisfied;* and indeed, were there but one farthing of that debt unpaid that Christ was engaged to satisfy, it would not have stood with the unspotted justice of God to have let him come into heaven and sit down at his own right hand. But all our debts, by his death, being discharged, we are freed, and he is exalted to sit down at the right hand of his Father, which is the top of his glory, and the greatest pledge of our felicity: 'For he hath made him to be sin for us that knew no sin, that we might be made the righteousness of God in him,' saith the apostle, 2 Cor. v. 21.[1] All our sins were made to meet upon Christ, as that evangelical prophet hath it: 'He was wounded for our transgressions, he was bruised for our iniquities, the chastisement of our peace was upon him, and with his stripes we are healed. All we like sheep have gone astray, we have turned every one to his own way, and the Lord hath laid on him the iniquity of us all;' or, as the Hebrew hath it, 'He hath made the iniquity of us all to meet in him,' Isa. liii. 5, 6. In law, we know that all the debts of the wife are charged upon the husband. Saith the wife to one and to another, If I owe you anything, go to my husband. So may a believer say to the law, and to the justice of God, If I owe you anything, go to my Christ, who hath undertaken for me. I must not sit down discouraged, under the apprehension of those debts, that Christ, to the utmost farthing, hath fully satisfied. Would it not argue much weakness, I had almost said much madness, for a debtor to sit down discouraged upon his looking over those debts that his surety hath readily, freely, and fully satisfied? The sense of his great love should engage a man for ever to love and honour his surety, and to bless that hand that hath paid the debt, and crossed the books, &c. But to sit down discouraged when the debt is satisfied, is a sin that bespeaks repentance.[2]

Christ hath cleared all reckoning betwixt God and us. You remember the scapegoat. Upon his head all the iniquities of the children of Israel, and all their transgressions in all their sins, were confessed and put, and the goat did bear upon him all their iniquities, &c., Lev. xvi. 21. Why! the Lord Jesus is that blessed scapegoat, upon whom all our sins were laid, and who alone hath carried ' our sins away into the land of forgetfulness, where they shall never be remembered more.'[3]

participle, and notes a constant, a continued act of God. I, I am he, blotting out thy transgressions to-day and to-morrow, &c.

[1] Christ was *peccatorum maximus*, the greatest of sinners by imputation and reputation.

[2] Christ hath the greatest worth and wealth in him. As the worth and value of many pieces of silver is in one piece of gold, so all the excellencies scattered abroad in the creatures are united in Christ. All the whole volume of perfections which are spread through heaven and earth are epitomised in him.

[3] Christ is *canalis gratiæ*, the channel of grace from God.

A believer, under the guilt of his sin, may look the Lord in the face, and sweetly plead thus with him : It is true, Lord, I owed thee much, but thy Son was my ransom, my redemption. His blood was the price; he was my surety and undertook to answer for my sins ; 1 know thou must be satisfied, and Christ hath satisfied thee to the utmost farthing : not for himself, for what sins had he of his own ? but for me ; they were my debts that he satisfied for ; be pleased to look over the book, and thou shalt find that it is crossed by thy own hand upon this very account, that Christ hath suffered and satisfied for them.[1]

Remedy (5). The fifth remedy against this device of Satan is, solemnly to consider, *Of the reasons why the Lord is pleased to have his people exercised, troubled, and vexed with the operations of sinful corruptions;* and they are these : partly to keep them humble and low in their own eyes;[2] and partly to put them upon the use of all divine helps, whereby sin may be subdued and mortified ; and partly, that they may live upon Christ for the perfecting the work of sanctification ; and partly, to wean them from things below, and to make them heart-sick of their absence from Christ, and to maintain in them bowels of compassion towards others that are subject to the same infirmities with them ; and that they may distinguish between a state of grace and a state of glory, and that heaven may be more sweet to them in the close. Now doth the Lord upon these weighty reasons suffer his people to be exercised and molested with the operations of sinful corruptions ? Oh then, let no believer speak, write, or conclude bitter things against his own soul and comforts, because that sin troubles and vexes his righteous soul, &c.; but lay his hand upon his mouth and be silent, because the Lord will have it so, upon such weighty grounds as the soul is not able to withstand.[3]

Remedy (6). The sixth remedy against this device of Satan is, solemnly to consider, *That believers must repent for their being discouraged by their sins.* Their being discouraged by their sins will cost them many a prayer, many a tear, and many a groan ; and that because their discouragements under sin flow from ignorance and unbelief. It springs from their ignorance of the richness, freeness, fulness, and everlastingness of God's love ; and from their ignorance of the power, glory, sufficiency, and efficacy of the death and sufferings of the Lord Jesus Christ ; and from their ignorance of the worth, glory, fulness, largeness, and completeness of the righteousness of Jesus Christ ; and from their ignorance of that real, close, spiritual, glorious, and inseparable union that is between Christ and their precious souls. Ah ! did precious souls know and believe the truth of these things as they should, they would not sit down dejected and overwhelmed under the sense and operation of sin, &c.[4]

---

[1] The bloods of Abel, for so the Hebrew hath it, as if the blood of one Abel had so many tongues as drops, cried for vengeance against sin; but the blood of Christ cries louder for the pardon of sin.

[2] Augustine saith, that the first, second, and third virtue of a Christian is humility. [Cf. under Humilitas in Conf., and De C. D. Epist. 56 ad Diosc.—G.]

[3] *Lilme Blelammed,* we therefore learn, that we may teach, is a proverb among the Rabbins. After the Trojans had been wandering and tossing up and down the Mediterranean sea, as soon as they espied Italy, they cried out with exulting joy, Italy, Italy ! So will saints when they come to heaven.

[4] God never gave a believer a new heart that it should always lie a-bleeding, and that it should always be rent and torn in pieces with discouragements.

The second device that Satan hath to keep souls in a sad, doubting, and questioning condition is,

Device (2). *By working them to make false definitions of their graces.* Satan knows, that as false definitions of sin wrong the soul one way, so false definitions of grace wrong the soul another way.

I will instance only in faith : Oh how doth Satan labour might and main to work men to make false definitions of faith ! Some he works to define faith too high, as that it is a full assurance of the love of God to a man's soul in particular, or a full persuasion of the pardon and remission of a man's own sins in particular. Saith Satan, What dost thou talk of faith ? Faith is an assurance of the love of God, and of the pardon of sin ; and this thou hast not ; thou knowest thou art far off from this ; therefore thou hast no faith. And by drawing men to make such a false definition of faith, he keeps them in a sad, doubting, and questioning condition, and makes them spend their days in sorrow and sighing, so that tears are their drink, and sorrow is their meat, and sighing is their work all the day long, &c.

The philosophers say there are eight degrees of heat; we discern three. Now, if a man should define heat only by the highest degree, then all other degrees will be cast out from being heat. So if men shall define faith only by the highest degrees, by assurance of the love of God, and of the pardon of his sins in particular, what will become of lesser degrees of faith?

If a man should define a man to be a living man, only by the highest and strongest demonstrations of life, as laughing, leaping, running, working, walking, &c., would not many thousands that groan under internal and external weaknesses, and that cannot laugh, nor leap, nor run, nor work, nor walk, be found dead men by such a definition, that yet we know to be alive? It is so here, and you know how to apply it, &c.

Now the remedies against this device are these :

Remedy (1). The first remedy against this device of Satan is, solemnly to consider, *That there may be true faith, yea, great measures of faith, where there is no assurance.* The Canaanite woman in the Gospel had strong faith, yet no assurance that we read of. 'These things have I written unto you,' saith John, 'that believe on the name of the Son of God, that ye may know that ye have eternal life, and that ye may believe on the name of the Son of God,' 1 John v. 13. In these words you see that they did believe, and had eternal life, in respect of the purpose and promise of God, and in respect of the seeds and beginnings of it in their souls, and in respect of Christ their head, who sits in heaven as a public person, representing all his chosen ones, ' Who hath raised us up together, and made us sit together in heavenly places in Christ Jesus,' Eph. ii. 6 ; and yet they did not know that they had eternal life. It is one thing to have a right to heaven, and another thing to know it; it is one thing to be beloved, and another thing for a man to know that he is beloved. It is one thing for God to write a man's name in the book of life, and another thing for God to tell a man that his name is written in the book of life ; and to say to him, Luke x. 20, ' Rejoice, because thy name is written in heaven.' So Paul, ' In whom ye also trusted, after ye heard the word of truth, the gospel of your salvation :

in whom also, after ye believed, ye were sealed with that Holy Spirit of promise,' Eph. i. 13. So Micah: 'Rejoice not against me, O my enemy: for when I shall fall, I shall rise ; when I shall sit in darkness, the Lord shall be a light unto me. I will bear the indignation of the Lord, because I have sinned,' &c., or, 'the sad countenance of God,' as the Hebrew hath it, Micah vii. 8, 9. This soul had no assurance, for he sits in darkness, and was under the sad countenance of God; and yet had strong faith, as appears in those words, ' When I fall, I shall rise ; when I sit in darkness, the Lord shall be a light unto me.' He will bring me forth to the light, and I shall behold his righteousness. And let this suffice for the first answer.[1]

Remedy (2). The second remedy against this device of Satan is, solemnly to consider, *That God in the Scripture doth define faith otherwise.* God defines faith to be a receiving of Christ—'As many as received him, to them he gave this privilege, to be the sons of God,' John i. 12. 'To as many as believed on his name,' Acts xi. 23—to be a cleaving of the soul unto God, though no joy, but afflictions, attend the soul. Yea, the Lord defines faith to be a coming to God in Christ, and often to a resting and staying, rolling of the soul upon Christ. It is safest and sweetest to define as God defines, both vices and graces. This is the only way to settle the soul, and to secure it against the wiles of men and devils, who labour, by false definitions of grace, to keep precious souls in a doubting, staggering, and languishing condition, and so make their lives a burden, a hell, unto them.[2]

Remedy (3). The third remedy against this device of Satan is, seriously to consider this, *That there may be true faith where there is much doubtings.* Witness those frequent sayings of Christ to his disciples, ' Why are ye afraid, O ye of little faith ?'[3] Persons may be truly believing who nevertheless are sometimes doubting. In the same persons that the fore-mentioned scriptures speak of, you may see their faith commended and their doubts condemned, which doth necessarily suppose a presence of both.

Remedy (4). The fourth remedy against this device of Satan is, solemnly to consider, *That assurance is an effect of faith; therefore it cannot be faith.* The cause cannot be the effect, nor the root the fruit. As the effect flows from the cause, the fruit from the root, the stream from the fountain, so doth assurance flow from faith. This truth I shall make good thus :

The assurance of our salvation and pardon of sin doth primarily arise from the witness of the Spirit of God that we are the children of God, Eph. i. 13 ; and the Spirit never witnesseth this till we are believers : 'For we are sons by faith in Christ Jesus,' Gal. iv. 6. Therefore assurance is not faith, but follows it, as the effect follows the cause.

Again, no man can be assured and persuaded of his salvation till he be united to Christ, till he be ingrafted into Christ ; and a man cannot be ingrafted into Christ till he hath faith. He must first be ingrafted into Christ by faith before he can have assurance of his salvation ; which doth clearly evidence, that assurance is not faith, but an effect and fruit of faith, &c.

[1] So those in Isa. l. 10 had faith, though they had no assurance.
[2] Mat. xi. 23, John vi. 37, Heb. vii. 25, 26.   [3] Mat. vi. 30, xiv. 31, xvi. 8 ; Luke xii. 28.

Again, faith cannot be lost, but assurance may; therefore assurance is not faith.[1] Though assurance be a precious flower in the garden of a saint, and is more infinitely sweet and delightful to the soul than all outward comforts and contents; yet it is but a flower that is subject to fade, and to lose its freshness and beauty, as saints by sad experience find, &c.

Again, a man must first have faith before he can have assurance, therefore assurance is not faith. And that a man must first have faith before he can have assurance, is clear by this, a man must first be saved before he can be assured of his salvation; for he cannot be assured of that which is not. And a man must first have a saving faith before he can be saved by faith, for he cannot be saved by that which he hath not; therefore a man must first have faith before he can have assurance, and so it roundly follows that assurance is not faith, &c.[2]

The third device that Satan hath to keep the soul in a sad, doubting, and questioning condition is,

Device (3). *By working the soul to make false inferences from the cross actings of Providence.* Saith Satan, Dost thou not see how Providence crosses thy prayers, and crosses thy desires, thy tears, thy hopes, thy endeavours?[3] Surely if his love were towards thee, if his soul did delight and take pleasure in thee, he would not deal thus with thee, &c.

Now, the remedies against this device are these:

Remedy (1). The first remedy against this device of Satan is, solemnly to consider, *That many things may be cross to our desires that are not cross to our good.* Abraham, Jacob, David, Job, Moses, Jeremiah, Jonah, Paul, &c., met with many things that were contrary to their desires and endeavours, that were not contrary to their good; as all know that have wisely compared their desires and endeavours and God's actings together. Physic often works contrary to the patients' desires, when it doth not work contrary to their good.

I remember a story of a godly man, who had a great desire to go to France, and as he was going to take shipping he broke his leg; and it pleased Providence so to order it, that the ship that he should have gone in at that very same time was cast away, and not a man saved; and so by breaking a bone his life was saved. Though Providence did work cross to his desire, yet it did not work cross to his good, &c.[4]

Remedy (2). The second remedy against this device of Satan is, solemnly to consider, *That the hand of God may be against a man, when the love and heart of God is much set upon a man.* No man can conclude how the heart of God stands by his hand. The hand of God was against Ephraim, and yet his love, his heart, was dearly set upon Ephraim: 'I have surely heard Ephraim bemoaning himself thus: Thou hast chastised me, and I was chastised, as a bullock unaccustomed

---

[1] Ps. li. 12, xxx. 6, 7; Cant. v. 6; Isa. viii. 17.

[2] There is many thousand precious souls, of whom this world is not worthy, that have the faith of reliance, and yet want assurance and the effects of it; as high joy, glorious peace, and vehement longings after the coming of Christ.

[3] Ps. lxxvii. 7, *et seq.*, xxxi. 1, *ult.*, lxxiii. 2, 23.

[4] The Circumcellians being not able to withstand the preaching and writing of Augustine, sought his destruction, having beset the way he was to go to his visitation, but by God's providence he, missing his way, escaped the danger. [See *ante*, Conf.—G.]

to the yoke. Turn thou me, and I shall be turned; for thou art the Lord my God. Surely, after that I was returned, I repented; and after that I was instructed, I smote upon my thigh; I was ashamed, yea, even confounded, because I did bear the reproach of my youth. Ephraim is my dear Son, he is a pleasant child; for since I spake against him, I do earnestly remember him still. Therefore my bowels are troubled for him; I will surely have mercy upon him, saith the Lord,' Jer. xxxi. 18–20.[1]

God can look sourly, and chide bitterly, and strike heavily, even where and when he loves dearly. The hand of God was very much against Job, and yet his love, his heart, was very much set upon Job, as you may see by comparing chaps. i. and ii. with xli. and xlii. The hand of God was sore against David and Jonah, when his heart was much set upon them. He that shall conclude that the heart of God is against those that his hand is against, will condemn the generation of the just, whom God unjustly would not have condemned.

Remedy (3). The third remedy against this device of Satan, is, to consider, *That all the cross providences that befall the saints are but in order to some noble good that God doth intend to prefer[2] upon them.* Providence wrought cross to David's desire, in taking away the child sinfully begotten, but yet not cross to more noble good; for was it not far better for David to have such a legitimate heir as Solomon was, than that a bastard should wear the crown, and sway the sceptre?

Joseph, you know, was sold into a far country by the envy and malice of his brethren, and afterwards imprisoned because he would not be a prisoner to his mistress's lusts; yet all these providences did wonderfully conduce to his advancement, and the preservation of his father's family, which was then the visible church of Christ. It was so handled by a noble hand of providence, that what they sought to decline,[3] they did promote. Joseph was therefore sold by his brethren that he might not be worshipped, and yet he was therefore worshipped because he was sold.[4]

David was designed to a kingdom, but oh! the straits, troubles, and deaths that he runs through before he feels the weight of the crown; and all this was but in order to the sweetening of his crown, and to the settling of it more firmly and gloriously upon his head. God did so contrive it that Jonah's offence, and those cross actings of his that did attend it, should advantage that end which they seemed most directly to oppose. Jonah he flies to Tarshish, then cast into the sea, then saved by a miracle. Then the mariners, as it is very probable, who cast Jonah into the sea, declared to the Ninevites what had happened; therefore he must be a man sent of God, and that his threatenings must be believed and hearkened to, and therefore they must repent and humble themselves, that the wrath threatened might not be executed, &c.[5]

Remedy (4). The fourth remedy against this device of Satan is,

---

[1] God's providential hand may be with persons when his heart is set against them. God's providential hand was for a time with Saul, Haman, Asshur, and Jehu, and yet his heart was set against him. 'No man knoweth love or hatred by all that is before him,' Eccles. ix. 1, 2.   [2] = confer.—G.   [3] 'Lower' = injure.—G.

[4] Cf. Genesis xxxvii. 7, &c.—G.

[5] The motions of divine providence are so dark, so deep, so changeable, that the wisest and noblest souls cannot tell what conclusions to make.

seriously to consider, *That all the strange, dark, deep, and changeable providences that believers meet with, shall further them in their way to heaven, in their journey to happiness.* Divine wisdom and love will so order all things here below, that they shall work for the real, internal, and eternal good of them that love him. All the rugged providences that David met with, did contribute to the bringing of him to the throne ; and all the rugged providences that Daniel and the 'three children' met with, did contribute to their great advancement. So all the rugged providences that believers meet with, they shall all contribute to the lifting up of their souls above all things, below God. As the waters lifted up Noah's ark nearer heaven, and as all the stones that were about Stephen's ears did but knock him the closer to Christ, the corner-stone, so all the strange rugged providences that we meet with, they shall raise us nearer heaven, and knock us nearer to Christ, that precious corner-stone.[1]

The fourth device that Satan hath to keep souls in a sad, doubting, and questioning condition is,

Device (4). *By suggesting to them that their graces are not true, but counterfeit.* Saith Satan, All is not gold that glitters, all is not free grace that you count grace, that you call grace. That which you call faith is but a fancy, and that which you call zeal, is but a natural heat and passion ; and that light you have, it is but common, it is short, to what many have attained to that are now in hell, &c. Satan doth not labour more mightily to persuade hypocrites that their graces are true when they are counterfeit, than he doth to persuade precious souls that their graces are counterfeit, when indeed they are true, and such as will abide the touchstone of Christ, &c.[2]

Now the remedies against this device are these :

Remedy (1). The first remedy against this device of Satan is, seriously to consider, *That grace is taken two ways.*

[1.] It is taken for *the gracious good-will and favour of God*, whereby he is pleased of his own free love to accept of some in Christ for his own. This, some call the first grace, because it is the fountain of all other graces, and the spring from whence they flow, and it is therefore called grace, because it makes a man gracious with God, but this is only in God.

[2.] Grace is taken for *the gifts of grace*, and they are of two sorts, common or special.

Some are common to believers and hypocrites, as a gift of knowledge, a gift of prayer, &c.

Some are special graces, and they are proper and peculiar to the saints, as faith, humility, meekness, love, patience, &c., Gal. v, 22, 23.

Remedy (2). The second remedy against this device of Satan is, wisely to consider, *The differences betwixt renewing grace and restraining grace, betwixt sanctifying grace and temporary grace* ; and this I will shew you in these ten particulars.

[1.] True grace *makes all glorious within and without* : 'The King's

---

[1] Orosius, speaking of Valentinian, saith : He that for Christ's name's sake had lost a tribuneship, within a while after succeeded his persecutor in the empire.

[2] Yet it must be granted that many a fair flower may grow out of a stinking root, and many sweet dispositions and fair actions may be where there is only the corrupt root of nature.

daughter is all glorious within ; her raiment is of wrought gold,' Ps. xlv. 13. True grace makes the understanding glorious, the affections glorious. It casts a general glory upon all the noble parts of the soul : ' The King's daughter is all glorious within.' And as it makes the inside glorious, so it makes the outside glorious : ' Her clothing is of wrought gold.' It makes men look gloriously, and speak gloriously, and walk and act gloriously, so that vain souls shall be forced to say that these are they that have seen Jesus.[1] As grace is a fire to burn up and consume the dross and filth of the soul, so it is an ornament to beautify and adorn the soul. True grace makes all new, the inside new and the outside new : ' If any man be in Christ, he is a new creature,' 2 Cor. v. 17,[2] but temporary grace doth not this. True grace changes the very nature of a man. Moral virtue doth only restrain or chain up the outward man, it doth not change the whole man. A lion in a grate is a lion still ; he is restrained, but not changed, for he retains his lion-like nature still. So temporary graces restrain many men from this and that wickedness, but it doth not change and turn their hearts from wickedness. But now true grace, that turns a lion into a lamb, as you may see in Paul, Acts ix., and a notorious strumpet into a blessed and glorious penitent, as you may see in Mary Magdalene, &c., &c., Luke vii.[3]

[2.] *The objects* of true grace are *supernatural*. True grace is conversant about the choicest and the highest objects, about the most soul-ennobling and soul-greatening objects, as God, Christ, precious promises that are more worth than a world, and a kingdom that shakes not, a crown of glory that withers not, and heavenly treasures that rust not. The objects of temporary grace are low and poor, and always within the compass of reason's reach.[4]

[3.] True grace enables a Christian, *when he is himself, to do spiritual actions with real pleasure and delight*, To souls truly gracious, Christ's yoke ' is easy, and his burden is light ;' ' his commandments are not grievous, but joyous.' ' I delight in the law of God after the inward man,' saith Paul.[5] The blessed man is described by this, that he ' delights in the law of the Lord,' Ps. i. 2. ' It is joy to the just to do judgment,' saith Solomon, Prov. xxi. 15. To a gracious soul, ' All the ways of the Lord are pleasantness, and his paths are peace, Prov. iii. 17 ; but to souls that have but temporary grace, but moral virtues, religious services are a toil, not a pleasure ; a burden, and not a delight. ' Wherefore have we fasted,' say they, ' and thou seest not ? Wherefore have we afflicted our souls, and thou takest no knowledge ?' Isa. lviii. 3, &c. ' Ye have said,' say those in Malachi, ' It is vain to serve God ; and what profit is it that we have kept his ordinances, and that we have walked mournfully before the Lord of hosts ?' Mal. iii. 14. ' When will the new moon be gone,' say those in Amos, ' that we may sell corn, and the Sabbath, that we may set forth wheat, making the ephah small,

---

[1] God brings not a pair of scales to weigh our graces, but a touchstone to try our graces. Purity, preciousness, and holiness is stamped upon all saving graces, Acts xv. 9, 2 Peter iv. 1, Jude 20.

[2] καινη κτισις, a new creation : new Adam, new covenant, new paradise, new Lord, new law, new hearts, and new creatures go together.

[3] It seems right to question this admittedly common mode of speaking of Mary of Magdala. It is not certain that the two were identical.—G.

[4] 2 Cor. iv. 18. Prov. xiv. A saint hath his feet where other men's heads are, Mat. vi.

[5] Mat. xi. 30 ; 1 John v. 3 ; Rom. vii. 22.

and the shekel great, and falsifying the balances by deceit,' Amos viii. 5.

[4.] True grace makes *a man most careful, and most fearful of his own heart*.[1] It makes him most studious about his own heart, informing that, examining that, and watching over that; but temporary grace, moral virtues, make men more mindful and careful of others, to instruct them and counsel them, and stir up them, and watch over them, &c. Which doth with open mouth demonstrate that their graces are not saving and peculiar to saints, but that they are temporary, and no more than Judas, Demas, and the pharisees had, &c.

[5.] Grace will *work a man's heart to love and cleave to the strictest and holiest ways and things of God, for their purity and sanctity, in the face of all dangers and hardships.* ' Thy word is very pure, therefore thy servant loveth it,' Ps. cxix. 140. Others love it, and like it, and follow it, for the credit, the honour, the advantage that they get by it; but I love it for the spiritual beauty and purity of it. So the psalmist, ' All this is come upon us; yet have we not forgotten thee, neither have we dealt falsely in thy covenant. Our heart is not turned back, neither have our steps declined from thy way : though thou hast sore broken us in the place of dragons, and covered us with the shadows of death,' Ps. xliv. 17–19. But temporary grace, that will not bear up the soul against all oppositions and discouragements in the ways of God, as is clear by their apostasy in John vi. 60, 66, and by the stony grounds falling away, &c., Mat. xiii. 20, 21.[2]

[6.] True grace will *enable a man to step over the world's crown, to take up Christ's cross ; to prefer the cross of Christ above the glory of this world.* It enabled Abraham, and Moses, and Daniel, with those other worthies in Heb. xi., to do so.

Godfrey of Bullen [Bouillon], first king of Jerusalem, refused to be crowned with a crown of gold, saying, ' That it became not a Christian there to wear a crown of gold, where Christ had worn a crown of thorns.' Oh ! but temporary grace cannot work the soul to prefer Christ's cross above the world's crown ; but when these two meet, a temporary Christian steps over Christ's cross to take up, and keep up, the world's crown. ' Demas hath forsaken us to embrace this present world,' 2 Tim. iv. 10. So the young man in the Gospel had many good things in him ; he bid fair for heaven, and came near to heaven ; but when Christ set his cross before him, he steps over that to enjoy the world's crown, Mat. xix. 19-22. When Christ bid him, ' go and sell all that he had, and give to the poor,' &c., ' he went away sorrowful, for he had great possessions.' If heaven be to be had upon no other terms, Christ may keep his heaven to himself, he will have none, &c.[3]

[7.] Sanctifying grace, renewing grace, *puts the soul upon spiritual duties, from spiritual and intrinsecal motives,* as from the sense of divine love, that doth constrain the soul to wait on God, and to act for

---

[1] Ps. li. 10, and cxix. 36, 80, and cxxxix. 23, and lxxxvi. 11.

[2] Grace is a panoply against all trouble, and a paradise of all pleasures.

[3] Few are of Jerome's mind, that had rather have St Paul's coat with his heavenly graces, than the purple of kings with their kingdoms. The king of Navarre told Beza, that in the cause of religion he would launch no further into their sea, than he might be sure to return safe to the haven. [Henry IV., afterwards the Apostate from Protestantism.—G.]

God ;[1] and the sense of the excellency and sweetness of communion with God, and the choice and precious discoveries that the soul hath formerly had of the beauty and glory to [sic] God, whilst it hath been in the service of God. The good looks, the good words, the blessed love-letters, the glorious kisses, and the sweet embraces that gracious souls have had from Christ in his service, do provoke and move them to wait upon him in holy duties. Ah ! but restraining grace, temporary grace, that puts men upon religious duties only from external motives, as the care of the creature, the eye of the creature, the rewards of the creature, and the keeping up of a name among the creatures, and a thousand such like considerations, as you may see in Saul, Jehu, Judas, Demas, and the scribes and pharisees, &c.[2]

The abbot in Melancthon lived strictly, and walked demurely, and looked humbly, so long as he was but a monk, but when, by his seeming extraordinary sanctity, he got to be abbot, he grew intolerable proud and insolent ; and being asked the reason of it, confessed, ' That his former lowly look was but to see if he could find the keys of the abbey.' Such poor, low, vain motives work temporary souls to all the service they do perform, &c.

[8.] Saving grace, renewing grace, will *cause a man to follow the Lord fully in the desertion of all sin, and in the observation of all God's precepts.* Joshua and Caleb followed the Lord fully,[3] Num. xiv. 24 ; Zacharias and Elizabeth were righteous before God, and walked in all the commandments and ordinances of the Lord blameless, Luke i. 5, 6. The saints in the Revelation are described by this, that ' they follow the Lamb whithersoever he goes,' Rev. xiv. 4 ; but restraining grace, temporary grace, cannot enable a man to follow the Lord fully. All that temporary grace can enable a man to do, is to follow the Lord partially, unevenly, and haltingly, as you may see in Jehu, Herod, Judas, and the scribes and pharisees, who paid tithe of ' mint, and anise, and cummin, but omitted the weighty matters of the law, judgment, mercy, and faith,' &c., Mat. xxiii. 23.

True grace works the heart to the hatred of all sin, and to the love of all truth ; it works a man to the hatred of those sins that for his blood he cannot conquer, and to loathe those sins that he would give all the world to overcome, Ps. cxix. 104, 128.[4] So that a soul truly gracious can say, Though there be no one sin mortified and subdued in me, as it should, and as I would, yet every sin is hated and loathed by me. So a soul truly gracious can say, Though I do not obey any one command as I should, and as I would, yet every word is sweet, every command of God is precious, Ps. cxix. 6, 119, 127, 167. I dearly prize and greatly love those commands that I cannot obey; though there be

---

[1] As what I have, if offered to thee, pleaseth not thee, O Lord, without myself, so the good things we have from thee, though they may refresh us, yet they satisy us not without thyself.—*Bern[ard]*.

[2] It is an excellent speech of Bernard, *Bonus es Domine animæ quærenti ; quid invenienti ?* Good art thou, O Lord, to the soul that seeks thee, what art thou then to the soul that finds thee ?

[3] ויִמַלֵּא, hath fulfilled after me. A metaphor taken from a ship under sail, that is strongly carried with the wind, as fearing neither rocks nor sands.

[4] I had rather go to hell pure from sin, than to heaven polluted with that filth, saith Anselm. *Da quod jubes et jube quod vis*, Give what thou commandest, and command what thou wilt. [Augustine.—G].

many commands that I cannot in a strict sense fulfil, yet there is no command I would not fulfil, that I do not exceedingly love. 'I love thy commandments above gold, above fine gold:' 'My soul hath kept thy testimonies, and I love them exceedingly,' Ps. cxix. 117, and xcix. 7.

[9.] True grace *leads the soul to rest in Christ, as in his* summum bonum, *chiefest good.* It works the soul to centre in Christ, as in his highest and ultimate end. 'Whither should we go? thou hast the words of eternal life,' John vi. 68. 'My beloved is white and ruddy, the chiefest of ten thousand; I found him whom my soul loved, I held him and would not let him go,' Cant. v. 10, iii. 4. That wisdom a believer hath from Christ, it leads him to centre in the wisdom of Christ, 1 Cor. i. 30; and that love the soul hath from Christ, it leads the soul to centre in the love of Christ; and that righteousness the soul hath from Christ, it leads the soul to rest and centre in the righteousness of Christ, Philip. iii. 9.[1] True grace is a beam of Christ, and where it is, it will naturally lead the soul to rest in Christ. The stream doth not more naturally lead to the fountain, nor the effect to the cause, than true grace leads the soul to Christ. But restraining grace, temporary grace, works the soul to centre and rest in things below Christ. Sometimes it works the soul to centre in the praises of the creature; sometimes to rest in the rewards of the creature: 'Verily they have their reward,' saith Christ, Mat. vi. 1, 2: and so in an hundred other things. &c., Zech. vii. 5, 6.

[10.] True grace will *enable a soul to sit down satisfied and contented with the naked enjoyments of Christ.* The enjoyment of Christ without honour will satisfy the soul; the enjoyment of Christ without riches, the enjoyment of Christ without pleasures, and without the smiles of creatures, will content and satisfy the soul. 'It is enough; Joseph is alive,' Gen. xlv. 28. So saith a gracious soul, though honour is not, and riches are not, and health is not, and friends are not, &c., it is enough that Christ is, that he reigns, conquers, and triumphs. Christ is the pot of manna, the cruse of oil, a bottomless ocean of all comfort, content, and satisfaction. He that hath him wants nothing; he that wants him enjoys nothing.[2] 'Having nothing,' saith Paul, 'and yet possessing all things,' 2 Cor. vi. 10. Oh! but a man that hath but temporary grace, that hath but restraining grace, cannot sit down satisfied and contented, under the want of outward comforts.[3] Christ is good with honours, saith such a soul; and Christ is good with riches, and Christ is good with pleasures, and he is good with such and such outward contents. I must have Christ and the world, or else with the young man in the Gospel, in spite of my soul, I shall forsake Christ to follow the world. Ah! how many shining professors be there in the world, that cannot sit down satisfied and contented, under the want of this or that outward comfort and content, but are like bedlams, fretting

---

[1] Grace is that star that leads to Christ; it is that cloud and pillar of fire that leads the soul to the heavenly Canaan, where Christ sits chief.

[2] *Cui cum paupertate bene convenit, pauper non est,* saith Seneca, a contented man cannot be a poor man. [Epistle i. and *De Constantia Sapientis,* vi.—G].

[3] Charles the Great his motto was, *Christus regnat, vincit, triumphat.* And so it is the saints.' St Austin upon Ps. xii. brings in God rebuking a discontented Christian thus: What is thy faith? have I promised thee these things? What! wert thou made a Christian that thou shouldst flourish here in this world?

and vexing, raging and madding,[1] as if there were no God, no heaven, no hell, nor no Christ to make up all such outward wants to souls. That a soul truly gracious can say, in having nothing I have all things, because I have Christ; having therefore all things in him, I seek no other reward, for he is the universal reward. Such a soul can say, Nothing is sweet to me without the enjoyment of Christ in it; honours, nor riches, nor the smiles of creatures, are not sweet to me no farther than I see Christ, and taste Christ in them.[2] The confluence of all outward good cannot make a heaven of glory in my soul, if Christ, who is the top of my glory, be absent; as Absalom said, 'What is all this to me so long as I cannot see the king's face?' 2 Sam. xiv. 32. So saith the soul, why do you tell me of this and that outward comfort, when I cannot see his face whom my soul loves? Why, my honour is not my Christ, nor riches is not Christ, nor the favour of the creature is not Christ; let me have him, and let the men of this world take the world, and divide it amongst themselves; I prize my Christ above all, I would enjoy my Christ above all other things in the world; his presence will make up the absence of all other comforts, and his absence will darken and embitter all my comforts; so that my comforts will neither taste like comforts, nor look like comforts, nor warm like comforts, when he that should comfort my soul stands afar off, &c., Lam. i. 16. Christ is all and in all to souls truly gracious, Col. iii. 11. We have all things in Christ, and Christ is all things to a Christian. If we be sick, he is a physician; if we thirst, he is a fountain; if our sins trouble us, he is righteousness; if we stand in need of help, he is mighty to save; if we fear death, he is life; if we be in darkness, he is light; if we be weak, he is strength; if we be in poverty, he is plenty; if we desire heaven, he is the way. The soul cannot say, this I would have, and that I would have; but saith Christ, it is in me, it is in me eminently, perfectly, eternally.[3]

The fifth device that Satan hath to keep souls in a sad, doubting, and questioning condition is,

Device (5). *By suggesting to them, That that conflict that is in them, is not a conflict that is only in saints, but such a conflict that is to be found in hypocrites and profane souls;* when the truth is, there is as much difference betwixt the conflict that is in them, and that which is in wicked men, as there is betwixt light and darkness, betwixt heaven and hell.[4] And the truth of this I shall evidence to you in the following particulars:

[1.] *The whole frame of a believer's soul is against sin.* Understanding, will, and affection, all the powers and faculties of the soul are in

---

[1] Going about as 'mad.'—G.

[2] Content is the deputy of outward felicity, and supplies the place where it is absent. As the Jews throw the book of Esther to the ground before they read it, because the name of God is not in it, as the Rabbins have observed; so do saints in some sense those mercies wherein they do not read Christ's name, and see Christ's heart. [With reference to the throwing down of the book of Esther, see Trapp's quaint remarks on it, under Esther i. 1.—G].

[3] Luther said, he had rather be in hell with Christ, than in heaven without him. None but Christ, none but Christ, said Lambert, lifting up his hands and his fingers' end flaming. [Clarke's 'Martyrologie,' as before, *sub nomine.*—G].

[4] John viii. 44, the devil is a liar, and the father of it. The devil's breasts (saith Luther) are very fruitful with lies.

arms against sin. A covetous man may condemn covetousness, and yet the frame and bent of his heart may be to it; a proud person may condemn pride, and yet the frame of his spirit may be to it; and the drunkard may condemn drunkenness, and yet the frame of his spirit may be to it; a man may condemn stealing and lying, and yet the frame of his heart may be to it.[1] 'Thou that preachest a man should not steal, dost thou steal? Thou that sayest a man should not commit adultery, dost thou commit adultery? thou that abhorrest idols, dost thou commit sacrilege? Thou that makest thy boast of the law, through breaking the law dishonourest thou God?' Rom. ii. 21–23. But a saint's will is against it. 'The evil that I would not do, that I do;' and his affections are against it, 'What I hate, I do,' Rom. vii. 19, 20.

[2.] A saint *conflicts against sin universally, the least as well as the greatest;* the most profitable and the most pleasing sin, as well as against those that are less pleasing and profitable. He will combat with all, though he cannot conquer one as he should, and as he would. He knows that all sin strikes at God's holiness, as well as his own happiness; at God's glory, as well as at his soul's comfort and peace.[2]

He knows that all sin is hateful to God, and that all sinners are traitors to the crown and dignity of the Lord Jesus. He looks upon one sin, and sees that that threw down Noah, the most righteous man in the world, and he looks upon another sin, and sees that that cast down Abraham, the greatest believer in the world, and he looks upon another sin, and sees that that threw down David, the best king in the world, and he looks upon another sin, and sees that that cast down Paul, the greatest apostle in the world. He sees that one sin threw down Samson, the strongest man in the world; another cast down Solomon, the wisest man in the world; and another Moses, the meekest man in the world; and another sin cast down Job, the patientest man in the world; and this raiseth a holy indignation against all, so that nothing can satisfy and content his soul but a destruction of all those lusts and vermin that vex and rack his righteous soul. It will not suffice a gracious soul to see justice done upon one sin, but he cries out for justice upon all. He would not have some crucified and others spared, but cries out, Lord, crucify them all, crucify them all. Oh! but now the conflict that is in wicked men is partial; they frown upon one sin and smile upon another; they strike at some sins yet stroke others; they thrust some out of doors but keep others close in their bosoms; as you may see in Jehu, Herod, Judas, Simon Magus, and Demas. Wicked men strike at gross sins, such as are not only against the law of God, but against the laws of nature and nations, but make nothing of less sins; as vain thoughts, idle words, sinful motions, petty oaths, &c.

---

[1] It was a good saying of him [Augustine, *Conf.*—G.] that said, *Domine libera me a malo homine, me ipso,* Lord, deliver me from an ill man, myself. Austin complains, That men do not tame their beasts in their own bosoms.

[2] Ps. cxix. 104, I hate every false way; *sincthi,* from שָׂנֵא, which signifies to hate with a deadly and irreconcileable hatred. He knows that all the parts of the old man hath, and doth play the part of a treacherous friend and a friendly traitor; therefore he strikes at all. The greater the combat is, the greater shall be the following rewards, saith Tertullian. True hatred is προς τα γίνη, against the whole kind. Plutarch reports of one who would not be resolved of his doubts, because he would not lose the pleasure in seeking for resolution. So wicked men will not be rid of some sins, because they would not lose the seeming pleasure of sinning.

They fight against those sins that fight against their honour, profits, pleasures, &c., but make truce with those that are as right hand and as right eyes to them, &c.

[3.] *The conflict that is in a saint, against sin, is maintained by several arguments:* by arguments drawn from the love of God, the honour of God, the sweetness and communion with God, and from the spiritual and heavenly blessings and privileges that are conferred upon them by God, and from arguments drawn from the blood of Christ, the glory of Christ, the eye of Christ, the kisses of Christ, and the intercession of Christ, and from arguments drawn from the earnest of the Spirit, the seal of the Spirit, the witness of the Spirit, the comforts of the Spirit. Oh! but the conflict that is in wicked men is from low, carnal, and legal arguments, drawn from the eye, ear, or hand of the creature, or drawn from shame, hell, curses of the law, &c., 2 Cor. xii. 7-9.[1]

[4.] The conflict that is in saints is *a constant conflict.* Though sin and grace were not born in the heart of a saint together, and though they shall not die together, yet, whilst a believer lives, they must conflict together. Paul had been fourteen years converted, when he cried out, ' I have a law in my members rebelling against the law of my mind, and leading me captive to the law of sin,' Rom. vii. 2, 3.

Pietro Candiano, one of the dukes of Venice, died fighting against the Nauratines with the weapons in his hands. So a saint lives fighting and dies fighting, he stands fighting and falls fighting, with his spiritual weapons in his hands.[2] But the conflict that is in wicked men is inconstant: now they fall out with sin, and anon they fall in with sin; now it is bitter, anon it is sweet; now the sinner turns from his sin, and anon he turns to the wallowing in sin, as the swine doth to the wallowing in the mire, 2 Pet. ii. 19, 20. One hour you shall have him praying against sin, as if he feared it more than hell, and the next hour you shall have him pursuing after sin, as if there were no God to punish him, no justice to damn him, no hell to torment him.

[5.] The conflict that is in the saints, *is in the same faculties;* there is the judgment against the judgment, the mind against the mind, the will against the will, the affections against the affections, that is, the regenerate part against the unregenerate part, in all the parts of the soul; but now, in wicked men, the conflict is not in the same faculties, but between the conscience and the will. The will of a sinner is bent strongly to such and such sins, but conscience puts in and tells the sinner, God hath made me his deputy, he hath given me a power to hang and draw, to examine, scourge, judge and condemn, and if thou dost such and such wickedness, I shall be thy jailor and tormenter. I do not bear the rod nor the sword in vain, saith conscience; if thou sinnest, I shall do my office, and then thy life will be a hell: and this raises a tumult in the soul.[3]

---

[1] Though to be kept from sin brings comfort to us, yet for us to oppose sin from spiritual and heavenly arguments, and God to pardon sin, that brings most glory to God.

[2] It was an excellent saying of Eusebius Emesenus, Our fathers overcame the torrents of the flames, let us overcome the fiery darts of vices. Consider that the pleasure and sweetness that follows victory over sin, is a thousand times beyond that seeming sweetness that is in sin.

[3] A heathen could say, their soul is in a mutiny; a wicked man is not friends with himself, he and his conscience are at difference.—*Arist*[*otle*].

[6.] The conflict that is in the saints, *is a more blessed, successful, and prevailing conflict.* A saint, by his conflict with sin, gains ground upon his sin : ' They that are Christ's,' saith the apostle, ' have crucified the world with the affections and lusts,' Gal. v. 24. Christ puts to his hand and helps them to lead captivity captive, and to set their feet upon the necks of those lusts that have formerly trampled upon their souls and their comforts. As the house of Saul grew weaker and weaker, and the house of David stronger and stronger, so the Lord, by the discoveries of his love, and by the influences of his Spirit, he causeth grace, the nobler part of a saint, to grow stronger and stronger, and corruption, like the house of Saul, to grow weaker and weaker. But sin in a wicked heart gets ground, and grows stronger and stronger, notwithstanding all his conflicts. His heart is more encouraged, emboldened, and hardened in a way of sin, as you may see in the Israelites, Pharaoh, Jehu, and Judas, who doubtless found many strange conflicts, tumults, and mutinies in their souls, when God spake such bitter things against them, and did such justice upon them, 2 Tim. iii. 13.[1]

But remember this by way of caution : Though Christ hath given sin its death-wound, by his power, Spirit, death, and resurrection, yet it will die but a lingering death.[2] As a man that is mortally wounded dies by little and little, so doth sin in the heart of a saint. The death of Christ on the cross was a lingering death, so the death of sin in the soul is a lingering death ; now it dies a little, and anon it dies a little, &c., as the psalmist speaks, ' Slay them not, lest my people forget : scatter them by thy power ; and bring them down, O Lord our shield,' Ps. lix. 11. He would not have them utterly destroyed, but some relics preserved as a memorial. So God dealeth in respect of sin ; it is wounded and brought down, but not wholly slain ; something is still left as a monument of divine grace, and to keep us humble, wakeful, and watchful, and that our armour may be still kept on, and our weapons always in our hands.

The best men's souls in this life hang between the flesh and the spirit, as it were like Mahomet's tomb at Mecca, between two loadstones ; like Erasmus, as the papists paint him, betwixt heaven and hell ; like the tribe of Manasseh, half on this side of Jordan, in the land of the Amorites, and half on that side, in the Holy Land ; yet, in the issue, they shall overcome the flesh, and trample upon the necks of their spiritual enemies.[3]

The sixth device that Satan hath to keep souls in a sad, doubting, questioning condition is,

Device (6). *By suggesting to the soul, that surely his estate is not*

---

[1] These two, grace and sin, are like two buckets of a well, when one is up, the other is down. They are like the two laurels at Rome, when one flourishes the other withers. The more grace thrives in the soul, the more sin dies in the soul. From naught they grow to be very naught, and from very naught to be stark naught. Lactant[ius] said of Lucian, *Nec Diis, nec hominibus pepercit,* he spared neither God nor man.

[2] Mortification is a continued act, it is a daily dying to sin, ' I die daily.' A crucified man will strive and struggle, yet, in the eyes of the law, and in the account of all that see him, he is dead. It is just so with sin.

[3] There is no such pleasure, saith Cyprian, as to have overcome an offered pleasure ; neither is there any greater conquest than that that is gotten over a man's corruptions. The Romans lost many a battle, and yet in the issue were conquerors in all their wars ; it is just so with the saints.

good, because he cannot joy and rejoice in Christ as once he could; because he hath lost that comfort and joy that once was in his spirit. Saith Satan, Thou knowest the time was when thy heart was much carried out to joying and rejoicing in Christ; thou dost not forget the time when thy heart used to be full of joy and comfort; but now, how art thou fallen in thy joys and comforts! Therefore, thy estate is not good; thou dost but deceive thyself to think that ever it was good, for surely if it had, thy joy and comfort would have continued. And hereupon the soul is apt to take part with Satan, and say, It is even so; I see all is naught, and I have but deceived my own soul, &c.

Now the remedies against this device are these:

Remedy (1). The first remedy against this device of Satan is, to consider, *That the loss of comfort is a separable adjunct from grace.* The soul may be full of holy affections when it is empty of divine consolations.[1] There may be, and often is, true grace, yea, much grace, where there is not a drop of comfort, nor dram of joy. Comfort is not of the being, but of the well-being, of a Christian. God hath not so linked these two choice lovers together, but that they may be put asunder. That wisdom that is from above will never work a man to reason thus: I have no comfort, therefore I have no grace; I have lost that joy that once I had, therefore my condition is not good, was never good, &c. But it will enable a man to reason thus: Though my comfort is gone, yet the God of my comfort abides; though my joy is lost, yet the seeds of grace remain. The best men's joys are as glass, bright and brittle, and evermore in danger of breaking.[2]

Remedy (2). The second remedy against this device of Satan is, solemnly to consider, *That the precious things that thou still enjoyest are far better than the joys and comforts that thou hast lost.* Thy union with Christ, thy communion with Christ, thy sonship, thy saintship, thy heirship, thou still enjoyest by Christ, are far better than the comforts thou hast lost by sin. What though thy comforts be gone, yet thy union and communion with Christ remains, Jer. xxxi. 18, 19, 20. Though thy comforts be gone, yet thou art a son, though a comfortless son; an heir, though a comfortless heir; a saint, though a comfortless saint. Though the bag of silver, thy comforts, be lost, yet the box of jewels, thy union with Christ, thy communion with Christ, thy sonship, thy saintship, thy heirship, which thou still enjoyest, is far better than the bag of silver thou hast lost; yea, the least of those precious jewels is more worth than all the comforts in the world. Well! let this be a cordial to comfort thee, a star to lead thee, and a staff to support thee, that thy box of jewels are safe, though thy bag of silver be lost.[3]

Remedy (3). The third remedy against this device of Satan is, to consider, *That thy condition is no other than what hath been the condition of those precious souls whose names were written upon the heart of Christ, and who are now at rest in the bosom of Christ.* One day

[1] Ps. lxiii. 1, 2, 8, Isa. l. 10, Micah vii. 8, 9, Ps. xlii. 5.

[2] Spiritual joy is a sun that is often clouded; though it be as precious a flower as most paradise affords, yet it is subject to fade and wither.

[3] When one objected to Faninus his cheerfulness to Christ's agony and sadness, he answered, Christ was sad, that I might be merry; he had my sins, and I have his righteousness. [Clarke's 'Martyrologie,' as before, *sub nomine.*—G.]

you shall have them praising and rejoicing, the next day a-mourning and weeping. One day you shall have them a-singing, 'The Lord is our portion;' the next day a-sighing and expostulating with themselves, 'Why are ye cast down, O our souls?' 'Why is our harp turned to mourning? and our organ into the voice of them that weep?' &c.[1]

Remedy (4). The fourth remedy against this device of Satan is, solemnly to consider, *That the causes of joy and comfort are not always the same.* Happily, thy former joy and comfort did spring from the witness of the Spirit, he bearing witness to thy soul, that thy nature was changed, thy sins pardoned, thy soul reconciled, &c.[2] Now, the Spirit may, upon some special occasion, bear witness to the soul, that the heart of God is dearly set upon him, that he loves him with an everlasting love, &c., and yet the soul may never enjoy such a testimony all the days of his life again. Though the Spirit be a witnessing Spirit, it is not his office every day to witness to believers their interest in God, Christ, heaven, &c.

Or, happily, thy former joy and comfort did spring from the newness and suddenness of the change of thy condition. For a man in one hour to have his night turned into day, his darkness turned into light, his bitter into sweet, God's frowns into smiles, his hatred into love, his hell into a heaven, must greatly joy and comfort him.[3] It cannot but make his heart to leap and dance in him, who, in one hour, shall see Satan accusing him, his own heart condemning him, the eternal God frowning upon him, the gates of heaven barred against him, all the creation standing armed, at the least beck of God, to execute vengeance on him, and the mouth of the infernal pit open to receive him. Now, in this hour, for Christ to come to the amazed soul, and to say to it, I have trod the wine-press of my Father's wrath for thee; I have laid down my life a ransom for thee; by my blood I have satisfied my Father's justice, and pacified his anger, and procured his love for thee; by my blood I have purchased the pardon of thy sins, thy freedom from hell, and thy right to heaven; oh! how wonderfully will this cause the soul to leap for joy!

Remedy (5). The fifth remedy against this device of Satan is, to consider, *That God will restore and make up the comforts of his people.*[4] Though thy candle be put out, yet God will light it again, and make it burn more light than ever. Though thy sun for the present be clouded, yet he that rides upon the clouds shall scatter those clouds, and cause the sun to shine and warm thy heart as in former days, as the psalmist speaks: 'Thou which hast shewed me great and sore troubles, shalt

---

[1] Ps. li. 12, xxx. 6, 7; Job xxiii. 6, 8, 9, 30, 31; Lamen. i. 16, Mat. xxvii. 46; Ps. xlii. 5, Lament. v. 15.

[2] The Spirit doth not every day make a feast in the soul; he doth not make every day to be a day of weaving the wedding robes.

[3] A pardon given unexpectedly into the hand of a malefactor, when he is on the last step of the ladder, ready to be turned off, will cause much joy and rejoicing. The newness and suddenness of the change of his condition will cause his heart to leap and rejoice; yet, in process of time, much of his joy will be abated, though his life be as dear to him still as ever it was.

[4] Hudson the martyr, deserted at the stake, went from under his chain, and, having prayed earnestly, was comforted immediately, and suffered valiantly. So Mr Glover, when he was within sight of the stake, cried out to his friend, He is come, he is come, meaning the Comforter that Christ promised to send. [On Thomas Hudson, see Clarke's 'Martyrologie,' as before, pp. 498, 499; on Glover, *ibid.* pp. 460–61.—G.]

quicken me again, and shalt bring me up again from the depths of the earth. Thou shalt increase my greatness, and comfort me on every side,' Ps. lxxi. 20, 21. God takes away a little comfort, that he may make room in the soul for a greater degree of comfort. This the prophet Isaiah sweetly shews : ' I have seen his ways, and will heal him ; I will lead him also, and restore comforts unto him, and to his mourners,' Isa. lvii. 18. Bear up sweetly, O precious soul ! thy storm shall end in a calm, and thy dark night in a sunshine day ; thy mourning shall be turned into rejoicing, and the waters of consolation shall be sweeter and higher in thy soul than ever ;[1] the mercy is surely thine, but the time of giving it is the Lord's. Wait but a little, and thou shalt find the Lord comforting thee on every side.

The seventh device that Satan hath to keep souls in a sad, doubting, and questioning condition, is,

Device (7). *By suggesting to the soul his often relapses into the same sin which formerly he hath pursued with particular sorrow, grief, shame, and tears, and prayed, complained, and resolved against.* Saith Satan, Thy heart is not right with God ; surely thy estate is not good ; thou dost but flatter thyself to think that ever God will eternally own and embrace such a one as thou art, who complainest against sin, and yet relapsest into the same sin ; who with tears and groans confessest thy sin, and yet ever and anon art fallen into the same sin.

I confess this is a very sad condition for a soul after he hath obtained mercy and pity from the Lord, after God hath spoken peace and pardon to him, and wiped the tears from his eyes, and set him upon his legs, to return to folly.[2] Ah ! how do relapses lay men open to the greatest afflictions and worst temptations ! How do they make the wound to bleed afresh ! How do they darken and cloud former assurances and evidences for heaven ! How do they put a sword into the hand of conscience to cut and slash the soul ! They raise such fears, terrors, horrors, and doubts in the soul, that the soul cannot be so frequent in duty as formerly, nor so fervent in duty as formerly, nor so confident in duty as formerly, nor so bold, familiar, and delightful with God in duty as formerly, nor so constant in duty as formerly. They give Satan an advantage to triumph over Christ ; they make the work of repentance more difficult ; they make a man's life a burden, and they render death to be very terrible unto the soul, &c.

Now the remedies against this device are these :

Remedy (1). The first remedy against this device of Satan is, solemnly to consider, *That there are many scriptures that do clearly evidence a possibility of the saints falling into the same sins whereof they have formerly repented.* ' I will heal their backslidings, I will love them freely : for mine anger is turned away from them,' saith the Lord by the prophet Hosea, chap. xiv. 4. So the prophet Jeremiah speaks : ' Go and proclaim these words toward the north, and say, Return, thou backsliding Israel, saith the Lord, and I will not cause mine anger to fall upon you : for I am merciful, saith the Lord, and I

---

[1] See Ps. cxxvi. 6, and xlii. 7, 8.

[2] A backslider may say, *Opera et impensa periit*, all my pains and charge is lost.

will not keep mine anger for ever. Turn, O backsliding Israel, saith the Lord ; for I am married unto you : and I will take you one of a city, and two of a family, and I will bring you to Zion,' chap. iii. 12, 14. So the psalmist : ' They turned back, and dealt unfaithfully with their fathers ; they were turned aside like a deceitful bow.' And no wonder, for though their repentance be never so sincere and sound, yet their graces are but weak, and their mortification imperfect in this life. Though by grace they are freed from the dominion of sin, and from the damnatory power of every sin, and from the love of all sin, yet grace doth not free them from the seed of any one sin ; and therefore it is possible for a soul to fall again and again into the same sin.   If the fire be not wholly put out, who would think it impossible that it should catch and burn again and again ?[1]

Remedy (2). The second remedy against this device of Satan is, seriously to consider, *That God hath nowhere engaged himself by any particular promise, that souls converted and united to Christ shall not fall again and again into the same sin after conversion.*   I cannot find in the whole book of God where he hath promised any such strength or power against this or that particular sin, as that the soul should be for ever, in this life, put out of a possibility of falling again and again into the same sins ; and where God hath not a mouth to speak, I must not have a heart to believe.   God will graciously pardon those sins to his people that he will not in this life effectually subdue in his people.   I would go far to speak with that soul that can shew me a promise, that when our sorrow and grief hath been so great, or so much, for this or that sin, that then God will preserve us from ever falling into the same sin.   The sight of such a promise would be as life from the dead to many a precious soul, who desires nothing more than to keep close to Christ, and fears nothing more than backsliding from Christ.[2]

Remedy (3). The third remedy against this device of Satan is, seriously to consider, *That the most renowned and now crowned saints have, in the days of their being on earth, relapsed into one and the same sin.*[3]   Lot was twice overcome with wine ; John twice worshipped the angel ; Abraham did often dissemble, and lay his wife open to adultery to save his own life, which some heathens would not have done : ' And it came to pass, when God caused me to wander from my father's house, that I said unto her, This is thy kindness which thou shalt shew unto me ; at every place whither we shall come, say of me, as he is my brother,' Gen. xx. 13.   David in his wrath was resolved, if ever man was, that he would be the death of Nabal, and all his innocent family ; and after this he fell into the foul murder of Uriah.   Though Christ told his disciples that his ' kingdom was not of this world,' yet again, and again, and again, three several times they

---

[1] The sin of backsliding is a soul-wounding sin, ' I will heal their backsliding.' You read of no arms for the back, though you do for the breast. When a soldier bragged too much of a great scar in his forehead, Augustus Cæsar (in whose time Christ was born) asked him if he did not get it as he looked back when he fled.

[2] In some cases the saints have found God better than his word. He promised the children of Israel only the land of Canaan, but besides that he gave them two other kingdoms which he never promised. And to Zacharias he promised to give him his speech at the birth of the child, but besides that he gave him the gift of prophecy.

[3] A sheep may often slip into a slough, as well as a swine.

would needs be on horseback; they would fain be high, great, and glorious in this world. Their pride and ambitious humour put them, that were but as so many beggars, upon striving for pre-eminence and greatness in the world, when their Lord and Master told them three several times of his sufferings in the world, and of his going out of the world. Jehoshaphat, though a godly man, yet joins affinity with Ahab, 2 Chron. xviii. 1–3, 30, 31; and though he was saved by a miracle, yet soon after he falls into the same sin, and 'joins himself with Ahaziah king of Israel, who did very wickedly,' 2 Chron. xx. 35–37. Samson is by the Spirit of the Lord numbered among the faithful worthies, yet he fell often into one gross sin, as is evident, Heb. xi. 32. Peter, you know, relapsed often, and so did Jonah; and this comes to pass that they may see their own inability to stand, to resist or overcome any temptation or corruptions, Jude 14, 15, 16.[1] And that they may be taken off from all false confidences, and rest wholly upon God, and only upon God, and always upon God; and for the praise and honour of the power, wisdom, skill, mercy, and goodness of the physician of our souls, that can heal, help, and cure when the disease is most dangerous, when the soul is relapsed, and grows worse and worse, and when others say, 'There is no help for him in his God,' and when his own heart and hopes are dying.[2]

Remedy (4). The fourth remedy against this device of Satan is, to consider, *That there are relapses into enormities, and there are relapses into infirmities.* Now it is not usual with God to leave his people frequently to relapse into enormities; for by his Spirit and grace, by his smiles and frowns, by his word and rod, he doth usually preserve his people from a frequent relapsing into enormities; yet he doth leave his choicest ones frequently to relapse into infirmities (and of his grace he pardons them in course), as idle words, passion, vain thoughts, &c.[3] Though gracious souls strive against these, and complain of these, and weep over these, yet the Lord, to keep them humble, leaves them frequently to relapse into these; and these frequent relapses into infirmities shall never be their bane, because they be their burden.

Remedy (5). The fifth remedy against this device of Satan is, to consider, *That there are involuntary relapses, and there are voluntary relapses.* Involuntary relapses are, when the resolution and full bent of the heart is against sin, when the soul strives with all its might against sin, by sighs and groans, by prayers and tears, and yet out of weakness is forced to fall back into sin, because there is not spiritual strength enough to overcome. Now, though involuntary relapses must humble us, yet they must never discourage nor defect us; for God will freely and readily pardon those, in course. Voluntary relapses are, when the soul longs and loves to 'return to the flesh-pots of Egypt,' Exod. xvi. 3; when it is a pleasure and a pastime to a man to return

---

[1] Perhaps the prodigal sets out unto us a Christian relapse, for he was a son before, and with his father, and then went away from him, and spent all; and yet he was not quite undone, but returned again.

[2] The prodigal saw the compassion of his father the greater, in receiving him after he had run away from him.

[3] Relapses into enormities are *peccata vulnerantia et divastantia*, wounding and wasting sins; therefore the Lord is graciously pleased to put under his everlasting arms, and stay his chosen ones from frequent falling into them.

to his old courses, such voluntary relapses speak out the man blinded, hardened, and ripened for ruin, &c.[1]

Remedy (6). The sixth remedy against this device of Satan is, to consider, *That there is no such power, or infinite virtue, in the greatest horror or sorrow the soul can be under for sin, nor in the sweetest or choicest discoveries of God's grace and love to the soul, as for ever to fence and secure the soul from relapsing into the same sin.* Grace is but a created habit, that may be prevailed against by the secret, subtle, and strong workings of sin in our hearts ; and those discoveries that God makes of his love, beauty, and glory to the soul, do not always abide in their freshness and power upon the heart ; but by degrees they fade and wear off, and then the soul may return again to folly, as we see in Peter, who, after he had a glorious testimony from Christ's own mouth of his blessedness and happiness, labours to prevent Christ from going up to Jerusalem to suffer, out of bare slavish fears that he and his fellows could not be secure, if his Master should be brought to suffer, Mat. xvi. 15–19, and ver. 22–24. And again, after this, Christ had him up into the mount, and there shewed him his beauty and his glory, to strengthen him against the hour of temptation that was coming upon him ; and yet, soon after he had the honour and happiness of seeing the glory of the Lord (which most of his disciples had not), he basely and most shamefully denies the Lord of glory, thinking by that means to provide for his own safety ;[2] and yet again, after Christ had broke his heart with a look of love for his most unlovely dealings, and bade them that were first acquainted with his resurrection to ' go and tell Peter that he was risen,' Mark xvi. 7 ; I say, after all this, slavish fears prevail upon him, and he basely dissembles, and plays the Jew with the Jews, and the Gentile with the Gentiles, to the seducing of Barnabas, &c., Gal. ii. 11–13.

Yet, by way of caution, know, it is very rare that God doth leave his beloved ones frequently to relapse into one and the same gross sin ; for the law of nature is in arms against gross sins, as well as the law of grace, so that a gracious soul cannot, dares not, will not, frequently return to gross folly. And God hath made even his dearest ones dearly smart for their relapses, as may be seen by his dealings with Samson, Jehoshaphat, and Peter. Ah, Lord ! what a hard heart hath that man, that can see thee stripping and whipping thy dearest ones for their relapses, and yet make nothing of returning to folly, &c.

The eighth device that Satan hath to keep souls in a sad, doubting, and questionable condition, is,

Device (8). *By persuading them that their estate is not good, their hearts are not upright, their graces are not sound, because they are so followed, vexed, and tormented with temptations.* It is his method, first to weary and vex thy soul with temptations, and then to tempt the soul, that surely it is not beloved, because it is so much tempted. And by this stratagem he keeps many precious souls in a sad, doubting,

---

[1] There is a great difference between a sheep that by weakness falls into the mire, and a swine that delights to wallow in the mire ; between a woman that is forced, though she strives and cries out, and an alluring adulteress.

[2] Christ upbraided his disciples for their unbelief and hardness of heart, who had seen his glory, ' as the glory of the only begotten Son of God, full of grace and truth.'

and mourning temper many years, as many of the precious sons of Sion have found by woful experience, &c.[1]

Now the remedies against this device are these :

Remedy (1). The first remedy against this device of Satan is, solemnly to consider, *That those that have been best and most beloved, have been most tempted by Satan.* Though Satan can never rob a Christian of his crown, yet such is his malice, that he will therefore tempt, that he may spoil them of their comforts. Such is his enmity to the Father, that the nearer and dearer any child is to him, the more will Satan trouble him, and vex him with temptations. Christ himself was most near and most dear, most innocent and most excellent, and yet none so much tempted as Christ. David was dearly beloved, and yet by Satan tempted to number the people.[2] Job was highly praised by God himself, and yet much tempted ; witness those sad things that fell from his mouth, when he was wet to the skin. Peter was much prized by Christ ; witness that choice testimony that Christ gave of his faith and happiness, and his shewing him his glory in the mount, and that eye of pity that he cast upon him after his fearful fall, &c., and yet tempted by Satan. ' And the Lord said, Simon, Simon, behold, Satan hath desired to have you, that he may sift you as wheat : but I have prayed for thee, that thy faith fail thee not,' &c., Luke xxii. 31, 32.

Paul had the honour of being exalted as high as heaven, and of seeing that glory that could not be expressed ; and yet he was no sooner stepped out of heaven, but he is buffeted by Satan, ' lest he should be exalted above measure,' 2 Cor. xii. 2, 7. If these, that were so really, so gloriously, so eminently beloved of God, if these, that have lived in heaven, and set their feet upon the stars, have been tempted, let no saints judge themselves not to be beloved, because they are tempted. It is as natural for saints to be tempted, that are dearly beloved, as it is for the sun to shine, or a bird to sing. The eagle complains not of her wings, nor the peacock of his train, nor the nightingale of her voice, because these are natural to them ; no more should saints of their temptations, because they are natural to them. ' For we wrestle not against flesh and blood, but against principalities, against powers, against the rulers of the darkness of this world, against spiritual wickedness in high places,' Eph. vi. 12.

Remedy (2). The second remedy against this device of Satan is, to consider, *That all the temptations that befall the saints shall be sanctified to them by a hand of love.* Ah ! the choice experiences that the saints get of the power of God supporting them, of the wisdom of God directing them (so to handle their spiritual weapons, their graces, as not only to resist, but to overcome), of the mercy and goodness of the Lord pardoning and succouring of them. And therefore, saith Paul, ' I received the messenger of Satan for to buffet me, lest I should be exalted, lest I should be exalted above measure,' 2 Cor. xii. 7.[3] Twice

---

[1] He may so tempt as to make a saint weary of his life : Job x. 1, ' My soul is weary of my life.'

[2] Pirates do not use to set upon poor empty vessels—[See ' Ep. Dedicatory.'—G.]; and beggars need not fear the thief. Those that have most of God, and are most rich in grace, shall be most set upon by Satan, who is the greatest and wisest pirate in the world.

[3] Vide Bezam, Grotium, et Estium [on the passage.—G.].

in that verse; he begins with it, and ends with it. If he had not been buffeted, who knows how his heart would have swelled; he might have been carried higher in conceit, than before he was in his ecstasy. Temptation is God's school, wherein he gives his people the clearest and sweetest discoveries of his love;[1] a school wherein God teaches his people to be more frequent and fervent in duty. When Paul was buffeted, then he prayed thrice, *i. e.* frequently and fervently; a school wherein God teaches his people to be more tender, meek, and compassionate to other poor, tempted souls than ever; a school wherein God teaches his people to see a greater evil in sin than ever, and a greater emptiness in the creature than ever, and a greater need of Christ and free grace than ever; a school wherein God will teach his people that all temptations are but his goldsmiths, by which he will try and refine, and make his people more bright and glorious. The issue of all temptations shall be to the good of the saints, as you may see by the temptations that Adam and Eve, and Christ and David, and Job and Peter and Paul met with. Those hands of power and love, that bring light out of darkness, good out of evil, sweet out of bitter, life out of death, heaven out of hell, will bring much sweet and good to his people, out of all the temptations that come upon them.

Remedy (3). The third remedy against this device of Satan is, wisely to consider, *That no temptations do hurt or harm the saints, so long as they are resisted by them, and prove the greatest afflictions that can befall them.* It is not Satan's tempting, but your assenting; not his enticing, but your yielding, that makes temptations hurtful to your soul. If the soul when it is tempted resists temptation, and saith with Christ, ' Get thee behind me, Satan,' Mat. xvi. 23; and with that young convert, ' I am not the man I was,'—*ego non sum ego*—or as Luther counsels all men to answer all temptations with these words—*Christianus sum*—I am a Christian. If a man's temptation be his greatest affliction, then is the temptation no sin upon his soul, though it be a trouble upon his mind. When a soul can look the Lord in the face, and say, Ah, Lord! I have many outward troubles upon me, I have lost such and such a near mercy, and such and such desirable mercies; and yet thou that knowest the heart, thou knowest that all my crosses and losses do not make so many wounds in my soul, nor fetch so many sighs from my heart, tears from my eyes, as those temptations do that Satan follows my soul with! When it is thus with the soul, then temptations are only the soul's trouble, they are not the soul's sin.

Satan is a malicious and envious enemy. As his names are, so is he; his names are all names of enmity; the accuser, the tempter, the destroyer, the devourer, the envious man; and this malice and envy of his he shews sometimes by tempting men to such sins as are quite contrary to the temperature of their bodies, as he did Vespasian and Julian, men of sweet and excellent natures, to be most bloody murderers.[2] And sometimes he shews his malice by tempting men to such things as will

---

[1] Luther said, there were three things that made a preacher, meditation, prayer, and temptation.

[2] Sometimes he shews his malice by letting those things abide by the soul, as may most vex and plague the soul, as Gregory observes in his leaving of Job's wife, which was not out of his forgetfulness, carelessness, or any love or pity to Job, but to vex and torment him, and to work him to blaspheme God, despair, and die, &c.

bring them no honour nor profit, &c. 'Fall down and worship me.' Mat. iv. 9, to blasphemy, and atheism, &c., the thoughts and first motions whereof cause the heart and flesh to tremble. And sometimes he shews his malice by tempting them to those sins which they have not found their natures prone to, and which they abhor in others. Now, if the soul resists these, and complains of these, and groans and mourns under these, and looks up to the Lord Jesus to be delivered from these, then shall they not be put down to the soul's account, but to Satan's, who shall be so much the more tormented, by how much the more the saints have been by him maliciously tempted, &c.

Make present and peremptory resistance against Satan's temptations, bid defiance to the temptation at first sight. It is safe to resist, it is dangerous to dispute. Eve lost herself and her posterity by falling into lists[1] of dispute, when she should have resisted, and stood upon terms of defiance with Satan. He that would stand in the hour of temptation must plead with Christ, 'It is written.' He that would triumph over temptations must plead still, 'It is written.[2] Satan is bold and impudent, and if you are not peremptory in your resistance, he will give you fresh onsets. It is your greatest honour, and your highest wisdom, peremptorily to withstand the beginnings of a temptation, for an after-remedy comes often too late.

Mrs Catherine Bretterege once, after a great conflict with Satan, said, ' Reason not with me, I am but a weak woman; if thou hast anything to say, say it to my Christ; he is my advocate, my strength, and my redeemer, and he shall plead for me.'[3]

Men must not seek to resist Satan's craft with craft, *sed per apertum Martem*, but by open defiance. He shoots with Satan in his own bow, who thinks by disputing and reasoning to put him off. As soon as a temptation shews its face, say to the temptation, as Ephraim to his idols, ' Get you hence, what have I any more to do with you?' Hosea xiv. 8. Oh ! say to the temptation, as David said to the sons of Zeruiah, ' What have I to do with you?' 2 Sam. xvi. 10. You will be too hard for me. He that doth thus resist temptations, shall never be undone by temptations, &c.[4]

Make strong and constant resistance against Satan's temptations. Make resistance against temptations by arguments drawn from the honour of God, the love of God, your union and communion with God; and from the blood of Christ, the death of Christ, the kindness of Christ, the intercession of Christ, and the glory of Christ ; and from the voice of the Spirit, the counsel of the Spirit, the comforts of the Spirit, the presence of the Spirit, the seal of the Spirit, the whisperings of the Spirit, the commands of the Spirit, the assistance of the Spirit, the witness of the Spirit; and from the glory of heaven, the excellency of grace,

---

[1] 'Artifices.' Cf. Halliwell, *sub voce.*—G.

[2] When Constantine the emperor was told that there was no means to cure his leprosy but by bathing his body in the blood of infants, he presently answered, *Malo semper ægrotare quam tali remedio convalescere*, I had rather not be cured than use such a remedy.

[3] See ' Two Funeral Sermons for Mrs Catherine Bretterege ;' the one by W. Harrison, the other by W. Legh. 1605.'—G.

[4] I have read of one, who, being tempted with offers of money to desert Christ, gave this excellent answer : Let not any man think that he will embrace other men's goods to forsake Christ, who hath forsaken his own proper goods to follow Christ.

the beauty of holiness, the worth of the soul, and the vileness or bitterness and evil of sin—the least sin being a greater evil than the greatest temptation in the world.

And look that you make constant resistance, as well as strong resistance ; be constant in arms. Satan will come on with new temptations when old ones are too weak.[1] In a calm prepare for a storm. The tempter is restless, impudent, and subtle ; he will suit his temptations to your constitutions and inclinations. Satan loves to sail with the wind. If your knowledge be weak, he will tempt you to error ; if your conscience be tender, he will tempt you to scrupulosity and too much preciseness, as to do nothing but hear, pray, read, &c.; if your consciences be wide and large, he will tempt you to carnal security ; if you are bold-spirited, he will tempt you to presumption; if timorous, to desperation ; if flexible, to inconstancy ; if proud and stiff, to gross folly ; therefore still fit for fresh assaults, make one victory a step to another. When you have overcome a temptation, take heed of unbending your bow, and look well to it, that your bow be always bent, and that it remains in strength. When you have overcome one temptation, you must be ready to enter the list[2] with another. As distrust in some sense is the mother of safety, so security is the gate of danger. A man had need to fear this most of all, that he fears not at all. If Satan be always roaring, we should be always a-watching and resisting of him. And certainly he that makes strong and constant resistance of Satan's temptations, shall in the end get above his temptations, and for the present is secure enough from being ruined by his temptations, &c.

For a close of this, remember, that it is dangerous to yield to the least sin to be rid of the greatest temptation. To take this course were as if a man should think to wash himself clean in ink, or as if a man should exchange a light cross, made of paper, for an iron cross, which is heavy, toilsome, and bloody. The least sin set home upon the conscience, will more wound, vex, and oppress the soul, than all the temptations in the world can ; therefore never yield to the least sin to be rid of the greatest temptation.[3] Sidonius Apollinarius relateth how a certain man named Maximus, arriving at the top of honour by indirect means, was the first day very much wearied, and fetching a deep sigh, said, ' Oh, Damocles ! how happy do I esteem of thee, for having been a king but the space of a dinner ! I have been one whole day, and can bear it no longer.'[4] I will leave you to make the application.

IV. The fourth thing to be shewed is,

The several ways and devices that Satan hath to destroy and ensnare all sorts and ranks of men in the world.

I shall begin with the honourable and the great, and shew you the devices that Satan hath to destroy them. I will only instance in those that are most considerable.

Device (1). His first device to destroy *the great and honourable of*

---

[1] Luke iv. 13, ' And when the devil had ended all the temptation, he departed from him for a season.' Christ had no rest until he was exactly tried with all kinds of temptations. [Calvin *in loc.*—G.]   [2] ' Course.'—G.

[3] He that will yield to sin to be rid of temptation, will be so much the more tempted, and the less able to withstand temptations.

[4] *Opera:* Sidonius C. S. Apollinaris, *sub nomine* (Paris, 1652, by Sirmond).—G.

the earth is, *By working them to make it their business to seek them-selves, to seek how to greaten themselves, to raise themselves, to enrich themselves, to secure themselves,* &c., as you may see in Pharaoh, Ahab, Rehoboam, Jeroboam, Absalom, Joab, Haman, &c.[1] But were the Scripture silent, our own experiences do abundantly evidence this way and method of Satan to destroy the great and the honourable; to bury their names in the dust, and their souls in hell, by drawing them wholly to mind themselves, and only to mind themselves, and in all things to mind themselves, and always to mind themselves. 'All,' saith the apostle, ' mind themselves,' Philip. ii. 21. All comparatively, in respect of the paucity of others, that let fall their private interests, and drown all self-respects in the glory of God and the public good, &c.

Now the remedies against this device are these,

Remedy (1). The first remedy against this device of Satan is, solemnly to consider, *That self-seeking is a sin that will put men upon a world of sins, upon sins not only against the law of God, the rules of the gospel, but that are against the very laws of nature, that are so much darkened by the fall of man.*[2] It puts the Pharisees upon opposing Christ, and Judas upon betraying Christ, and Pilate upon condemning Christ. It puts Gehazi upon lying, and Balaam upon cursing, and Saul and Absalom upon plotting David's ruin. It put Pharaoh and Haman upon contriving ways to destroy those Jews that God did pur-pose to save by his mighty arm. It puts men upon using wicked balances, and the bag of deceitful weights. It puts men upon ways of oppression, and ' selling the righteous for silver, and the poor for a pair of shoes,' &c., Amos ii. 6. I know not any sin in the world but this sin of self-seeking will put men upon it, though it be their eternal loss.

Remedy (2). The second remedy against this device of Satan is, seriously to consider, *That self-seeking doth exceedingly abase à man.* It strips him of all his royalty and glory. Of a lord it makes a man become a servant to the creature, ay, often to the worst of creatures; yea, a slave to slaves, as you may see in Judas, Demas, Balaam, and the Scribes and Pharisees.[3] Self-seekers bow down to the creatures, as Gideon's many thousands bowed down to the waters. Self-seeking will make a man say anything, do anything, and be anything, to please the lusts of others, and to get advantages upon others. Self-seeking transforms a man into all shapes and forms; now it makes a man ap-pear as an angel of light, anon as an angel of darkness.[4] Now self-seekers are seemingly for God, anon they are openly against God; now you shall have them crying, ' Hosanna in the highest,' and anon, ' Crucify him, crucify him;' now you shall have them build with the saints, and anon you shall have them plotting the overthrow of the saints, as those self-seekers did in Ezra and Nehemiah's time. Self-seekers are the basest of all persons. There is no service so base, so

[1] Self-seeking, like the deluge, overthrows the whole world.

[2] Self-love is the root of the hatred of others, 2 Tim. iii. 2. First, lovers of themselves, and then fierce, &c. The naturalists observe, that those beasts which are most cruel to others are most loving to their own.

[3] A self-seeker is a Cato without, but a Nero within. Domitian would seem to love them best whom he willed least should live, and that is the very temper of self-seekers.

[4] It was death in Moses' rites to counterfeit that ceremonial and figurative ointment, Ex. xxx. What shall it then be to counterfeit the spirit of life and holiness!

poor, so low, but they will bow to it. They cannot look neither above, nor beyond their own lusts, and the enjoyment of the creature, Rom. i. 25. These are the prime and ultimate objects of their intendments.

It is said of Tiberius, 'that whilst Augustus ruled, he was no way tainted in his reputation, and that while Drusus and Germanicus were alive, he feigned those virtues which he had not, to maintain a good opinion of himself in the hearts of the people; but after he had got himself out of the reach of contradiction and controlment, there was no fact in which he was not faulty, no crime to which he was not accessory.' My prayer shall be, that Tiberius his spirit may not be found in any of our rulers, lest it prove their ruin, as it did his; and that wherever it is, it may þe detected, loathed, and ejected, that so neither the state nor souls may be ruined by it, &c.

Remedy (3). The third remedy against this device of Satan is, solemnly *To dwell upon those dreadful curses and woes that are from heaven denounced against self-seekers*. 'Woe unto them that join house to house, that lay field to field, till there be no place, that they may be placed alone in the midst of the earth,' Isa. v. 8. So Habakkuk, ii. 6, 9–12, 'Woe to him that increaseth that which is not his, and to him that ladeth himself with thick clay!' 'Woe to him that coveteth an evil covetousness to his house, that he may set his nest on high, that he may be delivered from the power of evil! Thou hast consulted shame to thy house by cutting off many people, and hast sinned against thy soul. For the stone shall cry out of the wall, and the beam out of the timber shall answer it. Woe to him that buildeth a town with blood, and establisheth a city by iniquity!' The materials of the house built up by oppression shall come as joint witnesses. The stones of the wall shall cry, 'Lord, we were built up by blood and violence; and the beam shall answer, True, Lord, even so it is.' The stones shall cry, Vengeance, Lord! upon these self-seekers! and the beam shall answer, Woe to him, because he built his house with blood![1] So Isaiah, 'Woe unto them that decree unrighteous decrees, and that write grievousness which they have prescribed; to turn aside the needy from judgment, and to take away the right from the poor of my people, that widows may be their prey, and that they may rob the fatherless,' Isa. x. 1, 2. So Amos, 'Woe unto them that are at ease in Zion, and trust in the mountain of Samaria, which are named chief of the nations, to whom the house of Israel came; that put far away the evil day, and cause the seat of violence to come near; that lie upon beds of ivory, and stretch themselves upon their couches, and eat the lambs out of the flock, and the calves out of the middle of the stall; that drink wine in bowls, and anoint themselves with the chief ointments: but they are not grieved for the afflictions of Joseph,' Amos vi. 1, 3–6. So Micah, 'Woe to them that devise iniquity, and work evil upon their beds! when the morning is light, they practise it, because

---

[1] Crassus, a very rich Roman, and a great self-seeker, for greedy desire of gold, he managed war against the Parthians, by whom both he and thirty thousand Romans were slain. And because the barbarians conjectured that he made this assault upon them for their gold, therefore they melted gold, and poured it into his dead body, saying, *Satura te auro*, Satisfy thyself with gold. [The above was done by Orodes, who said, 'Sate thyself now with that metal of which in life thou wert so greedy.'—*Dion. Cass.* xl. 27; *Florus*, iii. 11.—G.]

it is in the power of their hand.   And they covet fields, and take them
by violence, and houses, and take them away.   So they oppress a man
and his house, even a man and his heritage,' Micah ii. 1, 2.

By these scriptures, you see that self-seekers labour like a woman
in travail, but their birth proves their death, their pleasure their pain,
their comforts their torment, their glory their shame, their exaltation
their desolation.   Loss, disgrace, trouble and shame, vexation and confusion, will be the certain portion of self-seekers.

When the Tartarians had taken in battle the Duke of Muscovia, they
made a cup of his skull, with this inscription, ' All covet, all lose.'[1]

Remedy (4). The fourth remedy against this device of Satan is,
solemnly to consider, *That self-seekers are self-losers and self-destroyers.*
Absalom and Judas seek themselves, and hang themselves.   Saul seeks
himself, and kills himself.   Ahab seeks himself, and loses himself, his
crown and kingdom.   Pharaoh seeks himself, and overthrows himself and his mighty army in the Red Sea.   Cain sought himself, and
slew two at once, his brother and his own soul.   Gehazi sought change
of raiment, but God changed his raiment into a leprous skin.   Haman
sought himself, and lost himself.   The princes and presidents sought
themselves, in the ruin of Daniel, but ruined themselves, their wives
and children.   That which self-seekers think should be a staff to support them, becomes by the hand of justice an iron rod to break them ;
that which they would have as springs to refresh them, becomes a gulf
utterly to consume them.   The crosses of self-seekers shall always
exceed their mercies : their pain their pleasure ; their torments their
comforts.   Every self-seeker is a self-tormentor, a self-destroyer ; he
carries a hell, an executioner, in his own bosom, &c.[2]

Remedy (5). The fifth remedy against this device of Satan is, *To
dwell much upon the famous examples of those worthy saints that
have denied themselves and preferred the public good before their own
particular advantage.*[3]   As Moses, ' And the Lord said unto Moses,
Let me alone, that I may destroy them, and blot out their name from
under heaven : and I will make of thee a nation mightier and greater
than they,' Deut. ix. 14.   Oh ! but this offer would not take with Moses,
he being a man of a brave public spirit.   It is hot in his desires and
prayers that the people might be spared and pardoned ; saith he, ' Pardon, I beseech thee, the iniquity of this people, unto the greatness of
thy mercy, and as thou hast forgiven this people from Egypt until now.
And the Lord said, I have pardoned according to thy word,' ix. 26, *et
seq.*   Ah ! should God make such an offer to many that write themselves
Moses, and are called by many, Moses, I am afraid they would prefer
their own advantage above the public good ; they would not care what
become of the people, so they and theirs might be made great and

---

[1] Tacitus the Roman emperor's word was. *Sibi bonus, aliis malus,* He that is too much
for himself, fails to be good to others.

[2] Adam seeks himself, and loses himself, paradise, and that blessed image that God
had stamped upon him.   Lot seeks himself, Gen. xiii. 10, 11, and loses himself and his
goods.   Peter seeks to save himself, and miserably loses himself.   Hezekiah, in the business of the ambassadors, seeks himself, and lost himself and his life too, had not God
saved him by a miracle.

[3] It is good to be of his opinion and mind, who was rather willing to beautify Italy
than his own house.   The ancients were wont to place the statues of their princes by
their fountains, intimating they were (or at least should be) fountains of the public good.

glorious in the world ; they would not care so they might have a Babel
built for them, though it was upon the ashes and ruin of the people.
Baser spirits than these are not in hell ; no, not in hell ; and I am sure
there are no such spirits in heaven.   Such men's hearts and principles
must be changed, or they will be undone for ever.   Nehemiah was a
choice soul, a man of a brave public spirit, a man that spent his time,
his strength, and his estate, for the good and ease of his people.
' Moreover,' saith he, ' from the time that I was appointed to be their
governor in the land of Judah, from the twentieth year even unto the
two and thirtieth year of Artaxerxes the king, that is, twelve years, I
and my brethren have not eaten the bread of the governor.   Yea, also
I continued in the work of this wall: and all my servants were gathered
hither unto the work.   Moreover, there were at my table an hundred
and fifty of the Jews and rulers, besides those that came unto us from
among the heathen that are about us.   Now, that which was prepared
for me daily was one ox, and six choice sheep; also fowls were prepared
for me, and once in ten days store of all sorts of wine : yet for all this
required I not the bread of the governor, because the bondage was
heavy upon the people.   Think upon me, O my God, for good, according to all that I have done for this people,' Neh. v. 14–19.   So Daniel
was a man of a brave public spirit : ' Then the presidents and princes
sought to find occasion against Daniel concerning the kingdom ; but
they could find no occasion nor fault ; forasmuch as he was faithful,
neither was there any error or fault found in him.   Then said these
men, We shall not find any occasion against this Daniel, except we
find it against him concerning the law of his God,' Daniel vi. 4, 5.[1]

Christ had a public spirit, he laid out himself, and laid down himself
for a public good.   Oh ! never leave looking and meditating upon these
precious and sweet examples till your souls are quickened and raised
up, to act for the public good, more than for your own particular
advantage.   Many heathens have been excellent at this.[2]

Macrobius writes of Augustus Cæsar, in whose time Christ was born,
that he carried such an entire and fatherly affection to the commonwealth, that he called it *filiam suam,* his own daughter ; and therefore
refused to be called *Dominus,* the lord or master of his country, and
would only be called *Pater patriæ,* father of his country, because he
governed it not by fear, *per timorem, sed per amorem,* but by love ;
the senate and the people of Rome jointly saluting him by the name of
Pater patriæ, father of his country.   The people very much lamented
his death, using that speech, ' Would he had never been born, or never
died.'[3]

So Marcus Regulus, to save his country from ruin, exposed himself
to the greatest sufferings that the malice and rage of his enemies could
inflict.

So Titus and Aristides, and many others, have been famous for their
preferring the public good above their own advantage.   My prayer is,

[1] A certain great emperor coming into Egypt, to shew the zeal he had for the public
good, saith to the Egyptians, Draw from me as from your river Nilus.   The Counsellor
saith, a statesman should be thus tripartited : his will to God, his love to his master, his
heart to his country, his secret to his friend, his time to business.

[2] Solomon's tribunal was underpropped with lions, to shew what spirit and metal a
magistrate should be made of.   [3] *Utinam aut non nasceretur, aut [non] moreretur.*

and shall be, that all our rulers may be so spirited by God, that they may be willing to be anything, to be nothing, to deny themselves, and to trample their sinful selves under feet, in order to the honour of God, and a public good ; that so neither saints nor heathens may be witnesses against them in that day, wherein the hearts and practices of all the rulers in the world shall be open and bare before him that judges the world in righteousness and judgment.

Remedy (6). The sixth remedy against this device of Satan is, seriously to consider, *That self is a great let to divine things ; therefore the prophets and apostles were usually carried out of themselves, when they had the clearest, choicest, highest, and most glorious visions.* Self-seeking blinds the soul that it cannot see a beauty in Christ, nor an excellency in holiness ; it distempers the palate that a man cannot taste sweetness in the word of God, nor in the ways of God, nor in the society of the people of God. It shuts the hand against all the soul-enriching offers of Christ ; it hardens the heart against all the knocks and entreaties of Christ ; it makes the soul as an empty vine, and as a barren wilderness : 'Israel is an empty vine, he bringeth forth fruit to himself,' Hosea x. 1. There is nothing that speaks a man to be more empty and void of God, Christ, and grace, than self-seeking. The Pharisees were great self-seekers, and great undervaluers of Christ, his word and Spirit. There is not a greater hindrance to all the duties of piety than self-seeking. Oh ! this is that that keeps many a soul from looking after God and the precious things of eternity. They cannot wait on God, nor act for God, nor abide in those ways wherein they might meet with God, by reason of self. Self-seeking is that which puts many a man upon neglecting and slighting the things of his peace. Self-seekers will neither go into heaven themselves, nor suffer others to enter, that are ready to take the kingdom by violence, as you may see in the Scribes and Pharisees. Oh ! but a gracious spirit is acted quite other ways, as you may see in that sweet scripture, Cant. vii. 13, 'At our gates are all manner of pleasant fruits, new and old, which I have laid up for thee, O beloved.' All the church hath and is, is only for him. Let others bear fruit to themselves, and lay up for themselves, gracious spirits will hide for Christ and lay up for Christ.[1] All the divine endeavours and productions of saints fall into God's bosom, and empty themselves into his lap. As Christ lays up his merits for them, his graces for them, his comforts for them, his crown for them, so they lay up all their fruits, and all their loves, all their graces, and all their experiences, and all their services, only for him who is the soul of their comforts, and the crown and top of all their royalty and glory, &c.

The second device that Satan hath to ensnare and destroy the great and honourable of the earth is,

Device (2). *By engaging them against the people of the Most High, again those that are his jewels, his pleasant portion, the delight of his eye and the joy of his heart.* Thus he drew Pharaoh to engage against the children of Israel, and that was his overthrow, Exod. xiv. So he

---

[1] Self-seekers, with Esau, prefer a mess of pottage above their birthright, and with the men of Shechem, esteem the bramble above the vine, the olive, and the fig-tree, yea, empty things above a full Christ, and base things above a glorious Christ. The saints' motto is, *Propter te, Domine, propter te.* The saints' motto is, *Non nobis, Domine.*

engaged Haman against the Jews, and so brought him to hang upon that gallows that he had made for Mordecai, Esther vii. So he engaged those princes and presidents against Daniel, which was the utter ruin of them and their relations, Dan. vi. So in Rev. xx. 7–9, ' And when the thousand years are expired, Satan shall be loosed out of his prison. And he shall go out to deceive the nations which are in the four quarters of the earth, Gog and Magog, to gather them together to battle, whose number is as the sand of the sea. And they went up upon the breadth of the earth, and compassed the camp of the saints about, and the beloved city ; and fire came down from heaven and consumed them.'

Now the remedies against this device are these :

Remedy (1). The first remedy against this device of Satan is, solemnly to consider, *That none have engaged against the saints, but have been ruined by the God of saints.* Divine justice hath been too hard for all that have opposed and engaged against the saints, as is evident in Saul, Pharaoh, Haman, &c : ' He reproved kings for their sakes, saying, Touch not mine anointed, nor do my prophets no harm,' Ps. cv. 15. When men of Balaam spirits and principles have been engaged against the saints, how hath the angel of the Lord met them in the way, and justled their bones against the wall ! how hath he broke their backs and necks, and by his drawn sword cut them off in the prime of their days, and in the height of their sins !¹ Ah ! what a harvest hath hell had in our days, of those who have engaged against the Lamb, and those that are called chosen and faithful ! Ah ! how hath divine justice poured out their blood as water upon the ground ! how hath he laid their honour and glory in the dust, who, in the pride and madness of their hearts, said, as Pharaoh, ' We will pursue, we will overtake, we will divide the spoil, our lusts shall be satisfied upon them. We will draw our sword, our hand shall destroy them,' Exod. xv. 9. In the things wherein they have spoken and done proudly, justice hath been above them. History abounds in nothing more than in instances of this kind, &c.

Remedy (2). The second remedy against this device of Satan is, *To dwell some time every morning upon the following scriptures, wherein God hath engaged himself to stand by his people and for his people, and to make them victorious over the greatest and wisest of their enemies.*² Associate yourselves, saith the Lord by the prophet, ' O ye people, and ye shall be broken in pieces ; and give ear, all ye of far countries : gird yourselves, and ye shall be broken in pieces. Take counsel together, and it shall come to nought ; speak the word, and it shall not stand : for God is with us.' ' Fear not, thou worm Jacob, and ye men of Israel : I will help thee, saith the Lord, and thy Redeemer, the holy One of Israel. Behold, I will make thee a new sharp threshing instrument having teeth : thou shalt thresh the mountains, and beat them small, and shalt make the hills as chaff. Thou shalt fan them, and the wind shall carry them away, and the whirlwind shall scatter them, and thou shalt rejoice in the Lord, and shalt glory in the holy One of Israel.' ' No weapon that is formed against thee shall

¹ As they said once of the Grecians in the epigram, whom they thought invulnerable, We shoot at them, but they fall not down ; we wound them, and not kill them, &c. *Tanto plus gloriæ referemus, quoniam eo plures superabimus.* The number of opposers makes the Christian's conquest the more illustrious, said Pedarelus in Erasmus.

² *Occidi poterant, sed vinci non poterant*, said Cyprian of the Christians in his time.

prosper, and every tongue that shall rise against thee in judgment thou shalt condemn. This is the heritage of the servants of the Lord, and their righteousness is of me, saith the Lord.' 'Now also many nations are gathered together against thee that say, Let us be defiled, and let our eye look upon Sion. But they know not the thoughts of the Lord, neither understand they his counsel ; for he shall gather them as sheaves into the floor. Arise and thresh, O daughter of Sion : I will make thy horn iron, and I will make thy hoof brass, and thou shalt beat in pieces many people, and I will consecrate their gain unto the Lord, and their substance unto the Lord of the whole earth.' 'Behold, I will make Jerusalem a cup of trembling unto all the people round about, when they shall be in the siege, both against Judah and against Jerusalem. And in that day will I make Jerusalem a burdensome stone for all people : all that burden themselves with it shall be cut in pieces, though all the people of the earth be gathered together against it.'[1]

Remedy (3). The third remedy against this device of Satan is, to consider, *That you cannot engage against the saints, but you must engage against God himself, by reason of that near and blessed union that is between God and them.* You cannot be fighters against the saints, but you will be found in the casting up of the account to be fighters against God himself.[2] And what greater madness than for weakness itself to engage against an almighty strength ! The near union that is between the Lord and believers, is set forth by that near union that is betwixt a husband and his wife. 'They two shall be one flesh. This is a great mystery : but I speak concerning Christ and the church ; we are members of his body, of his flesh, and of his bones,' saith the apostle, Eph. v. 32. This near union is set forth by that union that is between the head and the members, which make up one body, and by that union that is betwixt the graff and the stock, which are made one by insition.[3] The union between the Lord and a believer is so near, that you cannot strike a believer, but the Lord is sensible of it, and takes it as done to himself. 'Saul, Saul, why persecutest thou me ?' Acts ix. 4 ; and 'in all their afflictions he was afflicted,' &c., Isa. lxiii. 9. Ah, souls ! who ever engaged against God and prospered ? who ever took up the sword against him but perished by it ? God can speak you to hell and nod you to hell at pleasure. It is your greatest concernment to lay down your weapons at his feet, and to ' Kiss the Son, lest he be angry, and you perish in the midway,' Ps. ii. 12.

Remedy (4). The fourth remedy against this device of Satan is, solemnly to consider, *That you are much engaged to the saints, as instruments for the mercies that you do enjoy, and for the preventing and removing of many a judgment that otherwise might have been your ruin before this day.* Were it not for the saints' sake, God would quickly make the heavens to be as brass and the earth as iron ; God would quickly strip thee of thy robes and glory, and set thee upon the dunghill with Job. They are the props that bear the world from falling about thy ears, and that keep the iron rod from breaking of thy bones.

[1] Isa. viii 9, 10 ; xli. 14, 15, and liv. 17 ; Micah iv. 11–13 ; Zech. xii. 2, 3.—G.

[2] Acts v. 39. It seems to be drawn from the fable of the giants, which were said to make war with the gods.

[3] The soul's happiness consists not in anything, but in its union with God ; nor its misery lies not so much in anything, as in its disunion from God.

' Therefore he said that he would destroy them, had not Moses his chosen stood before him in the breach, to turn away his wrath, lest he should destroy them,' Ps. cvi. 23.

Ah ! had not the saints many a time cast themselves into the breach betwixt God's wrath and you, you had been cut off from the land of the living, and had had your portion with those whose names are written in the dust.[1]   Many a nation, many a city, and many a family, is surrounded with blessings for the Josephs' sakes that live therein, and are preserved from many calamities and miseries for the Moseses', the Daniels', the Noahs', and the Jobs' sakes, that dwell amongst them. That is a sweet word, Prov. x. 25, ' As the whirlwind passeth, so is the wicked no more : but the righteous is an everlasting foundation, or is the foundation of the world.'[2]   The righteous is the foundation of the world, which but for their sakes would soon shatter and fall to ruin.   So the psalmist : Ps. lxxv. 3, ' The earth and all the inhabitants thereof are dissolved : I bear up the pillars of it.   Selah.'

The emperor Marcus Antoninus being in Almany[3] with his army, was enclosed in a dry country by his enemies, who so stopped all the passages that he and his army were like to perish for want of water.   The emperor's lieutenant seeing him so distressed, told him that he had heard that the Christians could obtain any thing of their God by their prayers, whereupon the emperor, having a legion of Christians in his army, desired them to pray to their God for his and the army's delivery out of that danger, which they presently did, and presently a great thunder fell amongst the enemies, and abundance of water upon the Romans, whereby their thirst was quenched, and the enemies overthrown without any fight.[4][5]   I shall close up this last remedy with those sweet words of the psalmist : ' In Judah is God known ; his name is great in Israel.   In Salem also is his tabernacle, and his dwelling-place in Zion. There brake he the arrows of the bow, the shield, and the sword, and the battle.   Selah,' Ps. lxxvi. 1–3.

Secondly, Satan hath his devices to ensnare and destroy *the learned and the wise*, and that sometimes *by working them to pride themselves in their parts and abilities; and sometimes by drawing them to rest upon their parts and abilities; and sometimes by causing them to make light and slight of those that want their parts and abilities, though they excel them in grace and holiness; and sometimes by drawing them to engage their parts and abilities in those ways and things that make against the honour of Christ, the joy of the Spirit, the advancement of the gospel, and the liberty of the saints, &c.*[6][7]

Now the remedies against this device are these.

Remedy (1).   The first remedy against this device of Satan is, seriously to consider, *That you have nothing but what you have received, Christ*

---

[1] *Hic homo potuit apud Deum quod voluit*, said one concerning Luther.   He could have what he would of God.   Prayer is *Porta cœli, clavis paradisi*, the gate of heaven, a key to let us into paradise.   When the danger is over, the saint is forgotten, is a French proverb, and that which many saints in England have found by experience.

[2] יסוד עולם *Jsodh Gnolam* from *Jasedh*.   [3] Germany.—G.

[4] The famous mythical ' Thundering Legion.'—G.

[5] Mary, Queen of Scots, that was mother to King James, was wont to say, That she feared Mr Knox's prayers more than an army of ten thousand men.

[6] John v. 44 ; 1 Kings xxii. 22–25 : 1 Cor. i. 18–29.

[7] The truth of this you may see in the learned Scribes and Pharisees.

being as well the fountain of common gifts as of saving grace. 'What hast thou,' saith the apostle, 'that thou hast not received? And if thou hast received it, why dost thou glory as though thou hadst not received it?' 1 Cor. iv. 7.[1] There are those that would hammer out their own happiness, like the spider climbing up by the thread of her own weaving. Of all the parts and abilities that be in you, you may well say as the young man did of his hatchet, 'Alas, master! it was but borrowed,' 2 Kings vi. 5. Alas, Lord! all I have is but borrowed from that fountain that fills all the vessels in heaven and on earth, and it overflows. My gifts are not so much mine as thine: 'Of thine own have we offered unto thee,' said that princely prophet, &c., 1 Chron. xxix. 14.

Remedy (2). The second remedy against this device of Satan is, solemnly to consider, *That men's leaning and trusting to their own wits, parts, and abilities, have been their utter overthrow and ruin;* as you may see in Ahithophel, and those presidents and princes that engaged against Daniel, and in the Scribes and Pharisees. God loves to confute men in their confidences.[2] He that stands upon his parts and abilities, doth but stand upon a quicksand that will certainly fail him. There is nothing in the world that provokes God more to withdraw from the soul than this; and how can the soul stand, when his strength is departed from him? Everything that a man leans upon but God, will be a dart that will certainly pierce his heart through and through. Ah! how many in these days have lost their estates, their friends, their lives, their souls, by leaning upon their admired parts and abilities! The saints are described by their leaning upon their beloved, the Lord Jesus, Cant. viii. 5. He that leans only upon the bosom of Christ, lives the highest, choicest, safest, and sweetest life. Miseries always lie at that man's door that leans upon anything below the precious bosom of Christ; such a man is most in danger, and this is none of his least plagues, that he thinks himself secure. It is the greatest wisdom in the world to take the wise man's counsel: 'Trust in the Lord with all thine heart, and lean not to thine own understanding,' Prov. iii. 5.

Remedy (3). The third remedy against this device of Satan is, to consider, *That you do not transcend others more in parts and abilities, than they do you in grace and holiness.* There may be, and often is, great parts and abilities, where there is but little grace, yea, no grace; and there may be, and often is, a great deal of grace, where there is but weak parts and abilities.[3] You may be higher than others in gifts of knowledge, utterance, learning, &c., and those very souls may be higher than you in their communion with God, in their delighting in God, in their dependence upon God, in their affections to God, and in their humble, holy, and unblameable walking before God.[4] Is it folly and madness in a man, to make light and slight of another, because he is

---

[1] *Quicquid es debes creanti; quicquid potes debes redimenti,* said Bernard. Whatsoever thou art, thou owest to him that made thee; and whatsoever thou hast, thou owest to him that redeemed thee.

[2] General councils were seldom successful, because men came with confidence, leaning to their own understanding, and seeking for victory rather than verity, saith one.

[3] Judas and the Scribes and Pharisees had great parts, but no grace. The disciples had grace, but weak parts.   [4] Luke xi. 1; xxiv. 19–28.

not so rich in lead or iron as he, when he is a thousand thousand times richer in silver and gold, in jewels and in pearls, than he? And is it not madness and folly with a witness, in those that have greater parts and abilities than others, to slight them upon that account, when that those very persons that they make light and slight of have a thousand times more grace than they? And yet, ah! how doth this evil spirit prevail in the world!

It was the sad complaint of Austin in his time : 'The unlearned,' saith he, 'rise up and take heaven by violence, and we with all our learning are thrust down to hell.'[1] It is sad to see how many of the rabbis of these times do make an idol of their parts and abilities, and with what an eye of pride, scorn, and contempt do they look upon those that want their parts, and that do not worship the idol that they have set up in their own hearts. Paul, who was the great doctor of the Gentiles, did wonderfully transcend in all parts and abilities the doctors and rabbis of our times, and yet, ah! how humbly, how tenderly, how sweetly, doth he carry himself towards the meanest and the weakest! 'To the weak I became as weak, that I might win the weak : I am made all things to all men, that I might by all means save some,' 1 Cor. ix 22. 'Who is weak, and I am not weak? Who is offended, and I burn not? Wherefore, if meat make my brother to offend, I will eat no flesh while the world standeth, lest I make my brother to offend,' 1 Cor. viii. 13. But, ah! how little of this sweet spirit is to be found in the doctors of our age, who look sourly and speak bitterly against those that do not see as they see, nor cannot speak as they speak. Sirs! the Spirit of the Lord, even in despised saints, will be too hard for you, and his appearance in them, in these latter days, will be so full of spiritual beauty and glory, as that they will darken that, that you are too apt to count and call your glory. The Spirit of the Lord will not suffer his choicest jewel grace to be always buried under the straw and stubble of parts and gifts, Isa. lx. 13–17.

Remedy (4). The fourth remedy against this device of Satan is, to consider, *That there is no such way for men to have their gifts and parts blasted and withered, as to pride themselves in them, as to rest upon them, as to make light and slight of those that want them, as to engage them against those persons, ways, and things, that Jesus Christ hath set his heart upon.* Ah! how hath God blasted and withered the parts and abilities of many among us, that have once been famous shining lights![2] How is their sun darkened, and their glory clouded! 'How is the sword of the Lord upon their arm, and upon their right eye! how is their arm clean dried up, and their right eye utterly darkened!' as the prophet speaks, Zech. xi. 17. This is matter of humiliation and lamentation. Many precious discerning saints do see this, and in secret mourn for it; and oh! that they were kindly sensible of God's withdrawing from them, that they may repent, keep humble, and carry it sweetly towards God's jewels, and lean only upon the Lord,

---

[1] Surgunt indocti et rapiunt cœlum, et nos cum doctrina nostra detrudimur in gehennam. [More accurately as follows : 'Surgunt indocti et cœlum rapiunt, et nos cum doctrinis nostris sine corde, ecce ubi volutamur in carne et sanguine.' Confess. l. viii. c. 8.—G.]

[2] Becanus saith, that the tree of knowledge bears many leaves, and little fruit. Ah! that it were not so with many in these days, who once did outshine the stars, &c.

and not upon their parts and understanding, that so the Lord may delight to visit them with his grace at such a rate as that their faces may shine more gloriously than ever, and that they may be more serviceable to the honour of Christ, and the faith of the saints, than formerly they have been, &c.

Thirdly, Satan hath his devices to destroy the saints; and one great device that he hath to destroy the saints is,

By working them first to be strange, and then to divide, and then to be bitter and jealous, and then ' to bite and devour one another,' Gal. v. 15. Our own woful experience is too great a proof of this. The Israelites in Egypt did not more vex one another than Christians in these days have done, which occasioned a deadly consumption to fall upon some.[1]

Now the remedies against this device are these :

Remedy (1). The first remedy against this device of Satan is, *To dwell more upon one another's graces than upon one another's weaknesses and infirmities.* It is sad to consider that saints should have many eyes to behold one another's infirmities, and not one eye to see each other's graces, that they should use spectacles to behold one another's weaknesses, rather than looking-glasses to behold one another's graces.[2]

Erasmus tells of one who collected all the lame and defective verses in Homer's works, but passed over all that was excellent. Ah! that this were not the practice of many that shall at last meet in heaven, that they were not careful and skilful to collect all the weaknesses of others, and to pass over all those things that are excellent in them. The Corinthians did eye more the incestuous person's sin than his sorrow, which was like to have drowned him in sorrow.

Tell me, saints, is it not a more sweet, comfortable, and delightful thing to look more upon one another's graces than upon one another's infirmities ? Tell me what pleasure, what delight, what comfort is there in looking upon the enemies, the wounds, the sores, the sickness, the diseases, the nakedness of our friends? Now sin, you know, is the soul's enemy, the soul's wound, the soul's sores, the soul's sickness, the soul's disease, the soul's nakedness ; and ah! what a heart hath that man that loves thus to look! Grace is the choicest flower in all a Christian's garden ; it is the richest jewel in all his crown ; it is his princely robes; it is the top of royalty ; and therefore must needs be the most pleasing, sweet, and delightful object for a gracious eye to be fixed upon. Sin is darkness, grace is light; sin is hell, grace is heaven; and what madness is it to look more at darkness than at light, more at hell than at heaven![3]

Tell me, saints, doth not God look more upon his people's graces than upon their weaknesses ? Surely he doth. He looks more at David's and Asaph's uprightness than upon their infirmities, though they were great and many. He eyes more Job's patience than his passion. 'Re-

---

[1] If we knock, we break. Dissolution is the daughter of dissension.

[2] Flavius Vespasian, the emperor, was more ready to conceal the vices of his friends than their virtues. Can you think seriously of this, Christians, that a heathen should excel you, and not blush ?

[3] *Non gens, sed mens, non genus sed genius,* Not race or place, but grace truly sets forth a man.

member the patience of Job,' not a word of his impatience, James v. 11. He that drew Alexander whilst he had a scar upon his face, drew him with his finger upon the scar. God puts his fingers upon his people's scars, that no blemish may appear. Ah! saints, that you would make it the top of your glory in this, to be like your heavenly Father. By so doing, much sin would be prevented, the designs of wicked men frustrated, Satan outwitted, many wounds healed, many sad hearts cheered, and God more abundantly honoured, &c.[1]

Remedy (2). The second remedy against this device of Satan is, solemnly to consider, *That love and union makes most for your own safety and security.* We shall be *insuperabiles* if we be *insepara-biles*, invincible if we be inseparable. The world may frown upon you, and plot against you, but they cannot hurt you. Unity is the best bond of safety in every church and commonwealth.[2]

And this did that Scythian king in Plutarch represent lively to his eighty sons, who, being ready to die, he commanded a bundle of arrows fast bound together to be given to his sons to break; they all tried to break them, but, being bound fast together, they could not; then he caused the band to be cut, and then they broke them with ease. He applied it thus: 'My sons, so long as you keep together, you will be invincible; but if the band of union be broke betwixt you, you will easily be broken in pieces.'[3]

Pliny writes of a stone in the island of Scyros, that if it be whole, though a large and heavy one, it swims above water, but being broken, it sinks.[4] So long as saints keep whole, nothing shall sink them; but if they break, they are in danger of sinking and drowning, &c.

Remedy (3). The third remedy against this device of Satan is, *To dwell upon those commands of God that do require you to love one another.* Oh! when your hearts begin to rise against each other, charge the commands of God upon your hearts, and say to your souls, O our souls! hath not the eternal God commanded you to love them that love the Lord? And is it not life to obey, and death to rebel?[5] Therefore look that you fulfil the commands of the Lord, for his commands are not like those that are easily reversed; but they are like those of the Medes, that cannot be changed. Oh! be much in pondering upon these commands of God. 'A new commandment I give unto you, that ye love one another, as I have loved you, that ye also love one another,' John xiii. 34. It is called a new commandment, because it is renewed in the gospel, and set home by Christ's example, and because it is rare, choice, special, and remarkable above all others.[6]

---

[1] Sin is Satan's work, grace is God's work; and is it not most meet that the child should eye most and mind most his father's work?

[2] There was a temple of Concord amongst the heathens; and shall it not be found among Christians, that are temples of the Holy Ghost?

[3] Pancirollus [Guy] saith, that the most precious pearl among the Romans was called *unio*, union.

[4] Lib. xxxvi. c. 26, and elsewhere: no doubt a volcanic, porous product.—G.

[5] To act, or run cross to God's express command, though under pretence of revelation from God, is as much as a man's life is worth, as you may see in that sad story, 1 Kings xiii. 24.

[6] Some conceive it to be an Hebraism, in which language *new, rare,* and *excellent,* are synonimals.

'This is my commandment, That ye love one another, as I have loved you.' 'These things I command you, that ye love one another.' 'Owe no man any thing, but love one another: for he that loveth another, hath fulfilled the law.' 'Let brotherly love continue.' 'Love one another, for love is of God, and every one that loveth is born of God, and knoweth God.' 'See that ye love one another with a pure heart fervently.' 'Finally, be ye all of one mind, having compassion one of another. Love as brethren, be pitiful, be courteous.' 'For this is the message that ye heard from the beginning, that we should love one another.' 'And this is his commandment, that we should believe on the name of his Son Jesus Christ, and love one another, as he gave us commandment.' 'Beloved, if God so loved us, we ought to love one another.'[1] Oh! dwell much upon these precious commands, that your love may be inflamed one to another.

In the primitive times, it was much taken notice of by the heathens, that in the depth of misery, when fathers and mothers forsook their children, Christians, otherwise strangers, stuck one to another, whose love of religion proved firmer than that of nature. Ah! that there were more of that spirit among the saints in these days. The world was once destroyed with water for the heat of lusts, and it is thought it will be again destroyed with fire for the coldness of love.[2]

Remedy (4). The fourth remedy against this device of Satan is, *To dwell more upon these choice and sweet things wherein you agree, than upon those things wherein you differ.* Ah! did you but thus, how would sinful heats be abated, and your love raised, and your spirits sweetened one to another. You agree in most, you differ but in a few; you agree in the greatest and weightiest, as concerning God, Christ, the Spirit, the Scripture, &c. You differ only in those points that have been long disputable amongst men of greatest piety and parts. You agree to own the Scripture, to hold to Christ the head, and to walk according to the law of the new creature.[3] Shall Herod and Pilate agree? Shall Turks and pagans agree? Shall bears and lions, tigers and wolves, yea, shall a legion of devils, agree in one body? And shall not saints agree, who differ only in such things as have least of the heart of God in them, and that shall never hinder your meeting in heaven? &c.

Remedy (5). The fifth remedy against this device of Satan is, solemnly to consider, *That God delights to be styled* Deus pacis, *the God of peace; and Christ to be styled* Princeps pacis, *the Prince of peace, and King of Salem, that is, King of peace; and the Spirit is a Spirit of peace.* 'The fruit of the Spirit is love, joy, peace,' Gal. v 22. Oh! why then should not the saints be children of peace? Certainly, men of froward, unquiet, fiery spirits, cannot have that sweet evidence of their interest in the God of peace, and in the Prince of peace, and in the Spirit of

---

[1] John xv. 12, 17; Rom. xiii. 8; Heb. xiii. 1; 1 John iv. 7; 1 Peter i. 22, and iii. 8; 1 John iii. 11, 23; iv. 11.—G.

[2] The ancients use to say commonly, that Alexander and Ephestion [*i. e.* Hephaestion] had but one soul in two distinct bodies, because their joy and sorrow, glory and disgrace, was mutual to them both. [Cf. Note on above frequently recurring saying, in Sibbes, Vol. II., page 194: where the reference is misprinted to page 35 for page 37.—G.].

[3] What a sad thing was it that a heathen should say, No beasts are so mischievous to men as Christians are one to another.

peace, as those precious souls have that follow after the things that make for love and peace. The very name of peace is sweet and comfortable; the fruit and effect thereof pleasant and profitable, more to be desired than innumerable triumphs; it is a blessing that ushers in a multitude of other blessings,[1] 2 Cor. xiii. 11 ; Isa. ix. 6.

The ancients were wont to paint peace in the form of a woman, with a horn of plenty in her hand.[2] Ah ! peace and love among the saints, is that which will secure them and their mercies at home; yea, it will multiply their mercies ; it will engage the God of mercy to crown them with the choicest mercies ; and it is that that will render them most terrible, invincible, and successful abroad. Love and peace among the saints is that which puts the counsels of their enemies to a stand, and renders all their enterprises abortive ; it is that which doth most weaken their hands, wound their hopes, and kill their hearts, &c.

Remedy (6). The sixth remedy against this device of Satan is, *To make more care and conscience of keeping up your peace with God.* Ah! Christians, I am afraid that your remissness herein is that which hath occasioned much of that sourness, bitterness, and divisions that be among you.[3] Ah ! you have not, as you should, kept up your peace with God, and therefore it is that you do so dreadfully break the peace among yourselves. The Lord hath promised, ' That when a man's ways please him, he will make his enemies to be at peace with him,' Prov. xvi. 7. Ah ! how much more then would God make the children of peace to keep the peace among themselves, if their ways do but please him ! All creatures are at his beck and check. Laban followed Jacob with one troop. Esau met him with another, both with hostile intentions ; but Jacob's ways pleasing the Lord, God by his mighty power so works that Laban leaves him with a kiss, and Esau met him with a kiss ; he hath an oath of one, tears of the other, peace with both. If we make it our business to keep up our league with God, God will make it his work and his glory to maintain our peace with men ; but if men make light of keeping up their peace with God, it is just with God to leave them to a spirit of pride, envy, passion, contention, division, and confusion, to leave them ' to bite and devour one another, till they be consumed one of another,'[4] &c.

Remedy (7). The seventh remedy against this device of Satan is, *To dwell much upon that near relation and union that is between you.* This consideration had a sweet influence upon Abraham's heart : ' And Abraham said unto Lot, Let there be no strife, I pray thee, between me and thee, and between my herdsmen and thy herdsmen ; for we are brethren,' Gen. xiii. 8.[5] That is a sweet word in the psalmist, ' Behold, how good and how pleasant it is for brethren to live together in unity,'

---

[1] *Ubi pax ibi Christus, quia Christus pax,* where peace is, there is Christ, because Christ is peace. *Dulce nomen pacis,* said the orator.

[2] The Grecians had the statue of Peace, with Pluto, the god of riches, in her arms.

[3] There is no fear of knowing too much, but there is much fear in practising too little.

[4] Pharnaces sent a crown to Cæsar at the same time he rebelled against him ; but he returned the crown and this message back, *Faceret imperata prius,* let him return to his obedience first. There is no sound peace to be had with God or man, but in a way of obedience. [Pharnaces II. Appian, *Mithr.* 120 ; Dion. Cass. xlii. 45–48 ; Plutarch, *Cæsar,* 50 ; *Suet. Jul.* 35.—G.]

[5] מריבה, Oh ! let there be no bitterness between us, for we are brethren.

Ps. cxxxiii. 1. It is not *good and not pleasant,* or *pleasant and not good,* but *good and pleasant.* There be some things that be *bona sed non jucunda,* good and not pleasant, as patience and discipline ; and there be some things that are pleasant but not good, as carnal pleasures, voluptuousness, &c. And there are some things that are neither good nor pleasant, as malice, envy, worldly sorrow, &c. ; and there are some things that are both good and pleasant, as piety, charity, peace, and union among brethren ; and oh ! that we could see more of this among those that shall one day meet in their Father's kingdom and never part. And as they are brethren, so they are all fellow-members : ' Now ye are the body of Christ, and members in particular,' 1 Cor. xii. 27. And again : ' We are members of his body, of his flesh, and of his bones,' Eph. v. 30. Shall the members of the natural body be serviceable and useful to one another, and shall the members of this spiritual body cut and destroy one another ? Is it against the law of nature for the natural members to cut and slash one another ?[1] And is it not much more against the law of nature and of grace for the members of Christ's glorious body to do so ? And as you are all fellow-members, so you are fellow-soldiers under the same Captain of salvation, the Lord Jesus, fighting against the world, the flesh, and the devil. And as you are all fellow-soldiers, so you are all fellow-sufferers under the same enemies, the devil and the world. And as you are all fellow-sufferers, so are you fellow-travellers towards the land of Canaan, ' the new Jerusalem that is above.' ' Here we have no abiding city, but we look for one to come.' The heirs of heaven are strangers on earth. And as you are all fellow-travellers, so are you all fellow-heirs of the same crown and inheritance.[2]

Remedy (8). The eighth remedy against this device of Satan is, *To dwell upon the miseries of discord.* Dissolution is the daughter of dissension. Ah ! how doth the name of Christ, and the way of Christ, suffer by the discord of saints ! How are many that are entering upon the ways of God hindered and sadded, and the mouths of the wicked opened, and their hearts hardened against God and his ways, by the discord of his people ! Remember this, the disagreement of Christians is the devil's triumph ; and what a sad thing is this, that Christians should give Satan cause to triumph ![3]

It was a notable saying of one, ' Take away strife, and call back peace, lest thou lose a man, thy friend ; and the devil, an enemy, joy over you both,' &c.

Remedy (9). The ninth remedy against this device of Satan is, seriously to consider, *That it is no disparagement to you to be first in seeking peace and reconcilement, but rather an honour to you, that you have begun to seek peace.* Abraham was the elder, and more worthy than Lot, both in respect of grace and nature also, for he was uncle unto Lot, and yet he first seeks peace of his inferior, which God hath

---

[1] The parti-coloured coats were characters of the king's children : so is following after peace now.

[2] Rev. xii. 7, 8; Heb. ii. 10; Rev. ii. 10; John xv. 19, 20; Heb. xii. 14, xiii. 4; Rom. viii.15–17.

[3] Our dissensions are one of the Jews' greatest stumbling-blocks. Can you think of it, and your hearts not bleed ?

recorded as his honour.[1]   Ah! how doth the God of peace, by his Spirit and messengers, pursue after peace with poor creatures.   God first makes offer of peace to us : 'Now then we are ambassadors for Christ, as though God did beseech you by us : we pray you in Christ's stead, be ye reconciled to God,' 2 Cor. v. 20.   God's grace first kneels to us, and who can turn their backs upon such blessed and bleeding embracements, but souls in whom Satan the god of this world kings it?   God is the party wronged, and yet he sues for peace with us at first : 'I said, Behold me, behold me, unto a nation that was not called by my name,' Isa. lxv. 1.[2]   Ah! how doth the sweetness, the freeness, and the riches of his grace break forth and shine upon poor souls.   When a man goes from the sun, yet the sunbeams follow him ; so when we go from the Sun of righteousness, yet then the beams of his love and mercy follow us.   Christ first sent to Peter that had denied him, and the rest that had forsaken him : 'Go your ways, and tell his disciples and Peter, that he goeth before you into Galilee : there shall ye see him, as he said unto you,' Mark xvi. 7.   Ah! souls, it is not a base, low thing, but a God-like thing, though we are wronged by others, yet to be the first in seeking after peace.   Such actings will speak out much of God with a man's spirit, &c.

Christians, it is not matter of liberty whether you will or you will not pursue after peace, but it is matter of duty that lies upon you ; you are bound by express precept to follow after peace ; and though it may seem to fly from you, yet you must pursue after it : 'Follow peace with all men, and holiness, without which no man can see the Lord,' Heb. xii. 14.[3]   Peace and holiness are to be pursued after with the greatest eagerness that can be imagined.   So the psalmist : 'Depart from evil, and do good ; seek peace and pursue it,' Ps. xxxiv. 14. The Hebrew word that is here rendered *seek*, is in *Piel*, and it signifies to seek earnestly, vehemently, affectionately, studiously, industriously.   'And pursue it.'   That Hebrew word signifies earnestly to pursue, being a metaphor taken from the eagerness of wild beasts or ravenous fowls, which will run or fly both fast and far rather than be disappointed of their prey.   So the apostle presses the same duty upon the Romans : 'Let us follow after the things that make for peace, and things wherein one may edify another,' Rom. xiv. 19.   Ah! you froward, sour, dogged Christians, can you look upon these commands of God without tears and blushing?

I have read a remarkable story of Aristippus. though but a heathen, who went of his own accord to Æschines his enemy, and said, 'Shall we never be reconciled till we become a table-talk to all the country?' and when Æschines answered he would most gladly be at peace with him, 'Remember, then, said Aristippus, that though I were the elder and better man, yet I sought first unto thee.'   Thou art indeed, said Æschines, a far better man than I, for I began the quarrel, but thou the reconcilement.[4]   My prayer

---

[1] They shall both have the name and the note, the comfort and the credit, of being most like unto God, who first begin to pursue after peace.

[2] Behold me! behold me! It is geminated [doubled] to shew God's exceeding forwardness to shew favour and mercy to them.

[3] Διωκετε, It signifies to follow after peace, as the persecutor doth him whom he persecuteth.

[4] Plutarch.   [Cf. Diogenes Laërtius, ii. 65 ; also Horace, Ep. i. l. 18, and i. 17, 23.—G.]

shall be that this heathen may not rise in judgment against the flourishing professors of our times : ' Who whet their tongues like a sword, and bend their bows to shoot their arrows, even bitter words,' Ps. lxiv. 3.

Remedy (10). The tenth remedy against this device of Satan is, *For saints to join together and walk together in the ways of grace and holiness so far as they do agree, making the word their only touchstone and judge of their actions.* That is sweet advice that the apostle gives : ' I press toward the mark for the prize of the high calling of God in Christ Jesus,' Philip. iii. 14–16. ' Let us therefore, as many as be perfect,—comparatively or conceitedly[1] so,—be thus minded. And if in anything ye be otherwise minded, God shall reveal even this unto you. Nevertheless, whereto we have already attained, let us walk by the same rule, let us mind the same thing.' Ah ! Christians, God loses much, and you lose much, and Satan gains much by this, that you do not, that you will not, walk lovingly together so far as your ways lie together. It is your sin and shame that you do not, that you will not, pray together, and hear together, and confer together, and mourn together, &c., because that in some far lesser things you are not agreed together. What folly and madness is it in those whose way of a hundred miles lies fourscore and nineteen together, yet will not walk so far together, because that they cannot go the other mile together ; yet such is the folly and madness of many Christians in these days, who will not do many things they may do, because they cannot do everything they should do.[2] I fear God will whip them into a better temper before he hath done with them. He will break their bones, and pierce their hearts, but he will cure them of this malady, &c.

And be sure you make the word the only touchstone and judge of all persons and actions : ' To the law and to the testimony, if they speak not according to this word, it is because there is no light in them,' Isa. viii. 20. It is best and safest to make that to be the judge of all men and things now that all shall be judged by in the latter day : ' The word, saith Christ, that I have spoken, the same shall judge him in the last day,' John xii. 48. Make not your dim light, your notions, your fancies, your opinions, the judge of men's action, but still judge by rule, and plead, ' It is written.'

When a vain importunate soul cried out in contest with a holy man, ' Hear me, hear me,' the holy man answered, ' Neither hear me, nor I thee, but let us both hear the apostle.'[3]

Constantine, in all the disputes before him with the Arians, would still call for the word of God as the only way, if not to convert, yet to stop their mouths, &c.

Remedy (11). The eleventh remedy against this device of Satan is, *To be much in self-judging* : ' Judge yourselves, and you shall not be judged of the Lord,' 1 Cor. xi. 31. Ah ! were Christians' hearts more taken up in judging themselves and condemning themselves, they would not be so apt to judge and censure others, and to carry it sourly and

[1] Those who have reason to *conceive* themselves ' perfect.'—G.
[2] Great is the power of joint prayer. Mary Queen of Scots, that was mother of king James, was wont to say that she feared Master Knox's prayer more than an army of ten thousand men. [Already used in this treatise : cf. page 125.—G.]
[3] *Nec ego te, nec tu me, sed ambo audiamus Apostolum.*

bitterly towards others that differ from them.[1] There are no souls in the world that are so fearful to judge others as those that do most judge themselves, nor so careful to make a righteous judgment of men or things as those that are most careful to judge themselves. There are none in the world that tremble to think evil of others, to speak evil of others, or to do evil to others, as those that make it their business to judge themselves. There are none that make such sweet constructions and charitable interpretations of men and things, as those that are best and most in judging themselves.[2] One request I have to you that are much in judging others and little in judging yourselves, to you that are so apt and prone to judge rashly, falsely, and unrighteously, and that is, that you will every morning dwell a little upon these scriptures :

'Judge not, that ye be not judged ; for with what judgment ye judge, ye shall be judged ; and with what measure ye mete, it shall be measured to you again,' Mat. vii. 1, 2. 'Judge not according to appearance, but judge righteous judgment,' John vii. 24. 'Let not him that eateth not judge him that eateth, for God hath received him. Why dost thou judge thy brother ? or why dost thou set at nought thy brother ?' Rom. xiv. 3, 10, 13. 'We shall all stand before the judgment-seat of Christ. Let us not judge one another any more, but judge this rather, that no man put a stumbling-block or an occasion to fall in his brother's way.' 'Judge nothing before the time, until the Lord come, who both will bring to light the hidden things of darkness, and will manifest the counsels of the heart, and then shall every man have praise of God,' 1 Cor. iv. 5. 'Speak not evil one of another, brethren : he that speaketh evil of his brother, and judgeth his brother, speaketh evil of the law, and judgeth the law ; but if thou judgest the law, thou art not a doer of the law, but a judge. There is one lawgiver, who is able to save and to destroy,' James iv. 11, 12. 'Who art thou that judgest another man's servant ? to his own master he standeth or falleth ; yea, he shall be holden up, for God is able to make him stand,' Rom. xiv. 4.

One Delphidius accusing another before Julian about that which he could not prove, the party denying the fact, Delphidius answers, If it be sufficient to deny what is laid to one's charge, who shall be found guilty ? Julian answers, And if it be sufficient to be accused, who can be innocent ? You are wise, and know how to apply it.

Remedy (12). The twelfth remedy against this device of Satan is this, above all, *Labour to be clothed with humility.* Humility makes a man peaceable among brethren, fruitful in well-doing, cheerful in suffering, and constant in holy walking, 1 Pet. v. 5. Humility fits for the highest services we owe to Christ, and yet will not neglect the lowest service to the meanest saint, John xiii. 5. Humility can feed upon the meanest dish, and yet it is maintained by the choicest delicates, as God, Christ, and glory. Humility will make a man bless him that curses him, and pray for those that persecute him. An humble heart is an habitation for God, a scholar for Christ, a companion of angels, a preserver of grace, and a fitter for glory. Humility is the nurse of our graces, the preserver of our mercies, and the great pro-

---

[1] It is storied of Nero, himself being unchaste, he did think there was no man chaste.

[2] In the Olympic games, the wrestlers did not put their crowns upon their own heads, but upon the heads of others. It is just so with souls that are good at self-judging.

moter of holy duties. Humility cannot find three things on this side heaven : it cannot find fulness in the creature, nor sweetness in sin, nor life in an ordinance without Christ. An humble soul always finds three things on this side heaven : the soul to be empty, Christ to be full, and every mercy and duty to be sweet wherein God is enjoyed.[1] Humility can weep over other men's weaknesses, and joy and rejoice over their graces. Humility will make a man quiet and contented in the meanest condition, and it will preserve a man from envying other men's prosperous condition, 1 Thes. i. 2, 3. Humility honours those that are strong in grace, and puts two hands under those that are weak in grace, Eph. iii. 8. Humility makes a man richer than other men, and it makes a man judge himself the poorest among men. Humility will see much good abroad, when it can see but little at home. Ah, Christian ! though faith be the champion of grace, and love the nurse of grace, yet humility is the beautifier of grace ; it casts a general glory upon all the graces in the soul. Ah ! did Christians more abound in humility, they would be less bitter, froward, and sour, and they would be more gentle, meek, and sweet in their spirits and practices. Humility will make a man have high thoughts of others and low thoughts of a man's self ; it will make a man see much glory and excellency in others, and much baseness and sinfulness in a man's self ; it will make a man see others rich, and himself poor ; others strong, and himself weak ; others wise, and himself foolish.[2] Humility will make a man excellent at covering others' infirmities, and at recording their gracious services, and at delighting in their graces ; it makes a man joy in every light that outshines his own, and every wind that blows others good. Humility is better at believing than it is at questioning other men's happiness. I judge, saith an humble soul, it is well with these Christians now, but it will be far better with them hereafter. They are now upon the borders of the New Jerusalem, and it will be but as a day before they slide into Jerusalem. An humble soul is willinger to say, Heaven is that man's, than mine ; and Christ is that Christian's, than mine ; and God is their God in covenant, than mine. Ah ! were Christians more humble, there would be less fire and more love among them than now is, &c.

Fourthly, As Satan hath his device to destroy gracious souls, so he hath his devices to destroy *poor ignorant souls*, and that sometimes,

By drawing them to affect ignorance, and to neglect, slight, and despise the means of knowledge. Ignorance is the mother of mistake, the cause of trouble, error, and of terror ; it is the highway to hell, and it makes a man both a prisoner and a slave to the devil at once.[3] Ignorance unmans a man ; it makes a man a beast, yea, makes him more miserable than the beast that perisheth.[4] There are none so easily nor so frequently taken in Satan's snares as ignorant souls. They are easily drawn to dance with the devil all day, and to dream of supping with Christ at night, &c.

---

[1] Humility is *conservatrix virtutum*, said Bernard, that which keeps all graces together.

[2] The humble soul is like the violet, which grows low, hangs the head downwards, and hides itself with its own leaves ; and were it not that the fragrant smell of his many virtues discovered him to the world, he would choose to live and die in his self-contenting secrecy.   [3] Hosea iv. 6, Mat. xxii. 29.

[4] Ignorants have this advantage, *ut mitius ardeant*, they have a cooler hell.

Now the remedies against this device are these :

Remedy (1). The first remedy against this device of Satan is, seriously to consider, *That an ignorant heart is an evil heart.* 'Without knowledge the mind is not good,' Prov. xix. 2. As an ignorant heart is a naughty heart, it is a heart in the dark ; and no good can come into a dark heart, but it must pass through the understanding : 'And if the eye be dark, all the body is dark,' Mat. vi. 22. A leprous head and a leprous heart are inseparable companions. Ignorant hearts are so evil that they let fly on all hands, and spare not to spit their venom in the very face of God, as Pharaoh did when thick darkness was upon him.[1]

Remedy (2). The second remedy against this device of Satan is, to consider, *That ignorance is the deformity of the soul.* As blindness is the deformity of the face, so is ignorance the deformity of the soul. As the want of fleshly eyes spoils the beauty of the face, so the want of spiritual eyes spoils the beauty of the soul. A man without knowledge is as a workman without his hands, as a painter without his eyes, as a traveller without his legs, or as a ship without sails, or a bird without wings, or like a body without a soul.

Remedy (3). The third remedy against this device of Satan is, solemnly to consider, *That ignorance makes men the objects of God's hatred and wrath.* 'It is a people that do err in their hearts, and have not known my ways. Wherefore I sware in my wrath, they should never enter into my rest,' Heb. iii. 10, 11. 'My people are a people of no understanding, therefore he that made them will have no mercy on them,' Isa. xxvii. 11. Christ hath said, 'That he will come in flaming fire, to render vengeance on them that know not God,' 2 Thes. i. 8. Ignorance will end in vengeance. When you see a poor blind man here, you do not loathe him, nor hate him, but you pity him. Oh ! but soul-blindness makes you abominable in the sight of God. God hath sworn that ignorant persons shall never come into heaven. Heaven itself would be a hell to ignorant souls.[2]

' My people are destroyed for want of knowledge ; because thou hast rejected knowledge, I will reject thee,' Hosea, iv. 6 ; [אמאסאן, cut off].

Chilo, one of the seven sages, being asked what God had done, answered, 'He exalted humble men, and suppressed proud ignorant fools.[3]

Remedy (4). The fourth remedy against this device of Satan is, to consider, *That ignorance is a sin that leads to all sins.* All sins are seminally in ignorance. 'You do err, not knowing the Scriptures,' Mat. xxii. 29. It puts men upon hating and persecuting the saints. 'They shall hate you, and put you out of the synagogues : yea, the time cometh, that whosoever killeth you will think that he doth God service. And these things will they do unto you, because they have not known the Father, nor me,' John xvi. 2, 3. Paul thanks his ignorance for all his cruelties to Christians. 'I was a blasphemer, and a persecutor, and injurious : but I obtained mercy, because I did it

---

[1] *Ignorat sane improbus omnis*, saith Aristotle.

[2] They must needs err that know not God's ways, yet cannot they wander so wide as to miss of hell.

[3] Rome saith, ignorance is the mother of devotion, but the Scripture saith, it is the mother of destruction.

ignorantly,' 1 Tim. i. 13.[1] It was ignorance that put the Jews upon crucifying Christ : 'Father, forgive them,' saith Christ of his murderers, 'for they know not what they do,' Luke xxiii. 34 : 'for if the princes of this world had known, they would not have crucified the Lord of glory,' 1 Cor. ii. 8.[2] Sin at first was the cause of ignorance, but now ignorance is the cause of all sin. 'Swearing, and lying, and killing, and stealing, and whoring abound,' saith the prophet, 'because there is no knowledge of God in the land.' There are none so frequent, and so impudent in the ways of sin, as ignorant souls ; they care not, nor mind not what they do, nor what they say against God, Christ, heaven, holiness, and their own souls. 'Our tongues are our own, who shall control us? They are corrupt, and speak wickedly concerning oppression : they speak loftily. They set their mouth against the heavens ; and their tongue walketh through the earth. Have all the workers of iniquity no knowledge? who eat up my people as they eat bread, and call not upon the Lord ?'[3] [4]

---

[1] It seems right to note that the apostle does not allege his ignorance, for which he was responsible, as the ground of the 'mercy' shewn him, but only as the source and explanation of his sin and violence   The clause, ' but I obtained mercy,' is parenthetic, and it is of importance to note this.—G.

[2] Aristotle makes ignorance the mother of all the misrule in the world.

[3] Ps. xiv. 4 ; lxxiii. 8, 9.

[4] They did like Œdipus, who killed his father Laius, king of Thebes, and thought he killed his enemy. [Euripides, *Phoen.* 39.—G.]

AN APPENDIX

TOUCHING FIVE MORE OF SATAN'S DEVICES,

Whereby he keepeth poor souls from believing in Christ, from receiving of Christ, from embracing of Christ, from resting, leaning, or relying upon Christ, for everlasting happiness and blessedness, according to the gospel; and remedies against these devices.

His first device to keep the soul from believing in Christ is,

Device (1). *By suggesting to the soul the greatness and vileness of his sins.* What! saith Satan, dost thou think that thou shalt ever obtain mercy by Christ, that hast sinned with so high a hand against Christ? that hast slighted the tenders[1] of grace? that hast grieved the Spirit of grace? that hast despised the word of grace? that hast trampled under feet the blood of the covenant, by which thou mightest have been pardoned, purged, justified, and saved? that hast spoken and done all the evil that thou couldest? No! no! saith Satan, he hath mercy for others, but not for thee; pardon for others, but not for thee; righteousness for others, but not for thee, &c., therefore it is in vain for thee to think of believing in Christ, or resting and leaning thy guilty soul upon Christ, Jer. iii. 5.

Now the remedies against this device are these :—

Remedy (1). The first remedy against this device of Satan is, to consider, *That the greater your sins are, the more you stand in need of a Saviour.* The greater your burden is, the more you stand in need of one to help to bear it. The deeper the wound is, the more need there is of the chirurgeon; the more dangerous the disease is, the more need there is of the physician. Who but madmen will argue thus: My burden is great, therefore I will not call out for help; my wound is deep, therefore I will not call out for balm; my disease is dangerous, therefore I will not go to the physician. Ah! it is spiritual madness, it is the devil's logic to argue thus: My sins are great, therefore I will not go to Christ, I dare not rest nor lean on Christ, &c.; whereas the soul should reason thus: The greater my sins are, the more I stand in need of mercy, of pardon, and therefore I will go to Christ, who delights in mercy,

[1] ' Offers.'—G.

who pardons sin for his own name's sake, who is as able and as willing
to forgive pounds as pence, thousands as hundreds, Micah vii. 18, Isa.
xliii. 25.

Remedy (2). The second remedy against this device of Satan is,
solemnly to consider, *That the promise of grace and mercy is to returning souls.* And, therefore, though thou art never so wicked, yet if thou
wilt return, God will be thine, and mercy shall be thine, and pardon
shall be thine : 2 Chron. xxx. 9, 'For if you turn again unto the Lord,
your brethren and your children shall find compassion before them that
lead them captive, so that they shall come again into this land : for the
Lord our God is gracious and merciful, and will not turn away his face
from you, if ye return unto him.' So Jer. iii. 12, 'Go and proclaim
these words towards the north, and say, Return, thou backsliding Israel,
saith the Lord, and I will not cause my anger to fall upon you : for I
am merciful, saith the Lord, and I will not keep anger for ever.' So
Joel ii. 13, 'And rend your hearts, and not your garments, and turn
unto the Lord your God : for he is gracious and merciful, slow to anger,
and of great kindness, and repenteth him of the evil.' So Isa. lv. 7,
'Let the wicked forsake his ways, and the unrighteous man his
thoughts : and let him return unto the Lord, and he will have mercy
upon him ; and to our God, for he will abundantly pardon,' or, as the
Hebrew reads it, 'He will multiply pardon :' so Ezek. xviii.

Ah ! sinner, it is not thy great transgressions that shall exclude thee
from mercy, if thou wilt break off thy sins by repentance and return to
the fountain of mercy. Christ's heart, Christ's arms, are wide open to
embrace the returning prodigal. It is not simply the greatest[1] of thy
sins, but thy peremptory persisting in sin, that will be thy eternal
overthrow.

Remedy (3). The third remedy against this device of Satan is,
solemnly to consider, *That the greatest sinners have obtained mercy,
and therefore all the angels in heaven, all the men on earth, and all
the devils in hell cannot tell to the contrary, but that thou mayest
obtain mercy.* Manasseh was a notorious sinner ; he erected altars for
Baal, he worshipped and served all the host of heaven ; he caused his
sons to pass through the fire : he gave himself to witchcraft and sorcery ;
he made Judah to sin more wickedly than the heathen did, whom the
Lord destroyed before the children of Israel ; he caused the streets of
Jerusalem to run down with innocent blood, 2 Kings xxi. Ah ! what a
devil incarnate was he in his actings ! Yet when he humbled himself,
and sought the Lord, the Lord was entreated of him and heard his
supplication, and brought him to Jerusalem, and made himself known
unto him, and crowned him with mercy and loving-kindness, as you
may see in 2 Chron. xxxiii.[2] So Paul was once a blasphemer, a persecutor and injurious, yet he obtained mercy, 1 Tim. i. 13. So Mary
Magdalene was a notorious strumpet, a common whore, out of whom
Christ cast seven devils, yet she is pardoned by Christ, and dearly beloved of Christ, Luke vii. 37, 38. So Mark xvi. 9, 'Now, when Jesus
was risen early the first day of the week, he appeared first to Mary
Magdalene, out of whom he had cast seven devils.'[3]

[1] Qu. 'greatness'?—G.
[2] The Hebrew doctors writ that he slew Isaiah the prophet, who was his father-in-law.
[3] See footnote on page 100.—G.

Jansenius on the place saith, it is very observable that our Saviour after his resurrection first appeared to Mary Magdalene and Peter, that had been grievous sinners; that even the worst of sinners may be comforted and encouraged to come to Christ, to believe in Christ, to rest and stay their souls upon Christ, for mercy here and glory hereafter. That is a very precious word for the worst of sinners to hang upon, Ps. lxviii. 18. The psalmist speaking of Christ saith, 'Thou hast ascended on high, thou hast led captivity captive; thou hast received gifts for men; yea, for the rebellious also, that the Lord might dwell amongst them.'

What though thou art a rebellious child, or a rebellious servant! What though thou art a rebellious swearer, a rebellious drunkard, a rebellious Sabbath breaker! Yet Christ hath received gifts for thee, 'even for the rebellious also.' He hath received the gift of pardon, the gift of righteousness, yea, all the gifts of the Spirit for thee, that thy heart may be made a delightful house for God to dwell in.

Bodin[1] hath a story concerning a great rebel that had made a strong party against a Roman emperor. The emperor makes proclamation, that whoever could bring the rebel dead or alive, he should have such a great sum of money. The rebel hearing of this, comes and presents himself before the emperor, and demands the sum of money. Now, saith the emperor, if I should put him to death, the world would say I did it to save my money. And so he pardons the rebel, and gives him the money.

Ah, sinners! Shall a heathen do this, that had but a drop of mercy and compassion in him: and will not Christ do much more, that hath all fulness of grace, mercy, and glory in himself? Surely his bowels do yearn towards the worst of rebels. Ah! if you still but come in, you will find him ready to pardon, yea, one made up of pardoning mercy. Oh! the readiness and willingness of Jesus Christ to receive to favour the greatest rebels! The father of mercies did meet, embrace, and kiss that prodigal mouth which came from feeding with swine and kissing of harlots, Col. i. 19, ii 3, 4.[2]

Ephraim had committed idolatry, and was backslidden from God; he was guilty of lukewarmness and unbelief, &c., yet saith God, 'Ephraim is my dear son, he is a pleasant child, my bowels are troubled for him, I will have mercy,' or rather as it is in the original, 'I will have mercy, mercy upon him, saith the Lord,'[3]

Well! saith God, though Ephraim be guilty of crimson sins, yet he is a son, a dear son, a precious son, a pleasant child; though he be black with filth, and red with guilt, yet my bowels are troubled for him; I will have mercy, mercy upon him. Ah sinners, if these bowels of mercy do not melt, win, and draw you, justice will be a swift witness against you, and make you lie down in eternal misery for kicking against the bowels of mercy.

Christ hangs out still, as once that warlike Scythian did, a white flag of grace and mercy to returning sinners that humble themselves at his feet for favour; but if sinners stand out, Christ will put forth his red

---

[1] John Bodin died 1596: for above see *Universæ Naturæ Theatrum*, &c., &c., 1579; and *Les six Livres de la Republique*, &c., 1593.—G.

[2] Neh. ix. 15, Hebrew, But thou a God of pardons.

[3] Hosea iv. 17; v. 3; vi. 8, 11; xii. 12, 14; xiii. 12. *Vide* Jer. xxxi. 20.

flag, his bloody flag, and they shall die for ever by a hand of justice. Sinners! there is no way to avoid perishing by Christ's iron rod, but by kissing his golden sceptre.

Remedy (4). The fourth remedy against this device of Satan is, to consider, *That Jesus Christ hath nowhere in all the Scripture excepted against the worst of sinners that are willing to receive him, to believe in him, to rest upon him for happiness and blessedness.* Ah! sinners, why should you be more cruel and unmerciful to your own souls than Christ is? Christ hath not excluded you from mercy, why should you exclude your own souls from mercy? Oh that you would dwell often upon that choice Scripture, John vi. 37, 'All that the Father giveth me, shall come to me; and him that cometh to me I will in no wise cast out,' or as the original hath it, 'I will not not cast out.' Well! saith Christ, if any man will come, or is coming to me, let him be more sinful or less; more unworthy or less; let him be never so guilty, never so filthy, never so rebellious, never so leprous, &c., yet if he will but come, I will not not cast him off. So much is held forth in 1 Cor. vi. 9–11, 'Know ye not that the unrighteous shall not inherit the kingdom of God? Be not deceived: neither fornicators, nor idolaters, nor adulterers, nor effeminate, nor abusers of themselves with mankind, nor thieves, nor covetous, nor drunkards, nor revilers, nor extortioners, shall inherit the kingdom of God. And such were some of you: but ye are washed, but ye are sanctified, but ye are justified in the name of the Lord Jesus, and by the Spirit of our God.'

Ah! sinners, do not think that he that hath received such notorious sinners to mercy will reject you. 'He is yesterday, and to-day, and the same for ever,' Heb. xiii. 8. Christ was born in an inn, to shew that he receives all comers; his garments were divided into four parts, to shew that out of what part of the world soever we come, we shall be received. If we be naked, Christ hath robes to clothe us; if we be harbourless, Christ hath room to lodge us. That is a choice scripture, Acts x. 34, 35, 'Then Peter opened his mouth and said, Of a truth I perceive that God is no respecter of persons. But in every nation, he that feareth him, and worketh righteousness, is accepted with him.'

The three tongues that were written upon the cross, Greek, Latin, and Hebrew, John xix. 19, 20, to witness Christ to be the king of the Jews, do each of them in their several idiom avouch this singular axiom, that Christ is an all-sufficient Saviour; and 'a threefold cord is not easily broken.' The apostle puts this out of doubt: Heb. vii. 25, 'Wherefore he is able also to save them to the uttermost that come unto God by him, seeing he ever liveth to make intercession for them.' Now, he were not an all-sufficient Saviour if he were not able to save the greatest, as [well as] the least of sinners. Ah! sinners, tell Jesus Christ that he hath not excluded you from mercy, and therefore you are resolved that you will sit, wait, weep, and knock at the door of mercy, till he shall say, Souls, be of good cheer, your sins are forgiven, your persons are justified, and your souls shall be saved.

Remedy (5). The fifth remedy against this device of Satan is, to consider, *That the greater sinner thou art, the dearer thou wilt be to Christ, when he shall behold thee as the travail of his soul:* Isa. liii. 11, 'He shall see of the travail of his soul, and be satisfied.' The dearer we pay for anything, the dearer that thing is to us.   Christ hath paid most, and prayed most, and sighed most, and wept most, and bled most for the greatest sinners, and therefore they are dearer to Christ than others that are less sinful.   Rachel was dearer to Jacob than Leah, because she cost him more ; he obeyed, endured, and suffered more by day and night for her than for Leah.   Ah ! sinners, the greatness of your sins does but set off the freeness and riches of Christ's grace, and the freeness of his love.   This maketh heaven and earth to ring of his praise, that he loves those that are most unlovely, that he shews most favour to them that have sinned most highly against him, as might be shewed by several instances in Scripture, as Paul, Mary Magdalene, and others. Who sinned more against Christ than these ?   And who had sweeter and choicer manifestations of divine love and favour than these?

Remedy (6). The sixth remedy against this device of Satan is, seriously to consider, *That the longer you keep off from Christ, the greater and stronger your sins will grow.*   All divine power and strength against sin flows from the soul's union and communion with Christ, Rom. viii. 10, 1 John i. 6, 7.   While you keep off from Christ, you keep off from that strength and power which is only able to make you trample down strength, lead captivity captive, and slay the Goliaths that bid defiance to Christ.   It is only faith in Christ that makes a man triumph over sin, Satan, hell, and the world, 1 John v. 4.   It is only faith in Christ that binds the strong man's hand and foot, that stops the issue of blood, that makes a man strong in resisting, and happy in conquering, Mat. v. 15 to 35.   Sin always dies most where faith lives most.   The most believing soul is the most mortified soul.   Ah ! sinner, remember this, there is no way on earth effectually to be rid of the guilt, filth, and power of sin, but by believing in a Saviour.   It is not resolving, it is not complaining, it is not mourning, but believing, that will make thee divinely victorious over that body of sin that to this day is too strong for thee, and that will certainly be thy ruin, if it be not ruined by a hand of faith.

Remedy (7). The seventh remedy against this device of Satan is, wisely to consider, *That as there is nothing in Christ to discourage the greatest sinners from believing in him, so there is everything in Christ that may encourage the greatest sinners to believe on him, to rest and lean upon him for all happiness and blessedness,* Cant. i. 3. If you look upon his nature, his disposition, his names, his titles, his offices as king, priest, and prophet, you will find nothing to discourage the greatest sinners from believing in him, but many things to encourage the greatest sinners to receive him, to believe on him.[1]   Christ is the greatest good, the choicest good, the chiefest good, the most suitable good, the most necessary good.   He is a pure good, a real good, a total good, an eternal good, and a soul-satisfying good, Rev. iii. 17, 18. Sinners, are you poor? Christ hath gold to enrich you.   Are you naked ? Christ hath royal robes, he hath white raiment to clothe you. Are you blind? Christ hath eye-salve to enlighten you.   Are you hungry? Christ will be manna to feed you.   Are you thirsty ? He will be a well of living water to refresh you.   Are you wounded ? He hath a balm under his wings to heal you.   Are you sick ? He is a physician

[1] Col. i. 19, ii. 3, Cant. v. 10.

to cure you. Are you prisoners? He hath laid down a ransom for you.
Ah, sinners! tell me, tell me, is there anything in Christ to keep you
off from believing? No. Is there not everything in Christ that may
encourage you to believe in him? Yes. Oh, then, believe in him, and
then, 'Though your sins be as scarlet, they shall be as white as snow,
though they be red like crimson, they shall be as wool,' Isa. i. 18.
Nay, then, your iniquities shall be forgotten as well as forgiven, they
shall be remembered no more. God will cast them behind his back, he
will throw them into the bottom of the sea, Isa. xliii. 25, xxxviii. 17,
Micah vii. 19.

Remedy (8). The eighth remedy against this device of Satan is,
seriously to consider, *The absolute necessity of believing in Christ.*
Heaven is too holy and too hot to hold unbelievers; their lodging is
prepared in hell: Rev. xxi. 8, 'But the fearful and unbelieving, &c.,
shall have their part in the lake which burneth with fire and brim-
stone, which is the second death.' 'If ye believe not that I am he,'
saith Christ, 'you shall die in your sins,' John viii. 24. And he that
dies in his sins must to judgment and to hell in his sins. Every un-
believer is a condemned man: 'He that believeth not,' saith John, 'is
condemned already, because he hath not believed in the name of the
only begotten Son of God. And he that believeth not the Son, shall
not see life, but the wrath of God abideth on him,' John iii. 18, 36.
Ah, sinners! the law, the gospel, and your own consciences, have passed
the sentence of condemnation upon you, and there is no way to reverse
the sentence but by believing in Christ. And therefore my counsel is
this, Stir up yourselves to lay hold on the Lord Jesus, and look up to
him, and wait on him, from whom every good and perfect gift comes,
and give him no rest till he hath given thee that jewel faith, that is
more worth than heaven and earth, and that will make thee happy in
life, joyful in death, and glorious in the day of Christ, Isa. lxiv. 7,
James i. 17, Isa. lxii. 7.

And thus much for the remedies against this first device of Satan,
whereby he keeps off thousands from believing in Christ.

The second device that Satan hath to keep poor sinners from believing, from closing with a Saviour, is,

Device (2). *By suggesting to them their unworthiness.* Ah! saith
Satan, as thou art worthy of the greatest misery, so thou art unworthy of the least crumb of mercy. What! dost thou think, saith
Satan, that ever Christ will own, receive, or embrace such an unworthy
wretch as thou art? No, no; if there were any worthiness in thee,
then, indeed, Christ might be willing to be entertained by thee. Thou
art unworthy to entertain Christ into thy house, how much more unworthy art thou to entertain Christ into thy heart, &c.

Now the remedies against this device are these.

Remedy (1). The first remedy against this device of Satan is,
seriously to consider, *That God hath nowhere in the Scripture required
any worthiness in the creature before believing in Christ.* If you
make a diligent search through all the scripture, you shall not find,
from the first line in Genesis to the last line in the Revelations, one
word that speaks out God's requiring any worthiness in the creature
before the soul's believing in Christ, before the soul's leaning and rest-

ing upon Christ for happiness and blessedness; and why, then, should
that be a bar and hindrance to thy faith, which God doth nowhere
require of thee before thou comest to Christ, that thou mayest have
life? Mat. xix. 8, John v. 29. Ah, sinners! remember Satan objects
your unworthiness against you only out of a design to keep Christ and
your souls asunder for ever; and therefore, in the face of all your unworthiness, rest upon Christ, come to Christ, believe in Christ, and you
are happy for ever, John vi. 40, 47.

Remedy (2). The second remedy against this device of Satan is,
wisely to consider, *That none ever received Christ, embraced Christ,
and obtained mercy and pardon from Christ, but unworthy souls.*
Pray, what worthiness was in Matthew, Zaccheus, Mary Magdalene,
Manasseh, Paul, and Lydia, before their coming to Christ, before their
faith in Christ? Surely none. Ah, sinners! you should reason thus:
Christ hath bestowed the choicest mercies, the greatest favours, the
highest dignities, the sweetest privileges, upon unworthy sinners, and
therefore, O our souls, do not you faint, do not you despair, but patiently
and quietly wait for the salvation of the Lord. Who can tell but that
free grace and mercy may shine forth upon us, though we are unworthy,
and give us a portion among those worthies that are now triumphing
in heaven.

Remedy (3). The third remedy against this device of Satan is, *That
if the soul will keep off from Christ till it be worthy, it will never
close with Christ,* it will never embrace Christ. It will never be one
with Christ, it must lie down in everlasting sorrow, Isa. l. 11. God
hath laid up all worthiness in Christ, that the creature may know where
to find it, and may make out after it. There is no way on earth to
make unworthy souls worthy, but by believing in Christ, James ii. 23.
Believing in Christ, of slaves, it will make you worthy sons; of enemies,
it will make you worthy friends. God will count none worthy, nor
call none worthy, nor carry it towards none as worthy, but believers,
who are made worthy by the worthiness of Christ's person, righteousness, satisfaction, and intercession, &c., Rev. iii. 4.

Remedy (4). The fourth remedy against this device of Satan is
solemnly to consider, *That if you make a diligent search into your
own hearts, you shall find that it is the pride and folly of your own
hearts that puts you upon bringing of a worthiness to Christ.* Oh! you
would fain bring something to Christ that might render you acceptable
to him; you are loath to come empty-handed. The Lord cries out, 'Ho,
every one that thirsteth, come ye to the waters, and he that hath no
money: come ye, buy and eat; yea, come, buy wine and milk without
money, and without price. Wherefore do ye spend your money upon
that which is not bread, and your labour for that which satisfieth not?'
Isa. lv. 1, 2. Here the Lord calls upon moneyless, upon penniless
souls, upon unworthy souls, to come and partake of his precious favours
freely. But sinners are proud and foolish, and because they have no
money, no worthiness to bring, they will not come, though he sweetly
invites them. Ah, sinners! what is more just than that you should
perish for ever, that prefer husks among swine before the milk and
wine, the sweet and precious things of the gospel, that are freely and

sweetly offered to you, &c. Well, sinners! remember this, it is not so much the sense of your unworthiness, as your pride, that keeps you off from a blessed closing with the Lord Jesus.

The third device that Satan hath to keep poor sinners from believing, from closing with a Saviour, is,

Device (3). *By suggesting to them the want of such and such preparations and qualifications.* Saith Satan, Thou art not prepared to entertain Christ; thou art not thus and thus humbled and justified; thou art not heart-sick of sin; thou hast not been under horrors and terrors as such and such; thou must stay till thou art prepared and qualified to receive the Lord Jesus, &c.

Now, the remedies against this device are these:

Remedy (1). The first remedy against this device of Satan is, solemnly to consider, *That such as have not been so and so prepared and qualified as Satan suggests, have received Christ, believed in Christ, and been saved by Christ.* Matthew was called, sitting at the receipt of custom, and there was such power went along with Christ's call, that made him to follow him, Mat. ix. 9. We read not of any horrors or terrors, &c., that he was under before his being called by Christ. Pray, what preparations and qualifications were found in Zaccheus, Paul, the jailor, and Lydia, before their conversion, Luke xix. 9, Acts xvi. 14, *seq.* God brings in some by the sweet and still voice of the gospel, and usually such that are thus brought into Christ are the sweetest, humblest, choicest, and fruitfullest Christians. God is a free agent to work by law or gospel, by smiles or frowns, by presenting hell or heaven to sinners' souls. God thunders from mount Sinai upon some souls, and conquers them by thundering. God speaks to others in a still voice, and by that conquers them. You that are brought to Christ by the law, do not you judge and condemn them that are brought to Christ by the gospel; and you that are brought to Christ by the gospel, do not you despise those that are brought to Christ by the law. Some are brought to Christ by fire, storms, and tempests, others by more easy and gentle gales of the Spirit. The Spirit is free in the works of conversion, and, as the wind, it blows when, where, and how it pleases, John iii. 8. Thrice happy are those souls that are brought to Christ, whether it be in a winter's night or in a summer's day.

Remedy (2). The second remedy against this device of Satan is, solemnly *To dwell upon these following scriptures, which do clearly evidence that poor sinners which are not so and so prepared and qualified to meet with Christ, to receive and embrace the Lord Jesus Christ, may, notwithstanding that, believe in Christ; and rest and lean upon him for happiness and blessedness, according to the gospel.* Read Prov. i. 20-33, and chap. viii. 1-11,.and chap. ix. 1-6; Ezek. xvi. 1-14; John iii. 14-18, 36; Rev. iii. 15-20. Here the Lord Jesus Christ stands knocking at the Laodiceans' door; he would fain have them to sup with him, and that he might sup with them; that is, that they might have intimate communion and fellowship one with another.

Now, pray tell me, what preparations or qualifications had these Laodiceans to entertain Christ? Surely none; for they were lukewarm, they were 'neither hot nor cold,' they were 'wretched, and miserable, and poor, and blind, and naked;' and yet Christ, to shew his free grace and his condescending love, invites the very worst of sinners to open to him, though they were no ways so and so prepared or qualified to entertain him.

Remedy (3). The third remedy against this device of Satan is, seriously to consider, *That the Lord does not in all the Scripture require such and such preparations and qualifications before men come to Christ, before they believe in Christ, or entertain, or embrace the Lord Jesus.* Believing in Christ is the great thing that God presses upon sinners throughout the Scripture, as all know that know anything of Scripture.

Obj. But does not Christ say, ' Come unto me all ye that labour and are heavy laden, and I will give you rest ' ? Mat. xi. 28.

To this I shall give these three answers :

(1.) That though the invitation be to such that 'labour and are heavy laden,' yet the promise of giving rest, it is made over to 'coming,' to 'believing.'

(2.) I answer, that all this scripture proves and shews is, that such as labour under sin as under a heavy burden, and that are laden with the guilt of sin and sense of God's displeasure, ought to come to Christ for rest ; but it doth not prove that only such must come to Christ, nor that all men must be thus burdened and laden with the sense of their sins and the wrath of God, before they come to Christ.

Poor sinners, when they are under the sense of sin and wrath of God, they are prone to run from creature to creature, and from duty to duty, and from ordinance to ordinance, to find rest ; and if they could find it in any thing or creature, Christ should never hear of them ; but here the Lord sweetly invites them : and to encourage them, he engages himself to give them rest : ' Come,' saith Christ, ' and I will give you rest.' I will not *shew* you rest, nor barely *tell* you of rest, but ' I will *give* you rest.' I am faithfulness itself, and cannot lie, ' I *will* give you rest.' I that have the greatest power to give it, the greatest will to give it, the greatest right to give it, ' Come, *laden sinners*, and I will give you rest.' Rest is the most desirable good, the most suitable good, and to you the greatest good. ' Come,' saith Christ, that is, ' believe in me, and I will give you rest ;' I will give you peace with God, and peace with conscience ; I will turn your storm into an everlasting calm; I will give you such rest, that the world can neither give to you nor take from you.

(3.) I answer, No one scripture speaks out the whole mind of God ; therefore do but compare this one scripture with those several scriptures that are laid down in the second remedy last mentioned, and it will clearly appear, that though men are thus and thus burdened and laden with their sins and filled with horror and terror, if they may come to Christ, they may receive and embrace the Lord Jesus Christ.

Remedy (4). The fourth remedy against this device of Satan is, to consider, *That all that trouble for sin, all that sorrow, shame, and mourning which is acceptable to God, and delightful to God, and prevalent with God, flows from faith in Christ, as the stream doth from the fountain, as the branch doth from the root, as the effect doth from the cause.* Zech. xii. 10, ' They shall look on him whom they have pierced, and they shall mourn for him.' All gospel mourning flows from believing; they shall first look, and then mourn. All that know anything know this, that 'whatever is not of faith is sin,' Rom. xiv 33. Till men have faith in Christ, their best services are but glorious sins.

The fourth device that Satan hath to keep poor sinners from believing, from closing with a Saviour, is,

Device (4). *By suggesting to a sinner Christ's unwillingness to save.* It is true, saith Satan, Christ is able to save thee, but is he willing? Surely, though he is able, yet he is not willing to save such a wretch as thou art, that has trampled his blood under thy feet, and that has been in open rebellion against him all thy days, &c.

The remedy against this device of Satan is, briefly to consider these few things.

Remedy (1). *First, The great journey that he hath taken, from heaven to earth, on purpose to save sinners, doth strongly demonstrate his willingness to save them.* Mat. ix. 13, ' I came not to call the righteous, but sinners to repentance.' 1 Tim. i. 15, ' This is a faithful saying, and worthy of all acceptation, that Jesus Christ came into the world to save sinners, of whom I am chief.'

Secondly, His divesting himself of his glory in order to sinners' salvation, speaks out his willingness to save them. He leaves his Father's bosom, he puts off his glorious robes, and lays aside his glorious crown, and bids adieu to his glistering courtiers the angels; and all this he doth, that he may accomplish sinners' salvation.[1]

Thirdly, That sea of sin, that sea of wrath, that sea of trouble, that sea of blood that Jesus Christ waded through, that sinners might be pardoned, justified, reconciled, and saved, doth strongly evidence his willingness to save sinners, 1 Cor. v. 19, 20.

Fourthly, His sending his ambassadors, early and late, to woo and entreat sinners to be reconciled to him, doth with open mouth shew his readiness and willingness to save sinners.

Fifthly, His complaints against such as refuse him, and that turn their backs upon him, and that will not be saved by him, doth strongly declare his willingness to save them: John i. 11, ' He came to his own, and his own received him not.' So in John v. 40, ' But ye will not come to me, that ye may have life.'

Sixthly, The joy and delight that he takes at the conversion of sinners, doth demonstrate his willingness that they should be saved: Luke xv. 7, ' I say unto you, That likewise joy shall be in heaven over one sinner that repenteth, more than over ninety and nine just persons that need no repentance.' God the Father rejoiceth at the return of his prodigal son; Christ rejoices to see the travail of his soul; the Spirit rejoices that he hath another temple to dwell in; and the angels rejoice that they have another brother to delight in, &c., Isa. liii. 11.

The fifth device that Satan hath to keep poor sinners from believing, from closing with a Saviour, is,

Device (5). *By working a sinner to mind more the secret decrees and counsels of God, than his own duty.* What needest thou to busy thyself about receiving, embracing, and entertaining of Christ? saith

---

[1] From the cradle to the cross, his whole life was a life of sufferings.

Satan; if thou art elected, thou shalt be saved; if not, all that thou canst do will do thee no good. Nay, he will work the soul not only to doubt of its election, but to conclude that he is not elected, and therefore let him do what he can, he shall never be saved.

Now the remedies against this device are these:

Remedy (1). The first remedy against this device of Satan is, seriously to consider, *That all the angels in heaven, nor all the men on earth, nor all the devils in hell, cannot tell to the contrary, but that thou mayest be an elect person, a chosen vessel.* Thou mayest be confident of this, that God never made Satan one of his privy council, God never acquainted him with the names or persons of such that he hath set his love upon to eternity, &c.

Remedy (2). The second remedy against this device of Satan is, *To meddle with that which thou hast to do.* 'Secret things belong to the Lord, but revealed things belong to thee,' Deut. xxix. 29. Thy work, sinner, is, to be peremptory in believing, and in returning to the Lord; thy work is to cast thyself upon Christ, lie at his feet, to wait on him in his ways, and to give him no rest till he shall say, Sinner, I am thy portion, I am thy salvation, and nothing shall separate between thee and me.

Here followeth seven characters of false teachers, which let me add for a close, viz.:—

That Satan labours might and main, by false teachers, which are his messengers and ambassadors, to deceive, delude, and for ever undo the precious souls of men:' Jer. xxiii. 13, 'I have seen folly in the prophets of Samaria; they prophesied in Baal, and caused my people Israel to err;' Micah iii. 5, 'The prophets make my people to err.' They seduce them, and carry them out of the right way into by-paths and blind thickets of error, blasphemy, and wickedness, where they are lost for ever. 'Beware of false prophets, for they come to you in sheep's clothing, but inwardly they are ravening wolves,' Mat. vii. 15. These lick and suck the blood of souls: Philip. iii. 2, 'Beware of dogs, beware of evil workers, beware of the concision.' These kiss and kill; these cry, Peace, peace, till souls fall into everlasting flames, &c., Prov. vii.

Now, the best way to deliver poor souls from being deluded and destroyed by these messengers of Satan is, to discover them in their colours, that so, being known, poor souls may shun them, and fly from them as from hell itself.

Now you may know them by these characters following:

[1.] *The first character.* False teachers *are men-pleasers.*[2] They preach more to please the ear than to profit the heart: Isa. xxx. 10, 'Which say to the seers, See not; and to the prophets, Prophesy not unto us right things: speak to us smooth things; prophesy deceits.' Jer. v. 30, 31, 'A wonderful and horrible thing is committed in the land: the prophets prophesy falsely, and the priests bear rule by their means, and my people love to have it so. And what will you do in the end thereof?' They handle holy things rather with wit and dalliance than with fear and reverence. False teachers are soul-undoers. They

---

[1] Acts xx. 28–30, 2 Cor. xi. 13–15, Eph. iv. 14, 2 Tim. iii. 4–6, Titus i. 11, 12, 2 Peter ii. 18, 19.   [2] But so are not true teachers, Gal. i. 10, 1 Thes. ii. 1–4.

are like evil chirurgeons, that skin over the wound, but never heal it.
Flattery undid Ahab and Herod, Nero and Alexander. False teachers
are hell's greatest enrichers. *Non acerba, sed blanda*, Not bitter, but
flattering words do all the mischief, said Valerian, the Roman emperor.
Such smooth teachers are sweet soul-poisoners, &c., Jer. xxiii. 16, 17.[1]

[2.] *The second character.* False teachers *are notable in casting
dirt, scorn, and reproach upon the persons, names, and credits of
Christ's most faithful ambassadors.* Thus Korah, Dathan, and Abiram
charged Moses and Aaron that they took too much upon them, seeing
all the congregation was holy, Num. xvi. 3. You take too much state,
too much power, too much honour, too much holiness upon you ; for
what are you more than others, that you take so much upon you ? And
so Ahab's false prophets fell foul on good Micaiah, paying of him with
blows for want of better reasons, 1 Kings xxii. 10–26. Yea, Paul, that
great apostle of the Gentiles, had his ministry undermined and his reputation blasted by false teachers : ' For his letters,' say they, ' are weighty
and powerful, but his bodily presence is weak and contemptible,' 2 Cor.
x. 10. They rather contemn him than admire him ; they look upon
him as a dunce rather than a doctor. And the same hard measure had
our Lord Jesus from the Scribes and Pharisees, who laboured as for life
to build their own credit upon the ruins of his reputation.[2] And never
did the devil drive a more full trade this way than he does in these
days, Mat. xxvii. 63. Oh ! the dirt, the filth, the scorn that is thrown
upon those of whom the world is not worthy. I suppose false teachers
mind not that saying of Austin, *Quisquis volens detrahit famæ, nolens
addit mercedi meæ*, He that willingly takes from my good name, unwillingly adds to my reward.

[3.] *The third character.* False teachers are *venters of the devices
and visions of their own heads and hearts.*[3] Jer. xiv. 14, ' Then the
Lord said unto me, The prophets prophesy lies in my name : I sent
them not, neither have I commanded them, neither spake unto them :
they prophesy unto you a false vision and divination, and a thing of
nought, and the deceit of their heart ;' chap. xxiii. 16, ' Thus saith the
Lord of hosts, Hearken not unto the words of the prophets that prophesy unto you ; they make you vain : they speak a vision of their own
heart, and not out of the mouth of the Lord.' Are there not multitudes
in this nation whose visions are but golden delusions, lying vanities,
brain-sick phantasies ? These are Satan's great benefactors, and such as
divine jüstice will hang up in hell as the greatest malefactors, if the
physician of souls do not prevent it, &c.

[4.] *The fourth character.* False teachers *easily pass over the great
and weighty things both of law and gospel, and stand most upon those
things that are of the least moment and concernment to the souls of
men.*[4] 1 Tim. i. 5–7, ' Now the end of the commandment is charity

---

[1] Whilst an ass is stroked under the belly, you may lay on his back what burden you
please.
[2] The proverb is, *Oculus et fama non patiuntur jocos*, a man's eye and his good name can
bear no jests. Yea, and Lucian, that blasphemous atheist, termeth him the crucified cozener.
[3] Mat. xxiv. 4, 5, xi. 14, Titus i. 10, Rom. xvi. 18.
[4] Luther complained of such in his time as would strain at a gnat, and swallow a camel.
This age is full of such teachers, such monsters. The high priest's spirit, Mat. xxiii. 24,
lives and thrives in these days.

out of a pure heart, and of a good conscience, and of faith unfeigned ; from which some having swerved, have turned aside unto vain jangling, desiring to be teachers of the law, and understand neither what they say nor whereof they affirm.' Mat. xxiii. 2, 3, 'Woe unto you, scribes and Pharisees, hypocrites ! for ye pay tithe of mint, and anise and cummin, and have omitted the weightier matters of the law, judgment, mercy, and faith ; these ought ye to have done, and not to leave the other undone.' False teachers are nice in the lesser things of the law, and as negligent in the greater. 1 Tim. vi. 3–5, 'If any man teach otherwise, and consent not to wholesome words, even the words of our Lord Jesus Christ, and to the doctrine which is according to godliness, he is proud, knowing nothing, but doting about questions and strife of words, whereof cometh envy, strife, railings, evil surmisings, perverse disputings of men of corrupt minds, and destitute of the truth, supposing that gain is godliness : from such withdraw thyself.' If such teachers are not hypocrites in grain, I know nothing, Rom. ii. 22. The earth groans to bear them, and hell is fitted for them, Mat. xxiv. 32.

[5.] *The fifth character.* False teachers *cover and colour their dangerous principles and soul-impostures with very fair speeches and plausible pretences, with high notions and golden expressions.* Many in these days are bewitched and deceived by the magnificent words, lofty strains, and stately terms of deceivers, viz. illumination, revelation, deification, fiery triplicity, &c. As strumpets paint their faces, and deck and perfume their beds, the better to allure and deceive simple souls,[1] so false teachers will put a great deal of paint and garnish upon their most dangerous principles and blasphemies, that they may the better deceive and delude poor ignorant souls. They know sugared poison goes down sweetly ; they wrap up their pernicious, soul-killing pills in gold. Weigh the scriptures in the margin.[2]

In the days of Hadrian the emperor, there was one Ben-Cosbi gathered a multitude of Jews together, and called himself *Ben-cocuba*, the son of a star, applying that promise to himself, Num. xxiv. 17; but he proved *Bar-chosaba*, the son of a lie. And so will all false teachers, for all their flourishes prove at the last the sons of lies.

[6.] *The sixth character.* False teachers *strive more to win over men to their opinions, than to better them in their conversations.* Mat. xxiv. 17, 'Woe unto you, scribes and Pharisees, hypocrites ! for ye compass sea and land to make one proselyte, and when he is made, ye make him twofold more the child of hell than yourselves.' They busy themselves most about men's heads. Their work is not to better men's hearts, and mend their lives ; and in this they are very much like their father the devil, who will spare no pains to gain proselytes.[3]

[7]. *The seventh character.* False teachers *make merchandise of their followers :* 2 Peter ii. 1–3, 'But there were false prophets also among the people, even as there shall be false teachers among you, who privily shall bring in damnable heresies, even denying the Lord that bought them, and bring upon themselves swift destruction. And many shall

---

[1] Gal. vi. 12 ; 2 Cor. xi. 13–15 ; Rom. xvi. 17, 18 ; Mat. xvi. 6, 11, 12 ; vii. 15.

[2] See footnote *supra.*—G.

[3] For shame, says Epictetus to his Stoics ; either live as Stoics, or leave off the name of Stoics. The application is easy.

follow their pernicious ways; by reason of whom the way of truth shall be evil spoken of.   And through covetousness shall they with feigned words make merchandise of you : whose judgment now of a long time lingereth not, and their damnation slumbereth not.'   They eye your goods more than your good ; and mind more the serving of themselves, than the saving of your souls.   So they may have your substance, they care not though Satan has your souls, Rev. xviii. 11–13.   That they may the better pick your purse, they will hold forth such principles as are very indulgent to the flesh.   False teachers are the great worshippers of the golden calf, Jer. vi. 13.[1]

Now, by these characters you may know them, and so shun them, and deliver your souls out of their dangerous snares; which that you may, my prayers shall meet-yours at the throne of grace.

And now, to prevent objections, I shall lay down some propositions or conclusions concerning Satan and his devices, and then give you the reasons of the point, and so come to make some use and application of the whole to ourselves.

Propositions concerning Satan and his devices :

Proposition (1).   The first proposition is this, *That though Satan hath his devices to draw souls to sin, yet we must be careful that we do not lay all our temptations upon Satan, that we do not wrong the devil, and father that upon him that is to be fathered upon our own base hearts.*   I think that oftentimes men charge that upon the devil that is to be charged upon their own hearts.   'And the Lord said unto the woman, What is this that thou hast done? And the woman said, The serpent beguiled me, and I did eat,' Gen. iii. 13.   Sin and shifting came into the world together.[2]   This is no small baseness of our hearts, that they will be naught, ay, very naught, and yet will father that naughtiness upon Satan.   Man hath an evil root within him ; that were there no devil to tempt him, nor no wicked men in the world to entice him, yet that root of bitterness, that cursed sinful nature that is in him, would draw him to sin, though he knows beforehand that 'the wages of sin is eternal death,' Rom. vi. 23   'For out of the heart proceed evil thoughts, murders, adulteries, fornication, thefts, false witnesses, blasphemies,' Mat. xv. 19.   The whole frame of man is out of frame.   The understanding is dark, the will cross, the memory slippery, the affections crooked, the conscience corrupted, the tongue poisoned, and the heart wholly evil, only evil, and continually evil.   Should God chain up Satan, and give him no liberty to tempt or entice the sons of men to vanity or folly, yet they would not, yet they could not but sin against him, by reason of that cursed nature that is in them, that will still be a-provoking them to those sins that will provoke and stir up the anger of God against them, Jude 15, 16.   Satan hath only a persuading sleight, not an enforcing might.   He may tempt us, but without ourselves he cannot conquer us ; he may entice us, but without ourselves

---

[1] Crates threw his money into the sea, resolving to drown it, lest it should drown him. But false teachers care not who they drown, so they may have their money.   [It may be well to distinguish above among the different persons of the name, as Crates of Thebes, son of Ascondus.   Diog. Laërtius, vi. 85, 93, 96–98.—G.]

[2] *Cum primum nascimur in omni continuo pravitate versamur,* We are no sooner born, than buried in a bog of wickedness.—*Tully.*

he cannot hurt us.   Our hearts carry the greatest stroke in every sin.
Satan can never undo a man without himself; but a man may easily
undo himself without Satan.   Satan can only present the golden cup,
but he hath no power to force us to drink the poison that is in the cup;
he can only present to us the glory of the world, he cannot force us to
fall down and worship him, to enjoy the world; he can only spread his
snares, he hath no power to force us to walk in the midst of his snares.
Therefore do the devil so much right, as not to excuse yourselves, by
your accusing him, and laying the load upon him, that you should lay
upon your own hearts.[1]

Prop. (2). The second proposition is, *That Satan hath a great hand
and stroke in most sins.*   It was Satan that tempted our first parents
to rebellion; it was Satan that provoked David to number the people;
it was Satan that put Peter upon rebuking Christ; therefore saith
Christ, 'Get thee behind me, Satan;' it was Satan that put Cain upon
murdering of righteous Abel, therefore it is that he is called 'a murderer
from the beginning;' it was Satan that put treason into the heart of
Judas against Christ, 'And supper being ended, the devil having put
into the heart of Judas Iscariot, Simon's son, to betray him;' it was
Satan that put Ananias upon lying, Peter said, 'Ananias, why hath
Satan filled thine heart to lie to the Holy Ghost?'[2]   As the hand of Joab
was in the tale of the woman of Tekoah, so Satan's hand is usually in
all the sins that men commit.   Such is Satan's malice against God, and
his envy against man, that he will have a hand one way or other in all
the sins, though he knows that all the sins he provokes others to shall
be charged upon him to his greater woe, and eternal torment.[3]

Ambrose brings in the devil boasting against Christ and challenging
Judas as his own: 'He is not thine, Lord Jesus, he is mine; his thoughts
beat for me; he eats with thee, but is fed by me; he takes bread from
thee, but money from me; he drinks wine with thee, and sells thy
blood to me.'   Such is his malice against Christ, and his wrath and rage
against man, that he will take all advantages to draw men to that, that
may give him advantage to triumph over Christ and men's souls for
ever.

Prop. (3). The third proposition is, *That Satan must have a double
leave before he can do anything against us.*   He must have leave from
God, and leave from ourselves, before he can act anything against our
happiness.   He must have his commission from God, as you may see
in the example of Job, Job i. 11, 12, ii. 3–5.   Though the devil had
malice enough to destroy him, yet he had not so much as power to
touch him, till God gave him a commission.

They could not so much as enter into the swine without leave from
Christ, Luke viii. 32.   Satan would fain have combated with Peter, but
this he could not do without leave.   'Satan hath desired to have you,
to winnow you,' Luke xxii. 31.   So Satan could never have overthrown
Ahab and Saul, but by a commission from God, 1 Kings xxii.   Ah!
what a cordial, what a comfort should this be to the saints, that their

---

[1] Τὸ πῦρ παρ' ἡμῶν δὶ φλοξ διαβόλου σώματα, the fire is our wood, though it be the devil's
flame.—*Nazianzen.*

[2] Gen. iii. 1–5; 1 Chron. xxi. 1; Mat. xvi. 22, 23; John viii. 44, xiii. 2; Acts v. 3.—G.

[3] *Diabolus tentat, Deus probat.*—Tertullian.

greatest, subtlest, and watchfullest enemy cannot hurt nor harm them, without leave from him who is their sweetest Saviour, their dearest husband, and their choicest friend.

And as Satan must have leave from God, so he must have leave of us. When he tempts, we must assent ; when he makes offers, we must hearken ; when he commands, we must obey, or else all his labour and temptations will be frustrate, and the evil that he tempts us to shall be put down only to his account.[1] That is a remarkable passage in Acts v. 3, ' Why hath Satan filled thy heart to lie to the Holy Ghost ?' He doth not expostulate the matter with Satan ; he doth not say, Satan, ' Why hast thou filled Ananias's heart to make him lie to the Holy Ghost ?' but he expostulates the case with Ananias ; Peter said, ' Ananias, why hath Satan filled *thine* heart to lie to the Holy Ghost ?' Why hast thou given him an advantage to fill thy heart with infidelity, hypocrisy, and obstinate audacity, to lie to the Holy Ghost ? As if he had said, Satan could never have done this in thee, which will now for ever undo thee, unless thou hadst given him leave. If, when a temptation comes, a man cries out, and saith, Ah, Lord ! here is a temptation that would force me, that would deflower my soul, and I have no strength to withstand it ; oh ! help ! help ! for thy honour's sake, for thy Son's sake, for thy promise' sake ; it is a sign that Satan hath not gained your consent, but committed a rape upon your souls, which he shall dearly pay for.[2]

Prop. (4). The fourth proposition is, *That no weapons but spiritual weapons will be useful and serviceable to the soul in fighting and combating with the devil.* This the apostle shews : ' Wherefore take unto you,' saith he, ' the whole armour of God, that ye may be able to stand in the evil day, and having done all, to stand,' Eph. vi. 13. So the same apostle tells you, ' That the weapons of your warfare are not carnal, but mighty through God, to the casting down of strongholds,' 2 Cor. x. 4. You have not to do with a weak, but with a mighty enemy, and therefore you had need to look to it, that your weapons are mighty, and that they cannot be, unless they are spiritual. Carnal weapons have no might nor spirit in them towards the making of a conquest upon Satan.[3] It was not David's sling nor stone that gave him the honour and advantage of setting his feet upon Goliah, but his faith in the name of the Lord of hosts. ' Thou comest to me with a sword, with a spear, and with a shield, but I am come to thee in the name of the Lord of hosts, the God of the armies of Israel, whom thou hast defied,' 1 Sam. xvii. 45. He that fights against Satan, in the strength of his own resolutions, constitution or education, will certainly fly and fall before him. Satan will be too hard for such a soul, and lead him captive at his pleasure. The only way to stand, conquer, and triumph, is still to plead, ' It is written,' as Christ did, Mat. iv. 10. There is no sword but the two-edged sword of the Spirit, that will be

---

[1] *Adversaria potestas non habet vim cogendi sed persuadendi.*—Isidore.

[2] They are the worst and greatest liars who pretend religion, and the Spirit, and yet are acted only by carnal principles to carnal ends.

[3] We read of many that, out of greatness of spirit, could offer violence to nature, but were at a loss when they came to deal with a corruption or a temptation. Heraclitus [Heraclius] his motto was, *A Deo victoria*, It is God that gives victory ; and that should be every Christian's motto.

found to be metal of proof when a soul comes to engage against Satan ; therefore, when you are tempted to uncleanness, plead, 'It is written, be ye holy, as I am holy,' 1 Peter i. 16 ; and, 'Let us cleanse ourselves from all filthiness of the flesh and spirit, perfecting holiness in the fear of the Lord,' 2 Cor. vii. 1.   If he tempts you to distrust God's providence and fatherly care of you, plead, 'It is written,' 'They that fear the Lord shall want nothing that is good,' Ps. xxxiv. 9.

It is written, 'The Lord will give grace and glory, and no good thing will he withhold from them that purely live,' Ps. lxxxiv. 11.   If he tempt you to fear, that you shall faint, and fall, and never be able to run to the end of the race that is set before you, plead, It is written, 'The righteous shall hold on his way, and he that hath clean hands shall be stronger and stronger,' Job xvii. 9.

It is written, 'I will make an everlasting covenant with them, that I will not turn away from them, to do them good, but I will put my fear in their hearts, that they may not depart from me,' Jer. xxxii. 40.

It is written, 'They that wait upon the Lord, they shall renew their strength ; they shall mount up with wings as eagles; they shall run, and not be weary; and they shall walk, and not faint,' Isa. xl. 31.   If Satan tempt you to think that because your sun for the present is set in a cloud, that therefore it will rise no more, and that the face of God will shine no more upon you ; that your best days are now at an end, and that you must spend all your time in sorrow and sighing; plead, It is written, 'He will turn again, he will have compassion upon us, and cast all our sins into the depth of the sea,' Micah vii. 19.

It is written, 'For a small moment have I forsaken thee, but with great mercies will I gather thee.   In a little wrath I hid my face from thee for a moment, but with everlasting kindness will I have mercy on thee, saith the Lord, thy Redeemer,' Isa. liv. 7, 8, 10.

It is written, 'The mountains shall depart, and the hills be removed, but my kindness shall not depart from thee, neither shall the covenant of my peace be removed, saith the Lord that hath mercy on thee.'

It is written, 'Can a woman forget her sucking child, that she should not have compassion on the son of her womb ?   Yea, they may forget, yet will not I forget thee.   Behold, I have graven thee upon the palms of my hands, thy walls are continually before me,' Isa. xlix. 15, 16.

If ever you would be too hard for Satan, and after all your assaults, have your bow abide in strength, then take to you the word of God, which is 'the two-edged sword of the Spirit, and the shield of faith, whereby you shall be able to quench the fiery darts of the devil,' Eph. vi. 17.   It is not spitting at Satan's name, nor crossing yourselves, nor leaning to your own resolutions, that will get you the victory.

Luther reports of Staupitius, a German minister, that he acknowledged himself, that before he came to understand aright the free and powerful grace of God, that he vowed and resolved an hundred times against some particular sin, and never could get power over it.   At last he saw the reason to be his trusting to his own resolution.   Therefore be skilful in the word of righteousness, and in the actings of faith upon Christ and his victory, and that crown of glory that is set before you, and Satan will certainly fly from you, &c., James iv. 7.

Prop. (5). The fifth proposition is, *That we may read much of Satan's nature and disposition by the divers names and epithets that are given him in the Scripture.* Sometimes he is called Behemoth, which is *Bruta,* whereby the greatness and brutishness of the devil is figured, Job xl. 15. Those evil spirits are sometimes called Διαβολοι, *accusers,* for their calumnies and slanders; and πονηροι, *evil ones,* for their malice. Satan is *Adversarius,* an adversary, that troubleth and molesteth, 1 Pet. v. 8. *Abaddon* is a destroyer. They are *tempters,* for their suggestion; *lions,* for their devouring; *dragons,* for their cruelty; and *serpents,* for their subtilty, &c. As his names are, so is he; as face answers to face, so do Satan's names answer to his nature. He hath the worst names and the worst nature of all created creatures, &c.

Prop. (6). The sixth proposition is, *That God will shortly tread down Satan under the saints' feet.* Christ, our champion, hath already won the field, and will shortly set our feet upon the necks of our spiritual enemies. Satan is a foiled adversary. Christ hath led him captive, and triumphed over him upon the cross. Christ hath already overcome him, and put weapons into your hands, that you may overcome him also, and set your feet upon his neck. Though Satan be a roaring lion, yet Christ, who is the lion of the tribe of Judah, will make Satan fly and fall before you. Let Satan do his worst, yet you shall have the honour and the happiness to triumph over him.[1] Cheer up, you precious sons of Sion, for the certainty and sweetness of victory will abundantly recompense you for all the pains you have taken in making resistance against Satan's temptations. The broken horns of Satan shall be trumpets of our triumph and the cornets of our joy, &c.

Now I shall come to the reasons of the point, and so draw to a close, &c.

Reason (1). The first reason is, *That their hearts may be kept in an humble, praying, watching frame.* Oh! hath Satan so many devices to ensnare and undo the souls of men? How should this awaken dull, drowsy souls, and make them stand upon their watch! A saint should be like a seraphim, beset all over with eyes and lights, that he may avoid Satan's snares, and stand fast in the hour of temptation.

The Lord hath in the Scripture discovered the several snares, plots, and devices that the devil hath to undo the souls of men, that so, being forewarned, they may be forearmed; that they may be always upon their watch-tower, and hold their weapons in their hands, as the Jews did in Nehemiah's time.[2]

Reason (2). The second reason is, *From that malice, envy, and enmity that is in Satan against the souls of men.* Satan is full of envy and enmity, and that makes him very studious to suit his snares and plots to the tempers, constitutions, fancies, and callings of men, that so he may make them as miserable as himself.[3]

The Russians are so malicious, that you shall have a man hide some of

---

[1] Rom. xvi. 20, συντρίψει, from συντρίβω. The Greek word signifies to break or crush a thing to pieces. Being applied to the feet, it noteth that breaking or crushing which is by stamping upon a thing.

[2] The philosopher had a ball of brass in his hand, which, if he chanced to sleep with, the fall into a basin awaked him to his studies. You are wise, and know how to apply it.

[3] Malice cares not what it saith or doth, so it may kill or gall.

his own goods in the house of him whom he hateth, and then accuse him for the stealth of them.[1]   So doth Satan, out of malice to the souls of men, hide his goods, his wares, as I may say, in the souls of men, and then go and accuse them before the Lord ; and a thousand, thousand other ways Satan's malice, envy, and enmity puts him upon, eternally to undo the precious souls of men, &c.

Reason (3). The third reason is drawn from *that long experience that Satan hath had.* He is a spirit of mighty abilities ; and his abilities to lay snares before us are mightily increased by that long standing of his.   He is a spirit of above five thousand years' standing. He hath had time enough to study all those ways and methods which tend most to ensnare and undo the souls of men.   And as he hath time enough, so he hath made it his whole study, his only study, his constant study, to find out snares, depths, and stratagems, to entangle and over-throw the souls of men.   When he was but a young serpent, he did easily deceive and outwit our first parents, Gen. iii. ; but now he is grown that 'old serpent,' as John speaks, Rev. xii. 9, he is as old as the world, and is grown very cunning by experience.

Reason (4). The fourth reason is, *In judgment to the men of the world, that they may stumble and fall, and be ensnared for ever.* Wicked men that withstand the offers of mercy, and despise the Spirit of grace, that will not open, though God knocks never so hard by his word and rod, by his Spirit and conscience, are given up by a hand of justice, to be hardened, deceived, and ensnared by Satan, to their ever-lasting ruin, 1 Kings xxii. 23.   And what can be more just than that they should be taken and charmed with Satan's wiles, who have fre-quently refused to be charmed by the Spirit of grace, though he hath charmed never so wisely, and never so sweetly, &c. ?

Reason (5). The fifth reason is, *That the excellency and power of God's grace may be more illustrated and manifested, by making men able to grapple with this mighty adversary, and that notwithstanding all the plots, devices, and stratagems of Satan, yet he will make them victorious here, and crown them with glory hereafter.* The greater and the subtler the enemies of the children of Israel were, the more did divine power, wisdom, and goodness, sparkle and shine ; and that, notwithstanding all their power, plots, and stratagems, &c., yet to Canaan he would bring them at last.   When Paul had weighed this, he sits down and glories in his infirmities and distresses and Satan's buffetings, that the power of Christ might rest upon him, 2 Cor. xii. 7–9.

The use of the point.

If Satan hath such a world of devices and stratagems to ensnare and undo the souls of men, then, instead of wondering that so few are saved, sit down and wonder that any are saved, that any escape the snares of this cunning fowler, who spreads his nets and casts forth his baits in all places, in all cases and companies.

But this is not the main thing that I intend to speak to ; my main business shall be, to set before you some special rules and helps against all his devices.

[1] An envious heart and plotting head are inseparable companions.

The first help. If you would not be taken by any of Satan's devices, then *walk by rule.*[1] He that walks by rule, walks most safely ; he that walks by rule, walks most honourably ; he that walks by rule, walks most sweetly. When men throw off the word, then God throws off them. and then Satan takes them by the hand, and leads them into snares at his pleasure. He that thinks himself too good to be ruled by the word, will be found too bad to be owned by God ; and if God do not, or will not own him, Satan will by his stratagems overthrow him. Them that keep to the rule, they shall be kept in the hour of temptation. 'Because thou hast kept the word of my patience, I also will keep thee from the hour of temptation, which shall come upon all the world, to try them that dwell upon the earth,' Rev. iii. 10.

The second help. As you would not be taken with any of Satan's devices, *take heed of vexing and grieving the Holy Spirit of God.*[2] It is the Spirit of the Lord Jesus Christ that is best able to discover Satan's snares against us ; it is only he that can point out all his plots, and discover all his methods, and enable men to escape those pits that he hath digged for their precious souls. Ah ! if you set that sweet and blessed Spirit a-mourning, that alone can secure you from Satan's depths, by whom will you be secured ? Man is a weak creature, and no way able to discover Satan's snares, nor to avoid them, unless the Spirit of the Lord gives skill and power ; therefore, whoever be grieved, be sure the Spirit be not grieved by your enormities, nor by your refusing the cordials and comforts that he sets before you, nor by slighting and despising his gracious actings in others, nor by calling sincerity hypocrisy, faith fancy, &c., nor by fathering those things upon the Spirit, that are the brats and fruits of your own hearts.[3] The Spirit of the Lord is your counsellor, your comforter, your upholder, your strengthener. It is only the Spirit that makes a man too great for Satan to conquer. 'Greater is he that is in you, than he that is in the world,' 1 John iv. 4.

The third help. If you would not be taken with any of Satan's devices, then *labour for more heavenly wisdom.*[4] Ah, souls ! you are much in the dark, you have but a little to that others have, and to that you might have had, had you not been wanting to yourselves. There are many knowing souls, but there are but a few wise souls. There is oftentimes a great deal of knowledge, where there is but a little wisdom to improve that knowledge. Knowledge without wisdom is like mettle in a blind horse, which often is an occasion of the rider's fall, and of his bones being jostled against the walls.[5] It is not the most knowing Christian, but the most wise Christian, that sees, avoids, and escapes Satan's snares. 'The way of life is above to the wise,' saith Solomon, ' that he may depart from hell beneath,' Prov. xv. 24. Heavenly wisdom makes a man delight to fly high ; and the higher any man flies, the more he is out of the reach of Satan's snares.[6] Ah, souls ! you

---

[1] Prov. xii. 24 ; Gal. vi. 16.

[2] *Spiritus sanctus est res delicata.* the Divine Spirit is a very tender thing : if you grieve him, he will certainly grieve and vex your precious souls, Lam. i. 16.

[3] Isa. lxiii. 10 ; Ps. lxxiii. 23 ; 1 Thes. v. 19 ; Acts ii. 13.

[4] If men could but see the fair face of wisdom with mortal eyes, they would be in love with her, saith Plato.   [5] *Sine prudentia simplicitas stultitia est.*—Drusius.

[6] *Malim prudentiæ guttam quam fœcundioris fortunæ pelagus,* said Nazianzen. A serpent's eye is a singular ornament in a dove's head.

had need of a great deal of heavenly wisdom, to see where and how Satan lays his baits and snares; and wisdom to find out proper remedies against his devices, and wisdom to apply those remedies seasonably, inwardly, and effectually to your own hearts, that so you may avoid the snares which that evil one hath laid for your precious souls.

The fourth help. If you would not be taken with any of Satan's devices, then *make present resistance against Satan's first motions.* It is safe to resist, it is dangerous to dispute. Eve disputes, and falls in paradise, Gen. iii.; Job resists, and conquers upon the dunghill. He that will play with Satan's bait, will quickly be taken with Satan's hook. The promise of conquest is made over to resisting, not to disputing: 'Resist the devil, and he will fly from you,' James iv. 7. Ah, souls! were you better at resisting than at disputing, though happily you were not very expert at either, your temptations would be fewer, and your strength to stand would be greater than now it is, &c.

The fifth help. If you would not be taken with any of Satan's devices, then *labour to be filled with the Spirit.* The Spirit of the Lord is a Spirit of light and power; and what can a soul do without light and power 'against spiritual wickedness in high places'? Eph. vi. 12. It is not enough that you have the Spirit, but you must be filled with the Spirit, or else Satan, that evil spirit, will be too hard for you, and his plots will prosper against you. That is a sweet word of the apostle, 'Be filled with the Spirit, Eph. v. 18;[1] *i.e.* labour for abundance of the Spirit. He that thinks he hath enough of the Holy Spirit, will quickly find himself vanquished by the evil spirit. Satan hath his snares to take you in prosperity and adversity, in health and sickness, in strength and weakness, when you are alone and when you are in company, when you come on to spiritual duties and when you come off from spiritual duties, and if you are not filled with the Spirit, Satan will be too hard and too crafty for you, and will easily and frequently take you in his snares, and make a prey of you in spite of your souls. Therefore labour more to have your hearts filled with the Spirit than to have your heads filled with notions, your shops with wares, your chests with silver, or your bags with gold; so shall you escape the snares of this fowler, and triumph over all his plots, &c.[2]

The sixth help. If you would not be taken in any of Satan's snares, then *keep humble.* An humble heart will rather lie in the dust than rise by wickedness, and sooner part with all than the peace of a good conscience. Humility keeps the soul free from many darts of Satan's casting, and snares of his spreading; as the low shrubs are free from many violent gusts and blasts of wind, which shake and rend the taller trees. The devil hath least power to fasten a temptation on him that is most humble. He that hath a gracious measure of humility, is neither affected with Satan's proffers nor terrified with his threatenings.[3] I

---

[1] πληροῦσθε. To be filled with the Spirit, as the sails of a ship is filled with wind.

[2] Luther saith, a holy gluttony is to lay on, to feed hard, and to fetch hearty draughts, till they be even drunk with loves, and with the abundance of the Spirit. Oh that there were more such holy gluttony in the world!

[3] It is reported of Satan that he should say thus of a learned man, *Tu me semper vincis,* thou dost always overcome me; when I would exalt and promote thee, thou keepest thyself in humility; and when I would throw thee down, thou liftest up thyself in assurance of faith.

have read of one who, seeing in a vision many snares of the devil spread
upon the earth, he sat down, and mourned, and said in himself, *Quis
pertransiet ista?* who shall pass through these? whereunto he heard a
voice answering, *Humilitas pertransiet*, humility shall. God hath
said, that 'he will teach the humble,' and that 'he will dwell with the
humble,' and that 'he will fill and satisfy the humble.'[1] And if the
teachings of God, the indwellings of God, if the pourings in of God, will
not keep the soul from falling into Satan's snares, I do not know what
will. And therefore as you would be happy in resisting Satan, and
blessed in triumphing over Satan and all his snares, keep humble; I
say again, keep humble, &c.

The seventh help. If you would not be taken in any of Satan's snares,
then *keep a strong, close, and constant watch*, 1 Thes. v. 6.[2] A secure
soul is already an ensnared soul. That soul that will not watch against
temptations, will certainly fall before the power of temptations. Satan
works most strongly on the fancy when the soul is drowsy. The soul's
security is Satan's opportunity to fall upon the soul and to spoil the
soul, as Joshua did the men of Ai. The best way to be safe and secure
from all Satan's assaults is, with Nehemiah and the Jews, to watch and
pray, and pray and watch. By this means they became too hard for
their enemies, and the work of the Lord did prosper sweetly in their
hands. Remember how Christ chid his sluggish disciples, 'What! could
you not watch with me one hour?' what, cannot you watch with me?
how will you then die with me? if you cannot endure words, how will
you endure wounds? &c. Satan always keeps a crafty and malicious
watch, 'seeking whom he may devour (καταπίῃ), or whom he may drink
or sip up, as the apostle speaks in that 1 Peter v. 8. Satan is very
envious at our condition, that we should enjoy that paradise out of
which he is cast, and out of which he shall be for ever kept.

Shall Satan keep a crafty watch, and shall not Christians keep a holy
spiritual watch?[3] Our whole life is beset with temptations. Satan
watches all opportunities to break our peace, to wound our consciences,
to lessen our comforts, to impair our graces, to slur our evidences, and
to damp our assurances, &c. Oh! what need then have we to be
always upon our watch-tower, lest we be surprised by this subtle serpent. Watchfulness includes a waking, a rousing up of the soul. It
is a continual, careful observing of our hearts and ways, in all the turn-
ings of our lives, that we still keep close to God and his word.

Watchfulness is nothing else but the soul running up and down, to
and fro, busy everywhere; it is the heart busied and employed with
diligent observation of *quid inde*, what comes from within us, and of
quid inde, what comes from without us and into us. Ah, souls! you
are no longer safe and secure than when you are upon your watch.
While Antipater kept the watch, Alexander was safe; and while we

---

[1] Ps. xxv. 9; Isa. lvii. 15; James iv. 6.

[2] We must not be like Agrippa's dormouse, that would not awake till cast into boil-
ing lead, but effectually mind these following scriptures, wherein this duty of watchfulness is so strictly enjoined:—Mat. xxvi. 40; Mark xiii. 33, 34, 36, 37; 1 Cor. xvi. 13;
Col. iv. 2; 1 Peter iv. 7; Rev. ii. 3.

[3] Hannibal never rested, whether he did conquer or was conquered. It is so with
Satan. Learn, for shame of the devil, said blessed Latimer, to watch, seeing the devil is
so watchful.

keep a strict watch, we are safe. A watchful soul is a soul upon the wing, a soul out of gun-shot, a soul upon a rock, a soul in a castle, a soul above the clouds, a soul held fast in everlasting arms.

I shall conclude this seventh head with this advice, Remember the dragon is subtle, and bites the elephant's ear, and then sucks his blood, because he knows that to be the only place which the elephant cannot reach with his trunk to defend ; so our enemies are so subtle, that they will bite us, and strike us where they may most mischief us, and therefore it doth very much concern us to stand always upon our guard.

The eighth help. If you would not be taken with any of Satan's snares and devices, then *keep up your communion with God.*[1] Your strength to stand and withstand Satan's fiery darts is from your communion with God. A soul high in communion with God may be tempted, but will not easily be conquered. Such a soul will fight it out to the death. Communion with God furnisheth the soul with the greatest and the choicest arguments to withstand Satan's temptations. Communion is the result of union. Communion is a reciprocal exchange between Christ and a gracious soul. Communion is Jacob's ladder, where you have Christ sweetly coming down into the soul, and the soul, by divine influences, sweetly ascending up to Christ. Communion with Christ is very inflaming, raising and strengthening. While Samson kept up his communion with God, no enemy could stand before him, but he goes on conquering and to conquer ; but when he was fallen in his communion with God, he quickly falls before the plots of his enemies. It will be so with your souls. So long as your communion with God is kept up, you will be too hard for ' spiritual wickedness in high places ;' but if you fall from your communion with God, you will fall, as others, before the face of every temptation.[2] David, so long as he kept up his communion with God, he stands, and triumphs over all his enemies ; but when he was fallen in his communion with God, then he falls before the enemies that were in his own bosom, and flies before those that pursued after his life. It will be so with your souls, if you do not keep up your communion with God. Job keeps up his communion with God, and conquers Satan upon the dunghill ; Adam loses his communion with God, and is conquered by Satan in paradise. Communion with God is a shield upon land, as well as an anchor at sea ; it is a sword to defend you, as well as a staff to support you ; therefore keep up your communion.

The ninth help. If you would not be taken in any of Satan's snares, then *engage not against Satan in your own strength, but be every day drawing new virtue and strength from the Lord Jesus.*[3] Certainly that soul that engages against any old or new temptation without

---

[1] 1 Cor. vi. 19. The words are very significant in the original. There are two *ins*, as though God could never have near enough communion with them.

[2] The sea ebbs and flows, the moon increases and decreases; so it is with saints in their communion with God. Plutarch tells of Eudoxus, that he would be willing to be burnt up presently by the sun, so he might be admitted to come so near it as to learn the nature of it. What! should not we be content to suffer for the keeping up communion with Christ?—[Eudoxus : Delambre, *Hist. Astron. Anc.*, I. 107.—G.]

[3] There is a remarkable saying of Moses, Exod. xv., God is *fortitudo mea, et laus mea, et salus mea,* my strength, and my praise, and my salvation, all in the abstract. It is but look up and live ; look unto me, and be saved, from the ends of the earth, Isa. xlv. 22.

new strength, new influences from on high, will fall before the power of the temptation. You may see this in Peter; he rested upon some old received strength—'Though all men should deny thee, yet will not I,' Mat. xxvi. 35—and therefore he falls sadly before a new temptation. He curses and swears, and denies him thrice, that had thrice appeared gloriously to him. Ah, souls! when the snare is spread, look up to Jesus Christ, who is lifted up in the gospel, as the brazen serpent was in the wilderness, and say to him, Dear Lord! here is a new snare laid to catch my soul, and grace formerly received, without fresh supplies from thy blessed bosom, will not deliver me from this snare. Oh! give me new strength, new power, new influences, new measures of grace, that so I may escape the snares. Ah, souls! remember this, that your strength to stand and overcome must not be expected from graces received, but from the fresh and renewed influences of heaven.[1] You must lean more upon Christ than upon your duties; you must lean more upon Christ than upon spiritual tastes and discoveries; you must lean more upon Christ than upon your graces, or else Satan will lead you into captivity, &c.

The tenth help. If you would not be taken in any of Satan's snares, then *be much in prayer.* Prayer is a shelter to the soul; a sacrifice to God and a scourge to the devil. David's heart was oft more out of tune than his harp. He prays, and then, in spite of the devil, cries, ' Return unto thy rest, O my soul.' Prayer is *porta cœli, clavis paradisi,* the gate of heaven, a key to let us into paradise. There is nothing that renders plots fruitless like prayer; therefore saith Christ, 'Watch and pray that ye enter not into temptation,' Mat. xxvi. 41. You must watch and pray, and pray and watch, if you would not enter into temptation.[2] When Sennacherib and Haman had laid plots and snares to have destroyed the Jews, they prayed, and their souls were delivered, and Sennacherib and Haman destroyed. David had many snares laid for him, and this puts him upon prayer. ' Keep me,' saith he, ' from the snares which they have laid for me, and the gins of the workers of iniquity.' ' Let the wicked fall into their own nets, whilst that I escape,' Ps. cxli. 9, 10. 'The proud,' saith he, ' have hid a snare for me, and cords: they have spread a net by the wayside; they have set gins for me. Selah. I said unto the Lord, Thou art my God : hear the voice of my supplication, O Lord !' Ps. cxl. 5, 6. Saul and many others had laid snares for David, and this puts him upon prayer, and so the snares are broken and he is delivered.[3] Ah, souls! take words to yourselves, and tell God that Satan hath spread his snares in all places and in all companies; tell God that he digs deep, and that he hath plot upon plot, and device upon device, and all to undo you; tell God that you have neither skill nor power to escape his snares; tell God that it is a work too high and too hard for any created creature to work your

---

[1] John xv. 5, χωρὶς ἐμοῦ, is *seorsim a me,* separate from me, or apart from me, ye can do nothing.

[2] Of Carolus Magnus it was spoken, *Carolus plus cum Deo quam cum hominibus loquitur,* that he spake more with God than with men. Ah! that I could say so of the Christians in our days.

[3] *Nunquam abs te, absque te recedo.*— Bernard. O Lord! saith he, I never go away from thee, without thee. Let us, saith Basil, with a holy impudence, make God ashamed, that he cannot look us in the face, if he do deny our importunity: Jacob-like, ' I will not let hee go, unless thou bless me.'

deliverance, unless he put under his own everlasting arms ; tell God how his honour is engaged to stand by you, and to bring you off, that you be not ruined by his plots ; tell God how the wicked would triumph, if you should fall into Satan's snares ; tell God of the love of Christ, of the blood of Christ, and of the intercession of Christ for you, that a way may be found for your escape ; tell God if he will make it his honour to save you from falling into Satan's snares, you will make it your glory to speak of his goodness and to live out his kindness.   Christians must do as Dædalus, that when he could not escape by a way upon earth, went by a way of heaven,[1] and that is, the way of prayer, which is the only way left to escape Satan's snares, &c.

Use. The next use is a use *of thankfulness to those that escape Satan's snares, that are not taken by him at his will.* Ah ! Christians, it stands upon you with that princely prophet David, to call upon your souls, and say, ' Bless the Lord, O our souls ; and all that is within us, bless his holy name ! Bless the Lord, O our souls, and forget not all his benefits !' Ps. ciii. 1, 2 ; who hath not given us to be a prey to Satan, and to be ensnared by those snares that he hath laid for our souls. The sense of this great favour did work up David's heart to praises : ' Blessed be the Lord,' saith he, ' who hath not given us a prey to their teeth. Our soul is escaped as a bird out of the snares of the fowlers : the snare is broken, and we are escaped,' Ps. cxxiv. 7. Ah ! Christians, remember that the greatest part of the world, yea, the greatest part of professors, are taken in Satan's snares. Can you think seriously of this, and not blush to be unthankful ? What are you better than others ? and what have ye deserved of God, or done for God more than others, that you should by the help of a divine hand escape the snares, when others are taken and held in the snares of the devil to their eternal overthrow ? &c.

Will you be thankful for the escaping the snares that men spread for your lives or estates, &c., and will you not be much more thankful for escaping those snares that Satan hath laid for your precious souls ? Ps. lxxi. 14.[2]

Remember this, that deliverance from Satan's snares doth carry with it the clearest and the greatest evidence of the soul and heart of God to be towards us. Many a man by a common hand of providence escapes many a snare that man hath laid for him, but yet escapes not the snares that Satan hath laid for him. Saul, and Judas, and Demas, doubtless escaped many snares that men had laid for them, but none of them escaped the snares that the devil had laid for them. Many men are lifted up above the snares of men by a common hand of providence, that are left to fall into the snares of the devil by a hand of justice ; your deliverance from Satan's snares is a fruit of special love. Can you thus look upon it and not be thankful, O precious soul ? I judge not.

Use. The last use of this point is, *To bespeak Christians to long to be at home.*[3] Oh ! long to be in the bosom of Christ ! long to be in the

---

[1] The well-known legend of the ' wax-fixed wings' of Dædalus and Icarus. —G.

[2] The ancients use to say, *Ingratum dixeris, omnia dixeris,* say a man is unthankful, and say he is anything. Ps. lxxi. 14, ' I will yet praise thee more and more.' In the original it is, I will add to thy praise. The stork is said to leave one of her young ones where she hatcheth them ; and the elephant to turn up the first sprig toward heaven, when he cometh to feed, out of some instinct of gratitude. Ah ! souls, that these may not bear witness against you in the day of Christ.

[3] Austin wished that he might have seen three things : Rome flourishing, Paul preach-

land of Canaan ! for this world, this wilderness, is full of snares, and all employments are full of snares, and all enjoyments are full of snares. In civil things, Satan hath his snares to entrap us ; and in all spiritual things, Satan hath his snares to catch us. All places are full of snares, city and country, shop and closet, sea and land ; and all our mercies are surrounded with snares. There are snares about our tables and snares about our beds, &c. ; yea, Satan is so powerful and subtle that he will oftentimes make our greatest, nearest, and dearest mercies to become our greatest snares. Sometimes he will make the wife that lies in the bosom to be a snare to a man, as Samson's was, and as Job's was. Sometimes he will make the child to be a snare, as Absalom was and Eli's sons were ; and sometimes he will make the servant to be a snare, as Joseph was to his mistress. Ah ! souls, Satan is so cunning and artificial[1] that he can turn your cups into snares, and your clothes into snares, and your houses into snares, and your gardens into snares, and all your recreations into snares, &c. And oh ! how should the consideration of these things work all your souls to say with the church, 'Make haste, my beloved, and be like a roe, or a young hart upon the mountain of spices,' and to love, and look, and long for the coming of Christ, Cant. viii. 14.[2] Shall the espoused maid long for the marriage day ? the servant for his freedom ? the captive for his ransom ? the traveller for his inn ? and the mariner for his harbour ? and shall not the people of the Lord long much more to be in the bosom of Christ ? there being nothing below the bosom of Christ that is not surrounded with Satan's snares, Philip. i. 23, and 2 Cor. v. 2, 4.

What Paul once spake of bonds and afflictions, that they attended him in every place, Acts xx. 23, that may all the saints say of Satan's snares, that they attend them in every place, which should cause them to cry out, *Migremus hinc, migremus hinc*, let us go hence, let us go hence ; and to say with Monica, Austin's mother, What do we here ? why depart we not hence ? why fly we no swifter ?[3] Ah ! souls, till you are taken up into the bosom of Christ, your comforts will not be full, pure, and constant ; till then, Satan will still be thumping of you, and spreading snares to entangle you ; therefore you should always be crying out with the church, ' Come, Lord Jesus !' Rev. xxii. 20. Is not Christ the star of Jacob, that ' giveth light to them that are in darkness ?' that Prince of peace who brings the olive branch to souls that are perplexed ? Is not the greatest worth and wealth in him ? Is not the petty excellencies and perfections of all created creatures epitomized in him ? Is not he the crown of crowns, the glory of glories, and the heaven of heavens ? Oh then, be still a-longing after a full, clear, and constant enjoyment of Christ in heaven ; for till then, Satan will still have plots and designs upon you. He acts by an united[4] power, and will never let you rest till you are taken up to an everlasting rest in the bosom of Christ.[5]

ing, and Christ conversing with men upon the earth. Bede comes after, and, correcting this last wish, saith, Yea, but let me see the King in his beauty, Christ in his heavenly kingdom.

[1] ' Artful.'—G.   [2] ברח דודי, *berach dodi ;* flee away speedily, my beloved.

[3] Quid hic faciamus ? cur non ocius migramus ? cur non hinc avolamus ?

[4] Qu. ' untired ' ?—G.

[5] It is as easy to compass the heavens with a span, and contain the sea in a nutshell, as to relate fully Christ's excellencies, or heaven's happiness.

THE EPISTLE DEDICATORY.

To his honoured friends, Sir JOHN MORE, Knight and Alderman of the City of London ; and to his good Lady, MARY MORE, his most affectionate Consort.[1]

The Father of all mercies, and the God of all blessings, bless you both with grace and peace here, and glory hereafter.

Honoured Friends,—Christian friendship makes such a knot, that great Alexander cannot cut. It was well observed by Sir Francis Bacon,[2] 'That old wood is best to burn, and old books best to read, and old friends best to trust. It was a witty saying of the Duke of Buckingham to Bishop Morton,[3] in Richard the III. his time, ' Faithful friends,' saith he, 'are in this age for the most part gone all in pilgrimage, and their return is uncertain.' 'They seem to take away the sun out of the world,' said the heathen orator,[4] 'who take away friendship from the life of men, and we do not more need fire and water than true friendship.[5] In this epistle I shall endeavour so to acquit myself as becomes a real friend, a cordial friend, a faithful friend, and a soul-friend, as to your great and everlasting concernments, that it may go well with you for ever and ever.

Sir, The points that are handled in this following treatise, and in the first part, are of as high, choice, necessary, noble, useful, and comfortable a nature, as any that can be treated on by mortal man. The

[1] More, or Moore, was elected Alderman of Walbrook in 1671 ; served the office of Sheriff in 1672, and that of Lord Mayor in 1682. See Northoack's ' History of London,' (1773.) He was of the Grocers' Company. Buried in St Dunstan's-in-the-East, Thames Street.—Herbert's ' History of the Twelve Companies of London,' i. 330.—G.

[2] Bacon's Works, by Spedding, vii. 139. Apophthegms, No. 97 of edition of 1625, and 75 of those printed in the *Resuscitatio.* Brooks quotes evidently from memory. The following is the passage :—'Alonso of Arragon was wont to say in commendation of age, that age appeared to be best in four things : old wood best to burn ; old wine to drink ; old friends to trust ; and old authors to read.'—G.

[3] Misprinted ' Monton.' A full account of Morton is to be found in Godwin *de Præsulibus,'* (ed.: Richardson, p. 130.) He was John Morton, then Bishop of Ely, but afterwards Archbishop of Canterbury : and the above saying was probably uttered while the bishop was under Buckingham's wardship at Brecon, by command of Richard III. See Foss's 'Judges of England,' v. 59.—G.   [4] Cicero : de Amicitiâ.—G.

[5] It is the saying of Euripides, ' That a faithful friend is better than a calm sea to a weather-beaten mariner.' [Orestes 717 chorus, ed. Porson ; cf. also two passages of the Andromache, 748, 749, and in 891.—G.]

four things which God minds most and loves most are, (1.) His honour. (2.) His worship. (3.) His people. (4.) His truth. Surely their souls must needs be of a very sad complexion who can read the great truths that are here opened and applied, and not (1.) dearly love them, (2.) highly prize them, (3.) cordially bless God for them, (4.) seriously ponder and meditate upon them, (5.) and not frequently and diligently study them, and make a gracious and daily improvement of them.

The covenant of grace, and the covenant of redemption, are a rich armoury, out of which you may furnish yourselves with all sorts of spiritual weapons, wherewith you may encounter Satan's temptations, wiles, devices, methods, depths, stratagems. Nothing of Satan's can stand before the covenant of grace and the covenant of redemption, well understood and well applied, Eph. vi. 11 ; 2 Cor. ii. 11 ; Rev. ii. 24.

In the covenant of grace and the covenant of redemption that is passed betwixt God the Father and our Lord Jesus Christ,[1] you will find many rich and rare cordials, which have a strong tendency to preserve all gracious souls from desponding and fainting : (1.) in times of afflictions ; (2.) in times of temptations ; (3.) in times of desertion ; (4.) in times of sufferings for Christ's sake and the gospel's sake ; (5.) in times of opposition ; (6.) and at the time of death and dissolution. There are no comforts nor cordials that can reach the souls of Christians in their deep distresses, but such as flow from these two covenants. The more it concerns all such Christians to study these two covenants, and to be well acquainted with them, that so they may the more readily have recourse to such cordials as their present estate and condition calls for.

In these two covenants you will find much matter which has a strong tendency (1.) to inflame your love to God and Christ, and all in the covenant of grace ; (2.) to strengthen your faith ; (3.) to raise your hopes ; (4.) to cheer your souls ; (5.) to quiet and satisfy your consciences ; (6.) to engage you to a close and holy walking with God ; (7.) to provoke you to triumph in free grace, and in the Lord Jesus Christ ; (8.) to sit loose from this world.[2] The riches and treasures that are wrapt up in both these covenants are so great, so sure, so durable, and so suitable to all believers, as may well deaden their hearts to all the riches and glories of this lower world, Rev. xii. 1.

In these two covenants every sincere Christian will find (1.) a special salve for every spiritual sore ; (2.) a special remedy against every spiritual malady ; (3.) a special plaster against every spiritual wound ; (4.) a spiritual magazine to supply all their spiritual wants ; and (5.) a spiritual shelter under every spiritual storm. In these two covenants you will find food to nourish you, a staff to support you, a guide to lead you, a fire to warm you, and springs of life to cheer and refresh you.

In this covenant of grace and the covenant of redemption, you may clearly see the wisdom, counsel, love, and transactions between the Father and the Son sparkling and shining, there being nothing under

[1] 2 Sam. xxiii. 5 ; Isa. liv. 9, 10 ; Jer. xxxii. 38–41 ; Zech. ix. 11 ; Heb. xiii. 20.
[2] Ps. cxvi. 1–9, 16, and iii. ; 2 Sam. xxiii. 5 ; Ps. ciii. 17, 18, and cxi. 5, 9, 17 ; 2 Cor. ii. 14 ; Gal. vi. 14.

heaven that contributes more to the peace, comfort, assurance, settlement, and satisfaction of sincere Christians than such a sight.[1] The main reason why so many gracious souls are so full of fears, doubts, darkness, and disputes about their internal and eternal estates, is because they have no more clear and full understanding of these two covenants; and if such Christians would but more seriously buckle to the study of those two covenants, as they are opened and applied in the following treatise, their fears and doubts, &c., would quickly vanish ; and they would have their triumphant songs : their mourning would soon be turned into rejoicing, and their complaints into hallelujahs. Neither do I know anything in all this world that would contribute more to seriousness, spiritualness, heavenliness, humbleness, holiness, and fruitfulness, than a right understanding of these two covenants, and a divine improvement of them. There are many choice Christians who have always either tears in their eyes, complaints in their mouths, or sighs in their breasts ; and oh that these, above all all others, would make these two covenants their daily companions ! Let these few hints[2] suffice concerning the following treatise.

Now, Sir John, I shall crave leave to put you and your lady a little in mind of your deceased and glorified father.[3] ' He is a true friend,' saith the Smyrnean poet of old, ' who continueth the memory of his deceased friend.'[4] When a friend of Austin's died, he professed he was put into a great strait, whether he himself should be willing to live or willing to die : he was unwilling to live, because one half of himself was dead ; yet he was not willing to die, because his friend did partly live in him, though he was dead. Let you and I make the application as we see cause : your glorified father's name and memory remains to this day as fresh and fragrant as the Rose of Sharon— Cant. ii. 1—among all those that fear the Lord, and had the happiness of inward acquaintance with him. ' The memory of the just is blessed, but the name of the wicked shall rot,' Prov. x. 7. In the original it is, ' The memory of the just לברכה *in benedictionem*, shall be for a blessing ;' the very remembering of them shall bring a blessing to such as do remember them.[5] The moralists say of fame, or of a man's good name—

> Omnia si perdas famam servare memento,
> Quà semel amissà postea nullus eris;[6]

i.e, Whatsoever commodity you lose, be sure yet to preserve that jewel of a good name.[7] This jewel, among others, your honoured father

---

[1] It was the saying of an eminent saint, on his death-bed, that he had much peace and quietness, not so much from a greater measure of grace than other Christians had, or from any immediate witness of the Spirit, but because he had a more clear understanding of the covenant of grace than many others, having studied it and preached it so many years as he had done. [Qu. William Strong?—G.]

[2] Misprinted ' kinds.'—G.

[3] Ponder upon that Deut. xiii. 6 : Thy friend which is as thine own soul.

[4] Qu. Homer ? Smyrna was one of the seven cities which claimed him. Strabo, *l. c.* Cicero, Arch. 8.—G.

[5] *Memoria justi erit celebris*, So Barn. [Qu. Bernard ?—G.] *Ego si bonam famam servasso, sat dives ero.* If I may but keep a good name, I have wealth enough, saith the heathen—Plautus.   [6] Claudian, De. Cons. Mall. Theod. v. 3.—G.

[7] Heb. xi. 13, 39. A good renown is better than a golden girdle, saith the French proverb.

carried with him to the grave—yea, to heaven. There is nothing raises a man's name and fame in the world like holiness. The seven deacons that the church chose were 'holy men,' Acts vi. 5; and they were men of 'good report,' ver. 3. They were men well witnessed unto, well testified of, as the Greek word imports.[1] Cornelius was a 'holy man,' Acts x. 1–4; and he was a man of 'good report' among all the nation of the Jews, ver. 22. Ananias was a 'holy man,' Acts ix. 10, 20; and he was a man of a 'good report,' Acts xxii. 12. Caius and Demetrius were both 'holy men,' and of a 'good report;' witness that Third Epistle of John. The patriarchs and prophets were 'holy men,' and they were men of a 'good report,' Heb. xi. 1, 2—'For by it the elders obtained a good report;' their holiness did eternalise their names. The apostles were 'holy men,' 1 Thes. ii. 10; and they were men of 'good report,' 2 Cor. vi. 8. Now certainly it is none of the least of mercies to be well reputed and reported of. Next to a good God and a good conscience, a good report, a good name, is the noblest blessing. It is no great matter, if a man be great and rich in the world, to obtain a great report; but without holiness you can never obtain a good report. Holiness, uprightness, righteousness, will embalm your names; it will make them immortal: Ps. cxii. 6, 'The righteous shall be in everlasting remembrance.' Wicked men many times outlive their names, but the names of the righteous outlive them. Holy Abel hath been dead above this five thousand years, and yet his name is as fresh and fragrant as it was the first day he was made a martyr, 1 John iii. 12. When a sincere Christian dies, he leaves his name as a sweet and as a lasting scent behind him; his fame shall live when he is dead. This is verified in your precious father, who is now 'asleep in Jesus,' 1 Thes. iv. 14.

Now you both very well know that there was no Christian friend that had so great a room in his heart, in his affections, as I had, and you can easily guess at the reasons of it. Neither can you forget how frequently, both in his health, sickness, and before his death, he would be pressing of me to be a soul-friend to you, and to improve all the interest I had in heaven for your internal and eternal good, that he might meet you both in that upper world, Mat. xxv. 33, and that you might both be found with him at the right hand of Christ in the great day of the Lord. I know that your glorified father, whilst he was on earth, did lay up many a prayer for you in heaven. My desire and prayer is, that those prayers of his may return in mighty power upon both your hearts; and having a fair opportunity now before me, I shall endeavour to improve it for the everlasting advantage of both your souls; and therefore let my following counsel be not only accepted, but carefully, faithfully, and diligently followed by you, that so you may be happy here and blessed hereafter.

1. The first word of counsel is this: Let it be the principal care of both of you *to look after the welfare of your precious and immortal souls.* If your souls are safe, all is safe; if they are well, all is well;

[1] The Persians seldom write their king's name but in characters of gold. Throughout the Old and New Testaments God has written the names of just men in golden characters, as I may speak.

but if they are lost, all is lost, and you lost and undone in both worlds.[1]
Christ, that only went to the price of souls, hath told us that one soul
is more worth than all the world. Chrysostom well observeth, 'that
whereas God hath given us many other things double—viz., two eyes
to see with, two ears to hear with, two hands to work with, and two
feet to walk with, to the intent that the failing of the one might be
supplied with the other—he hath given us but one soul; if that be
lost, hast thou,' saith he, 'another soul to give in recompense for it?' Ah,
friends! Christ left his Father's bosom and all the glory of heaven for
the good of souls; he assumed the nature of men for the happiness of
the soul of man; he trod the wine-press of his Father's wrath for souls;
he prayed for souls; he paid for souls, and he bled out his heart-blood
for souls.[2] The soul is the breath of God, the beauty of man, the
wonder of angels, and the envy of devils. It is of an angelical nature;
it is a heavenly spark, a celestial plant, and of a divine offspring,
1 Pet. v. 8. Again, weigh well τὸ λύτρον, 'the incomparable price,'
which Christ paid for the redemption of the soul, 1 Pet. i. 18, 19.
What are the riches of the East or West Indies, the spoil of the
richest nations, rocks of diamonds, mountains of gold, or the price of
Cleopatra's draught, to the price that Christ laid down for souls!
1 John i. 4, 12, and Heb. xxii. 23. The soul is a spiritual substance,
capable of the knowledge of God, of union with God, of communion
with God, and of an eternal fruition of God. There is nothing can
suit the soul below God, nor nothing that can satisfy the soul without
God, nor nothing that can save the soul but God. The soul is so
choice, so high, and so noble a piece, that it divinely scorns all the
world in point of acceptation, justification, satisfaction, delectation, and
salvation. Christ made himself an offering for sin, that souls might
not be undone by sin. The Lord died that slaves might live; the Son
died that servants might live; the natural Son died that adopted sons
might live; the only-begotten Son died that bastards might live; yea,
the judge died that malefactors might live, Heb. ix. 11–14, and x. 10, 14;
Gal. iv. 4–6; Heb. ii. 8. Ah, friends! as there was never sorrow like
Christ's sorrow, so there was never love like Christ's love, and of all
his love none to that of soul-love, Isa. liii. 3, and Gal. ii. 20. To
say much in a little room, the spiritual enemies which daily war
against the soul, the glorious angels which hourly guard the soul, and
the precious ordinances which God hath appointed as means both to
convert and nourish the soul, [shew forth that love,] Eph. vi. 11, 12;
1 Pet. ii. 11; Rom. x. 17; 1 Cor. xi. 23–27. The soul is capable of
'a crown of life,' Rev. ii. 10; of 'a crown of glory,' 1 Pet. v. 4; of 'a
crown of righteousness,' 2 Tim. iv. 8; of 'an incorruptible crown,'
1 Cor. ix. 25. The crowns of earthly princes stand as a sophister's[3]
cap, on one side of the head. Many may say of their crowns as that
king said of his, O crown, more noble than happy![4] In the time of
Galienus the emperor, Anno Christo 260, there were thirty competi-

---

[1] Mat. xvi. 26. The soul is a greater miracle in man than all the miracles wrought
amongst men, saith Augustine.

[2] Isa. lxiii. 3; John xvii.; Luke xxiii. 34; Mat. xxvi. 28.

[3] 'Sophister,' a 'pretender to wisdom,' but here probably a University term for an
undergraduate of a given (early) standing.—G.

[4] Queen Elizabeth was said to swim to her crown through a sea of sorrow.

tors on foot for the Roman crown and throne, who confounded and destroyed one another. A princely crown is oftentimes the mark for envy and ambition to shoot at. Henry the Sixth was honoured with the crowns of two kingdoms, France and England ; the first was lost through the faction of his nobles, the other was twice plucked from his head. Earthly crowns have so many cares, fears, vexations, and dangers that daily attend them, that oftentimes they make the heads and hearts of monarchs ache, which made Cyrus say, ' You look upon my crown and my purple robes, but did you but know how they were lined with thorns, you would not stoop to take them up.'[1] But the crowns that immortal souls are capable of are crowns without crosses ; they are not attended with care of keeping or fear of losing ; there are no evil persons nor evil spirits that haunt those crowns. Darius, that great monarch, fleeing from his enemies, he threw away the crown of gold from his head that he might run the faster ; but a sincere Christian is in no danger of losing his crown, 2 Tim. iv. 8. His crown is laid up in a safe hand, in an omnipotent hand, 1 Pet. i. 5. Now what do all these things speak out but the preciousness and excellency of the soul ? Once more, the excellency of the case or cabinet—viz., the body—intimates a more than ordinary excellency of this jewel. The body is of all materials the most excellent. How does David admire the rare texture and workmanship of his body ! ' I am wonderfully made ; I was curiously wrought in the lowest parts of the earth,' Ps. cxxxix. 13, 15. When curious workmen have some choice piece in hand, they perfect it in private, and then bring it forth to the light for men to gaze at. So here, the greatest miracle in the world is man, in whose very body—how much more in his soul !—are miracles enough, betwixt head and feet, to fill a volume. One complains that men much wonder at the high mountains of the earth, the huge waves of the sea, the deep falls of rivers, the vastness of the ocean, and at the motions of the stars, &c., but wonder not at all at their wonderful selves.[2] Galen, a profane physician and a great atheist, writing of the excellent parts of man's body, he could not choose but sing an hymn to that God, whosoever he were, that was the author of so excellent and admirable a piece of work ; he could not but cry out, 'Now I adore the God of nature.'[3] Now if the cabinet be so curiously wrought, what is the jewel that is contained in it ! Oh, how richly and gloriously is the soul embroidered ! How divinely inlaid and enamelled is that ! Princes impress their images or effigies upon the choicest metals, viz., gold and silver. God hath engraven his own image with his own hand upon angels and men, Gen. i. 26, [Damascene.] The soul is the glory of the creation, a beam of God, a spark of celestial brightness, a vessel of honour, a bird of paradise, a habitation for God. The soul is spiritual in its essence ; God breathed it in ; God hath invested it with many noble endowments ; he hath made it a mirror of beauty, and printed upon it a surpassing excellency. The soul is

[1] Prov. xxvii. 4, ' Doth the crown endure to all generations'—*Heb.*, to generation and generation !'
[2] Austin. The Stoic thought it was better to be a fool in the form of a man than wise in the shape of a beast.

spiritual in its object; it contemplates God and heaven. God is the orb and centre where the soul doth fix.[1] God is the *terminus ad quem*, the soul moves to him as to his rest, ' Return to thy rest, O my soul.' This dove can find no rest but in this heavenly ark.[2] Nothing can fill the soul but God, nothing can quiet the soul but God, nothing can satisfy the soul but God, nothing can secure the soul but God, nothing can save the soul but God. The soul being spiritual, God only can be the adequate object of it. The soul is spiritual in its operations. It being immaterial, doth not depend upon the body in its working. The rich and rare endowments, and the noble operations of the soul, speak out the excellency of the soul. The soul, saith one, [Aristotle.] hath a nature distinct from the body; it moves and operates of itself, though the body be dead, and hath no dependence upon, or co-existence with, the body. The soul hath an intrinsecal principle of life and motion, though it be separate from the body. And doth not the immortality of the soul speak out the excellency of the soul, against that dangerous notion of the soul's mortality? Consult the scriptures in the margin,[3] and seriously and frequently think of this one argument, among a multitude of arguments that might be produced to prove the immortality of the soul. That which is not capable of killing is not capable of dying; but the soul is not capable of killing, *ergo.* Our Lord Jesus proves the minor proposition, that it is not capable of killing: Luke xii. 4, ' Fear not them that kill the body, and after that have no more that they can do.' Therefore the soul, not being capable of killing, is not in a possibility of dying. The essence of the soul is metaphysical: it hath a beginning, but no end; it is eternal *à parte post;* it runs parallel with eternity. The soul doth not wax old; it lives for ever, which we cannot affirm of any sublunary created glory. To conclude this first word of counsel, what Job saith of wisdom, I may fitly apply to the soul, ' Man knows not the price thereof ; it cannot be valued with the gold of Ophir, with the precious onyx, or the sapphire, the gold and crystal cannot equal it, and the exchange of it shall not be for jewels of fine gold,' Job xxviii. 13, 16, 17. O my friends, it is the greatest wisdom, policy, equity, and justice, to provide for your precious souls, to secure your precious souls; for they are jewels of more worth than ten thousand worlds. All the honours, riches, greatness, and glory of this world are but chips, toys, and pebbles to these glorious pearls. But,

2. The second word of counsel is this, as you would be safe here, and saved in the great day of the Lord, as you would be happy here, and blessed hereafter, *take up in nothing below a gracious acquaintance with Christ, a choice acceptation of Christ, a holy reliance upon Christ, a full resignation of yourselves to Christ, and a real and glorious union with Christ,* Acts ii. 20; Job xxii. 21; 1 Tim. i. 15; Job xiii. 15; 2 Cor. ii. 11. If you do, you are lost and undone in both worlds.

[1.] First, *Some take up in a name to live when they are dead,* Rev.

[1] Gen. ii. 7; Heb. xii. 9; Eccles. xii. 7; Zech. xii. 1; Ps. cxvi. 7; John xiv. 8; Ps. xvii. 16.

[2] ' Lord,' saith Austin, ' thou hast made us for thyself, and our heart is unquiet till it comes unto thyself.' [Confessions, as before.—G.]

[3] Luke xxiii. 43; 1 Thes. iv. 17, 18; Phil. i. 23; Acts vii. 59.

iii. 1, dead in trespasses and sins, Eph. ii. 1, dead Godwards, and dead Christwards, and dead heavenwards, and dead holinesswards. The Sadducees derive their name from Zeduchim or Zadducæus, a just man. But the worst men, saith the historian, got the best names. The Alcoran of the Turks hath its name from brightness, *Al,*[1] in the Arabic, being as much as *Kazan* in the Hebrew, 'to shine' or 'cast forth in brightness,' when it is full of darkness, and fraught with false-hoods. It will be but a poor comfort to any for the world to commend them as gracious, if God condemn them as graceless; for the world to commend them as pious, if God condemn them as impious; for the world to commend them as sincere, if God condemn them as hypocrites. But,

[2.] Secondly, Some take up *in a form of godliness when they are strangers to the power,* 2 Tim. iii. 5; *when they deny, yea, when they oppose and persecute, the power.* Such monsters this age hath abounded with; but their seeming goodness is but a religious cheat, Acts xiii. 45, 50.

[3.] Thirdly, There are some that take up *in their religious duties and services;* in their praying, fasting, prophesying, hearing, receiving; they make a God, a Christ, a Saviour of their own duties and services. This was the undoing and damning sin of the Scribes and Pharisees, and is the undoing and damning sin of many thousands in our days, Mat. vii. 22; Luke xviii. 12, xiii. 26, and xvi. 15; Ezek. xxxiii. 31, 32.

[4.] Fourthly, There are many that take up *in their common gifts and parts;* in a gift of knowledge, and in a gift of teaching, and in a gift of utterance, and in a gift of memory, and in a gift of prayer, and this proves ruinous and destructive to them, Mat. vii. 22; Rom. ii. 17–24; 1 Cor. xii.; Heb. vi. 4, 5.

[5.] Fifthly, There are many that take up *in their riches, prosperity, and worldly grandeur and glory:* Prov. xviii. 11, 'The rich man's wealth is his strong city.' It is hard to have wealth, and not trust to it, Mat. xix. 24. Wealth was never true to those that trusted it. There is an utter uncertainty in riches, 1 Tim. vi. 17; a nonentity, Prov. xxiii. 5, 6; an impotency to help in an evil day, Zeph. i. 18; an impossibility to stretch to eternity, unless it be to destroy the owner for ever,[2] Prov. x. 15; Ps. lxxiii. 19; Mat. xx. 26. There is nothing more clear in Scripture and history than that riches, prosperity, and worldly glory hath been commonly their portion who never have had a God for their portion, Luke xvi. 25. It was an excellent saying of Lewis of Bavaria, emperor of Germany: *Hujusmodi comparandæ sunt opes, quæ cum naufragio simul enatent,* Such goods are worth getting and owning as will not sink or wash away if a shipwreck happen.[3] *Solus sapiens dives,* Only the wise man is the rich man, saith the philosopher. Another saith, [Augustine,] *Divitiæ corporales paupertatis plenæ sunt,* That earthly riches are full of poverty, they cannot enrich the soul; for oftentimes under silken apparel there is a threadbare soul.

---

[1] Query, '*Koran*'? *Al* is simply the definite article, *the.*—ED.

[2] *Divitibus ideo pietas deest, quia nihil deest,* Rich men's wealth proves an hindrance to their happiness, Eccles. v. 13; James v. 1, 2.

[3] Riches are called thick clay, Hab. ii. 6, which will sooner break the back than lighten the heart.

He that is rich in conscience sleeps more soundly than he that is richly clothed in purple.

No man is rich which cannot carry hence that which he hath; that which we must leave behind us is not ours but some other's, [Ambrose, lib. 8, ep. 10.]

The shortest cut to riches is by their contempt. It is great riches not to desire riches, and he hath most that covets least. If there were any happiness in riches, the gods would not want them, saith the same author, [Seneca.]

When one was a-commending the riches and wealth of merchants: I do not love that wealth, said a poor heathen, which hangs upon ropes; for if they break, the ship miscarrieth, and then where is the merchant's riches?

If I had an enemy, saith one, whom it was lawful to wish evil unto, I would chiefly wish him great store of riches, for then he should never enjoy quiet, [Latimer.]

The historian [Tacitus] observes, that the riches of Cyprus invited the Romans to hazard many dangerous fights for the conquering of it.

Earthly riches, saith one, [Augustine,] are an evil master, a treacherous servant, fathers of flattery, sons of grief, a cause of fear to those that have them, and a cause of sorrow to those that want them.

I have read a famous story of Zelimus, emperor of Constantinople, that after he had taken Egypt, he found a great deal of treasure there; and the soldiers coming to him, and asking of him what they should do with the citizens of Egypt, for that they had found great treasure among them, and had taken their riches? Oh, saith the emperor, hang them all up, for they are too rich to be made slaves; and this was all the thanks they had for the riches they were spoiled of.[1] What more contemptible than a rich fool, a golden beast, as Caligula called his father-in-law Syllanius?[2] Not but that some are great and gracious, rich and righteous, as Abraham, Lot, Job, David, Hezekiah, &c.

It is said of Shusa in Persia, saith Cassiodorus, that it was so rich that the stones were joined together with gold; and that in it Alexander found seventy thousand talents of gold. If you can take this city, saith Aristagorus[3] to his soldiers, you may vie with Jove himself for riches. The riches of Shusa did but make the soldiers the more desperate in their attempt to take it.

By these short hints you may see the folly and vanity of those men who take up in their riches. But,

[6.] Sixthly, Many there are that take up *in their own righteousness, which at best is but as filthy rags*, Isa. lxiv. 6. This was the damning sin of the Jews, and of the scribes and Pharisees; and is the undoing sin of many of the professors of this age, Rom. x. 2, 3; Mat. v. 20.

---

[1] [Knolles] The Turkish History. The poets feigned Pluto to be the god of riches and hell, as if they were inseparable.—*Homer.*

[2] Rather 'Silanus:' Dion Cass, lviii. 25.—G.

[3] Rather 'Aristagoras' Herod:' iv. 138, v. 37, 38: for Shusa rather 'Susa.'—G.

[7.] Seventhly, Many there are that take up *in their external church privileges*, crying out, ' The temple of the Lord, the temple of the Lord,' Jer. vii. 4, 8–11, when they have no union nor communion with the Lord of the temple. These forget that there will come a day, when the ' children of the kingdom shall be cast out,' Mat. viii. 12. It would be very good for such persons to make these five scriptures their daily companions, Mat. xxii. 10, 12–14; Luke xiii. 25–28; Rom. ii. 28, 29; Gal. vi. 15; Jer. ix. 25, 26. That they may never dare to take up in their outward church privileges, which can neither secure them from hell, nor secure them of heaven. But,

[8.] Eighthly, Many there be that take up *in common convictions.* Judas had mighty convictions of his sin, but they issued in desperation, Mat. xxvii. 4, 5. Balaam was mightily enlightened and convinced, insomuch that he desired to die the death of the righteous; but under all his convictions he died Christless and graceless, Num. xxiii. and xxiv. Nebuchadnezzar had great convictions, Dan. iv. 31, 32, yet we do not read that ever he was converted before he was driven from the society of men, to be a companion with the beasts of the field, Dan. iv. 31, 32. He had strong convictions, (1.) by Daniel's interpreting of his dream, Dan. ii. 47. (2.) He told Daniel, that ' his God was the God of gods, and a Lord of kings, and a revealer of secrets;' and yet presently he fell into gross idolatry, Dan. iii., and strictly commanded to worship the golden image that he had set up; and as if he had lost all his former convictions, he was so swelled up with pride and impudence, as to say to the three children, when they divinely scorned to worship the image he had set up, ' What God is there that can deliver you out of my hand?' ver. 15. Saul had great convictions, ' I have sinned, return, my son David, I will no more do thee harm,' &c. And Saul lifted up his voice and wept; and he said unto David, ' Thou art more righteous than I, for thou hast rewarded me good, whereas I have rewarded thee evil,' 1 Sam. xxvi. 21, 25, and xxiv. 16–19. But these convictions issued in no saving change, for after these he lived and died in the height of his sins. Pharaoh had great convictions: ' And Pharaoh sent, and called for Moses and Aaron, and said unto them, I have sinned this time: the Lord is righteous, and I and my people are wicked.' And again, ' Then Pharaoh called for Moses and Aaron in haste; and he said, I have sinned against the Lord your God, and against you,' Exod. ix. 27, and x. 16. But these convictions issued in no reformation, in no sound conversion, and therefore drowning and damning followed. Cain was under convictions, but went and built a city, and lost his convictions in a crowd of worldly business, Gen. iv. Herod and Felix were under convictions, but they went off, and never issued in any saving work upon their souls, Mark vi. 20; Acts xxiv. 25. Oh, how many men and women have fallen under such deep convictions, that they have day and night cried out of their sins, and of their lost and undone estates, and that they should certainly go to hell and be damned for ever, so that many good people have hoped that these were the pangs of the new birth; and yet either merry company, or carnal pleasures and delights, or much worldly business, or else length of time, have wrought off all their convictions, and they have grown more profane and wicked than ever they were before.   As water heated, if taken off the fire, will soon return to its natural coldness, yea, becomes colder after heating than before, [Aristotle,] this hath been the case of many under convictions. I shall forbear giving of particular instances.   But,

[9.] Ninthly, Many take up *in an outward change and reformation;* they have left some old courses and sinful practices which formerly they walked in, &c., and therefore they conclude and hope that their condition is good, and that all is well, and shall be for ever well with them.   They were wont to swear, whore, be drunk, profane Sabbaths, reproach saints, &c.; but now they have left all these practices, and therefore the main work is done, and they are made for ever.   I confess sin is that abominable thing which God hates, Jer. xliv. 4, and therefore it is a very great mercy to turn from it.   To leave one sin is a greater mercy than to win the whole world, Mat. xvi. 26; and it is certain that he that doth not outwardly reform shall never go to heaven, Job xxii. 23, 26.   He that doth not leave his sins, he can never be happy here nor blessed hereafter; and yet it is possible for a man, with Herod, to reform many things, and yet be a lost and undone man for ever, as he was, Mark vi. 20.   Judas was a very reformed man, but he was never inwardly changed nor throughout sanctified, Mat. xxvi. 20-22; 1 Thes. v. 23.   The scribes and Pharisees were outwardly reformed, but they were not inwardly renewed.   A man may be another man than what once he was, and yet not be a new man, a new creature.   When a sinner is sermon-sick, oh, then he will leave his sins; but when that sickness is off, he returns with the dog to his vomit, and with the sow to her wallowing in the mire, 2 Cor. v. 17; 2 Pet. ii. 20, 22.   Sometimes conscience is like the handwriting upon the wall, Dan. v. 5-8: it makes the sinner's countenance to change, and his thoughts to be troubled, and the joints of his loins to be loosed, and his knees to smite one against another.   And now the sinner is all for reforming, and turning over a new leaf; but when these agonies of conscience are over, the sinner returns to his old courses again, and oftentimes is twofold more a child of hell than before, Mat. xxiii. 15.   There was a man in this city who was given up to the highest wickednesses; on his sick-bed conscience made an arrest of him, and he was filled with such wonderful horror and terror, that he cried out day and night that he was damned, he was damned, he was damned; and when he had some small intervals, oh, what large promises did he make! what a new man, a reformed man, he would be! but when in time his terrors and sickness wrought off, he was sevenfold worse than before. Sometimes the awakened sinner parts with some sins to make room for others, and sometimes the sinner seems to give a bill of divorce to this sin and that, but it is only because his bodily strength fails him, or because he wants an opportunity, or because there is a more strict eye and watch upon him, or because the sword of the magistrate is more sharpened against him, or because he wants fuel, James iv. 3; he wants a purse to bear it out, or because some company, or some relations, or some friends lie between him and his sins, so that he must either tread over them, or else keep from his sins; or because he has deeply smarted for this sin, and that his name has been blotted, his credit and reputation stained, his trade decayed, his health impaired, his body wasted, &c., Prov. vi. 32–35. By these short hints it is evident that men may attain to some outward reformation, whose states and hearts were never changed, and who were never taken into marriage union with Christ. But,

[10.] Tenthly and lastly, Many take up *in a party.* As of old some cried up Paul as the only deep preacher, and others cried up Apollos as the only eloquent preacher, and many cried up Cephas as the most zealous preacher, 1 Cor. i. 10–13. We are for the Church of England, say some; we are for the Baptized people, say others; we are for the Presbyterian government, cry some; we are for the Congregational way, cry others. I have so much ingenuity and charity, as to judge that some of all these several parties and persuasions are really holy and will be eternally happy, are gracious and will be glorious, are sanctified and will be saved, are now governed by Christ and will be hereafter glorified with Christ. Judas was one of Christ's party, if I may so speak, and yet he had no part nor portion in Christ, Mat. xxvi. 20–26. Demas was one of Paul's party, and yet he played the apostate, and turned an idolatrous priest at Thessalonica, as Dorotheus saith, 2 Tim. iv. 10.[1] And Phygellus and Hermogenes were of Paul's party, but were only famous for their recidivation[2] and apostasy, 2 Tim. i. 15. Hymeneus and Alexander were of Paul's party, but they made shipwreck of faith and a good conscience, 1 Tim. i. 19, 20. The five foolish virgins were in society with the wise, and were accounted as members of their association, and yet the door of heaven was shut against them, Mat. xxv. 1, 2, 12. Many light, slight, and vain persons went with the children of Israel out of the land of Egypt, even a mixed multitude that embarked in the same bottom with them, and yet never arrived at the land of promise, Exod. xii. 38; Num. xi. 4. O my friends, it is not a man's being of this party or that, this church or that, this way or that, this society or that, that will bring him to heaven, without a spiritual conjunction with Christ, 1 Pet. i. 4; Heb. i. 2. He that would enjoy the heavenly inheritance must be espoused to Christ, the heir of all things: 'For he that hath the Son hath life, and he that hath not the Son hath not life,' 1 John v. 12. This marriage-union between Christ and the soul is set forth to the life throughout the book of Solomon's Song, Cant. ii. 16. Though the marriage-union between Christ and the soul be imperceptible to the eye of reason, yet it is real, 1 Cor. vi. 17. Things in nature often work insensibly, yet really. We do not see the hand move on the dial, yet it moves. The sun exhales and draws up the vapours of the earth insensibly, yet really, Eccles. xi. 6. Now this marriage-union between Christ and the soul includes and takes in these following particulars:—

First, This marriage-union between Christ and the soul does include and take in *the soul's giving a present bill of divorce to all other lovers;* sin, the world, and Satan.[3] Are you seriously and sincerely willing for ever to renounce these, and be divorced from these? There is no compounding betwixt Christ and them. Sin and your souls

[1] As before, see foot-note and Index *sub nomine.*—G.
[2] 'Relapse'=backsliding.—G.
[3] Consult these scriptures: Hosea xiv. 8; Isa. ii. 20, and xxx. 22; Ps. xlv. 10; Exod. xii. 33; Isa. lix. 20.

must part, or Christ and your souls can never meet; sin and your souls must be two, or Christ and your souls can never be one; you must in good earnest fall out with sins, or else you can never in good earnest fall in with a Saviour; the heart must be separated from all other lovers, before Christ will take the soul into his bed of loves. Christ takes none into marriage-union with himself, but such as are cordially willing that all old former leagues with sin and the world shall be for ever broken and dissolved. Your cordial willingness to part with sin, is your parting with sin in divine account. . You may as soon bring east and west together, light and darkness together, heaven and hell together, as bring Christ to espouse himself to such a soul, as has no mind, no will, no heart to be divorced from his former lovers. It is a foolish thing for any to think of keeping both Christ and their lusts too. It is a vain thing for any to think of saving the life of his sins, and the life of his soul too. If sin escape, your soul cannot escape; if thou art not the death of thy sins, they will be the death and ruin of thy soul. Marriage is a knot or tie, wherein persons are mutually limited and bound each to other, in a way of conjugal separation from all others, and this in Scripture is called a covenant, Prov. ii. 7. So when any one marries Christ, he doth therein discharge himself in affection and subjection from all that is contrary unto Christ, and solemnly covenants and binds himself to Christ alone; he will have no Saviour and no Lord but Christ, and to him will he cleave for ever, Ps. lxiii. 8; Acts xi. 23. But,

Secondly, This marriage-union with Christ doth include and take in *a hearty willingness, to take, to receive the Lord Jesus Christ for your Saviour and sovereign.*[1] Are you willing to consent to the match. It is not enough that Christ is willing to enter into a marriage-union with us, but we must be willing also to enter into a marriage-union with him.[2] God will never force a Christ, nor force salvation upon us, whether we will or no. Many approve of Christ, and cry up Christ, who yet are not willing to give their consent, that he, and he alone shall be their Prince and Saviour. Though knowledge of persons be necessary and fit, yet it is not sufficient to marriage, without consent, for marriage ought to be a voluntary transaction of persons. In marriage we do in a sort give away ourselves, and elect and make choice for ourselves, and therefore consent is a necessary concurrence to marriage. Now this consent is nothing else but a free and plain act of the will, accepting of Jesus Christ before all others to be its head and Lord, and in the soul's choice of him to be its Saviour and sovereign. Then a man is married to Christ, when he doth freely and absolutely and presently receive the Lord Jesus; not, I would have Christ if it did not prejudice my worldly estate, ease, friends, relations, &c., or hereafter, I will accept of him when I come to die, and be in distress, but now when salvation is offered, now while Christ tenders himself, I now yield up my heart and life unto him. But,

Thirdly, This marriage-union with Christ includes and takes in

---

[1] John i. 12; Acts v. 31; Col. ii. 6: weigh well these scriptures: Ps. cxii. 3, and xxv. 5; Hosea ii. 7.

[2] Many can choose Christ as a refuge to hide them from danger, and as a friend to help them in their need, who yet refuse him as a husband.

a universal and perpetual consent for all time and in all states and conditions. There is, you know, a great difference between a wife and a strumpet; a wife takes her husband upon all terms, to have and to hold, for better and for worse, for richer and for poorer, in sickness and in health, whereas a strumpet is only for hire and lust. When the purse is emptied, or the body wasted and strength consumed, the harlot's love is at an end: so here. That acceptance and consent which ties the marriage-knot between Christ and the soul, must be an unlimited and indefinite acceptance and consent, when we take the Lord Jesus Christ wholly and entirely, without any secret reservations or exceptions. That soul that will have Christ, must have all Christ or no Christ, 'for Christ is not divided,' 1 Cor. i. 13. That soul must entertain him to all purposes and intents, he must follow the Lamb wheresoever he goeth, Rev. xiv. 4, though it should be through fire and water, over mountains and hills. He must take him with his cup of affliction as well as his cup of consolation, Ps. lxvi. 12, with his shameful cross as well as his glorious crown, with his great sufferings as well as his great salvation, Heb. ii. 3, with his grace as well as his mercy, with his Spirit to lead and govern them, as well as his blood to redeem and justify them, to suffer for him as well as to reign with him, to die for him as well as to live to him, 2 Tim. ii. 12; Acts xxi. 13; Rom. xiv. 7, 8. Christianity, like the wind *Cæcias*, doth ever draw clouds and afflictions after it.[1] 'All that will live godly in Christ Jesus shall suffer persecution,' 2 Tim. iii. 12. A man may have many faint wishes and cold desires after godliness, and yet escape persecution, yea, he may make some essays and attempts, as if he would be godly, and yet escape persecution; but when a man is thoroughly resolved to be godly, and sets himself in good earnest upon pursuing after holiness, and living a life of godliness, then he must expect to meet with afflictions and persecutions. Whoever escapes, the godly man shall not escape persecution in one kind or another, in one degree or another.[2] He that is peremptorily resolved to live up to holy rules, and to live out holy principles, must prepare for sufferings. All the roses of holiness are surrounded with pricking briars. The history of the Ten Persecutions, and that little Book of Martyrs, the 11th of the Hebrews, and Mr Foxe his Acts and Monuments, with many other treatises that are extant, do abundantly evidence that from age to age, and from one generation to another, they that have been born after the flesh have persecuted them that hath been born after the spirit, and that the seed of the serpent have been still a-multiplying of troubles upon the seed of the woman, Gal. iv. 29; but a believer's future glory and pleasure will abundantly recompense him for his present pain and ignominy. But such as will have Christ for their Saviour and sovereign, but still with some proviso or other—viz., that they may keep such a beloved lust, or enjoy such carnal pleasures and delights, or raise such an estate for them and theirs, or comply with the times, and such and such great men's humours, or that they may follow the Lamb only

---

[1] The north-east wind, (καικίας,) Pl. 2, 46, 47; Vitr. 1, 6; Sen. Q. N. 5, 16.—G.

[2] The common cry of persecutors have been, *Christianos ad Leones*: within the first three hundred years after Christ, upon the matter all that made a profession of the apostle's doctrine, were cruelly murdered.

in sunshine weather, &c., these are still Satan's bond-slaves, and such as Christ can take no pleasure nor delight to espouse himself unto. But,

3. The third word of advice and counsel is this, viz.—' *Put off the old man, and put on the new,*' Col. iii. 9, 10. Consult the scriptures in the margin.[1] You must be new creatures, or else it had been better you had been any creatures than what you are: 2 Cor. v. 17, ' If any man be in Christ he is a new creature, old things are passed away, behold all things are become new.' The new creature includes a new light, a new sight, a new understanding. Now the soul sees sin to be the greatest evil, and Christ and holiness to be the chiefest good, Ps. xxxviii. 4, and Cant. v. 10. When a man is a new creature he has a new judgment and opinion, he looks upon God as his only happiness, and Christ as his all in all, Col. iii. 11, and upon the ways of God as ways of pleasantness, Prov. iii. 17. The new man has new cares, new requests, new desires. Oh that my soul may be saved! Acts ii. 37, and xvi. 30; Oh that my interest in Christ may be cleared! Oh that my heart may be adorned with grace! Oh that my whole man may be secured from wrath to come! 1 Thes. i. 10. The new man is a man of new principles. If you make a serious inspection into his soul, you shall find a principle of faith, of repentance, of holiness, of love, of contentment, of patience, &c.[2] There is not any one spiritual and heavenly principle respecting salvation, but may be found in the new creature. The new man experiences a new combat and conflict in his soul. ' The flesh lusteth against the spirit, and the spirit lusteth against the flesh.' ' I see another law in my members warring against the law of my mind,' Gal. v. 17, and Rom. vii. 23. The new man experiences a combat in every faculty. Here is the judgment against the judgment, and the will against the will, and the affections against the affections. And the reason is this; because there is flesh and spirit, sin and grace co-existent and cohabiting in every faculty of the soul; renewing grace is in every faculty, and remaining corruption is also in every faculty, like Jacob and Esau struggling in the same womb, or like heat and cold in the same water, and in every part of it. The new man also combats with all sorts of known sins, whether they be great or small, inward or outward, whether they be the sins of the heart or the sins of the life; and besides, the conflict in the new man is a daily conflict, a constant conflict. The new creature can never, the new creature will never, be at peace with sin; sin and the new creature will fight it out to the death. The new creature will never be brought into a league of friendship with sin. The new man is a man of a new life and conversation. Always a new life attends a new heart. You see it in Paul, Mary Magdalene, Zaccheus, the jailor, and all the others that are upon Scripture record.[3] The new man has new society, new company: Ps. cxix. 63, ' I am a companion of all them that fear thee, and of them that keep thy precepts.' Ps. xvi. 3, ' My goodness extends not to thee, but to the saints that are in the earth, and to the excellent, in whom is all my delight.' Holy society is the only society for persons of holy hearts, and in that society can no man delight until God renew

---

[1] Eph. iv. 22–24; Gal. vi. 15; 1 Pet. ii. 2.
[2] Phil. i. 29; Acts xi. 18; 1 Thes. iv. 9; Phil. iv. 11; 1 Cor. iv. 12.
[3] See 1 John iii. 14; 2 Cor. vi. 14; Ps. cxx. 5, cxxxix. 21, and xlii. 4.

his heart by grace. Many men be as the planet Mercury, good in conjunction with those that are good, and bad with those that are bad; these are they that do *Virtutis stragulam pudefacere*, Put honesty to an open shame.[1] Clothes and company do oftentimes tell tales in a mute but significant language. Tell me with whom thou goest, and I will tell thee what thou art, saith the Spanish proverb. Algerius, an Italian martyr, had rather be in prison with Cato than with Cæsar in the senate-house.[2] But to conclude this word of counsel, the new man walks by a new rule. As soon as ever God has made a man a new creature, he presently sets up a new rule of life to walk by, and that is no other but that which God himself sets up for his people to walk by, and that is his written word: Isa. viii. 20, ' To the law and to the testimony;' Ps. cxix. 105, ' Thy word is a lamp unto my feet, and a light unto my path;' ver. 133, ' Order my steps in thy word;' Gal. vi. 16, ' And as many as walk according to this rule, peace be on them and mercy, and upon the Israel of God.' This rule he sets up for all matters of faith, and for all matters of fact. The word is like the stone *Garamantides*, that hath drops of gold within itself, enriching of every soul that makes it his rule to walk by. Alexander kept Homer's Iliads in a cabinet, embroidered with gold and pearls;[3] and shall not we keep the word in the cabinet of our hearts, that it may be always ready at hand as a rule for us to walk by? Well, friends, whatever you do forget, be sure that for ever you remember this—viz., that none can or shall be glorious creatures, but such as by grace are made new creatures. But,

4. The fourth word of advice and counsel is this, *Labour to be more inwardly sincere than outwardly glorious.* ' The king's daughter is all glorious within,' Ps. xlv. 13. Oh labour rather to be good than to be thought to be good, to live than to have a name to live, Rev. iii. 1, 15–17. Whatever you let go, be sure you hold fast your integrity. A man were better to let friends go, relations go, estate go, liberty go, and all go, than let his integrity go. ' God forbid that I should justify you; till I die I will not remove my integrity from me; my righteousness I will hold fast, and I will not let it go: my heart shall not reproach me so long as I live,' Job xxvii. 5, 6. Job is highly and fully resolved to keep his integrity close against all assaults of enemies or suspicions of friends. Job's integrity was the best jewel he had in all the world, and this jewel he was resolved to keep to his dying day. It was neither good men, nor bad men, nor devils that should baffle Job out of his integrity; and though they all pulled, and pulled hard, at his integrity, yet he would not let it go, he would hold fast this pearl of price whatever it cost him. The sincere Christian, like John Baptist, will hold his integrity though he lose his head for it, Mark vi. The very heathens loved a candid and sincere spirit, as he that wished that there was a glass in his breast, that all the world might see what was in his heart. Integrity will be a sword to defend you, a staff to support you, a star to guide you, and a cordial to cheer you; and therefore, above all gettings get sincerity, and above all keepings keep sincerity, as your crown, your comfort, your life. But,

---

[1] Cicero had rather have no companion than a bad one.
[2] Clarke, as before, p. 187.—G.   [3] As before.—G.

5. The fifth word of comfort and counsel is this, *Be true to the light of your consciences, and maintain and keep up a constant tenderness in your consciences.* A tender conscience is a mercy more worth than a world. Conscience is God's spy in our bosoms: keep this clear and tender, and then all is well, Acts xxiv. 16; 2 Cor. i. 12. Act nothing against the dictates of conscience, rebel not against the light of conscience. You were better that all the world should upbraid you and reproach you, than that your consciences should upbraid you and reproach you, Job xxvii. 5, 6. Beware of stifling conscience, and of suppressing the warnings of conscience, lest a warning conscience prove a gnawing conscience, a tormenting conscience. The blind man in the Gospel, Mark viii., newly recovering his sight, imagined trees to be men: and the Burgundians, as Comines reports, expecting a battle, supposed long thistles to be lances. Thus men under guilt are apt to conceit every thistle a tree, and every tree a man, and every man a devil. Take heed of tongue-tied consciences; for when God shall untie these strings, and unmuzzle your consciences, conscience will then be heard, and ten concerts of music shall not drown her clamorous cries. Hearken to the voice of conscience, obey the voice of conscience, and when conscience shall whisper you in the ear, and tell you there is this and that amiss in the house, in the habit, in the heart, in the life, in the closet; don't say to conscience, Conscience be quiet, be still, make no noise now, I will hear thee in a more convenient season, Acts xxiv. 24, 25. The heathen orator could say, *A recta conscientia ne latum quidem unguem discedendum*, A man may not depart a hair's-breadth all his life long from the dictates of a good conscience.[1] Will not this heathen one day rise in judgment against those who daily crucify the light of their own consciences? But,

6. The sixth word of advice and counsel is this, *Make it the great business of your lives to make sure such things as will go with you beyond the grave.*[2] Riches and honours and offices, and all worldly grandeur, won't go with us beyond the grave. Saladin, a Turkish emperor—he was the first of that nation that conquered Jerusalem—lying at the point of death, after many glorious victories, commanded that a white sheet should be borne before him to his grave, upon the point of a spear, with this proclamation: 'These are the rich spoils which Saladin carrieth away with him, of all his triumphs and victories, of all his riches and realms that he had; now nothing at all is left for him to carry with him but this sheet.' It is with us in this world as it was in the Jewish fields and vineyards, pluck and eat they might what they would while they were there, but they might not pocket nor put up aught to carry with them, Deut. xxiii. 24, 25. Death, as a porter, stands at the gate, and strips men of all their worldly wealth and glory. Athenæus speaks of one that, at the hour of death, devoured many pieces of gold, and sewed the rest in his coat, commanding that they should be buried with him. Hermocrates, being loath that any man should enjoy his goods after him, made himself by will heir of his own goods. These muck-worms would fain live

[1] Cicero: in Offic.
[2] See my Treatise on Assurance, and there you will find how you may secure something that will go with you beyond the grave.—[Vol. ii., p. 301, *seq.*—G.]

still on this side Jordan; having made their gold their god, they
cannot think of parting with it. They would, if possible, carry the
world out of the world. But what saith the apostle? ' We brought
nothing with us into this world, and it is certain'—see how he asse-
vereth and assureth it, as if some rich wretches made question of it—
' we can carry nothing out,' nothing but a winding-sheet, 1 Tim. vi. 7.
Oh, how should this alarm us to make sure our calling and election,[1] to
make sure our interest in Christ, to make sure our covenant-relation, to
make sure a work of grace in power upon our souls, to make sure the
testimony of a good conscience, Gal. iv. 5-7, to make sure our sonship, our saintship, our heirship, &c., Rom. viii. 15, 16; for these are
the only things that will go with us into another world. In the
Marian persecution there was a woman who, being convened before
Bonner, then Bishop of London,[2] upon the trial of religion, he threatened
her that he would take away her husband from her. Saith she, Christ
is my husband. I will take away thy child. Christ, saith she, is
better to me than ten sons. I will strip thee, saith he, of all thy outward comfort. Yea, but Christ is mine, saith she, and you cannot
strip me of him. Assurance that Christ was hers, and that he would
go with her beyond the grave, bore her heart up above the threats of
being spoiled of all, Heb. x. 34. When a great lord had shewed a
sober, serious, knowing Christian his riches, his stately habitation, his
pleasant gardens, his delightful walks, his rich grounds, and his
various sorts of pleasure, the serious Christian, turning himself to this
great lord, said: My lord, you had need to make sure Christ and
heaven, you had need make sure something that will go with you
beyond the grave, for else when you die you will be a very great loser.
O my friends, I must tell you, it highly concerns you to make
sure something that will go with you beyond the grave, or else you
will be very great losers when you come to die, God having given
you an abundance of the good things and of the great things of this
world, beyond what he has given to many thousands of others. But,

7. The seventh word of advice and counsel is this, *Look upon all
the things of this world, and value all the things of this world now,
as you will certainly look upon them and value them when you come
to lie upon a sick-bed, a dying-bed*, 1 Cor. vii. 29-31. When a
man is sick in good earnest, and when death knocks at the door in
good earnest, oh, with what a disdainful eye, with what a weaned eye,
with what a scornful eye does a man then look upon the honours,
riches, dignities, and glories of this world! If men could but thus
look upon them now, it would keep them from being fond of them,
from trusting in them, from doting upon them, from being proud of
them, and from venturing a damning either in getting or in keeping
of them. But,

8. The eighth word of advice and counsel is this, *In all places and
companies carry your soul-preservatives still about you*—viz., a holy
care, a holy fear, a holy jealousy, a holy watchfulness over your own
thoughts, hearts, words, and ways, Prov. iv. 23, and xxviii. 14; Gen.
vi. 9, and xxxix. 9, 10; Ps. xvii. 4, xviii. 23, and xxxix. 1, &c. You

---

[1] 2 Pet. i. 10; 2 Cor. v. 17; 2 Sam. xxiii. 5; 1 Thes. v. 23; 2 Cor. i. 12.
[2] Foxe's Acts and Monuments.

know that in infectious times men and women carry their several preservatives about them, that they may be kept from the infection of the times. Never were there more infectious times than now. Oh the snares, the baits, the infections that attend us at all times, in all places, in all companies, in all employments, and in all enjoyments, so that if we do not carry our soul-preservatives about us, we shall be in imminent danger of being infected with the pride, ill customs, and vanities of the times wherein we live. But,

9. The ninth word of advice and counsel is this, *Live not at uncertainties as to your spiritual and eternal estates.*[1] There are none so miserable as those that are strangers to the state of their own souls. It is good for a man to know the state of his flock, the state of his family, the state of the nation, the state of his body; but above all to know the state and condition of his own soul. How many thousands are there that can give a better account of their lands, their lordships, their riches, their crops, their shops, their trades, their merchandise, yea, of their hawks, their hounds, their misses, than they can of the estate of their own souls! O my friends, your souls are more worth than ten thousand worlds, Mat. xvi. 26, and therefore it must be the greatest prudence, and the choicest policy in the world, to secure their everlasting welfare, and to know how things stands between God and your souls, what you are worth for eternity, and how it is like to go with you in that other world. Whilst a Christian lives at uncertainties as to his spiritual and everlasting estate, as whether he has grace or no grace, or whether his grace be true or counterfeit, whether he has an interest in Christ or not, a work in power upon his soul or not, or whether God loves him or loathes him, whether he will bring him to heaven or throw him to hell—how can any Christian who lives at so great an uncertainty delight in God, rejoice evermore, triumph in Christ Jesus, be ready to suffer, and desirous to die? Job xxvii. 10; Phil. iv. 4; 2 Cor. ii. 14; Phil. i. 23. All men love to be at a certainty in all their outward concernments; and yet how many thousands are there that are at a marvellous uncertainty as to the present and future state of their precious and immortal souls! But,

10. The tenth word of advice and counsel is this, *Set the highest Scripture examples and patterns before you, of grace and holiness, for your imitation,* 1 Cor. iv. 16. In the point of faith and obedience set an Abraham before you, Gen. xii. and xxii.; in the point of meekness set a Moses before you, Num. xii. 3; in the point of courage set a Joshua before you, Josh. i.; in the point of uprightness set a David before you, Ps. xviii. 23; in the point of zeal set a Phinehas before you; and in the point of patience set a Job before you. Make Christ your main pattern, ' Be ye followers of me, as I am of Christ,' James v. 11, 12, and 1 Cor. xi. 1. And next to him set the patterns of the choicest saints before you for your imitation.[2] The nearer you come to those blessed copies that they have set before you, the more will be your joy and comfort, and the more God will be honoured, Christ

---

[1] See my ' Box of Precious Ointment.' In that glass you may read the state of your souls.—[Vol. iii. p. 233, *seq.*—G.]

[2] *Præcepta docent, exempla movent,* Precepts may instruct, but examples do persuade.—[As before.—G.]

exalted, the Spirit pleased, religion adorned, the mouths of sinners stopped, and the hearts of saints rejoiced. He that shooteth at the sun, though he shoot far short, yet will shoot higher than he that aimeth at a shrub. It is safest, it is best, to eye the highest and worthiest examples. Examples are, (1.) More awakening than precepts; (2.) More convincing than precepts; (3.) More encouraging than precepts, Heb. xi. 8; and that because in them we see that the exercise of godliness, though difficult, yet is possible; when we see men subject to like passions with ourselves to be so and so mortified, self-denying, humble, holy, &c.; what should hinder but that it may be so with us also? Such as begin to work with the needle, look much on their sampler and pattern: it is so in learning to write, and indeed in learning to live also. Observe the gracious conversations and carriages of the choicest saints, keep a fixed eye upon the wise, prudent, humble, holy, and heavenly deportment; write after the fairest copy you can find, labour to imitate those Christians that are most eminent in grace. I shall conclude this head with that of the heathen: *Optimum est majorum sequi vestigia, si rectè præcesserint*, It is best to tread in the steps of those who are gone in a safe and good way before us, [Seneca.] But,

11. The eleventh word of advice and counsel is this, *Be much in the most spiritual exercises of religion.* There are external exercises, such as hearing, praying, singing, receiving, holy conference, &c., Isa. i. 11–14, and 1 Tim. iv. 8, and Mat. vi. Now custom, conviction, education, and a hundred other external considerations, may lead persons to these external exercises: but then there are the more spiritual exercises of religion, such as loving of God, delighting in God, prizing of Christ, compliance with the motions, counsels, and dictates of the Spirit, living in an exercise of grace, triumphing in Christ Jesus, setting our affections upon things above, meditation, self-examination, self-judging, &c. Now the more you live in the exercise of these more spiritual duties of religion, the more you glorify God—the more you evidence the power of grace, and the in-dwellings of the Spirit—and the more you difference and distinguish yourselves from hypocrites and all unsound professors, and the better foundation you lay for a bright, strong, and growing assurance. But,

12. The twelfth and last word of advice and counsel I shall give you is, *To make a wise, a seasonable, a sincere, a daily, and a thorough improvement of all the talents that God has intrusted you with.* There is a talent of time, of power, of riches, of honour, of greatness, that some are more intrusted with than others are. The improvement of these is your great wisdom, and should be your daily works, 1 Cor iv. 1, 2. You know you are but stewards, and that you must shortly give an account of your stewardship, Luke xvi. 1–4. And oh that you may make such a faithful and full improvement of all the great talents that God has intrusted you with, that you may give up your account at last with joy, and not with grief! Some princes have wished upon their beds that they had never reigned, because they have not improved their power for God and his people, but against God and his people; and some rich men have wished that they had never been rich, because they have not improved their riches for the glory of God, nor for the

succour and relief of his suffering saints. A beggar upon the way asked something of an honourable lady: she gave him sixpence, saying, This is more than ever God gave me. Oh! says the beggar, Madam, you have abundance, and God hath given you all that you have; say not so, good madam. Well, says she, I speak the truth, for God hath not given but lent unto me what I have, that I may bestow it upon such as thou art. And it is very true, indeed, that poor Christians are Christ's alms-men, and the rich are but his stewards, into whose hands God hath put his moneys, to distribute to them as their necessities require. It is credibly reported of Mr Thomas Sutton, the sole founder of that eminent hospital commonly known by his name, that he used often to repair into a private garden, where he poured forth his prayers unto God, and, amongst other passages, was frequently overheard to use this expression: Lord, thou hast given me a liberal and large estate, give me also a heart to make good use of it; which was granted to him accordingly.[1] Riches are a great blessing, but a heart to use them aright is a far greater blessing. Every rich man is not so much a treasurer as a steward, whose praise is more how to lay out well than to have received much. I know I have transgressed the bounds of an epistle, but love to your souls, and theirs into whose hands this treatise may fall, must be my apology.

Sir, if you and your lady were both my own children, and my only children, I could not give you better nor more faithful counsel than what I have given you in this epistle; and all out of a sincere, serious, and cordial desire and design, that both of you may be happy here, and found at Christ's right hand in the great day of account, Mat. xxv. 33, 34.

Now the God of all grace fill both your hearts with all the fruits of righteousness and holiness, and greatly bless you both with all spiritual blessings in heavenly places, and make you meet-helps to each other heaven-ward, and at last crown you both with ineffable glory in the life to come. 1 Pet. v. 1; Gal. v. 22, 23; Eph. i. 3.

So I take leave, and rest your assured friend, and soul's servant,

THOMAS BROOKS.

---

[1] Fuller's Church History of Britain. [The founder of the Charter-house, London.—G.]

THE COVENANT OF GRACE PROVED
AND OPENED.

BELOVED IN OUR LORD,—In the first part of my Golden Key, I have shewed you seven several pleas, that all sincere Christians may form up, as to those several scriptures in the Old and New Testament, that refer either to the great day of account, or to their particular days of account. In this second part, I shall go on where I left, and shew you several other choice pleas, that all believers may make in the present case.

VIII. The eighth plea that a believer may form up as to the ten scriptures in the margin,[1] that refer to the great day of account, or to a man's particular account, may be drawn up from *the consideration of the covenant of grace, or the new covenant that all believers are under.* It is of high concernment to understand the tenure of the covenant of grace, or the new covenant, which is the law you must judge of your estates by, for if you mistake in that you will err in the conclusion. That person is very unfit to make a judge, who is ignorant of the law, by which himself and others must be tried. For the clearing of my way, let me premise these six things :—

1. First, Premise this with me, that *God hath commonly dealt with man in the way of a covenant ;* that being a way that is most suitable to man, and most honourable for man, and the most amicable and friendly way of dealing with man. No sooner was man made, but God entered into covenant with him, ' In the day thou eatest thereof, thou shalt die the death,' Gen. ii. 17; and after this, he made a covenant with the world, by Noah, Gen. ix. 11–15, and vi. 18; and after this, he made a covenant with Abraham, Gen. xvii. 1, 2; and after this, he made a covenant with the Jews at Mount Sinai, Exod. xix. Thus you see that God has commonly dealt with man in the way of a covenant. But,

2. Secondly, Premise this with me, *All men are under some covenant or other ;* they are either under a covenant of works, or they are under a covenant of grace. All persons that live and die without an interest in Christ, they live and die under a covenant of works ; such as live and die with an interest in Christ, they live and die under a

---

[1] Eccles. xi. 9, and xii. 14 ; Mat. xii. 14, and xviii. 23 ; Luke xvi. 2 ; Rom. xiv. 10 ; 2 Cor. v. 10 ; Heb. ix. 27, and xiii. 17 ; 1 Pet. iv. 5.

covenant of grace. There is but a twofold standing taken notice of in the blessed Scriptures; the one is under the law, the other is under grace. Now he that is not under grace, is under the law, Rom vi. 14. It is true, in the Scripture you do not read, *in totidem syllabis*, of the covenant of works and the covenant of grace; but that of the apostle comes near it: Rom. iii. 27, 'Where is boasting then? It is excluded. By what law? of works? Nay, but by the law of faith.' [1] Here you have the law of works, opposed to the law of faith; which holds out as much as the covenant of works and the covenant of grace. The apostle sets forth this twofold condition of men, by a very pertinent resemblance, namely, by that of marriage, Rom. vii. 1–3. All Adam's seed are married to one of these two husbands; either to the law, or to Christ. He that is not spiritually married to Christ, and so brought under his covenant, is still under the law as a covenant of works; even as a wife is under the law of her husband while he is yet alive. Certainly there were never any but two covenants made with man, the one legal, the other evangelical; the one of works, the other of grace; the first in innocency, the other after the fall: ponder upon Rom. iv. 13. But,

3. Thirdly, Let me premise this, that *the covenant of grace was so legally dispensed to the Jews, that it seems to be nothing else but the repetition of the covenant of works;* in respect of which legal dispensations of it, the same covenant, under the law, is called a covenant of works; under the gospel, in regard of the clearer manifestation of it, it is called a covenant of grace: but these were not two distinct covenants, but one and the same covenant diversely dispensed. The covenant of grace is the same for substance now to us since Christ was exhibited, as it was to the Jews before he was exhibited; but the manner of administration of it is different, because it is:—(1.) Now clearer: things were declared then in types and shadows, heaven was then typed out by the land of Canaan, but now we have things more plainly manifested, 2 Cor. iii. 12; Heb. vii. 22. In this respect it is called ' a better testament or covenant,' Heb. viii. 6; not in substance, but in the manner of revealing it; and the promises are said to be ' better promises' upon the same account, Acts x. 35. (2.) The covenant of grace, is now more largely extended; then it extended only to the Jews, but now to all that know the Lord, and that choose him, fear him, love him, and serve him in all nations, Col. iii. 11; Neh. vii. 2; Job i. 1, 8; Acts xiii. 22, *seq.;* Rom. iv. 18–20. (3.) There is more abundance of the Spirit, of grace, of light, of knowledge, of holiness, poured out generally upon the people of God now, than there was in those times. Though then some few eminent saints had much of the Spirit, and much of grace and holiness, both in their hearts and lives; but now the generality of the saints have more of the Spirit, and more grace and holiness, than the generality of the saints had in those times. But,

4. Fourthly, Premise this with me, that *a right notion of the covenant, according to the originals of the Old and New Testament, will*

---

[1] I am not of Cameron's mind, that there were three covenants; but of the apostle's mind, who expressly tells us that there are two testaments, and no more, in that Gal. iv. 24.

conduce much to a right understanding of God's covenant.[1] The derivation of the Hebrew word, and of the Greek, may give us great light,
and is of special use to shew the nature of the covenant which they
principally signify, and what special things are therein required.   (1.)
The Hebrew word, ברית, *Berith,* a covenant, is by learned men derived from several roots:

[1.] First, Some derive it from ברר, *Barar,* to purify, make clear,
and to purge out dross, chaff, and all uncleanness; and to select,
and choose out, and separate the pure from the impure, the gold
and silver from the dross, and the pure wheat from the chaff.
The reasons of this derivation are these two :—(1.) Because by covenants open and clear amity is confirmed, and faithfulness is plainly
and clearly declared and ratified, without deceit or sophistication,
betwixt covenanters ; and things are made plain and clear betwixt
them in every point and article.   (2.) Because God, in the covenant of works, did choose out man especially, with whom he made
the covenant; and because in the covenant of grace he chooseth
out of the multitude his elect, even his church and faithful people,
whom he did separate by predestination and election from all eternity,
to be a holy people to himself in Christ, Eph. i. 4. (3.) Some derive
it from ברה, and verily, the Lord, when he makes a covenant with
any, he doth separate them from others, he looks on them, and takes
them, and owns them for his ' peculiar people,' 1 Pet. ii. 9, for his
' peculiar treasure,' Exod. xix. 5, and agrees with them as the chosen
and choicest of all others.   The first staff in Zech. xi. 10, is called
' Beauty,' and this was the covenant ; and certainly it must be a high
honour for a people to be in covenant with God ; for by this means
God becomes ours, and we are made nigh unto him, Jer. xxxi. 38, 40, 41.
He is ours, and we are his, in a very peculiar way of relation ; and by
this means God opens his love and all his treasures of grace unto us.
In his covenant he tells us of his special care, love, kindness, and great
intentions of good to us; and by this means his faithfulness comes to
be obliged to make good all his covenant relations and engagements
to us, Deut. vii. 9.   Now in all this God puts a great favour and
honour upon his people.   Hence, when the Lord told Abraham that
he would make a covenant with him, Abraham fell upon his face ; he
was amazed at so great a love and honour, Gen. xvii. 2, 3.

[2.] Secondly, Some derive the word from ברה, *Barah, comedit,* to
eat, because usually they had a feast at the making of covenants.   In
the Eastern countries they commonly established their covenants by
eating and drinking together.   Herodotus tells us that the Persians
were wont to contract leagues and friendship, *inter vinum et epulas,*
in a full feast, whereat their wives, children, and friends, were present.
The like, Tacitus reports of the Germans.   Amongst the Greeks and
other nations, the covenanters ate bread and salt together.   The
Emperor of Russia, at this day, when he would shew extraordinary

---

[1] The word *covenant* in our English tongue, signifies, as we all know, a mutual promise,
bargain, and obligation, between two persons ; and so likewise doth the Hebrew *Berith,*
and the Greek διαθηκη.   A covenant is a solemn compact or agreement between two
chosen parties, or more ; whereby, with mutual, free, and full consent, they bind and
oblige themselves one to another. A covenant is *Amicus status inter fœderatos :* so Martin
[Luther?] ' A friendly state between allies.'

grace and favour unto any, sends him bread and salt from his
table ; and when he invited Baron Sigismund, the Emperor Ferdin-
and's ambassador, he did it in this form : *Sigismunde, comedes sal
et panem nostrum nobiscum :* Sigismund, you shall eat our bread
and salt with us. Hence that symbol of Pythagoras, Ἄρτον μὴ
καταγνύειν, ' break no bread,' is interpreted by Erasmus and others to
mean, ' break no friendship.' [1] Moreover, the Egyptians, Thracians,
and Lybians in special, are said to have used to make leagues, and
contract friendship, by presenting a cup of wine one to another ; which
custom we find still in use amongst our western nations.   It has been
the universal custom of mankind, and still remains in use, to contract
covenants, and make leagues and friendship, by eating and drinking
together.   When Isaac made a covenant with Abimelech, the king of
Gerar, the text saith, ' He made him, and those that were with him,
a feast ; and they did eat and drink, and rose up betimes in the morning, and sware one to another,' Gen. xxvi. 30, 31.   When Jacob
made a covenant with Laban, after they had sworn together, he
made him a feast, ' and called his brethren to eat bread,' saith the
text, Gen. xxxi. 54.   When David made a league with Abner, upon
his promise of bringing all Israel unto him, David made ' Abner and
the men that were with him a feast,' saith the text, 2 Sam. iii. 20.
Hence, in the Hebrew tongue a covenant is called ברית, *Berith*, of
ברה, *Barah*, to eat, as if they should say an eating ; which derivation
is so natural, that it deserves, say some, to be preferred before that,
from the other signification of the same verb, which is to choose ; of
which before.   Now they that derive *Berith* from *Barah*, which signifies to eat and refresh one's self with meat, they give this reason for
that derivation, viz., because the old covenant of God, made with man
in the creation, was a covenant wherein the condition or law was about
eating ; that man should eat of all the trees and fruits, except of the
tree of knowledge of good and evil, Gen. ii. 16, 17 ; and in the solemn
making and sealing of the covenant of grace in Christ, the blessed
seed, the public ceremony was slaying and sacrificing of beasts, and
eating some part of them, after the fat and the choice parts were
offered up and burned on the altar.   For God, by virtue of that covenant, gave man leave to eat the flesh of beasts, Deut. xii. 27, which
he might not do in the state of innocency, Gen. i. 29, being limited to
fruits of trees, and herbs bearing seed, for his meat.   So, also, in
solemn covenants between men, the parties were wont to eat together,
Gen. xxxi. 46.

[3.] Thirdly, Others derive the word *Berith* from ברא, *Bara*, or
ברה, *Barah*, to smite, strike, cut, or divide, as both these words signify.
The word also signifies to elect or choose ; and the reasons they give
for this derivation, are these two :—*First*, Because covenants are not
made, but by choice persons, chosen one by another, and about
choice matters, and upon choice conditions, chosen out, and agreed
upon by both parties.   *Secondly*, Because, in making of covenants,
commonly sacrifices were stricken and slain, for confirmation and
solemnity.   Of old, God sealed his covenants by sacrifices of beasts
slain, divided, and cut asunder, and the choice fat, and other parts,

[1] Vide Turcium ritum opud Busbequium, epist. i. 11.

offered upon the altar. And in making of great and solemn covenants, men, in old time, were wont to kill and cut asunder sacrificed
beasts; and to pass between the parts divided, for a solemn testimony,
or for the confirmation of the covenants that they had made, Gen. xv.
9, 10, 17.[1] And as, learned men have long since observed, that the
very heathen, in their covenanting, used sacrifices, and divided them,
passing between the parts; and this they did, as some conjecture, in
imitation of God's people. This third is the common opinion, about
the original of this name; and therefore preferred before all other.
So this word ברית, Berith, covenant, seems to sound as much as
כרית, Kerith, a smiting or striking, because of sacrifices slain in covenanting. Hence the word covenant is often joined with כרת, Karath,
which signifies striking of covenant. An example of this beyond all
exception, saith my author,[2] is in that sacrifice, wherein God by
Moses, made a covenant with all the people of Israel, and bound them
to obey his law: the description of it is in Exod. xxiv. 4–8, ' And
Moses wrote all the words of the Lord, and rose up early in the morning and builded an altar under the hill, and twelve pillars, according to
the twelve tribes of Israel. And he sent young men of the children
of Israel, which offered burnt-offerings, and sacrificed peace-offerings
of oxen unto the Lord. And Moses took half of the blood, and put it
in basins; and half of the blood he sprinkled on the altar. And he
took the book of the covenant and read it in the audience of the
people; and they said, All that the Lord hath said will we do, and be
obedient. And Moses took the blood, and sprinkled it on the people,
and said, Behold the blood of the covenant, which the Lord hath made
with you concerning all these words.'[3] I shall not trouble my reader
with that mystical and too curious a sense, that some of the ancients
put upon these words:[4] the historical sense is here more fit: for in this
ceremony of dividing the blood in two parts, and so besprinkling the
altar with the one half, which represented God; and the people with
the other, between whom the covenant was confirmed, the old use
in striking of covenants is observed. For the ancient custom was,
that they which made a league or covenant, divided some beasts, and
put the parts asunder, walking in the midst; signifying that as the
beast was divided, so they should be which brake the covenant. So
when Saul went against the Ammonites, coming out of the field, he
hewed two oxen, and sent them into all the coasts of Israel, 1 Sam.
xi. 7; expressing the like signification, that so should his oxen be served
that came not forth after Saul and Samuel. After the same manner,
when God made a covenant with Abraham, Gen. xv. 12–19, and he had
divided certain beasts, as God had commanded him, and laid one part
against another, a smoking firebrand went between, representing
God, signifying, that so he should be divided, which violated the covenant. So in this place, not much unlike; the blood is parted in twain,
shewing that so should his blood be shed, which kept not the covenant.

[1] Jer. xxxiv. 18–20, and Lev. xxvi. 25. Weigh well these two scriptures. Covenant breakers may well look upon them as flaming swords, as terrible thunderbolts.
[2] And. Rivetus in Gen. xxxi; Exercitat 135. [Misprinted ' Riven.'—G.]
[3] Anciently covenants were made with blood, to betoken constancy in the covenant,
even to the shedding of blood, and loss of life.
[4] Rupertus, Ambrose, Cajetan, &c.

[4.] Fourthly, Some derive the word *Berith* from ברא, *Bara*, to create; and the reason they give for this derivation is this, because the first state of creation was confirmed by the covenant which God made with man, and all creatures were to be upheld by means of observing of the law and condition of the covenant; and that covenant being broken by man, the world, made subject to ruin, is upheld, yea, and as it were created anew, by the covenant of grace in Christ.

[5.] Fifthly, Some derive the word *Berith* from ברת, *Berath*, which signifies firmness, sureness, because covenants are firm and sure, and all things agreed on are confirmed and made sure by them. God's covenant is a sure covenant: Deut. vii. 9, ' The Lord thy God, he is the faithful God,' or the God of Amen, ' which keepeth covenant with them that love him:' Ps. lxxxix. 34, ' My covenant will I not break '—Hebrew, ' I will not profane,' ' nor alter the thing that is gone out of my lips.'[1]   All God's precepts, all God's predictions, all God's menaces, and all God's promises, are the issue of a most just, faithful, and righteous will.   There are three things that God cannot do:—(1.) He cannot die. (2.) He cannot lie: Titus i. 2, ' In hope of eternal life, which God, that cannot lie, promised before the world began.' (3.) He cannot deny himself.   Now the derivation of *Berith*, from the several roots specified, and not from one only, doth give much light to the point under consideration; and doth reconcile in one, all the several opinions of the learned, and justifies their several derivations, without rejecting or offering any wrong or disgrace to any.

(2.) Secondly, The Greek name Διαθήκη, *Diatheke*, a covenant or a testament.   By this Greek word the Septuagint, in their Greek translation, do commonly express the Hebrew word *Berith;* and it is observable that this is the only word by which the Hebrew word *Berith* is rendered in the New Testament.   This Greek word, Διαθήκη, is translated *covenant* in the New Testament about twenty times; and the same word is translated *testament* in the New Testament about twelve times.[2]   Wherever you find the word *covenant* in the New Testament, there you shall find *Diatheke;* and wherever you find the word *testament* in the New Testament, there you shall find *Diatheke;* so that it is of importance for us to understand this word aright. Now this Greek word, Διαθήκη, is derived from Διατίθημι, *Diatithemi*, which hath divers of the significations of the Hebrew words of which *Berith* is derived; for it signifies to set things in order and frame, to appoint orders, and make laws, to pacify and make satisfaction, and to dispose things by one's last will and testament.   Now to compose and set things in order is to uphold the creation; to walk by orders and laws made and appointed is to walk by rule, and to live, to deal plainly and faithfully without deceit.   To pacify and make satisfaction includes sacrifices and sin-offerings.   To dispose by will and testament implies choice of persons and gifts; for men do commonly by will give their best and most choice things to their most dear and most choice friends.   Thus the Greek which the apostles use in the New Testament to signify a covenant, to express the Hebrew

[1] Jer. xxxi. 31, 33, 35-37; Ps. xix. 7; Rev. iii. 14; Isa. liv. 10.
[2] Heb. viii. 6-10, and i. 4; Luke i. 72 ; Rom. ix. 4, &c.; Mat. xxvi. 28; Luke xxii. 20, &c.

word *Berith,* which is used in the law and the prophets, doth confirm our derivation of it from all the words before named. And this derivation of the Hebrew and Greek names of a covenant being thus laid down, and confirmed by the reasons formerly cited, is of great use. The various acceptation and use of these two names in the Old and New Testament is very considerable for the opening of the covenant: *First,* To shew unto us the full signification of the word *covenant,* and what the nature of a covenant is in general. *Second,* To justify the divers acceptations of the word, and to shew the nature of every word in particular, and so to make way for the knowledge of the agreement and difference between the old and new covenant. Here, as in a crystal glass, you may see that this word *Berith,* and this word *Diatheke,* signify all covenants in general, whether they are religious or civil; for there is nothing in any true covenant which is not comprised in the signification of these words, being expounded according to the former derivations. Here also we may see what is the nature of a covenant in general, and what things are thereunto required; as, *first,* every true covenant presupposeth a division or separation; *secondly,* it comprehends in it a mutual promising and binding between two distinct parties; *thirdly,* there must be faithful dealing, without fraud, or dissembling on both sides; *fourthly,* this must be between choice persons; *·fifthly,* it must be about choice matters and upon choice conditions, agreed upon by both; *sixthly* and lastly, it must tend to the well-ordering and composing of things between them. Now all these are manifest by the several significations of the words from which *Berith* and *Diatheke* are derived. And thus much for the word *covenant* according to the originals of the Old and New Testament.

5. Fifthly, Premise this with me, that there was *a covenant of works, or a reciprocal covenant, betwixt God and Adam, together with all his posterity.* Before Adam fell from his primitive holiness, beauty, glory, and excellency, God made a covenant with Adam as a public person, which represented all mankind. The covenant of works was made with all men in Adam, who was made and stood as a public person, head and root, in a common and comprehensive capacity. I say, it was made with him as such, and we all in him; he and all stood and fell together. (1.) Witness the imputation of Adam's sin to all mankind: Rom. v. 12, ' In whom,' or forasmuch as, ' all have sinned;' they sinned not all in themselves, therefore in Adam; see ver. 14, ' In him all died.' (2.) Witness the curse of the covenant that all mankind are directly under; consult the scriptures in the margin.[1] Those on whom the curse of the covenant comes, those are under the bond and precept of the covenant. But all mankind are under the curse of the covenant, and therefore all mankind are under the bond and precept of the covenant. Adam did understand the terms of the covenant, and did consent to the terms of the covenant; for God dealt with him in a rational way, and expected from him a reasonable service. The end of this covenant was the upholding of the creation, and of all the creatures in their pure natural estate, for the comfort of man continually, and for the special manifestation of God's free grace;

[1] 1 Cor. xv. 47; Deut. xxix. 21; Rom. viii. 20, 21; Gal. iii. 10, 13.

and that he might put the greater obligation upon Adam to obey his Creator and to sweeten his authority to man; and that he might draw out Adam to an exercise of his faith, love, and hope in his Creator; and that he might leave Adam the more inexcusable in case he should sin; and that so a clear way might be made for God's justification and man's conviction. Upon these grounds God dealt with Adam, not only in a way of sovereignty, but in a way of covenant.

Quest. But how may it be evidenced that God entered into a covenant of works with the first Adam before his fall, there being no mention of such a covenant in the Scripture that we read of?

Ans. Though the name be not in the Scripture, yet the thing is in the Scripture, as will evidently appear by comparing scripture with scripture.[1] Though it be not positively and plainly said in the blessed Scripture that God made a covenant of works with Adam before his fall, yet, upon sundry scripture grounds and considerations, it may be sufficiently evidenced that God did make such a covenant with Adam before his fall; and therefore it is a nice cavil, and a foolish vanity, for any to make such a noise about the word covenant, and for want of the word covenant, boldly to conclude that there was no such covenant made with Adam, when the thing is lively set down in other words, though the word covenant be not expressed; and this I shall make evident by an induction of particulars, thus:—

[1.] First, God, to declare his sovereignty and man's subjection, gave Adam, though innocent, *a law*. God's express prescription of a positive law unto Adam in his innocent state, is clearly and fully laid down in that Gen. ii. 16, 17, 'And the Lord God commanded the man, saying, Of every tree of the garden thou mayest freely eat; but of the tree of the knowledge of good and evil, thou shalt not eat of it: for in the day that thou eatest thereof thou shalt surely die;' Hebrew, 'dying thou shalt die.' Mark how God bounds man's obedience with a double fence: *first*, He fenced him with a free indulgence to eat of every tree in the garden but one, the less cause he had to be liquorish after forbidden fruit; but 'stolen waters are sweet.' *Secondly*, By an exploratory[2] prohibition, upon pain of death. By the first, the Lord woos him by love; by the second, he frights him by the terror of his justice, and bids him touch and taste if he durst. The *fœderati* were God and Adam; God the Creator, and man, the creature, made 'after God's image and likeness;' and so not contrary to God, nor at enmity with him, but like unto God, though far different and inferior to God in nature and substance. Here are also terms agreed on, and matters covenanted reciprocally, by these parties. Adam, on his part, was to be obedient to God, in forbearing to eat of the tree of knowledge only. God's charge to our first parents was only negative, not to eat of the tree of knowledge; the other, to eat of the trees, was left unto their

[1] Socinians call for the word 'Satisfaction,' others call for the word 'Sacrament,' others call for the word 'Trinity,' and others call for the word 'Sabbath,' for Lord's day, &c.; and thence conclude against Satisfaction, Sacraments, Trinity, Sabbath, for want of express words, when the things themselves are plainly and lively set down, in other words, in the blessed Scriptures; so it is in this case of God's covenant with Adam. The vanity and folly of such ways of reasoning is sufficiently demonstrated by all writers upon those subjects that are sound in the faith, &c.

[2] Qu. 'explanatory'?—G.

choice. Eve confesseth that God spake unto them both, and said, 'Ye shall not eat of it,' Gen. iii. 2; and God speaks unto both of them together in these words, 'Behold, I have given unto you every herb, and every tree,' &c., Gen. i. 19. At which time also it is very like that he gave them the other prohibition of not eating of that one tree; for if God had made that exception before, he would not have given a general permission after; or if this general grant had gone before, the exception coming should seem to abrogate the former grant. The Septuagint seem to be of this mind, that this precept was given both to Adam and Eve, reading thus in the plural number, 'In what day ye shall eat thereof ye shall die.' [1] And though, in the original, the precept be given in the name of Adam only, that is only (1.) Because Adam was the more principal, and he had the charge of the woman; and (2.) Because that the greatest danger was in his transgression, which was the cause of the ruin of his posterity; (3.) Because, as Mercerus well observes, Adam was the common name both of the man and woman, Gen. v. 2, and so is taken, ver. 15. And God, on his part, for the present, permits Adam to eat of all other trees of the garden; and for the future, in his explicit threatening of death in case of disobedience, implicitly promiseth life in case of obedience herein.

[2.] Secondly, *The promises of this covenant on God's part were very glorious—First,* That heaven, and earth, and all creatures should continue in their natural course and order wherein God had created and placed them, serving always for man's use, and that man should have the benefit and lordship of them all. *Secondly,* As for natural life, in respect of the body, Adam should have had perfection without defect, beauty without deformity, labour without weariness. *Thirdly,* As for spiritual life, Adam should never have known what it was to be under terrors and horrors of conscience, nor what a wounded spirit means, Prov. xviii. 14; he should never have found 'the arrows of the Almighty sticking fast in him, nor the poison thereof drinking up his spirits, nor the terrors of God to set themselves in array against him,' Job vi. 4; nor he should never have tasted of death. Death is a fall that came in by a fall. Had Adam never sinned, Adam had never died; had Adam stood fast in innocency, he should have been translated to glory without dissolution. Death came in by sin, and sin goeth out by death. As the worm kills the worm that bred it, so death kills sin that bred it. Now where there are parties covenanting, promising, and agreeing upon terms, and terms mutually agreed upon by those parties, as here, there is the substance of an express covenant, though it be not formally and in express words called a covenant. This was the first covenant which God made with man, and this is called by the name *Berith,* Jer. xxxiii. 20, where God saith, 'If you can break my covenant of the day and night, and that there shall not be day and night in their season,' ver. 21, 'then may also my covenant with David be broken.' In these words he speaks plainly of the promise in the creation, that day and night should keep their course, and the sun, moon, and stars, and all creatures, should serve for man's use, Gen. i. 14–16. Now though man did break the covenant on his part, yet God, being immutable, could not break covenant

---

[1] So doth Gregory read as the Septuagint does.—*Greg. Moral.* lib. **xxxv.** cap. 10.

on his part, neither did he suffer his promise to fail; but, by virtue of Christ promised to man in the new covenant, he will keep touch with man so long as mankind hath a being on the earth. In this first covenant, God promised unto man life and happiness, lordship over all the creatures, liberty to use them, and all other blessings which his heart could desire, to keep him in that happy estate wherein he was created. And man was bound to God to walk in perfect righteousness, to observe and keep God's commandments, and to obey his will in all things which were within the reach of his nature, and so far as was revealed to him. In the first covenant, God revealed himself to man as one God, Creator, and Governor of all things, infinite in power, wisdom, goodness, nature, and substance. God was man's good Lord, and man was God's good servant; God dearly loved man, and man greatly loved God with all his heart. There was not the least shadow or occasion of hatred or enmity between them; there was nothing but mutual love, mutual delight, mutual content, and mutual satisfaction between God and man. Man, in his primitive glory, needed no mediator to come between God and him. Man was perfect, pure, upright, and good, created after God's own image; and the nearer he came to God, the greater was his joy and comfort. God's presence now was man's great delight, and it was man's heaven on earth to walk with God. But,

[3.] Thirdly, Consider *the intention and use of the two eminent trees in the garden, that are mentioned in a more peculiar manner*—viz., the tree of life and the tree of knowledge. The intended use of these two trees in paradise was sacramental. Hence they are called *symbolical* trees, and *sacramental* trees, by learned writers, both ancient and modern. By these the Lord did signify and seal to our first parents that they should always enjoy that happy state of life in which they were made, upon condition of obedience to his commandments; *i.e.*, in eating of the tree of life, and not eating of the tree of knowledge.[1] The tree of life is so called, not because of any native property and peculiar virtue it had in itself to convey life, but symbolically, morally, and sacramentally. It was a sign and obligation to them of life, natural and spiritual, to be continued to them as long as they continued in obedience to God. The seal of the first covenant was the tree of life, which if Adam had received by taking and eating of it, whilst he stood in the state of innocency before his fall, he had certainly been established in that estate for ever; and the covenant being sealed and confirmed between God and him on both parts, he could not have been seduced and supplanted by Satan, as some learned men do think, and as God's own words seem to imply, Gen. iii. 22, 'And now, lest he put forth his hand, and take also of the tree of life, and eat, and live for ever.' 'The tree of knowledge of good and evil' was spoken from the sad event and experience they had of it, as Samson had of God's departing from him when he lost his Nazaritish hair by Delilah. 'The tree of life' was a sacrament of life; 'the tree of knowledge' a sacrament of death. 'The tree of life' was for confirmation of man's obe-

---

[1] The tree of life was the sign and seal which God gave to man for confirmation of this first covenant; and it was to man a sacrament and pledge of eternal life on earth and of all blessings needful to keep man in life.

dience, and 'the tree of knowledge' was for caution against disobedience. Now if those two trees were two sacraments, the one
assuring of life in case of obedience, the other assuring of death in case
of disobedience, then hence we may collect that God not only entered
into a covenant of works with the first Adam, but also gave him this
covenant under sacramental signs and seals. But,

[4.] Fourthly, Seriously consider that *a covenant of works lay clear,
in that commandment*, Gen. ii. 16, 17, which may thus be made evident:—(1.) Because that was the condition of man's standing and life,
as it was expressly declared; (2.) Because, in the breach of that commandment given him, he lost all, and we in him. God made the
covenant of works primarily with Adam, and with us in him, as our
head, inclusively; so that when he did fall we did fall, when he lost
all we lost all. There are five things we lost in our fall:—(1.) Our
holy image, and so became vile; (2.) Our sonship, and so became
slaves; (3.) Our friendship, and so became enemies; (4.) Our communion with God, and so became strangers; (5.) Our glory, and so
became miserable. Sin and death came into the world by Adam's
fall. In Adam's sinning we all sinned, and in Adam's dying we all
died; as you may see, by comparing the scriptures in the margin
together.[1] In Adam's first sin, we all became sinners by imputation:
Adam being a universal person, and all mankind one in him, by God's
covenant of works with him. *Omnes ille unus homo fuerunt*, All were
that one man, [Augustine,] viz., by federal consociation. God covenanted with Adam, and in him with all his posterity; and therefore
Adam's breach of covenant fell not only upon him, but upon all his
posterity. But,

[5.] Fifthly and lastly, We read of *a second covenant*, Heb. x. 9;
Rom. ix. 4; Gal. iv. 24; Eph. ii. 12, and we read of a ' new covenant:'
Jer. xxxi. 31, ' Behold the days come, saith the Lord, that I will make
a new covenant with the house of Israel, and with the house of Judah.'
So Heb. viii. 8, ' I will make a new covenant,' &c.; ver. 13, ' In that
he saith a new covenant, he hath made the first old,' &c.; chap. xii.
24, ' And to Jesus the mediator of the new covenant,' &c. Now if
there be a ' second covenant,' then we may safely conclude there was a
' first;' and if there be a ' new covenant,' then we may boldly conclude
that there was an ' old covenant.' A covenant of grace always sup-
poseth a covenant of works, Heb. viii. 7-9. I know there is a repetition
of the covenant of works with Adam, in the law of Moses; as in that
of the apostle to the Galatians, ' The law is not of faith, but the man
that doth these things, shall live in them,' Gal. iii. 10-12. The law
requires works, and promiseth no life to those that will be justified by
faith. In the first covenant, three things are observable:—(1.) The
precept, that ' continueth not in all things;' the precept requires perfect, personal, and perpetual obedience; (2.) The promise, ' live;'
' the man that doth them shall live;' live happily, blessedly, cheerfully, everlastingly; (3.) The curse in case of transgression, ' Cursed
is every one that continueth not in all things which are written in the
book of the law, to do them.' One sin, and that but in thought, broke
the angels' covenant, and hath brought them into everlasting chains,

[1] 1 Cor. xv. 22; Rom. v. 12 to the end, &c.

Jude 6. So the same apostle to the Romans further tells us, that 'Moses describeth the righteousness which is of the law, that the man that doth those things shall live by them,' Rom. x. 5. Thus it was with Adam, principally and properly, therefore he was under a covenant of works, when God gave him that command, Gen. ii. 16, 17. This first covenant is called a covenant of works, because this covenant required working on our part as the condition of it, for justification and happiness, 'The man that doth these things shall live.' Under this covenant God left man to stand upon his own bottom, and to live upon his own stock, and by his own industry. God made him perfect and upright, and gave him power and ability to stand, and laid no necessity at all upon him to fall. In this first covenant of works, man had no need of a mediator, God did then stipulate with Adam immediately; for seeing he had not made God his enemy by sin, he needed no daysman to make friendly intercession for him, Job ix. 33.

Adam was invested and endowed with righteousness and holiness in his first glorious estate; with righteousness, that he might carry it fairly, justly, evenly, and righteously towards man; and with holiness, that he might carry it wisely, lovingly, reverentially, and holily towards God, and that he might take up in God as his chiefest good, as in his great all.[1] I shall not now stand upon the discovery of Adam's beauty, authority, dominion, dignity, honour, and glory, with which he was adorned, invested, and crowned in innocency. Let this satisfy, that Adam's first estate was a state of perfect knowledge, wisdom, and understanding; it was a perfect state of holiness, righteousness, and happiness. There was nothing within him but what was desirable and delectable; there was nothing without him but what was amiable and commendable; nor nothing about him but what was serviceable and comfortable. Adam, in his innocent estate, was the wonder of all understanding, the mirror of wisdom and knowledge, the image of God, the delight of heaven, the glory of the creation, the world's great lord, and the Lord's great darling. Upon all these accounts, he had no need of a mediator. And let thus much suffice to have spoken concerning the first covenant of works, that was between God and Adam in innocency. But,

6. Sixthly, Premise this with me—viz., that there is *a new covenant, a second covenant, or a covenant of grace betwixt God and his people*, Heb. viii. 6-13. Express scriptures prove this: Deut. vii. 9, 'Know therefore, that the Lord thy God, he is God; the faithful God, which keepeth covenant and mercy with them that love him, and keep his commandments, to a thousand generations;' 2 Sam. xxiii. 5, 'Although my house be not so with God, yet he hath made with me an everlasting covenant, ordered in all things, and sure: for this is all my salvation, and all my desire; although he make it not to grow;'[2] Neh. i. 5, 'I beseech thee, O Lord God of heaven, the great and terrible God; that keepeth covenant and mercy for them that love him, and keep his commandments;' Isa. liv. 10, 'For the mountains shall depart, and the hills be removed; but my kindness shall not

---

[1] Eph. iv. 22–24. In this scripture, the apostle speaks plainly of the renovation of that knowledge, holiness, and righteousness that Adam sometimes had, but lost it by his fall, Ps. viii. 4–6; Gen. ii. 20.

[2] See this, 2 Sam. xxiii. 5, opened in my 'Box of Precious Ointments,' pp. 369–374. [Vol. iii. p. 491, *seq.*—G.]

depart from thee, neither shall the covenant of my peace be removed, saith the Lord, that hath mercy on thee;' Jer. xxxii. 40, ' And I will make an everlasting covenant with them, that I will not turn away from them, to do them good; but I will put my fear in their hearts, that they shall not depart from me;' Ezek. xx. 37, ' And I will cause you to pass under the rod, and I will bring you into the bond of the covenant;' Deut. xxix. 12, ' That thou shouldest enter into covenant with the Lord thy God; and into his oath, which the Lord thy God maketh with thee to-day.' Consult the scriptures in the margin also, for they cannot be applied to Christ, but to us.[1] But for the further evidencing of that covenant that is between the Lord and his people —now that there is a covenant betwixt God and his people may be further evinced by unanswerable arguments—let me point at some among many.

[1.] First, *Christ is said to be ' the mediator of this covenant:'* Heb. ix. 15, ' And for this cause he is the mediator of the new testament, that by means of death, for the redemption of the transgressions that were under the first testament, they which are called might receive the promise of eternal inheritance.' Certainly that covenant, of which Christ is the testator, must needs be a covenant made with us; for else, if the covenant were made only with Christ, as some would have it, then it will roundly follow that Jesus Christ is both testator and the party to whom the testaments and legacies are bequeathed; which sounds harsh, yea, which to assert is very absurd. Since the creation of the world, was it ever known that ever any man did bequeath a testament and legacies to himself? Surely no. Christ is the testator of the new covenant, and therefore we may safely conclude that the new covenant is made with us. The office of mediator, you know, is to stand betwixt two at variance. The two at variance were God and man. Man had offended and incensed God against him. God's wrath was an insupportable burden, and a consuming fire; no creature was able to stand under it, or before it. Therefore Christ, to rescue and redeem man, becomes a mediator. Christ, undertaking to be a mediator, both procured a covenant to pass betwixt God and man, and also engaged himself for the performance thereof on both parts; and to assure man of partaking of the benefit of God's covenant, Christ turns the covenant into a testament, that the conditions of the covenant, on God's part, might be as so many legacies, which, being confirmed by the death of the testator, none might disannul: Heb. viii. 6, ' He is the mediator of a better covenant, which was established upon better promises.' The promises of the new covenant are said to be better in these six respects:—(1.) All the promises of the law were conditional; ' Do this, and thou shalt live.' The promises of the new covenant are absolute, of grace, as well as to grace. (2.) In this better covenant God promiseth higher things. Here God promiseth Himself, his Son, his Spirit, a higher righteousness and a higher sonship. (3.) Because of their stability; those of the old covenant were ' swallowed up in the curse.' These are the ' sure mercies of David.' (4.) They are all bottomed upon faith, they

[1] Deut. iv. 23; Isa. lv. 1–3; Jer. xxiv. 7, xxx. 22, xxxi. 31, 33, and xxxii. 38; Heb. viii. 8–10.

all depend upon faith.[1]   (5.) They are all promised upon our interest in Christ.   This makes the promises sweet, because they lead us to Christ, the fountain of them, whose mouth is most sweet, and in whose person all the sweets of all created beings do centre.   (6.) Because God hath promised to pour out a greater measure of his Spirit, under the new covenant, than he did under the old covenant: Heb. xii. 24, 'And to Jesus, the mediator of the new covenant.'   Thus you see that Christ is called ' the mediator of the covenant' three several times.   Now he could not be the mediator of that covenant that is betwixt God and himself, of which more shortly, but of that covenant that is betwixt God and his people.   But,

[2.] Secondly, *The people of God have pleaded the covenant that is betwixt God and them:* 'Remember thy covenant.'   Now how could they plead the covenant betwixt God and them if there were no such covenant ?   See the scriptures in the margin.[2]   But,

[3.] Thirdly, *God is often said to remember his covenant:*[3] Gen. ix. 15, 'I will remember my covenant, which is between you and me ;' Exod. vi. 5, 'I have remembered my covenant ;' Lev. xxvi. 42, 'I remember my covenant with Jacob, and also my covenant with Isaac, and also my covenant with Abraham will I remember ;' Ezek. xvi. 60, ' I will remember my covenant with thee, and I will establish unto thee an everlasting covenant.'   Now how can God be said to remember his covenant with his people, if there were no covenant betwixt God and them ?   But,

[4.] Fourthly, *The temporal and spiritual deliverances that you have by the covenant do clearly evidence that there is a covenant betwixt God and you:* Zech. ix. 11, ' As for thee also, by the blood of thy covenant, I have sent forth thy prisoners out of the pit, wherein there was no water.'[4]   These words include both temporal and spiritual deliverances.   So that now, if there be not a covenant betwixt God and you, what deliverances can you expect, seeing they all flow in upon the creature by virtue of the covenant, and according to the covenant ? By the blood of the covenant believers are delivered from the infernal pit, where there is not so much water as might cool Dives his tongue, Luke xvi. 24, 25 ; and by the blood of the covenant they are delivered from those deaths and dangers that do surround them, 2 Cor. i. 8–10. When sincere Christians fall into desperate distresses and most deadly dangers, yet they are prisoners of hope, and may look for deliverance by the blood of the covenant.   This does sufficiently evince a covenant betwixt God and his people.   But,

[5.] Fifthly, *God has threatened severely to avenge and punish the quarrel of his covenant:* Lev. xxvi. 25, ' And I will bring a sword upon you, that shall avenge the quarrel of my covenant ;' or which shall avenge the vengeance of the covenant, &c.   Consult the scriptures in the margin.[5]   Breach of covenant betwixt God and man, breaks

---

[1] Rom. iv. 15, 16 ; Gal. iii. 16, 17 ; 2 Cor. i. 20 ; Cant. v. 16 ; Col. i. 19, and ii. 3 ; Isa. xliv. 3 ; Joel ii. 28 ; Acts ii. 16, 17 ; Gal. iii. 2.
[2] Jer. xiv. 21 ; Luke i. 72 ; Ps. xxv. 6.
[3] Ponder upon these scriptures, Ps. cv. 8, cvi. 45, and cxi. 5.
[4] Gen. ix. 11 ; Isa. liv. 9; Ps. cxi. 9 ; Isa. lix. 21.
[5] Deut. xxix. 20, 21, 24, 25, and xxxi. 20, 21 ; Josh. vii. 11, 12, 15, and xxiii. 15, 16 Judges ii. 20 ; 2 Kings xviii. 9–12.

the peace, and breeds a quarrel betwixt them ; in which he will take vengeance of man's revolt, except there be repentance on man's side, and pardoning grace on his. For breach of covenant, Jerusalem is long since laid waste, and the seven golden candlesticks broken in pieces ; and many others, this day, lie a-bleeding in the nations who have made no more of breaking covenant with the great God than if therein they had to do with poor mortals, with dust and ashes like themselves. Now how can there be such a sin as breach of covenant, for which God will be avenged, if there were no covenant betwixt God and his people? But,

[6.] Sixthly, *The seals of the covenant are given to God's people.* Now to those to whom the seals of the covenant are given, with them is the covenant made ; for the seals of the covenant, and the covenant, go to the same persons : but the seals of the covenant are given to believers. 'Abraham receives the sign of circumcision, a seal of the righteousness of faith,' Rom. iv. 11, *ergo*, the covenant is made with believers. Circumcision is a sign, in regard of the thing signified, and a seal, in regard of the covenant made betwixt God and man. Seal is a borrowed word, taken from kings and princes, who add their broad seal, or privy-seal, to ratify and confirm the leagues, edicts, grants, covenants, charters, that are made with their subjects or confederates. God had made a covenant with Abraham, and by circumcision signs and seals up that covenant.[1] But,

[7.] Seventhly, *The people of God are said sometimes to keep covenant with God :* Ps. xxv. 10, ' All the paths of the Lord are mercy and truth unto such as keep his covenant and his testimonies.' Mercies flowing in upon us, through the covenant, are of all mercies the most soul-satisfying, soul-refreshing, soul-cheering mercies ; yea, they are the very cream of mercy. Oh, how well is it with that saint that can look upon every mercy as a present sent him from heaven by virtue of the covenant! Oh, this sweetens every drop, and sip, and crust, and crumb of mercy that a Christian enjoys, that all flows in upon him through the covenant! The promise last cited is a very sweet, choice, precious promise, a promise more worth than all the riches of the Indies. Mark, ' all the paths of the Lord' to his people, they are not only ' mercy,' but they are ' mercy and truth ;' that is, they are sure mercies that stream in upon them, through the covenant. Solomon's dinner of green herbs, Prov. xv. 17 ; Daniel's pulse, Dan. i. 12 ; barley loaves and a few fishes, John vi. 9 ; swimming in upon a Christian, through the new covenant, are far better, greater and sweeter mercies, than all those great things are that flow in upon the great men of the world, through that general providence that feeds the birds of the air, and the beasts of the field : Ps. xliv. 17, ' Yet have we not forgotten thee, neither have we dealt falsely in thy covenant ;' that is, we have kept covenant with thee, by endeavouring to the uttermost of our power to keep off from the breach of thy covenant, and to live up to the duties of thy covenant, suitable to that of the prophet Micah, ' We will walk in the name of the Lord our God for

[1] In reason, the covenant and the seals must go together. Were it not a fond and foolish thing in any man to make a covenant with one, and to give the seals to another ! In equity and justice, the covenant and the seals must go to the same persons.

ever and ever,' Micah iv. 5. Persons in covenant with God will not only take a turn or two in his ways, as temporaries and hypocrites do, who are hot at hand, but soon tire and give in, but they will hold on in a course of holiness, and not fail to follow the Lamb, whithersoever he goes: Rev. xiv. 4, and xvii. 14; Ps. ciii. 17, ' The mercy of the Lord is from everlasting to everlasting :' ver. 18, ' To such as keep his covenant,' &c. All sincere Christians they keep covenant with God:—(1.) In respect of their cordial desires to keep covenant with God; (2.) In respect of their habitual purposes and resolutions to keep covenant with God; (3.) In respect of their habitual and constant endeavours to keep covenant with God, Neh. i. 11; Ps. cxix. 133, and xxxix. 1, 2. This is an evangelical and incomplete keeping covenant with God, which in Christ God owns and accepts, and is as well pleased with it as he was with Adam's keeping of covenant with him before his fall. From what has been said, we may thus argue: Those that keep covenant with God, those are in covenant with God, those have made a covenant with God; but all sincere Christians they do keep covenant with God, *ergo.* But,

[8.] Eighthly and lastly, *The Lord hath, by many choice, precious, and pathetical promises, engaged himself to make good that blessed covenant that he has made with his people, yea, with his choice and chosen ones,* 2 Pet. i. 4. Take a few instances, ' If ye hearken to these judgments,'[1] saith God to Israel, ' and keep and do them, the Lord thy God shall keep unto thee the covenant and the mercy which he sware unto thy fathers,' Deut. vii. 12. This blessed covenant is grounded upon God's free grace; and therefore in recompensing their obedience God hath a respect to his own mercy, and not to their merits. So Judges ii. 1, ' I made you to go up out of Egypt, and have brought you into the land which I sware unto your fathers; and I said, I will never break my covenant with you.' God is a God of mercy, and his covenant with his people is a covenant of mercy; and therefore he will be sure to keep touch with them. So Ps. lxxxix. 34, ' My covenant will I not break, nor alter the thing that is gone out of my mouth ;' as if he should have said, Though they break my statutes, yet will I not break my covenant; for this seems to have reference to the 31st verse, ' If they break my statutes,' &c. Though they had profaned God's statutes, yet God would not profane his covenant, as the Hebrew runs, ' My covenant will I not break ;' that is, I will stand steadfastly to the performance of it, and to every part and branch of it, I will never be inconstant, I will never be off and on with my people, I will never change my purpose, nor eat my words, nor unsay what I have said. So Jer. xxxiii. 20, ' Thus saith the Lord, If ye can break my covenant of the day, and my covenant of the night,[2] and that there shall not be day and night in their season ;' ver. 21, ' Then may also my covenant be broken with my servant David,' &c. It is impossible for any created power to break off the intercourse of night and day, so it is impossible for me to break the covenant that

---

[1] Under the name judgments, the commandments and statutes of God are contained.

[2] That is, the order that I have set upon the courses and the revolutions of day and night.

I have made with David, my servant ; the day and night shall as soon
fail as my covenant shall fail.   So Isa. liv. 10, ' The mountains shall
depart, and the hills be removed ; but my kindness shall not depart
from thee, neither shall the covenant of my peace be removed, saith
the Lord that hath mercy on thee.'   Though great and huge mountains
should remove, yea, though heaven and earth should meet, Ps. xlvi. 2,
yet the covenant of God with his people shall stand unmovable.
The covenant of God, the mercy of God, and the loving-kindness
of God to his people, shall last for ever, and remain constant and immutable, though all things in the world should be turned upside
down.   So Ps. cxi. 4, ' The Lord is gracious, and full of compassion ;'
ver. 5, ' He will ever be mindful of his covenant.'   God looks not
at his people's sins, but at his own promise ; he will pass by their
infirmities, and supply all their necessities.   God will never break his
covenant, he will never alter his covenant, he will still keep it, he will
for ever be mindful of it.   The covenant of God with his people shall
be as inviolable as the course and revolution of day and night, and
more immovable than the very hills and mountains.   From what has
been said, we may thus argue : If God hath, by many choice, precious,
and pathetical promises, engaged himself to make good that blessed
covenant that he has made with his people, then certainly there is a
covenant between God and his people ; but God hath, by many choice,
precious, and pathetical promises, engaged himself to make good his
covenant to his people.   *Ergo.* . . .

I might have laid down several other unanswerable arguments to
have evinced this blessed truth, that there is a covenant betwixt God
and his people ; but let these eight suffice for the present.

7. Seventhly and lastly, Premise this with me—viz., *that it is a
matter of high importance and of great concernment, for all mortals to
have a clear and a right understanding of that covenant under which
they are*, 2 Sam. xxiii. 3, 4.   God deals with all men according to
the covenant under which they stand.   We shall never come to understand our spiritual estate and condition, till we come to know under
what covenant we are, Ps. cv. 8, cxi. 5 ; 1 Cor. xi. 28 ; Gal. iv. 23–25.
If we are under a covenant of works, our state is miserable ; if we are
under a covenant of grace, our state is happy ; if we die under a
covenant of works, we shall be certainly damned ; if we die under a
covenant of grace, we shall be certainly saved.   Until we come to
understand under what covenant we are, we shall never be able to put
a right construction, a right interpretation, upon any of God's actions,
dealings, or dispensations towards us.   When we come to understand
that we are under the covenant of grace, then we shall be able to put
a sweet, a loving, and a favourable construction upon the most sharp,
smart, severe, and terrible dispensations of God, knowing that all
flows from love, and shall work for our external, internal, and eternal
good, and for the advancement of God's honour and glory in the
world.[1]   When we come to understand that we are under a covenant
of works, then we shall know that there is wrath, and curses, and
woes wrapped up in the most favourable dispensations, and in the

[1] Rev. iii. 19 ; Job i. 21 ; Jer. xxiv. 4, 5 ; Rom. viii. 28 ; Heb. xii. 10, 11 ; 2 Cor.
iv. 15–18.

greatest outward mercies and blessings that Christ confers upon us.[1] If a man be under a covenant of grace, and doth not know it, how can he rejoice in the Lord ? How can he sing out the high praises of God ? How can he delight himself in the Almighty ? How can he triumph in Christ Jesus ? How can he cheerfully run the race that is before him ? How can he bear up bravely and resolutely in his sufferings for the cause of Christ ? How can he besiege the throne of grace with boldness ? How can he be temptation-proof ? How can he be dead to this world ? How can he long to be with Christ in that other world ? And if a man be under a covenant of works, and doth not know it, how can he lament and bewail his sad condition ? How can he be earnest with God to bring him under the bond of the new covenant ? How can he make out after Christ ? How can he choose the things that please God ? How can he cease from doing evil, and learn to do well ? How can he lay hold on eternal life ? How can he be saved from wrath to come ? &c. If we are under a covenant of grace, and do not know it, how can we manage our duties and services with that life, love, seriousness, holiness, spiritualness, and upright-ness, as becomes us ?[2] &c. If we are under a covenant of works,[3] and do not know it, how rare shall we be in religious duties ! How weary shall we be of religious duties, and how ready shall we be to cast off religious duties ! By ·these few things I have been hinting at, you may easily discern how greatly it concerns all sorts of persons to know what covenant they are under ; whether they are under the first or second covenant ; whether they are under a covenant of works or a covenant of grace. Now having premised these seven things, my way is clear to that I would be at, which is this—viz., 1. *That there are but two famous covenants that we must abide by.* In one of them, all men and women in the world must of necessity be found—either in the covenant of grace or in the covenant of works. The covenant of works is a witness of God's holiness and perfection ; the covenant of grace is a witness of God's goodness and commiseration. The cove-nant of works is a standing evidence of man's guiltiness ; the covenant of grace is the standing evidence of God's righteousness. The cove-nant of works is the lasting monument of man's impotency and changeableness ; the covenant of grace is the everlasting monument of God's omnipotency and immutability. Now no man can be under both these covenants at once. If he be under a covenant of works, he is not under a covenant of grace ; and if he be under a covenant of grace, he cannot be under a covenant of works. Such as are under a covenant of works, they have the breach of that covenant to count for, they being the serpentine brood of a transgressing stock ; but such as are under a covenant of grace shall never be tried by the law of works, because Christ, their surety, hath fulfilled it for them, Acts xiii. 38, 39 ; Rom. viii. 2-4 ; Gal. iv. 4-6. But let me open myself more fully thus :—

That all unbelievers, all Christless, graceless persons, are under a covenant of works, which they are never able safely to live under.

[1] Prov. i. 32 ; Mal. ii. 2 ; Deut. xxviii. 15–20 ; Lev. xxvi. 14–24 ; 2 Cor. ii. 14 ; Heb. xii. 1.
[2] Ps. xvi. 4 ; Amos viii. 5 ; Mal. i. 13 ; Hosea vi. 4, and iv. 10 ; Ps. xxxvi. 3.
[3] Query, 'grace ?'—Ed.

Should they live and die under a covenant of works, they were surely lost and destroyed for ever; for the covenant of works condemns and curses the sinner: Gal. iii. 10, 'Cursed is every one that continueth not in all things which are written in the book of the law to do them.' Neither hath the sinner any way to escape that curse of the law, nor the wrath of God revealed against all unrighteousness and ungodliness, but in the covenant of grace, Rom. i. 18. This covenant of works the apostle calls 'the law of works,' Rom. iii. 27. This is the covenant which God made with man in the state of innocency before the fall, Gen. ii. 16, 17. In this covenant God promised to Adam, for himself and his posterity, life and happiness, upon the condition of perfect, personal, and perpetual obedience; and it is summed up by the apostle, 'Do this and live,' Gal. iii. 12. God having created man upright, after his own image, Eccles. vii. 29; Gen. i. 26, 27, and so having furnished him with all abilities sufficient for obedience, thereupon he made a covenant with him for life upon the condition of obedience; I say, he made such a covenant with Adam, as a public person, as the head of the covenant; and as he promised life to him and his posterity in case of obedience, so he threatened death and a curse unto him and his posterity in case of disobedience: 'In the day thou eatest thereof thou shalt surely die;' or, 'dying thou shalt die,' Gen. ii. 17.[1] God, in this covenant of works, did deal with Adam and his posterity in a way of supremacy and righteousness, and therefore there is mention made only of the threatenings: 'In the day thou eatest thereof thou shalt die the death.' And it is further observable, that in this covenant that God made with Adam and his posterity, he did promise unto them eternal life and happiness in heaven, and not eternal life in this world only, as some would have it; for hell was threatened in these words, 'In the day thou eatest thereof thou shalt die the death;' and therefore heaven and happiness, salvation and glory, was promised on the contrary. We must necessarily conclude that the promise was as ample, large, and full as the threatening was; yet this must be remembered, that when God did at first enter into covenant with us, and did promise us heaven and salvation, it was upon condition of our personal, perfect, and perpetual obedience, and therefore called a covenant of works. 'Do this and live' was not only a command, but a covenant, with a promise of eternal happiness upon perfect and perpetual obedience. All that are under a covenant of works, are under the curse of the covenant, and they are all bound over unto eternal wrath; but the Lord Christ has put an end to this covenant, and abolished it unto all that are in him, being himself made under it; and satisfying the precept and the curse of it, and so he did cancel it, 'as a handwriting against us, nailing it unto his cross,' Col. ii. 14. So that all they that are in Christ are freed from the law as a covenant; but unto all other men it remains a covenant still, and they remain under the curse of it for ever, and the wrath of God abides upon them, John iii. 36. Though the covenant of works, as it is a

[1] Gal. iii. 10. Not only the covenant of grace, but the covenant of works also, is an eternal covenant; and therefore the curse of the covenant remains upon men unto eternity. There is an eternal obligation upon the creature, he being bound to God by an eternal law; and the transgression of that law carries with it an eternal guilt, which eternal guilt brings sinners under an eternal curse.

covenant for life, ceaseth unto believers, yet it stands in force against all unbelievers.

Now, oh how sad is it for a man to be under a covenant of works! For,

First, The covenant of works, in the nature of it, requires perfect, personal, and perpetual obedience, under pain of the curse and death, according to that of the apostle, 'As many as are of the works of the law, are under the curse,' Gal. iii. 10—presupposing man's fall, and, consequently, his inability to keep it—'For it is written, Cursed is every one that continueth not in all things that are written in the book of the law to do them,' Deut. xxvii. 26. The covenant of works, therefore, affords no mercy to the transgressors of it, but inflicts death and curse for the least delinquency: 'For whosoever shall keep the whole law, and yet offend in one point, he is guilty of all,' James ii. 10. The whole law is but one copulative; he that breaketh one commandment habitually, breaketh all. A dispensatory conscience keeps not any commandment. When the disposition of the heart is qualified to break every command, then a man breaks every command in the account of God. Every one sin contains virtually all sin in it. He that dares contemn the lawgiver in any one command, he dares contemn the lawgiver in every command. He that allows himself in any one known sin, in any course, way, or trade of sin, he lays himself under that curse which is threatened against the transgressors of the law.

They that are under this covenant of works must of necessity perish. The case stands thus: Adam did break this covenant, and so brought the curse of it both upon himself and all his seed to the end of the world; in his sin all men sinned, Rom. v. 12. Now if we consider all men as involved in the first transgression of the covenant, they must all needs perish without a Saviour. This is the miserable condition that all mortals are in that are under a covenant of works. But,

Secondly, Such as are under a covenant of works, their best and choicest duties are rejected and abhorred, for the least miscarriages or blemishes that do attend them or cleave to them. Observe the dreadful language of that covenant of works, 'Cursed is he that continueth not in all things that are written in the law of God to do them,' Gal. iii. 10. Hence it is that the best duties of all unregenerate persons are loathed and abhorred by God; as you may clearly see by comparing the scriptures in the margin together.[1] The most glorious duties and the most splendid performances of those that are under a covenant of works, are loathsome to God, for the least mistake that doth accompany them. The covenant of works deals with men according to the exactest terms of strict justice. It doth not make nor allow any favourable or gracious interpretation as the covenant of grace doth; the very least failure exposes the soul to wrath, to great wrath, to everlasting wrath. This covenant is not a covenant of mercy, but of pure justice. But,

Thirdly, This covenant admits of no mediator. There was no daysman betwixt God and man, none to stand between them, neither was there any need of a mediator; for God and man were at no dis-

[1] Isa. i. 11-15; Jer. vi. 20; Isa. lxvi. 3; Amos v. 21; Micah vi. 6; Mal. i. 10.

tance, at no variance.[1] Man was then righteous, perfectly righteous.
Now the proper work of a mediator is to make peace and reconciliation between God and us.   At the first, in the state of innocency, there
was peace and friendship between God and man, there was no enmity
in God's heart towards man, nor no enmity in man's heart towards
God: but upon the fall a breach and separation was made between
God and man; so that man flies from God, and hides from God, and
trembles at the voice of God, Gen. iii. 8–10.   Fallen man is now
turned rebel, and is become a desperate enemy to God; yea, his heart
is full of enmity against God.' 'The wisdom of the flesh is enmity
against God,' Rom. viii. 7; not an 'enemy,' as the Vulgar Latin read-
eth it, but 'enmity,' in the abstract; noting an excess of enmity: as
when we see a proud man, we say, There goes pride, so here is enmity.[2]
Nothing can be said more; for an 'enemy' may be reconciled, but
'enmity' can never; a vicious man may become virtuous, but vice
cannot.   There are natural antipathies between some creatures, as
between the lion and the cock, the elephant and the boar, the camel
and the horse, the eagle and the dragon, &c.   But what are all these
antipathies to that antipathy and enmity that is in the hearts of all
carnal men against God?   Now whilst men stand under a covenant
of works, there is none to interpose by way of mediation, but fallen
man lies open to the wrath of God, and to all the curses that are
written in this book.   When breaches are made between God and
man, under the covenant of grace, there is a mediator to interpose and
to make up all such breaches; but under the covenant of works there
is no mediator to interpose between God and fallen man.   These three
things I have hinted a little at, on purpose to work my reader, if under
a covenant of works, to be restless till he be got from under that covenant, into the covenant of grace, where alone lies man's safety, felicity,
happiness, and comfort.   Now this consideration leads me by the
hand to tell you,

2. Secondly, *That there is a covenant of grace, that all believers,
all sincere Christians, all real saints are under;* for under these two
covenants all mankind fall.   The apostle calls this covenant of grace,
'the law of faith,' Rom. iii. 17.   Now, first, this covenant of grace is
sometimes styled an 'everlasting covenant:' Isa. lv. 3, 'And I will
make an everlasting covenant with you, even the sure mercies of
David.'   You need not question my security, in respect of the great
things that I have propounded and promised in my word, for the encouragement of your faith and hope; for I will give you my bond for
all I have spoken, which shall be as surely made good to you as the
mercies that I have performed to my servant David, 2 Sam. xxiii. 5.
The word *everlasting* hath two acceptations; it doth denote, (1.)
Sometimes a long duration; in which respect the old covenant, clothed
with figures and ceremonies, is called everlasting, because it was to
endure, and did endure, a long time, Ps. cv. 9, 10; (2.) Sometimes it
denotes a perpetual duration, a duration which shall last for ever, Heb.
xiii. 20, &c.   In this respect the covenant of grace is everlasting; it

---

[1] Hence this covenant is called by some, *Pactum amicitiæ*, a covenant of friendship.
[2] The word signifies the act of a carnal mind, comprehending thoughts, desire, dis-
course, &c.   *Vide* Pareus, on the words.

shall never cease, never be broken, nor never be altered. Now the covenant of grace is an everlasting covenant in a twofold respect.

First, Ex parte fœderantis, in respect of God, who will never break covenant with his people; but is their God, and will be their God, for ever and ever, Titus i. 2; Ps. xc. 2, and xlviii. 14, ' For this God is our God, for ever and ever; he will be our God even unto death;' ay, and after death too: for this is not to be taken exclusively; oh no! for ' he will never, never leave them, nor forsake them,' Heb. xiii. 5. There are five negatives in the Greek, to assure God's people that he will never forsake them. According to the Greek it may be rendered thus, ' I will not, not leave thee, neither will I not, not forsake thee.'[1] Leave us! God may, to our thinking, leave us; but forsake us he will not. So Ps. lxxxix. 34, ' My covenant will I not break'— *Heb.*, I will not profane my covenant—' nor alter the thing that is gone out of my mouth'—*Heb.*, the issue of my lips I will not alter. Though God's people should profane his statutes, ver. 31, yet God will not profane his covenant; though his people often break with him, yet he will never break with them; though they may be inconstant, yet God will be constant to his covenant: Isa. liv. 10, ' For the mountains shall depart, and the hills be removed; but my kindness shall not depart from thee, neither shall the covenant of my peace be removed, saith the Lord that hath mercy on thee.' Though huge mountains should remove, which is not probable, or though heaven and earth should meet, which is not likely, yet his covenant shall stand immovable; and his mercy and kindness to his people shall be immutable. This new covenant of grace is like the new heavens and new earth, which will never wax old or vanish away, Isa. lxvi. 22. But,

Secondly, The covenant of grace is called an everlasting covenant: *Ex parte confœderatorum;* in respect of the people of God, who are brought into covenant, and shall continue in covenant for ever and ever, Mal. iii. 6; Hosea ii. 19; Gen. xvii. 7. You have both these expressed in that excellent scripture, Jer. xxxii. 40, ' I will make an everlasting covenant with them '—*Heb.*, I will cut out with them a covenant of perpetuity—' that I will not turn away from them, to do them good; but'—*Heb.*, and—' I will put my fear into their hearts, that they shall not depart from me.' Seriously dwell upon the place; it shews that the covenant is everlasting on God's part, and also on our part.[2] On God's part, ' I will never turn away from them to do them good;' and on our part, ' they shall never depart from me.' How so? ' I will put my fear into their hearts, that they shall not depart from me.' That they may continue constant with me, and not constrain me, by their apostasy, to break again with them: I will so deeply rivet a reverent dread of myself in their souls, as shall cause them to cling, and cleave, and keep close to me for ever. In the covenant of grace, God undertakes for both parts; for his own, that he ' will be their God'—*i.e.*, that all he is, and all he has, shall be employed for their external, internal, and eternal good;

[1] Five times in Scripture is this precious promise renewed : Josh. i. 5; Deut. xxxi. 8; 1 Kings viii. 57; Gen. xxviii. 15, that we may be still a-pressing of it till we have pressed all the sweetness out of it, Isa. lxvi. 11.

[2] God will never surcease to pursue and follow his covenant-people with favours and blessings incessantly.

and for ours, that we ' shall be his people'—*i.e.*, that we shall believe, love, fear, repent, obey, serve him, and walk with him, as he requires, Jer. xxxii. 38; Ezek. xxxvi. 26, 27; and thus the covenant of grace becomes an ' everlasting covenant;' yea, such a covenant as hath the sure or unfailable mercies of David wrapped up in it.   The covenant of grace is a new compact or agreement, which God hath made with sinful man, out of his mere mercy and grace, wherein he undertakes, both for himself and for fallen man, and wherein he engages himself to make fallen man everlastingly happy.   In the covenant of grace there are two things considerable: *first*, the covenant that God makes for himself to us, which consists mainly of these branches: (1.) That he will be our God; that is as if he said, You shall have as true an interest in all my attributes for your good, as they are mine for my own glory, Jer. xxxi. 38; Ps. cxliv. 15; 2 Cor. vi. 16-18.   My grace, saith God, shall be yours to pardon you, and my power shall be yours to protect you, and my wisdom shall be yours to direct you, and my goodness shall be yours to relieve you, and my mercy shall be yours to supply you, and my glory shall be yours to crown you. This is a comprehensive promise, for God to be our God: it includes all, *Deus meus et omnia*, said Luther.   (2.) That he 'will give us his Spirit.'   Hence the Spirit is called 'the Holy Spirit of promise.' The giving of the Holy Ghost is the great promise which Christ, from the Father, hath made unto us.   It is the Spirit that reveals the promises, that applies the promises, and that helps the soul to live upon the promises, and to draw marrow and fatness out of the promises.   The great promise of the Old Testament was the promise of Christ, Gen. iii. 16, and the great promise of the New Testament is the promise of the Spirit, as you may see by the scriptures in the margin.[1]   That in this last age of the world there may be a more clear and full discovery of Christ, of the great things of the gospel, of Antichrist, and of the glorious conquests that are in the last days to be made upon him, the giving of the Spirit is promised as the most excellent gift.   (3.) That he ' will take away the heart of stone, and give a heart of flesh,' *i.e.*, a soft and tender heart, Ezek. xxxvi. 26.   (4.) That he ' will not turn away his face from us, from doing of us good;' and that ' he will put his fear into our hearts,' Jer. xxxii. 40.   (5.) That he ' will cleanse 'us from all our filthiness, and from all our idols,' Ezek. xxxvi. 25.   (6.) That he ' will rejoice over us, to do us good,' Jer. xxxiii. 9, 10, and xxxii. 41.   The *second* thing considerable in the covenant of grace is the covenant which God doth make for us to himself, which consists mainly in these things: (1.) That we ' shall be his people.'   (2.) That we ' shall fear him for ever.'   (3.) That we ' shall walk in his statutes, keep his judgments, and do them.'   (4.) That we ' shall never depart from him.'   (5.) That we ' shall persevere, and hold out to the end.'   (6.) That we ' shall grow, and flourish in grace.'   (7.) A true right to the creatures.   (8.) That all providences, changes, and conditions shall work for our good.   (9.) Union and communion with Christ.   (10.) That we shall have a kingdom, a crown, and glory at last.   And what

[1] Isa. xliv. 3; Jer. xxxi. 33; Joel ii. 28; John xiv. 16, 20; Acts ii. 23; Luke xxiv. 49; John xv. 26, and xvi. 7.

would we have more?[1] By these short hints it is most evident that
the covenant of grace is an entire covenant, an everlasting covenant,
made by God both for himself and for us.   O sirs ! this is the glory
of the covenant of grace, that whatsoever God requires of us, that he
stands engaged to give unto us.   Whatever in the covenant of grace
God requires on man's part, that he undertakes to perform for man.
That this covenant of grace is an 'everlasting covenant' may be made
further clear,

[1.] First, *From God's denomination, who hath often styled it an
' everlasting covenant.'*   In the Old Testament he frequently calls
it, in *Heb.*, עלם ברית, *Bereth Gnolam*, a covenant of eternity.   In
the New Testament he calls it, in Greek, Διαθήκη αἰώνιος, the eternal
covenant, or the everlasting covenant.   And those whom God has taken
into covenant with himself, they have frequently acknowledged it to
be an everlasting covenant, as is evident up and down the Scripture.
The covenant of works was not everlasting, it was soon overthrown by
Adam's sin; but the covenant of grace is everlasting.   The joy that
is wrapped up in the covenant is an everlasting joy, Isa. xxxv. 10;
and the righteousness that is wrapped up in the covenant is an everlasting righteousness, Dan. ix. 24; and the life that is wrapped up in
the covenant is an everlasting life, John iii. 16; and all the happiness,
and glory, and salvation that is wrapped up in the covenant is everlasting, John xii. 2; Mat. xix. 29; 1 Pet. v. 4; Isa. xlv. 17.   The
covenant-relation that is betwixt God and his people is everlasting;
and the mediator of the covenant is everlasting—viz., 'Jesus Christ,
yesterday, and to-day, and the same for ever,' Heb. xiii. 8.   Though the
covenant, in respect of our own personal entering into it, is made
with us now in time, and hath a beginning; yet for continuance it
is everlasting and without end; it shall remain for ever and ever.
But,

[2.] Secondly, This covenant of grace, under which the saints stand,
is sometimes styled *a covenant of life :* Mal. ii. 5, 'My covenant was
with him of life and peace.'   Life is restored, and life is promised, and
life is settled by the covenant.   There is no safe life, no comfortable
life, no easy life, no happy life, no honourable life, no glorious life, for
any sinner that is not under the bond of this covenant.[2]   All mankind
had been eternally lost, and God had lost all the glory of his mercy
for ever, had he not, of his own free grace and mercy, made a covenant
of life with poor sinners.   A man, in the covenant of grace, hath three
degrees of life : the first in this life, when Christ lives in him ; the
second, when his ' body returns to the earth, and his soul to God that
gave it ;' the third, at the end of the world, when body and soul re-
united shall enjoy heaven.

[3.] Thirdly, This covenant of grace, under which the saints or
faithful people of Christ stand, is sometimes styled *a holy covenant.*
Daniel, describing the wickedness of Antiochus Epiphanes, saith, 'His

---

[1] Jer. xxxii. 38, 40; Ezek. xxxvi. 27; Job xvii. 9; Prov. iv. 18; Ps. i. 3; Hosea xiv.
5-7 ; Zech. xii. 18; Mal. iv. 2; Jer. xxiv. 5; Rom. viii. 28; Luke xii. 32; Rev. ii. 10;
Ps. lxxxiv. 11 ; John x. 28.   See the truth of this fully evidenced in twelve particulars,
in my ' Box of Precious Ointment,' pp. 364-367.—[Vol. iii., p. 487, *seq.*—G.]

[2] *Omnis vita est propter delectationem.*   Philosophers say that a fly is more excellent
than the heavens, because the fly has life, which the heavens have not.

heart shall be against the holy covenant,' Dan. xi. 28, 30; he shall have indignation against the holy covenant, and have intelligence with them that forsake the holy covenant. So the psalmist, ' For he remembered his holy promise, and Abraham his servant,' Ps. cv. 42, 43; [1] promise here being put for covenant by a synecdoche; Luke i. 72, 'To perform the mercy promised to our fathers, and to remember his holy covenant.' The parties interested in this covenant are holy. Here you have a holy God and a holy people in covenant together. Holiness is one of the principal things that is promised in the covenant. The covenant commands holiness, and encourages to holiness, and works souls up to a higher degree of holiness, and fences and arms gracious souls against all external and internal unholiness.[2] The author of this covenant is holy; the mediator of this covenant is holy; the great blessings contained in this covenant are holy blessings; and the people taken into this covenant are sometimes styled holy brethren, holy men, holy women. 'An holy temple, an holy priesthood, an holy nation, an holy people,' as you may see by comparing the scriptures in the margin together.[3] Whenever God brings a poor soul under the bond of the covenant, he makes him holy, and he makes him love holiness, and prize holiness, and delight in holiness, and press and follow hard after holiness. A holy God will not take an unholy person by the hand, as Job speaks, chap. viii.; neither will he allow of such to take his covenant into their mouths, as the psalmist speaks, Ps. xx. 6.

[4.] Fourthly, This covenant of grace, under which the saints stand, is sometimes styled *a covenant of peace:* Num. xxv. 12, ' Behold, I give unto him my covenant of peace.' Peace is the comprehension of all blessings and prosperity. All sorts of peace, viz., peace with God, and peace with conscience, and peace with the creatures, flows from the covenant of grace, Mal. ii. 5. There is (1.) An external peace, and that is with men; (2.) There is a supernatural peace, and that is with God; (3.) There is an internal peace, and that is with conscience; (4.) There is an eternal peace, and that is in heaven. Now all these sorts of peace flow in upon us through the covenant of grace. The Hebrew word for peace comes from a root which denotes perfection. The end of the upright man is perfection of happiness, Ps. xxxvii. 37.[4] Hence the Rabbins say, that ' the holy blessed God finds not any vessel that will contain enough of blessings for Israel, but the vessel of peace.' Peace is a very comprehensive word. It carries in the womb of it all outward blessings. It was the common greeting of the Jews, ' Peace be unto you:' and thus David, by his proxy, salutes Nabal, ' Peace be to thee, and thy house.' The ancients were wont to paint peace in the form of a woman, with a horn of plenty in her hand. The covenant of grace is that hand, by which God gives out all sorts of peace unto us: Isa. liv. 10, ' Neither shall the covenant of my peace

---

[1] *Heb.,* The word of his holiness, that is, his sacred and gracious covenant that he had made with Abraham and his posterity.

[2] See my Treatise of Holiness. [Vol. iv.—G.]

[3] Ps. l. 5; Heb. iii. 1; 1 Thes. v. 27; 2 Peter i. 21; 1 Peter iii. 5; 1 Cor. iii. 17; 1 Peter ii. 9, &c.

[4] This covenant is styled a covenant of peace, because it breeds, settles, quiets, and establisheth our hearts in perfect peace, it stills all fears and doubts and thoughts of heart.

be removed, saith the Lord that hath mercy on thee.' The covenant is here called the covenant of peace, because the Lord therein offers us all those things that may make us completely happy ; for under this word peace the Hebrews comprehend all happiness and felicity : Ezek. xxxiv. 25, 'And I will make with them a covenant of peace ;' the Hebrew is, 'I will cut with them a covenant of peace.' This expression of cutting a covenant is taken from the custom of the Jews in their making of covenants. The manner of this ceremony or solemnity, Jeremiah declares, saying, 'I will give the men that have transgressed my covenant, which have not performed the words of the covenant which they had struck before me, when they cut the calf in twain, and passed between the parts thereof,' Jer. xxxiv. 18. Their manner was to kill sacrifices, to cut these sacrifices in twain, to lay the two parts thus divided in the midst, piece against piece, exactly one over against another, to answer each other : then the parties covenanting passed betwixt the parts of the sacrifices so slit in twain, and laid answerably to one another : the meaning of which ceremonies and solemnities is conceived to be this—viz., as part answered to part, so there was a harmonious correspondency and answerableness of their minds and hearts that struck covenant : and as part was severed from part, so the covenanters implied, if not expressed, an imprecation or curse ; wishing the like dissection and destruction to the parties covenanting, as most deserved, if they should break the covenant, or deal falsely therein.[1] To this custom God alludes, when he saith, 'I will cut with them a covenant of peace,' Isa. xlii. 6 ; and this he did by making Christ a sacrifice, by shedding his blood, and dividing his soul and body, who is said to be given for a covenant of the people, that is, to be the mediator of the covenant between God and his people. So Ezek. xxxvii. 26, 'Moreover, I will make a covenant of peace with them ; it shall be an everlasting covenant with them,' &c. The word for peace is *Shalom*, by which the Hebrews understand not only outward quietness, but all kind of outward happiness. Others, by the covenant of peace here, do understand the gospel, wherein we see Christ hath pacified all things by the blood of his cross. And Lavater saith, it is called a covenant of peace, *Quia Christi merito, pax inter Deum et nos constituta est.* Not only outward, but inward peace, between God and us, is merited by our Lord Jesus Christ, Col. i. 20. But,

[5.] Fifthly, This covenant of grace, under which the saints stand, is sometimes styled a *new covenant :* Jer. xxxi. 31, 'Behold, the days come, saith the Lord, that I will make a new covenant with the house of Israel, and with the house of Judah :' Heb. xii. 24, 'And to Jesus, the mediator of the new covenant,' &c., Heb. viii. 8, 13, and ix. 15. Now the covenant of grace is styled a new covenant in several respects. (1.) In opposition to the former covenant, that was old, and being old, vanished away, Heb. viii. 13. It is called a new covenant in opposition to the covenant that was made with Adam in the state of innocency, and in opposition to the covenant that was made with the Jews in the time of the Old Testament. (2.) To shew the excellency of the covenant of grace. New things are rare and excellent things.

---

[1] This ceremony or solemnity of covenanting, the Romans and other nations used. Some judge the heathens borrowed this custom from the Jews. But of this before.

In the blessed Scriptures excellent things are frequently called 'new;' as a 'new testament,' a 'new Jerusalem,' 'new heavens,' and 'new earth;' 'a new name,' that is, an excellent name; a 'new commandment,' that is, an excellent commandment; a 'new way,' that is, an excellent way; a 'new heart,' is an excellent heart; a 'new spirit,' is an excellent spirit; and a 'new song,' is an excellent song.[1] (3.) In regard of the succession of it in the room of the former. (4.) In regard of the dilation and enlargement of it, it being in the days of old confined to the Jewish nation and state, and some few proselytes that adjoined themselves thereunto; whereas now it is propounded and extended, without respect of persons or places, unto all indifferently, of all people and nations that shall embrace the faith of Christ. (5.) Sometimes that is styled new, which is diverse from what it was before: 2 Cor. v. 17, 'If any man be in Christ, he is a new creature,' that is, he is not such a man as he was before; a man must be either a new man or no man in Christ.[2] The substance of the soul is not changed, but the qualities and operations of it are altered; in regeneration our natures are changed, not destroyed. This word 'new,' in Scripture, signifieth as much as 'another;' not that it is essentially new, but new only in regard of qualities. A new creature is a changed creature: 2 Cor. iii. 18, 'But we all, with open face beholding as in a glass the glory of the Lord, are changed into the same image, from glory to glory,' that is, from grace to grace. In this respect also, is the covenant styled new, not only because it is diverse from the covenant of works, but also because it is diverse from itself in respect of the administration of it, after that Christ was manifested in the flesh, and died and rose again. From the different administration it is called old and new. This new covenant hath not those seals of circumcision and the passover; nor those manifold sacrifices, ceremonies, types, and shadows, &c., to the observation whereof the Jews were strictly obliged; but now all these things are taken away upon the coming of Christ, and a service of God, much more spiritual, substituted in the room of them; upon which accounts the covenant of grace is called a 'new covenant.' (6.) It is styled new, because it is fresh, and green, and flourishing, it is like unto Aaron's rod, which continued new, fresh, and flourishing, Num. xvii. 8.[3] All the choice blessings, all the great blessings, all the internal and all the eternal blessings of the new covenant, are as new, fresh, and flourishing, as they were when God brought your souls first under the bond of the new covenant. But, (7.) Such things are sometimes styled new which are strange, rare, wonderful, marvellous, and unusual, the like not heard of before. So Jer. xxxi. 22, 'The Lord hath created a new thing in the earth, a woman shall compass a man;' as the nut encloseth the kernel, not receiving aught from without, but conceiving and breeding of herself, by the power of

---

[1] Mat. xxvi. 28; Rev. xxi. 2; 2 Pet. iii. 13; Rev. ii. 17; John xiii. 34; Ezek. xxxvi. 26, 27; Ps. xl. 3.

[2] A new creature has a new light, a new judgment, a new will, new affections, new thoughts, new company, new choice, new Lord, new law, new way, new work, &c. A new creature is a changed creature throughout, 1 Thes. v. 23.

[3] Austin, and others, think that the commandment of love is called a new commandment, because it is always fresh, and green, and flourishing; and why may not the covenant of grace be called a new covenant upon the same account?

the Almighty, from within.   That a virgin should conceive and bring forth a man-child, this was indeed a new thing, a strange thing, a wonderful thing, a thing that was never thought of, never heard of, never read of, from the creation of the world to that very day.   So Isa. xliii. 19, ' Behold, I will do a new thing, I will make a way in the wilderness, and rivers in the desert.'[1]   This was a new work, that is, a wonderful and unusual work; for God to make a plain or free way in the wilderness, where the ways are wont to be uneven, with hills and dales, and obstructed with thickets, and overgrown with brambles and briars, is a strange and marvellous work indeed.   In this respect also, the covenant of grace is styled new, that is, it is a wonderful covenant.   O sirs ! what a wonder is this, that the great God, who was so transcendently dishonoured, despised, provoked, incensed, and injured by poor base sinners, should yet so freely, so readily, so graciously, condescend to vile forlorn sinners, as to treat with them, as to own them, as to love them, and as to enter into a covenant of grace and mercy with them !   This may well be the wonder of angels, and the astonishment of men.   (8.) and lastly, It is called a new covenant, because it is never to be antiquated, as the apostle explains himself, Heb. viii. 13.   But,

[6.] Sixthly, This covenant of grace, under which the saints stand, is sometimes styled *a covenant of salt:* Lev. ii. 13, ' Neither shalt thou suffer the salt of the covenant of thy God to be lacking from the meat-offering,' &c.[2]   The salt of the covenant signifies that covenant that God hath made with us in Christ, who seasoneth us, and makes all our services savoury.   The meaning of the words, say some, is this, The salt shall put thee in mind of my covenant, whereby thou standest engaged to endeavour always for an untainted and uncorrupted life and conversation.   By this salting, say others, was signified the covenant of grace in Christ, which we by faith apprehend unto incorruption, wherefore our unregenerate estate is likened to a child new born and not salted, Ezek. xvi. 4.   Others say it signifies the eternal and perpetual holiness of the covenant between God and man ; and some there be that say that this salt of the covenant signifies the grace of God, whereby they are guided and sanctified that belong unto the covenant of grace.   So Num. xviii. 19, ' It is a covenant of salt for ever before the Lord, unto thee, and to thy seed with thee.'   A covenant of salt is used for an inviolable, incorruptible, and perpetual covenant.   This covenant which the Lord made with the priests is called a covenant of salt, because, as salt keepeth from corruption, so that covenant was perpetual, authentical, and inviolable [3]—as anciently the most solemn ceremony that was used in covenants was to take and eat of the same salt, and it was esteemed more sacred and firm than to eat at the same table and drink of the same cup.   This covenant, in regard of its perpetuity, is here called a ' covenant of salt,' that is, a sure and

---

[1] The word ' new ' doth intimate some more excellent mercies than God had formerly conferred upon his people.

[2] Salt they were bound as by a covenant to use in all sacrifices, or it meaneth a sure and pure covenant.   Some, by the salt of the covenant, do mystically understand the grace of the New Testament.

[3] Of old, amity and friendship was symbolised by salt, for its consolidating and conserving property, saith Pierius.

stable, a firm and incorruptible covenant.   So 2 Chron. xiii. 5, ' Ought
you not to know that the Lord God of Israel gave the kingdom over
Israel to David for ever, even to him and to his sons by a covenant of
salt ?'—i. e., perpetual and inviolable, solemn and sure.   By this
metaphor of salt, a perpetuity is set forth, for salt makes things last.[1]
The covenant therefore here intended is by this metaphor declared to
be a perpetual covenant, that was not to be abrogated or nulled.   In
this respect these two phrases, ' a covenant of salt,' and ' for ever,' are
joined together.   Some take this metaphor of salt to be used in relation to their manner of making their covenant with a sacrifice, on which
salt was always sprinkled, and thereby is implied that it was a most
solemn covenant not to be violated.[2]   But,

    [7.] Seventhly, The covenant of grace, under which the saints stand,
is sometimes styled *a sure covenant, a firm covenant, a covenant that
God will punctually and accurately perform.*   In this regard, the covenant of grace is in the Old Testament styled שמורה, *Shemurah*, that is,
kept, observed, performed.   The word imports care, diligence, and
solicitude lest anything be let go, let slip, &c.   God is ever mindful of
his covenant, and will have that singular care and that constant and
due regard to it, that not the least branch of it shall ever fail, as you
may clearly see by consulting the special scriptures in the margin.[3]
Hence it is called the mercy and the truth: Mic. vii. 20, ' Thou wilt
perform the truth to Jacob'—*Heb.*, ' thou wilt give,' for all is of free
gift—' and the mercy to Abraham.'   The covenant is called mercy,
because mercy only drew this covenant ; it was free mercy, it was
mere mercy, it was only mercy which moved God to enter into covenant with us.   And it is called truth, because the great God who has
made this covenant will assuredly make good all that mercy and all
that grace and all that favour that is wrapped up in it.   God having
made himself a voluntary debtor to his people, he will come off fairly
with them, and not be worse than his word.   Hence Christ is said to
have a rainbow upon his head, to shew that he is faithful and constant
in his covenant, Rev. x. 1.   God hath hitherto kept promise with
nights and days, that one shall succeed the other, Isa. liv. 9, 10 ; therefore much more will he keep promise with his people, Jer. xxxiii. 20,
25.[4]   Hence also the covenant is called the oath : Luke i. 73, ' The
oath which he sware unto our father Abraham.'   You never read of
God's oath in a covenant of works.   In that first covenant you read
not of a mediator nor of an oath.; but in the covenant of grace you
read both of a mediator and of an oath, the more effectually to confirm
us as touching the immutability of his will and purpose, for the accomplishment of all the good and the great things that are mentioned in the
covenant of grace.   The covenant of grace is incomparably more firm,
sure, immutable, and irrevocable than all other covenants in the world.

---

[1] Zanchy's [Zanchius] exposition of the place is strange and farfetched.
[2] Num. xviii. 19, but now opened, Lev. ii. 13.
[3] 2 Sam. xxiii. 5 ; Deut. vii. 9 ; 2 Chron. vi. 14 ; Ps. xix. 7, and lxxxix. 28 ; Titus i.
2 ; Ps. cxxxii. 11 ; Isa. liv. 10.   See my 'Box of Precious Ointment,' pp. 367, 368,
371-373.   [Vol. iii., as before.—G.]
[4] The stability of God's covenant is compared to the unvariable course of the day and
the night, and to the firmness and unmovableness of the mighty mountains, Isa. liv.
9, 10.

Therefore it is said, Heb. vi. 17, 18, ' God willing more abundantly to shew unto the heirs of promise the immutability of his counsel, confirmed it by an oath; that by two immutable things, in which it was impossible for God to lie, we might have strong consolation,'[1] ἰσχυραν παρακλησιν, that is, a valiant, strong, prevailing consolation, such as swalloweth up all worldly griefs, as Moses his serpent did the sorcerers' serpents, or as the fire doth the fuel. God's word, his promise, his covenant, is sufficient to assure us of all the good that he has engaged to bestow upon us; yet God, considering of our infirmity, hath bound his word with an oath. His word cannot be made more true, but yet it may be made more credible. Now two things make a thing more credible: (1.) The quality of the person speaking; (2.) The manner of the speech. If God doth not simply speak, but solemnly swear, we have the highest cause imaginable to rest assured and abundantly satisfied in the word and oath of God. An oath amongst men is the strongest, surest, most sacred, and inviolable bond; ' For men verily swear by the greater, and an oath for confirmation is to them an end of all strife,' Heb. vi. 16. The end of an oath among men is to help the truth in necessity, and to clear men's innocency, Exod. xxii. 11. O sirs! God doth not only make his covenant, but swears his covenant; ' My covenant,' saith the psalmist, ' will I not break, nor alter the thing that is gone out of my lips; once have I sworn by my holiness that I will not lie unto David,' Ps. lxxxix. 34, 35. This is as great and deep an oath as God could take; for his holiness is himself, who is most holy, and the foundation of all holiness.[2] God is essentially holy, unmixedly holy, universally holy, transcendently holy, originally holy, independently holy, constantly holy, and exemplarily holy. Now for so holy a God to swear once for all by his holiness that he will keep covenant, that he will keep touch with his people, how abundantly should it settle and satisfy them! Ah! my friends, hath God said it, and will he not do it? Yea, hath he sworn it, and will he not bring it to pass? Dare we trust an honest man upon his bare word, much more upon his oath; and shall we not much more trust a holy, wise, and faithful God upon his word, upon his covenant, when confirmed by an oath? The covenant of grace is sure in itself; it is a firm covenant, an unalterable covenant, an everlasting covenant, a ratified covenant; so that heaven and earth may sooner pass away, than the least branch or word of his covenant should pass away unfulfilled, Mat. v. 18.

(1.) *Let us but cast our eyes upon the several springs from whence the covenant of grace flows*, and then we cannot but strongly conclude that the covenant of grace is a sure covenant. Now if you cast your eye aright, you shall see that the covenant of grace flows from these three springs.

First, From *the free grace and favour of God.* There was nothing in fallen man to invite God to enter into covenant with him; yea, there was everything in fallen man that might justly provoke God to abandon man, to abhor man, to revenge himself upon man. It was mere

---

[1] Who shall doubt when God doth swear, who cannot possibly deny himself or forswear himself?

[2] See my Treatise of Holiness, p. 585 to p. 595. [Vol. iv., as before.—G.]

grace that made the covenant, and it is mere grace that makes good the covenant. Now that which springs from mere grace must needs be unexceptionably sure. The love of God is unchangeable; 'whom he loves he loves to the end,' John xiii. 3; whom God loves once he loves for ever. He is not as man, soon in and soon off again, Mal. iii. 6; James i. 17; soon in, and as soon out, as Joab's dagger was! Oh no! his love is like himself, lasting, yea, everlasting: 'I have loved thee with an everlasting love,' Jer. xxxi. 3. Though we break off with him, yet he abides faithful, 2 Tim. ii. 13. Now what can be more sure than that which springs from free love, from everlasting love? Rom. iv. 16. Hence the covenant must be sure. The former covenant was not sure, because it was of works; but this covenant is sure, because it is of grace, and rests not on any sufficiency in us, but only on grace.

Secondly, The covenant of grace springs from *the immutable counsel of God:* Heb. vi. 17, ' God, willing more abundantly to shew unto the heirs of promise the immutability of his counsel, confirmed it by an oath.' Times are mutable, and all sorts of men are mutable, and the love and favour of the creature is mutable; but the counsel of God, from which the covenant of grace flows, is immutable, and therefore it must needs be sure, Isa. xl. 6; Ps. cxlvi. 3, 4; Jer. xxxiii. 14. The manifestation of the immutability of God's counsel is here brought in, as one end of God's oath. God swears, that it might evidently appear that what he had purposed, counselled, determined, and promised to Abraham and his seed should assuredly be accomplished; there should be, there could be, no alteration thereof. His counsel was more firm than the laws of the Medes and Persians, which altereth not, Dan. vi. 13. Certainly God's counsel is inviolable: ' My counsel shall stand,' Isa. xlvi. 10; Ps. xxxiii. 11, ' The counsel of the Lord standeth for ever, the thoughts of his heart to all generations;' Prov. xix. 21, ' Nevertheless the counsel of the Lord, that shall stand.' The immutability of God's counsel springs from the unchangeableness of his essence, the perfection of his wisdom, the infiniteness of his goodness, the absoluteness of his sovereignty, the omnipotency of his power. God in his essence being unchangeable, his counsel also must needs be so. Can darkness flow out of light, or fulness out of emptiness, or heaven out of hell? No! no more can changeable counsels flow from an immutable nature. Now the covenant of grace flows from the immutable counsel of God, which is most firm and inviolable, and therefore it must needs be a sure covenant. But,

Thirdly, The covenant of grace springs from *the purpose of God, resolving and intending everlasting good unto us.* Now this purpose of God is sure; so the apostle, 2 Tim. ii. 19, ' The foundation of God standeth sure.'[1] That foundation of God is his election, which is compared to a foundation; because it is that upon which all our good and happiness is built, and because as a foundation it abides firm and sure. The gracious purpose of God is the fountain-head of all our spiritual blessings. It is the impulsive cause of our vocation,

---

[1] Our graces are imperfect, our comforts ebb and flow; but God's foundation stands sure.

justification, glorification; it is the highest link in the golden chain of salvation. What is the reason that God has entered into a covenant with fallen man? it is from his eternal purpose. What is the reason that one man is brought under the bond of the covenant and not another? it is from the eternal purpose of God, Ezek. xx. 37. In all the great concerns of the covenant of grace, the purpose of God gives the casting voice. The purpose of God is the sovereign cause of all that good that is in man, and of all that external, internal, and eternal good that comes to man. Not works past, for men are chosen from everlasting; not works present, for Jacob was loved and chosen before he was born; nor works foreseen, for men were all corrupt in Adam. All a believer's present happiness, and all his future happiness, springs from the eternal purpose of God; as you may see, by comparing the scriptures in the margin together.[1] This purpose of God speaks our stability and certainty of salvation by Christ, God's eternal purpose never changes, never alters; 'Surely, as I have thought, so shall it come to pass, and as I have purposed,' saith God, 'so shall it stand.' God's purposes are immutable, so is his covenant. God's purposes are sure, very sure, so is his covenant. The covenant of grace that flows from the eternal purpose of God, is as sure as God is sure; for God can neither deceive nor be deceived. That covenant that is built upon this rock of God's eternal purpose, must needs be sure; and therefore all that are in covenant with God need never fear falling away. There is no man, no power, no devil, no violent temptation, that shall ever be able to overturn those that God has brought under the bond of the covenant, John x. 28–31; 1 Pet. i. 5. But,

(2.) Secondly, Consider that the covenant of grace *is confirmed and made sure by the blood of Jesus Christ*, which is called 'the blood of the everlasting covenant,' Heb. xiii. 20. Christ, by his irrevocable death, hath made sure the covenant to us, Heb. ix. 16, 17. The covenant of grace is to be considered under the notion of a testament; and Christ, as the testator of this will and testament.[2] Now look, as a man's will and testament is irrevocably confirmed by the testator's death;—' For where a testament is, there must also, of necessity, be the death of the testator; for a testament is of force, after men are dead; otherwise, it is of no strength at all whilst the testator liveth;'— these two verses are added as a proof of the necessity of Christ's manner of confirming the new testament as he did, namely, by his death. The argument is taken from the common use and equity of confirming testaments, which is by the death of the testator. A testament is only and wholly at his pleasure that maketh it, so that he may alter it, or disannul it while he liveth, as he seeth good; but when he is dead, he not remaining to alter it, none else can do it. In the seventeenth verse, the apostle declareth the inviolableness of a man's last will, being ratified as before by the testator's death. This he sheweth two ways: (1.) Affirmatively; in these words, ' A testa-

---

[1] Rom. viii. 28, and ix. 11; Eph. i. 11, and iii. 11; 2 Tim. i. 9.

[2] The main point which the apostle intended, by setting down the inviolableness of men's last wills after their death, is to prove that Christ's death was very requisite for ratifying of the New Testament: consult the scriptures, Mat. xvi. 21; Luke xxiv. 26; Heb. ii. 10, 17.

ment is of force after men are dead.' (2.) Negatively, in these words, 'Otherwise it is of no strength.' Now from the affirmative and the negative, it plainly appears that a testament is made inviolable by the testator's death ; so Jesus Christ hath unalterably confirmed this will and testament—viz., the new covenant, by his blood and death, 'that by means of death, for the redemption of the transgressions that 'were under the first testament, they which are called might receive the promise of eternal inheritance,' Heb. ix. 15. Christ died to purchase an eternal inheritance ; and on this ground eternal life is called an eternal inheritance ; for we come to it as heirs, through the good-will, grace, and favour of this purchaser thereof, manifested by the last will and testament. Hence you read, 'This is my blood of the new testament, which is shed for many, for the remission of sins,' Mat. xxvi. 28. Again, 'This cup is the new testament in my blood, which is shed for you,' Luke xxii. 20 ; 1 Cor. xi. 25. The covenant is called both a covenant and a testament, because his covenant and testament is founded, established, ratified, and immutably sealed up, in and by his blood. Christ is the faithful and true witness, yea, truth itself ; his word shall not pass away, Rev. iii. 14 ; John xiv. 6 ; Mark xiii. 31. If the word of Christ be sure, if his promise be sure, if his covenant be sure, then surely his last will and testament, which is ratified and confirmed by his death, must needs be very sure. Christ's blood is too precious a thing to be spilt in vain ; but in vain is it spilt if his testament, his covenant, ratified thereby, be altered. If the covenant of grace be not a sure covenant, 1 Cor. xv. 14, then Christ died in vain, and our preaching is in vain, and your hearing, and receiving, and believing is all in vain. Christ's death is a declaration and evidence of the eternal counsel of his Father, which is most stable and immutable in itself. But how much more it is so when it is ratified by the death of his dearest Son, 'In whom all the promises are yea and amen,' 2 Cor. i. 20 ; that is, in Christ they are made, performed, and ratified. By all this we may safely conclude that the covenant of grace is a most sure covenant. There can be no addition to it, detraction from it, or alteration of it, unless the death of Jesus Christ, whereby it is confirmed, be frustrated and overthrown. Certainly the covenant is as sure as Christ's death is sure. The sureness and certainty of the covenant is the ground and bottom of bottoms for our faith, hope, joy, patience, peace, &c. Take this corner, this foundation-stone away, and all will tumble. Were the covenant uncertain, a Christian could never have a good day all his days, his whole life would be filled up with tears, doubts, disputes, distractions, &c. ; and he would be still a-crying out, Oh, I can never be sure that God will be mine, or that Christ will be mine, or that mercy will be mine, or that pardon of sin will be mine, or that heaven will be mine ! Oh, I can never be sure that I shall escape 'the great damnation, the worm that never dies, the fire that never goes out, or an eternal separation from the presence of the Lord and from the glory of his power,' 2 Thes. i. 9. The great glory of the covenant is the certainty of the covenant ; and this is the top of God's glory, and of a Christian's comfort, that all the mercies that are in the covenant of grace are 'the sure mercies of David,' and that all the grace that is in the covenant is sure grace, and that all the glory that is in the covenant is sure glory, and that all the external, internal, and eternal blessings of the covenant are sure blessings.

I might further argue the sureness of the covenant of grace from all the attributes of God, which are deeply engaged to make it good, as his wisdom, love, power, justice, holiness, faithfulness, righteousness, &c. ; and I might further argue the certainty of the covenant of grace from the seals which God hath annexed to it. You know what was sealed by the king's ring could not be altered, Esth. viii. 8. God hath set his seals to this covenant: his broad seal in the sacraments, and his privy seal in the witness of his Spirit; and therefore the covenant of grace is sure, and can never be reversed. But upon several accounts I may not now insist on these things. And therefore,

[8.] Eighthly and lastly, The covenant of grace is styled *a well-ordered covenant:* 2 Sam. xxiii. 5, 'He hath made with me an ever-lasting covenant, ordered in all things, and sure.' Oh, the admirable counsel, wisdom, love, care, and tenderness of the blessed God, that sparkles and shines in the well-ordering of the covenant of grace![1] Oh, how comely and beautiful, with what symmetry and proportion, are all things in this covenant ordered and prepared! Oh, what head can conceive, or what tongue can express, that infinite understanding that God has manifested in ordering the covenant of grace, so as it may most and best suit to all the wants, and straits, and necessities, and miseries, and desires, and longings of poor sinners' souls! Here are fit and full supplies for all our spiritual wants, so excellently and orderly hath God composed and constituted the covenant of grace. In the covenant of grace every poor sinner may find a suit-able help, a suitable remedy, a suitable succour, a suitable support, a suitable supply, Jer. xxxiii. 8; Ezek. xxxvi. 25; Ps. xciv. 19. The covenant of grace is so well ordered by the unsearchable wisdom of God, that you may find in it remedies to cure all your spiritual diseases, and cordials to comfort you under all your soul-faintings, and a spiritual armoury to arm you against all sorts of sins, and all sorts of snares, and all sorts of temptations, and all sorts of oppositions, and all sorts of enemies, whether inward or outward, open or secret, subtle or silly, Eph. vi. 10–18. Dost thou, O distressed sinner, want a loving God, a compassionate God, a reconciled God, a sin-pardoning God, a tender-hearted God? Here thou mayest find him in the covenant of grace, Exod. xxxiv. 5–7. Dost thou, O sinner, want a Christ, to counsel thee by his wisdom, and to clothe thee with his righteousness, and to enrich thee with his grace, and to enlighten thee with his eyesalve, and to justify thee from thy sins, and to recon-cile thee to God, and to secure thee from wrath to come, and after all, to bring thee to heaven? Rev. iii. 17, 18; Acts xiii. 39; 1 Thes. i. 10; John x. 28–31. Here thou mayest find him in a covenant of grace. Dost thou, O sinner! want the Holy Spirit to awaken thee, and to convince thee of sin, of righteousness, and of judgment? or to enlighten thee, and teach thee, and lead thee, and guide thee in the way everlasting? or to cleanse thee, or comfort thee, or to seal thee

---

[1] Rom. xi. 33–36; 1 Cor. ii. 7; Eph. i. 8, and iii. 10; Ps. cxlvii. 5; Isa. xl. 28; Rev. vii. 12.

up to the day of redemption? Ezek. xxxvi. 25-27; Luke xi. 13;
Eph. i. 13. Here thou mayest find him in the covenant of grace.
Dost thou, O sinner! want grace, all grace, great grace, abundance of
grace, multiplied grace? Here thou mayest find it in the covenant
of grace? Dost thou, O sinner! want peace, or ease, or rest, or quiet
in thy conscience? Here thou mayest find it in the covenant of grace.
Dost thou want, O sinner! joy, or comfort, or content, or satisfaction? Here thou mayest have it in a covenant of grace. O sinner,
sinner! whatever thy bodily wants are, or whatever thy soul wants
are, they may all be supplied out of the covenant of grace. God, in
his infinite wisdom and love, has laid into the covenant of grace, as
into a common store, all those good things, and all those great things,
and all those suitable things; that either sinners or saints can either
beg or need. Now the adequate suitableness of the covenant of grace
to all a sinner's wants, straits, necessities, miseries, and desires, does
sufficiently demonstrate the covenant of grace to be a well-ordered
covenant. Look, as that is a well-ordered commonwealth, where there
are no wholesome laws wanting to govern a people, and where there
are no wholesome remedies wanting to relieve a people, and where
there are no defences wanting to secure a people; so that must needs
be a well-ordered covenant, where there is nothing wanting to govern
poor souls, or to secure poor souls, or to save poor souls; and such a
covenant is the covenant of grace. I might easily lay down other
arguments to evince the covenant of grace to be a well-ordered covenant. As for the right placing of all persons and things in the covenant of grace, and from the outward dispensation of it, God revealed
it but gradually. First, he discovered it more darkly, remotely, and
imperfectly, as we see things a great way off; but afterwards the Lord
did more clearly, fully, immediately, frequently, and completely discover it, as we discern things at hand. God did not at once open all
the riches and rarities of the covenant to his people, but in the opening of those treasures that were there laid up, God had a respect to
the non-age and full-age of his people; and from God's dispensing
and giving out all the good and all the great things of the covenant
in their fittest time, in a right and proper season, when his people
most need them, and when they can live no longer without them.
But I must hasten to a closing up of this particular. Thus you see
in these eight particulars how gloriously the covenant of grace, under
which the saints stand, is set out in the blessed Scriptures.

Concerning the covenant of grace, or the new covenant, that all
sincere Christians are under, and by which at last they shall be
judged, let me further say, besides what I have already said, *All mankind had been eternally lost, and God had lost all the glory of his
mercy for ever, had he not, of his own free grace and mercy, made a
new covenant with sinful man.* The fountain from whence this new
covenant flows is the grace of God: Gen. xvii. 22, 'I will make'
(*Heb.*, 'I will') 'my covenant.' This covenant is called a covenant of
grace, because it flows from the mere grace and mercy of God. There
was nothing out of God, nor nothing in God, but his mere mercy and
grace, that moved him to enter into covenant with poor sinners,
who were miserable, who were loathsome, and polluted in their

blood, and who had broken the covenant of their God, and were actually in arms against him.[1] This must needs be of mere favour and love, for God to enter into covenant with man, when he lay wallowing in his blood, and no eye pitied him, no, not his own. As there was nothing in fallen man to draw God's favour or affection towards him, so there was everything in fallen man that might justly provoke God's wrath and indignation against him; and therefore it must be a very high act of favour and grace, for the great, the glorious, the holy, the wise, and the all-sufficient God, to enter into covenant with such a forlorn creature as fallen man was. Nothing but free grace was the foundation of the covenant of grace with poor sinners. Now let us seriously mind how this covenant of grace, or this new covenant, runs both in the Old and in the New Testament:[2] Jer. xxxi. 31, ' Behold, the days come, saith the Lord, that I will make a new covenant with the house of Israel, and with the house of Judah;' ver. 32, ' Not according to the covenant that I made with their fathers, in the day that I took them by the hand to bring them out of the land of Egypt; which my covenant they brake, although I was an husband unto them, saith the Lord;' ver. 33, ' But this shall be the covenant that I will make with the house of Israel; After those days, saith the Lord, I will put my law in their inward parts, and write it in their hearts, and will be their God, and they shall be my people;' ver. 34, ' And they shall teach no more every man his neighbour, and every man his brother, saying, Know the Lord; for they shall all know me, from the least of them unto the greatest of them, saith the Lord: for I will forgive their iniquities, and I will remember their sin no more.' Now let us see how Paul doth exegetically explain this new covenant in that Heb. viii. 6, ' But now hath he obtained a more excellent ministry, by how much also he is the mediator of a better covenant, which was established upon better promises;' ver. 7, ' For if that first covenant had been faultless, then should no place have been sought for the second; but finding fault with them, he saith,' ver. 8, ' Behold, the days come, saith the Lord, when I will make a new covenant with the house of Israel, and the house of Judah': ver. 9, ' Not according to the covenant that I made with their fathers, in the day when I took them by the hand to lead them out of the land of Egypt; because they continued not in my covenant, and I regarded them not, saith the Lord;' ver. 10, ' But this is the covenant that I will make with the house of Israel, after those days, saith the Lord; I will put my laws into their mind, and write them in their hearts: and I will be to them a God, and they shall be to me a people;' ver. 11, ' And they shall not teach every man his neighbour, and every man his brother, saying, Know the Lord: for all shall know me, from the least to the greatest;' ver. 12, ' For I will be merciful

---

[1] Isa. xli. 1, 2; Eph. i. 5-7, and ii. 5, 7, 8; 2 Sam. vii. 21; Rom. ix. 18, 23; Jer. xxxii. 38-41; Ezek. xxxvi. 25-27, and xvi. 1-10. Surely if a woman commit adultery, it is a mere act of favour if her husband accept of her again, Jer. iii. 7. The application is easy.

[2] Though the covenant of redemption made to the fathers, and this which was given after, seem diverse, yet they are all one, and grounded on Jesus Christ, save that this is called ' new;' because of the manifestations of Christ, and the abundant graces of the Holy Ghost, given to his church under the gospel, 2 Cor. iii. 1-3.

to their unrighteousness, and their sins and their iniquities will I remember no more;' ver. 13, ' In that he saith, A new covenant, he hath made the first old. Now that which decayeth and waxeth old is ready to vanish away.' This is the substance of the new covenant; and thus the Lord did fore-promise it by Jeremiah, and afterwards expounded it by Paul. Some small difference there is in their words, but the sense is one and the same. Now this covenant is styled the new covenant, because it is to continue new, and never to wax old or wear away, so long as this world shall continue. Neither doth the Holy Scriptures anywhere reveal another covenant, which shall succeed this covenant.[1] If any covenant should succeed this, it must be either a covenant of works, or a covenant of grace; not a covenant of works, for that would bring us all under a curse, and make our condition utterly desperate; not a covenant of grace, because more grace cannot be shewn in any other covenant than in this; here is all grace and all mercy, here is Jesus Christ with all his righteousness, mediatorship, merits, purchase. This covenant is so full, so ample, so large, so perfect, so complete, and is every way so accommodated to the condition of lost sinners, that nothing can be altered, nor added, nor mended: and therefore it must needs be the last covenant, that ever God will make with man. So Heb. x. 16, ' This is the covenant that I will make with them, after those days, saith the Lord; I will put my laws into their hearts, and' in their minds will I write them;' ver. 17, ' And their sins and iniquities will I remember no more.' Rom. xi. 26, ' There shall come out of Zion the Deliverer, and shall turn away ungodliness from Jacob.' The person delivering is Christ, described here by his office and by his original; his office, the deliverer; the original word ῥυόμενος, which Paul useth, signifies delivering by a strong hand, to rescue by force, as David delivered the lamb out of the lion's paw; ver. 27, ' For this is my covenant unto them, when I shall take away their sin.' This covenant concerning the pardon of believers' sins, and their deliverance by Christ, God will certainly make good to his people.

Now from the covenant of grace, or the new covenant that God has made with sincere Christians, a believer may form up this eighth plea to the ten scriptures cited in the margin,[2] that refer to the great day of account, or to a man's particular account, viz., *O blessed God, thou hast, in the covenant of grace, by which I must be tried, freely and fully engaged thyself that thou wilt pardon mine iniquities, and remember my sins no more;* so runs the new covenant: Jer. xxxi. 34, ' I will forgive their iniquity, and I will remember their sin no more;' so again, Heb. viii. 12, ' I will be merciful to their unrighteousness, and their sins and their iniquities will I remember no more;' so Heb. x. 17, ' Their sins and iniquities will I remember no more;' Isa. xliii. 25, ' I, even I, am he that blotteth out thy transgressions

---

[1] Where then is the fire of purgatory, and that popish distinction of the fault and the punishment? As for the fiction of purgatory, it deserves rather to be hissed at, than by arguments refuted. And to punish sin in purgatory, as popish doctors teach, what is this, but to call sin to mind and memory, to view and sight, to reckoning and account? which is contrary to the doctrine of the new covenant.

[2] Eccles. xi. 9, and xii. 14; Mat. xii. 14, and xviii. 23; Luke xvi. 2; Rom. xiv. 10 2 Cor. v. 10; Heb. ix. 27, and xiii. 17; 1 Pet. iv. 5.

for mine own sake, and will not remember thy sins;' Ezek. xviii. 22, 'All his transgressions that he hath committed, they shall not be mentioned unto him;' Jer. l. 20, 'In those days, saith the Lord, the iniquity of Israel shall be sought for, and there shall be none; and the sins of Judah, and they shall not be found; for I will pardon them whom I reserve.' *Now, O holy God, I cannot but observe that in the new covenant thou hast made such necessary, choice, absolute, and blessed provision for thy poor people, that no sin can disannul the covenant, or make a final separation between thee and thy covenant-people.*[1] Breaches made in the first covenant were irreparable, but breaches made in the new covenant are not so, because this new covenant is established in Christ. Christ lies at the bottom of the covenant. The new covenant is an everlasting covenant; and all the breaches that we make upon that covenant are repaired and made up by the blood and intercession of dear Jesus. Every jar doth not break the marriage covenant between husband and wife; no more doth every sin break the new covenant that is between God and our souls. Every breach of peace with God is not a breach of covenant with God. That free, that rich, that infinite, that sovereign, and that glorious grace of God that shines in that covenant of grace, tells us that our eternal estates shall never be judged by a covenant of works; and that the want of an absolute perfection shall never damn a believing soul; and that the obedience that God requires at our hands is not a legal, but an evangelical obedience. So long as a Christian doth not renounce his covenant with God, so long as he doth not wilfully, wickedly, and habitually break the bond of the covenant, the main, the substance, of the covenant is not yet broken, though some articles of the covenant may be violated; as among men, there be some trespasses against some particular clauses in covenants, which, though they be violated, yet the whole covenant is not forfeited; it is so here between God and his people.

And, O blessed God, I cannot but observe that in the new covenant thou hast engaged thyself to pardon all my sins: 'I will be merciful to their unrighteousness, and their sins and their iniquities will I remember no more,' Heb. viii. 12; Jer. xxxi. 34.[2] Here are two things worthy of our notice: (1.) The reconciliation of God with his people, 'I will be merciful to their unrighteousness;' he will be merciful or propitious, appeased and pacified towards them; which hath respect to the ransom and satisfaction of Christ. (2.) That God will pardon the sins of his people fully, completely, perfectly. Here are three words, 'unrighteousness,' 'sins,' and 'iniquities,' to shew that he will forgive all sorts, kinds, and degrees of sins. The three original words here expressed are all in the plural number; 1. Ἀδικίαις, *unrighteousnesses*. This word is by some appropriated to the wrongs and injuries that are done against men; 2. Ἁμαρτιῶν, *sins*, is a general word, and according to the notation of the Greek, may imply a not following of that which is set before us; for he sinneth that followeth not the rule

[1] The new covenant can never be broken. 2 Chron. xiii. 5; Ps. lxxxix. 34; Isa. l. 7 2 Sam. xxiii. 5; Heb. vii. 25; 1 John ii. 1, 2; Isa. liv. 10.
[2] He is a forgiving God, Neh. ix. 31. None like him for that, Micah vii. 18. He forgives naturally, Exod. ii. 2; abundantly, Isa. lv. 7, 3; constantly, Ps. cxxx. 4; Mal. iii. 6.

that is set before him by God. The third word, Ανομιῶν, *iniquities*, according to the notation of the Greek, signifies in general, transgressions of the law. This word is by some appropriated to sins against God. The Greek word Ἀνομία, that is frequently translated 'iniquity,' is a general word, which signifieth a transgression of the law, and so it is translated, 1 John iii. 4. The word iniquity is of as large an extent as the word unrighteousness, and implieth an unequal dealing, which is contrary to the rule or law of God. And all this heap of words is to intimate to us that it is neither the several sorts of sins, nor degrees of sin, nor aggravations of sin, nor yet the multitude of sins, that shall ever prejudice those souls that are in covenant with God. God hath mercy enough, and pardons enough, for all his covenant-people's sins, whether original or actual, whether against the law or against the gospel, whether against the light of nature or the rule of grace, whether against mercies or judgments, whether against great means of grace or small means of grace. The covenant remedy against all sorts and degrees of sin, doth infinitely transcend and surpass all our infirmities and enormities, our weaknesses and wickednesses, our follies and unworthinesses, &c. What is our unrighteousness to Christ's righteousness, our debts to Christ's pardons, our unholiness to Christ's holiness, our emptiness to Christ's fulness, our weakness to Christ's strength, our poverty to Christ's riches, our wounds to that healing that is under the wings of the Sun of Righteousness! 1 Cor. i. 30; Ps. i. 3, 9, 10; Mal. iv. 2. Parallel to this, Heb. viii. 12, is that noble description that Moses gives of God in that Book of Exodus: chap. iii. 4, 6, 7, 'The Lord, the Lord merciful and gracious; forgiving iniquity, transgression, and sin.' Some, by these three words, do understand such sins as are committed against our neighbour, against God, or against ourselves. A merciful God, a gracious God will pardon all sorts of sinners, and all sorts and degrees of sin, by what names or titles soever they may be styled or distinguished. Some by *iniquity* do understand sins of infirmity; and by *transgression* they understand sins of malice; and by *sin* they understand sins of ignorance. God is said to keep mercy, and to forgive all sorts of sins, as if his mercy were kept on purpose for pardoning all sorts of sinners and all sorts of sins. The Hebrew word עָוֹן, *Gnavon*, that is here translated *iniquity*, signifies that which is unright, unequal, crooked or perverse; it notes the vitiosity or crookedness of nature; it notes crooked offences, such as flow from malice, hatred, and are committed on purpose. Secondly, the Hebrew word וָפֶשַׁע, from פָּשַׁע, *Pashang*, that is here translated *transgression*, signifies to deal unfaithfully; it notes such sins as are treacherously committed against God, such sins as flow from pride and contempt of God. Thirdly, the Hebrew word וְחַטָּאָה, *Chataah*, generally signifieth sin, but is more especially here taken for sins of ignorance and infirmity. Oh, what singular mercy, what rich grace is here: that God will not only pardon our light, our small offences, but our great and mighty sins! &c.

And I cannot, O dear Father, but further observe that in the new covenant thou hast frequently and deeply engaged thyself, that thou wilt remember the sins of thy people no more! O my God, thou hast told me six several times in thy word, that thou wilt remember my sins no more. In the new covenant thou hast engaged thyself not only to forgive but also to forget, and that thou wilt cross thy debt-book, and never question or call me to an account for my sins ; that thou wilt pass an eternal act of oblivion upon them, and utterly bury them in the grave of oblivion, as if they had never been. The sins that are forgiven by God are forgotten by God, the sins that God remits he removes from his remembrance, Heb. x. 13–19, and 1–15. Christ hath so fully satisfied the justice of God for the sins of all his seed, by the price of his own blood and death, that there needs no more expiatory sacrifices to be offered for their sins for ever. Christ hath, by the sacrifice of himself, blotted out the remembrance of his people's sins with God for ever. The new covenant runs thus, ' And their sinful error,' לא אזכר־עוד, *Lo escar guhod*, ' I will not remember any more,' Jer. xxxi. 34 ; but the Greek runs thus, ' And their sinful errors and their unrighteousnesses, I will not remember again, or any more,' Heb. viii. 12; οὐ μὴ μνησθῶ ἔτι. Here are two negatives, which do more vehemently deny, according to the propriety of the Greek language; that is, I will never remember them again, I will in no case remember them any more, I will so forgive as to forget : not that in propriety of phrase, God either remembers or forgets, for all things are present to him ; he knows all things, he beholds, he sees, he observes all things, by one eternal and simple act of his know-ledge, which is no way capable of change, as now knowing and anon forgetting ; but it is an allusion to the manner of men, who, when they forgive injuries fully and heartily, do also forget them, blot them out of mind ; or rather, as some think, it is an allusion to the manner of the old covenant's administration in the sacrifices, where there was a remembrance again of sins every year, there was a fresh indictment and arraignment of the people for sin continually, Heb. x. 1–3, &c. ; but under this new covenant our Lord Jesus Christ hath, ' by one offering, perfected for ever them that are sanctified,' [see from ver. 5 to ver. 20 ;] Christ hath, for ever, taken away the sins of the elect ; there needs no more expiatory sacrifice for them ; they that are sprinkled with the blood of this sacrifice shall never have their sins remembered any more against them. God's not remembering or forgetting a thing is not simply to be taken of his essential knowledge, but respectively of his judicial knowledge, to bring the same into judgment. Not to remember a thing that was once known, and was in mind and memory, is to forget it ; but this properly is not incident to God, it is an infirmity. To him all things past and future are as present. What he once knoweth he always knoweth. His memory is his very essence, neither can anything that hath once been in it slip out of it. For God to remit sin is not to remember it ; and not to remember it is to remit it. These are two reciprocal propositions, therefore they are thus joined together. ' I will forgive their iniquity, and I will remember their sin no more : I, even I, am he that blotteth out thy transgressions for mine own sake, and will not remem-ber thy sins,' Jer. xxxi. 34 ; Isa. xliii. 25. To remember implieth a fourfold act ; (1.) To lay up in the mind what is conceived thereby ; (2.) To hold it fast ; (3.) To call it to mind again ; (4.) Oft to think of it. Now in that God saith, ' I will remember their iniquities no more ;' he implieth that he will neither lay them up in his mind, nor there hold them, nor call them again to mind, nor think on them, but that they shall be to him as if they had never been committed. God's discharge of their sins shall be a full discharge. Such sinners shall never be called to account for them. Both the guilt and the punishment of them shall be fully and everlastingly removed. Let the sins of a believer be what they will for nature, and never so many for number, they shall all be blotted out, they shall never be mentioned more ;[1] (1.) God will never remember, he will never mention their sins, so as to impute them or charge them upon his people ; (2.) God will never remember, he will never mention their sins any more, so as to upbraid his people with their follies or miscarriages. He will never hit them in the teeth with their sins, he will never cast their weaknesses into their dish. When persons are justified, their sins shall be as if they had not been ; God will bid them welcome into his presence, and embrace them in his arms, and will never object to them their former unkindness, unfruitfulness, unthankfulness, vileness, stubbornness, wickedness, as you may plainly see in the return of the prodigal, and his father's deportment towards him: Luke xv. 20–23, ' When he was a great way off.' The prodigal was but conceiving a purpose to return, and God met him. The very intention, and secret motions, and close purposes of our hearts, are known to God. The old father sees a great way off. Dim eyes can see a great way when the son is the object; ' his father saw him, and had compassion.' His bowels roll within him. The father not only sees, but commiserates and compassionates the returning prodigal, as he did Ephraim of old, ' My bowels are troubled for him, I will surely have mercy on him ;' or, as the Hebrew runs, ' I will, having mercy, have mercy, have mercy on him, or I will abundantly have mercy on him,' Jer. xxxi. 20. Look, saith God, here is a poor prodigal returning to me, the poor child is come back, he hath smarted enough, he hath suffered enough. I will bid him welcome, I will forgive him all his high offences, and will never hit him in the teeth with his former vanities. ' And ran.' The feet of mercy are swift to meet a returning sinner. It had been sufficient for him to have stood, being old, and a father; but the father runs to the son. ' And fell on his neck.' He cannot stay and embrace him, or take him by the hand ; but he falls upon him, and incorporates himself into him. How open are the arms of mercy to embrace the returning sinner, and lay him in the bosom of love ! ' And kissed him.' Free, rich, and sovereign mercy hath not only feet to meet us, and arms to clasp us, but also lips to kiss us. One would have thought that he should rather have kicked him or killed him, than have kissed him. But God is *Pater miserationum*, he is all bowels. All this while the father speaks not one word. His joy was too great to be uttered. He ran, he fell on his neck, and kissed him, and so sealed up to him mercy and peace, love and reconciliation, with the kisses of his lips. And the son said

---

[1] Mat. xii. 31 ; Isa. lv. 7 ; Jer. xxxi. 12 ; Ezek. xviii. 22 ; Ps. xxxii. 2 ; Rom. iv. 8. Now if God will not remember nor mention his people's sins, then we may safely and roundly infer that either there is no purgatory, or else that God severely punishes those sins in purgatory which he remembers not.

unto him, 'Father, I have sinned against heaven, and in thy sight.' Sincerely confess, and the mends[1] is made; acknowledge but the debt, and he will cross the book. 'And am no more worthy to be called thy son.' *Infernus sum, Domine,* said that blessed martyr,[2] 'Lord, I am hell, but thou art heaven; I am soil and a sink of sin, but thou art a gracious God,' &c. But the father said to his servants, 'Bring forth the best robe, and put it on him, and put a ring on his hands, and shoes on his feet. And bring hither the fatted calf, and kill it, and let us eat and be merry.' Here you have, (1.) The best robe; (2.) The precious ring;[3] (3.) The comely shoes; and (4.) The fatted calf. The returning prodigal hath garments, and ornaments, and necessaries, and comfortables. Some understand by the robe the royalty which Adam lost; and by the ring they understand the seal of God's Holy Spirit; and by the shoes the preparation of the gospel of peace; and by the fatted calf they understand Christ, who was slain from the beginning. Christ is that fatted calf, saith Mr Tyndale the martyr, slain to make penitent sinners good cheer withal, and his righteousness is the goodly raiment to cover the naked deformities of their sins.[4] The great things intended in this parable is to set forth the riches of grace, and God's infinite goodness, and the returning sinner's happiness. When once the sinner returns in good earnest to God, God will supply all his wants, and bestow upon him more than ever he lost, and set him in a safer and happier estate than that from which he did fall in Adam; and will never hit him in the teeth with his former enormities, nor never cast in his dish his old wickednesses. You see plainly in this parable that the father of the prodigal does not so much as mention or object the former pleasures, lusts, or vanities wherein his prodigal son had formerly lived. All old scores are quit, and the returning prodigal embraced and welcomed, as if he had never offended. And now, O Lord, I must humbly take leave to tell thee further that thou hast confirmed the new covenant by thy word, and by thy oath, and by the seals that thou hast annexed to it, and by the death of thy Son, and therefore thou canst not but make good every tittle, word, branch, and article of it. Now this new covenant is my plea, O holy God, and by this plea I shall stand. Hereupon God declares, this plea, I accept as holy, just, and good. I have nothing to say against thee; enter thou into the joy of thy Lord.

IX. The ninth plea that a believer may form up as to the ten scriptures that are in the margin,[5] that refer to the great day of account, or to a man's particular account, may be drawn up from the consideration of that *evangelical obedience that God requires, and that the believer yields to God.* There is a legal, and there is an evangelical account. Now the saints, in the great day, shall not be put to give up a legal account; the account they shall be put to give up is an evangelical account. In the covenant of works, God required perfect obedience in our own persons; but in the covenant of grace God

---

[1] 'Amends.'—G.   [2] Mr Hooper, at his death.—[Foxe,] Act. and Mon., 1374.
[3] Among the Romans the ring was an ensign of virtue, honour, and especially nobility, whereby they were distinguished from the common people.
[4] [Foxe,] Act. and Mon., fol. 986.
[5] Eccles. xi. 9, and xii. 14; Mat. xii. 14, and xviii. 23; Luke xvi. 2; Rom. xiv. 10 2 Cor. v. 10; Heb. ix. 27, and xiii. 17; 1 Pet. iv. 5.

will be content if there be but uprightness in us, if there be but
sincere desires to obey, if there be faithful endeavours to obey, if
there be a hearty willingness to obey. Well, saith God, though I
stood upon perfect obedience in the covenant of works, 2 Cor. viii.
12; yet now I will be satisfied with the will for the deed; if there
be but uprightness of heart, though that be attended with many
weaknesses and infirmities, yet I will be satisfied and contented
with that. God, under the covenant of grace, will for Christ's sake
accept of less than he requires in the covenant of works. He requires perfection of degrees, but he will accept of perfection of parts;
he requires us to live without sin, but he will accept of our sincere
endeavours to do it. Though a believer, in his own person, cannot
perform all that God commands, yet Jesus Christ, as his surety
and in his stead, hath fulfilled the law for him. So that Christ's
perfect righteousness is a complete cover for a believer's imperfect
righteousness. Hence the believer flies from the covenant of works
to the covenant of grace; from his own unrighteousness to the
righteousness of Christ.[1] If we consider the law in a high and rigid
notion, so no believer can fulfil it; but if we consider the law in a
soft and mild notion, so every believer does fulfil it: Acts xiii. 22, ' I
have found David the son of Jesse, a man after mine own heart, which
shall fulfil all my will;' πάντα τὰ θελήματα, ' All my wills,' to note
the universality and sincerity of his obedience. David had many slips
and falls, he often transgressed the royal law; but being sincere in the
main bent and frame of his heart, and in the course of his life, God
looked upon his sincere obedience as perfect obedience. A sincere
Christian's obedience is an entire obedience to all the commands of
God, though not in respect of practice, which is impossible, but in
disposition and affection.[2] A sincere obedience is a universal obedience. It is universal in respect of the subject, the whole man; it is
universal in respect of the object, the whole law; and it is universal
in respect of durance, the whole life; he who obeys sincerely obeys
universally. There is no man that serves God truly that doth not
endeavour to serve God fully: sincerity turns upon the hinges of
universality; he who obeys sincerely endeavours to obey thoroughly,
Num. xiv. 24. A sincere Christian does not only love the law, and
like the law, and approve of the law, and delight in the law, and consent to the law, that it is holy, just, and good, but he obeys it in part,
Rom. vii. 12, 16, 22; which, though it be but in part, yet he being
sincere therein, pressing towards the mark, and desiring and endeavouring to arrive at what is perfect, Phil. iii. 13, 14, God accepts of
such a soul, and is as well pleased with such a soul, as if he had perfectly fulfilled the law. Where the heart is sincerely resolved to obey,
there it does obey. A heart to obey, is our obeying; a heart to do, is
our doing; a heart to believe, is our believing; a heart to repent, is
our repenting; a heart to wait, is our waiting; a heart to suffer, is
our suffering; a heart to pray, is our praying; a heart to hear, is our
hearing; a heart to give, feed, clothe, visit, is our giving, feeding,

---

[1] Luke i. 5, 6; Mat. xxviii. 20; Acts xxiv. 16; 1 Pet. i. 14, 15; Heb. xiii. 18. *Lex
data est ut gratia quæreretur; gratia data est ut lex impleretur.*—Augustine.
[2] Ps. cxix. 6. Heb., When my eye is to all thy commandments.

clothing, visiting; a heart to walk circumspectly, is our walking circumspectly; a heart to work righteousness, is our working righteousness; a heart to shew mercy, is our shewing mercy; a heart to sympathise with others, is our sympathising with others. He that sincerely desires and resolves to keep the commandments of God, he does keep the commandments of God, and he that truly desires and resolves to walk in the statutes of God, he does walk in the statutes of God. In God's account and God's acceptation, every believer, every sincere Christian, is as wise, holy, humble, heavenly, spiritual, watchful, faithful, fruitful, useful, thankful, joyful, &c., as he desires to be, as he resolves to be, and as he endeavours to be; and this is the glory of the new covenant, and the happiness that we gain by dear Jesus. And, my friends, it is remarkable that our inchoate, partial and very imperfect obedience is frequently set forth in the blessed Scriptures by our fulfilling of the law, Luke x. 25–27. Take a few places for a taste: Rom. ii. 27, ' And shall not uncircumcision, which is by nature, if it fulfil the law, judge thee?' &c.; Rom. xiii. 8, ' He that loveth another, hath fulfilled the law;' ver. 10, ' Love is the fulfilling of the law.' Not to love is to do ill and to break the law, but love is the fulfilling of it; *Non potest peccari per illam, quæ legis est perfectio;* we cannot do ill by that which is the perfection and the fulfilling of the law.[1] Love is the sum of the law, love is the perfection of the law; and were love perfect in us, it would make us perfect keepers of the law. Love works the saints to keep the law in desires and endeavours, with care and study to observe it in perfection of parts, though not in perfection of degrees: Gal. v. 14, ' All the law is fulfilled in one word, even in this, Thou shalt love thy neighbour as thyself;' Gal. vi. 2, ' Bear ye one another's burdens, and so fulfil the law of Christ.' Now in this sense that is under consideration, the saints in themselves, even in this life, do keep the royal law. Now, from what has been said, a believer may form up this plea:—

O blessed God, in Christ my head I have perfectly and completely kept thy royal law; and in my own person I have evangelically kept thy royal law, in respect of my sincere desires, purposes, resolutions, and endeavours to keep it: and this evangelical keeping in Christ, and in the new covenant, thou art pleased to accept of, and art well satisfied with it. I know that breaches made in the first covenant were irreparable, but breaches made in the covenant of grace are not so; because this covenant is established in Christ; who is still a-making up all breaches. Now this is my plea, O holy God, and by this plea I shall stand. Well, saith God, I cannot in honour or justice but accept of this plea, and therefore enter thou into the joy of thy Lord.

X. The tenth plea that a believer may form up, as to the ten scriptures that are in the margin,[2] that refer to the great day of account, or to a man's particular account, may be drawn up from the consideration of that *compact, covenant, and agreement, that was solemnly made between God and Christ, touching the whole business of man's salvation*

---

[1] Ambrose, *in loco.*
[2] Eccles. xi. 9, and xii. 14; Mat. xii. 14, and xviii. 23; Luke xvi. 2; Rom. xiv. 10; 2 Cor. v. 10; Heb. ix. 27, and xiii. 17; 1 Pet. iv. 5.

or redemption. We may present it to our understanding in this form:
God the Father saith to Christ the mediator, I look upon Adam and
his posterity as a degenerate seed, ' a generation of vipers,' of apostates
and backsliders, yea, traitors and rebels ; liable to all temporal, spiritual,
and eternal judgments ; yet I cannot find in my heart to damn them
all ; ' Mine heart is turned within me, my repentings are kindled together ; I will not execute the fierceness of mine anger : for I am God,
and not man,' Hosea xi. 8, 9 : and therefore I have determined to
shew mercy upon many millions of them, and save them from wrath
to come, and to bring them to glory, Rev. vii. 9, 10 ; but this I must
do with a salvo to my law, justice, and honour. If, therefore, thou wilt
undertake for them, and become a curse for their sakes, Gal. iii. 10,
13, and so make satisfaction to my justice for their sins ; I will give
them unto thee, John xvii. 2, 6, 11, to take care of them, and to bring
them up to my kingdom, for the manifestation of the glory of my
grace. Well, saith Christ, I am content, I will do all thou requirest
with all my heart, and so the agreement is made between thee and
me. This may be gathered from the scriptures in the margin.[1] Christ
the Son speaks in both places. In the first he publisheth the decree
or ordinance of heaven, touching himself, and bringeth in the Father,
installing him into the priesthood or office of mediator ; for so the
apostle applieth that text, Heb. v. 5, ' Thou art my son,' &c., and
also avoucheth this covenant and agreement in the two main parts
of it.

1. First, *The condition which he will have performed on Christ's
part, as mediator ; or what Christ must do, as mediator,* ' He must
ask of God ;' that is, not only verbally, by prayers and supplications,
beg mercy, pardon, righteousness, and salvation for poor lost sinners ;
but also really, by fulfilling the righteousness of the law, both in doing
and suffering ; and so by satisfaction and merit, purchasing acceptation for them at his hands.[2] The Father engaged so and so to Christ,
and Christ reciprocally engaged so and so to the Father ; a considerable part of the terms and matter of which covenant is set down : Isa.
liii. 10, ' When thou shalt make his soul an offering for sin, he shall
see his seed,' &c. The Father covenants to do thus and thus for fallen
man ; but first in order thereunto the Son must covenant to take
man's nature, therein to satisfy offended justice, to repair and vindicate
his Father's honour, &c. Well, he submits, assents to these demands,
indents and covenants to make all good ; and this was the substance
of the covenant of redemption. But,

2. Secondly, Let us consider *the promise which the Father engageth to perform on his part ;* the Son must ask, and the Father will
give : ' He will give him the heathen for his inheritance, and the
uttermost parts of the earth for his possession,' Ps. ii. 8. An allusion
to great princes, when they would shew great affection to their
favourites, they bid them ask what they will, as Ahasuerus did, and
as Herod did ; that is, he shall both be the Lord's salvation to the ends
of the earth, and ' have all power given him in heaven and earth ;

---

[1] Ps. ii. 7–9, and xl. 6–8.
[2] Consider Christ in the capacity of a mediator, for so only he covenanted with the
Father, for the salvation of mankind.

so that all knees shall bow to him, and every tongue shall confess him to be Lord.'[1] In the other text before mentioned, Ps. xl., Christ declares his compliance to the agreement, and his subscribing the covenant on his part, when he came into the world, as the apostle explains it, Heb. x. 5, &c. ; ' Mine ears,' saith he, ' hast thou digged or pierced : Lo, I come to do thy will ;' as if he had said, O Father, thou dost engage me to be thy servant in this great work of saving sinners. Lo, I come to do the work, I here covenant and agree to yield up myself to thy disposing, and to serve thee for ever. It seems to be an allusion to the master's ' boring through the servant's ear,' Exod. xxi. 6. Among the Jews only one ear was bored, but in this Ps. xl. 6, here are ears in the plural number, a token of that perfect and desirable subjection, which Christ, as mediator, was in to his Father. But for a more clear, distinct, and full opening of the covenant of redemption, or that blessed compact between God the Father and Jesus Christ, which is a matter of grand importance to all our souls ; and considering that it is a point that I have never yet treated of in pulpit or press, I shall therefore take the liberty at this time to open myself as clearly and as fully as I can. And therefore thus :—

Quest. If you ask me, What this covenant of redemption is ?

Ans. 1. I answer, in the general, that a covenant is a mutual agreement between parties, upon articles or propositions on both sides, so that each party is tied and bound to perform his own conditions. This description holds the general nature of a covenant, and is common to all covenants, public and private, divine or human. But,

Ans. 2. Secondly, and more particularly, I answer, the covenant of redemption is that federal transaction or mutual stipulation that was betwixt God and Christ from everlasting, for the accomplishment of the work of our redemption, by the mediation of Jesus Christ, to the eternal honour, and unspeakable praise, of the glorious grace of God. Or, if you please, take it in another form of words, thus :—

It is a compact, bargain, and agreement between God the Father and God the Son, designed mediator, concerning the conversion, sanctification, and salvation of the elect, through the death, satisfaction, and obedience of Jesus Christ, which in due time was to be given to the Father. But for the making good the definition I have laid down, I must take leave to tell you that there are many choice scriptures which give clear intimation of such a federal transaction between God the Father and Jesus Christ, in order to the recovery, and everlasting happiness, and salvation of his elect. I shall instance in the most considerable of them :—

(1.) The first is this, Gen. iii. 15, ' And I will put enmity between thee and the woman, and between thy seed and her seed ; it shall bruise thy head, and thou shalt bruise his heel.' Here begins the book of the Lord's wars, God's battles.[2] This is spoken of that holy enmity that is between Christ and the devil, and of Christ's destroying the kingdom and power of Satan : ' Forasmuch then as the children are partakers of flesh and blood, he also himself likewise took part of the same; that through death he might destroy him that had the power of death, that

---

[1] Esth. v. 3; Mark vi. 23; Isa. xlix. 6; Mat. xxviii. 18; Phil. ii. 10, 11; Ps. xl. 6–8.
[2] The Scriptures are called the Book of the Battles of the Lord, Num. xxi.—*Rupertus.*

is, the devil,' Heb. ii. 14. God, by way of threatening, told Satan that the seed of the deceived woman should overmatch him at last, and should break in pieces his power and crafty plots. He gives Satan leave to do his worst, and proclaims an open and an utter enmity between Christ and him. From this scripture some conclude that Christ covenanted from eternity to take upon him the seed of the woman, and the sinless infirmities of our true human nature; and under those infirmities to enter the lists with Satan, and to continue obedient through all his afflictions, temptations, and trials, to the death, even to the death of the cross, Phil. ii. 8, 9. And that God the Father had covenanted with Christ, that in case Christ did continue obedient through all his sufferings, temptations, and trials, that then his obedience to the death should be accounted as full satisfaction to divine justice for all those wrongs and injuries that were done to God by the sins of man. Christ must die, or else he could not have been the mediator of the new covenant through death, Heb. ix. 15, 16. But,

(2.) The second scripture is that, Isa. xlii. 6, ' The Lord hath called thee in righteousness, and will hold thine hand, and will keep thee, and give thee for a covenant of the people, for a light of the Gentiles.' Thus God speaks of Christ. In this chapter we have a glorious prophecy of Christ our Redeemer. Here are four things prophesied of him: (1.) The divine call, whereby he was appointed to the work of our redemption: ver. 1, ' Behold my servant whom I uphold, mine elect in whom my soul delighteth; I have put my Spirit upon him: he shall bring forth judgment to the Gentiles.' Jesus Christ would not, yea, he could not, he durst not, thrust himself upon this great work, or engage in this great work, till he had a clear call from heaven. (2.) Here you have the gracious carriage and deportment of Christ, in the work to which he was called; this is fully set down, vers. 2–4, ' He shall not cry, nor lift up, nor cause his voice to be heard in the street.' He shall come clothed with majesty and glory, and yet full of meekness: ' a bruised reed shall he not break, and the smoking flax shall he not quench; he shall bring forth judgment unto truth.' In the words there is a *meiosis*,[1] ' he will not break,' that is, he will bind up the bruised reed, he will comfort the bruised reed, he will strengthen the bruised reed. Christ will acknowledge and encourage the least degrees of grace; he will turn a spark of grace into a flame, a drop into a sea, &c.: ' He shall not fail, nor be discouraged.' These words shew his kingly courage and magnanimity. Though he should meet with opposition from all hands, yet nothing should daunt him, nothing should dismay him; no afflictions, no temptations, no sufferings should in the least abate his courage and valour. (3.) The divine assistance he should have from him that called him. This is set down in two expressions: ver. 6, ' I will hold thy hand, I will keep thee.' Divine assistance doth usually concur with a divine call. When God sets his servants on work, he uses to defend and uphold them in the work. (4.) The work itself to which Christ was called. This is expressed under divers phrases: ver. 6, 7, ' To be a light to the Gentiles, to open the blind eyes, to bring out the prisoners from the prison, and to be a covenant to the people.' In these last words you have two things

---

[1] Same as *litotes*, as before.—G.

observable; the first is one special part of Christ's office: 'He was given for a covenant.' Second, The persons in reference to whom this office was designed: 'a covenant of the people.' One end why God the Father gave Christ out of his bosom, was, that he might be a covenant to his people. Christ is given for a covenant both to the believing Jews and Gentiles. As he is 'the glory of the people of Israel,' so he is 'a light to lighten the Gentiles.' In this scripture last cited, you have the Father's designation and sealing of Christ to the mediatorial employment, promising him much upon his undertaking it, and his acceptation of this office, and voluntary submission to the will of the Father in it: 'Lo, I come to do thy will,' Heb. v. 4, 5; Ps. xl. 7, 8; John x. 17, 18. And these together amount to the making up of a covenant between God the Father and his Son; for what more can be necessary to the making up of a covenant than is here expressed? But,

(3.) The third scripture is that, Isa. xlix. 1, 'Listen, O isles, unto me; and hearken, ye people, from far; The Lord God hath called me from the womb; from the bowels of my mother hath he made mention of my name.'[1] These words are spoken in the person of Christ; he tells us how he is called by his Father to be a mediator and Saviour of his people. Jesus Christ would not take one step in the work of our redemption till he was called and commissionated by his Father to that work. God the Father, who from eternity had fore-assigned Christ to this office of a mediator, a Redeemer, did, both while he was in the womb, and as soon as he was come out of it, manifest and make known this his purpose concerning Christ both to men and angels. Christ did not thrust himself, he did not intrude himself at random into the office of a Redeemer: 'No man takes this honour to himself, but he that is called of God, as was Aaron,' Heb. v. 4, 5. So Christ took not upon himself the office of a mediator, a Saviour, but upon a call and a commission from God. The sum is, that Christ took up the office of a Redeemer by the ordinance of his Father, that he might fulfil the work of our redemption unto which he was destinated. Ver. 2, 'And he made my mouth like a sharp sword; in the shadow of his hand hath he hid me, and made me a polished shaft; in his quiver hath he hid me.' Christ having avouched his Father's calling of him to the work of man's redemption, he gives you a relation in this verse of God's fitting and furnishing of him with abilities sufficient for so important a work, together with his sustaining and supporting of him in the performance of the same. Here are two similitudes or comparisons: (1.) That of a 'sharp sword;' that of a bright and 'sharp arrow,' to shew the efficacy of Christ's doctrine.[2] The word of Christ is a sword of great power and efficacy for the subduing of the souls of men to the obedience of it, and for the cutting off of whomsoever or whatsoever shall oppose or withstand it. Christ was not sent of the Father to conquer by force of arms, as earthly princes do; but he conquers all sorts of sinners, even the proudest and stoutest of them,

[1] This prophecy is applied to Christ, Luke ii. 32; Acts xiii. 47; Gal. iii. 16; Heb. v. 4, 5. And many of the Jews do confess that this place is to be understood of Christ only, Mat. i. 21, 22; Luke ii. 10, 11; Heb. i. 6.

[2] See Eph. vi. 17; Heb. iv. 12; Rev. i. 16, and vi. 2.

by the sword of the Spirit, which is the word of God, as you may see by comparing the scriptures in the margin together.[1] Having spoken of the efficacy of Christ's doctrine, he tells us that he will take care of the security of his person: ' In the shadow of his hand hath he hid me, and in his quiver hath he hid me.' God the Father undertakes to protect the Lord Jesus Christ against all sorts of adversaries that should band themselves against him, and to maintain his doctrine against all enemies that should conspire to suppress it.[2] God so protected his dear Son against all the might and malice of his most capital enemies that they neither could lay hold on him, or do aught, before the time by God fore-designed was come. Christ was sheltered under the wing of God's protection till that voluntarily he went to his passion ; neither could they keep him under when that time was once over, though they endeavoured with all their might to do it. Now in the third verse, God the Father tells Jesus Christ what a glorious reward he should have for undertaking the great work of redemption: ' And said unto me, Thou art my servant, O Israel, in whom I will be glorified.'[3] God having called Christ, set him apart, sanctified him, and sent him into the world for the execution of the office of a Redeemer, he doth in this third verse encourage him to set upon it, and to go on cheerfully, resolutely, and constantly in it, with assurance of good and comfortable success, notwithstanding all the plots, designs, and oppositions that Satan and his imps might make against him. Ver. 4, ' Then I said, I have laboured in vain, I have spent my strength for nought, and in vain ; yet surely my judgment is with the Lord, and my work with my God.' In these words Jesus Christ complains to his Father of the incredulity, wickedness, and obstinate rebellion of the greatest part of the Jews against that blessed word which he had clearly and faithfully made known to them. When Christ looked upon the paucity and small number of those that his ministry had any saving and powerful work upon, he pours out his complaints before the Father: not that Christ's pains in his ministry among the Jews were wholly in vain, either in regard of God that sent him, or in regard of the persons unto whom he was sent, as if not any at all were converted. Oh no! for some were called, converted, and sanctified, as you may see by the scriptures in the margin.[4] Or in regard of himself, as if any loss or prejudice should thereby redound unto him. Oh no! but in regard of the small, the slender effect, that his great labours had hitherto found. ' Yet surely my judgment is with the Lord.' Christ, for the better support and re-encouraging of himself to persist in his employment, opposeth unto the want of the chiefly desired success of his labours with men, the gracious acceptance of them with God. It is as if Christ had said, Although my labour hath not produced such fruits and effects as I

[1] Acts ii. 37, 41, iv. 1–4, and xvi. 29–35; 2 Cor. x. 4, 6.

[2] John vii. 30, 44 ; Luke xxii. 53 ; Mat. xxvii. 62–66, and 2–6; Acts ii. 23, 24.

[3] Or, as some render the words, Thou art my servant to Israel, or for Israel; that is, for Israel's good, for my people's behoof.—Few, saith Sasbont, to this day do consider Christ's labour in preaching, prayer, fasting, and suffering a cruel death for us; for if they did, they would be more affected with love towards him that loved them so dearly. [By ' Sasbont' is probably intended Adam Sasbouth, or Sasbouthius. See his Commentarius in Isaiam. 1563 : 8vo.—G.]

[4] Isa. vi. 13, and viii. 18, &c.

indeed desired, yet I do comfort and bear up my heart with this, that my heavenly Father knows that in the office and place wherein he hath set me, I have faithfully done all that could be done for the salvation of poor sinners' souls, and for the securing of them from wrath to come: 'And my work,' or reward, 'with my God;' that is, the reward of my work, or my wages for my work, which God will render unto me, not according to the issue or success of my labours, but according to my pains therein taken, and the faithful discharge of my office and duty therein. What, saith Christ, though the Jews believe not, repent not, return not to the Most High, yet my labour is not lost, for my God will really, he will signally reward me. Upon this, God the Father comes off more freely and roundly, and opens his heart more abundantly to Jesus Christ, and tells him in the fifth and sixth verses following, that he will give him full, complete, and honourable satisfaction for all his pains and labours in preaching, in doing, in suffering, in dying, that he might bring many sons to glory. Ver. 5, 'And now, saith the Lord, that formed me from the womb to be his servant, to bring Jacob again to him, Though Israel is not gathered, yet shall I be glorious in the eyes of the Lord, and my God shall be my strength.' In this verse you have a further encouragement to our Lord Jesus Christ, God the Father engaging himself not only to support him and protect him in the work of his ministry, but of making him glorious in it and by it also; and that though his work should not prove so successful among his own people as he desired, yet his ministry should become very glorious and efficacious upon the Gentiles, far and near, throughout the whole world.[1] Jesus Christ is very confident of his being high in the esteem of his Father for the faithful discharge of his duty; and that, notwithstanding all the hard measure that he met with from the body of the Jews, that yet his Father would crown him with honour and glory, and that he would enable him to go through the work that is incumbent upon him, and that he would protect him and defend him in his work, against all might and malice, all power and policy, that should make head against him. Ver. 6, 'And he said, It is a light thing that thou shouldest be my servant, to raise up the tribes of Jacob, and to restore the preserved of Israel; I will also give thee for a light to the Gentiles, that thou mayest be my salvation to the ends of the earth.' Thus you see that God the Father still goes on to shew that the labours of Christ should be very glorious, not only in the eyes of God, but in the eyes of all the world. You know elsewhere Christ is called 'the way, the truth, and the life,' John xiv. 6; and here he is called the light and salvation of the Gentiles. God the Father, speaking to Jesus Christ, tells him that it was but a small matter, a mean thing—*Heb.*, it is too light—for him to have such happy and ample success as to reduce and win the Jews, in comparison of that further work that he intended to effect by him, even the salvation of the Gentiles unto the ends of the earth. God the Father seems to say thus to Jesus Christ, The dignity and worthiness of thy person, thou being the eternal and only Son of God, as also the high office whereunto I have called thee, requireth more excellent things than that thou shouldest only raise up and restore the people of Israel

[1] John v. 20, 23, x. 15, 17, and xvii. 1, 5; Phil. ii. 9.

to their right; I have also appointed and ordained thee for a Saviour
to the Gentiles, even to the ends of the earth; therefore though the
greatest part among the Jews will not receive thee nor submit unto
thee, yet the Gentiles they shall own thee and honour thee, they shall
embrace thee and give themselves up unto thee. I shall be briefer
in the remaining proofs; and therefore,

(4.) The fourth scripture is that, Isa. lii. 13, 14, 'Behold, my servant shall deal prudently, he shall be exalted and extolled, and be
very high.'[1] The three last verses of this chapter, with the next
chapter, do jointly make up an entire prophecy concerning Christ his
person, parentage, condition, manner of life, sufferings, humiliation,
exaltation, &c., with the noble benefits that redound to us, and the
great honour that redounds to himself. In these two verses you
have—(1.) The two parties contracting, viz., God the Father, and
Jesus Christ: 'Behold my servant,' saith God the Father. This title
is several times given by the Father to Jesus Christ, because he did
the Father great service in the work of man's redemption, freeing
fallen man from the thraldom of sin and Satan. (2.) Both parties are
very sure and confident of the event of the paction, and of the accomplishment of the whole work of redemption: 'Behold, my servant
shall deal prudently, he shall be exalted and extolled, and be very
high.' Here are divers terms heaped up to express in part the transcendent and unexpressible advancement of Jesus Christ. When men
are raised from a mean and low estate to some honourable condition,
when men are furnished with such parts and endowments of prudence,
wisdom, and understanding as makes them admirable in the eyes of
others, and when they are enabled to do and suffer great things
whereby they become famous and renowned far and near, then we say
they are highly exalted. Now in all these respects our Lord Jesus
Christ was most eminently exalted above all creatures in heaven and
earth, as is most evident throughout the Scriptures. (3.) He tells
you of the price which Jesus Christ should pay for the redemption of
his people, agreed upon by paction, viz., the humbling of himself to
the death of the cross, as you may see in ver. 14: 'As many were
astonished at thee; his visage was so marred, more than any man's,
and his form more than the sons of men.' This is the speech of the
Father to Jesus Christ; his visage was so marred that the Jews were
ashamed to own him for their King and Messiah. The astonishment
here spoken of is such an astonishment as ariseth from the contemplation of some strange, uncouth, and rueful spectacle of desolation, deformity, and misery. And no wonder if many were astonished at the
sight of our Saviour's condition, in regard of those base, disgraceful,
and despiteful usages that were offered and done to him in the time of
his humiliation here on earth, when his own followers were so amazed
at the relation of them when they were foretold of them, Mat. x.
32–34. O sirs! the words last cited are not so to be understood as if
our blessed Saviour had, in regard of his bodily person or presence,
been some strange, deformed, or misshapen creature, Isa. liii. 3, but
in regard of his outward estate, coming of mean and obscure parents,

[1] The Chaldee paraphrast, and some of [the] Jewish doctors, expound this place of the
Messiah, Isa. xlii. 1, and liii. 11, &c.

living in a low, despicable condition, exposed to scorn and contempt, and to much affliction, through the whole course of his life, and more especially yet in regard of what he was also in his personal appearance, through the base and scornful usages that he sustained at the hands of his malicious and mischievous adversaries, when they had gotten him into their power; besides his watchings, draggings to and fro from place to place, buffetings, scourgings, carrying his cross, and other base usages, could not but much alter the state of his body, and impair, yea, deface all the sightliness of it. And yet all this he suffered, to make good the compact and agreement that he had made with his Father about the redemption of his elect. But,

(5.) The fifth scripture is that 53d of Isaiah. This scripture, among many others, gives us very clear intimations of a federal transaction between God the Father and Jesus Christ, in order to the recovery and everlasting happiness of poor sinners. The glorious gospel seems to be epitomized in this chapter. The subject-matter of it is the grievous sufferings and dolorous death of Christ, and the happy and glorious issue thereof. Of all the prophets, this prophet Isaiah was the most evangelical prophet, and of all the prophecies of this prophet, that which you have in this chapter is the most evangelical prophecy.[1] In this chapter you have a most plain, lively, and full description and representation of the humiliation, death, and passion of Jesus Christ; which indeed is so exact, and so consonant to what hath fallen out since, that Isaiah seems here rather to pen a history than a prophecy.[2] The matter contained in this chapter is so convictive, from that clear light that goes along with it, that several of the Jews, in reading of this chapter, have been converted, as not being able to stand any longer out against the shining light and evidence of it. Out of this chapter, which is more worth than all the gold of Ophir, yea, than ten thousand worlds, observe with me these eight things:

[1.] First, Observe that *God and Christ are sweetly agreed, and infinitely pleased in the conversion of the elect:* ver. 10, 'He shall see his seed,' that is, he shall see them called, converted, changed, and sanctified: 'he shall see his seed,' that is, an innumerable company shall be converted to him by his word and Spirit, in all countries and nations, through the mighty workings of the Spirit, and the incorruptible seed of the word, Ps. cx. 3; 1 Pet. i. 23; infinite numbers of poor souls should be brought in to Jesus Christ, which he should see to his full content and infinite satisfaction, Rev. vii. 9; Heb. ii. 10, 13. 'He shall see his seed,' that is, he shall see them increase and multiply; he shall see believers brought in to him from all corners and quarters, and he shall see them greatly increase and grow by the preaching of the everlasting gospel, especially after his ascension into heaven, and a more glorious pouring forth of the Holy Ghost upon his apostles and others, Acts ii. 37, 41, iv. 1–4, and viii. No accountants on earth can count or reckon up Christ's spiritual seed and issue. But,

[1] Jerome calls him Isaiah the evangelist.
[2] In this chapter you have the compact and agreement between God the Father and Jesus Christ plainly asserted and proved.

[2.] Secondly, Observe with me, that *in the persons redeemed by Jesus Christ there was neither weight nor worth, neither portion nor proportion, neither inward nor outward excellencies or beauties, for which the punishment due to them should be transferred upon dear Jesus*, Ezek. xvi. 1–10; for if you look upon them in their sins, in their guilt, you shall find them despisers and rejecters of Christ: ver. 4, 'Surely he hath borne our griefs, and carried our sorrows; yet we did esteem him stricken, smitten of God, and afflicted.' Christ took upon him not our nature alone, but the infirmities also of it, and became liable to such sorrows, and afflictions, and pains, and griefs, as man's sinful nature is exposed and subject unto. They are called ours because they were procured to him by our sins, and sustained by him for the discharge of our sins; unto the guilt whereof, out of love to us undertaken by him, they were deservedly due, Rom. viii. 3; Heb. iv. 15. Christ, for our sakes, hath taken all our spiritual maladies, that is, all our sins, upon him, to make satisfaction for them; and as our surety, to pay the debt that we had run into. Christ, in the quality of a pledge for his elect, hath given full satisfaction for all their sins, bearing all the punishments due for them, in torments and extreme griefs, both of body and soul.[1] The reason why they so much disesteemed of Christ was, because they made no other account, but that all those afflictions that befell him were by God inflicted upon him for his own evil deserts. They accounted him to be one out of grace and favour with God, yea, to be one pursued by him with all those evils, for his sins. When the Jews saw what grievous things Christ suffered, they wickedly and impiously judged that he was thus handled by God, in way of vengeance for his sins. By all which, you may see, that in the persons redeemed by Christ, there was nothing of worth or honour to be found, for which the punishment, due to them, should be transferred upon our Lord Jesus Christ. But,

[3.] Thirdly, Observe with me, that *no sin, nor meritorious cause of punishment, is found in Jesus Christ, our blessed Redeemer, for which he should be stricken, smitten, and afflicted by God:* ver. 5, 9, 'He was wounded for our transgressions, he was bruised for our iniquities; the chastisement of our peace was upon him, and with his stripes we are healed. He had done no violence, neither was any deceit in his mouth.' Sin had cast God and us at infinite distance. Now Christ is punished that our sins may be pardoned; he is chastised that God and we may be reconciled. Guilt stuck close upon us, but Christ, by the price of his blood, hath discharged that guilt, pacified divine wrath, and made God and us friends.[2] God the Father laid upon dear Jesus all the punishments that were due to the elect, for whom he was a pledge; and by this means they come to be acquitted, and to obtain peace with God. 'Christ was holy, harmless, and undefiled.' No man could convince him of sin; yea, the devil himself could find nothing amiss in him, either as to word or deed. Christ was without original blemish or actual blot.[3] All

---

[1] You know they traduced him as a notorious deceiver, a drunkard, a friend of publicans and sinners, and one that wrought by the devil.

[2] 1 Pet. i. 18, 19; Rom. iii. 25, and v. 1, 10; 2 Cor. v. 19, 21; Col. i. 19, 20.

[3] Heb. vii. 26; John viii. 46, and xiv. 30; 1 John iii. 5.

Christ's words and works were upright, just, and sincere. Christ's innocency is sufficiently vindicated, ver. 9. It is true, Christ suffered great and grievous things, but not for his own sins; 'For he had done no violence, neither was any deceit found in his mouth;' but for ours. Christ had now put himself in the sinner's stead, and was become his surety, and so obnoxious to whatever the sinner had deserved in his own person; and upon this account, and no other, was he wounded, bruised, and chastised. The Lord Jesus had no sin in him by *inhesion*, but he had a great deal of sin upon him by *imputation:* 'He was made sin that knew no sin, that we might be made the righteousness of God in him,' 2 Cor. v. 21. It pleased our Lord Jesus Christ to put himself under our guilt, and therefore it pleased the Father to wound him, bruise him, and chastise him. But,

[4.] Fourthly, Observe with me, that *peace and reconciliation with God, and the healing of all our sinful maladies, and our deliverance from wrath to come, are all such noble favours as are purchased for us by the blood of Christ:*[1] ver. 5, 'The chastisement of our peace was upon him, and with his stripes we are healed.' Christ was chastised to procure our peace, by removal of our sins, that set God and us asunder; the guilt thereof being discharged with the price of his blood, and we reconciled to God by the same price. Christ was punished that we by him might obtain perfect peace with God, who was at enmity with us by reason of our sins. By Christ's stripes we are freed both from sin and punishment. Now because some produce this scripture to justify that corrupt doctrine of universal redemption, give me leave to argue thus from it. That chastisement for sin that was laid upon the person of Jesus Christ procured peace for them for whom he was so chastised, Isa. lvii. 21; Eph. ii. 14; but there was no peace procured for the reprobates, or those who should never believe, *ergo*. . . . Further, 'By his stripes we are healed.' Whence I reason thus: the stripes inflicted upon Christ are intended, and do become healing medicines for them for whom they are inflicted; but they never become healing medicines for reprobates or unbelievers: Nahum iii. 9, 'There is no healing of their bruise.' *Ergo*. . . But,

[5.] Fifthly, Observe with me, that *the great and the grievous sufferings that were inflicted upon Jesus Christ he did endure freely, willingly, meekly, patiently, according to the covenant and agreement that was made between the Father and himself:* ver. 7, 'He was oppressed and he was afflicted, yet he opened not his mouth: he is brought as a lamb to the slaughter, and as a sheep before her shearers is dumb, so he opened not his mouth.' This is a very pregnant place to prove the satisfaction made by Christ's sufferings for our sins; if we look upon the words as they run in the original, for thus they run; ' It was exacted, and he answered;' that is, the penalty due to God's justice for our sins was exacted of Christ, and he sustained the same for us. The prophet doth not speak of one and the same party or parties, both sinning and suffering or sustaining penalties for their own defaults; but as one suffering, for the sins of another, and sustaining grievous penalties for faults made and faults committed by

[1] 1 Thes. i. 10; 1 Pet. i. 18, 19; Rom. iii. 25, and v. 1, 16; 2 Cor. v. 19, 21.

other persons. The words, rightly read and understood, do sufficiently confirm the doctrine of satisfaction, made to God's justice by Christ's sufferings, for our sins. The penalty due to us was, in rigour of justice, exacted of him, and he became a sponsor or surety for us, by undertaking in our behalf the discharge of it. Christ did voluntarily undertake and engage himself unto God his Father in our behalf, as a surety for the payment of all our debts. They were exacted of him, and he answered for them all; that is, he not only undertook them, but he also discharged us of them. So we use the word commonly in our English tongue; to answer a debt, for to discharge it; and this is most true of our dear Lord Jesus, for he answered our debt, and caused our bond to be cancelled, that it might never come to be put in suit against us, either in this or that other world, John xix. 30; Rom. iv. 25; Col. ii. 14. 'Yet he opened not his mouth:' this has respect to his patience; for the oppressions and afflictions that he sustained for others, and that in regard of those by whom he suffered them unjustly, yet was he silent. He neither murmured or repined at God's disposal of things in that manner, nor used any railing or reviling speeches against those that dealt so despitefully with him, but carried himself calmly and quietly under them; Christ having an eye to his voluntary obedience and submission to the will of his Father, and agreement thereunto, Mat. xxvi. 39, 42; Mark xiv. 36; John xviii. 23; 1 Pet. ii. 23. He undertook willingly what his Father required of him, and as willingly, when the time came, underwent it; neither hanging back or opposing aught in way of contradiction thereunto, when it was by his Father propounded to him at first; nor afterward seeking to shift it off, when he was to perform what he had engaged himself unto, by pleading aught for himself, and the releasement of him from their most unjust proceedings in whose hands he then was. 'He opened not his mouth' to confute the slanders and false accusations of his enemies; neither did he utter anything to the prejudice of them that put him to death, but prayed for them that crucified him, Luke xxiii. 34; Mat. xxvi. 63, and xxvii. 12, 14. 'He was led as a lamb to the slaughter,'—properly, as a ewe-lamb, or she-lamb; the ewe is mentioned as the quieter of that kind, because the rams are sometimes more unruly,—'and as a sheep that is dumb before the face of her shearers.' A lamb doth not bite nor push him that is going about to kill it, but goeth as quietly to the shambles or the slaughter-house as if it were going to the fold wherein it is usually lodged, or the field where it is wont to feed. But,

[6.] Sixthly, Observe with me, that *the original cause of this compact or covenant between the Father and the Son, by virtue of which God the Father demands a price, and Jesus Christ pays the price according to God's demands, is only from the free grace and favour of God:* ver. 10, 'It pleased the Lord to bruise him, he hath put him to grief.' God the Father looks upon Jesus Christ as sustaining our person and cause; he looks upon all our sins as laid upon him, and to be punished in him. Sin could not be abolished, the justice of God could not be satisfied, the wrath of God could not be appeased, the terrible curse could not be removed, but by the death of Christ; and therefore God the Father took a pleasure to bruise him, and to put him to grief, according to the agreement between him and his Son. It must be readily granted that God did not incite or instigate the wicked Jews to those vile and cruel courses and carriages of theirs to Jesus Christ. But yet that his sufferings were by God pre-determined for the salvation of mankind is most evident by the scriptures in the margin ;[1] and, accordingly, it pleased the Lord to bruise him, and to put him to grief. The singular pleasure that God the Father takes in the work of our redemption is a wonderful demonstration of his love and affection to us.

[7.] Seventhly, Observe with me, that *it is agreed between the Father and the Son that our sins should be imputed unto him, and that his righteousness should be imputed unto us, and that all the redeemed should believe in him, and so be justified :* ver. 11, ' He shall see of the travail of his soul, and shall be satisfied : by his knowledge (or faith in him) shall my righteous servant justify many; for he shall bear their iniquities ;' or, as some render it, ' He shall see the fruit of the travail of his soul, and shall be satisfied '—that is, Jesus Christ shall receive and enjoy that, as the effect and issue of all the great pains that he hath taken, and of all the grievous things that he hath suffered, as shall give him full content and satisfaction. When Christ hath accomplished the work of redemption, he shall receive a full reward for all his sufferings. Christ takes a singular pleasure in the work of our redemption, and doth herein, as it were, refresh himself, as with the fruits, of his own labours. God the Father engages to Jesus Christ that he should not travail in vain, but that he should survive to see with great joy a numerous issue of faithful souls begotten unto God. You know when women, after sore, sharp, hard labour, are delivered, they are so greatly refreshed, delighted, gladded, and satisfied, that they forget their former pains and sorrow, ' for joy that a man-child is born into the world,' John xvi. 21. God the Father undertakes that Jesus Christ should have such a holy seed, such a blessed issue, as the main fruit and effect of his passion, as should joy him, please him, and as he should rest satisfied in. Certainly there could be no such joy and satisfaction to Christ as for him to see poor souls reconciled, justified, and saved by his sufferings and satisfaction ; as it is the highest joy of a faithful minister to see souls won over to Christ, and to see souls built up in Christ, 1 Thes. ii. 19, 20 ; Gal. iv. 19. Christ did bear the guilt of his people's sins, and thereby he made full satisfaction ; and therefore he is said here ' to justify many ;' not all promiscuously, but those only whose sins he undertook to discharge, and for whom he laid down his life.[2] Christ's justifying of many is his discharging of many from the guilt of sin, by making satisfaction to God for the same. But,

[8.] Eighthly, Observe with me, that *it is agreed between the Father and the Son, that for those persons for whom Jesus Christ should lay down his life, he should stand intercessor for them also, that so they may be brought to the possession of all those noble favours and blessings that he has purchased with his dearest blood :* ver. 12, ' He bare the sins of many, and made intercession for the trans-

---

[1] Acts ii. 23, and iv. 28.
[2] Besides the elect, he intercedes for none, John xvii. 9, 10.

gressors,' saying, 'Father, forgive them; for they know not what they do,' Luke xxiii. 34.   For those very transgressors, by whom he suffered, he does intercede; for the article here is emphatical, and seems to point unto that special act, and those particular persons. Not but that these words have relation also to Christ's intercession for all those sinners that belong to him, and that have an interest in him; which intercession continues still, and shall do to the end of the world, Heb. vii. 25.   But,

(6.) The sixth scripture is that, Isa. lix. 20, 21, 'And the Redeemer shall come to Zion, and unto them that turn from transgression in Jacob, saith the Lord.   As for me, this is my covenant with them, saith the Lord; My spirit that is upon thee, and my words which I have put in thy mouth, shall not depart out of thy mouth, nor out of the mouth of thy seed, nor out of the mouth of thy seed's seed, saith the Lord, from henceforth, and for ever.'   Out of this blessed scripture you may observe these following things: *First*, The parties covenanting and agreeing, and they are God the Father and Jesus Christ: God the Father in those words, 'Saith the Lord;' and Jesus Christ in those words, 'The Redeemer shall come to Zion.' *Secondly*, You have God the Father, first covenanting with Jesus Christ, and then with his seed, as is evident in the 21st verse. *Thirdly*, You have the persons described, that shall be sharers in redemption mercies, and they are the Zionites, the people of God, the citizens of Zion.   But lest any should think that all Zion should be saved, it is added by way of explication, that only such of Zion 'as turn from transgression in Jacob,' shall have benefit by the Redeemer.   The true citizens of Zion, the right Jacobs, the sincere Israelites, in whom there is no guile, Rom. xi. 26, are they and only they that turn from their sins.   None have interest in Christ, none have redemption by Christ. but converts, but such as cast away their transgressions, as Ephraim did his idols, saying, 'What have I any more to do with you?' Hosea xiv. 8.   *Fourthly*, You have the way and manner of the elect's delivery, and that is, not only by paying down upon the nail, the price agreed on, but also by a strong and powerful hand, as the original imports in the scriptures cited in the margin.[1]   The Greek word that is used by Paul, and the Hebrew word that is used by Isaiah, do both signify delivering 'by strong hand,' to rescue by force, as David delivered the lamb out of the lion's paw.   *Fifthly*, You have the special blessings that are to be conferred upon the elect—viz., redemption, conversion, faith, repentance, reconciliation, turning from their iniquity; all comprehended under that term 'the redeemed.'   *Sixthly*, You have the Lord Jesus Christ considered as the head of the church, from whom all spiritual gifts—sanctification, salvation and perseverance do flow and run, as a precious balsam, upon the members of his body: 'My Spirit that is in me,' saith God the Father, to Christ the Redeemer, 'and my word which I have put into thy mouth, shall not depart out of thy mouth; nor out of the mouth of thy seed,' &c.   In these words, God the Father engages, that his Spirit and word should continue with his church to direct and instruct it, and the children of it, in all necessaries, throughout all ages successively, even unto the world's end.   But,

[1] Rom. xi. 26; Isa. lix. 20.

(7.) The seventh scripture is that, Zech. vi. 12, 13, ' And speak unto him, saying, Thus speaketh the Lord of hosts, saying, Behold the man whose name is the Branch; and he shall grow up out of his place, and he shall build the temple of the Lord: even he shall build the temple of the Lord; and he shall bear the glory, and shall sit and rule upon his throne; and he shall be a priest upon his throne: and the counsel of peace shall be between them both.' Now that the business of man's redemption was transacted betwixt the Father and the Son, is very clear from this text, ' And the counsel of peace shall be between them both,' that is, the two persons spoken of—viz., the Lord Jehovah, who speaks, and the man, whose name is the Branch, Jesus Christ. This counsel was primarily about the reconciliation of the riches of God's grace, and the glory of his justice. The design and counsel, both of the Father and the Son, was our peace.[1] The counsel of reconciliation, how man, that is now an enemy to God, may be reconciled to God, and God to him; this counsel or consultation shall be ' betwixt them both,' that is Jehovah and the Branch. There were blessed transactions between the Father and the Son, in order to the making of peace between an angry God and sinful men. I know several learned men interpret it of Christ's offices—viz., of his kingly and priestly office; for both conspire to make peace betwixt God and man. Now if you will thus understand the text, yet it will roundly follow, that there was a consultation at the council-board in heaven, concerning the reconciliation of fallen man to God; which reconciliation Christ, as king and priest, was to bring about. Look, as there was a counsel taken, touching the creation of mankind, between the persons in the blessed Trinity, ' Let us make man after our image,' Gen. i. 26; Col. iii. 19; Eph. iv. 24; so there was a consultation held concerning the restoration of mankind out of their lapsed condition: ' The counsel of peace shall be between them both.' Certainly there was a covenant of redemption made with Christ; upon the terms whereof he is constituted to be a reconciler and a redeemer, to say to the prisoners, ' Go forth, to bring deliverance to the captives, and to proclaim the year of release or jubilee, the acceptable year of the Lord,' as it is, Isa. lxi. 1, 2. But,

(8.) The eighth scripture is that, Ps. xl. 6-8, ' Sacrifice and offering thou didst not desire; mine ears hast thou opened: burnt-offering and sin-offering hast thou not required. Then said I, Lo, I come: in the volume of the book it is written of me, I delight to do thy will, O my God; yea, thy law is within my heart'—*Heb.*, ' in the midst of my bowels.' Compared with that, Heb. x. 5-7, ' Wherefore, when he cometh into the world, he saith, Sacrifice and offering thou wouldest not, but a body hast thou prepared for me: in burnt-offerings and sacrifices for sin thou hast had no pleasure: then said I, Lo, I come, in the volume of the book it is written of me, to do thy will, O God.' In these two scriptures, two things are concluded:—(1.) The impotency of legal sacrifices, ver. 5, 6; (2.) The all-sufficiency of Christ's sacrifice, ver. 7. There is some difference in words and phrases betwixt the apostle and the prophet, but both agree in sense, as we shall

[1] Whatever Socinians say, it is most certain that reconciliation is not only on the sinner's part, but on God's also.

endeavour to demonstrate. Penmen of the New Testament were not translators of the Old, but only quoted them for proof of the point in hand, so as they were not tied to syllables and letters, but to the sense. That which the prophet speaketh of himself, the apostle applieth to Christ, say some. This may be readily granted ; for David being a special type of Christ, that may in history and type be spoken of David, which, in mystery and truth, is understood of Christ. But that which David uttered in the aforesaid text, is questionless, uttered by the way of prophecy, concerning Christ, as is evident by these reasons.

First, In David's time, God required sacrifices and burnt-offerings, and took delight therein, 1 Chron. xxi. 26 ; 1 Sam. xxvi. 19 ; for God answered David from heaven by fire, upon the altar of burnt-offering ; and David himself advised Saul to offer a burnt-offering that God might accept of it.

Secondly, David was not able so ' to do the will of God,' as by doing it, to make all sacrifices void ; therefore this must be taken as a prophecy of Christ.

Thirdly, In the verse before, namely, Ps. xl. 5, such an admiration of God's goodness is premised, as cannot fitly be applied to any other evidence, than of his goodness in giving Christ ; in reference to whom, it may be truly said, ' That eye hath not seen, nor ear heard, neither have entered into the heart of man, the things which God hath prepared for them that love him,' 1 Cor. ii. 9.

Fourthly, These words used by the apostle, ' when he cometh into the world, he saith,' are meant of Christ ; which argue that that which followeth was an express prophecy of Christ. These things being premised, out of the texts last cited we may observe these following particulars that make to our purpose.

[1.] First, *That the Holy Spirit opens and expounds the covenant of redemption, bringing in the Father and the Son, as conferring and agreeing together about the terms of it ;* and the first thing agreed on between them is the price ; and the price that God the Father stands upon is ' blood ;' and that not ' the blood of bulls and goats, but the blood of his Son ;' which was the best, the purest, and the noblest blood, that ever ran in veins.[1] Now Christ, to bring about the redemption of fallen man, is willing to come up to the demands of his Father, and to lay down his blood. The scripture calls the blood of Christ, τίμιον αἷμα, precious blood. Oh, the virtue in it, the value of it ! Through this red sea we must pass to heaven ; *Sanguis Christi clavis cœli,* Christ's blood is heaven's key. ' Precious in the sight of the Lord is the blood of the saints,' Ps. cxvi. 15, and truly ' precious in the sight of the saints is the blood of Christ.' *Una guttula plus valet quam cœlum et terra,* One little drop is more worth than heaven and earth, [Luther.] Christ's blood is ' precious blood,' in regard of the dignity of his person. It is ' the blood of God himself,' Acts xx. 28, it is the blood of that person, who is very God as well as very man. Christ's blood was noble blood, and therefore precious. He came of the race of kings, as touching his manhood ; but being withal the Son of God. This renders his nobility matchless and peerless. It was

[1] Heb. x. 4, and ix. 22 ; John x. 11, 15, 17, 18, and i. 29 ; 1 Pet. i. 18, 19.

Pharaoh's brag that he was the son of ancient kings, Isa. xix. 11. Who can lay claim to this more than Christ? Who can challenge this honour before him? He is the Son of the ancientest king in the world, he was begot a king from all eternity, Dan. vii. 9, 13, 27; and the blood of good kings is precious; ' Thou are worth ten thousand of us,' said David's subjects to him, 2 Sam. xviii. 3; and therefore they would not suffer him to hazard himself in the battle. The nobleness of his person did set a high rate upon his blood. And whom doth this argument more commend unto us than Christ? And the blood of Christ is precious blood in regard of the virtues of it. By this blood, God and man are reconciled; by this blood, the chosen of God are redeemed. It was an excellent saying of Leo, ' The effusion of Christ's blood is so rich and available, that if the whole multitude of captive sinners would believe in their Redeemer, not one of them should be detained in the tyrant's chains.'[1] This precious blood justifies our persons in the sight of God, it frees us from the guilt of sin, and it frees us from the reign and dominion of sin, and it frees us from the punishments that are due to sin, it saves us, $\dot{\alpha}\pi\dot{o}$ $\tau\hat{\eta}s$ $\dot{o}\rho\gamma\hat{\eta}s$ $\tau\hat{\eta}s$ $\dot{\epsilon}\rho\chi o\mu\acute{\epsilon}\nu\eta s$, ' from that wrath that is to come,' Acts xiii. 38, 39; Rom. iii. 24, 25; 1 John i. 7; 1 Thes. i. 10. Now were not Christ's blood of infinite value and virtue, it could never have produced such glorious effects. The blood of Christ is precious, beyond all account; and yet our Lord Jesus did not think it too dear a price to pay down for his saints. God the Father would be satisfied with no other price; and therefore God the Son comes up to his Father's price, that our redemption might be sure. But,

[2.] Secondly, Observe that *God rejects all ways of satisfaction by men.* Could men make as many prayers as there be stars in heaven and drops in the sea, and could they weep as much blood as there is water in the ocean, and should they 'give all their goods to the poor, and their bodies to be burned,' 1 Cor. xiii. 3, as some have done, yet all this would not satisfy for the least sin, not for an idle word, not for a vain thought: Heb. x. 5, 'Sacrifice and offering thou wouldest not;' that is, thou wilt not accept of them for an expiation and satisfaction for sin, as the Jews imagined. The apostle shews the impotency and insufficiency of legal sacrifices by God's rejecting of them. The things here set down not to be regarded by God—as sacrifices, offerings, burnt-offerings, and sacrifices for sin, together with other legal ordinances comprised under them—do evidently demonstrate that God regards none of those things in a way of satisfaction; they are no current price, they are no such pay that will be accepted of in the court of heaven. Remission of sin could never be obtained by sacrifices and offerings, nor by prayers, tears, humblings, meltings, watchings, fastings, penances, pilgrimages, &c. Remission of sins cost Christ dear, though it cost us nothing. Remission of sins drops down from God to us through Christ's wounds, and swims to us in Christ's blood. It was well said by one of the ancients: ' I have not whence I may glory in my own works, I have not whence I may boast myself, and therefore I will glory in Christ; I will not glory that I am righteous, but I will glory that I am redeemed; I will glory, not

[1] Leo de pas., serm. xii. c. 4.

because I am without sin, but because my sins are forgiven; I will not glory because I have profited, or because any hath profited me, but because Christ is an advocate with the Father for me, but because the blood of Christ is shed for me.'[1] Certainly the popish doctrine of man's own satisfaction in part for his sins is most derogatory to the blood, and to the plenary and complete satisfaction, of Jesus Christ. But,

[3.] Thirdly, Observe that *nothing below the obedience and suffer-ings of Christ, our mediator, could satisfy divine justice :* Heb. x. 5, 'But a body hast thou prepared me.' The Hebrew text, Ps. xl. 7, saith, 'Thou hast bored through mine ears ;' but the apostle follows the Greek translation, seeing the same sense is contained in both. Christ having declared what his Father delighteth not in, he further sheweth affirmatively what it was wherein he rested well pleased, in these words, 'But a body hast thou prepared me.' In this phrase, ' A body hast thou prepared me,' Christ is brought in, speaking to his Father. By body is meant the human nature of Christ. Body is synecdochically put for the whole human nature, consisting of body and soul; the body was the visible part of Christ's human nature. A body is fit for a sacrifice, fit to be slain, fit to have blood shed out of it, fit to be offered up, fit to be made a price, and a ransom for our sins, and fit to answer the types under the law. Pertinently there-fore, to this purpose, is it said of Christ, 'He himself bare our sins in his own body,' 1 Pet. ii. 24; and those infirmities wherein he was 'made like unto us,' Heb. ii. 9, 14, 17, were most conspicuously evi-denced in his body; and hereby Christ was manifested to be a true man : he had a body like ours, a body subject to manifold infirmities, yea, to death itself. That body which Christ had is said to be 'pre-pared by God;' the Greek word, κατηρτίσω, which is translated *pre-pared*, is a metaphor from mechanics, who do artificially fit one part of their work to another, and so finish the whole. God fitted his Son's body to be joined with the deity, and to be an expiatory sacrifice for sin. The word 'prepared' implies that God the Father ordained, formed, and made fit and able, Christ's human nature to undergo, suffer, and fulfil that for which he was sent into the world. God the Father is here said to have prepared Christ a body; because Christ having received of his Father the human nature out of the flesh and blood of the Virgin Mary by the power of the Holy Ghost, Mat. i. 20; Luke i. 31, 35, here gives up the same unto the service of his Father, to do, to suffer, to die, that he might be a sacrifice of expiation for our sins. As for the words of the psalmist, Ps. xl. 6, 'Mine ear hast thou opened,'—*Heb.*, 'digged open,' it is a proverbial manner of speech, whereby there is implied the qualifying or fitting a man unto obedience in service—the ear, or the opening of the ear, being an emblem, or symbol, or a metaphorical sign of obedience, Isa. lv. 5; Job xxxiii. 16. Now St Paul, following the translation of the Septuagint, and being directed by the Spirit of God, expounds this of God's sanctifying and fitting a body unto Christ, wherein he was obedient, even unto the shame-ful death of the cross.. These words, 'Thou hast bored through mine ears,' do import that Christ, now becoming man, gives up himself to

[1] Ambrose de Jacob, et Vita beat. lib. i. cap. vi. pp. 290, 291.

be a willing servant of his Father, to obey him unto the death of the cross. And it is a similitude taken from the servants of the Hebrews, who, after that they had served their masters six years, would not depart out of their masters' service the seventh year, but abide in it continually until death; for a testimony whereof their ear was bored through on the posts of the door, as may be seen, Exod. xxi. 6. It is therefore as much as if he should say, Thou hast given me a body that is willing and ready in thy service, even unto death. But to conclude this head, the apostle speaking of disannulling the sacrifice of the law, he uses this word *body* to set out a sacrifice which should come instead of the legal sacrifices, to effect that which the legal sacrifices could not effect. But,

[4.] Fourthly, Observe that *Christ, our mediator, freely and readily offers himself to be our pledge and surety.* ' Then said I, Lo, I come,' to wit, as surety, to pay the ransom, and to do thy will, O God. Every word carrieth a special emphasis as, (1.) The time, ' then,' even so soon as he perceived that his Father had prepared his body for such an end, then, without delay. This speed implieth forwardness and readiness ; he would lose no opportunity. (2.) His profession in this word, ' said I ;' he did not closely, secretly, timorously, as being ashamed thereof, but he maketh profession beforehand. (3.) This note of observation, ' Lo ;' this is a kind of calling angels and men to witness, and a desire that all might know his inward intention, and the disposition of his heart ; wherein was as great a willingness as any could have to anything. (4.) An offering of himself without any enforcement or compulsion ; this he manifesteth in this word, ' I come.' (5.) That very instant set out in the present tense, ' I come ;' he puts it not off to a future and uncertain time, but even in that moment, he saith, ' I come.' (6.) The first person twice expressed, thus, ' I said,' ' I come.' He sendeth not another person, nor substituteth any in his room ; but he, even he himself in his own person, cometh. All which do abundantly evidence Christ's singular readiness and willingness, as our surety, to do his Father's will, though it were by suffering, and by being made a sacrifice for our sins. God's will was the rule of Christ's active and passive obedience. Jesus Christ, our only mediator and surety, by free and ready obedience and death, did make a proper, real, and full satisfaction to God's justice for the sins of all the elect. Christ hath, by his death and blood, as an invaluable price of our redemption, made sure the favour of God, the pardon of our sins, and the salvation of our souls. Christ hath freed his chosen from all temporal, spiritual, and eternal punishments, properly so called ; so that now the mercy of God may embrace the sinner without the least of wrong to his truth or justice. But,

[5.] Fifthly, Observe that *Jesus Christ, our surety, does not only agree with his Father about the price that he was to lay down for our redemption, but also agrees with his Father about the persons that were to be redeemed, and their sanctification :* Heb. x. 10, ' By the which will '—that is, by the execution of which will, by the obedience of Christ to his heavenly Father—' we are sanctified, through the offering of the body of Jesus Christ, once for all.' Jesus Christ agrees with the Father that all those shall be sanctified for whom he has suffered and satisfied. The virtue, efficacy, and benefit of that which ariseth from the aforesaid will of the Father and of the Son is expressed under this word, 'sanctified.' To pass by the notation and divers acceptations of this word 'sanctified,' let it suffice to tell you it is not here to be taken, as distinguished from justification or glorification, as it is elsewhere taken, 1 Cor. i. 30, and vi. 11 ; but so as comprising under it all the benefits of Christ's sacrifice, Heb. x. 14, and ii. 11; Acts xxvi. 18. In this general and large extent it is sometimes taken ; only this word, sanctified, here gives us to understand that perfection consisteth especially in holiness ; for he expresseth the perfection of Christ's sacrifice under the word 'sanctified,' which implieth 'a making holy.' This was that special part of perfection wherein man was made at first, Eccles. vii. 31 ; and whereunto the apostle alludeth, where he exhorteth, 'To put on that new man, which after God is created in righteousness and true holiness,' Eph. iv. 24 ; for this end, Christ gave himself even unto death, for his church, 'that he might sanctifiy it,' Eph. v. 25. The principal thing under this word 'sanctified' in this place is, that Christ's sacrifice maketh perfect. In this respect, Christ's sacrifice is here opposed to the legal sacrifices, which could not make perfect ; so that Christ's sacrifice was offered up to do that which they could not do ; for this end was Christ's sacrifice surrogated in the room of the legal sacrifices. Now this surrogation had been in vain, if Christ's sacrifice had not made us perfect. If the dignity of his person that was offered up, and his almighty power, and unsearchable wisdom, and other divine excellencies of his, be duly weighed, we cannot but acknowledge, that as his sacrifice is perfect in itself, so it is sufficient to make us perfect also. Christ's body was given up as a price and ransom, and offered up as a sacrifice for our sins ; and that we might be sanctified and made holy, Christ, by the offering of his body once for all, has purchased of his Father grace and holiness for all his redeemed ones. Christ agrees with his Father that he will lay down an incomparable price for his chosen ones ; and then he further agrees with his Father that all those shall be sanctified for whom he has laid down an invaluable price. The will of God the Father was, that Jesus Christ should have a body, and that that body of his should be offered up, that his elect might be sanctified and saved. Now to this Christ readily answers, ' Lo, I come to do thy will.' From what hath been said from Ps. xl., compared with Heb. x., we may very safely and roundly conclude that it is most clear and evident that there was a covenant, compact, or agreement, between God the Father and Jesus Christ, concerning the redemption of fallen man. This I shall more abundantly clear up before I have said all I have to say about the covenant of redemption that is under our present consideration. But,

(9.) The ninth scripture is that, Ps. lxxxix. 28, 'My mercy will I keep for him for evermore, and my covenant shall stand fast with him.' With whom ? why, with our dear Lord Jesus, of whom David was a singular type. There are many passages in this psalm which do clearly evidence that it is to be interpreted of Christ ; yea, there are many things in this psalm that can never be clearly, pertinently, and appositely applied to any but Jesus Christ. For a taste, see ver. 19, 'I have laid help upon one that is mighty,' mighty to pardon, to reconcile, to justify, to save, to bring to glory; suitable to that of the apostle, Heb. vii. 25, 'He is able to save unto the uttermost'—that is, to all ends and purposes, perfectly, completely, fully, continually, perpetually.[1] Christ is a thorough Saviour, a mighty Saviour: Isa. lxiii. 1, 'Mighty to save.' There needs none to come after him to finish the work which he hath begun: ver. 19, 'I have exalted one, chosen out of the people,' which is the very title given to our Lord Jesus: Isa. xlii. 1, 'Behold my servant whom I uphold, mine elect,' or chosen one, 'in whom my soul delighteth: ver. 20, 'I have found David my servant.' Christ is very frequently called by that name, as being most dearly beloved of God, and most highly esteemed and valued by God, and as being typified by him both as king and prophet of his church: ver. 10, 'With my holy oil have I anointed him;' suitable to that of Christ: Luke iv. 18, 'The Spirit of the Lord is upon me, because he hath anointed me to preach the gospel to the poor;' and therefore we need not doubt of the excellency, authority, certainty, and sufficiency of the gospel: ver. 27, 'I will make him my firstborn, higher than the kings of the earth.'[2] Christ is the firstborn of every creature, and in all things hath the pre-eminence: ver. 29, 'His seed also will I make to endure for ever, and his throne as the days of heaven.'[3] This is chiefly spoken of Christ and his kingdom. The aspectable heaven is corruptible, but the kingdom of heaven is eternal; and such shall be Christ's seed, throne and kingdom: ver. 36, 'His seed shall endure for ever, and his throne as the sun before me.' 'Christ shall see his seed, he shall prolong his days, and the pleasure of the Lord shall prosper in his hands,' Isa. liii. 10. 'And his throne as the sun before me;' that is, perpetual and glorious, as the Chaldee explaineth it, 'shall shine as the sun.' Other kingdoms and thrones have their times and their turns, their rise and their ruins, but so hath not the kingdom and throne of Jesus Christ. Christ's dominion is 'an everlasting dominion,' which shall not pass away; 'and his kingdom that which shall not be destroyed,' Dan. vii. 13, 14. I might give further instances out of this Psalm, but enough is as good as a feast. Now saith God, 'I have made a covenant with him;' so then there is a covenant that God the Father hath made with Christ the mediator; which covenant, the Father engages to the Son, shall stand fast, there shall be no cancelling or disannulling of it. God the Father hath not only made a covenant of grace with the saints in Christ, of which before; but he has also made a covenant of redemption, as we call it for distinction sake, with Jesus Christ himself, 'My covenant shall stand fast with him;' that is, with Christ, as we have fully and clearly demonstrated. But,

(10.) The tenth scripture is that, Zech. ix. 11, 'As for thee also, by the blood of thy covenant,' or whose covenant is by blood, 'I have

---

[1] Ad plenum, *Erasmus;* ad perfectum, [*Faber*] *Stapulensis.*
[2] See Jer. xxx. 9; Hosea iii. 5; Ezek. xxxiv. 23.
 cannot be understood of David's seed, for Solomon's throne was overthrown.

sent forth thy prisoners out of the pit, wherein is no water.'[1]   Here
God the Father speaks to Christ, with relation to some covenant between them both ; and what covenant can that be but the covenant of
redemption ?   All the temporal, spiritual, and eternal deliverances
which we enjoy, they swim to us through the blood of that covenant
that is passed between the Father and the Son.   By virtue of the
same blood of the covenant, wherewith we are reconciled, justified,
and saved, were the Jews delivered from their Babylonish captivity.
The Babylonish captivity, thraldom, and dispersion, was that waterless
pit, that dirty dungeon, that uncomfortable and forlorn condition, out
of which they were delivered by virtue of the blood of the covenant ;
that is, by virtue of the blood of Christ, figured by the blood that was
sprinkled upon the people, and by virtue of the covenant confirmed
thereby, Exod. xxiv. 8 ; Ps. lxxiv. 20 ; Heb. xiii. 20.   Look, as all
the choice mercies, the high favours, the noble blessings that the
saints enjoy, are purchased by the blood of Christ ; so they are made
sure to the saints by the same blood ; by the blood of thy covenant ' I
have sent forth thy prisoners.'   Whatever desperate distresses, and
deadly dangers, the people of God may fall into, yet they are ' prisoners
of hope,' and may look for deliverance by the blood of the covenant.

By these ten scriptures it is most clear and evident that there was
a covenant, a compact, and agreement between God the Father and
our Lord Jesus Christ, concerning the work of our redemption.
Christ's being called ' the surety of the better covenant,' Heb. vii. 21,
shews that there was a covenant between God the Father and him,
as there is between a creditor and a surety.   Christ gave bonds, as it
were, to God the Father, and paid down the debt upon the nail, that
breaches might be made up between God and us, and we restored to
divine favour for ever.   But for the further clearing up of the covenant of redemption, I shall, in the second place, lay down these propositions.   And,

(1.) The first is this, *That the covenant of redemption differs from
the covenant of grace.*   It is true, the covenant of redemption is a
covenant of grace, but it is not properly that covenant of grace which
the Scripture holds out in opposition to the covenant of works ; which
I shall thus evidence :—

[1.] The covenant of redemption differs from the covenant of grace
in regard of the federates.   In the covenant of redemption, it is God
the Father and Jesus Christ that mutually covenant ; but in the
covenant of grace the confederates are God and believers.

[2.] In the covenant of redemption, God the Father requires of
Jesus Christ that he should suffer, shed his blood, die, and make himself an offering for our sins.   In the covenant of grace, God requires
of us that we should believe and embrace the Lord Jesus.

[3.] In the covenant of redemption, God the Father has made many
great, precious, and glorious promises to Jesus Christ.   As, ' Sit on my
right hand, till I make thine enemies thy footstool,' Heb. i. 13 ; and,
' He shall see his seed, he shall prolong his days, the pleasure of the
Lord shall prosper in his hands,' Isa. liii. 10 ; and, ' Ask of me, and I

---

[1] And thou also died with the blood of thy covenant, when I have sent out thy prisoners
out of the cistern in which there are no waters.—*Tremellius.*

will give thee the heathen for thine inheritance, and the uttermost parts of the earth for thy possession,' Ps. ii. 8; and, 'I will be to him a Father, and he shall be to me a Son,' Heb. i. 5. But in the covenant of grace, God promises to us grace and glory, holiness and happiness, both the upper and the lower springs, Ps. lxxxiv. 11; Ezek. xxxvi. 26, 27.

[4.] The covenant of redemption betwixt God and Christ secures the covenant of grace betwixt God and believers; for what God promises to us, he did, before the foundation of the world, promise to Jesus Christ, Titus i. 2; and therefore, if God the Father should not make good his promises to his saints, he would not make good his promises to his dearest Son, which for any to imagine would be high blasphemy. God will be sure to keep touch with Jesus Christ; and therefore we may rest fully assured that he will not fail to keep touch with us.

[5.] The covenant of redemption is the very basis or bottom of the covenant of grace. God made a covenant with Christ, the spiritual David, that he might make a covenant with all his elect in him, Ps. lxxxix. 3, 4; Rom. xi. 26, 27. He made this agreement with Christ, as the head, and on this is reared up the whole frame of precious promises comprised in the covenant of grace, as a goodly building upon a sure foundation. But,

(2.) The second proposition is this, *God the Father, in order to man's redemption and salvation, stands stiffly and peremptorily upon complete satisfaction.* Without full satisfaction, no remission, no salvation. Satisfaction God will have to the utmost, though it cost Christ his life and blood. Man is fallen from his primitive purity, glory, and excellency, and by his fall he hath provoked divine justice, transgressed God's righteous law, and cast a deep dishonour upon his name, Rom. viii. 32. The case standing thus, God is resolved to have ample satisfaction in the reparation of his honour, in the manifestation of his truth, and in the vindication of his holiness and justice. All the attributes of God are alike dear to him, and he stands as much upon the advance of his justice as he does upon the glory of his grace; and therefore he will not remit one sin, yea, not the least sin, without entire satisfaction. In this God the Father is fixed, that he will have 'an offering for sin,' in an expiatory and propitiatory way; 'a price and a ransom' he will have paid down upon the nail, or else the captive sinner shall never be released, pardoned, saved, Isa. liii. 10; 1 Tim. ii. 6. Now lost man being wholly incapable of giving such a satisfaction to divine justice, Christ must give it, or fallen man must perish for ever. Sin and sorrow, iniquity and misery, always go hand in hand. 'The wages of sin is death,' Rom. vi. 23. Every sinner is worthy of death. 'They which commit such things are worthy of death,' Rom. i. 32. If God be a just and righteous God, then sin cannot absolutely escape unpunished; for it is but 'a just and righteous thing with God' to punish the sinner, who is worthy of punishment. 'It is a righteous thing with God,' saith the apostle, 'to recompense tribulation to them that trouble you,' 2 Thes. i. 6. And as God cannot but be just, so he cannot but be true; and if he cannot but be true, then he cannot but make good his threatenings against sin and sinners. The word is

gone out of his mouth, ' In the day that thou eatest thereof thou shalt
surely die; and the soul which sins shall die,' Gen. ii. 17. Look, as
there is not a promise of God but shall take place in time, so there is
not a threatening of God but shall take place in time, Ezek. xviii. 4.
The faithfulness of God, and the honour of God, is as much concerned
in making good of terrible threatenings, as they are concerned in making good of precious promises, 2 Pet. i. 4. God has given it under
his own hand, that ' he will by no means clear the guilty;' and that
' the soul that sinneth shall surely die;' and that ' the wickedness of
the wicked shall be upon him;' and that ' he will render to every man
according to his deeds,' Exod. xxxiv. 7; Ezek. xviii. 20; Rom. ii. 6.
And will God abrogate his own laws, or will he dare men to sport and
play with his threatenings? Will not every wise and prudent prince
look to the execution of their own laws? and shall not that God, who is
wonderful in wisdom, and whose understanding is infinite, see all his
laws put in execution against offenders? Isa. xl. 28; Ps. cxlvii. 5.
Surely yes. Thus you see that God stands upon full satisfaction, and
will admit of no treaty of peace with fallen man without it. Now
sorry man is never able, either by doing or suffering, to compensate
and make God amends for the wrong and injury that he has done to
God by his sin; and therefore one that is able, by doing and suffering,
to give complete satisfaction, must undertake it, or else we are lost,
cast, and undone in both worlds. Concerning that full and complete
satisfaction that Jesus Christ has given to God's enraged justice, I
have in part discovered already, and shall say no more to it before I
close up the covenant of redemption. But,

(3.) The third proposition is this, *The business transacted between
those two great and glorious persons, God the Father,* ' *whose greatness
is unsearchable,*' Ps. cxlv. 3, *and Jesus Christ,* ' *who is the prince of
the kings of the earth,*' Rev. i. 5, *was the redemption and salvation of
the elect.* Our everlasting blessedness was now fresh in their eyes, and
warm upon their hearts. How lost man might be found, and how fallen
man might be restored, and how miserable man might be made happy,
how slaves might be made sons, and how enemies might be made
friends, Luke xv. 30, and how those that ' were afar off might be
made nigh,' Eph. ii. 12–17, without the least prejudice to the honour,
holiness, justice, wisdom, and truth of God, was the grand business,
the thing of things, that lay before them. Upon the account of the
covenant, compact, and agreement that was between the Father and the
Son, it is that Christ is called ' the second Adam,' 1 Cor. xv. 25; for
as with the first Adam God plighted a covenant concerning him and
his posterity, so also he did indent with Jesus Christ, concerning that
eternal redemption, that he was to obtain and secure for his seed, Heb.
ix. 12. For the clearing of this, let us a little consider of the excellent properties of that redemption that we have by Jesus Christ.

[1.] First, *It is a great redemption.* The work of redemption was
a great work. The greatness of the person employed in this work
speaks out the work to be a great work. This was a work too high,
too hard, too great for all the angels in heaven, and all the men on
earth to undertake. None but that Jesus who is ' mighty to save,'

Isa. lxiii. 1, was ever able to bring about the redemption of man. Hence Christ is called the Deliverer, Rom. xi. 26 : ' And their redeemer is mighty,' Prov. xxiii. 11; Isa. xliv. 6, ' And his redeemer, the Lord of hosts ;' Isa. xlvii. 4, ' As for our redeemer, the Lord of hosts is his name ;' Isa. xlix. 26, ' And thy redeemer, the mighty one of Jacob ;' Jer. l. 34, ' Their redeemer is strong, the Lord of hosts is his name.' Again, the great and invaluable price that was paid down for our redemption speaks it out to be a great redemption. The price that we are bought with is a price beyond all compute. 1 Pet. i. 18, 19, ' Forasmuch as ye know that ye were not redeemed with corruptible things, as silver and gold, from your vain conversation ; but with the precious blood of Christ, as of a lamb without blemish and without spot,' 1 Cor. vi. 19, 20, and vii. 23. Christ was a lamb (1.) for harmlessness; (2.) for patience and silence in afflictions; (3.) for meekness and humility; (4.) for sacrifice. This lamb was ' without blemish,' Isa. liii. 7, that is, free from actual sin, and 'without spot,' that is, free from original sin, Jer. xi. 19, [Aquinas.] That the most absolute and perfect purity of Christ—prefigured in the lambs of the Old Testament, that were to be sacrificed—might be better expressed, the apostle calls him ' a lamb without blemish, and without spot,' Eph. v. 27. The price that this lamb without a spot has laid down is sufficient to pay all our debts; it is a price beyond all compute. All the silver, gold, pearls, jewels in the world, are of no value, in respect of this price ; a price in itself infinite, and of infinite value. Among the Romans, the goods and estates which men had gotten in the wars, with hazard of their lives, were called *peculium castrense*, or a field-purchase.[1] Oh how well then may the elect be called Christ's *peculium castrense*, his purchase, gotten not only by the jeopardy of his life, but with the loss of his life and blood, John x. 11, 15, 17, 18, and Acts xx. 28. Again, if you compare the work of redemption with other great works, you must necessarily conclude that the work of redemption is a great work. The making of the world was a great work of God, but yet that did but cost him a word of his mouth, a ' let it be ;' he spake the word, and it was done ; ' He said, Let there be light, and there was light,' &c., Gen. i. 3-6, 9, 11, 14, 20, 24 ; but the work of redemption cost Christ's dearest blood. Much matter of admiration doth the work of redemption afford us. The work of creation is many ways admirable, yet not to be compared with the work of redemption, wherein the power, wisdom, justice, mercy, and other divine attributes of God do much more shine forth ; and wherein the redeemed reap much more good than Adam did by his creation, which will evidently appear by observing these particular differences :

First, In the creation God brought something out of nothing ; but in the work of redemption, out of one contrary he brought another ; out of death he brought life. This was a work of far greater power, wisdom, mercy. Death must first be destroyed, and then life brought forth.

Secondly, In creation there was but a word ; and thereupon the

[1] Neither God nor Christ could lay down a greater price. All things in heaven and earth are not to be compared to this blood, to this price.

work followed; in redemption there was doing and dying. The work of redemption could be brought about by none but God. God must come down from heaven, God must be made man, God must be made sin, God must be made a curse, 2 Cor. v. 21; Gal. iii. 13.

Thirdly, In the creation God arrayed himself with majesty, power, and other like properties, fit for a great work ; in the work of redemption he put on weakness, he assumed a nature subject to infirmities, and the infirmities of that nature. He did as David did when he fought against Goliah, he ' put off all armour, and took his staff in his hand, and drew near to the Philistine,' 1 Sam. xvii. 39, 40.

Fourthly, In the work of creation there was nothing to withstand God, to make opposition against God; but in the work of redemption there was justice against mercy, wrath against pity; death, and he that had the power of death, was vanquished, Heb. ii. 14, 15; Col. ii. 14, 15.

Fifthly, By creation man was made after God's image, like him, Gen. i. 26, 27; by redemption man was made a member of the same mystical body 'whereof Christ is the head,' Eph. i. 22, 23.

Sixthly, By creation man received a natural being, by redemption a spiritual.

Seventhly, By creation man received a possibility to stand, by redemption a certainty of standing and impossibility of falling, John x. 28-31; 1 Pet. i. 5; Jer. xxxii. 40, 41.

Eighthly, By creation man was placed in an earthly paradise, but by redemption he is advanced to an heavenly paradise.

Thus you see how the work of redemption transcends the work of creation. Again, the works of providence are great, very great, in the eye of God, of angels, of men; but what are the works of providence to the works of redemption? For in order to the accomplishment of that great work, Christ must put off his royal robes, take a journey from heaven to earth, assume our nature, do and die, &c. Again, the work of redemption by Christ will be found a great work, if you will but compare it with those redemptions that were but types of this. Israel's redemption from their Egyptian bondage, and from their Babylonish bondage, were very great redemptions, that were brought about by a strong hand, a mighty hand, and an out-stretched arm, as the Scripture speaks; but, alas! what were those redemptions to our being redeemed from the love of sin, the guilt of sin, the dominion of sin, the damnatory power of sin, and to our being redeemed from the power of Satan, the curse of the law, hell and wrath to come? 1 Thes. i. 10. Lastly, the great things that are wrapped up in the womb, in the belly, of redemption, speak out our redemption by Christ to be a very great redemption. In the womb of this redemption you shall find reconciliation, justification, adoption, eternal salvation, &c. ; and are not these great, very great, things ? Surely yes. But,

[2.] A second excellent property of that redemption that we have by Christ is this, that it is *a free and gracious redemption*. All the rounds in this ladder of redemption are made up of free, rich, and sovereign grace. Though our redemption cost Christ dear, as has been before hinted, yet as to us it is most free: Eph. i. 7, 'In whom we have redemption through his blood, the forgiveness of sins, according to the riches of his grace;' that is, according to his exceeding great and abundant grace: 'Being justified freely by his grace, through the redemption that is in Christ Jesus.'[1] Our redemption is from the free love and favour of God. It was free grace that put God the Father upon finding out a way for the redemption of lost sinners. It was free grace that put God upon providing of such a surety, as should undertake the work of redemption, as should carry on the work of redemption, and as should accomplish and complete the work of redemption; and it was free grace that moved God the Father to accept of what Christ did and suffered, in order to the bringing about of our redemption; and it is free grace that moves God to make an application of this redemption to the souls of his people. Ah, poor souls! the Lord looks not, neither for money nor money's worth from you, towards the purchase of your redemption, and therefore always look upon your redemption as the mere fruit of rich grace, Isa. lii. 3. But,

[3.] The third excellent property of that redemption that we have by Jesus Christ is this, it is *a full and plenteous redemption*: Ps. cxxx. 7, 'Let Israel hope in the Lord; for with the Lord there is mercy, and with him is plenteous redemption.' Christ redeems us from all sin, and from all the consequences of sin. He redeems from death, and from the power of the grave; he redeems us from the law, and from the malediction of the law. Christ took that off; he was made a curse for all that believe on him.[2] He did not only stand in the room of eminent believers, but he stood in the room of all believers, and endured the wrath of God to the uttermost for every one that believeth on him. Every believer is freed from a cursed estate by the least faith. Every degree of true faith makes the condition to be a state of life, and passeth us from death and condemnation: 'There is no condemnation to them that are in Christ Jesus.' And Christ redeems us from this present evil world, and from the earth, and from among men, and from wrath to come, and from 'the hands of all our enemies.'[3] Jesus Christ hath gone thorough-stitch[4] with the work of our redemption. Christ does not his work by halves; all his works are perfect; there is no defect or flaw in them at all. Christ does not redeem us from some of our sins, and leave us to grapple with the rest; he doth not work out some part of our redemption, and leave us to work out the rest; he doth not bear the heat and burden of divine wrath in part, and leave us to wrestle with other parts of divine wrath. Oh, no; Christ makes most complete work of it. He redeems us from 'all our iniquities; he delivers us out of the hands of all our enemies,' Heb. vii. 25. He pays all debts, he cuts all scores, he delivers from all wrath, he takes off the whole curse, he saves to the uttermost, and will settle us in a state of full and perfect freedom, when grace shall be turned into glory. In heaven our redemption shall be entire and perfect.

[4.] The fourth excellent property of that redemption that we have

[1] ἀπολύτρωσιν. This word properly signifies a deliverance, which is brought to pass by paying of a ransom and price. See Mat. xx. 28; 1 Cor. vi. 20; 1 Pet. i. 18.
[2] Hosea xiii. 14; Titus ii. 14; Rom. vii. 6; Gal. iv. 5, and iii. 13.
[3] Rom. viii. 1; Gal. i. 4; Rev. xiv. 3, 4; 1 Thes. i. 10; Luke i. 71, 74.
[4] 'Completely.'—G.

by Jesus Christ, is this, it is *an eternal, a permanent, a lasting, yea, an everlasting redemption:* Heb. ix. 12, 'Neither by the blood of goats and calves, but by his own blood, he entered in once into the holy place, having obtained eternal redemption for us.' Redemption is in general a freeing one out of thraldom, Exod. vi. 6. Now this is done three ways—(1.) By interceding and pacifying wrath. Thus the prophet Oded, 2 Chron. xxviii. 9, &c., procured redemption for the captives of Judah by his intercession. (2.) By force and might. Thus Abraham redeemed his brother Lot, and the people that were captives with him, by overcoming their enemies, Gen. xiv. 16. (3.) By ransom, or paying a price. Thus a Hebrew that was sold a slave to a stranger might be redeemed by one of his brethren, Lev. xxv. 48, 49. The last of these is most agreeable to the notation of the several words, which in the three learned languages do signify to redeem, though the last be especially intended. In that, mention is made of a price, namely, Christ's blood; yet the other two are not altogether exempted, for Christ hath all those three ways redeemed his people. This will more clearly appear if we duly weigh the distinct kinds of bondage in which we were by reason of sin—(1.) We were debtors to divine justice, Mat. vi. 12; (2.) We were children of wrath, Eph. ii. 3; (3.) We were slaves to Satan, Heb. ii. 14, 15. (1.) As debtors, Christ hath paid a ransom for us; (2.) As children of wrath, Christ makes intercession for us; (3.) But though divine justice be satisfied and divine wrath pacified, yet the devil will not let his captives go; therefore Christ by a strong hand wrests us out of Satan's power, 'and destroys him that had the power of death, that is, the devil,' Heb. ii. 14, 15. The ransom which Christ paid was the ground of man's full and eternal redemption, for by satisfaction of justice way was made to pacify wrath; both which being accomplished, the devil lost his right and power over such as he held in bondage. This redemption is a full freedom from all misery, and compriseth under it reconciliation, justification, sanctification, and salvation. By this redemption divine justice is satisfied, wrath pacified, grace procured, and all spiritual enemies vanquished. The perfection of this redemption is hinted in this word *eternal.* The eternity here meant hath a special respect to the continual duration thereof without end, yet also it respecteth the time past, so as it looks backward and forward. It implieth a virtue and efficacy from the beginning of the world, for Christ was 'a lamb slain from the foundation of the world,' Rev. xiii. 8. Christ himself is, Rev. i. 8, 'Alpha and Omega, the beginning and the ending, which is, and which was, and which is to come.' Now that which is spoken of the person of Christ may very well be applied to our redemption by Christ. This epithet *eternal* is here added to redemption, in opposition to the legal purifications, which were momentary and temporary. They had a day, and endured no longer than the 'time of reformation.' On this ground, by just and necessary consequence, it followeth that the redemption wrought by Christ is absolutely perfect, and that there is no need of any other. This being eternal, all that have been, all that shall be redeemed, have been and shall be redeemed by it; and they who are redeemed by it need no other means. The liberty whereinto Christ Jesus brings the elect is permanent and lasting, it abides irremoveable and unchangeable to all eternity. The Jews which had sold themselves to be servants were to be set free at the jubilee, yet the jubilee lasted but for one year; therefore the same persons might afterwards become bondmen again, Lev. xxv. But this 'acceptable year of the Lord's redeemed,' Isa. lxi. 2, and lxiii. 4, is an everlasting year, it shall never end; therefore they shall never be subject to bondage any more. It is observable that when the Lord would comfort the Jews with hopes of a return from Babylon, he usually annexed evangelical promises respecting the deliverance of poor sinners from the slavery of Satan, whereof that captivity was a type, some of which promises do plainly express the perpetuity of that spiritual freedom which they shall enjoy. Take a taste: [1] Isa. xxxv. 10, 'And the ransomed of the Lord shall return, and come to Zion with songs and everlasting joy upon their heads: they shall obtain joy and gladness, and sorrow and sighing shall flee away.' Isa. li. 6, 'Lift up your eyes to the heavens, and look upon the earth beneath; for the heavens shall vanish away like smoke, and the earth shall wax old like a garment, and they that dwell therein shall die in like manner: but my salvation shall be for ever, and my righteousness shall not be abolished.' Isa. lx. 19, 20, 'The sun shall be no more thy light by day; neither for brightness shall the moon give light unto thee: but the Lord shall be unto thee an everlasting light, and thy God thy glory. Thy sun shall no more go down; neither shall thy moon withdraw itself: for the Lord shall be thine everlasting light, and the days of thy mourning shall be ended.' Jer. xxxi. 11, 12, 'For the Lord hath redeemed Jacob, and ransomed him from the hand of him that was stronger than he. Therefore they shall come and sing in the height of Zion, and their soul shall be as a watered garden, and they shall not sorrow any more at all.' But,

[5.] The fifth excellent property of that redemption that we have by Jesus Christ is this—viz., it is *an enriching redemption;* it is a redemption that makes men rich in 'spiritual blessings in heavenly places,' Eph. i. 3. There are many choice and rare spiritual benefits that 'wait and attend on redemption, that go hand in hand with redemption: as reconciliation, remission of our sins, justification of our persons, adoption, sanctification, full glorification, Rom. v. 1, and iii. 24, 25. We have some foretastes of it in this life. Here we have the 'first-fruits of the Spirit,' Rom. viii. 23, 30; but in the morning of the resurrection we shall reap the whole harvest of glory. It is called, by way of eminency, 'the salvation of our souls,' 1 Pet. i. 9. Redemption, and the noble benefits attending on it, are salvation begun; but in heaven this shall be salvation consummate. Redemption is a rich mine, containing a mass of treasure that cannot be valued. Could we dig into it, could we pry into it, we might find variety of the choicest jewels and pearls, in comparison whereof all the riches of the Indies, all the gold of Ophir, and all the precious jewels and most orient pearls that are in the world, are no better than dross. I have read of Tiberius the emperor, that passing by a place where he saw a cross lying in the ground upon a marble stone, and causing the stone to be digged up, he found a great treasure under

[1] See also Jer. xxxii. 39; Ezek. xxxvii. 25-28, and xxxix. 29.

the cross: but what was this treasure but a great nothing to that treasure that is wrapped up in our redemption by Christ! What the Lord said once to his anointed Cyrus, a temporal deliverer of his people, the same he hath spoken, and much more, to his anointed Jesus, the greater Saviour and Redeemer of his church: 'I will give thee the treasures of darkness, the hidden riches of secret places,' Isa. xliii. 3. There are 'unsearchable riches' in Jesus Christ.[1] In him are riches of grace, of all grace; in him are riches of justification, and riches of sanctification, and riches of consolation, and riches of glorification. Would you share in the best of riches, would you share in the most durable riches, would you share in soul riches, would you share in heavenly riches? Oh, then, secure your interest in the redemption that is by Jesus Christ. But,

[6.] The sixth, and last, excellent property of that redemption that we have by Jesus Christ is this—viz., it is a *redemption-sweetening redemption;* it is such a redemption as sweetens all other redemptions. It is redemption by Christ that sweetens our redemption out of this trouble and that, out of this affliction and that, out of this danger and that, out of this sickness and that, out of this bondage and that. Redemption by Christ is like that tree which Moses cast into the bitter waters of Marah, that made them sweet, Exod. xv. 23. This water became sweet for the use and service of the Israelites for a time only, and remained not always sweet after, as appears by Pliny's Natural History, who makes mention of those bitter waters in his time.[2] But the redemption that we have by Jesus Christ does for ever sweeten all the bitter trials and afflictions that we meet with in this world. The Jewish doctors say that this tree was bitter, and they give us this note upon it, 'that it is the manner of the blessed God to sweeten that which is bitter by that which is bitter.' I shall not dispute about the truth of their notion; but this I may safely say, that it is the manner of the blessed God to sweeten our greatest troubles, and our sharpest trials, by that redemption that we have by Jesus Christ. And thus you see the excellent properties of that redemption that Jesus Christ, by covenant or compact with his Father, was engaged to work for us. But,

(4.) The fourth proposition is this—viz., *That the blessed and glorious titles that are given to Jesus Christ, in the Holy Scriptures, do clearly and strongly evidence that there was a covenant of redemption passed between God the Father and Jesus Christ.* He is called a 'mediator of the covenant' of reconciliation, interceding for and procuring of it; and that not by a simple entreaty, but by giving himself over to the Father, calling for satisfaction to justice, that reconciliation might go on, for paying a compensatory price sufficient to satisfy divine justice for the elect. 'There is one God, and one mediator between God and men'—to wit, God incarnate—'the man Christ Jesus, who gave himself a ransom for all'—to wit, his elect children—'to be testified in due time,' 1 Tim. ii. 5, 6. Let me glance a little upon the words, 'one mediator between God and men.' In the Greek, it is one mediator of God and men; which may

---

[1] See my treatise called 'The Unsearchable Riches of Christ.' — [Vol. iii. p. 1, *seq.*—G.]   [2] Plin. Natural History, lib. vi., cap. 29.

refer either to the two parties betwixt which he deals, pleading for God to men and for men to God, or to the two natures, mediator of God, having the divine nature, and of men, having the human nature upon him; one mediator, not of redemption only, as the papists grant, but of intercession too. We need no other master of requests in heaven, but the man Christ Jesus, who being so near us, in the matter of his incarnation, will never be strange to us in the business of intercession. 'A ransom,' the Greek ἀντίλυτρον, is *a counter-price* such as we could never have paid, but must have remained and even rotted in prison, but for our all-sufficient surety and Saviour. The ransom that Christ paid was a real testimony of his mediatorship betwixt God and men, whereby he reconciled both. 'The man Christ Jesus.' Paul speaks not this to exclude his divinity from this office of mediatorship, for he is 'God manifested in the flesh,' 1 Tim. iii. 16, and 'God hath purchased his church by his own blood,' Acts xx. 28; but to shew that, in his human nature, he paid the ransom for us, and that, as man, he is like unto us, Heb. ii. 10; and therefore all sorts and ranks of men have a free access by faith unto him, and to his sacrifice. He is also called a Redeemer, 'I know that my Redeemer liveth,' Job xix. 25. The word redeemer in the Hebrew is very emphatical, *Goel;* for it signifieth a kinsman, near allied unto him; one that was bone of his bone, and flesh of his flesh.[1] Christ is of our kindred by incarnation, and redeems us by his passion. The words are an allusion to the ceremonial law, where the nearest kinsman was to take the wife and buy the land, Ruth iii. 9, 12, 13, and iv. 4, 5. We were Satan's by nature, but Christ our brother, our kinsman, hath redeemed us by the price of his own blood, and will deliver us from hell, and bring us 'to the inheritance of the saints in light,' John xx. 17; and therefore deserves the name of a redeemer, 1 Pet. i. 3, 4; Col. i. 12. Jesus Christ is near, very near, yea, nearest of kin to us, Eph. v. 30; he is flesh of our flesh, and bone of our bone, and blood of our blood: 'Forasmuch as the children are partakers of flesh and blood, he also himself took part of the same,' Heb. ii. 14. Now it is evident, by the old law of redemption, that the nearest kinsman was under a special obligation to redeem; as you may see by comparing Ruth iii. 12, 13 with iv. 4, 5. Boaz was a kinsman, and had right to redeem; yet because there was a nearer kinsman, he would not engage himself, but upon his refusal: 'If thou wilt redeem it, redeem it; but if thou wilt not redeem it, then tell me, that I may know; for there is none to redeem it besides thee, and I am after thee.' Now Jesus Christ is nearest of kin to us, and therefore, upon the strictest terms and laws of redemption, he is *Goel*, our Redeemer. If we consider Jesus Christ as a kinsman, a brother, we must say, that he had not only a right to redeem us; but that he was also under the highest obligation to redeem us. There is a double way of redeeming persons:—(1.) By force and power: thus when Lot was taken prisoner by those four kings that came against Sodom, 'Abraham armed his servants,' and by force and power redeemed them, Gen. xiv. 14, 16. We were all Satan's prisoners, Satan's captives, but Christ our nearest

---

[1] Some read the words thus, 'I know that my kinsman, or he that is near to me, liveth.'

kinsman, our brother, ' by spoiling principalities and powers,' Col. ii. 15, rescues us out of that tyrant's hand.   (2.) There is a redemption by price or ransom; to redeem is to buy again, 1 Cor. vi. 20, ' Ye are bought with a price ;' vii. 23, ' Ye are bought with a price.'   The word price is added, not by a *pleonasmus*, but κατ᾽ ἐξοχὴν, to intimate the excellency and dignity of the price wherewith they were bought, which was not ' silver or gold; but the precious blood of Christ, as of a lamb without blemish, and without spot,' 1 Pet. i. 18, 19.   ' Ye are bought with a price;' that is, ye are dearly bought, by a price of inestimable value; but of this before.   Again, sometimes Christ is called ' the surety of a better covenant.'   Heb. vii. 22, ' By so much was Jesus made a surety of a better testament,' so called from the manner of the confirmation of it—viz., by the death of Christ.   Look, as Christ was our surety to God, for the discharge of our debt—the surety and debtor, in law, are reputed as one person—so he is God's surety to us, for the performance of his promises.   The office of a surety being applied to Christ sheweth that he hath so far engaged himself for us, as that he neither can nor will start from his engagement.   You shall as soon remove the earth, stop the sun in his course, empty the sea with a cockle-shell, make a world, and unmake yourselves, as any power on earth, or in hell, shall ever be able to hinder Christ from the performance of the office of a surety.   A perfect fulfilling of all righteousness, according to the tenor of the law, is required of man.   Now Christ our surety, by a voluntary subjection of himself to the law, and by being made under the law, he hath fulfilled all righteousness, Gal. iv. 4; Mat. iii. 15; and that he did this for us is evident by that phrase of the apostle, Rom. v. 19, ' By the obedience of one shall many be made righteous.'   The contents of the law must be accomplished by our surety, or else we can never escape the curse of the law, Gal. iii. 10, 13 ; there must be a translation of the law from us in our persons, unto the person of our surety, or we are undone, and that for ever.   Christ is the end of the law for righteousness, and hath made us just by his obedience ; ' We are made the righteousness of God in him,' Rom. x. 4.   Our surety became subject to the law, that he might redeem us that were obnoxious to the law, 2 Cor. v. 21.   Again, full satisfaction for every transgression is required of man.   Now Christ our surety hath made satisfaction for all our sins, he was made a curse for us,' Gal. iii. 13 ; and by that means he hath redeemed us from the curse of the law.   To exact a debt which is fully satisfied, is a point of injustice.   Now Christ our surety having made full satisfaction for all our sins, we need not fear to stand before the face of God's justice.   A debtor that hath a surety that is able and willing to pay his debt, yea, who hath fully paid it, need fear no colours.   This title, ' a surety of a better covenant,' does necessarily import a blessed covenant between Jesus Christ and his dear Father, to whom he freely and readily becomes surety for us ; for what is suretyship but a voluntary transferring of another's debt upon the surety, he obliging to pay the debt for which he engageth as surety ? Thus you see, by the blessed and glorious titles that are given to Jesus Christ in the Scriptures, that there was a covenant of redemption passed between God the Father and Jesus Christ.   But,

(5.) The fifth proposition is this, *That the work of our redemption and salvation, was transacted between God the Father and Jesus Christ, before the foundation of the world.* This federal transaction between the Father and the Son was from eternity. Upon this account the Lord Jesus is said to be ' the Lamb slain from the foundation of the world,' Rev. xiii. 8, because that it was agreed and covenanted between God the Father and Jesus Christ, that he should, in the fulness of time, be made flesh and die for sinners; and therefore it was said to be done from the foundation of the world.[1] Though Christ was not actually slain, but when he suffered for us upon the cross, yet he was slain from the beginning in God's purpose, in God's decrees, in God's promises, in the sacrifices, in the faith of the elect, and in the martyrs; for Abel, the first that ever died, died a martyr, he died for religion. This compact betwixt the Father and the Son bears date from eternity. This the apostle asserts: 2 Tim. i. 9, 'Who hath saved us and called us with an holy calling; not according to our works, but according to his own purpose and grace, which was given us in Christ Jesus, before the world began.'[2] Here is grace given us in Christ Jesus before the world began. But what grace was that which was given us in Christ Jesus before the world began? Doubtless it was the grace of redemption, which God, in his purpose and decree, had given us in Christ Jesus, before the world began. The scripture last cited does clearly shew that God the Father and Jesus Christ dealt together about the redemption of souls before the world began; and that all our everlasting concernments were agreed on and made sure between them: so that Titus i. 2 gives the same sound, ' In hope of eternal life; which God, that cannot lie, promised before the world began.' How was this life promised before the world began, but in this covenant of redemption, wherein God the Father promised and engaged to Jesus Christ that he would give eternal life to all his seed? So the apostle tells us, ' He hath chosen us in him,' that is, in Christ, 'before the foundation of the world.' There was an eternal contrivance, compact, covenant, or agreement between God the Father and Jesus Christ, concerning the sanctification, holiness, and salvation of the elect. God agrees with Christ about the everlasting happiness of his chosen before the world began.[3] So John x. 16, ' And other sheep I have, which are not of this fold; them also I must bring.' Why must he bring them home? how was he bound, how was he engaged to bring home his other sheep, that he puts a *must* upon it? ' Them also I *must* bring.' Doubtless it was from this covenant and agreement which he had made with God the Father, wherein he had engaged himself to bring home all his elect. Christ takes a great deal of pains to bring home his sheep; being bound in the covenant of redemption, to present all that are given him by charter blameless

---

[1] God loved his people and provided for them, and contrived all their happiness before they were, yea, before the world was.

[2] The grace here spoken of cannot be understood of infused grace, unless we will say that it could be infused into us before either the world was, or we were in it.

[3] The whole business of our salvation was first transacted between the Father and Christ before it was revealed to us, John vi. 27. The Apostle Peter, speaking of our redemption by the precious blood of Christ, saith that ' Christ was foreordained, thereunto, before the foundation of the world,' 1 Pet. i. 20.

before the Father; therefore, saith he, I bring them, and ' I *must* bring them;' the matter not being left arbitrary, even in respect of his obligation to God the Father, Col. i. 22.   Certainly the decree, cove- nant, and agreement between God the Father and Jesus Christ about the whole way of redemption, about all things belonging to the salva- tion of the elect, to be brought about in due time, was fixed and settled before the world began.[1]   Ponder seriously on this, it may be a loadstone to draw out your hearts more than ever, to love the Father and the Son, and to delight in the Father and the Son, and to act faith upon the Father and the Son, and to long to be with the Father and the Son, and all your days to admire at the love of the Father and the Son, who have from eternity, by compact and agreement, secured your souls and your everlasting concern- ments.   But,

(6.) The sixth proposition is this, *That God the Father had the first and chief hand in this great work of saving sinners, by virtue of this covenant of redemption, wherein he and his Son had agreed to bring ' many sons to glory,'* Heb. ii. 10.   Weak Christians many times have their thoughts and apprehensions more busied and taken up with the love of the Son, than with the love of the Father; but they must remember, that in the great and glorious work of redemption, God the Father had a great hand, an eminent hand, yea, the first and chief hand.   God the Father first laid the foundation-stone of all our happi- ness and blessedness.   His head and heart was first taken up about that heaven-born project, the salvation of sinners: Isa. xxviii. 16, ' Therefore thus saith the Lord God, Behold, I lay in Zion for a foundation a stone, a tried stone, a precious corner-stone, a sure foundation;' Heb., ' I am he that foundeth a stone in Zion.'   It is God the Father that hath long since laid Christ as a sure foundation, for all his people to build their hopes of happiness upon; it is he that first laid Christ, the true corner-stone, whereby Zion is for ever secured against death, hell, and wrath.   Hence it is said, ' The pleasure of the Lord shall prosper in his hand,' that is, God's eternal decree about the work of our redemption and salvation, shall be powerfully, faithfully, and completely executed by Jesus Christ; who, by his word and Spirit, shall communicate unto all his elect the fruit of his death, to life and salvation, Rom. ix. 33; 1 Pet. ii. 6; Isa. liii. 10.   Again: Job xxxiii. 24,[2] ' Deliver him from going down into the pit, for I have found a ransom.'   The Hebrew word signifies a price paid to redeem a man's life or liberty, ' I have found a ransom,' or an atonement, a cover for man's sin.   Angels and men could never have found a ran- som, but by my deep, infinite, and unsearchable wisdom, saith God the Father, ' I have found a ransom,' I have found out a way, a means for the redeeming of mankind, from going down to the infernal pit, viz., the death and passion of my dearest Son.   But where, O blessed God, didst thou find a ransom?   Not in angels, not in men, not in

---

[1] Ps. ii. 7; Acts xv. 18, and ii. 23; Eph. i. 9; Prov. viii. 22–32.

[2] This is a full place against all Socinians, who boldly assert that God removes the curse of the law, by a free and absolute pardon, without satisfaction. Grotius's exposi- tion on the place is but flat and dull. When God saith, ' I have found a ransom,' we are to understand it of a real ransom, of full pay or satisfaction, and not of a ransom by favour and acceptation.

legal sacrifices, not in gold or silver, not in tears, humblings, and meltings of my people ; but in my own bosom.   That Jesus, that Son of
my love, who has lain in my bosom from all eternity, John i. 18, he is
that ransom, that by my own matchless wisdom and singular goodness,
' I have found.'   I have not called a council to inquire where to find
a ransom, that fallen man might be preserved from falling into the
fatal pit of destruction ; but I have ' found a ransom' in my own
heart, my own breasts, my own bosom ; without advising or consulting
with others, I have found out a way how to save sinners with a salvo
to my honour, justice, holiness, and truth.   Had all the angels in
heaven, from the first day of their creation, to this very day, sat in
serious council, to invent, contrive, or find out a way, a means, whereby lost man might be secured against the curse of the law, hell, condemnation, and wrath to come, and whereby he might have been made
happy, and blessed for ever ; and all this without the least wrong or
prejudice to the justice and righteousness of God, they could never
have found out any way or means to have effected those great things.
Our redemption, by a ransom, is God's own invention, and God's only
invention.   The blessed ransom which the Lord has found out for
poor sinners, is the blood of his own dearest Son—a ransom which
never entered into the thoughts or hearts of angels and men, till God
had revealed it—which is called ' the blood of the covenant,' Heb. x.
29, because thereby the covenant is confirmed, and all covenant-
mercies assured to us.   Again,—' God so loved the world, that he gave
his only-begotten Son,' John iii. 16 ; Hosea xiv. 4.   Here is a *sic*,
without a *sicut*, that *sic, so,* signifies the firstness of the Father's love,
and the freeness of the Father's love, and the vehemency of the Father's
love, and the admirableness of the Father's love, and the matchless-
ness of the Father's love.   Oh ! what manner of love is this, for God to
give his Son, not his servant ; his begotten Son, not his adopted Son,
his only Son, and not one son of many ; his only Son by eternal generation, and communication of the same essence ; to be a ransom and
mediator for sinners !   God the Father loving lost man, sent his Son
to suffer and to do the office of a mediator, that through his mediation,
he might communicate the effects of his love, in a way agreeable to
his justice ! for God loved the world, and that antecedently to his
giving Christ, and as a cause of it.   The design, the project of
saving sinners, was first contrived and laid by God the Father ; therefore Christ says, ' The Son can do nothing of himself, but what he sees
the Father do.'   God the Father sent his Son, and God the Father
sealed his Son a commission to give life to lost sinners.   ' Him hath
God the Father sealed ;' that is, made his commission authentical, as
men do their deeds by their seals.   It is a metaphor taken from them
who ratify their authority whom they send ; that is, approve of them,
as it were, by setting to their seal.   Christ is to be acknowledged to
be he whom the Father hath authorised and furnished to be the
Saviour and Redeemer of lost sinners, and the storehouse from whence
they are to expect all spiritual supplies.   Look, as kings give sealed
warrants and commissions to their ministers of state, who are sent
out or employed in great affairs, 1 Kings xxi. 8 ; Eph. iii. 12, and
viii. 8, so Christ is the Father's great 'ambassador, authorised and sent

out by him to bring about the redemption and salvation of lost man. And look, as a seal represents in wax that which is engraven on it, so the Father hath communicated to him his divine essence and properties, and stamped upon him all divine perfection, for carrying on the work of redemption. And look, as a seal annexed to a commission is a public evidence of the person's authority, so Christ's endowments are visible marks whereby to know him, and clear evidences that he was the true Messiah, and of the Father's installing him into that office of a Redeemer. So John vi. 38, 'I came down from heaven, not to do mine own will, but the will of him that sent me.'[1] In this verse Christ declares in the general that his errand into the world is to do his Father's will who sent him, and not his own; which is not to be understood that, as God, he hath a different and contrary will to the Father's, though, as man, he hath a distinct and subordinate will to his; but the meaning is, he came not to do his own will only, as the Jews alleged against him, but the Father's also; and that in this work he was the Father's commissioner, sent to do what he had intrusted him with, and not, as the Jews gave out, that he was one who did that for which he had no warrant. Christ, in entertaining them that come to him, as in ver. 37, is not only led thereunto by his own mercy, and bounty, and love towards them, as the reward of all his sufferings, but doth also stand obliged thereunto by virtue of a commission and trust laid upon him by the Father, and accepted and undertaken by him; therefore he doth mention ' the will of him that sent him' as a reason of his fidelity in this matter. By what has been said, it is most evident that God the Father had the first and chief hand in the great work of our redemption. It is good to look upon God the Father as the first projector of our happiness and blessedness, that we may honour the Father as we honour the Son, and love the Father as we love the Son, and value the Father as we value the Son, and admire the Father as we admire the Son, and exalt the Father as we exalt the Son, and cleave to the Father as we cleave to the Son, &c. I have a little the longer insisted on this proposition, because commonly we are more apprehensive of the love of the Son than we are of the love of the Father, and that I may the more heighten your apprehensions of the Father's love in the great work of redemption. Ah! what amazing love is this, that the thoughts of the Father, that the eye of the Father, that the heart of the Father, should be first fixed upon us, that he should begin the treaty with his Son, that he should make the first motion of love, that he should first propose the covenant of redemption, and thereby lay such a sure foundation for man's recovery out of his slavery and misery. To speak after the manner of men, the business from eternity lay thus: Here is man, saith God the Father to his Son, fallen from his primitive purity, glory, and excellency, into a most woeful gulf of sin and misery; he that was once a son is now become a slave; he that was once a friend is now become an enemy, Eph. ii. 12, 13; he that was once near us is now afar off; he that was once in favour is now cast off; he that was once made in our image has now the image of Satan stamped upon him, Gen. i. 26, 27; he who had once sweet communion with us has now fellowship

---

[1] See John x. 17, and xvi. 27.

with the devil and his angels. Now out of this forlorn estate he can never deliver himself, neither can all the angels in heaven deliver him. Now this being his present case and state, I make this offer to thee, O my Son: If, in the fulness of time, Phil. ii. 7, 8, thou wilt assume the nature of man, 'tread the winepress of my wrath alone,' Isa. lxiii. 3, bear the curse, Gal. iii. 13, shed thy blood, die, suffer, satisfy my justice, fulfil my royal law, then I can, upon the most honourable terms imaginable, save fallen man, and put him into a safer and happier condition than ever that was from whence Adam fell, and give thee a noble reward for all thy sufferings. Upon this Jesus Christ replies: O my Father! I am very ready and willing to do, to suffer, to die, to satisfy thy justice, to comply with thee in all thy noble motions, and in all thy gracious and favourable inclinations, that poor sinners may be sanctified and saved, made gracious and glorious, holy and happy; that poor sinners may never perish, that poor sinners may be secured from wrath to come, and be brought into a state of light, life, and love, 1 Thes. i. 10; Heb. x. 10, 14; I am willing to make myself an offering; and, 'Lo, I am come to do thy will, O God,' Ps. xl. 6, 7. Thus you see how firstly, and greatly, and graciously, the thoughts of God have been set at work, that poor sinners may be for ever secured and saved. But,

(7.) The seventh proposition is this, *It was agreed between the Father and the Son that Jesus Christ should be incarnate, that he should take on him the nature of those whom he was to save, and for whom he was to satisfy, and to bring to glory.*[1] Christ's incarnation was very necessary in respect of that work of redemption, that he, by agreement with the Father, had undertaken. He had engaged himself to his Father that he would redeem lost sinners, and, as their surety, make full satisfaction. By the fall of Adam, God and man was fallen out, they were at variance, at enmity, at open hostility, Rom. viii. 7; so that by this means all intercourse between heaven and earth was stopped, and all trading between God and us ceased. Now to redress all this, and to make an atonement, a mediator was necessary; now this office belonged unto Jesus Christ, both by his Father's ordination and his own voluntary susception, Heb. x. 5-7; and for discharge of it a human nature was very requisite. There was an absolute necessity that Christ should suffer, partly because he was pleased to substitute himself in the sinner's stead, and partly because his sufferings only could be satisfactory. But now, unless Christ be incarnate, how can he suffer? The whole lies thus: without satisfaction no redemption, without suffering no satisfaction, without flesh no suffering; *ergo*, Christ must be incarnate. The Word must be made flesh, John i. 14: and so Heb. ii. 14, 16, 'Forasmuch then as the children are partakers of flesh and blood, he also himself likewise took part of the same; that through death he might destroy him that had the power of death, that is, the devil; for verily he took not on him the nature of angels; but he took on him the seed of Abraham:' 1 Tim. iii. 16, 'Without controversy, great is the mystery of godliness: God was manifested in the flesh, justified in the Spirit, seen of angels, preached unto the Gentiles,

[1] Gen. iii. 15; 1 John iii. 8; Acts ii. 30, and iii. 22; Isa. vii. 14, and ix. 6; Deut. xviii. 15-18; Gal. iv. 4 Rom. viii. 3.

believed on in the world, received up into glory.' This is only applicable to the person of Christ. He that by his office is to be Emmanuel, God with us, he must, in regard of his person, be Emmanuel also, that is, God-man in one person.   He that by office is to make peace between God and man, he must be God-man ; he that by office is to stand and minister between God and men, he must be God and man, that so he might not be only zealously faithful towards God's justice, but also tenderly merciful towards men's errors, Heb. ii. 17, 18, and iv. 15, 16.   Look, as he must be more than man that he may be able so to suffer, that his sufferings may be meritorious, that he may go through-stitch with the work of redemption, and triumph over death, devils, difficulties, discouragements, curse, hell, wrath, &c., all which Christ could never have done had he been but a mere man, so it was requisite that he should be man, that he might be in a capacity to suffer, die, and obey ; for these are not works for one who is only God.   A God only cannot suffer, a man only cannot merit.   God cannot obey, man is bound to obey.   Wherefore Christ, that he might obey and suffer, he was man ; and that he might merit by his obedience and suffering, he was God-man.   Now such a person, and only such a person, did the work of redemption call for.   That is a mighty scripture, Phil. ii. 6, 7, ' Who being in the form of God thought it no robbery to be equal with God'—here's Christ's preexisting in the nature of the Godhead, and then after comes his manhood—' but made himself of no reputation :' Greek, he ' emptied himself,' as it were, of his divine dignity and majesty ; he did disrobe himself of his glory, and became a sinner, both by imputation and reputation, for our sakes, for our salvation—' and took upon him the form of a servant, and was made in the likeness of men,' Isa. liii. 6, 9. All this Christ did upon his Father's prescription, and in pursuit of the great work of redemption.   The blessed Spirit fitted the man Christ Jesus to be a meet mediator and redeemer for poor sinners.   The Spirit formed the nature of man, of the substance of the virgin, after an extraordinary manner for the service of the Lord Christ, Luke i. 35 ; he sanctified the human nature which Christ assumed, after such a perfect manner, that it was free from all sin, Gal. iv. 4 ; Luke i. 35 ; in the very moment of conception he united this pure human nature with the divine in the same person, the person of the Son of God, that he might be a fit head, mediator, and redeemer for us, Heb. x. 5.   But,

(8.) The eighth proposition is this,—viz., *That there were commandments from the Father to the Son which he must obey and submit to.* God the Father did put forth his paternal authority, and lay his commands upon his Son, to engage in this great work of redeeming and saving poor sinners' souls.   He had a command from the Father what to teach his people, as the prophet of the church : ' For I have not spoken of myself,' saith Christ ; ' but the Father which sent me, he gave me a commandment, what I should say, and what I should speak,' John xii. 49.   Christ declares that he had received a commission from the Father, who sent him, concerning his doctrine, and what to say and speak ; and that he was persuaded that this doctrine delivered to him by the Father points out the true way to eternal life ; and that he had exactly followed this commission in preaching, both for matter and manner. The two words of saying and speaking may be taken comprehensively, pointing out all the ways of delivering his commission, by set and solemn preaching, or occasional conferences, and the whole subject-matter of his preaching, in precepts, promises, and threatenings; and so it will import that his commission from the Father was full, both for matter and manner, and his discharge thereof answerable.[1] Christ is a true prophet, who speaks neither more or less in the doctrine of the gospel than what was the Father's will should be delivered to us: 'For whatsoever I speak, even as the Father said unto me, so I speak.' Christ keeps close to his commission, without adding or diminishing; and herein Christ's practice should be every faithful minister's pattern. Again, Christ had a command to lay down his life for those that were given him: 'No man taketh it from me, but I lay it down of myself; I have power to lay it down, and I have power to take it again; this commandment have I received of my Father,' John x. 18. The Father is so well pleased with the reconciliation of lost sinners, that he loveth Christ for the undertaking thereof, and is fully satisfied with his suffering for attaining that end. In both these respects it holds good: 'Therefore doth my Father love me, because I lay down my life,' ver. 17. The Father is pleased with him that he undertook this service, and is content with his death as a sufficient ransom. Christ having laid down his life for the redemption of lost man, did take it again, as a testimony that the Father was satisfied with his sufferings. Now the way of the accomplishment of our redemption was agreed on betwixt the Father and the Son before the accomplishment thereof; therefore saith he, 'This commandment have I received of my Father,' which makes it clear that he came into the world fully instructed about carrying on the work of redemption, [Ps. xl. 6, 7 with Heb. x. 6–8.] It pleased Christ to suffer death, not only voluntarily, but in a way of subjection to his Father's command, that so the merit thereof might every way be full and acceptable to the Father: 'For this commandment have *I received.*' He was content to be a servant by paction, that so his sufferings might be accepted for his people. And so when Christ was going to die, he saith, 'That the world may know that I love the Father; and as the Father gave me commandment, even so I do: arise, let us go hence,' John xiv. 31. As if he had said, Power is permitted to Satan and his accomplices to persecute me to death, that dying for man's redemption, the world may see the obedience and love I bear to the Father, who hath thus determined. All that Christ suffered for the redemption of sinners was by the order, and at the command, of the Father, who did covenant with him concerning this work: 'For as the Father gave me a commandment, even so do I.' In this scripture, as in a crystal glass, you may see that Christ did enter the lists in his sufferings with much willingness and alacrity, with much courage and resolution, that so he might commend his love to us, and encourage us to do the like through him. Therefore, saith he, 'Arise, and let us go hence.' I am very free and ready, by my death and sufferings, to complete the work of man's redemption, according to the covenant and agreement that long since was made

---

[1] Between saying and speaking there is this difference, saith à Lapide: that to say, is to teach and publish a thing gravely; to speak, is familiarly to utter a thing.

between the Father and myself. If Christ should fail in complying
with his Father's commands about suffering and dying for us, then
not only the breach of articles, but high disobedience too, might be
justly charged upon him; but from all such charges Christ has bravely
quitted himself. There was a special law laid upon Christ as he was
our mediator, which law he was willing and ready to obey, in order to
our redemption. That Christ should die was no part of the moral
law, but it was a positive special law laid upon Christ. Well, this
law he obeys, he complies with: 'I lay down my life for my sheep;
this commandment have I received of my Father,' John x. 11, 15,
17, 18. Christ, as mediator, had a command from his Father to die,
and he observes it; hence God calls him his servant: 'Behold my
servant whom I uphold,' Isa. xlii. 1. And in pursuance of God's royal
law, will, and pleasure, he takes upon him the form of a servant; and
frequently proclaims before all the world, that he 'came to do the will
of him that sent him,' Phil. ii. 6, 7. Again, God the Father lays a
special command upon Jesus Christ, to preserve and bring to glory all
those that come unto him. Jesus Christ has not only leave to save
the elect, but a charge to save the elect: 'All that the Father giveth
me, shall come to me; and him that cometh to me, I will in no wise
cast out'—where the doubled negatives, in the original, serve to make
the assertion strong, and to carry their faith over all their doubts and
fears—'for I came down from heaven, not to do mine own will, but
the will of him that sent me. And this is the Father's will which
hath sent me, that of all which he hath given me, I should lose nothing, but should raise it up again at the last day. And this is the
will of him that sent me, that every one which seeth the Son, and
believeth on him, may have everlasting life; and I will raise him up
at the last day.' [1] Christ is to be answerable for all those that are
given to him, at the last day, and therefore we need not doubt but that
he will certainly employ all the power of his Godhead to secure and
save all those that he must be accountable for. In this blessed scripture there are several special things that we may take notice of, that
are pat to our present purpose:—

[1.] As *first*, that it is the great dignity and happiness of the elect,
that they are, *from eternity, given to Christ in the covenant of redemption, as the reward of his sufferings, to come to him in due time;* and
that they are given to him in trust, and that he must be accountable
for them, as being given by the Father to him, Ps. xxiv. 1. They
were the Father's first, not only by the right of creation, but by particular election also; and being thus the Father's, they are given to
Christ from eternity, to be redeemed by him, and as the reward of his
sufferings. Again, such as are elected and given to Christ, will certainly, in due time, come to him. Their being given from eternity,
produceth their being given and coming in time; for God is faithful,
who will not frustrate Christ of what he hath purchased; and the
power that draweth them is invincible and irresistible; therefore, saith
he, 'All that the Father giveth me, shall come to me.' Again, Christ
in entertaining them that come to him is not only led thereunto by
his own mercy, and bounty, and love towards them as the reward of

---

[1] John vi. 37–40.   Here you have Christ's commission to save the elect, &c.

his sufferings, but doth also stand obliged thereunto by virtue of a commission and trust laid upon him by the Father, and accepted and undertaken by him; therefore doth he mention 'the will of him that sent me,' as a reason of his fidelity in this matter. Further, from ver. 39, we may observe that the gospel contains an extract of the deep counsels of God, and of the eternal transactions betwixt the Father and the Son concerning lost man, so far as is for our good; for he brings out and reads in the gospel his very commission, and some articles of the covenant, passed betwixt the Father and him. Again, the first fountain and rise of the salvation of any of lost mankind, is in the absolute and sovereign will and pleasure of God; for here he mentions the will of him that sent him, as the first original of all; from whence their giving to Christ, their coming and safety, do flow. Again, these, whose salvation the Father willeth, are given over to Christ in his eternal purpose, to be brought to him in due time; for so it is here held out. Again, such as are given to Christ by the Father, and do in time come to him, are put in his keeping, and he hath a care of them, not to lose the least of them, 'For this is the will of him that sent me, that of all he hath given me, I should lose nothing,' John x. 28, 29; wherein the Father doth so commit the trust to him, as that he still keeps them in his own hand also. Again, Christ's charge and care of these that are given to him, extends even to the very day of their resurrection, that there he may make a good account of them, when all perils and hazards are now over, and that he may not so much as lose their dust, but gather it together again, and raise it up in glory, to be a proof of his fidelity; for, saith he, 'I should lose nothing, but raise it up again at the last day;' and so death and dissolution proves no loss.

[2.] Again, from ver. 40, we may observe, *that such as are given to Christ, to be under his charge, and to participate of his benefits, are drawn to believe on him: and it is the Father's will, and a part of the transaction betwixt him and his Son, that faith be the way to partake of these benefits, and not the fulfilling of the impossible condition of the works of the law;* for they who are given to Christ, are expounded to be they who believe on him; and it is the Father's will that such partake of these benefits here mentioned, as of the rest of his purchase. Albeit mortification, holiness, &c., do prepare for the possession of these benefits, and do evidence a right thereunto, and the begun possession thereof; yet it is only faith in Christ that giveth the right and title, that so it may be of grace, Eph. ii. 6–8. Again, it is covenanted betwixt the Father and the Son, that believers shall be made partakers of everlasting life; for it is explained, that not to lose them, ver. 39, is 'that they may have everlasting life.' For the further assurance of believers of their eternal happiness, it is also covenanted that they shall have this life in present possession, in the earnest, and firstfruits thereof; for they have everlasting life even here, and before their raising up. They have everlasting life—(1.) *In promisso;* (2.) *In pretio;* (3.) *In primitiis.* He stands already on the battlements of heaven, he hath one foot in the porch of paradise. Again, Christ having given an earnest-penny of salvation, will not suffer it to be lost, by any difficulty or impediment in the way, but will carry believers through all difficulties, till he destroy death and the grave, and raise up their very dust, that in body and soul they may partake of that bliss; and that he may make it manifest, that death and rotting in the grave doth not make void his interest, nor cause his affection to cease. Therefore it is added, ' And I will raise him up at the last day.' Thus you see that God the Father did lay his commands upon his Son, to engage in this great work of redeeming and saving poor sinners' souls, &c.

[3.] In the third place, I shall shew you that *the manner or quality of the transaction between God the Father and Jesus Christ, was by mutual engagements and stipulations; each person undertaking to perform his part in order to our recovery and eternal felicity.* We find each person undertaking for himself by solemn promise. The Father promiseth that he will hold Christ's hand and keep him, Isa. xlii. 6. God the Father engages himself to direct and assist Christ, and to keep him from miscarrying; and that he will give him all necessary strength and ability for the execution of his mediatory office, and work wonders by him and with him, according to that word, ' My Father hitherto worketh, and I work,' John v. 17. And the Son engages himself that he will obey the Father's call, and not be rebellious: Isa. l. 5, 'I was not rebellious, neither turned away back;' that is, I did not hang back, as Moses once and again did, Exod. iii. 11, 13, and iv. 1, 10, 13; nor refuse to go when God sent me, as once Jonah did, chap. i. 3; but I offered myself freely and readily to my Father's call. There was no affliction, no opposition, no persecution, no evil usage that I met with in carrying on the work of redemption that did ever startle me or discourage me, or make me flinch or shrink back from that great and blessed work that I had undertaken. I was dutiful and obedient to the calls and commands of my Father, in all things that he required of me or set me about. Now the Father and the Son being thus mutually engaged by promise one to another in honour and faithfulness, it highly concerned them to keep one another close to the terms of the covenant that was made between them, and accordingly they did; for God the Father peremptorily stands upon that complete and full satisfaction that Christ had promised to give to his justice; and therefore, when the day of payment came, he would not abate Jesus Christ one penny, one farthing of the many ten thousand talents that he was to pay down upon the nail for us, Mat. xviii. 24: Rom. viii. 32, ' God spared not his own Son;' that is, he abated nothing of that full price that, by agreement with his Father, he was to lay down for us. Other fathers give their all to spare and redeem their children; but the heart of God the Father is so fully and strongly set upon satisfaction that he will not spare his Son, his own Son, his only Son, but give him up to death, yea, to an accursed death, that we might be spared and saved for ever. I have read of a Roman emperor—Mauritius, who died most miserably [1]—who chose rather to spare his money than to redeem his soldiers being taken prisoners. But to redeem us God would not spare, no, not his own Son; because

---

[1] Rather Mauricius, [Μαυρίκιος.] He was murdered in the church of St Autonomus, Chalcedon, A.D. 602—a commonplace of history.—G.

no money nor treasure would serve the turn, but only the blood, yea, the heart-blood of his dear Son, 1 Pet. i. 18, 19.

And as God the Father keeps Christ close to the terms of the covenant, so Jesus Christ keeps his Father close to the terms of the covenant also: John xvii. 4, 5, 'I have glorified thee on the earth,' saith Christ to his Father, 'I have finished the work which thou gavest me to do. And now, O Father, glorify thou me with thine own self, with the glory which I had with thee before the world was.' O my Father, I have finished the work of redemption; but where is the wages, where is the glory, where is the reward that thou hast promised me? There was nothing committed to Christ by the Father, to be done on earth for the purchasing of our redemption, but he did finish it; so that the debt is paid, justice satisfied, and sin, Satan, and death spoiled; so that nothing remains but that Christ be glorified, according to the promise of the Father to him. The sum of Christ's petition is this, that since he had finished the work of redemption, that therefore the Father, according to his engagement, would advance him to the possession of that glory that he enjoyed from all eternity. Now for the clearing of this we must consider, that as Christ was from eternity the glorious God, so we are not to conceive of any real change in this glory of his godhead; as if by his estate of humiliation he had suffered any diminution; or by his state of exaltation any real accession were made to his glory as God. But the true meaning is this, that Christ having, according to the paction passed betwixt the Father and him, obscured the glory of his godhead for a time, under the veil of the form of a servant, and our sinless infirmities, Phil. ii. 5-8, doth now expect, according to the tenor of the same paction, after he had done his work, to be exalted and glorified, and 'openly declared to be the Son of God,' Rom. i. 4; the veil of his estate of humiliation, though not of our nature, being taken away. It is further to be considered that however this eternal glory be proper to him as God, yet he prays to be glorified in his whole person. 'Glorify me,' because not only his human nature was to be exalted to what glory finite nature was capable of, but the glory of his godhead was to shine in the person of Christ, God-man, and in the man Christ, though without confusion of his natures and properties. Christ did so faithfully discharge his trust, and perfect the work of redemption, as that the Father was engaged by paction to glorify him; and accordingly Christ, God incarnate, is exalted with the Father in glory and majesty; so that believers may be as sure that all things necessary for their redemption are done, as it is sure that Christ is glorified. But,

[4.] In the fourth place, let us seriously consider of the *articles agreed on between the Father and the Son*,—let us weigh well the promises that God the Father makes to Jesus Christ, and the promises that Jesus Christ makes to the Father, for the bringing about our reconciliation and redemption, that so we may the more clearly see how greatly both the heart of the Father and the heart of the Son is engaged in the salvation of poor sinners' souls. Now there are seven things which God the Father promiseth to do for Jesus Christ, upon his undertaking the work of our redemption.

First, That he will give him the Spirit in an abundant measure

' The Spirit of the Lord shall rest upon him, the spirit of wisdom and understanding, the spirit of counsel and might, the spirit of knowledge and of the fear of the Lord,' Isa. xi. 2. God the Father fits Jesus Christ for the work of redemption by a large effusion of the graces and gifts of the Spirit upon him. The Spirit of the Lord shall not only come upon Christ, but rest and abide with him. The Holy Spirit shall take up in a more special, yea, singular, manner its perpetual and never-interrupted or eclipsed residence with him and in him. God the Father promises that Christ shall, in his human nature, be filled with all the gifts and graces of the Holy Ghost, that he may be as an everlasting treasure, and as an overflowing fountain, to all his people. So Isa. xlii. 1, ' Behold my servant, whom I uphold; mine elect, in whom my soul delighteth : I have put my Spirit upon him, he shall bring forth judgment to the Gentiles.' So Isa. lxi. 1, ' The Spirit of the Lord is upon me.' So John iii. 34, ' God giveth not the Spirit by measure unto him.' Christ, as mediator, is endued with the Spirit for the discharge of that office ; and though Christ as man hath not an infinite measure of the Spirit, though indeed in that person the fulness of the Godhead dwells, as being God also, for that were to be no more man, but God, yet the gifts and graces of the Spirit are poured out upon the man Christ in a measure far above all creatures, Col. ii. 10 ; for though every believer be complete in him, yet, for what is inherent in him, they have but some gifts of the Spirit, 1 Cor. xii. 4 ; Eph. iv. 7 ; but Jesus Christ had all sorts of gifts. They had gifts for some particular uses, but he had gifts for all uses ; they have a measure of gifts which are capable of increase, he above measure, so much as the human nature is capable of, which, though it be finite in itself, yet it cannot be measured nor comprehended by us. So much is imported in that, ' God giveth not the Spirit by measure to him,' being understood of his manhood ; though, as we said, if we speak of his person, he hath the Spirit infinitely and without measure, Col. i. 19, and ii. 3, 9. This fulness became Christ as man, that he might be a fit temple for the Godhead, and as a mediator, that he might be the universal head of his church and storehouse of his people, that from him, as from a common person, spiritual root or principle, the Holy Ghost with his gifts and graces might be communicated to us. ' He received gifts for men, yea, for the rebellious also, that the Lord God might dwell among them,' Ps. lxviii. 18 ; ' Of his fulness we receive grace for grace,' John i. 16 ; ' The first Adam was a living soul, but the second Adam is a quickening spirit,' 1 Cor. xv. 45. In the man Christ Jesus there is a treasury and fulness of grace and glory for us ; he is the lord-keeper of all our lives, of all our souls, of all our comforts, and of all our graces ; and he is the lord-treasurer of all our spiritual, durable, and eternal riches, 2 Tim. i. 12. We lost our first stock by the fall of Adam, Prov. viii. 18. God put a stock into our own hands, and we soon proved bankrupts and run out of stock and block. Now since that fatal fall, God will trust us no more ; but he hath out of his great love and noble bounty put a new stock of grace and glory for us into the hands of Jesus Christ, who is mighty, who is able to save to the uttermost, and in whom are hid all the treasures of wisdom and knowledge, Isa. ix. 6 ; Heb. vii. 25 ; Col.

ii. 3. Christ was more capable, by infinite degrees, of the fulness of
the Holy Ghost than mere men were or could be; and his employment
being also infinitely beyond the employment of men, the measure of
the Holy Ghost's fulness in him must needs be accordingly beyond all
measure. Hence, by way of emphasis, Christ is called ' the anointed
one of God,' John xii. 15; Acts iii. 22, 23. The kings, priests, and
prophets among the Jews, who were anointed, were in their unction
but types of Christ, who is the great king, priest, and prophet of his
church, and anointed above them all, yea, and above all the apostles,
prophets, evangelists, pastors, teachers, and believers under the new
testament ministration. In Christ there is all kind of grace, and it
is in him in the highest and utmost degree, that he might be able to
manage all his offices, and finish ' that work which God gave him to
do,' John xvii. 4; and God hath filled him with his Spirit, that he
might successfully bring about the redemption and salvation of sinners. But,

*Secondly, God the Father promiseth to invest Jesus Christ with
a threefold office, and to anoint him and furnish him with whatever was requisite for the discharge of those three offices*—viz., his
prophetical, priestly, and kingly offices, Isa. lxi. 1–3, and xxxiii. 22.
Christ never forced himself into any of these offices, he never intruded
himself into any one office, he never run before he was sent, he never
assumed any office till his Father had signed and sealed his commission, John vi. 17. Whatever Jesus Christ had acted without a
commission under his Father's hand had been invalid and lost, and
God would one day have said to him, ' Who hath required this at thy
hand?'[1] Isa. i. 12. In order to our spiritual and eternal recovery
out of sin and misery, it was absolutely necessary that whatever
Christ did act as a priest, prophet, or king, he should act by the
authority of his Father, by a commission under the broad seal of
heaven: Heb. v. 5, ' So also Christ glorified not himself to be made
an high-priest; but he that said unto him, Thou art my Son.' These
two conjunctions, οὕτω καὶ, ' so also,' being joined together, are notes
of a reddition, or later part of a comparison, which is the application
thereof. This application may have reference either to the general
proposition, thus, ' As no man taketh this honour unto himself,' so
also, nor Christ; or to the particular instance of Aaron, thus, ' As
Aaron took not to himself that honour; so, nor Christ.' Both tend to
the same end. The high-priesthood was an honour; for Christ to
have taken that to himself, without a commission from his Father,
had been to glorify himself, by conferring glory and honour upon
himself. This negative, that ' Christ glorified not himself,' is a clear
evidence that Christ arrogated no honour to himself. Christ would
not arrogate honour to himself, but rather wait upon his Father, that
he might confer upon him what honour he saw meet. Christ glorified not himself to be made a high-priest; but his Father glorified
him, in ordaining or commissionating him to be the high-priest.
In short, to be made a high-priest is to be deputed or appointed

---

[1] Melchizedek was a king and a priest; Christ was more—a priest, a prophet, and a
king; Samuel was a priest and a prophet; David was a king and a prophet: but never
met all three in any but in Christ alone.

and set apart to that function ; and thus was our Lord Jesus Christ made a high-priest.   He had never undertaken that office had he not been ordained to it by his Father.   But, that you may see Christ's threefold commission to his threefold office, consider,

[1.] First, that God the Father promiseth to Jesus Christ *an excellent, royal and eternal priesthood :* Heb. vii. 21, ' For those priests were made without an oath ; but this with an oath by him that said unto him, The Lord sware and will not repent, Thou art a priest for ever after the order of Melchisedec ;' Heb. ii. 17, 18 ; Ps. cx. 4.   Among the Jews, in the times of the old testament, they had a high-priest, that was in all things to stand between God and them ; and in case any sinned, to make an atonement for them.   Now look, as the Jews had their high-priest, so the Lord Jesus Christ, he was to be, and he is, the apostle and the high-priest of our Christian profession, as Aaron was of the Jews' profession.   The priestly office of Jesus Christ is erected and set up, on purpose for the relief of poor distressed sinners.[1]   The work of the high-priest, is to make reconciliation for the sins of the people.   In the times of the old testament, the high-priest made an atonement for the people.   In case any man had sinned, he brought a sacrifice, and his sins were laid upon the head of the sacrifice.   Once every year, the high-priest did enter into the Holy of holies, and with the blood of the sacrifice, did sprinkle the mercy-seat, and laid the sins of the people upon the head of the scape-goat, and so made an atonement for the people, as is clear in that, Lev. xvi. 14, ' He shall take of the blood of the bullock, and sprinkle it with his finger, upon the mercy-seat eastward : and before the mercy-seat shall he sprinkle of the blood with his finger seven times ;' and at ver. 21, ' Aaron shall lay both his hands upon the head of the live goat, and confess over him all the iniquities of the children of Israel, and all their transgressions, and all their sins, putting them upon the head of the goat, and shall send him away by the hand of a fit man into the wilderness ; and so he shall make an atonement.'   This was the work of the high-priest, in case any had sinned, to make an atonement and satisfaction, by the way of type, for the sins of the people   The main scope of the apostle in that, Heb. vii., is to advance Christ his priesthood above the Levitical priesthood, in order to which he premiseth this, that those ' priests were made without an oath,' ver. 20.   The apostle's third argument to prove the excellency of Christ's priesthood above the Levitical, is taken from the different manner of instituting the one and the other.   Christ's institution was more solemn than the

---

[1] Heb. iii. 1. By the way, you may take notice that the whole body of Antichristianism is but an invasion upon the priestly office of Christ. What is the popish mass, that unbloody sacrifice, but a derogation from the sacrifice of Jesus Christ, once upon the cross ; and so a derogation from his priestly office ? What are all those popish penances and satisfactions enjoined, but a derogation unto the satisfaction of Christ ; and so unto the priestly office of Christ ? What is all their praying to saints and angels, but a derogation unto the intercession of Christ ; and so unto the priestly office ? God deputes Christ to his priestly office, as God and man ; yet papists say that Christ is a priest only in his human nature. God saith to his Son, ' Thou art a priest ;' yet they make many priests. God makes his Son a priest for ever ; yet they substitute others in his room. God gave Christ to offer up but one sacrifice, and that but once ; but they every day offer up many sacrifices in the mass. God gave Christ to offer up himself ; but they offer up bread and wine, upon pretence that it is the body and blood of Christ. Christ's sacrifice was a bloody sacrifice ; but they style theirs an unbloody sacrifice.

Levites'; their institution was without an oath, Christ's institution was with an oath. The argument may be thus framed: that priesthood which is established by an oath, is more excellent than that which is without an oath; but Christ's priesthood is with an oath, and theirs without, *ergo*. . . . It is here taken for granted that Christ was most solemnly instituted a priest, even by an oath; yea, by the oath of God himself, which is the greatest and most solemn manner of institution that can be. God's oath imports two things:—(1.) An infallible certainty of that which he sweareth; (2.) A solemn authority and dignity conferred upon that which he instituted by oath. Great and weighty matters of much concernment use to be established by oath. Hereby it appeareth that Christ's priesthood is a matter of great moment, and of much concernment. This will appear the more evident, if we consider the person who was made priest, viz., our Lord Jesus Christ, who was the greatest person that could be; Heb. vii. 28; therefore he is fitly called 'a great high-priest,' Heb. iv. 14. Or if we consider the ends of Christ's priesthood, which were very weighty, and that in reference both to God and man; to God, for the manifestation of his perfect justice, infinite mercy, almighty power, unsearchable wisdom, and other divine attributes, which never were, nor ever can be so manifested, as in and by Christ's priesthood; to man, that God's wrath might be averted, his favour procured, man's sin purged, and he freed from all evil, and brought to eternal happiness. Or if we consider the benefits of Christ's priesthood, which are answerable to the foresaid ends. Jesus Christ was appointed and made by the Father, ' The apostle and high-priest of the church's profession:' Heb. iii. 1, 2, 'Wherefore, holy brethren, partakers of the heavenly calling, consider the apostle and high-priest of our profession, Christ Jesus, who was faithful to him that appointed him.' Christ had a divine call to the execution of all those offices, which he sustained as our mediator, he did not run before he was sent, he did not act without a commission and warrant, he was lawfully constituted by him who had power to undertake that great charge he hath over the church; this we shall find asserted of all his three offices. As for his priestly office, he was made a priest by an immediate call and ordination from God, Heb. v. 4–6. The scope of the apostle is to set out the excellency of Christ's priesthood, by comparing it with the Levitical. His priesthood had a concurrence of all things necessary to the Levitical; and it had many excellencies above that. Now among other things required in the priesthood of Aaron, this was one, there must be a divine regular call. This was in the priesthood of Christ; ' He was called of God, a high-priest, after the order of Melchisedec.'[1] That Ps. cx. 4, is God's sure and irrevocable promise to Christ, touching that excellent and eternal priesthood, whereby the recovery of his seed was to be meritoriously obtained. This priestly office of Christ is sure, because it is confirmed by God's oath, of which before as well as his promise. The promise makes it sure, the oath doubly sure, irrevocable; and certainly the Lord neither can nor will

[1] Ps. cx. 4. The Hebrew is, ' Thou a priest,' &c., *i.e.*, ' Thou shalt be a priest for ever;' it being the manner of the Hebrew tongue, sometimes for brevity sake, to leave out a word, which is to be understood and supplied.

ever repent himself of this promise and oath. The priesthood of
Christ is the most noble part of all his mediation. In the priesthood
of Christ, and in that especially, lies the latitude and longitude, the
profundity and sublimity of God's love towards us; and in respect of
this especially, is the whole mystery of our redemption by Christ
called μεγαλεῖα τοῦ θεοῦ, the magnificent works of God. Christ as
man, and as mediator between God and man, was, by his Father,
deputed unto his priestly office. Concerning the dignity and excellency of Christ's priestly office, above the Levitical priesthood, I have
spoken elsewhere. But,

[2.] Secondly, God the Father promises to Jesus Christ *to make
him a prophet, a great prophet, yea, the prince of prophets.* Christ
is a prophet, in way of eminency and excellency, above all other prophets; he was the chief, the head of them all. Christ was made a
prophet by an immediate call and ordination from God. Christ, in
respect of his prophetical office, can plead the authority of his Father;
he can shew a commission for this office, under his Father's own
hand. Deut. xviii. 18, ' I will raise them a prophet from among their
brethren like unto thee, and will put my words in his mouth; and he
shall speak unto them all that I shall command them.'[1] Christ does
not raise himself up to the prophetical office, but God the Father
raises him up to this great office. He was anointed of God to preach
glad tidings. Weigh that, Isa. xlii. 6, ' I will give thee for a light to
the Gentiles; to open the blind eyes, to bring out the prisoners from
their prison, and them that sit in darkness out of the prison-house.'
' The Spirit of the Lord God is upon me, because the Lord hath anointed
me, to preach good tidings unto the meek; he hath sent me to bind
up the broken-hearted,' &c., Luke iv. 18. Thus you see that this
prophetical dignity of Christ, that he is the grand doctor of the church,
is built upon the authority of his Father, who hath authorised and
commissionated him to that great office: Isa. l. 4, ' The Lord hath given
me the tongue of the learned, that I should know how to speak a word
in season to him that is weary: he wakeneth morning by morning;
he wakeneth mine ear to hear as the learned.'[2] Thus you see that
God the Father promiseth to invest Christ with a prophetic office for
the opening the eyes of the blind, &c. This great prophet is richly
furnished with all kinds of knowledge; ' In him are hid all the
treasures of wisdom and knowledge.' They are hid in him as gold
and silver are *in suo loco*, as the philosopher speaks, hid in the veins
of the earth. ' Treasures of *knowledge*,' that is, precious knowledge,
saving knowledge; ' *Treasures* of knowledge,' that is, plentiful knowledge, abundance of knowledge; ' Treasures,' that is, hidden and stored
knowledge, was laid up in him. All the angels in heaven, and all
the men on earth, do not know all that is in the heart of God; but
now Jesus Christ, ' who lies in the bosom of the Father,' John i. 18,
he knows all that is in his Father's heart. All those secret mysteries,
that were laid up in the bosom of eternity, are fully known to this
great prophet of the church; John v. 20, ' The Father loveth the Son,

---

[1] See Acts iii. 22, and vii. 37; Deut. xviii. 15; Isa. lxi. 1.
[2] Christ displaces all Rabbis, by assuming this title to himself, ' one is your doctor and
master, even Christ,' Mat. xxiii. 8-10.

and sheweth him all things that himself doth,' by a divine and unspeakable communication. God the Father shews to Jesus Christ all things that he doth. God's love is communicative, and will manifest itself in effects, according to the capacity of the party beloved; so much appeareth in that unspeakable love of the Father to the Son, 'The Father loveth the Son, and sheweth him all things,' &c., or communicateth his nature, wisdom, and power, for operation with him; which is expressed in terms taken from among men, because of our weakness: and ought to be spiritually, and not carnally conceived of. And therefore these terms of the Father's 'shewing,' and the Son's 'seeing,' are made use of to prevent all carnal and gross conceptions of this inexpressible communication from the Father, and participation by the Son. In the blessed Scripture, Jesus Christ is sometimes called 'the' prophet, and 'that' prophet; because he is one that came from the bosom of the Father, and lives and lies in the bosom of the Father, and understands the whole mind, will, heart, counsels, designs, ways, and workings of the Father. Jesus Christ is anointed by God the Father to be the great prophet and teacher of his elect; and accordingly Jesus Christ has taken that office upon himself. God the Father has laid a charge upon Jesus Christ, to teach and instruct all those that he has given him, in his whole mind and will, so far as is necessary to their salvation, edification, consolation, &c. 'Moses was faithful as a servant, but Christ as a Son,' Heb. iii. 2, 5, 6. Christ cannot be unfaithful in his prophetical office. Those that God the Father hath charged him to teach and instruct, he will teach and instruct, in the great things of their peace; and no wonder, for the knowledge that is communicated to Jesus Christ, the great prophet of his church, is not by dreams, or visions, or revelations of angels, as to the prophets of old, but by a clear, full, intimate view, and beholding of the Godhead, the fountain of all sacred knowledge; Rev. v. 6, 'And I beheld, and, lo, in the midst of the throne and of the four beasts, and in the midst of the elders, stood a lamb as it had been slain, having seven horns and seven eyes, which are the seven spirits of God sent forth into all the earth.'[1] The lamb slain opens the prophecies, and foretells what shall befall the church, to the end of the world. The discovery of the secrets of God in his word, are the fruit of Christ slain, ascended, and anointed as the great prophet of the church. The lamb wanted neither power nor wisdom to open the seven seals, and therefore he is said to have 'seven horns and seven eyes.' Seven is a number of perfection. Horns signify power, eyes signify knowledge or wisdom;[2] both joined together, argue a fulness and perfection of power and wisdom in Christ; so that we have here a lively representation of the threefold office of Christ: his sacerdotal or priestly office in the lamb as slain, his royal or princely office in the horns, and his prophetical office in the eyes. But,

[3.] Thirdly, God the Father promises to make him *a king, yea, a mighty king also.* The kingly office speaks might and power. Christ is a king above all other kings; he is a king 'higher than the

---

[1] The Lamb stands, because (1.) prepared to perfect the work of redemption; (2.) to help; (3.) to judge; (4.) to intercede.

[2] Dan. vii. 24; Isa. xxxv. 5; Mat. xxviii. 18; Col. ii. 3, 9.

kings of the earth; he is the prince of the kings of the earth; he is Lord of lords, and King of kings,' Ps. lxxxix. 27; Rev. i. 5, and xvii. 14. I remember Theodosius the emperor and another emperor did use to call themselves the vassals of Christ; and it is most certain that all the emperors, kings, and princes of the world are but the vassals of this great king.   Christ is not only 'King of saints,' but he is also 'King of nations.' 'There was given him dominion and glory, and a kingdom; that all people, nations, and languages should serve him,' Rev. xv. 3, 4, and xii. 5; Dan. vii. 17.   God, by promise, hath 'given him the heathen for his inheritance, and the utmost parts of the earth for his possession,' Ps. ii. 8.   The monarchs of the world have stretched their empires far.   Nebuchadnezzar's kingdom in Strabo reached as far as Spain; the Persians reached farther, Alexander farther than they, and the Romans farther than them all; but none of all these has subdued the whole habitable world, as Christ has and will. 'All power is given unto him both in heaven and in earth.   The Father loveth the Son, and hath given all things into his hand, and the Father also hath put all things under his feet,' Rom. x. 18; Rev. xi. 15; Mat. xxviii. 18; John iii. 35; 1 Cor. xv. 27.   The government of all the world is given to Jesus Christ as God-man.   All the nations of the earth are under the government of Christ.   He is to govern them, and rule them, and judge them, and make what use he pleases of them, as may make most for his own glory, and the good of his chosen.   Now God the Father promiseth to invest Jesus Christ with his kingly office: Ps. ii. 6, 'Yet have I set my king upon my holy hill of Zion.' [1] These words are spoken by God the Father, of his Son Jesus Christ.   In a promissory way, God the Father anoints Jesus Christ as Zion's king; and therefore it cannot but be the highest madness, folly, and vanity, for any sort or number of men under heaven to seek or attempt to pull that king of saints down, whom God the Father hath set up.   Christ rules for his Father, and from his Father, and will so rule in despite of all the rage and wrath, malice and madness, of men and devils: 'yet have I set my king'—*Heb.*, 'I have anointed'—where the sign of Christ's inauguration, or entrance into his kingdom, is put for the possession and enjoying thereof.   Christ was anointed and appointed by his Father to the office and work of a mediator, and is therefore here called his king.   There is an emphasis in the word 'I,' 'Yet have I set my king upon my holy hill of Zion:' 'I,' before whom all the nations of the earth are but as a drop of a bucket, and as the small dust of the balance, Isa. xl. 15, 17; I, before whom all nations are as nothing, yea, less than nothing; I, by whom princes rule, and nobles, even all the judges of the earth, Prov. viii. 16; I, that rule the kingdoms of men, and give them to whomsoever I will, and who set over them the basest of men, Dan. iv. 17; I, that change times and seasons, and that remove kings and set up kings, Dan. ii. 21; I, that can kill and make alive, save and damn, bring to heaven and throw down to hell, Deut. xxxii. 39; I am he that hath set up Christ as king, and therefore let me see the nation, the council, the princes, the nobles, the judges, the family, the person, that dare oppose or run counter-cross

[1] 'My king,' in a peculiar way, *Decretum, Scriptum, Promulgatum.*

to what I have done. Again, the Lord, in a promissory way, approves and establisheth this king by a firm decree: Ps. ii. 7, ' I will declare the decree,' not the secret decree, but the decree manifested in the word. I, the Son of God, will, by my everlasting gospel, proclaim my Father's counsel, concerning the establishment of my kingdom. I will declare that irrevocable decree of the Father, for the setting up of his Son's sceptre, *contra gentes*, point-blank, opposite to that decree of theirs, ver. 3. The decree of God, concerning the kingly office and authority of Christ, is immutable, and in effect as irrevocable—so much may be collected out of the propriety of the word חק—as those things are that are most irrevocable in the course of nature. Again, the Lord, in a promissory way, extends the dominion of Christ to the Gentiles, and to the uttermost parts of the earth, ver. 8. So far should the enemies of Christ be from ruining his kingdom, that God the Father promiseth that all the inhabitants of the earth should be his, and brought into subjection to him, not only the Jews, but all the inhabitants of the earth shall be subjected to Christ's kingdom, the elect he shall save, and the refractory he shall destroy. ' He shall have dominion from sea to sea, and from the river even to the ends of the earth.' Again, the Lord, in a promissory way, declares the power, prevalency, and victory of Christ over all his enemies: ver. 9, ' Thou shalt break them with a rod of iron: thou shalt dash them in pieces like a potter's vessel.' This signifies their utter destruction, so that there is no hope of recovery. A potter's vessel, when it is once broken, cannot be made up again. This proverb also signifies facility in destroying them. As for such that plot, bandy, and combine together against the Lord Jesus Christ, he shall as easily and as irrecoverably by his almighty, eternal, and unresistible power, dash them in pieces, as a potter breaks his vessels in pieces: Jer. xix. 11, ' I will break this people and this city, as one breaketh a potter's vessel, that cannot be made whole again:' so Isa. xxx. 14, ' And he shall break it, as the breaking of the potter's vessel, that is broken in pieces, he shall not spare ; so that there shall not be found in the burstings of it, a sherd to take fire from the hearth, or to take water withal out of the pit.' The Jews, you know, were Christ's obstinate enemies ; and he hath so dashed them in pieces, that they are scattered abroad all the world over. The Lord hath made another promise, that Christ shall king it, Ps. cx. 1–6. And no wonder, when we consider that God the Father hath called Christ to the kingly office. The sceptre is given into his hand, and the crown is put upon his head, and the key of government is laid upon his shoulder by God himself. Isa. xxii. 22, it is written thus of Eliakim, ' The key of the house of David will I lay upon his shoulder ; so he shall open, and none shall shut ; and he shall shut, and none shall open.' Now herein was this precious soul a lively figure and type of Christ. The words of the prophecy are applied to Christ, in his advertisement to Philadelphia, Rev. iii. 7 ; and the sense is this, that look, as Eliakim was made steward or treasurer under Hezekiah, that is, the next under the king in government all over the land, to command, to forbid, to permit, to reward, to punish, to do justice, and to repress all disorder ; of which authority the bearing of a key on the shoulder was a badge ; so Christ, as mediator under his Father, hath regal power and authority over his Church, where he commands in chief, as I may say, and no man may lift up his hand or foot without him ; he hath the key of the house of David upon his shoulder, to prescribe, to inhibit, to call, to harden, to save, and to destroy at his pleasure. Such a monarch and king is Christ, neither hath any such rule and sovereignty beside him. And if you look into Dan. vii. 13, 14, you may observe, that after the abolishing of the four monarchies, Christ's monarchy is established by the Ancient of days, giving to Jesus Christ dominion, and glory, and a kingdom, that all people, nations, and languages should serve him ; and his dominion is an everlasting dominion, which shall not pass away, and his kingdom that which shall not be destroyed. Christ did not thrust himself into the throne, as some have done ; neither did he swim to his crown through a sea of blood, as others have done ; nor yet swam he through a sea of sorrow to this crown, as Queen Elizabeth is said to do ; no, he stayed till authority was given him by his Father. But,

Thirdly, God the Father hath promised, that he will give to Jesus Christ assistance, support, protection, help, and strength to carry on the great work of redemption. God the Father promises and covenants with Jesus Christ, to carry him through all dangers, difficulties, perplexities, trials, and oppositions, &c., that he should meet with in the accomplishing our redemption ; upon which accounts Jesus Christ undertakes to go through a sea of trouble, a sea of sorrow, a sea of blood, and a sea of wrath : Isa. xlii. 1, ' Behold my servant whom I uphold, mine elect in whom my soul delighteth ;' ver. 4, ' He shall not fail nor be discouraged, till he have set judgment in the earth; and the isles shall wait for his law ;' ver. 6, ' I, the Lord, have called thee in righteousness, and will hold thine hand, and will keep thee.' [1] What is that ? Why, I will support, strengthen, and preserve thee with my glorious power ; I will so hold thy hand, that thou shalt not be discouraged, but finish that great work of redemption, which, by agreement with me, thou hast undertaken. God the Father agreed with Jesus Christ about the power, strength, success, and assistance that he should have to carry on the work of redemption, all which God the Father made good to him till he had sent forth judgment unto victory; as Christ himself acknowledgeth, saying, ' Listen, O isles, unto me ; and hearken, ye people, from far ; the Lord hath called me from the womb; from the bowels of my mother hath he made mention of my name; and he hath made my mouth like a sharp sword; in the shadow of his hand hath he hid me, and made me a polished shaft; in his quiver hath he hid me ; and said unto me, Thou art my servant, O Israel, in whom I will be glorified,' Isa. xlix. 1–3. The work of redemption was so high, so hard, so great, so difficult a work, that it would have broken the hearts, backs, and necks of all the glorious angels in heaven, and mighty men on earth, had they engaged in it ; and therefore God the Father engages himself to stand close to Jesus Christ, and mightily to assist him, and to be singularly present with him, and wonderfully to strengthen him in all his mediatory administrations, John xvii. 2 ; upon which accounts Jesus Christ despises his

---

[1] Christ is our Lord, but in the work of redemption he was the Father's servant.

enemies, bears up bravely under all his sore temptations and trials, and 'triumphs over principalities and powers,' Mat. iv. 11; Luke xxii. 43; Col. ii. 15. And certainly if Christ ·had not had singular support, and an almighty strength from the Godhead, he could never have been able to have bore up under that mighty wrath, and to have drunk of that bloody cup that he did drink of. Now upon the account of God the Father's engaging himself to own Christ, and stand by him in the great work of our redemption, Jesus Christ acts faith against all his deepest discouragements, which he should meet with in the discharge of his mediatory office, as the prophet tells us: 'The Lord God will help me; therefore shall I not be confounded; therefore have I set my face like a flint, and I know that I shall not be ashamed. He is near that justifieth me, who will contend with me?' Isa. l. 7, 8. From the consideration of God's help, Jesus Christ strengthens and encourages himself, in the execution of his office, against all oppositions. God's presence and assistance made Jesus Christ victorious over all wrongs and injuries. Jesus Christ knew that God the Father would clear up his innocency and integrity, and this made him patient and constant to the last. But,

Fourthly, God the Father promiseth to Jesus Christ that he shall not labour in vain, and that the work of redemption shall prosper in his hand, and that he will give a blessed success to all his undertakings, and crown all his endeavours.[1] 'He shall see his seed, and he shall see the travail of his soul.' Another promise of the Father to the Son you have in that, Isa. lv. 5, 'Nations that know thee not, shall run unto thee.' The Gentiles, that never heard of Christ, nor ever were acquainted with Christ, nor ever had any notice of Christ; when Christ calls, they shall readily and speedily repair unto him and submit unto him. Christ shall one day see and reap the sweet and happy fruit of his blood, sufferings, and undertakings; 'The pleasure of the Lord shall,' certainly,. 'prosper in his hand.' Christ's sufferings were as a woman's travail, sharp though short. Now though a woman suffers many grievous pains and pangs, yet, when she sees a man-child brought into the world, she joys and is satisfied. So when nations shall run to Christ, he shall see his seed and be satisfied. God the Father promiseth that Jesus Christ shall have a numerous spiritual posterity, begetting and bringing many thousands to the obedience of his Father; 'Nations shall run unto thee;' and this shall fill the heart of Jesus Christ with abundance of joy and comfort, contentment and satisfaction, when he shall see the fruit of his bitter sufferings, when he shall see abundance of poor, filthy, guilty, condemned sinners pardoned, justified, and accepted with his Father, 'his soul shall be satisfied as with marrow and fatness,' Ps. lxiii. 5. The numerous body of believers, past, present, and to come, that God the Father had promised to Jesus Christ, was the life of his life. That is a sweet promise, Ps. cx. 2, 'Rule thou in the midst of thine enemies.' They that will not bend must break; those that will not stoop to his government shall feel his power. 'Thy people' —the people of God are Christ's five ways: (1.) By donation; (2.) By purchase; (3.) By conquest; (4.) By covenant; (5.) By com-

---

[1] See Isa. liii. 10, and xlix. 6–12; Micah iv. 3.

munication — 'shall be willing in the day of thy power' — Heb.,
willingnesses in the abstract and in the plural number, as if the Holy
Ghost could not sufficiently set forth their exceeding great willingness
to submit to all the royal commands of the Lord ; John xvii. 6 ; 1 Pet.
ii. 9 ; Luke i. 57 ; 1 Cor. iii. 23.   All Christ's subjects are volunteers,
free-hearted, like those isles that wait for God's law, Isa. xlii. 4, and
lvi. 6 ; Zech. viii. 21, 'And the inhabitants of one city shall go to
another, saying, Let us go speedily to pray before the Lord, and to
seek the Lord of hosts: I will go also;' 'From the womb of the
morning, thou hast the dew of thy youth,' Ps. cx. 3.   Here is the
success of Christ's office promised, both in the victorious subduing of
his enemies, and in the cheerful willingness of his subjects, and in the
wonderful numerousness of his people brought over to him, even like
the innumerable drops of the morning dew.   Another promise of that
great and complete success that God the Father hath made for Jesus
Christ in his mediatory office, you have in that Isa. xlix. from the 6th
verse to the 14th verse : Christ shall have a people gathered to him,
and a seed to serve him, 'because he hath made his soul an offering
for their sins.'   The multitude of sinners brought over to Jesus Christ,
is the product of the satisfaction which he hath made for them, and
the trophies of the victory that he hath got by dying the death of the
cross.   Thus you see that God the Father hath not only engaged himself by compact to preserve Jesus Christ in his work, but he hath also
made to him several precious promises of preservation, protection, and
success, so that the work of redemption shall be sure to prosper in his
hand.   And, to make these glorious promises the more valid and binding, God confirms them solemnly by an oath: Heb. vii. 21, 'This priest,'
Christ, 'was made with an oath by him that said unto him, The Lord
sware, and will not repent, Thou art a priest for ever.'   God the
Father foresaw from everlasting that Jesus Christ would so infinitely
satisfy him and please him by his incarnation, obedience, and death,
that thereupon he swears.   But,

*Fifthly, God the Father promiseth to Jesus Christ rule, dominion,
and sovereignty*, Ps. ii. 8, 9.   This sovereignty and rule is promised to
Jesus Christ in Isa. xl. 10, 'His arm shall rule for him.'   'He shall
sit in judgment in the earth, and the isles shall wait for his law,' Isa.
xlii. 4 — not the Jews only, but the Gentiles also, the people of divers
countries and nations shall willingly and readily receive and embrace
his doctrine, and submit to his laws, and give up themselves to his
rule.   Micah iv. 3, He shall judge among many nations,' that is,
rule, order, command, and direct as a judge and a ruler among many
nations.   The conquests that Christ shall gain over the nations shall
not be by swords and arms, but he shall bring them to a voluntary
obedience and spiritual subjection by his Spirit and Gospel: John iii.
35. 'The Father loveth the Son, and hath given all things into his
hand,' that is, God the Father hath given the rule and power over all
things in heaven and earth to Jesus Christ.   In carrying on the redemption of sinners, as the matter is accorded betwixt the Father and
the Son, so the redeemed are not left to themselves, but are put under
Christ's charge and custody, who has 'purchased them with his blood,'
God the Father having given him dominion over all that may contri-

bute to help or hinder his people's happiness, that he may order them so as may be for their good. And this power he hath as God with the Father, and as man and mediator by donation and gift from the Father, Mat. xxviii. 18, and ii. 3; and thus every believer's happiness is most firm and sure, all things being wisely and faithfully transacted between the Father and the Son. As long as Jesus Christ has all power to defend his people, and all wisdom and knowledge to guide and govern his people, and all dominion to curb the enemies of his people, and a commission and charge to be answerable for them, we may roundly conclude of their eternal safety, security, and felicity, Col. i. 19, and ii. 1. But,

Sixthly, God the Father promiseth to accept of Jesus Christ, in his mediatory office, according to that of Isaiah, 'Though Israel be not gathered, yet shall I be glorious in the eyes of the Lord,' Isa. xlix. 5; that is as if he had said, notwithstanding the infidelity, obstinacy, and impenitency of the greatest part of the Jews, yet my faithful labour and diligence in the execution of my mediatory office is, and shall be, greatly accepted, and highly esteemed of by my heavenly Father. Artaxerxes, the king of Persia, lovingly accepted of the poor man's present of water, because his good will was in it, and put it into a golden vessel, and gave him the vessel of gold, accounting it the part of a truly noble and generous spirit to take in good part small presents offered with a hearty affection. Oh, how much more will God the Father kindly accept of Jesus Christ in his mediatory office: ver. 7, 'Thus saith the Lord, the Redeemer of Israel, and his Holy One, to him whom man despiseth, to him whom the nation abhorreth, to a servant of rulers, Kings shall see and arise, princes also shall worship, because of the Lord that is faithful, and the Holy One of Israel, and he shall choose thee.'[1] God the Father, comforting of Christ, tells him that though he were contemptible to many, yea, to the nation of the Jews, and used basely, like a servant, by their princes, Herod, Annas, Caiaphas, and Pontius Pilate, yet other kings and princes should see his dignity and glory, and submit to him, and honour him as the Saviour and Redeemer of the world. God the Father chose Jesus Christ to be his servant, and to be a mediator for his elect; he designed him to that office of being a Saviour, both to the Jew and Gentile, and accordingly he accepted of him, 'Thus saith the Lord, In an acceptable time have I heard thee, and in a day of salvation have I helped thee; and I will preserve thee, and give thee for a covenant of the people, to establish the earth, to cause to inherit the desolate heritage.' Here you see that God the Father still goes on to speak more and more comfortably and encouragingly to Jesus Christ; for he tells him that he will be at hand to hear, and help, and assist him; and he tells him that he will preserve him, both in his person, and in the execution of his office; and he tells him that he will accept of his person, and of his services, and of his suits and intercession for himself and his people. So Mat. iii. 17, 'And, lo, a

---

[1] Jerome saith that the Jews cursed Christ in their synagogues three times a day. They so greatly abhorred the name *Jesus* that they would not pronounce it; but if they did unawares happen to pronounce it, then they would punish themselves with a blow on their faces, &c.

voice from heaven, saying, This is my beloved Son, in whom I am
well pleased.' The voice from heaven was doubtless the voice of his
Father, in that he saith, ' This is my beloved Son,' my natural Son,
by eternal and incomprehensible generation, and therefore dearest to
me, and most acceptable with me; my judgment is satisfied in
him, my love is settled upon him, and I have an inestimable value
for him; and therefore I cannot but declare my approbation and
acceptation both of him and his work. I am well pleased in him, I
am infinitely pleased in him, I am only pleased in him, I am at
all times pleased in him, I am for ever pleased in him; I am so well
pleased in him, that, for his sake, I am fully appeased with all them
whom ' I have given him, and who come unto him,' John vi. 37–40.[1]
But,

*Seventhly, God the Father promiseth highly to exalt Jesus Christ,
and nobly to reward him, and everlastingly to glorify him.* ' And
nations that knew not thee shall run unto thee, because of the Lord
thy God, and for the Holy One of Israel; for he hath glorified thee,'
Isa. xlix. 4–6, and xl. 10. These are the words of God the Father to his
Son, promising of him to set such a crown of glory upon his head as
should make the nations of the world run unto him. God the Father
made Christ glorious in his birth, by the angels' doxology, ' Glory be
to God on high;' in his baptism, by his speaking of him from heaven,
' as his beloved Son;' in his transfiguration on the mount, in his
resurrection, and in his ascension into heaven.[2] So Isa. liii. 12,
' Therefore will I divide him a portion with the great, and he shall
divide the spoil with the strong, because he hath poured out his soul
unto death; and he was numbered with the transgressors, and he
bare the sin of many, and made intercession for the transgressors.'
The meaning is this: I will impart, saith God the Father, to my Son,
such honour, glory, renown, and riches, after his sufferings, as conquerors use to have; and he shall have them as a glorious reward of
all his conflicts with my wrath, with temptations, with persecutions,
with reproach, with contempt, with death, yea, and with hell itself.
The words are a plain allusion to conquerors in war, who are commonly exalted and greatly rewarded by their princes for venturing of
their lives, and obtaining of conquests, as all histories will tell you.
And, indeed, should not God the Father reward Jesus Christ for all
his hard services, and his matchless sufferings, he would express less
kindness to him than he has done to heathen princes; for he gave
Egypt to Nebuchadnezzar as his hire, for his service at Tyre; and to
Cyrus he gave hidden treasure, Ezek. xxix. 18, 19; Isa. xlv. 1–3.
But, alas, what were their services to Christ's services, or their sufferings to Christ's sufferings? I have read of Cyrus, how that in a
great expedition against his enemies, the better to encourage his
soldiers to fight, in an oration that he made at the head of his army,
he promised, upon the victory, to make every foot soldier a horseman,
and every horseman a commander, and that no officer that did vali-

---

[1] This Jerome applies to the time of Christ's hanging on the cross. He cried out,
' My God, my God, why hast thou forsaken me!' for God made it appear that he heard
him, and forsook him not, in that he raised him from the dead, &c. See Heb. v. 7.
[2] Luke ii. 13, 14; Mat. iii. 17, and xvii. 1-5; Rom. i. 4; Acts i. 9–11.

antly should be unrewarded. And will God the Father let the Son of his dearest love, who has fought against all infernal powers, and conquered them, go without his reward? Surely no! Col. ii. 14, 15. So in Ps. ii. 7, 'I will declare the decree; the Lord hath said unto me, Thou art my Son, this day have I begotten thee.' David was God's son by adoption and acceptation; but Christ was his Son, Ps. lxxxix. 26, 27, Prov. viii., and Heb. i. 5, (1.) By eternal generation; (2.) By hypostatical union; and so God had one only Son, as Abraham had one only Isaac, though otherwise he was the father of many nations. Some by 'this day' do understand the day of eternity, where there is no time past nor to come, no beginning nor ending, but always one present day. Others by 'this day' do understand it of the day of Christ's incarnation, and coming into the world. Some again do understand it of the whole time of his manifestation in the world, when he was sent forth as a prophet to teach them, and was declared evidently to be the Son of God, both by his miracles and ministry, John i. 14, and by that voice that was heard from heaven, 'This is my beloved Son, in whom I am well pleased.' Others do understand it of the day of Christ's resurrection, and with them I close, for this seems to be chiefly intended; partly because it seems to be spoken of some solemn time of Christ's manifestation to be the Son of God, and 'he was declared to be the Son of God with power, according to the Spirit of holiness, by the resurrection from the dead,' Rom. i. 4; that is, by the power and force of the Deity, sanctifying and quickening the flesh, he was raised from the dead, and so declared mightily to be the Son of God; but mainly because the apostle doth clearly affirm that this was in Christ's resurrection: 'He hath raised up Jesus again, as it is also written in the second psalm, Thou art my Son, this day have I begotten thee,' Acts xiii. 33. In the day of Christ's resurrection he seems to tell all the world, that though from the beginning he had been hid in the bosom of his Father, John i. 18, and that though in the law he had been but darkly shadowed out; yet in the day of his resurrection they might plainly see that he had fully satisfied divine justice, finished his sufferings, and completed the redemption of his elect; and that accordingly his Father had arrayed him with that glory that was suitable to him. Before the resurrection the godhead was veiled under the infirmity of the flesh; but in the resurrection, and after the resurrection, the godhead did sparkle and shine forth very gloriously and wonderfully, 2 Cor. xiii. 4. Lest the human nature of Christ, upon its assumption, should shrink at the approach of sufferings, God the Father engages himself to give Jesus Christ a full and ample reward, 'and to exalt him far above all principality and power, and to put all things under his feet, and to make him head over all things to the church:' and to 'give him a name above every name; that at the name of Jesus every knee should bow;' and all because, to give satisfaction to his Father, he 'made himself of no reputation, and became obedient unto death, even the death of the cross;' that is, to his dying day, Eph. i. 21, 22; Phil. ii. 9.[1] He went through many a little death, all his life long, and at length underwent that cursed and pain-

---

[1] Name is put for person, and bowing of the knee, a bodily ceremony, to express inward subjection.—*Estius, Beza.*

ful death of the cross; upon which account the Father rewards him highly by exalting him to singular glory and transcendent honour. Look, that as the assumption of the human nature is the highest instance of free mercy, so is the rewarding thereof in its state of exaltation the highest instance of remunerative justice. Oh, how highly is the human nature of Christ honoured by being exalted to a personal union with the Godhead! Though vain men may dishonour Christ, yet the Father hath conferred honour upon him as mediator, that it may be a testimony to us that he is infinitely pleased with the redemption of lost man. Although Christ be, in himself, God all-sufficient, 'God blessed for ever,' and so is not capable of any access of glory; yet it pleased him to condescend so far as to obscure his own glory under the veil of his flesh, and state of humiliation, till he had perfected the work of redemption; and to account of his office of mediator, and the dignity accompanying it, as great honour conferred upon him by the Father, John viii. 54: and it is observable that Christ having finished our redemption on earth, he petitions his Father to advance him to the possession of that glory that he enjoyed from all eternity; 'And now, O Father, glorify thou me with thine own self; with the glory which I had with thee before the world was,' John xvii. 5. Now for the clearing up of this text we are to consider, that as Christ was from all eternity the glorious God, the God of glory; so we are not to conceive of any real change in this glory of his godhead; as if by his estate of humiliation he had suffered any diminution, or by his state of exaltation any real accession were made to his glory as God. But the meaning is this, that Christ having, according to the paction passed betwixt the Father and him, obscured the glory of his godhead for a time, under the veil of the form of a servant, and our sinless infirmities, doth now expect, according to the tenor of the same paction, that, after he hath done his work as mediator, he be highly exalted and glorified in his whole person; that his human nature be exalted to what glory finite nature is capable of, and that the glory of his godhead might shine in the person of Christ, God-man, and in the man Christ Jesus.[1] Thus you see the promises, the encouragements, and rewards that God the Father sets before Jesus Christ. And let thus much suffice concerning the articles of the covenant on God's part.

In the last place, Let us seriously consider of *the articles of the covenant on Christ's part; and let us weigh well the promises that Jesus Christ has made to the Father for the bringing about the great work of our redemption,* that so we may see what infinite cause we have to love the Son as we love the Father, and to honour the Son as we honour the Father, and to trust in the Son as we trust in the Father, and to glorify the Son as we glorify the Father, &c. Now there are six observable things on Christ's part, on Christ's side, that we are to take special notice of, &c.

[1.] First, Christ having consented and agreed with the Father about our redemption, accordingly *he applies himself to the discharge*

---

[1] Jesus Christ is true God, and was infinitely glorious from all eternity, for he had glory with his Father before the world was; and therefore he was no upstart God, and of a later standing, as the Arians and Mohammedans make of him.

of that great and glorious work by taking a body, by assuming our nature: Heb. ii. 14, 'Forasmuch then as the children are partakers of flesh and blood, he also himself likewise took part of the same.' He who was equal with God did so far abase himself as to take on him the nature of man, and subjected himself to all manner of human frailties, so far as they are freed from sin, even such as accompany flesh and blood; and this is one of the wonders of mercy and love, that Christ our head should stoop so low, who was himself full of glory, as to take part of flesh and blood, that he might suffer for flesh and blood: ver. 16, 'For verily he took not on him the nature of angels; but he took on him the seed of Abraham.' Christ assumed the common nature of man, and not of any particular person. The apostle doth here purposely use this word 'seed,' to shew that Christ came out of the loins of man, as Jacob's children and their children are said to come out of his loins, Gen. xlvi. 26, and as all the Jews are said to come out of the loins of Abraham, Exod. i. 5; Heb. vii. 5; and as Solomon is said to come out of the loins of David, 1 Kings viii. 19. In a man's loins his seed is, and it is a part of his substance Thus it sheweth that Christ's human nature was of the very substance of man, and that Christ was the very same that was promised to be the Redeemer of man; for of old he was foretold under this word *seed*, as 'the seed of the woman,' 'the seed of Abraham,' 'the seed of Isaac,' 'the seed of David.'[1] This word, 'he took on him,' as it setteth out the human nature of Christ, so it gives us a hint of his divine nature; for it presupposeth that Christ was before he took on him the seed of Abraham. He that taketh anything on him must needs be before he do so. Is it possible for him that is not, to take anything on him? Now Christ, in regard of his human nature, was not before he assumed that nature; therefore that former being must needs be in regard of his divine nature. In that respect he ever was even the eternal God. Being God, he took on him a human nature. Christ's eternal deity shines in this 16th verse, and so does his true humanity; in that he took upon him the seed of man, it is most evident that he was a true man. Seed is the matter of man's nature, and the very substance thereof. The seed of man is the root, out of which Christ assumed his human nature, Isa. xi. 1. The human nature was not created of nothing, nor was it brought from heaven, but assumed out of the seed of man, Luke i. 35. The human nature of Christ never had a subsistence in itself. At or in the very first framing or making it, it was united to the divine nature; and at or in the first uniting it, it was framed or made. Philosophers say of the uniting of the soul to the body, in creating it it is infused, and in infusing it it is created, *Creando infunditur, et infundendo creatur.* Much more is this true, concerning the human nature of Christ, united to his divine. Fitly therefore is it here said, that he 'took on him the seed of Abraham.' So John i. 14, 'The Word was made flesh, and dwelt among us.' The evangelist having proved the divinity of Jesus Christ, comes now to speak of his humanity, incarnation, and manifestation in the flesh, whereby he became God and man in one person. 'Flesh' here signifies the whole man in Scrip-

---

[1] Gen. iii. 15; Rom. ix. 7; Heb. xi. 18; John viii. 58.

ture. Ye all know that man consisteth of two parts, which are sometimes called flesh and spirit, and sometimes called soul and body.
Now by a synecdoche, either of these parts may be put for the whole:
and so sometimes the soul is put for the whole man, and sometimes
the body is put for the whole man, as you may see by comparing the
scriptures in the margin together.[1] Christ did assume the whole
man, he did assume the soul as well as the body, and both under the
term *flesh*. And indeed, unless he had assumed the whole man, the
whole man could not have been saved. If Christ had not taken the
whole man, he could not have saved the whole man. Christ took the
nature of man that he might be a fit mediator. If he had not been
man, he could not have died; and if he had not been God, he could
not have satisfied. So great was the difficulty of restoring the image
of God in lost man, and of restoring him to God's favour, and the
dignity of sonship, that no less could do it than the natural Son of
God his becoming the Son of man, to suffer in our nature; and so
great was the Father's love and the Son's love to fallen man, as to lay
a foundation of reconciliation betwixt God and man in the personal
union of the divine and human nature of Christ. So much is imported in those words, ' the Word was made flesh.'[2] The person of the
godhead that was incarnate was neither the Father nor the Holy Ghost,
but the Son, the second person, for ' the *Word* was made flesh.' There
being a real distinction of the persons, that one of them is not another;
and each of them having their proper manner of subsistence, the one
of them might be incarnate, and not the other; and it is the Godhead,
not simply considered, but the person of the Son subsisting in that
Godhead, that was incarnate. And it was very convenient that the
second or middle person, in order of subsistence of the blessed Trinity,
should be the reconciler of God and man; and that ' he, by whom
all things were made,' Col. i. 16, 17, should be the restorer and
maker of the new world; and that he who was ' the express image of
his Father,' Heb. i. 2, 3, should be the repairer of the image of God in
us. Oh the admirable love and wisdom of God that shines in this,
that the second person in the Trinity is set on work to procure our
redemption! Though reason could never have found out such a way,
yet when God hath revealed it, reason, though but shallow, can see a
fitness in it; because there being a necessity that the Saviour of man
should be man, and an impossibility that any but God should save
him, and one person in the Trinity being to be incarnate, it agrees to
reason that the first person in the Trinity should not be the mediator;
for who should send him? he is of none, and therefore could not
be sent. There must be one sent to reconcile the enmity, and another
to give gifts to friends; two proceeding persons, the Son from the
Father, and the Holy Ghost from the Father and the Son. Accordingly the second person, which is the Son, he is sent upon the first
errand, to reconcile man to God; and the third person, the Holy
Ghost, he is sent to give gifts to men so reconciled; so as to reason it

---

[1] Acts xxvii. 37; Gen. xlvi. 27; Rom. xii. 1, and iii. 20.
[2] Christ put himself into a lousy, leprous suit of ours, to expiate our pride and robbery
in reaching after the Deity, and to heal us of our spiritual leprosy; for if he had not
assumed our flesh he had not saved us.—[*Gregory*] *Nazianzen*.

is suitable, and a very great congruity, that God, having made all things by his Son, should now repair all things by his Son; that he that was the middle person in the Trinity should become the mediator between God and man; that he that was 'the express image of the Father's person' should restore the image of God, defaced in man by his sins. Ah, Christians, how well does it become you to lose yourselves in the admiration of the wisdom of God in the contrivance of the work of our redemption! For the Son of God to take on him the nature of man, with all the essential properties thereof, and all the sinless infirmities and frailties thereof, is a wonder that may well take up our thoughts to all eternity. And Christ took the infirmities of our nature as well as the nature itself. To shew the truth of his humanity he had a nature that could hunger and thirst even as ours do, and to sanctify them to us; and that so he might sympathise with us as 'a merciful and faithful high priest,' Heb. ii. 16–18, and iv. 15, 16; and that we might confide the more in him, and have access to him with boldness. By reason of the personal union of the two natures in Christ, he is a fit mediator betwixt God and man. His sufferings are of infinite value, being the sufferings of one who is God, Acts xx. 28, and who is mighty to carry on the work of redemption, and to apply his own purchase, and repair all our losses, Isa. lxiii. 1; Heb. vii. 25. Oh, what an honour has Jesus Christ put upon fallen man by taking the nature of man on him! What is so near and dear to us as our own nature? and lo, our nature is highly preferred by Jesus Christ to a union in the Godhead. Christ now sits in heaven with our nature, and the same flesh that we have upon us, only glorified, Acts i. 9–11. It is that which all the world cannot give a sufficient reason, why the same word in the Hebrew, *Basher*, should signify both 'flesh' and 'good tidings.' Divinity will give you a reason, though grammar cannot. Christ's taking of flesh upon him was good tidings to all the whole world, therefore no wonder if one word signify both. Abundance of comfort may be taken from hence to poor souls, when they think God hath forgotten them, to consider, is it likely that Christ, who is man, should forget man, now he is at the right hand of the Father, clothed in that nature that we have? When we are troubled to think it is impossible God and man should ever be reconciled, let us consider that God and man did meet in Christ, therefore it is possible we may meet. What hath been may be again. The two natures met in Christ, therefore God may be reconciled to man; yea, they therefore met, that God might be reconciled to man. He was made Emmanuel, 'God with us,' that he might bring God and us together. When a man is troubled to think of the corruptions of his nature, that is so full of defilements, that it cannot be sanctified perfectly, let him withal think that his nature is capable of sanctification to the full. Christ received human nature which was not polluted, his nature is the same, therefore that nature is capable of sanctification to the uttermost. O sirs! if Christ, the second person in the Trinity, did put on man, how careful should men be to put on Christ! 'Put you on the Lord Jesus,' saith the apostle, Rom. xiii. 14. If Christ assumed our human nature, how should we wrestle with God to be made partakers of the divine nature: 2 Pet. i. 4, 'Whereby are given unto us exceeding great and precious promises ; that by these we may be made partakers of the divine nature.' If Christ became thus one flesh with us, how zealous should we be to become one spirit with Christ, 1 Cor. vi. 17. Even as man and wife is one flesh, so ' he that is joined to the Lord is one spirit.' Was the Word made flesh ? did Christ take our nature ? yea, did he take our nature at the worst, after the fall ? What high cause have we to bless his name for ever for this condescension of his ! Should all the princes of the world have come from their thrones, and have gone a-begging from door to door, it would not amount to so much as for Christ to become man for our sakes. Christ took our nature, not in the integrity of it, as in Adam before his fall, but in the infirmities of it, which came to it by the fall. What amazing love was this ! For Christ to have taken our nature as it was in Adam, while he stood clothed in his integrity, and stood right in the sight of God, had not been so much as when Adam was fallen and proclaimed traitor ; as Bernard saith, *Quo pro me vilior, eò mihi carior, Domine*, Lord, thou shalt be so much the more dear to me, by how much the more thou hast been vile for me. Here is condescension indeed, that Christ should stoop so low to take flesh, and flesh with infirmities. But,

[2.] Secondly, Jesus Christ *promiseth to God the Father that he will freely, readily, and cheerfully accept, undertake, and faithfully discharge his mediatory office, to which he was designed by him, in order to the redemption and salvation of all his chosen ones.* Consult the scriptures in the margin,[1] they having been formerly opened, and in them you will find that Christ did not take the office of mediatorship upon himself, but first the Father calls him to it, and then the Son accepts it : ' Christ glorified not himself, to be made a high-priest ; but he that said unto him, Thou art my Son, this day have I begotten thee,' Heb. x. 12, 14, he called him, and then the Son answered him, ' Lo, I come.' God the Father promiseth that upon the payment of such a price by his Son, such and such souls should be ransomed and set free from the curse, from wrath, from hell, &c. Jesus Christ readily consents to the price, and pays it down upon the nail at once, and so makes good his mediatory office. It pleased the glorious Son of God, in obedience to the Father, to humble himself and obscure the glory of his godhead, that he might be like his brethren, and a fit mediator for sympathy and suffering, and that he might engage his life and glory for the redeeming of the elect, and lay by his robes of majesty, and not be reassumed till he gave a good account of that work, till he was able to say, ' I have finished the work that thou gavest me to do.' Christ very freely and cheerfully undertakes to do and suffer whatever was the will of his Father that he should do or suffer, for the bringing about the redemption of mankind. Christ willingly undertakes to be his Father's servant in this great work, and accordingly he looks upon his Father as his Lord, ' Thou art my Lord,' Isa. l. 5–7 ; Ps. xvi. 2—that is, thou art he to whom I have engaged myself that I will satisfy all thy demands, I will fulfil thy royal law, I will bear the curse, I will satisfy thy justice, I will

[1] Compare Ps. xl. 6–11 with Heb. x. 5–11, and Isa. lxi. 1–3 ; Luke iv. 18–20 ; Acts xiii. 23, and vii. 22.

humble myself to the death of the cross, Phil. li. 8, I will 'tread the wine-press of my Father's wrath,' Isa. lxiii. 3, I will fully discharge all the bonds, bills, and obligations that lie in open court against any of those whom by compact thou hast given me, Col. ii. 13–15, let their debts be never so many or never so great, or of never so long continuance, I will pay them all. There is no work so high, nor no work so hard, nor no work so hot, nor no work so bloody, nor no work so low, in which I am not ready to engage upon the account of my chosen: 'Lo, I come, I delight to do thy will; yea, thy law is in my heart.' Christ freely submits, not only to the duty of the law, but also to the penalty of the law,—not only to do what the law enjoins, but also to suffer what the law threatens; the former he makes good by his active obedience, and the latter by his passive obedience, Gal. iv. 4, 5. This was the way wherein the Father, by an eternal agreement with his Son, would have the salvation of lost sinners brought about, and accordingly Jesus Christ very readily complies with his Father's will and way, Titus i. 2. Christ, as mediator, had a command from his Father to die, which command he readily closes with: John x. 11, 'I am the good shepherd: the good shepherd layeth down his life for the sheep;' ver. 15, 'I lay down my life for the sheep;' ver. 17, 'I lay down my life, that I might take it again;' ver. 18, 'No man taketh it from me, but I lay it down of myself; this commandment have I received of my Father.' Christ was content to be a servant by paction, that so his sufferings might be accepted for his people; and certainly whatever God the Father put Jesus Christ upon in his whole mediatory work, that Jesus Christ did freely, fully, and heartily comply with: 'Lo, I come; and I have finished the work that thou gavest me to do,' John xvii. 4. And had not Christ been free and voluntary in his active and passive obedience, his active and passive obedience would never have been acceptable, satisfactory, or meritorious. To go further to prove it, would be to light a candle to see the sun at noon. But,

[3.] Thirdly, Jesus Christ *promises and engages himself that he will confide, depend, rely, and trust upon his Father for help and for assistance to go through with his work a-notwithstanding all the wrath and rage, all the malice and oppositions, that he should meet with from men and devils:* Heb. ii. 13, 'And again, I will put my trust in him.' Christ's confidence in his Father was one great encouragement to him to hold out in the execution of his office; and his confidence in God speaks him out to be a true man, in that, as other men, he stood in need of God's aid and assistance; and thereupon, as others of the sons of men, his brethren, he puts his trust in God. The Greek phrase used by the apostle carrieth emphasis; it implieth trust on a good persuasion that he shall not be disappointed. It is translated 'confidence,' Phil. i. 6; word for word it may be here thus translated, 'I will be confident in him.'[1] The relative 'him' hath apparent reference to God, so as Christ himself, being man, rested on God to be supported in his works, and to be carried through all his undertakings, till the top-stone was laid, and the work of redemption accomplished. Christ had many great and potent enemies, and was brought to very

[1] ἔσομαι πεποιθὼς ἐπ' αὐτῷ, Ps. xviii. 2; Isa. viii. 18.

great straits; yea, he and his were 'for signs and wonders in Israel;' yet he fainted not, but put his trust in the Lord; yea, his greatest enemies gave him this testimony, that 'he trusted in God;' and though they spoke it in scorn and derision, yet it was a real truth, Ps. xviii. 3-5; Isa. viii. 18; Mat. xxvii. 43. Christ's confidence in his Father was further manifested by the many prayers which, time after time, he made to his Father, Heb. v. 7. Another proof of Christ's confidence in God's assistance, even in his greatest plunges and his sharpest sufferings, the prophet Isaiah will furnish us with: 'The Lord God hath opened mine ear,' saith the prophet, 'and I was not rebellious, neither turned away back. I gave my back to the smiters, and my cheeks to them that plucked off the hair: I hid not my face from shame and spitting. For the Lord God will help me; therefore shall I not be confounded: therefore have I set my face like a flint, and I know that I shall not be ashamed. He is near that justifieth me; who will contend with me? let us stand together; who is mine adversary? let him come near to me. Behold, the Lord God will help me; who is he that shall condemn me? lo, they all shall wax old as a garment; the moth shall eat them up,' Isa. l. 5-9. Christ, as mediator, trusted God the Father to carry him through all difficulties and oppositions, till he had completed the great work of his mediation. Christ strengthens and encourages himself in the execution of his office against all hardships and oppositions, from his confidence and assurance of God's aid and assistance; and by the same eye of faith, he looks upon all his opposites as worn out and weathered by him. Christ's faith, patience, and constancy gave him victory over all wrongs and injuries; so Isa. xlix. 5, 'My God shall be my strength.' Christ is very confident of his Father's assistance to carry him through that work that he had assigned him to. Christ, in the want of comfort, never wanted faith to hang upon God, and to call him his God: 'My God, my God, why hast thou forsaken me?' Mat. xxvii. 46. Christ was never forsaken in regard of the hypostatical union; the union was not dissolved, but the beams, the influence, was restrained.[1] Nor in regard of his faith; for though now he was sweltering under the wrath of God, as our surety, and left in the hands of his enemies, and deserted by his disciples and dearest friends, and under the loss of the comforting and solacing presence of his Father, yet, in the midst of all, such was the strength and power of his faith, that he could say, 'My God, my God.' Christ, before the world began, having promised and engaged to the Father that, in the fulness of time, he would come into the world, assume our nature, be made under the law, tread the winepress of the Father's wrath, bear the curse, and give satisfaction to his justice;[2] now upon the credit of this promise, upon this undertaking of Christ, God the Father takes up the patriarchs and all the old testament believers to glory. God the Father, resting upon the promise and engagement of his Son, admits many thousands into those mansions above, before Christ took flesh upon him, John xiv. 2, 3.

[1] As man he cries out, 'My God, my God,' &c., when as God he promiseth paradise to the penitent thief.—*Hilary.*

[2] Titus i. 2; Gal. iv. 4; Isa. lxiii. 3; Gal. iii. 13; Rom. viii. 3, 4.

Now as the Father of old hath rested and relied on the promise and engagement of Christ, so Jesus Christ doth, to this very day, rest and stay himself upon the promise of his Father, that he shall, in due time, ' see all his seed,' Isa. liii. 10, and reap the full benefit of that full ransom that he has paid down upon the nail for all that have believed on him, that do believe on him, and that shall believe on him. Christ knew God's infinite love, his tender compassions, and his matchless bowels, to all those for whom he died; and he knew very well the covenant, the compact, the agreement that passed between the Father and himself; and so trusted the Father fully in the great business of their everlasting happiness and blessedness, relying upon the love and faithfulness of God, his love to the elect, and his faithfulness to keep covenant with him. As the elect are committed to Christ's charge, to give an account of them, so also is the Father engaged for their conversion, and for their preservation, being converted; as being not only his own, given to Christ out of his love to them, but as being engaged to Christ, that he shall not be frustrate of the reward of his sufferings, but have a seed to glorify him for ever, John vi. 37; Isa. liii. 11. Therefore doth Christ not only constantly preserve them by his Spirit, but doth leave also that burden on the Father: ' Father, keep those whom thou hast given me,' John xvii. 11. But,

[4.] Fourthly, Jesus Christ *promises and engages himself to his Father that he would bear all and suffer all that should be laid upon him, and that he would ransom poor sinners, and fully satisfy divine justice by his blood and death,* as you may see by comparing the scriptures in the margin together.[1] The work of redemption could never have been effected by ' silver or gold,' or by prayers or tears, or by the ' blood of bulls or goats,' but by the second Adam's obedience, even to the death of the cross. Remission of sin, the favour of God, the heavenly inheritance, could never have been obtained but by the precious blood of the Son of God. The innocent Lamb of God was slain in typical prefigurations from the beginning of the world, and slain in real performance in the fulness of time, or else fallen man had lain under guilt and wrath for ever. The heart of Jesus Christ was strongly set upon all those that his Father had given him, and he was fully resolved to secure them from hell and the curse, whatever it cost him; and seeing no price would satisfy his Father's justice below his blood, he lays down his life at his Father's feet, according to the covenant and agreement of old that had passed between his Father and himself. But,

[5.] Fifthly, *The Lord Jesus Christ was very free, ready, willing, and careful to make good all the articles of the covenant on his side, and to discharge all the works agreed on for the redemption and salvation of the elect:* John xvii. 4, ' I have finished the work that thou gavest me to do,' John xii. 49, 50, and xvii. 6. There was nothing committed to Christ by the Father to be done on earth, for the purchasing of our redemption, but he did finish it; so that the debt is paid, justice satisfied, and sin, Satan, and death spoiled of all their

---

[1] Isa. l. 5, 6; John x. 17, 18, and xv. 10; Luke xxiv. 46; Heb. x. 5-7, 10. I have opened these scriptures already.

hurting and destroying power, Col. ii. 14, 15, and Heb. ii. 14.   By
the covenant of redemption Christ was under an obligation to die, to
satisfy to divine justice, to pay our debts, to bring in an everlasting
righteousness, Dan. ix. 24, to purchase our pardon, and to obtain
eternal redemption for us, Heb. ix. 12; all which he completed and
finished before he ascended up to glory : and, without a peradventure,
had not Jesus Christ kept touch with his Father, had not he made
good the covenant, the compact, the agreement on his part, his Father
would never have given him such a welcome to heaven as he did, nor
he would never have admitted him to have ' sat down on the right
hand of the Majesty on high,' as he did,[1] Acts i. 9–11.   The right
hand is a place of the greatest honour, dignity, and safety that any
can be advanced to.   But had not Jesus Christ ' first purged away
our sins,' he had never ' sat down on the right hand of his Father.'
Christ's advancement is properly of his human nature.   That nature
wherein Christ was crucified was exalted; for God, being the Most
High, needs not be exalted; yet the human nature in this exaltation, is not singly and simply considered in itself, but as united to
the deity; so that it is the person, consisting of two natures, even
God-man, which is thus dignified, Mat. xxvi. 64; Acts vii. 56.   For
as the human nature of Christ is inferior to God, and is capable of
advancement, so also is the person consisting of a divine and human
nature.   Christ, as the Son of God, the second person of the sacred
Trinity, is, in regard of his deity, no whit inferior to his Father, but
every way equal; yet he assumed our nature, and became a mediator
betwixt God and man; he humbled himself, and made himself inferior to his Father; his Father therefore hath highly exalted him,
and set him down on his right hand, Phil. ii. 8, 9; Eph. i. 20.   If
Christ had not expiated our sins, and completed the work of our
redemption, he could never have sat down on the right hand of God :
Heb. x. 12, ' But this man, after he had offered one sacrifice for sins,
for ever sat down on the right hand of God.'   This verse is added in
opposition to the former, as is evident by the first particle, δέ.   But
in the former verse it was proved that the sacrifices which were
offered under the law could not take away sins.   This verse proveth
that there is a sacrifice which hath done that that they could not do.
The argument is taken from that priest's ceasing to offer any more
sacrifices after he had offered one; whereby is implied that there
needed no other, because that one had done it to the full.   Sin was
taken away by Christ's sacrifice, for thereby a ransom was paid, and
satisfaction made to the justice of God for man's sin, and thereupon
sin taken away.   Now sin being taken away, Christ ' sits down on
the right hand of his Father.'   Look, as the humiliation of Christ
was manifested in offering a sacrifice, so his exaltation, in sitting at
God's right hand, was manifested after that he had offered that
sacrifice.   This phrase, ' set down,' is a note of dignity and authority;
and this dignity and authority is amplified by the place where he is
said to sit down—viz., on ' the right hand of God;' and this honour
and dignity is much illustrated by the continuance thereof, which
is without date, ' For ever sat down on the right hand of God.'   It

---

[1] Heb. i. 3; Rom. viii. 34; Col. iii. 1; Heb. viii. 1, and x. 12; 1 Pet. iii. 22.

is an eclipse of the lustre of any glory to have a date and a period. The very thought that such a glory shall one day cease, will cast a damp upon the spirit of him that enjoys that glory. Christ's constant sitting at the right hand of his Father is a clear evidence that he has finished and completed the work of our redemption. Christ could never have gone to his Father, nor never have sat down at the right hand of his Father, if he had not first fulfilled all righteousness, and fully acquitted us of all our iniquities: John xvi. 10, 'Of righteousness, because I go to my Father.' The strength of the argument lies in this, Christ took upon him to be our surety, and he must acquit us of all our sins, and satisfy his Father's justice, before he can go to his Father, and be accepted of his Father, and sit down on the right hand of his Father. If God had not been fully satisfied, or if any part of righteousness had been to be fulfilled, Christ should have been still in the grave, and not gone to heaven; his very going to his Father argues all is done, all is finished and completed. But,

[6.] Sixthly, *Christ having performed all the conditions of the covenant on his part, he now peremptorily insists upon it, that his Father should make good to him and his the conditions of the covenant on his part.* Christ having finished his work, looks for his reward: 'Father,' says he, 'I have glorified thee on earth, I have finished the work which thou gavest me to do. And now, O Father, glorify thou me with thine own self, with the glory which I had with thee before the world was,' John xvii. 4, 5. There was a most blessed transaction between God the Father and God the Son before the world began, for the everlasting good of the elect; and upon that transaction depends all the good, and all the happiness, and all the salvation of God's chosen ; [1] and upon this ground pleads with his Father, that all his members may behold his glory: John xvii. 24, 'Father, I will that they also which thou hast given me be with me where I am, that they may behold my glory ;' ' Father, *I will*,' not only I pray, I beseech, but ' I will ;' I ask this as my right, by virtue of the covenant betwixt us ; I have done thus and thus, and I have suffered thus and thus, and therefore I cannot but peremptorily insist upon it, that those that I have undertaken for, ' be where I am, that they may behold my glory ;' for though glory be a gift to us, yet it is a debt due to Christ. It is a part of Christ's joy that we should be where he is. Christ will not be happy alone. As a tender father, he can enjoy nothing if his children may not have part with him. The greatest part of our happiness that we shall have in heaven lies in this, that then we shall be with Christ, and have immediate communion with him. O sirs ! the great end of our being in heaven is to behold and enjoy the glory of Christ. Christ is very desirous, and much taken up with his people's fellowship and company, so that before he removes his bodily presence from them, his heart is upon meeting and fellowship again, as here we see in his prayer before his departure ; and this he makes evident from day to day, in that until that time of meeting come, two or three are not gathered in his name but he is in the midst of them, Mat. xviii. 20, to eye their behaviour, to hear their suits, to guide their way, to pro-

[1] This transaction between the Father and the Son is worthy of our most deep, serious, and frequent meditation.

tect their persons, to cheer their spirits, and to delight in their presence.   He delights to ' walk in the midst of the seven golden
candlesticks,' Rev. ii. 1.   The golden candlesticks are the churches,
which are ' the light of the world,' Mat. v. 14, 16, and excel all other
societies as much as gold doth other metals.   And he desires to dwell
in the low and little hill of Zion, Ps. lxviii. 16.   Zion is his resting-
place, his chosen place, his dwelling-place : Ps. cxxxii. 13, ' For the
Lord hath chosen Zion, he hath desired it for his habitation ; ' ver. 14,
' This is my rest for ever : here will I dwell, for I have desired it.'
Christ chose Zion for his love, and loves it for his choice ; and accordingly he delights to dwell there.   The Lamb stands on mount Zion,
Rev. xiv. 1.   Christ is ready prest for action ; and in the midst of all
antichrist's persecutions he hath always a watchful eye over mount
Zion, and will be a sure life-guard to mount Zion, Isa. iv. 5, 6 ; he stands
readily prepared to assist mount Zion, to fight for mount Zion, to communicate to mount Zion, and to be a refuge to mount Zion ; and no
wonder, for he 'dwells in mount Zion,' Isa. viii. 18.   Now if Christ take
so much delight to have spiritual communion with his people in this
world, no wonder that he can never rest satisfied till their gracious communion with him here issue in their perfect and glorious communion with
him in heaven.[1]   And certainly the glory and happiness of heaven to
the elect will consist much in being in Christ's company, in whom they
delight so much on earth.   To follow the Lamb whithersoever he
goes, to enjoy him fully, and to be always in his presence, is the heaven
of heaven, the glory of glory ; it is the sparkling diamond in the ring
of glory.   The day is coming wherein believers shall be completely
happy in a sight of Christ's glory, when he shall be conspicuously
glorified and admired in all his saints, and glorified by them ; and
when all veils being laid aside, and they fitted for a more full fruition,
shall visibly and immediately behold and enjoy him ;   therefore is
their condition in heaven described, as consisting in this, that they
' may behold my glory which thou hast given me.'   Thus I have
glanced at Christ's solemn demand on earth for the full accomplishment of that blessed compact, covenant, agreement, and promises that
were made to him when he undertook the office of a mediator ; and
now in heaven he appears ' in the presence of God for us,' Heb. ix.
25, as a lawyer appears in open court for his client, opens the case,
pleads the cause, and carries the day.   The verb, $\dot{\epsilon}\mu\phi\alpha\nu\iota\sigma\theta\tilde{\eta}\nu\alpha\iota$, translated ' to appear,' signifieth conspicuously ' to manifest.'   It is some-
times taken in a good sense, viz., to appear for one as a favourite
before a prince, or as an advocate or an attorney before a judge, or as
the high-priests appeared once a year in the holy of holies, to
make atonement for the people, Exod. xxx. 10.   Christ is the
great favourite in the court of glory, and is always at God's right
hand, ready on all occasions to present our petitions to his Father, to
pacify his anger, and to obtain all noble and needful favours for us,
Rom. viii. 34.   And Christ is our great advocate to plead our cause
effectually for us, 1 John ii. 1.   Look, as in human courts there is the

---

[1] 2 Cor. vi. 16, ' I will dwell in them.'   The words are very significant in the original,
$\dot{\epsilon}\nuοικήσω$ $\dot{\epsilon}\nu$ $\alpha\dot{\nu}\tauοῖς$, · ' I will in-dwell in them.'   So the words are.   There are two *ins* in
the original, as if God could never have enough communion with them, 2 Thes. i. 10.

guilty, the accuser, the court, the judge, and the advocate ; so it is here. Heaven is the court, man is the guilty person, Satan is the accuser, God is the judge, and Christ is the advocate. Now look, as the advocate appeareth in the court before the judge to plead for the guilty against the accuser, so doth Christ appear before God in heaven, to answer all Satan's objections and accusations that he may make in the court of heaven against us. 'He ever lives to make intercession for us,' Heb. vii. 25. The verb, ἐντυγχάνειν, translated 'intercession,' is a compound, and signifies 'to call upon one' It is a judicial word, and importeth a calling upon a judge to be heard in this or that, against another or for another ; so here Christ maketh intercession for them, Acts xxv. 24; Rom. xi. 2, and viii. 34. The metaphor is taken from attorneys or advocates who appear for men in courts of justice ; from counsellors, who plead their client's cause, answer the adversary, supplicate the judge, and procure sentence to pass on their client's side. This act of making intercession may also be taken from kings' favourites, who are much in the king's presence, and ever ready to make request for their friends. But remember, though this be thus attributed to Christ, yet we may not think that in heaven Christ prostrateth himself before him, or maketh actual prayers ; that was a part of his humiliation which he did in the days of his flesh ; but it implieth a presenting of himself a sacrifice, a surety, and one that hath made satisfaction for all our sins, together with manifesting of his will and desires, that such and such should partake of the virtue and benefit of his sacrifice, Heb. v. 7, so as Christ's intercession consisteth rather in the perpetual vigour of his sacrifice and continual application thereof, than in any actual supplication. The intendment of this phrase applied to Christ, 'to make intercession,' is to shew that Christ, being God's favourite, and our advocate, continually appeareth before God, to make application of that sacrifice which once he offered up for our sins. Christ appears in the presence of God for us; (1.) To present unto his Father himself, who is the price of our redemption ; (2.) To make application of his sacrifice to his church time after time, according to the need of the several members thereof ; (3.) To make our persons, prayers, services, and all good things acceptable to God. But,

[7.] Seventhly and lastly, *The whole compact and agreement between God the Father and our Lord Jesus Christ, about the redemption of poor sinners' souls, was really and solemnly transacted in open court; or, as I may say, in the high court of justice above, in the presence of the great public notary of heaven—viz., the Holy Ghost;* who being a third person of the glorious Trinity, of the same divine essence, and of equal power and glory, makes up a third legal witness with the Father and the Son. They being, after the manner of kings,[1] their own witnesses also: 1 John v. 7, 'For there be three that bear record in heaven, the Father, the Word, and the Holy Ghost, and these three are one.' Three, (1.) In the true and real distinction of their per-

[1] So the king writes, *Teste meipso.* This, 1 John v. 7, is a very clear proof and testimony of the Trinity of persons; in the unity of the divine essence; they are all one in essence and will. As if three lamps were lighted in one chamber, albeit the lamps be divers, yet the lights cannot be severed ; so in the Godhead, as there is a distinction of persons, so a simplicity of nature.

sons; (2.) In their inward properties, as to beget, to be begotten, and to proceed; (3.) In their several offices one to another, as to send and to be sent: 'And these three are one,' one in nature and essence, one in power and will, one in the act of producing all such actions as, without themselves, any of them is said to act; and one in their testimony concerning the covenant of redemption that was agreed on between the Father and the Son   Consent of all parties, the allowance of the judge, and public record, is as much as can be desired to make all public contracts authentic in courts of justice; and what can we desire more, to settle, satisfy, and assure our own souls that all the articles of the covenant of redemption shall, on all hands, be certainly made good, than this, that these three heavenly witnesses, God the Father, God the Son, and God the Holy Ghost, do all agree to the articles of the covenant, and are all witnesses to the same covenant? Thus you see that there was a covenant of redemption made with Christ; upon the terms whereof he is constituted to be a Redeemer; ' to say to the prisoners, go forth, to bring deliverance to the captives, and to proclaim the year of release (or jubilee) the acceptable year of the Lord,' as it is, Isa. lxi. 1, 2. I have been the longer in opening the covenant of redemption, partly because of its grand importance to all our souls, and partly because others have spoken so little to it, to the best of my observation, and partly because I have never before handled this subject, either in the pulpit or the press, &c.

Now from the serious consideration of this compact, covenant, and agreement, that was solemnly made between God and Christ, touching the whole business of man's salvation or redemption, I may form up this tenth plea as to the ten scriptures that are in the margin,[1] that refer to the great day of account, or to a man's particular day of account. *O blessed God! I have read over the articles of the covenant of redemption that were agreed on between thyself and thy dearest Son; and I find by those articles that dear Jesus has died, and satisfied thy justice, and pacified thy wrath, and bore the curse, and purchased my pardon, and procured thy everlasting favour: and I find by the same articles that whatever Jesus Christ acted or suffered, he did act or suffer as my surety, and in my stead and room.* O Lord! when I look upon my manifold weaknesses and imperfections, though under a covenant of grace, yet I am many times not only grieved, but also stumbled and staggered; but when I look up to the covenant of redemption, I am cheered, raised, and quieted; for I am abundantly satisfied that both thyself and thy dear Son are infinitely ready, able, willing, and faithful to perform whatever in that covenant is comprised, Isa. xxxviii. 16, 17; by these things men live, and in these is the life of my spirit. Men may fail, and friends may fail, and relations may fail, and trade may fail, and natural strength may fail, and my heart may fail, but the covenant of redemption can never fail, nor the federates, who are mutually engaged in that covenant, can never fail, Ps. lxxiii. 24, 25; and therefore I am safe and happy for ever. What though my sins have been great and heinous, yet they are not greater than Christ's satisfaction; he did bear the curse

---

[1] Eccles. xi. 9, and xii. 14; Mat. xii. 14, and xviii. 23; Luke xvi. 2; Rom. xiv. 10; 2 Cor. v. 10; Heb. ix. 27, and xiii. 17; 1 Pet. iv. 5; Isa. liii. 6; Rom. v. 6, 8; Gal. ii. 20.

for great sins as well as small, for sins against the gospel as well as for sins against the law, for omissions as well as for commissions. Assuredly the covenant of redemption is a mighty thing, and there are no mighty sins that can stand before that covenant. If we look upon Manasseh, in those black and ugly colours that the Holy Ghost paints him out in, we must needs conclude that he was a mighty sinner, a monstrous sinner, 1 Kings xxi. 1–16 ; and yet his mighty sins, his monstrous sins, could not stand before the covenant of redemption. The greatest sins are finite, but the merit of Christ's redemption is infinite. All the Egyptians were drowned in the Red Sea. There remained not so much as one of them ; there was not one of them left alive to carry the news ; the high and the low, the great and the small, the rich and the poor, the honourable and the base, were all drowned, Exod. xiv. 28 ; Ps. cvi. 11.   The red sea of Christ's blood drowns all our sins, whether they are great or small, high or low, &c., ' Though my sins be as scarlet, my Redeemer will make them as white as snow ; though they be as red as crimson, they shall be as wool,' Isa. i. 18. There is not one of my sins for which Jesus Christ hath not suffered and satisfied, Eph. i. 7 ; Col. i. 14 ; nor there is not one of my sins for which Jesus Christ hath not purchased a pardon, and for which he hath not made my peace.   Though my sins are innumerable, though they are more than the hairs of my head, Ps. xl. 12, or the sands on the sea-shore, yet they are not to be named in the day wherein the merits of Christ, the satisfaction of Christ, and the covenant of redemption, is mentioned and pleaded.   Be my sins ever so many ; yea, though they might fill a roll that might reach from east to west, from north to south, from earth to heaven, yet they could but bring me under the curse.   Now Christ my surety, that he might redeem me from the curse, hath taken upon him the whole curse, Gal. iii. 13. I know there is no summing up of my debts, but Christ has paid them all.   Woe had been to me for ever, had Christ left but one penny upon the score for me to pay.   As I have multiplied my sins, so he has multiplied his pardons, Isa. lv. 7.   Christ has cancelled all bonds, and therefore it is but justice in God to give me a full acquittance, and to throw down all bonds as cancelled, saying, ' Deliver him, I have found a ransom,' Col. ii. 13–15 ; Job xxxiii. 24.   O God, though my sins are very many, and very great, yet if thou dost not pardon them, the innocent blood of thy dearest Son will lie upon thee, and cry out against thee ; for he therefore died, that my sins might be pardoned ; so that now, in honour and justice, thou art obliged to ' pardon all my transgressions, and remember mine iniquities no more,' Isa. xliii. 25 ; Dan. ix. 24.   Now this is my plea, O holy God, which I make to all those scriptures that respect my last account, and by this plea I shall stand.   Well, saith God the Father, I accept of this plea, I am pleased with this plea, thy sins shall not be mentioned, Ezek. xviii. 22 ; ' Enter thou into the joy of thy Lord.'

I shall now make a little improvement of what has been said as to the covenant of redemption, and so draw to a conclusion.

First, [1.] This covenant of redemption, as we have opened it, looks sadly and sourly upon those that *make so great a noise about the doctrine of universal redemption.*   The covenant of redemption extends itself, not to every man in the world, but only to those that are 'given by God the Father to Jesus Christ.'[1] [2.] It looks sadly and sourly upon those that *make so great a noise about God's choosing or electing of men, upon the account of God's foreseeing their faith, good works, obedience, holiness, when our election is merely of grace and favour, and flows only from* 'the good will of him that dwelt in the bush;' and faith, good works, holiness, sanctification, are the fruits and effects of election, as the Scripture everywhere tells us,[2] and as has been made evident in my opening the gracious terms of the covenant of redemption. But because I have, in another place, treated of these things more largely, a touch here may suffice. But,

(2.) Secondly, *How should this covenant of redemption spirit animate and encourage all the redeemed of God, to do anything for Christ, to suffer anything for Christ, to venture anything for Christ, to part with anything for Christ, to give up anything to Christ, who, according to the covenant of redemption, hath done and suffered such great and grievous things, that he might bring us to glory, that are above all apprehensions, and beyond all expressions,* Mark viii. 34, 35, 38; Heb. x. 34, and xi. Who can tell me what is fully wrapped up in that one expression—viz., ' That he poured out his soul unto death,' Heb. ii. 10, 11. Let us not shrink, nor faint, nor grow weary under our greatest sufferings for Christ. When sufferings multiply, when they are sharp, when they are more bitter than gall or wormwood, yea, more bitter than death itself, then remember the covenant of redemption, and how punctually Christ made good all the articles of it on his side, and then faint and give out if you can. Well may I be afraid, but I do not therefore despair, for I think upon and remember the wounds of the Lord, saith one, [Austin.] *Nolo vivere sine vulnere, cum te video vulneratum ;* O my God, as long as I see thy wounds, I will never live without wound, saith another, [Bonaventura.] *Crux Christi clavis paradisi ;* The cross of Christ is the golden key that opens paradise to us, saith one, [Damascene.] I had rather, with the martyrs and confessors, have my Saviour's cross, than, with their persecutors, the world's crown. The harder we are put to it, the greater shall be our reward in heaven, saith another, [Tertullian.] Gordius the martyr hit the nail, when he said, it is to my loss.if you abate me anything in my sufferings, [Chrysostom.] If you suffer not for religion, you will suffer for a worse thing, saith one. Never did any man serve me better than you serve me, said another to his persecutors, [Vincentius.] *Adversus gentes, gratias agimus quod à molestis dominis liberemur ;* We thank you for delivering us from hard task-masters, that we may enjoy more sweetly the bosom of our Lord Jesus, said the martyr. It was a notable saying of Luther, *Ecclesia totum mundum convertit sanguine et oratione ;* The church converteth the whole world by blood and prayers. They may kill me, said Socrates of his enemies, but they cannot hurt me. So may the redeemed of the Lord say, they may take away my head, but they cannot take away my crown of life, of righteousness, of glory, of immortality, Rev. ii. 10; 2

---

[1] Mat. xxiv. 16 ; Luke xii. 32 ; Rom. ix. 11, 12, and xi. 5–8 ; Rom. viii. 39, 40.
[2] Deut. vii. 6–8, and xxxiii. 11 ; Rom. ix. 14 ; 2 Tim. i. 9 ; Eph. i. 4 ; Rom. viii. 29 30 ; 2 Thes. ii. 13 ; 1 Pet. i. 2.

Tim. iv. 8; 1 Pet. v. 4, 5. The Lacedemonians were wont to say, it is a shame for any man to fly in time of danger; but for a Lacedemonian, it is a shame for him to deliberate. Oh, what a shame is it for Christians, when they look upon the covenant of redemption, so much as to deliberate whether they were best to suffer for Christ or no. *Petrus Blesensis* has long since observed, that the courtiers of his time suffered as great trouble, and as many vexations, for vanity, as good Christians did for the truth. The courtiers suffered weariness and painfulness, hunger and thirst, with all the catalogue of Paul's afflictions; and what can the best saints suffer more? Now shall men that are strangers to the covenant of redemption, suffer such hard and great things for their lusts, for very vanity; and will not you, who are acquainted with the covenant of redemption, and who are interested in the covenant of redemption, be ready and willing to suffer anything for that Jesus, who, according to the covenant of redemption, has suffered such dreadful things for you, and merited such glorious things for you? But,

(3.) Thirdly, From this covenant of redemption, as we have opened it, you may see *what infinite cause we have to be swallowed up in the admiration of the Father's love in entering into this covenant, and in making good all the articles of this covenant on his side.* When man was fallen from his primitive purity and glory, from his holiness and happiness, from his freedom and liberty, into a most woeful gulf of sin and misery; when angels and men were all at a loss, and knew no way or means, whereby fallen man might be raised, restored and saved; that then God should firstly and freely propose this covenant, and enter into this covenant, that miserable man might be saved from wrath to come, and raised and settled in a more safe, high and happy estate than that was from which he was fallen in Adam,—oh, what wonderful, what amazing love is this![1] Abraham manifested a great deal of love to God in offering up of his only Isaac, Gen. xxii. 12; but God has shewed far greater love to poor sinners, in making his only Son an offering for their sins: for [1.] God loved Christ with a more transcendent love than Abraham could love Isaac; [2.] God was not bound by the commandment of a superior to do it, as Abraham was, John x. 18; [3.] God freely and voluntarily did it, which Abraham would never have done without a commandment, Heb. x. 10, 12; [4.] Isaac was to be offered after the manner of holy sacrifices, but Christ suffered an ignominious death, after the manner of thieves; [5.] Isaac was all along in the hands of a tender father, but Christ was all along in the hands of barbarous enemies; [6.] Isaac was offered but in show, but Christ was offered indeed and in very good earnest. Is not this an excess, yea, a miracle of love? It is good to be always a-musing upon this love, and delighting ourselves in this love. But,

(4.) Fourthly, From this covenant of redemption, as we have opened it, you may see *what signal cause we have to be deeply affected with the love of Jesus Christ, who roundly and readily falls in with this covenant, and who has faithfully performed all the articles of this covenant.* Had not Jesus Christ kept touch with his Father as to every article

[1] God so loved his Son, that he gave him all the world for his possession, Ps. ii. 8; but he so loved the world that he gave Son and all for its redemption.—*Bernard.*

of the covenant of redemption, he could never have saved us, nor have satisfied divine justice, nor have been admitted into heaven. That Jesus Christ might make full satisfaction for all our sins, ' he was made a curse for us, whereby he hath redeemed us from the curse of the law,' Gal. iii. 13. All his sufferings were for us. All that can be desired of God by man is mercy and truth ; mercy in regard of our misery, truth in reference to God's promises. That which moved Christ to engage himself as a surety for us was his respect to God and man : to God, for the honour of his name. Neither the mercy nor the truth nor the justice of God had been so conspicuously manifested, if Jesus Christ had not been our surety, to man, and that to help us in our succourless and desperate estate. No creature either would or could discharge that debt, wherein man stood obliged to the justice of God. This is a mighty evidence of the endless love of Christ, this is an evidence of the endless and matchless love of Christ. We count it a great evidence of love for a friend to be surety for us when we intend no damage to him thereupon ; but if a man be surety for that which he knoweth the principal debtor is not able to pay, and thereupon purposeth to pay it himself, this we look upon as an extraordinary evidence of love. But what amazing love, what matchless love is this, for a man to engage his person and life for his friend ! whenas ' skin for skin, and all that a man hath, will he give for his life,' Job ii. 4 ; and yet, according to the covenant of redemption, Jesus Christ has done all this and much more for us, as is evident, if you will but cast your eye back upon the articles of the covenant, or consult the scriptures in the margin.[1] If a friend, to free a captive, or one condemned to death, should put himself into the state and condition of him whom he freeth, that would be an evidence of love beyond all comparison. But now, if the dignity of Christ's person and our unworthiness, if the greatness of the debt and kind of payment, and if the benefit which we reap thereby, be duly weighed, we shall find these evidences of love to come as much behind the love of Christ, as the light of a candle cometh short of the light of the sun. Christ's suretyship, according to the covenant of redemption, is and ought to be a prop of props to our faith. It is as sure a ground of confidence that all is well, and shall be for ever well between God and us, as any the Scriptures does afford. By virtue hereof we have a right to appeal to God's justice, for this surety hath made full satisfaction ; and to exact a debt which is fully satisfied is a point of injustice. Christ knew very well what the redemption of fallen man would cost him, *Solus amor nescit difficultates;* he knew that his life and blood must go for it ; he knew that he must lay by his robes of majesty, and be clothed with flesh ; he knew that he must encounter men and devils ; he knew that he must tread the wine-press of his Father's wrath, bear the curse, and make himself an offering for our sins, for our sakes, for our salvation ; yet, for all this, he is very ready and willing to bind himself by covenant, that he will redeem us, whatever it cost him. Oh, what tongue can express, what heart can conceive, what soul can comprehend, ' the heights, depths, breadths, and lengths of this love' ?

[1] John x. 11, 15, 17, 18, 28 ; Rom. v. 6, &c. ; Eph. i. 5–7, &c. ; Col. ii. 13–15 ; Heb. ii. 13–15.

Eph. iii. 18, 19.[1] O blessed Jesus, what manner of love is this! that thou shouldst wash away my scarlet sins in thine own blood! that thou shouldst die that I may live! that thou shouldst be cursed that I might be blessed! that thou shouldst undergo the pains of hell that I might enjoy the joys of heaven! that the face of God should be clouded from thee, that his everlasting favour might rest upon me! that thou shouldst be an everlasting screen betwixt the wrath of God and my immortal soul! that thou shouldst do for me beyond all expression, and suffer for me beyond all conception, and gloriously provide for me beyond all expectation! and all this according to the covenant of redemption! What shall I say, what can I say to all this, but fall down before thy grace, and spend my days in wondering at that matchless, bottomless love, that can never be fathomed by angels or men! O Lord Jesus, saith one, *plusquam mea, plusquam meos, plusquam me;* I love thee more than all my goods, and I love thee more than all my friends, yea, I love thee more than my very self, [Bernard.] It is good to write after this copy. But,

XI. The eleventh and last plea that a believer may form up as to the ten scriptures that are in the margin,[2] that refer to the great day of account, or to a man's particular account, may be drawn up from *the consideration of the book of life, out of which all the saints shall be judged in the great day of our Lord:* Rev. xx. 11, ' And I saw a great white throne, and him that sat on it, from whose face the earth and the heaven fled away; and there was found no place for them :' ver. 12, ' And I saw the dead, small and great, stand before God : and the books were opened; and another book was opened, which is the book of life: and the dead were judged out of those things which were written in the books, according to their works :' ver. 13, ' And the sea gave up the dead which were in it; and death and hell delivered up the dead which were in them : and they were judged every man according to their works :' ver. 14, ' And death and hell were cast into the lake of fire. This is the second death. And whosoever was not found written in the book of life was cast into the lake of fire.' In the 11th verse John describes the judge with his preparation; in the 12th verse he describes the persons that should be judged; and then he describes the process and sentence; and lastly, he describes the execution of the sentence, viz., the casting of the reprobates into the lake of fire, and the placing and fixing of the elect in the heavenly Jerusalem, ver. 13-15.

In the five last verses cited you have a clear and full description of the last general judgment, as is evident by the native [3] context and series of this chapter, Rev. xx. 1-3. For having spoken of the devil's last judgment, which, by Jude, is called ' The judgment of the great day,' Jude 6 ; it is consentaneous, therefore, to understand this of such a judgment whereby he is judged. And, indeed, the expressions are so full, and the matter and circumstances so satisfying and convincing, that they leave no place for fears, doubts, or disputes. This

---

[1] Look where thou wilt, thou art surrounded with flames of his love; and it were strange if thou shouldst not be set on fire ; if not, sure thou must needs be a diabolical salamander, says Cusanus.

[2] Eccles. x. 9, and xii. 14; Mat. xii. 14, and xviii. 23 ; Luke xvi. 2; Rom. xiv. 10; 2 Cor. v. 10 ; Heb. ix. 27, and xiii. 17; 1 Pet. iv. 5. [3] ' Neighbouring.'—G.

scripture that is under our present consideration runs parallel with that Dan. xii. 1-3, and several other places of Scripture where the day of judgment is spoken of ; and let him that can, shew me at what other judgment all the dead are raised and judged, and all reprobates sent to hell, and all the elect brought to heaven, and death and hell cast into the lake ; all which are plainly expressed here.   He shall be an Apollo to me that can make these things that are here spoken of to agree with any other judgment than the last judgment.   Let me give a little light into this scripture, before I improve it to that purpose for which I have cited it.

' And I saw a great white throne, and him that sat on it :' a lively description of the last judgment, ' a great throne.' ' Great,' because it is set up for the general judgment of all, for the universal judgment of the whole world.   Before this throne all the great ones of the world must stand,—popes, emperors, kings, princes, nobles, judges, prelates, without their mitres, crowns, sceptres, royal robes, gold chains, &c.,— and before this throne all other sorts and ranks of men must stand. And he that sits upon this throne is a great King, and a great God above all gods ; he is ' Prince of the kings of the earth, who is King of kings, and Lord of lords,'[1] Rev. i. 5, xvii. 14, and xix. 16.   Upon all which accounts this throne may well be called a great throne; and it is called ' a white throne,' because of its celestial splendour and majesty, and to shew the uprightness and glory of the judge.   The white colour in Scripture is used to represent purity and glory.   Here it signifies that Christ, the judge, shall give most just and righteous judgment, free from all spot of partiality.

' From whose face the heaven and the earth fled away.' The splendour and majesty of the judge is such, as neither heaven nor earth is able to behold or abide the same; how then shall the wicked be able to stand before him ?   Augustine understands it, for the future renovation of heaven and earth ; and here he acknowledgeth an ὑστέρο-σις,[2] for the heaven and the earth fled not before, but after the judgment; to wit, saith he, the judgment being finished, then shall this heaven and earth cease to be, ' when the new heaven and earth shall begin ;' for this world shall pass away by a change of things, not by an utter destruction. ' The heaven and the earth shall flee away ;' that is, this shape of heaven and earth shall pass away ; because they shall be changed from vanity, through fire, that so they may be transformed into a much better and more beautiful estate ; according to that which the apostle Peter writeth, ' The heaven shall pass away with a great noise, and the elements melt with heat; but we expect new heavens and a new earth, wherein dwelleth righteousness,' 1 Pet. iii. 12.   How this passing away, or perishing of heaven and earth, shall come to pass, there are divers opinions of learned men.   Some think that the substance or essence itself of the world shall wholly perish and be annihilated.   Others are of opinion, that only the corruptible qualities thereof shall perish and be changed, and the substance or essence re-

[1] All the thrones of the kings of the earth, with Solomon's golden throne, are but petty thrones to this throne; yea, they are but footstools to this throne ; and therefore upon this single ground it may well be called a great throne.

[2] *Hysterosis* is, when a thing is before put down, which should come after, or con-trariwise.   Aug. lib. xx., de C. D., c. 14 ; 1 Pet. iii. 12.

main. There shall be a renovation of all things, say most, and that only the fashion of the world, that is, the outward form and corruptible qualities, shall be destroyed; and so the earth shall be found no more as it was, but shall be made most beautiful and glorious, being to be 'delivered into the glorious liberty,' as far as it is capable, 'of the sons of God,' Rom. viii. 19-22; being to be freed from corruption and bondage; and with these I close. The sum of the 21st verse is, that the creature shall not be always subject to vanity, but shall have a manumission from bondage; of the which deliverance, three things are declared; *First*, Who the creature [is], that is, 'the world;' *Secondly*, From what, from 'corruption,' which is a bondage; *Thirdly*, Into what estate, into 'the glorious liberty of the sons of God.' Some here note the time of the deliverance of the creature, namely, when the children of God shall be wholly set free; for though they have here a freedom unto righteousness, from the bondage of sin, yet they have not a freedom of glory, which is from the bondage of misery. But others take it for the state itself which shall be glorious, not the same with the children of God, but proportioned according to its kind with them; for it is most suitable to the liberty of the faithful, that as they are renewed, so also should their habitation. And as when a nobleman mourneth, his servants are all clad in black; so it is for the greater glory of man, that the creatures, his servants, should in their kind partake of his glory. And whereas some say that it is deliverance enough for the creature, if it cease to serve man, and have an end of vanity, by annihilation, I affirm, it is not enough, because this 21st verse notes, not only such deliverance, but also a further estate which it shall have after such deliverance—namely, to communicate in some degree, with the children of God in glory. Certainly the creatures, in their kind and manner, shall be made partakers of a far better estate than they had while the world endured; because that God shall fully and wholly restore the world, being fallen into corruption through the transgression and sin of mankind. And this doth more plainly appear by the apostle's opposing subsequent liberty against former bondage; which, that he might more enlarge, he calleth it not simply freedom or liberty, but liberty of glory, as it is in the Greek text,[1] meaning thereby, according to the phrase and propriety of the Hebrew tongue, glorious liberty, or liberty that bringeth glory with it; under which term of glory, he compriseth the excellent estate that they shall be in after their delivery from their former baseness and servitude. As for those words, of the 'sons of God,' to which we must refer the glorious liberty before mentioned, they must be understood by a certain proportion or similitude thus; that as in that great day, and not before, God's children shall be graciously freed from all dangers and distresses of this life whatsoever, either in body or soul, and on the other side, made perfect partakers of eternal blessedness; so the creatures then, and not before, shall be delivered from the vanity of man, and their own corruption, and restored to a far

---

[1] ἐλευθερίαν τῆς δόξης. If any shall inquire what shall be the particular properties, works, and uses of all and every creature after the last judgment, I answer, (1.) That as to these things the word is silent, and it is not safe to be wise above what is written; (2.) Here is place for that which Tertullian calls a learned ignorance.

better estate than at present they enjoy; which also may further appear by the words the apostle useth, setting glorious liberty, deliverance and freedom, against servile bondage and slavery. Chrysostom reads διὰ, *for* the glorious liberty of the sons of God: as if the end or final cause of their deliverance were pointed at, namely, that as God made the world for man, and for man's sin subdued it to vanity; so he would deliver it and restore it for men, even to illustrate and enlarge the glory of God's children. I could, by variety of arguments, prove that this deliverance of the creature that our apostle speaks of, shall not be by a reduction into nothing, but by an alteration into a better estate. But I must hasten to a close.

Ver. 12, 'And I saw the dead, small and great, stand before God.' The judge, before whom all do appear, is our dear Lord Jesus, 'who hath the keys of hell and death in his hands,' Rev. i. 18; Acts xvii. 30, 31, and who is designed and appointed by God the Father to be the judge of quick and dead. He hath authority, and a commission under his Father's hand, to sit and act as judge. Here you see that John calleth the judge absolutely God, but Christ is the judge; therefore Christ is God absolutely; and he will appear to be God in our nature in that great day.

The parties judged, who stand before the throne, are, (1.) Generally 'the dead,' all who had died from Adam to the last day. He calls them 'the dead,' after the common law of nature, but then raised from death to life by the power of God, Eph. ii. 5; Col. ii. 13. He speaks not of men dead in sins and trespasses, but of such as died corporally, and now were raised up to judgment. But shall not the living then be judged? Oh, yes! 'For we must all appear before the judgment-seat of Christ: that he may be judge of the quick and the dead, and be Lord both of the dead and the living,' 2 Cor. v. 10; Rom. xiv. 9, 10. Under this phrase, 'the dead,' are comprehended all those that then shall be found alive. By 'the dead' we are to understand the living also, by an argument from the lesser. If the dead shall appear before the judgment-seat, how much more the living! But the dead alone are named, either because the number of the dead, from Adam to the last day, shall be far greater than those that shall be found alive on earth in that day, or because those that remain alive shall be accounted as dead, because 'they shall be changed in the twinkling of an eye,' 1 Cor. xv. 52. Secondly, He describes them from their age and condition, for the words may be understood of both 'great and small,' which takes in all sorts of men, tyrants, emperors, kings, princes, dukes, lords, &c., as well as subjects, vassals, slaves, beggars; rich and poor, strong and weak, bond and free, old and young. All and every one, without exception, are to be judged; for the judgment shall be universal. No man shall be so great as to escape the same, nor none so small as to be excluded; but every one shall have justice done him, without respect of persons, as that great apostle Paul tells us, 'We must all appear before the judgment-seat of Christ, that every one may receive the things done in his body, according to that he hath done, whether it be good or bad,' 2 Cor. v. 10. I am no admirer of the schoolmen's notion, who suppose that all shall be raised about the age of thirty-three, which was Christ's age; but do judge that that perfection, which consisteth in the conforming them to Christ's glorious body, is of another kind than to respect either age, stature, or the like.[1]

'Stand before God,' that is, brought to judgment. The guilty standing ready to be condemned, and the saints standing ready in Christ's presence to be absolved and pronounced blessed, John iii. 18.

'And the books were opened.' Christ the judge being set on his throne, and having all the world before him, 'the books are opened.' (1.) In the general the books are said to be open. (2.) Here is a special book for the elect, 'The book of life was opened.' (3.) Here you have sentence passed and pronounced, 'according to what was written in these books, and according to their works: and the dead were judged out of those things which were written in the books, according to their works.' Here the judicial process is noted by imitation of human courts, in which the whole process is wont to be drawn up, and laid before the judge, from whence the judge determineth for or against the person, according to the acts and proofs that lie open before him. The equity, justice, and righteousness of Christ the judge, that sits on his white throne, is set forth by a metaphor taken from human courts, where the judge pronounceth sentence according to the written law, and the acts and proofs agreeing thereunto. 'All things are naked and bare before him, whose eyes are as a flame of fire,' Heb. iv. 13; Rev. i. 14. But to shew that the judgment shall be as accurate and particular in the trial, and just and righteous in the close, as if all were registered and put on record, nothing shall escape or be mistaken in its circumstances, but all things shall be so cleared and issued beyond all doubts and disputes, as if an exact register of them had been kept and published; in all which there is a plain allusion unto the words of Daniel, speaking thus of this judgment, 'The judgment was set, and the books were opened,' Dan. vii. 10. We find six several books mentioned in the Scripture.

[1.] *The book of nature*, that is mentioned by David, 'Thine eyes did see my substance, yet being unperfect; and in thy book all my members were written, which in continuance were fashioned, when as yet there was none of them,' Ps. cxxxix. 16.[2] It is a metaphor from curious workmen, that do all by the book, or by a model set before them, that nothing may be deficient or done amiss. Had God left out an eye in his commonplace-book, saith one, thou hadst wanted it. 'The heavens declare the glory of God, and the firmament sheweth his handiwork.' The psalmist looks upon that great volume of heaven and earth, and there reads in capital letters the prints and characters of God's glory. This book, saith one, was imprinted at the New Jerusalem by the finger of Jehovah; and is not to be sold, but to be seen, at the sign of glory, of every one that lifts up his eyes to heaven. In this book of nature, which is made up of three great leaves, heaven, earth, and sea, God hath made himself visible, yea, legible, 'even his eternal power and godhead,' Rom. i. 20. So that

---

[1] See General Index, under 'Resurrection,' for more on this point.—G.

[2] The world, saith Clemens Alexandrinus, is, *Dei Scriptura*, the first Bible that God made for the instruction of man.

all men are left without excuse. Out of this book the poor blind Gentiles might have learned many choice lessons, as, *first,* that they had a maker; *secondly,* that this maker, being before the things made, is eternal, without beginning or ending; *thirdly,* that he must needs be almighty, which made all things out of nothing, and sustained such a mass of creatures; *fourthly,* the order, variety, and distinction of creatures declare his marvellous wisdom; *fifthly,* in this book they might run and read the great goodness, and the admirable kindness of God to the sons of men, in making all the creatures for their good, for their service, and benefit; *sixthly* and lastly, in this book they might run and read what a most excellent, what a most admirable, what a most transcendent workman God was. What are the heavens, the earth, the sea, but a sheet of royal paper, written all over with the wisdom and power of God? Now, in the great day of account, this book shall be produced to witness against the heathen world, because they did not live up to the light that was held forth to them in this book, but crucified that light and knowledge by false ways of worship, and by their wicked manners, whereof the apostle gives you a bead-roll or catalogue, from verse 21st to the end of that 1st of the Romans. But,

[2.] Secondly, There is *the book of providence,* wherein all particulars are registered, even such as atheists may count trivial and inconsiderable: Mat. x. 30, ' But the very hairs of your head are all numbered.' And where is their number summed up? Even in the book of providence. The three worthies were taken out of the fiery furnace, with their hairs in full number, not one of them singed, Dan. iii. 27. Paul, encouraging the passengers to eat, who were in fear and danger of death, tells them that ' there should not a hair fall from the head of any of them,' Acts xxvii. 34. And when Saul would have put Jonathan to death, the people told him ' that there should not a hair of his head fall to the ground,' 1 Sam. xiv. 45. Christ doth not say that the hairs of your eyelids are numbered, but the hairs of your head, where there is the greatest plenty, and the least use. Though hair is but an excrement, and the most contemptible part of man, yet every hair of an elect person is observed and registered down in God's books, and not one of them shall be lost. Nor the Holy Ghost doth not say the hairs of your heads *shall be* numbered, but the hairs of your head *are* all numbered. God has already booked them all down, and all to shew us that special, that singular care that God takes of the smallest and least concernments of his chosen ones. This book of providence God will produce in the great day, to confute and condemn the atheists of the world, who have denied a divine providence, and whose hearts have swelled against his government of the world, ' according to the counsels of his own heart.' But,

[3.] Thirdly, There is *the book of men's afflictions.* This some account an entire book of itself: Ps. lvi. 8, ' Thou tellest my wanderings; put thou my tears into thy bottle; are they not in thy book?' [1] God told all those weary steps that David took in passing over those

---

[1] The Septuagint, for my wanderings or flittings, have Ζωὴν, 'my life,' to teach us, saith one, that our life is but a flitting.

two great forests, when he fled from Saul, or thou cipherest up my flittings, as the words may be read. Whilst David was hunted up and down like a partridge, and hushed[1] out of every bush, and had no certain dwelling-place, but driven from post to pillar, from one country to another, God was all this while a-noting down and a-numbering of his flittings, and a-bottling up his tears, and a-booking down his sighs: 'Put thou my tears into thy bottle;' *Heb.*, 'my tear,' that is, every tear of mine; let not one of them be lost, but kept safe with thee, as so much sweet water. God is said in Scripture to have a bag and a bottle: a bag for our sins, and a bottle for our tears. And oh that we would all labour to fill his bottle with our tears, as we have filled his bag with our sins; and certainly if the white tears of his servants be bottled up, the red tears of their blood shall not be cast away. If God keeps the tears of the saints in store, much more will he remember their blood, to avenge it; and though tyrants burn the bones of the saints,[2] yet they cannot blot out their tears and blood out of God's register: 'Are they not in thy book?' are they not in thy register, or book of accounts, where they cannot be blotted out by any time or tyrants? *i.e.*, yes, certainly they are; thou dost assuredly book them down, and wilt never forget one of them, according to the usual interrogatory that was used among the Hebrews when they affirmed a thing past all doubt. Let the great Nimrods and oppressors of the saints look to themselves, for God books down all the afflictions, sufferings, and persecutions of his servants; and in the great day he will bring in this book, this register, to witness against them. Ah, sinners, sinners! look to yourselves. In the great day of account, the Lord will reckon with you for every rod that he hath spent upon you; he will reckon with you, not only for all your mercies, but also for all your crosses; not only for all your sweets, but also for all your bitters; not only for all your cordials, but also for all your corrosives. In this book of afflictions there is not only *item* for this mercy and that, but *item* also for this affliction and that, this sickness and that, this cross and that, this loss and that. And will not the opening of this book of the saints' afflictions and sufferings, and of sinners' afflictions and sufferings, be as the handwriting upon the wall, to all the wicked of the earth, in the great day of account? Dan. v. 5, 6. Surely yes; for as they cannot answer for one mercy of ten thousand that they have enjoyed, so they cannot answer for one affliction of ten thousand that they have been exercised with. But,

[4.] Fourthly, There is *the book of conscience*. Conscience, saith Philo, is the little consistory of the soul. Conscience is *mille testes*, a thousand witnesses, for or against a man, Rom. ii. 14, 15. Conscience is God's preacher in the bosom. Conscience hath a good memory, saith one. The chief butler forgot the promise that he had made to Joseph, but conscience told him of it, Gen. xli. 9. *Fama propter homines, conscientia propter Deum*, saith Augustine: a good name will carry it amongst men, but it is a good conscience only that can acquit

---

[1] 'Startled,' as birds by a cry or shout.—G.

[2] Cf. Sibbes, ii., 370, and note *m*, 434.—G.

[3] The conscience is a domestic and true tribunal, saith [Gregory] Nazianzen.

us before God.   In this great day the book of every man's conscience shall be opened for their conviction, wherein they shall read their guilt in legible characters; for that is a book of record, wherein men's actions are entered.   And although now it be shut up close, and sinners will by no means be brought to look into it, and though many things that are written in this book seem to be so greatly obliterated and blotted that they can hardly be read, yet in that great day of accounts God will refresh and recover the lustre of those ancient writings; and sinners, in that day, shall find that conscience hath an iron memory.   In the last day God will bring the book of conscience out of the rubbish, as they did the book of the law in Josiah's time; and the very laying open of this book before sinners will even put them beside their wits, and fill them with unspeakable horror and terror, and be a hell on this side hell unto them.   In this book they shall find an exact account of every vain thought they have had, and of every idle word they have spoken, and of every evil action they have done; and oh, what amazement and astonishment will this fill them with !   By the *books* in this Rev. xx. 12, Origen does understand the books of conscience, which now are hid, not from God, but from most men; for the hidden things of the heart are not now known, but then they shall be opened, and manifested to the consciences of every sinner, so as there shall be no place, no room left for any excuse or plea.[1] Ambrose saith that the books that are here said to be opened are the books of men's consciences and God's omniscience.[2]   Oh, what dreadful challenges and accusations will every sinner be forced to read out of this book of conscience in the great day !   Oh, how in that great day will all wicked men wish that they had followed the counsel of the heathen orator when he said, *A recta conscientia ne latum quidem unguem discedendum;* A man may not depart an hair's-breadth all his life long from the dictates of a good conscience.[3]   The book of God's omniscience takes in all things past, present, and to come, as if he had kept a diary of every man's thoughts, words, and actions. But,

[5.] Fifthly, There is the *book of Scripture ;* and of all books this book is the most precious book.   The book of the creature is but as the inventory of the goods ; the book of the Scripture is the evidence, and conveyance, and assurance of all good to us.   The book of Scripture is the book of the statutes and ordinances of the King of heaven, which must be opened and consulted, and by which all must be judged in the great day: James ii. 12, 'So speak ye, and so do, as they that shall be judged by the law of liberty ;' *i.e.,* by the gospel of Jesus Christ, by the whole word of God, registered in the blessed Scriptures, James i. 23–25.   Now the whole word of God is called the law of liberty ; because thereby we are born again to a new spiritual life, and so freed from the bondage and slavery of sin and Satan.[4]   Our Lord Jesus Christ, in his proceedings in the great day of account, will judge us by

---

[1] Comm. ad Rom. xiv.   [2] Ambrose in Ps. i.   [3] Cic. in Offic.
[4] Let the word be president in all assemblies and judgments, saith Beza.   In the Nicene Council, Constantine caused the Bible to be set upon the desk as judge of all controversies.   The word shall be the judge of all men's estates at last ; every man shall stand or fall according as he holds weight in the balance of the sanctuary.

the Scriptures, and pass everlasting sentence upon us according to the tenor of the Scriptures. At the great and general assizes Christ will try all causes by the word of God, and pass judgment upon all sorts of persons according to the word: John xii. 48, 'He that rejecteth me, and receiveth not my words, hath one that judgeth him: the word that I have spoken, the same shall judge him in the last day.' The persons that are to be judged in the great day are not believers in Christ, they are not receivers of Christ, but such as reject his person, and receive not his doctrine. 'He that rejecteth me, and receiveth not my words, hath one that judgeth him,' &c. However the rejecters of Christ may escape judgment for a time, yet they shall never be able to escape the judgment of the last day; they shall assuredly, they shall unavoidably, be judged in the last day. Though the rejecters of Christ had none to witness against them, yet the word of the Lord shall be more than a thousand witnesses against them in the great day, 'The word that I have spoken, the same shall judge him in the last day.' The word of the Lord is so sure and infallible a word, that Christ's sentence in the great day, when heaven and earth shall pass away, 2 Pet. iii. 7, 10–12, shall proceed according to the verdict and testimony thereof, 'For the word that I have spoken shall judge him in the last day.' Christ will pronounce then according to what it saith now; and that as well in favour of believers as against unbelievers. Look, as Christ himself is 'ordained to be the judge of quick and dead,' Acts xvii. 31; so the word, the doctrines which he hath delivered, will be the rule of all his judicial proceedings, both in acquitting the righteous, and condemning the wicked. By the *books* in this Rev. xx. 12, Augustine understands the books of the Old and New Testament, which shall then be opened; because, according to them, the judge will pronounce sentence:[1] Rom. ii. 16, 'When God shall judge the secrets of men by Jesus Christ, according to my gospel,' which promiseth heaven and happiness to all believers. The sentence of the last day shall be but a more manifest declaration of that judgment, that the Lord, in this life, most-an-end[2] hath passed upon men. Heathens shall be judged by the law of nature; profligate professors by the written law, and the word preached; believers by the gospel, which saith, 'He that believeth shall be saved; he that believes shall not perish, but have eternal life; he that believeth on the Son hath everlasting life; he that believeth shall not come into condemnation, but is passed from death to life,' Mark xvi. 16; John iii. 15, 16, 36, and v. 24. Christ shall, in the great day, give sentence according to the doctrine of the gospel, which saith, 'If there be first a willing mind, it is accepted according to that a man hath, and not according to that he hath not.' The Jesuits report of a student at Paris who, coming to confession, and not being able, for tears and sobbings, to speak, was willed by his confessor to write down his sins, which he did; and when the confessor received it, the writing vanished, and there remained nothing but the white and clean paper; this, say they, was by a miracle, because of his great contrition. Let the credit of this

---

[1] Lib. xx. De C. Dei. c. 14; and Bede saith the same with Austin.
[2] 'Continually,' 'generally.'—G.

story be upon the reporter ; but upon the credit of the word of God, if we believe, really, savingly, and repent unfeignedly, all our sins shall be blotted out ; and a book of clean paper, in respect of sin, shall be presented to the judge.   But,

[6.] Sixthly and lastly, There is *a book of life:* Rev. xx. 12, 'And another book was opened, which is the book of life.'   The book of life is the book of all those that were elected and redeemed to life through Christ Jesus.[1]   This book of life containeth a register of such particular persons in whose salvation God from all eternity determined to have his mercy glorified, and for whom Christ merited faith, repentance, and perseverance, that they should repent, believe, and be finally saved.   'The book of life shall be opened;' that is to say, the decrees of God will be then published and made known, which now are sealed up in his breast and locked up in his archives.   Then it will be seen who are appointed to life for the glorifying of God's free, rich, and sovereign grace, and whom he purposed to leave in their sins, and to perish for ever, for the exaltation of his justice.   It is called 'a book of life,' not that God hath need of a book, but to note the certainty of predestination—viz., that God knows all and every of the elect, even as men know a thing which, for memory's sake, they set down in writing.   This book of life shall be opened in the great day, because then it shall appear who were elect, who reprobates ; who truly believed in Christ, who not ; who worshipped God in spirit and in truth, and who not ; who walked with God as Noah, and who not ; who set up God as the object of their fear, who not ; who followed the Lamb whither ever he went, and who not ; who were sincere, and who not ; who preferred Christ above ten thousand worlds, and who preferred Barabbas before Jesus, and their farms, and their oxen, and their swine, yea, their very lusts, before a Saviour, a Redeemer ; who are sheep, and who are goats, Mat. xxv. 32 ; who are sons, and who are slaves ; who have mourned for their own sins and the sins of the time, and who they are that have made a sport of sin, Ezek. ix. 4, 6, &c.   Of this book of life you read often in Scripture : Phil. iv. 3, 'And I entreat thee also, true yoke-fellow, help those women which laboured with me in the gospel, with Clement also, and with other my fellow-labourers, whose names are in the book of life.'   Vorsitus thinks it a speech taken from the custom of soldiers or cities, in which the chosen soldiers or citizens are by name written in a certain book or roll. This book or roll is called here 'the book of life,' because therein are written all the elect who are ordained to eternal life : Rev. iii. 5, 'He that overcometh, the same shall be clothed in white raiment, and I will not blot out his name out of the book of life.'   In this book of life all 'the just, that live by faith,' are written.   The elect are certain of eternal life, they shall never perish, nor none can ever pluck them out of the Father's hand, nor out of Christ's hand, John x. 28–31. God is said to have books metaphorically ; he needs no books to help

---

[1] God neither needeth nor useth books to judge by, but this is spoken after the manner of men.   Mordecai's name was registered in the chronicles of Persia, Esth. vi. 1–3 ; and Tamerlane had always by him a catalogue of his best servants and their good deserts, which he daily perused.

his memory; he does all things by his infinite wisdom, eternal fore-knowledge, counsel, government, and judgment. But thus men cannot do; for whatsoever is done in their councils, cities, families, contracts, &c., for memory's sake, is set down in writing, that so, as there is occasion, they may look it over, and call to mind such things as they desire.[1] Mark, not to have our names blotted out of the book of life is to have them always remain therein; that is, to enjoy eternal glory; and what can the soul desire more? The names of the elect are written in the book of life. They do not obtain salvation by chance, but were elected of God to life and happiness before the foundation of the world. Now their names being once written in the book of life, they shall never, never be blotted out of that book. In the book of predestination there is not one blot to be found—the salvation of the elect is most sure and certain: Rev. xiii. 8, 'And all that dwell on the earth shall worship him, whose names are not written in the book of life of the Lamb slain from the foundation of the world.' The names of the elect are said to be written in the book of life by a usual metaphor; for we commonly write down the names of such as are dear unto us, that we may continually remember them. So God having in his eternal counsel elected some to salvation, hath written their names in the book of life; as our Saviour tells us, 'Rejoice, because your names are written in heaven,' Luke x. 20. Some understand the metaphor of the sonship of the elect; so that to be written in the book of life shews that they are heirs of glory; for we know that such are to inherit whose names are written in the last will and testament of men. Of this book of life you may further read, Rev. xvii. 8, xx. 15, xxi. 27, and xxii. 19.

Now from this book of life, that shall be opened in the great day, when the other books shall be opened, as hath been shewed, every sincere Christian may form up this eleventh plea as to the ten scriptures that are in the margin,[2] that refer to the great day of account, or to a man's particular account. *Most holy and blessed Lord, cast thine eye upon the book of election, and there thou wilt find my name written.* Now my name being written in that book, I am exempt from all condemnation, and interested in the great salvation; my name being written in the book of life, I am secured from coming into the judgment of reprobation or condemnation, John v. 14; Rev. xxi. 27. Jesus Christ, who hath written my name in the book of life, hath made up my accounts for me; he hath satisfied thy justice, and pacified thy wrath, and borne the curse, and purchased my pardon, and put upon me an everlasting righteousness, and given me my *quietus est;* he has crossed out the black lines of my sins with the red lines of his blood; he has cancelled all the bonds wherein I stood obliged to divine justice. I further plead, O blessed Lord, that there is an immutable connexion betwixt being written in this book of life and the obtaining of eternal life; and if the connexion betwixt being

---

[1] The holy God, by an *anthropopatheia*, speaketh to our capacity; for he doth all things without the help of books.

[2] Eccles. xi. 9, and xii. 14; Mat. xii. 14, and xviii. 23; Luke xvi. 2; Rom. xiv. 10 2 Cor. v. 10; Heb. ix. 27, and xiii. 17; 1 Pet. iv. 5; Dan. ix. 24; Col. ii. 14.

written in this book of life and the obtaining of eternal life were not peremptory, what reason could there be of opening this book in the day of judgment? The book of life is a book of sovereign grace, upon which lies the weight of my salvation, my happiness, my all; and therefore by that book I desire to stand or fall. Well, saith the Lord, I cannot but accept of this plea as holy, honourable, just, and righteous; and therefore 'enter thou into the joy of thy Lord, inherit the kingdom prepared for thee,' Mat. xxv. 21, 34. Thus, by divine assistance, and by a special and a gracious hand of providence upon me, I have finished those select and important cases of conscience which I designed to speak to.

Soli Deo Gloria in Aeternum.

PAPERBACK CLASSICS

150-00083-2p	An Alarm to the Unconverted, Alleine	1.00
150-00072-8p	An Antidote to Arminianism, C. Ness	1.00
150-00153-8p	Atonement According to Christ, Smeaton	2.50
150-00154-xp	Atonement According to Apostles, Smeaton	2.50
150-00065-0p	Augustine's Confessions (Modern English)	1.00
150-00281-6p	Thomas Watson's Body of Divinity, 3 v. in 1	3.50
150-00142-3p	A Call to the Unconverted, R. Baxter	1.50
150-00062-5p	The Cause of God & Truth, John Gill	3.00
150-00272-5p	Christ Our Mediator, Thomas Goodwin	3.50
150-00158-7p	Christian Love & Its Fruits, Jon. Edwards	1.75
150-00158-7p	Christian's Great Interest, Wm. Guthrie	1.75
150-00310-9p	Communion with God, John Owen	2.50
150-00159-9p	The Crook in the Lot, Thomas Boston	1.00
150-00161-7p	The Dairyman's Daughter, Richmond, etc.	1.50
150-00080-7p	Death, Samuel Eyres Pierce	1.00
150-00078-9p	Divine Cordial—Romans 8:28, Thomas Watson	1.25
150-00165-4p	The Eternal Sonship of Christ, J. C. Philpot	1.00
150-00119-8p	The Five Points of Calvinism,	1.50
150-00261-0p	God's Grace & God's Mercy, C. H. Spurgeon	1.50
150-00077-7p	God's Sovereignty, Elisha Coles	1.75
150-00082-0p	Heaven Opened, Richard and Joseph Alleine	1.50
150-00076-5p	A History of Redemption, Jonathan Edwards	3.00
150-00049-2p	Holiness, J. C. Ryle	1.50
150-00172-1p	The Holy Spirit, John Owen	4.50
150-00279-8p	Exposition of Hosea, Hutcheson—Wright	1.75
150-00171-xp	Human Nature, Thomas Boston	1.75
150-00259-2p	Humility & How to Get It, Spurgeon	1.50
150-00114-9p	Institutes of the Christian Religion, Calvin	4.00
150-00177-0p	Justification by Faith, John Owen	2.50
150-00064-9p	Keeping the Heart, John Flavel	1.25
150-00123-xp	Life & Diary of David Brainerd, Jon. Edwards	1.50
150-00269-5p	Life & Times of Jesus, Edersheim, 2 vols. in 1	6.00
150-00096-0p	Morning & Evening, C. H. Spurgeon	2.50
150-00185-xp	Mute Christian Under the Rod, T. Brooks	1.50
150-00217-8p	Narrative of Surprising Conversions, Edwards	1.50
150-00105-8p	On the Bondage of the Will, Martin Luther	1.50
150-00187-3p	Person & Glory of Christ, John Owen	2.50
150-00092-3p	The Philadelphia Confession of Faith	1.50
150-00045-5p	Pilgrim's Progress in Modern English, Bunyan	1.00
150-00034-0p	Prayer & Return of Prayers, Bunyan—Goodwin	1.25
150-00036-4p	Precious Remedies Against Satan, T. Brooks	1.75
150-00035-2p	Rare Jewel of Christ. Cont., J. Burroughs	1.75
150-00056-xp	The Reformed Pastor, Richard Baxter	1.50
150-00043-1p	The Religious Affections, Jonathan Edwards	2.50
150-00225-7p	The Saint's Everlasting Rest, R. Baxter	1.75
150-00044-3p	The Soul-Winner, C. H. Spurgeon	1.50
150-00115-0p	Temptation & Sin, John Owen, 3 vols. in 1	2.50
150-00245-2p	The Ten Virgins, Thomas Shepherd	2.50
150-00107-1p	The Trinity, Edward Bickersteth	1.50
150-00073-xp	The Vanity of Thoughts, Thomas Goodwin	1.25
150-00209-9p	The Work of the Holy Spirit, Abraham Kuyper	3.00

Printed in the United States
698600001B